THINKING CRITICALLY ABOUT ABOUT MORAL PROBLEMS

Thomas F. Wall
Emmanuel College

THOMSON

WADSWORTH

Australia • Canada • Mexico • Singapore • Spain
United Kingdom • United States

To my parents, Dorothy and Thomas
May the winds of both time and eternity be always at your back

THOMSON
★ ™
WADSWORTH

Publisher: Holly J. Allen
Philosophy Editor: Steve Wainwright
Development Editor: Eric Carlson
Assistant Editor: Kara Kindstrom
Editorial Assistant: Anna Lustig
Technology Project Manager: Susan DeVanna
Marketing Manager: Worth Hawes
Advertising Project Manager: Bryan Vann
Print/Media Buyer: Robert King

Permissions Editor: Bob Kauser
Production Service: Shepherd Incorporated
Copy Editor: Patterson Lamb
Cover Designer: Yvo Riezebos
Cover Image: Getty Images
Cover Printer: Webcom, Limited
Compositor: Shepherd Incorporated
Printer: Webcom, Limited

1 2 3 4 5 6 7 05 04 03

For more information about our products, contact us at:
Thomson Learning Academic Resource Center
1-800-423-0563

For permission to use material from this text,
contact us by: **Phone:** 1-800-730-2214
Fax: 1-800-730-2215
Web: http://www.thomsonrights.com

Library of Congress Cataloging-in-Publication Data

Wall, Thomas F.
 Thinking critically about moral problems / Thomas Wall.
  p. cm.
 Includes bibliographical references and index.
 ISBN 0-534-57423-8
  1. Ethics. 2. Ethical problems. 3. Critical thinking. I. Title.

BJ1012 .W3512 2003
170—dc21
                                    2001057452

Wadsworth/Thomson Learning
10 Davis Drive
Belmont, CA 94002-3098
USA

Asia
Thomson Learning
60 Albert Complex, #15-01
Albert Complex
Singapore 189969

Australia
Nelson Thomson Learning
102 Dodds Street
South Melbourne, Victoria 3205
Australia

Canada
Nelson Thomson Learning
1120 Birchmount Road
Toronto, Ontario M1K 5G4
Canada

Europe/Middle East/South Africa
Thomson Learning
Berkshire House
168-173 High Holborn
London WC1 V7AA
United Kingdom

Latin America
Thomson Learning
Seneca, 53
Colonia Polanco
11560 Mexico D.F.
Mexico

Spain
Paraninfo Thomson Learning
Calle/Magallanes, 25
28015 Madrid, Spain

www.wadsworth.com

wadsworth.com is the World Wide Web site for Wadsworth and is your direct source to dozens of online resources.

At *wadsworth.com* you can find out about supplements, demonstration software, and student resources. You can also send email to many of our authors and preview new publications and exciting new technologies.

wadsworth.com
Changing the way the world learns®

Contents

Preface

This text is designed to be used in a moral problems course. Such a course will show you how to use ethical theories to solve a variety of moral problems. *Thinking Critically About Moral Problems* takes for granted that the two central **goals** of such a course are the following.

First, a moral problems course should provide information. By the time you complete such a course you should be familiar with a variety of ethical theories as well as many of the important facts and arguments that surround each moral problem. In other words, you should be current in the ongoing debates that the moral problems discussed in this book have generated in society at large. This text provides you with lots of information. In Part 1 there are detailed discussions of several important ethical theories. In Part 2, a number of moral problems are discussed, including abortion, euthanasia, capital punishment, economic justice, pornography, reproductive technology, and others that you will find listed in the table of contents.

The *second* goal of an adequate moral problems course is to help you to figure out and defend your own solutions to moral problems. The moral problems discussed in *Thinking Critically About Moral Problems* are all controversial issues. They all have more than one reasonable solution. Deciding upon and defending a particular solution as the most reasonable will not be easy. You will need information to perform this task, but information alone is not enough to do the job. You will soon discover that the facts may be interpreted and explained in a variety of ways, each favoring one solution over another.

In addition to providing information, this text will help you to solve moral problems by developing and having you practice a particular method of thinking. This method is called **critical thinking.** We think critically about many things, but in this text we will focus on thinking critically about moral problems. What it will mean for us to solve moral problems will be to follow this pattern of thinking step by step. It is a pattern that is outlined in Part 1 and used in the discussion of each moral problem found in Part 2. Repeating this pattern from chapter to chapter will help to establish a habit of thinking about moral problems.

Through various exercises and assignments, *Thinking Critically About Moral Problems* will encourage you to develop your critical thinking skills in the context of solving moral problems. You will practice identifying and clarifying problems, defining concepts, gathering information, examining assumptions and points of view, formulating and evaluating arguments, deciding upon solutions, and considering the consequences of such decisions. This method of critical thinking will encourage you to think through moral problems for yourselves, to become competent and confident moral decision makers. Because their use will help to develop your thinking skills in general, the skills developed here should also help you to think critically in other areas as well. In an age when information changes so rapidly, when careers are redefined every few years, and when change is the only constant in life, being able to think for yourself, and to think well, lies at the very heart of an adequate education.

In addition to weaving the skills of critical thinking into its subject matter, this text is distinctive in at least two additional ways, both of which concern ethical theories. An **ethical theory** clarifies basic moral concepts and provides guidance for moral decision making. Ethical theories are required to solve moral problems, just as a general knowledge of mechanics is required to fix automobiles. While many textbooks on moral problems discuss ethical theories, they often simply outline their basic points and add a comment or two about how philosophers disagree about which of them is the most adequate. This often creates confusion. It may lead you to believe that any theory is as good as any other. In this text, however, one ethical theory is defended as the most adequate of the many that are discussed in Part 1. This ethical theory is used exclusively throughout the many discussions of moral problems found in Part 2.

Another way in which this text is different from most is its insistence on spending a great deal of time and effort demonstrating how theories may be used to guide moral decision making. A moral problems course is sometimes called a course in "applied ethics," because it is supposed to apply general ethical theories to particular problems. If this is so, then you should be shown in some detail how this is to be accomplished. You should not be left to your own resources to figure out how general principles such as "Do good and avoid evil" or "Treat everyone fairly" are used to decide right from wrong in particular areas such as capital punishment or abortion. When this guidance is absent you may end up abandoning reference to ethical theories altogether and instead favor a visceral reaction to problems. This is why the application of our ethical theory to particular problems will be stressed throughout Part 2—so that you may see and understand clearly how ethical theories guide moral decision making. Once you see this it will become easier for you to transfer a moral theory from one type of problem to another. This is important because perceiving solutions to particular problems as following from general theories lies at the very heart of thinking critically about moral problems.

Finally, *Thinking Critically About Moral Problems* also contains a special section at the end of each chapter in Part 2 called "Another Perspective." The purpose of this section is to show you another way to view the problem under discussion. Often this means looking at the issue in the way that someone from another culture might. Sometimes it means personalizing the issue, seeing real people struggling to understand or to live with the problem. The general purpose of this section is not so much to provide additional support for one of the possible solutions defended in the chapter as to broaden and deepen your understanding of the problem under consideration.

Note to Instructors

Although the **content** of this text is similar to most, the **method** it employs to solve particular moral problems is quite different. It encourages students to think for themselves in three ways. First, it clearly outlines a pattern of critical thinking in Part 1, and uses this pattern to structure discussions of the moral problems that are found in Part 2. Repeating this process of thinking from chapter to chapter helps to establish it as a habit of thinking. Second, students are required to evaluate the arguments presented for and against various possible solutions to the many moral problems examined in Part 2. This hands-on evaluation process will require them to practice the reasoning skills required to solve moral problems in a rational manner.

Third, various exercises located throughout the text will require students to define concepts clearly, to discover relevant and reliable facts, to examine the assumptions and points of view which they bring to the problem, to construct their own arguments in defense of possible solutions, and to form reasoned judgments about which solutions are most adequate. Practicing these critical thinking skills will enable students to think through moral problems for themselves, so that once the course is over they may continue to exercise the skills of competent moral decision makers. Students need to practice thinking skills in order to develop them, so the exercises are important. There are probably too many of them to include all in a single course, so you may have to select the ones most suited to your needs.

The exercises may be performed in any number of ways, depending upon your style of teaching and the size of your class. I am a fan of small group discussions, so I have designed most of the exercises with that format in mind. However, most of them may also be performed by individuals either as in-class or out-of-class written assignments, or be used to form the basis for class discussions.

Acknowledgments

I wish to thank those who reviewed this text for their many helpful comments which made this book better than it would otherwise have been: Julia Bartkowiak, Clarion University; Sharon Crasnow, Riverside Community College; Albert Flores, California State University, Fullerton; Marie Friquegnon, William Paterson University; Krishna Mallick, Salem State College; Roger Paden, George Mason University; William Soderberg, Montgomery College. I also wish to thank the staff at Wadsworth for their guidance and encouragement as this book made its way from an idea to a completed manuscript, and the staff at Shepherd, Inc., for seeing to its safe journey from manuscript to published text. Most of all I wish to thank my wife Kathleen for her unwavering enthusiasm and encouragement, and my parents, Dorothy and Thomas. It is to my parents that this book is dedicated, and it is to them that I owe so very much and am so very grateful.

Introduction

Making Moral Decisions

We make moral decisions whenever we decide to perform a certain action because it is the right thing to do or to refrain from acting in certain ways because doing so would be wrong. We also judge the moral actions of others, either publicly or in the privacy of our own hearts, praising them for their good deeds and scolding them for their moral faults. We make moral decisions frequently and often with a good deal of confidence. We often simply know that a particular action is right or wrong, and no amount of discussion will convince us otherwise.

If we already make moral decisions and appear to know how to do so, then why do we need a book to tell us how we should make moral decisions? The short answer is that most of the time we do not need any such help. In the process of growing, of becoming civilized, most of us were fortunate to have instilled within us a sense of right and wrong. We learned from our parents, our religious leaders, our peers, and others what is acceptable moral behavior and what is not. Just as we learned the rules of language and arithmetic and baseball, so too we learned the rules of morality. We learned that it is wrong to lie, to steal, to cheat, to break promises, and to kill. We also learned that we should be kind and fair and respectful of others.

Making moral decisions often amounts to no more than judging whether the action in question conforms to the relevant moral rule. If a man lies, we know that he has done something wrong simply because we know it is wrong to lie. If a friend breaks her promise to meet you for lunch, then she also has done something wrong. It is not a terrible wrong, but it is wrong. This we know with great confidence, because we were taught the rule that breaking promises is wrong. Since most of the people we associate with learned the same rules we did, there is usually widespread agreement about such decisions.

Making decisions such as these does not require us to think very much, if at all. This is good, as it saves a great deal of time. If we had to think every time we made a moral judgment, we would all be much busier people. There is no great amount of "figuring out" required for the vast majority of moral judgments, because they require us only to determine whether a moral rule has been broken. This is how we know the difference between right and wrong, and this is why most of our moral judgments seem so simple and clear. Since these rules are now present in us as habits, it is accurate to say that for most of our moral lives we are simply creatures of moral habit.

It may be difficult sometimes to get ourselves to *do* what is right. We often struggle with ourselves to do the right thing, especially in those instances when there seems to be so much to gain by breaking a moral law. The true test of our moral character is how well we live up to what we know to be right. These struggles are the stuff of literature, art, and entertainment—the good person's triumph in the face of moral trials and tribulations. If we do not always do the right thing, still we usually *know* the right thing to do. Figuring that out is less frequently the problem. Once in a while, however, not knowing the right thing to do is precisely the problem. Our society has many such problems, such as capital punishment, abortion, euthanasia, censorship, war, cloning, gene splicing, and the like. These sorts of problems divide us and cause great turmoil in our lives. This book is about these sorts of moral decisions, ones that require us to solve **moral problems.**

The reason these issues are problems is because our moral rules often do not readily show us how to decide right from wrong. Our moral habits fail to show us the way. Problems arise from the failure of habitual ways of doing things. Your usual way of getting to class, for example, may be to drive. If your car will not start, however, you have a problem. You have to solve it by thinking of ways to get the car running, or by thinking of other ways to get to class. Moral problems are similar to these types of everyday problems. Our usual way of telling right from wrong fails us; our moral habits break down and so we end up with a problem. The problem is that we do not know what is the right thing to do.

We may attempt to solve such moral problems, as many people do, by appealing to our visceral reaction, by judging an action as right or wrong depending on how it feels to us. We may be against surrogate motherhood, for example, just because it does not seem right to us, even in the absence of our ability to say why. Feelings play an important role in morality; however, they do not serve us well as a basis for solving moral problems. We may feel very differently about surrogate motherhood, for example, if it becomes the only way that we can have a child of our own. Even if your feelings did not change with circumstances, others often have different feelings about the same matter. In the midst of conflicting feelings, very often problems do not get resolved.

Instead, when we are faced with a moral problem, we ought to *think*, not just feel. Much of this text deals with the kind of thinking that is required to solve moral problems. Though the sort of thinking required to solve moral problems is quite natural to most of us, we need help to show us how to go about it—the sort of help that this book was designed to provide. As the title states, this book attempts to show you how to think about moral problems in a critical way, in a way that does justice to all sides and to all of the relevant factors involved. Just what this means, just what solving moral problems amounts to, is discussed in Part 1 of this book. In Part 2 we will use what we learn to attempt to solve some of the most difficult and important moral problems of our times.

Part 1

Ethics

Chapter 1

The General Nature of Ethics

To investigate the nature of moral decision making in general, and especially the type of moral decision making that requires us to solve moral problems, we must learn something about **ethics.** This is because ethics, among other things, is the study of moral decision making, the study of how we ought to make moral decisions. So we begin our investigation of moral decision making by examining the nature of ethics and how it is similar to and different from related areas.

Ethics and Philosophy

Ethics is a branch of philosophy. Philosophy, at least Western philosophy, began in ancient Greece some twenty-five hundred years ago. The word 'philosophy' comes from two Greek words, 'philein' (to love) and 'sophia' (wisdom). So originally philosophy was the love of wisdom, and philosophers were people who spent their lives attempting to become wise. To be wise was to have a general understanding of all things—nature, ourselves, society, God, morality, and the meaning of life and death. Wisdom was not identified with any sort of practical knowledge, what we might call "professional training" or "career preparation" today. It was considered by ancient philosophers to be much more valuable than practical knowledge, even to the point of constituting the very goal of life itself. A person who was wise was as close to happiness as he or she could be.

Philosophy has retained some of this original meaning, at least insofar as it is still concerned with a general understanding of these basic issues. But most philosophers today draw a sharper distinction than did their predecessors between knowledge of the world and knowledge of how we think about the world. Most philosophers today, for example, do not think of what they do as acquiring factual knowledge. That task has long been relinquished to the various natural and behavioral sciences that have developed since the original definition of philosophy was introduced by the Greeks. Now philosophers see themselves as concerned with ideas, not things; with conceptual questions, not empirical ones; with understanding or interpreting facts, not discovering them. Philosophers do not perform experiments or send out surveys or make observations to settle their questions. They think.

One thing that philosophers often think about we will call **basic beliefs.** Basic beliefs constitute much of the subject matter of philosophy. A belief is basic if its truth or falsity determines the truth or falsity of other beliefs. As a weak foundation undermines the entire house, so a false basic belief undermines the structure of beliefs built on it. The basic belief of religion, for example, may be identified as the belief that God exists. If this belief is false, other religious beliefs that depend on its truth become false, or at least need to be reinterpreted. Morality based on God's word, for example, or liturgical celebrations of the special relationships between humans and God, no longer have firm support. Sometimes philosophers refer to these basic beliefs as "fundamental issues" or "big questions," ways that mean essentially the same thing as basic beliefs.

How philosophers think about basic beliefs will be called **critical thinking.** This is the method of philosophy. Thinking critically in philosophy is similar to thinking critically in science and everyday life. It may be thought of as solving problems, and it involves many different skills. Some of these skills include identifying problems and their possible solutions, clarifying concepts, gathering information, being aware of assumptions and points of view, drawing inferences, and evaluating competing solutions. We will have much more to say about critical thinking a little later. For now, the central point is that one of the main things philosophers do is to think critically about basic beliefs.

Ethics is a branch of philosophy that studies beliefs about **right and wrong, good and evil.** These beliefs are basic because they determine the truth or falsity of other beliefs. If you believe, for example, that the right thing to do is whatever is good for you (and the heck with the other person), then your moral life will be very different from that of someone who believes that we ought to be concerned with the good of others as well. If you believe that what is good, what ought to be the goal of your life, is simply pleasure, then your life will be quite different from the life of someone who believes that love, knowledge, freedom, and other values are as important as pleasure.

In ethics we think critically about these sorts of beliefs. We have to, because not everyone agrees as to what these beliefs ought to be. Ethics is a controversial field of study, as we will see later. There are many different ideas about right and wrong, good and evil. In studying ethics, we try to discover the best set of moral basic beliefs we can, so that we can use them to make moral decisions throughout our lives. This is hard work, but if we think critically about what our basic moral beliefs ought to be, then we make them our own; we take charge of them. They are no longer simply the products of someone else's thinking or the product of society. Once we see how we ought to think about right and wrong, and good and evil, we are no longer moral "robots," conditioned by others to think in one way or another. By thinking critically about what our moral beliefs ought to be, by taking control of them, we will be in a much better position to make real decisions about the serious moral problems that divide society in this rapidly changing world.

Ethics, Law, and Religion

In addition to making decisions about what is morally right and wrong, we also make decisions based upon what is **legally** right and wrong. There are many ways to distinguish between law and morality, but for our purposes it is especially important to distinguish between the content of law and morality, between what actions may be judged to be legal or illegal, on the one hand, and moral or immoral the other hand. Often what is morally wrong is also legally wrong. Breaking some promises (contracts), killing, stealing, and some forms of lying and cheating, for example, are both immoral and illegal. In general, when immoral actions lead to serious harms, they are also made illegal and enforced by the strong arm of the law. So much of what is legally accepted or prohibited overlaps with what is morally accepted or prohibited.

Although moral wrongs often overlap with legal wrongs, this is not always the case. For example, some immoral actions are not illegal. This is especially true in the case of actions that harm no one but yourself. You will not be thrown in jail for spending night after night getting drunk in the privacy of your apartment, for example, though such behavior is arguably immoral. The main job of the legal system is to protect us from each other and not to interfere with our private lives, even if doing so is good for us. So, many actions that may be immoral may not be illegal, especially if they harm only ourselves.

On the other hand, some actions accepted as perfectly legal are arguably immoral. For example, many believe that abortion, physician-assisted suicide, and capital punishment are immoral, even though all are legal in some states. Finally, some laws are morally neutral, especially those laws that specify what procedures are required to exercise certain legal privileges. For example, laws that specify what constitutes a legal marriage or spell out what is required to register a car or incorporate a business are laws that are neither moral nor immoral. The important point to make in drawing these many distinctions between what is legally right and morally right is that pointing out the legality or illegality of an action is insufficient to determine its moral status. Instead, we will judge the morality of our actions by standards different from those used to judge their legality.

It is also important to distinguish moral beliefs about right and wrong, good and evil from their counterparts found in **religion.** It is not always easy here to distinguish between religious and philosophical ethics on the basis of their content. Many times the views of religion and philosophy about right and wrong do not differ. Most religions are opposed to cloning humans, for example, while the same is true for most philosophical ethicists. Instead, the central difference between the two approaches to ethics is more a matter of method. Philosophical ethics, the subject of this book, is based solely on facts and reason. Religious ethics may also use facts and reason to develop its views, but its primary guiding principle for deciding between right and wrong, good and evil, is the word of God. In religion, what is right is what God says is right. We know what God says by consulting the scriptures or sacred writings of a religion, as well as the teachings of those vested with the authority to interpret these writings.

Sometimes, however, in addition to differences in method, there are also differences in content. For example, philosophical ethics may allow abortion under certain conditions, whereas some religions adamantly oppose it. What is a person to do who is a member of such a religion but also wants to follow reason? Should she think of herself as abandoning faith if she agrees with reason, or abandoning reason if she agrees with faith? I do not think such extreme measures are called for. Instead, the occasional conflicts that arise between religion and philosophy in the matter of moral beliefs may be understood not so much as irresolvable dilemmas as calls to live on a different plane.

Philosophical ethics is concerned with the obligations to ourselves and each other to which every reasonable person ought to agree. It presents us with an outline of the basic minimal duties that are required for our dealings with ourselves and others. It tells us what sorts of things we must not do to each other, and it tells us what we ought to do for those with whom we have special relationships, such as our families and those with whom we work. Our religions, however, often call us to a higher duty. We are called to love our neighbor, not just to avoid harming him. In the abortion situation, for example, while it may be morally acceptable according to human reason to terminate some pregnancies, according to some religions it would be kinder not to exercise that right. It would be an act of love, an act of respect for the life of the fetus, that goes beyond "the call of duty."

Aspirations to live beyond our minimum duties also arise from nonreligious sources. Whenever we strive to be like those whom we admire for their noble or heroic lives, we aspire to live beyond the call of duty, beyond what we have to do. Such aspirations are the stuff of heroes and saints and ought to be encouraged by our parents, by our religious leaders, and by many others who have a role in shaping our lives. It will be the central task of philosophical ethics, however, to focus less on our moral aspirations and instead to examine what facts and reason have to say about our obligations. Our aspirations may be the noble stuff of life, but our obligations are the province of philosophy.

The Divisions of Ethics

There are many different ways to study moral beliefs, many different branches on the tree of ethics, and it will be helpful for you to distinguish among them. Let us begin by distinguishing between the concepts of "morality" and "ethics." Though these terms are often used interchangeably in daily life, they will have different, though related, meanings for us. The simple thing to say is that ethics is the study of morality, and morality is a term that refers to certain behavior. Moral behavior includes actions we refer to as right or wrong, and actions that express our desires for the things we value. In short, morality is a type of behavior directed toward the right and the good, and ethics is the study of that behavior.

Ethics may study morality in several ways, leading to various types of ethics. First, it may be an empirical study of the obligations and values that people accept as a matter of fact. We may study these beliefs by sending out a questionnaire, for example, to gather information about what a representative sample of Americans believes to be the important values in their lives. We may discover that most Americans want fame and fortune, or we may discover that they want more meaning in their lives, or more freedom. We may also examine what a group or an individual believes about right and wrong. We may conduct a poll among Catholic Americans, for example, about their beliefs on abortion, capital punishment, and physician-assisted suicide, studying whether they reflect the beliefs of the general population or the teachings of their church. We may also study the obligations and values of a country by studying what its laws, religions, and professional groups have to say. This way of studying moral beliefs is called **descriptive ethics**. It describes the moral ideas of a group of people or an individual. It is the sort of study that is usually carried out by the empirical sciences, especially by social scientists.

Ethics studies morality in other ways as well. The most important way for us in this text is called **normative ethics.** Normative ethics is not a study of what our moral beliefs *are,* but of what they *ought* to be. It is a study of what we *should* consider to be our obligations, and what we *should* desire. Sometimes what we actually think of as right and wrong and what we actually desire are not very different from what we ought to think of as right and wrong and what we ought to desire. Sometimes, however, there is a great difference. In the United States, for example, even though most states and most religions and most medical codes are officially opposed to physician-assisted suicide, we could argue that we ought to consider it a right of all competent, dying people. And even though most people may value fame and fortune, we could argue that they ought to desire knowledge and virtue instead, or perhaps love and spiritual fulfillment.

So normative ethics is about ideals, about how we ought to live, and about what sorts of things we ought to value. Because it is about ideals, normative ethics is not an empirical study. Ideals, after all, cannot be observed. Instead, we should understand how normative ethics studies morality by analogy with how the rulebook in chess is a study of chess, or an arithmetic book is a study of adding and subtracting behavior. "Study" here means laying out the rules. As the rulebook of chess tells us what are the allowable moves in chess, and as a textbook on arithmetic gives us the rules for adding and subtracting, so normative ethics gives us the rules for determining right from wrong, and good from evil. We often will appeal to descriptive ethics in this text, and thus to what people's moral beliefs are, but we will always do so to help us develop better ideas of what they ought to be.

Another distinction may be drawn between normative ethics and **applied ethics.** Normative ethics is often referred to by philosophers as **ethical theory.** While ethical theories give us general guidelines for determining right from wrong, applied ethics is the study of how to use these general guidelines to make specific types of moral decisions. Courses in business ethics, health care ethics, and social ethics, for example, are courses in applied ethics. Normative ethics, which we will simply call ethics or ethical theory from now on, is the focus of Part 1 of this text; Part 2 is concerned with applied ethics.

Chapter 2

Ethical Theory

Ethics is especially concerned with two basic moral beliefs, two different but related ideals. On the one hand, it tries to discover what we should desire or value, what we ought to pursue to make our lives happy. This part of ethics is called **value theory.** Value theory is the critical examination of one of our basic moral beliefs, our belief about what is good. It attempts to give us a general idea of what are the really important goals of life, the sorts of things that we must acquire if we really are to lead the good life, to be happy. The other part of ethics, **theory of obligation,** tries to determine what our beliefs about right and wrong ought to be. It is called theory of obligation because those actions that are morally right for us to perform may be thought of as our obligations or duties. We could call it a "theory of right action" or a "theory of duty," but we will use the more conventional name, theory of obligation, in this text.

A theory of obligation provides us with a means to determine right from wrong by giving us a general definition of right and wrong behavior, and a set of instructions for how to apply this definition to particular cases. For example, a theory of obligation may claim that what makes any action wrong is that it harms another. If I held such a claim my general definition of right and wrong behavior would be, "Do whatever you want to, as long as it harms no one else." How would I use such a general definition to figure out right from wrong? I would consider the consequences of my actions on others. If they cause harm to others, they are wrong; if not, they are permissible.

We can make most of the moral decisions about right and wrong with which we are confronted without any formal training in ethics. This is because knowing right from wrong is usually a fairly routine matter. It simply requires us to follow well-established moral rules. To solve moral *problems,* however, we do need to be clear about our basic beliefs about right and wrong, good and evil. To be competent moral decision makers, then, we must think about these ideas, these basic moral beliefs, and learn how to apply them to concrete cases. As a chess player must know the general rules of chess as well as its general strategies, so moral decision makers must understand their basic beliefs about values and obligations, as well as the way that such beliefs are applied to concrete cases.

We turn now to a detailed examination of ethical theories, first to a brief discussion of theories of value and then to a discussion of theories of obligation. We will spend more time on theories of obligation because most of the moral problems we will encounter in Part 2 will be problems about right and wrong rather than problems about good and evil. Unfortunately, as we will soon see, there is no general consensus among philosophers about which theory of value or which theory of obligation is best. There are instead many competing theories. It will be our task in what remains of Part 1 to decide for ourselves which of these is superior to the rest.

Value Theory

We all have beliefs about what we ought to value in life. We may not be able to say right now just what these beliefs are, but they do exist and they do guide and sustain our daily choices. At important points of our lives many of us question the values that we have accepted and that determine the direction our lives have taken thus far. When you made a choice about college and a major, for example, you had to think about what you wanted to do with your life, especially what sort of a career you wanted to pursue and why. Perhaps after graduating, becoming competent in a field, and achieving what you want to, you will wake up some day and ask, Is that all there is? Do I really want to work seventy hours a week, despite my handsome salary? Am I missing out on other things that are more important? Value theory attempts to answer these sorts of questions by identifying those values that are truly important for our happiness.

Moral and Nonmoral Values

In value theory, one major distinction is drawn between moral values and nonmoral values. **Moral values** are things that are *morally* good. For the most part, they are properties of persons that are morally good. Some examples of morally good properties of persons include having a good moral character, or having good intentions, or having good motives for acting. **Nonmoral values** are anything that we value, anything that we desire or want. Sometimes this can include moral values, such as having a morally good character, but it also includes other things as well. In addition to wanting a good moral character I may want a certain type of car, for example, or desire to be married and to have children, or to acquire lots of money. So one way to think of nonmoral values, which we will simply call values from now on, is to think of them as what we want.

Another important distinction needs to be drawn here. Some things we want for the sake of other things. We want money to buy things, for example. If we were stuck on a desolate island and could have only one thing with us, we would not wish for money. If there were nothing to buy, money would have no value. It would simply be a pile of useless paper. Such goods as money are called **extrinsic** values, or sometimes "instrumental" values. They are good only for something else. A hammer is extrinsically valuable. It is good for something, not good in itself. If it did not work to drive or pull nails, we would discard it. If it had "sentimental" value, it would be good only because it reminded us of something else that was important to us—the one who gave it to us, perhaps.

Intrinsic values, on the other hand, are things that are good in themselves. We sometimes say that they have "inherent worth." One way to think of nonmoral intrinsic values is to think of them as the ultimate goals of life, the things that we really ought to want, the things that will satisfy our deepest desires. Happiness, of course, is always what we all want. Intrinsic values may be thought of as what will bring us happiness. Whereas descriptive ethics studies what we do value, ethics is concerned with discovering what sorts of things we ought to value, what sorts of things we ought to desire, what sorts of things we need to acquire in order to be truly happy. It is concerned with what philosophers call the good life or, for short, the good.

Monistic and Pluralistic Theories of Value

Some philosophers think that only one thing is valuable in itself. Their value theories are called **monistic.** There have been various monistic theories of value defended by philosophers. Some have claimed that knowledge alone makes us happy; others opt for a virtuous character, and still others for freedom, love, power, or a relationship with God. Perhaps the most famous version of a monistic theory of intrinsic value, however, equates the good life with a life of pleasure. Such a theory is called hedonism.

Hedonism claims that only pleasure is worthwhile in itself. Everything else is valuable only because it leads to pleasure. Knowledge would not be valued if it led to pain and suffering, nor would freedom, power, love, and so on. For the hedonist, all these other goods have merely extrinsic value. They are simply a means to more pleasure. For some hedonists, the important thing about pleasure is the amount of it. Whether you get your pleasure from drinking beer or listening to Beethoven matters little. For others, however, the type of pleasure is what is important. Pleasures may be ranked according to their quality. Sensual, bodily pleasures are ranked lowest, while pleasures of the mind and spirit are seen as more valuable. Even less pleasure of a higher type is to be valued over more pleasure of a lower type. For this sort of hedonist, a life of gluttony and drunkenness is surely not the good life, while a life filled with knowledge, art, music, love, and virtue leads to the sort of pleasures that make for a happy life.

Others think there are many things that comprise the good life. Anyone who claims that more than one thing is intrinsically valuable holds a **pluralistic** theory of value. For them, pleasure is merely one item on the list of intrinsically valuable things, not the only item. To defend their case, pluralists do two things. First, they point out how deeply we desire many things, such as the items listed previously. Second, they previously point out the errors of hedonism. Pluralists claim that hedonists make a fundamental error in considering the plurality of values as simply a means to pleasure.

For example, a hedonist may be correct to point out that understanding a complex theory in science, after much struggle, produces a sense of pleasure. Doing the right thing when it is difficult also makes us feel good, as does being free to do what we want to, or being in love or feeling connected to God. However, the pluralist thinks that the hedonist makes a mistake in arguing from the fact that pleasure may be the *result* of all these activities that we value, to the conclusion that it is only pleasure that we value. For the pluralist, while it is true that knowledge, love, virtue, and other things that we value do produce pleasure when we acquire them, this does not mean that they are valued only for the pleasure they produce.

One way to see this is to note that there is no one single state called "pleasure" that is produced by acquiring these various goods. Each good produces a different type of mental state, a state often quite different from those produced by other goods. The pleasure one gets from understanding a scientific theory is quite different from the pleasure that results from being in love, or doing the right thing, or feeling close to God. So at the very least, the hedonist himself must admit to a plurality of values—the various types of pleasure derived from other goods. From this perspective, hedonism looks almost the same in practice as a pluralistic theory of value. What does it matter in practice, for example, if I say that the good life is a collection of all the various types of pleasure that I get from knowledge, love, power, freedom, God, virtue, and so on; or I say that it consists of the possession of these qualities themselves? In either case, I need a plurality of values to be happy, and I cannot get the various states of pleasure that I desire without them.

Most of the moral problems discussed in Part 2 will not be problems that require us to decide on the nature of intrinsic values, but rather problems about right and wrong actions. It will turn out, however, that deciding between right and wrong will often require us to assess the good and evil produced by our actions. This is one of the ways that beliefs about values relate to beliefs about obligations. At least for some theories of obligation, we are obliged to act in ways that promote good and reduce evil. So it is important for us to acquire clear and correct beliefs about values. However, most of the time the difficulties that we face as we attempt to solve moral problems are not difficulties in understanding what we ought to value. For the most part, though not always, we will be able to tell fairly easily the good from the evil, and we will be able to tell lesser goods from more important ones. Most of the time the biggest obstacles in solving moral problems will lie with our beliefs about right and wrong, especially with how to apply these beliefs to the particular problem in question. So it is to a discussion of right and wrong that we now turn.

Theories of Obligation

A **theory of obligation** does two things. It provides us with a general definition of right and wrong, and it gives us a set of instructions explaining how to apply this general definition to concrete cases. This is the heart of a theory of obligation; this is what it means to say that such theories give us a set of guidelines with which to determine right from wrong. Several additional points will help us to be even clearer about their nature.

The first thing to note about theories of obligation is that they are used to judge *actions*, not persons. The terms "right" and "wrong" are adjectives, as are "red" and "yellow." As red and yellow refer to properties of physical objects, right and wrong refer to properties of actions. It will always be actions and not persons that are right or wrong. As we will see later, making moral judgments about the person behind the action requires that we know something about the person's intentions, motives, and circumstances. Because this sort of information is often not readily available, it becomes much more difficult to judge people than it is to judge their actions.

Next, it is important to point out that ethical theories contain various *levels of explanation*. On one level they explain why an action is right by appealing to a general **rule**. For example, we say that a particular action such as lying to Sarah on Tuesday is wrong, because it is wrong (in general) to lie. On another level ethical theories explain why rules such as "do not lie" ought to be followed, by reference to even more general statements, called **principles.** These principles amount to a general definition of right action. A very common principle that many accept is called the Golden Rule. The Golden Rule tells you to do unto others what you would like them to do unto you. According to this principle, we should not lie because we would not want others to lie to us. We may view the levels involved in a theory of obligation as follows:

To understand theories of obligation we must understand the role that both rules and principles play in moral decision making.

Moral Rules

Theories of obligation are called "theories" because they offer explanations. What a theory of obligation explains is why specific moral actions are thought of as right or wrong. The kinds of explanations it offers are similar in many respects to those offered by scientific theories. Scientific theories explain observable events by appealing to scientific laws. For example, I may explain why an object I happen to be holding falls to the ground if I let it go, by appealing to the law of gravity. In a similar way, moral rules are used to explain moral actions. For example, I may explain that it is wrong not to show up for lunch with Maria when you promised to meet her, by appealing to the "it is wrong to break promises" rule. Most of the time, appealing to rules is sufficient for explaining right from wrong. In fact, as we said above, this is what we usually mean by right and wrong—following moral rules.

These rules are "out there" in society, and we learn them as we are raised by our parents and teachers. They become part of us. They are present in us as habits of behavior. If we have good habits (virtues) we generally do not lie, steal, cheat, and so on. If we have developed bad habits (vices) we routinely do things that break these rules. The collection of all of our moral habits is called our moral character. Most of our moral decisions simply involve conforming our behavior to these rules. We do not have to think about it to know what is right or wrong. We know right away, just as we know that running a red light is illegal without having to think about it. Most of the time we are simply creatures of moral habit, conforming our behavior to the rules of society that we have been trained to follow.

Sometimes, as was said before, we have to struggle to *do* what is right, to get ourselves to follow rules, especially when doing so is difficult. However, we usually do not have to struggle to *know* what is right. When we know whose wallet it is that we have found, but we could really use the money, returning it is a struggle. When I need to pass a test, and the answers are on a piece of paper in my pocket, it is a struggle to avoid looking at it. Such struggles occur between our desires and what we know to be the right thing to do. They constitute much of the moral pathos that fills the pages of great literature. During these struggles, however, we usually know what is right and wrong, because "right" simply means "conforming to a moral rule," and "wrong" means "breaking a moral rule."

Moral Principles

Sometimes, however, there is a problem about knowing right from wrong itself. Sometimes simply appealing to rules is insufficient. Sometimes we are faced with a problem that requires us to think, as habits now fail us. To solve these problems we must think, and part of thinking requires that we appeal to moral principles. It is important for us to distinguish between moral principles and moral rules, because they play different roles in moral decision making, especially in deciding how to solve moral problems. One difference is that moral principles, such as the Golden Rule and "Do no harm," are more general in scope than are rules. Whereas any particular rule governs a specific type of action such as lying, stealing, killing, and the like, principles provide us with a general definition of any sort of right action, a definition to which all rules must conform. Another difference is in the roles played by rules and principles in moral decision making. While moral rules govern which actions are right or wrong, these rules are themselves governed by moral principles in several ways.

First, as rules explain why actions are right or wrong, principles *explain* why we have the rules that we do. Why should we have a rule, "Do not lie," for example? Why not have a rule that says "Lie if you wish?" The answer is because moral principles prohibit such a rule. The Golden Rule would prohibit such a rule, for example, since we would not want to be lied to. The "Do no harm" principle would also prohibit such a rule, as lying generally causes harm.

Second, we need principles to introduce *new rules*. Sometimes changes in society have important consequences for good or evil. This is especially true of new technologies that follow on the heels of scientific discoveries. For example, should we allow you to clone a copy of yourself, to have a child that is an exact genetic copy of you? This would be acceptable if we had a rule about cloning that allowed the cloning of human beings. Should we have such a rule? That depends on whether the principle or principles accepted by your ethical theory allow it. Would the Golden Rule allow it? It's not easy to say. It depends on your perspective, whether you are the clone or the cloned, for example. In fact, the Golden Rule will not be the principle we shall adopt especially for this reason, that whatever guidance it gives depends on whether you are the one acted against immorally, or you are the one acting immorally. Whatever principle we do choose will have to be able to give us more objective guidance in matters such as this, in matters that require the formation of new rules that may then be used to guide the day-to-day actions of everyone.

Third, we need principles to resolve *conflicts between rules*. Sometimes two or more perfectly acceptable rules apply at the same time. We cannot follow both, so we have to choose which is the most important. Principles help us to decide this. Suppose you have promised to meet someone for lunch. On your way to the restaurant, you witness an automobile accident. You are the only one around at the time, and if you do not stop to help, the injured driver may die. If you do stop to help, you will be late for your luncheon date, thus breaking your promise. What is the right thing to do?

It is pretty easy to determine what is right in this case. While some slight psychological harm may occur to your friend, especially if she gets angry or worried about your absence, it pales by comparison to the harm you could avoid by helping the accident victim, even if it is only to use your cell phone to call for emergency assistance. The point is that there are two rules operating here. One is "keep your promises," while the other is something like "help prevent harm to others." When they conflict, as they do in this case, principles help us to decide which has the highest priority, and thus which is our obligation to follow at the time. If our moral principle is "do good and avoid evil," then clearly we are obliged to help the victim instead of keeping our promise.

The idea that rules sometimes conflict and that judgments must be made as to which has the highest priority is an important one. Ignoring it has led some ethical theorists to reject the importance of rules in ethics. They mistakenly believe that if doing what is right is a matter of following rules, then moral rules *always* have to be followed, no matter what. If ethics is a matter of following rules, then if you keep a rule you have done something right; if you break the rule, on the other hand, then you have done something wrong. This becomes a problem because there clearly seem to be circumstances in which following well-established moral rules would be wrong. This leads some people to the view that each situation must be judged anew. Sometimes lying is right and sometimes wrong; it depends on the circumstances.

With the insight that rules sometimes conflict, and that the right thing to do is to follow the rule with the highest priority, we can agree that making moral decisions is a matter of following rules, and that rules appear to have exceptions. According to the view that will be developed here, when your behavior conforms to an acceptable moral rule you have done something right; when you break a rule you have done something wrong. What about exceptions to rules? There are no exceptions to rules. When there *seems* to be an exception, when breaking a rule seems to be the right thing to do, it is simply that the rule in question has been overridden by a rule with a higher priority. Some of the most stubborn moral dilemmas we face in applied ethics arise from conflicts between otherwise acceptable rules. It is when both sides of a moral dilemma claim to have "right" on their side that we face our most difficult problems in determining right from wrong.

A Few More Concepts

The basic concepts required to describe a theory of obligation are "right" (as an adjective, referring to a property of actions), "rule," and "principle." Everything that needs to be said about theories of obligation can be said using these terms. Actions have the property of being morally right when they follow a rule that conforms to an acceptable principle. In addition to these three, there are related moral concepts that allow us to say the same sorts of things about right and wrong actions in different ways. Chief among these concepts are those of "right" (used as a noun), "duty," and "obligation."

Let's begin with the concept of a right, such as the right to life or the right to own property. It is my view that to talk about rights such as these is simply a shorthand way to talk about what sorts of actions are right. "Right," used as a noun, is derived from "right," used as an adjective. To say, for example, that I have a right to life, means that it is right for me to preserve my life and wrong for you to destroy it. It is wrong for you to destroy it because you are breaking a widely accepted moral rule, "Do not kill." To say that homeowners have property rights is another way of saying that it is wrong for another person to enter their house without permission, or to destroy them, rent them to others, sell them, and so on. These actions are wrong because they violate, among other things, the rule "Do not steal." Many of today's moral problems are phrased in terms of rights and are especially seen as a conflict of rights. The abortion problem, for example, may be seen as conflict between the right to life of the unborn and the right to privacy of the pregnant woman. It is acceptable to speak in this manner as long as we realize that to talk about conflicting rights is just another way to talk about conflicting moral rules.

Other concepts often used to discuss moral problems are those of "duty" and "obligation." Let us assume that these two concepts mean the same thing. As with rights talk, talking about duties or obligations may also be replaced by talk about rules. To see this, note that rights and duties are often opposite sides of the same coin. If I have a right to life, you have a duty not to kill me. If I have property rights, you have a duty or obligation to keep off my property, and so on. Because rights and duties fall in the same class, and because rights may be understood as simply shorthand ways of speaking about rules, then duties may also be understood in the same manner. To say that we have a moral obligation or duty to do something is to say that an action is morally right for us to do because doing so keeps a moral rule. Moral rules describe our duties or obligations. "Do not lie," "do not steal," "keep your promises," and so on are all moral rules that define some of the moral duties that society expects us to accept and live up to.

In short, moral rules describe which actions are right and define what are our rights and our duties or obligations. As long as you remember that talking about rights and duties is just another way to talk about moral rules, there should be no trouble in discussing moral problems in terms of rights and duties or obligations. In fact, we shall often do this, if only to conform to the way many of these issues are discussed today. The only time this should be a problem is when you begin to think of rights and duties as having some sort of existence apart from rules. If you do, you will become as puzzled as the person who has read a statistical report of American families and wonders where the "average man" is to be found.

Judging the Adequacy of Theories

It is now time for us to examine some of the leading ethical theories of obligation and to select which one is best. To do this we will first explore the criteria for judging one theory to be superior to another. Then we will take each theory, one at a time, and see how well it measures up to these criteria. The rules or criteria that are used to judge the adequacy of theories of obligation are similar to those used to evaluate scientific theories. These criteria state that one theory is better than another if (1) it accounts for all the facts, or least for more facts than its rivals, (2) it is more consistent, and (3) it is simpler. Let us examine these criteria in turn.

Universality

A good scientific theory should be able to explain all the facts that it is supposed to, and also be able to predict future events on the basis of this knowledge. Let's use an example to see how this rule works in judging one scientific theory to be superior to another. According to this rule, the theory of evolution is superior to its creationist competitors for lots of reasons, but one of them is that it explains more known facts than creationism does. Creationism is the view that the world was created more or less as described in the biblical account of creation, an account which is found in the book of Genesis in the Old Testament. Here it says, in effect, that the world was created some six thousand years ago, with all the species that now exist having been created at that time. Unfortunately, this leaves unexplained all the fossils that have been unearthed by scientists, fossils that dramatically predate the biblical date of creation. The theory of evolution explains more facts than creationism, so at least according to rule (1) it is a better theory.

This criterion works in a similar way to evaluate philosophical theories, including ethical theories. One ethical theory is better than another, according to this first criterion, if it explains more facts than its competitors. If it explains "all" the facts that it is supposed to, we say that it is **universal.** Some theories of obligation will be rejected because they are not universal—they leave unexplained too many common facts of our moral lives.

Note that ethical theories usually are required to be universal in other ways as well. They may be required, for example, to apply to "all" people. They may also follow a principle such as the Golden Rule, which requires us to act toward all people the way we would want them to act toward us. These senses of universality will be discussed later when we talk about the theories that appeal to them. The important point for now is that universality, as one of the criteria for judging ethical theories, means that adequate ethical theories must explain all the facts they are supposed to explain.

Consistency

The second criterion says that one theory is better than another if it is more **consistent.** Consistency refers to two properties of a theory. First, in an acceptable theory the statements that constitute the theory are all consistent with one another. They contain no contradictions or inconsistencies. We will call this *internal* consistency. Second, the theory itself must be consistent with generally accepted facts. It must not contradict the moral beliefs that we all know to be true. We will call this *external* consistency. All the ethical theories we will examine are internally consistent, so we only have to worry about their external consistency, their consistency with the facts of our moral lives.

Adopting external consistency as a criterion does not mean to imply acceptance of the view that our moral beliefs are all correct as they stand. An adequate moral theory may correct some of our current moral beliefs; it may show us that some of them are simply wrong. So an ethical theory does not have to be consistent with *all* our moral beliefs to be acceptable. However, when a proposed ethical theory is very much at odds with our current moral beliefs, when it denies most or even many of them, this is a good reason for questioning its adequacy. If a theory of obligation tells us that we ought to steal, lie, kill, and break our promises, for example, then it is inconsistent with our ordinary moral beliefs about what sorts of actions are right or wrong. If an ethical theory of value claims that we ought to desire something that most of us despise, this also would be a good reason to reject it. Because moral theories are supposed to explain our moral beliefs, any theory that is inconsistent with enough of them will be inadequate.

Simplicity

The third criterion says that for any two theories that are equally universal and consistent, the one to be preferred is the simpler one. For a theory to be simpler than another means that it uses fewer items in its explanations. This criterion is often used in science. For example, Kepler used it to decide that the sun should be considered the center of the solar system because thinking that way made the mathematics of planetary motion much simpler.

In ethics, this criterion that requires a theory to be **simple** shows itself especially in monistic theories of value and in theories of obligation that contain only one principle. Some of our theories of obligation will do very well by this criterion, which always must be balanced against the other two. There is also another meaning to "simple" that is important in assessing ethical theories—"simple to use." Some theories that contain the fewest principles are the most difficult to apply to particular problems. Some even seem impossible to use, as we will soon see.

Armed with these three criteria for judging the adequacy of normative ethical theories, let us now turn to the main business of Part 1, selecting the best theory of obligation. Before we undertake this difficult task, however, it is important to consider a challenge to its very plausibility. For those of you who believe that no one set of moral beliefs may be judged to be more adequate than another, but instead believe that any set of moral beliefs may be "correct" for some, while a different set may be "correct" for others, it is important to read and reflect upon the following section.

Ethical Relativism

One threat to normative ethics comes from **ethical relativism.** Ethical relativism is the claim that there is no correct set of moral obligations and values. According to this view, our obligations and values are every bit as subjective as our tastes in food or music. There are no "best-tasting" foods, or any "best songs," only different ideas of what tastes best and what sounds best. In the same way, there is also no one correct set of obligations and values, just different ideas of what is right and wrong, good and evil. People born and raised in different times, different cultures, and different parts of the world have different moral beliefs. None of these is any better than any other. They are just different. So what people believe is right is right for them, though it may not be right for me, and vice versa. No one set of moral beliefs is "the" correct one, any more than a certain food or song is "the" best one.

Our first assumption, sometimes called **ethical absolutism,** vigorously denies the claims of ethical relativism. Ethical absolutism claims that there are moral "absolutes," that is, moral ideals that are valid for all peoples at all times. It claims that the goal of normative ethics, to find "the" correct set of obligations and values, is a legitimate one. Regardless of the fact that people have different moral beliefs, there is, nevertheless, a correct set of beliefs. Just as there is a correct chemistry, or physics, or mathematics—despite what people may believe—so too, there are correct moral beliefs—despite the different beliefs held by people of various cultures. The correct normative theory of obligation tells us what are the correct moral principles and rules that we ought to follow; the correct normative theory of value tell us which things we should strive for in life. That these are "correct" means that everyone ought to accept them, regardless of the time, or the place, or the circumstances of their lives.

Cultural Relativism

Defenders of ethical relativism often support their claims by appealing to a view called cultural relativism. **Cultural relativism** makes a factual claim. Briefly put, it claims that moral beliefs do differ from culture to culture. This surely seems to be true, at least at first glance. Moral diversity is a fact of life on this planet. It shows itself in the various moral belief systems held by different cultures and is especially evident within diverse societies, such as that of the United States. Ethical relativism, however, makes quite a stronger claim than does cultural relativism. It claims that each of these differing belief systems is correct. If in my culture, killing people under certain circumstances is accepted as the morally proper action, then it is morally correct, regardless of how things may be in your culture.

Ethical absolutism, however, claims that only one set of moral beliefs is correct. Beliefs that differ from it are simply incorrect. Perhaps such differing beliefs represent those of a less-educated culture, or those who are seriously misinformed about facts. The belief of some people that enslaving others is morally permissible, for example, may be based on incorrect conceptions of the humanity of slaves. Just as many who previously accepted slavery as legitimate have come to see it as an evil, so will others, once they understand that slaves are persons. For an ethical absolutist, cultural relativism will disappear with proper education. Ethical relativism will then disappear as well and with it will come the acceptance of *the* correct moral perspective. Just as science has replaced superstition, so too will the correct ethical theory replace more misinformed moral beliefs.

Kant's theory of obligation is one of the best examples of ethical absolutism. It says that any moral maxim that conforms to the categorical imperative is universally binding on all moral agents. It applies to all people because it is based on reason, something that does not vary from time to time, place to place, and culture to culture. In a similar way, Aristotle's virtue theory claims that human well-being is the goal of life, a goal that ought to be shared by all. Human beings all have the same human nature. They differ in their moral values only because they do not understand what is truly good for them, what allows us to live in accordance with this nature. If they understood that their true good lay in the fulfillment of their rational selves and not in pleasure, fame, fortune, power, and the like, they would all come to agree on the nature of the virtues.

Many sociologists and anthropologists who study various cultures are ethical relativists. Most philosophers, on the other hand, champion the possibility of normative ethics. Who is right? Are moral beliefs like scientific beliefs, and therefore correct or incorrect? Or are they more like judgments of taste, just different from each other, but with no one group of them any more "correct" than any other?

The Argument for Ethical Relativism

Ethical relativism is usually defended, as we have suggested, by appealing to cultural relativism. Such an argument, reduced to its essentials, looks like this:

> 1. If moral beliefs differ from culture to culture, then there is no one correct set of moral beliefs.
>
> 2. Moral beliefs do differ from culture to culture.

Therefore, 3. There is no one correct set of moral beliefs.

Premise (2) is simply cultural relativism, whereas the conclusion is a statement of ethical relativism. Let us evaluate how well cultural relativism supports ethical relativism by examining the truth of the premises. First, some have pointed out that cultural variation is not as widespread as it first appears. Granted, there are many different ideas of right and wrong, but there are also many commonly shared moral beliefs as well. No group of people would survive intact for very long unless they prohibited murder, rape, lying, breaking promises, stealing, and the like. In addition, while most cultures share rules prohibiting these practices, they also share fundamental moral principles. For example, some form of the principle "Do good, and avoid evil" is followed by all cultures. Their very survival depends upon it.[1]

The differences between cultures seems to lie in some rules that not all possess. Very often, however, different rules exist because various cultures have different factual beliefs. In some cultures, women may be forced to endure involuntary circumcision, for example. They are forced to do this because of the belief that such a procedure will remove sexual pleasure and thus make them more faithful spouses and more effective mothers. Both results will strengthen the unity of the society of which they are members, and thus the act is good for them in the long run. Another example is that children may kill their relatively youthful parents in some societies because of two beliefs. First, they may believe that their parents will survive for all eternity in a life after this one, and second, they may believe that their parents will be preserved in the condition they were when they died. From the perspective of the children, they are doing their parents a kindness.

Premise (2) may be false, then, since what varies from culture to culture has more to do with beliefs about factual matters, about things other than morality. For the most part, similar moral principles are held across cultures. What differs from one group to another is the manner in which such principles are applied. Because different groups have different histories, different religious beliefs, and different circumstances in which they must survive, they have developed different conceptions of what is a true harm and what is a true benefit for them. This does not mean that they have different moral principles, however.

Even if premise (2) is true, however, this does not mean that ethical relativism is correct. That is, even if cultural relativism is correct in its claim that basic moral principles vary from culture to culture, this does not prove (3). The reason is that premise (1) may be false. Premise (1) says, in effect, that if a group *believes* that a certain moral practice is correct, then it *is* correct for them. What is right is what someone believes is right; what is good is what someone believes is good.

To see the problems of holding (1), note that what it claims may be interpreted to include beliefs that differ from individual to individual *within* a group as well as beliefs that differ *between* groups. On this reading, (1) claims that what is right for me may not be right for you, and vice versa. If I believe that abortion is immoral, then it is immoral for me. If you believe the reverse, then abortion is right for you. No one should criticize others for their moral beliefs, no matter how strongly you disagree with them. Everyone has a right to hold the moral beliefs with which he or she is comfortable. Just as the beliefs of everyone about the foods and music they enjoy should not be criticized by others, what they believe about what is right and wrong, good and evil, is their own business. They are not wrong if they hold moral beliefs that are different from yours; they are just different. If someone killed your best friend or stole your money and thought that he was doing the right thing, would you agree that it was right for him to perform such actions?

It is important to note that the rejection of ethical relativism does not mean that the moral beliefs of all cultures are to be judged by your own. Your own group may contain immoral rules and values and must continually undergo moral criticism for there to be moral progress. The basis of such criticism, and the moral progress that it promotes, is how well the moral rules and values of a society conform to basic principles of right and wrong, good and evil. These principles, which we use to justify our particular moral beliefs, are what are universal. Though their application may vary according to time, place, and circumstance, they remain the same for all. This is what normative ethics searches for: the ideals that ought to guide the moral beliefs of all groups.

Consequentialism

A helpful strategy is to divide theories of obligation into two main groups—those that are consequentialist theories and those that are not. We will give names to theories in the second category later, but for now we will begin with various versions of consequentialism. The different consequentialist theories of obligation all have one property in common: they determine the rightness or wrongness of actions exclusively by reference to their consequences. They would all accept the following statement: "An action is right if it leads to a greater balance of good over evil consequences; it is wrong if it leads to a greater balance of evil over good." From here on, however, the various versions of consequentialism diverge.

One main area of difference between them concerns their various theories of value. For example, some consequentialists are hedonists whereas others believe that God is the only intrinsic value, and still others believe something else. It makes a great deal of difference to your ethical outlook, as you might imagine, whether you are trying to promote pleasure and the avoidance of pain by your actions or achieve a close relationship with God. Another way in which consequentialists differ is in what they consider to be the proper scope of the consequences that must be taken into account. Some say what is important are the consequences of my actions on myself alone; others require a broader concern. With this as an introduction, let us consider our first theory of obligation—ethical egoism.

Ethical Egoism

Ethical egoism is the view that what is right is what is good for me. This is the moral principle that it claims to be the best for all of us to follow. This is its definition of right action: "Do what's good for yourself." The way to use this principle in practice is for the moral decision maker to consider the consequences that the action in question will have on himself. Then he is to consider the consequences that alternative actions will have—again only on himself. The action that produces the most good or the fewest evil consequences for him is the morally right action for him to perform. This is clearly an extreme view of ethics, and several points of clarification are in order for us to grasp its full meaning.

First, since this is a *consequentialist* theory, what makes an action right is solely the consequences of the action. If it produces good outcomes, then it is right. Because moral choices are sometimes choices between two evils, we say that the right thing to do is whatever action produces more good or less evil than its alternatives. Even more accurately, since some actions produce both good and evil consequences, the right thing to do is to perform the action that produces a higher ratio of good over evil than its alternatives.

Second, only the consequences "for me" matter to an ethical egoist. It is not that an ethical egoist tries to harm others by her actions, it is just that she is indifferent to how they affect others. This is why it is called ethical *egoism*, because such a theory is concerned only with the self-interest of the moral agent herself. The other types of consequentialist theories that we will examine later will all require that we consider the consequences of our actions on others, as well as ourselves, in determining right from wrong. Such theories are versions of *altruism*, the view that we are required to do good for others as well as ourselves. Ethical egoism, on the other hand, is thought of as a theory of selfishness. It denies that we have any obligations to others.

Third, ethical egoism is presented as a theory that everyone ought to adopt. It claims that everyone ought to act only in his own self-interest. As such, it presents us with a *universal moral principle*, one that is to be used by everyone any time he makes a moral decision. In addition, it is important to point out that ethical egoism does not claim simply that we *do* sometimes act selfishly, but rather makes the much stronger moral claim that we *ought to* act selfishly, that we are obliged to do so, that to act for others at our own expense would be immoral or wrong.

Fourth, there are many ways to be an ethical egoist, depending on which *value theory* is incorporated into your definition of right action. A life of selfishness is a life of pursuing what you have identified as the intrinsically valuable, the good that will lead to your happiness. Because many things appear to be intrinsically valuable, there are many ways to be an ethical egoist. An ethical egoist could lead a life of pursuing pleasure for himself, for example, or a close relationship with God, or knowledge, or power, and so on.

Fifth, notice that no mention is made of rules by ethical egoism. For an ethical egoist, it is not true that it is wrong to lie, to kill, to steal, and to break promises. Doing the right thing is not a matter of following rules but of calculating for each situation what the outcomes for me of competing actions are likely to be. To determine the rightness or wrongness of any action, I simply use my basic principle, "Do what's good for me," and calculate the outcomes of the available alternative actions. If I see some money in your handbag, for example, it is by no means wrong for me to take it. It may be that it usually is wrong to do so, because most of the time it will not be in my interest. After all, I might get caught and that would produce more evil than good for me. If I were fairly certain that I could get away with it, however, it would be in my interest to take the money. In fact, I would be obliged to do so. If I am an ethical egoist, whenever it is in my interest to do so, it is right for me to break any commonly accepted moral law. Any action is acceptable if it leads to good results for me.

Exercise A

A case study in ethics is simply a description of a particular situation that calls for a moral decision. To better understand the theory of ethical egoism, it will be helpful for you to solve the following case study as an ethical egoist would. Examine all the factors in the following case that you think are relevant, then decide what is the right thing to do as an ethical egoist would. For this exercise, take the perspective of the mother.

Case Study

Mrs. Lucas has just been informed that her newborn baby has a serious birth defect. The infant suffers from Down's syndrome, a condition that produces mental retardation with various levels of severity. Some children go on to live very happy lives and bring much joy to their parents. If you have ever watched a Special Olympics event, you have seen how much such children mean to their families. For others, however, the condition is less kind. They are severely retarded and their lives are lived on a very minimal level. Baby Lucas has an additional complicating factor, a blocked esophagus. This condition may be corrected surgically. Left untreated, the child will not be able to ingest food or liquids orally. As a result, the infant will die within a couple of weeks. The doctor explains that the surgery is relatively simple and risk-free, and she asks the parents for their consent to the surgery.

The father is devastated. He and his wife are young and this is their first child. He is a college professor. Between day care and his flexible schedule, he and his wife planned to raise the child in such a way as to allow her to continue with her career plans. The mother has just graduated from law school three years earlier, joined a prestigious law firm, and could be a partner in the firm within five years if she worked at it. Though somewhere deep down the father feels that surgery is the right thing to do, he does not want to raise such a child. He is afraid that his life will be spent entirely on his work and caring for this child. His way of handling the problem is to defer the decision to his wife.

In speaking with the parents, the doctor points out that there is some evidence that the child will be more retarded than the average Down's child, though she cannot be certain of this. The mother is torn. On the one hand she, too, feels that it is wrong to let the child die. This child, however, would require much more of her time to raise than would a healthy child. She does not want this child, but she also wants to do what is right. The doctor asks again, will the parents consent to the surgery. What should the mother say? Be sure to give reasons for your answer.

Evaluating Ethical Egoism

Given this general description of ethical egoism, it is now time to evaluate how well it meets our three criteria of an acceptable theory. At first glance, it appears to do very poorly indeed. The first problem with ethical egoism is that it is not **simple** to use. For ethical egoism, no action is right or wrong in itself; it is only right or wrong because of its outcomes. For example, the results of lying may be good sometimes, bad at other times. If I can get away with a lie and it brings me great benefits, then I am obliged to lie according to ethical egoism. To determine right from wrong, each time I am in a moral situation I must calculate all the goods and evils that may befall me for each alternative course of action that is possible. The problem is, if we really were required to perform all the necessary calculations every time we made a moral decision, we would spend most of each day engaged in moral reasoning. At the very least, it would be very difficult to determine right from wrong.

If I follow the method of ethical egoism, sometimes it would be more than difficult to know what is right or wrong; it would be impossible. This is because it is sometimes impossible to know what the consequences of my actions will be. Sometimes the consequences of my actions continue well into the future. A woman may decide not to have an abortion, for example. How does she know whether she has done the right thing? It is the right thing to do if it enhances her good or diminishes evil for her. But there is a lifetime of consequences that lie beyond her knowledge, consequences that she needs to know if she is to decide correctly. How will having the child or not having it affect her life—will it be for good or evil? If she cannot know these consequences, then she cannot know whether she has done the right thing.

Even if I say that ethical egoism requires only that I consider what I *think* will happen as a result of my actions, not what actually does happen, it still faces major problems. For one, it violates the criterion of **universality**. It does not explain all the facts of our moral lives. In determining right from wrong we often consider the effects of our actions on others. We often act altruistically, and doing so seems to be an essential part of morality. So ethical egoism, concerned as it is only for the well-being of the acting individual, does not explain why we often consider altruistic actions to be morally right actions. In short, the objection is that ethical egoism as a theory of selfishness ignores what most of us think of as the heart of morality—acting for the well-being of others.

If ethical egoism has trouble meeting the criteria of simplicity and universality, it has even more difficulty with **consistency,** especially external consistency. Ethical egoism is inconsistent with many of our deeply held moral beliefs. Remember, ethical egoism is not simply a description of how people *do* behave. Whereas it may be true that many of us often behave selfishly, with little regard for others, it surely is not true that we believe the stronger claim of ethical egoism—that we *ought to* behave selfishly, that we are obliged to ignore the interests of others and consider only our own, that altruistic actions at our own expense are immoral. If we are obliged to do anything that we believe will increase our good or decrease evil for ourselves, then any actions—including lying, stealing, cheating, and even killing—are permitted whenever they result in such an outcome.

The ethical egoist will say that it may not be in our interest, most of the time, to perform such actions. After all, they are prohibited by law and by the prevailing moral rules of society. We might get caught and be punished or we might feel guilty about what we have done, as most of us have been raised to believe that such rules are binding. Because breaking customary moral rules would usually not be worth enduring the consequences, the actual behavior of an ethical egoist may differ little from one who holds an altruistic theory of right and wrong. However, if you were really true to the egoistic principle, then whenever you knew that you would not get caught or feel guilty, or otherwise suffer negative consequences—whenever you could get away with something that most people believe to be wrong—you would not only be permitted but obliged to do it. Not to lie, steal, cheat, and so on under such circumstances would be immoral. Clearly, if we are looking for the moral principle that we actually do use to guide our decision making, we will not find it in ethical egoism.

Psychological Egoism

Some defenders of ethical egoism try to rescue it from its critics by appealing to psychological egoism. **Psychological egoism** is the view that we humans are all selfish by nature, that everything we do is done for ourselves, that our sole motive for acting is always and only self-interest. Psychological egoism is a factual claim, a claim about what motivates behavior. It says that I never act for the well-being of anyone else, that it is not possible for me to do so. I can only act in my own self-interest. If psychological egoism is true, the argument goes, if I *can* only act selfishly, then ethical egoism, the view that I am *obliged* to act only in my own interest, must be true. If psychological egoism is true, then ethical egoism is the only ethical theory that makes any sense. In particular, no altruistic theory makes any sense at all. After all, what sense does it make to say that someone is *obliged* to act for the interest of others if he or she cannot do so?

At first glance the claims of psychological egoism appear to have no merit. We do things for others all the time, do we not? Do we not sometimes sacrifice our own self-interest for family and friends, for example? Does this not refute the claim that we are *always* selfish, that we *cannot* act altruistically? The psychological egoist says that such behavior may appear to be in the interest of others, but it is really performed for our own good. When we spend our last few dollars on a gift for a friend, for example, and thus appear to be doing something for another, we get a lot out of it ourselves. For example, it makes us feel good to see our friend happy with her gift. Besides, it was her birthday, and not to give her a gift would make us feel guilty, cheap, and otherwise unhappy with ourselves. Giving the gift also helps to keep our friendship strong, and friends do things for us in return. Besides, not to have friends, to be cut off from others, is too painful to bear.

So we can see that the gift-giving, which at first glance appears to be motivated by altruistic concerns, is really motivated by selfishness, or self-interest. Giving my friend a gift is simply the means that I use to achieve my own satisfaction. Similar remarks may be made for other forms of "apparent" altruism as well. In the end, because we get some satisfaction by doing things for others, we are really acting for ourselves—to achieve that satisfaction. Like most animals, we usually act in our own interest. The bulk of what we do is done for ourselves. When we are hungry, we eat; thirsty, we drink; tired, we sleep. We act in accordance with our own desires most of the time. The psychological egoist says that even when we appear to do things for others, especially when doing so seems to go against our interest, seems to involve a sacrifice on our part, we are still really acting only for ourselves.

Problems with Psychological Egoism

The attractiveness of psychological egoism arises from our knowledge, deep in our hearts, that we often enjoy doing things for others. It does lead to satisfaction for most of us, especially if things work out as planned. Where psychological egoism errs, however, is in confusing the *motive* for acting with the *results* of acting successfully. Because I get satisfaction from taking my young nephew to the ball game, for example, does not mean that my motive for going to the game is my own satisfaction. Suppose he has a terrible time, suppose he is miserable the whole day, and I feel just awful about taking him? Does that mean I took him so that I would feel awful? I hardly think so.

In both cases, whether the day was successful or not, my motive was to make him happy. If I succeed in doing so, then I am satisfied; if not, I am not. We are built by nature in such a way that we have a sense of satisfaction whenever our actions turn out as we planned. This is true for actions that are motivated by self-interest, by altruistic reasons alone, or by mixed motives. When a tired mother gets up at two in the morning to feed her crying infant, is that selfish? It may make her feel good to have done so, or it may allow her to avoid the inevitable feelings of guilt that would result from her ignoring her infant's cries. While it is true that she does get something out of it, still, she did it for the child. Many of our actions have altruistic motives. We do many things for the sake of others. That we feel good when we do things successfully for others may be the result of our action, but it is not its motive. Psychological egoism is simply false. If it is false, the last hope for rescuing ethical egoism falls with it.

The Role of Selfishness in Ethics

If selfishness, or self-interest, is not a basic moral principle (ethical egoism), and if it is not our exclusive motive for behavior (psychological egoism), it nevertheless plays a fundamental role in morality. It may be worth our while to take a moment here to examine just what that role might be. My claim is that self-interest is not the answer to the question: *What does it mean to be moral?* Rather, it is the answer to the question: *Why should we be moral?* It is not a moral principle, but it is the reason any of us believe that we should act morally at all. It says that we should be moral because it is good for us. It is in our long-range interest to relinquish our desires to lie, cheat, steal, kill, and otherwise do whatever we want to.

To see how selfishness lies at the root of morality we must ask ourselves the following question: Why is it in our interest to sometimes give up some of our interests, which is what morality requires? It is in our interest to be moral because such restraint is necessary for an orderly social existence. What would society be like if there were no rules against lying, stealing, breaking promises, and killing each other? Life would be hell. Life and limb, property and security, trust and peace would be in constant peril. If we all did what we wanted to do, regardless of the consequences to others, then most of our lives would not be worth living. So it is in our interest to live in a society that requires us to refrain from doing what we want to whenever such actions would harm others. It is much better for us, in the long run, to live among people who follow moral rules than with those who do not. Many more of our desires can be satisfied in such a world than in a world of constant strife and fear.

In addition to fostering a good society, living a morally good life also promotes personal happiness. Aristotle defines morality as promoting well-being, for example, and Kant sees moral behavior as the key to happiness. Utilitarianism defines moral behavior as that which leads to happiness. But while it may be true in general that acting in accordance with moral rules may be beneficial for ourselves, and while we can all agree that morality is necessary for a stable social order, on some occasions it is not easy to see that acting morally is in our own personal interest. One little lie, one little theft, one little bit of cheating—surely these will not bring down society. And sometimes such actions can be very beneficial to you. Then again, you may get caught or you may feel guilty. The action will not be worth doing in that case. But what about a situation when you will not get caught, when you will not feel guilty, when your action will not threaten the social order, and when your action will bring you much gain? Why should you refrain from doing something immoral then?

To answer this question let us pose a hypothetical example: Why should I be moral when not doing so does not threaten society and when it does not threaten my personal happiness? As long as most people keep their moral obligations most of the time, society will not collapse into a state of chaos. As long as I am morally good most of the time, my life will also be on the right track. Sometimes, when neither society nor personal happiness is threatened, it may be in my interest to do immoral things. For example, suppose I am poor and spend most of my time scraping together just enough resources to meet my family's basic needs.

Suppose further that I come upon an opportunity to make a lot of money if I do something immoral, if I lie about a back injury that I supposedly received on my minimum wage job, for example. I hire a seedy lawyer and doctor who go along with the scam, and I firmly believe that I will not get caught by others or feel guilty about my lie.

Suppose that the fake back injury leads to a very generous cash settlement from my very wealthy employer. With this money I can send my children to fine schools, open a business of my own, and have much more time and money to pursue what Aristotle and Mill think of as the good life. Society will not crumble because my act will look like the act of a righteous man, and thus it will not inspire others to do likewise. My life will not crumble, I will not be off on a life of moral ruin, because I have resolved never to do anything immoral ever again. In fact, if anything I will be more moral. So is it not in my interest to lie in this one case? Is it not good for me?

There are at least three ways to answer this question. One is to deny that you will get away with the action. Either someone will find you out, or you will end up feeling guilty, and in either case the deception will not have been worth the consequence. This answer, however, flies in the face of our experience. How many people do you know who have broken the rules and seem the happier for it? We do not admire them, but we do know that there are many who "get away with it."

Another way to answer the question is to say that it is always in your interest to be moral, even if you could achieve some great personal gain by breaking moral rules. Plato answers this way, as does Kant. For Plato, being immoral disrupts the "harmony" of the soul by allowing desire to conquer reason. In such harmony lies our true well-being, so it always goes against our true interest to be immoral, whatever the gain. Kant would agree, citing a good moral character as more valuable than any material riches. But could not a little immorality, such as the one-time lie mentioned above, even *enhance* the moral life? If it frees us up from misery and allows us to pursue the good life more fully, then it appears to be even morally good for us to perform this immoral action.

The third way to answer is to agree that it is in your interest to be immoral whenever it does not contribute to the break down of society and whenever you will not get caught. To accept this answer is to recognize selfishness as the root of morality, as the reason we are moral in the first place. We are moral because it is (usually) good for us. We can argue about how realistic are examples such as the one discussed above. We may disagree about its requirements—that it will not be harmful for society or the individual. We may think that someone who lies once when he is in a jam is likely to do so again, and that such behavior, if discovered, would have serious negative effects on society, and so on. But *if* the conditions required by our example are met, then it clearly shows the fundamental role that selfishness plays in shoring up the altruistic practices of morality. In showing that we would not do what is morally right if it were not in our interest to do so, it also shows that when we act morally it is because we see that it is in our interest to do so. It is important to recognize this and to teach the next generation that they ought to act morally because it is good for them as well as for the rest of us.

Utilitarianism

Utilitarianism is like ethical egoism insofar as it defines the right in terms of the good. It claims that an action is right if it produces a greater ratio of good over evil than do its alternatives. Where it differs from ethical egoism is in the scope of those who must be considered when calculating these consequences. The most famous versions of utilitarianism, those first introduced by Jeremy Bentham (1748–1832) and John Stuart Mill (1806–1873)[2], claim that the consequences that occur for *everyone* affected by the action must be considered. For them, the right thing to do is what produces "the greatest good (or least evil) for the most people." They called this central moral principle the **principle of utility.**

Act Utilitarianism

As a consequentialist theory, utilitarianism may take the form of either act utilitarianism or rule utilitarianism. **Act utilitarianism,** as introduced by Jeremy Bentham, does not consider ethics to be a matter of following rules. As with the ethical egoist, determining right from wrong is not simply a matter of conforming behavior to rules because there are no hard and fast rules that one always has to follow. There are no such rules because sometimes following a rule does not lead to the greatest good or the least evil. There are too many exceptions for rules to be good guides to correct behavior. Instead, each situation should be seen as different from all those that went before it. Because the circumstances are always different, every act of lying, for example, is different from every other. This way of thinking about moral problems is sometimes called **situation ethics.** For situation ethics, of which act utilitarianism is one form and ethical egoism another, there are not three levels to a theory of obligation, but only two. There is only the basic principle, "the greatest good for the greatest number," in the case of the act utilitarian, and the individual "act" or action to which it is applied.

Bentham was a hedonist, so for him, good is pleasure and evil is pain. To figure out right from wrong, to reason morally, is to weigh the amount of pleasure and pain that an action will produce and compare it to the pleasure and pain produced by its alternatives. For Bentham, the source of the pleasure and what type of pleasure it is does not matter in determining right from wrong—only the amount is important. So the principle of utility tells us that the right thing to do is to perform those actions that will "maximize pleasure, and minimize pain." Bentham makes clear that what is to be weighed are the pleasures and pains that the action actually produces, not simply those that we believe it will produce. Because of this conviction, he provides a method for determining such consequences, a method that some have called the **hedonic calculus.**

The hedonic calculus was very explicit in discussing the elements that enter into an analysis of the consequences of our actions. In explaining how to apply the principle of utility to concrete actions, Bentham outlined a series of steps that must be considered in order to weigh the pleasure and pain that our actions will produce. If these steps are followed correctly, then everyone ought to be able to calculate the same outcomes, just as everyone who uses the same scale should come up with the same weight for a specific physical object. Since outcomes are the only thing that matter in determining right from wrong, Bentham believed that using his principle and following his instructions for applying it should produce agreement among all in moral matters.

For Bentham, to determine in advance the amount of pleasure or pain that an act will produce we must consider the following properties of the consequences of our actions:

1. *intensity*—how strong the pleasure or pain will be

2. *duration*—how long it will last

3. *certainty*—how certain we are that pleasure or pain will follow

4. *propinquity*—how soon it will occur

5. *fecundity*—whether it will lead to more pleasure or pain

6. *purity*—whether it will lead to pleasure or pain of the same type

7. *extent*—the number of those affected

When a person is trying to figure out right from wrong, she should weigh these hedonic consequences of all her choices for all those affected, and then choose the action that produces the greatest balance of pleasure over pain for all.

Reasoning similar to Bentham's model exists today whenever anyone performs a cost-benefit analysis, whenever he weighs the pros and cons of a course of action. Politicians reason this way, for example, when they want to be sensitive to the wishes of their constituents. They may commission a "preference poll" to see what course of action their voters wish them to back. What the majority of their voters want is the course of action they will choose, because they believe it will produce the greatest good for the greatest number of people. Health care analysts also reason this way whenever they choose to fund one research program instead of another. The government may wish to spend more money on cancer research than research on cystic fibrosis, for example, because the money spent on cancer research (cost) will produce more lives saved (benefits) than that spent on cystic fibrosis research. Bentham's reasoning about right and wrong is a form of cost-benefit analysis, in which the costs are pains and the benefits are pleasures.

Rule Utilitarianism

John Stuart Mill also accepts the principle of utility, but he holds quite a different view from Bentham about how to apply it to concrete cases. Mill has three levels in his theory of obligation. There are actions, the rules that explain why actions are right or wrong, and the principle that explains why the rules that we have are the ones that we ought to follow. For Mill, doing the right thing means following rules. Which rules? Those that, if followed, will lead to greater pleasure and less pain than their alternatives.

So for Mill, the principle of utility gets applied to rules, not to particular actions. We do not have to calculate for each potential act of lying, for example, whether it will produce a greater balance of pleasure over pain than not lying in that particular situation. Imagine how much time it would take to run through Bentham's seven steps each time we had to decide if a simple lie was right or wrong. Instead, lying is wrong, plain and simply. Moreover, lying is always wrong. For Mill, a greater overall good will follow if we always tell the truth, always keep our promises, and so on, even if sometimes doing so leads to less good than breaking the rule. Clearly, Mill would benefit from our "conflict of rules" insight, mentioned previously, an insight that would allow him to override a particular rule whenever following another rule of higher priority would result in greater good. This is a change in Mill that we will introduce later.

The important point for now, however, is that rules are essential to ethics for the rule utilitarian, and thus his theory benefits from being much simpler to use. Another benefit of a rule-centered theory of obligation is that it explains how we teach our children right from wrong. What morality would Bentham teach the next generation—to calculate using the principle of utility as their guide? This is hardly what we teach our children when we teach them right from wrong. We teach them not to lie, not to steal, to be kind, to be fair, and so on. We teach them rules, not a method of reasoning. We also teach them that when a rule seems not to hold, it is because there is a conflict between competing rules, and in these situations the rule with higher priority must be followed. We do not follow Bentham's advice and tell them that rules cannot be relied upon to guide moral actions. Instead, we follow Mill in asserting that determining right from wrong is a matter of following those rules that promote the greatest good for the greatest number.

One way to see how the principle of utility might be applied directly to rules is to consider how new moral rules are introduced to society. Very typically, when we debate what a new rule of society should be (think of physician-assisted suicide and cloning human beings), we consider the harms and benefits of following various rules. If we allow physician-assisted suicide, for example, it will *benefit* suffering, terminally ill patients. On the other hand, it may have social *harms*, such as starting us down the slippery slope to killing incompetent patients and putting pressure on patients to end their lives prematurely. As to cloning humans, we all have visions of the brave new world it may lead to, with all of its potential harms. We also may have some idea of how it may be a benefit to some prospective parents who, for example, want a child who is biologically their own but might pass on a genetic defect of one of them if they proceeded to have a child in the natural way. The point is this. For Mill, correct rules are introduced by using the principle of utility, by considering the harms and benefits of following the rule. Once such a rule is justified as leading to a greater balance of good over evil, doing the right thing amounts to conforming your behavior to such a rule.

In addition to differing from Bentham by including rules in his theory of obligation, Mill also has a different theory of value. Though Mill uses the same terms—pleasure and pain—to refer to good and evil as does Bentham, he means something quite different by these terms. Mill believes that only pleasure is intrinsically valuable, but he values not so much the amount of pleasure our actions produce, its *quantity*, as he values the kind of pleasure that results, its *quality*. "How much" pleasure is not as important to Mill as "what kind" of pleasure it is.

A life with only bodily pleasures is not as good as one containing pleasures of the mind and spirit. The pleasure that one gets from acquiring love, having knowledge, being morally good, securing freedom, knowing God, and so on makes life much more worth living than a life that wallows in the mire of bodily pleasures alone. In claiming that the good life should include the pleasures derived from all of these activities, Mill presents us, in effect, with a pluralistic theory of value.

Exercise B

Using the same case study described in Exercise A, decide on the right thing to do first from the perspective of the act utilitarian, and then from the perspective of a rule utilitarian. This time you need not take the perspective of the mother. Instead, you are to be an impartial observer. What would the act and rule utilitarian say is the right thing to do? Be sure to give reasons for your answer.

Evaluating Utilitarianism

Act utilitarianism and rule utilitarianism have shared strengths and weaknesses, as well as those that are unique to each. One of the greatest strengths of utilitarianism lies in its appeal to the *consequences* of our actions as the primary way to determine their moral rightness or wrongness. Any theory of obligation that ignores consequences altogether will not be universal, as it denies one of the central elements of moral reasoning. We all consider consequences in solving moral problems, whether it is the consequences of individual actions or those of following one rule or another.

Another strength of utilitarianism lies with its *altruism*. By including the interests of others in calculating the consequences of our actions, the utilitarian presents us with a theory of obligation that is much more externally consistent with our moral experience than ethical egoism. After all, we usually do consider others when we act morally, even sometimes at the expense of our own interests. In fact, some consider this the very heart of morality—that you put your duty to others before your own personal gain.

One of the major weaknesses shared by both act utilitarianism and rule utilitarianism is their insistence that we have a *general* obligation to do good for others. It may at first seem harsh to say this, but such a general obligation to promote the welfare of *all* persons is **inconsistent** with our ordinary moral experience. While surely we do have obligations to do good for others, it is only for those with whom we have special moral relationships, such as our families, our students, our patients, and our clients. Although we have duties toward such individuals, we have no duty to do good for just "any and all" others. All that we are obliged to do in general is not to harm others. You may be mean or stingy or hard-hearted not to help those with whom you have no special moral relationships, especially if they are in great need, and especially when doing so is easy enough for you. However, unless you are in a position of moral responsibility toward a person, not to help her is surely not immoral. You have done something that is immoral if you do not feed *your* children; you have not, however, done something immoral if you do not feed the children of the world. You may be a better person for doing so, but you are not an immoral person if you do not do so.

Perhaps on this small planet we should begin to include all of our fellow citizens, and even all of humankind as belonging to the class of those for whom we are *obliged* to do good. This claim will lie at the heart of the moral problem discussed in Chapter 5 of Part 2, and is certainly what many religions encourage us to do—to love our fellow human beings and not simply to refrain from harming them. Maybe we should also include members of other species as well, an issue that is discussed in Chapter 6 of Part 2. As it stands now, however, our moral ideals locate loving our fellow human beings in general as what philosophers call a **supererogatory** act, an act that we may voluntarily accept or not. It is noble and worthwhile to live a life of dedication to the needs of others; such a life is the life of heroes and saints. It is kindhearted and charitable to give away some of your resources to help others, even others who are strangers to you. These sorts of actions ought to be promoted in any moral education, since they often represent the very highest forms of our love for others. They are not, however, a requirement of morality.

Although helping others is kind and compassionate, doing so is not a moral duty—except for those with whom we have special moral relationships. But we are not required to do good for *all* people. Imagine how much your life would change if you thought of yourself as obliged to help all others on the planet who are in need. You would be obliged to give up most of what you have, right down to the barest of resources required to meet your own basic needs. This certainly would be a noble act, but surely it is not a moral obligation.

The most serious objection to utilitarianism in general is that it is not **universal.** The most important fact of our moral lives that it leaves unexplained is *justice.* Act utilitarianism claims that morally right actions are those that result in the best consequences for yourself and all others affected by your action. It says nothing about what means are used to produce these good consequences. If we follow the utilitarian principle, it is possible to practice great acts of injustice and still do the right thing. It is possible to use people as a "means" to the good of others, something that most of us abhor. As long as it produces a greater balance of good over evil, any act is acceptable for the utilitarian. The results are all that matter, not the manner in which they were produced.

We consider slavery wrong, for example, even if it produces great economic benefits for the majority. We consider using prisoners, nursing home patients, and children as subjects in risky medical experiments as highly immoral—even if such experiments yield results that would benefit millions. Would you not be upset, for example, if you discovered that something as beneficial as the polio vaccine was developed by testing it on orphans, fifty of whom died as a result of overdoses? Or that an AIDS vaccine was developed by using elderly nursing home patients? So utilitarianism is not universal because it does not explain our condemnation of actions that produce good results through an immoral means. Another way to put this is to say that for the utilitarian, "the end justifies the means."

Rule utilitarianism suffers from the same "justice" objection as does act utilitarianism. Rules can be every bit as unjust as individual actions. A rule supporting slavery or gender preferences, for example, uses some for the good of others.

The same is true for any laws that discriminate among people on irrelevant grounds, such as their religion, national origin, or race. The lesson to be learned is that any acceptable moral theory will have to explain more than our obligation to do good and avoid evil; it will also have to explain why some actions that produce a greater balance of good over evil may be quite immoral.

In addition to the problems that it shares with rule utilitarianism, act utilitarianism has its own unique problems. First, the theory is not **simple** to use. Because it says that every moral action is known to be right or wrong only after calculating its consequences, then calculating the harms and benefits of our actions is essential for moral decision making. This calculation must be performed not simply for each type of action—lying, for example—but for each act of lying. For the act utilitarian, you never know if lying on a certain occasion is right or wrong until you calculate its consequences for good and evil.

Imagine how long it would take to do that for every simple moral act we perform each day. Even if we had a clear idea of what "good" and "evil" meant, and even if we had a good way to estimate the goods and evils that each possible action would produce, we would still end up spending most of our lives calculating the outcomes of our actions on ourselves and everyone else affected by them. We already mentioned this objection in discussing the weaknesses of ethical egoism. We will only add here that the problem of calculating the consequences of our actions on just ourselves is now multiplied many times by having to include everyone else who is affected by what we do. How impossible is that task?

Clearly rule utilitarianism is superior to both ethical egoism and act utilitarianism. With its focus on altruism, its insistence that rules be at the center of morality, and its pluralistic theory of value, it is much more universal, consistent, and simpler to use than its current rivals. However, it still suffers from the "justice" and "general obligation to do good for all" objections that it shares with act utilitarianism. Mill's rule utilitarianism will be an acceptable theory only if it can be suitably modified to avoid these weaknesses. Here are some suggestions for changes that would improve rule utilitarianism.

First, when we think of the principle of utility as obliging us to "avoid evil," we must understand this in a universal sense—that it is never right to deliberately harm anyone else. But we must not view the "do good" part of the principle in this manner. Instead, we must restrict it to include doing good only for those with whom we have special relationships, not everyone in general. We do not do something wrong when we do not produce all the conceivable goods that we might, for all the possible people who might benefit from our actions. After all, a morally good life could be one of withdrawal from society, a life of seclusion, a life in which good was done for no one else because it contained no special relationships with others.

There is also a second way in which the principle of utility needs to be modified, in order to avoid the "justice" objection. The principle of utility tells us that doing evil is wrong, so harming others is wrong. It also tells us to do good, but it does not tell us which means of producing good are allowable and which are not. It appears that we need another principle that forbids us from using some people to produce good consequences for others. The point for now, however, is that the outlines of an adequate moral theory of obligation are beginning to emerge. Such a theory will include rules and at least two principles: one that obliges us to do good and avoid evil, and another that obliges us not to use people in the process of producing such goods. Our next theory of obligation takes us one step further in this search.

Deontology

Some theories of obligation consider more than the consequences of an action in determining whether it is morally right. They may consider the person's intention, for example, or her motive, as well as the consequences. Or they may not consider consequences at all. For example, I may say that what is right is what God commands me to do, *whatever* the consequences. Such theories are nonconsequentialist theories because they consider more than the consequences of our actions to be important in determining their rightness or wrongness. Among such nonconsequentialist theories there are two sorts of interest to us here. One type is called virtue ethics, and will be discussed later. Another type is called **deontological** theories of obligation.

This rather awkward name derives from the Greek term *deon*, meaning 'duty'. Deontological theories come in "act" and "rule" versions, as did consequentialist theories, but we will talk only about rule deontological theories of obligation. Act versions of deontology suffer from the same sort of criticisms as their act utilitarian counterparts, especially the problem of not being simple to use. As with rule utilitarianism, rule deontological theories of obligation think of right and wrong as a matter of conforming your behavior to a set of moral rules that define your duties or obligations.

The main difference between deontological theories and rule utilitarianism is that for the deontologist, rules are not justified by appealing solely to the consequences of following them. They are justified by appealing either to something in addition to these consequences or something other than the consequences altogether. Perhaps the most famous version of rule deontological ethics is that of Immanuel Kant (1724–1804),[3] the famous German philosopher, whose influence in ethics is nearly impossible to exaggerate.

The Ethics of Kant

As utilitarianism contains an idea of both what is good and what is right, so Kantian ethics also contains an idea of what is good in itself and what sorts of actions are morally acceptable. However, Kant's concept of right action, as well as his idea of the ultimate good, differs sharply from those of the utilitarians. Kant's theories are complex and sometimes challenging to understand, but they so enrich our discussion that the effort is worth making.

The Good Will

For Kant, the highest good, that which alone is intrinsically valuable, is a moral good, not a nonmoral good as it was with utilitarians. Kant says that the only thing that is good in itself is what he calls a *good will*. The term 'will' is used by Kant to refer to our choices. To say that a person has a good will is to say that he or she makes good choices.

To make a good choice in moral matters is both to do what is right *and* to do so with the correct motive. To choose to perform a morally acceptable action because it might make you look good, for example, is to act from the wrong motive. The only correct motive for moral action is duty. One should do what is right simply because it is his or her duty to do so, simply because it is right. Doing what is right because it leads to something else—pleasure for example, or a good reputation, or avoidance of guilt—is to act from the wrong motive. Having a good will, then, should not be seen as a means to some other good. It is good in itself. It has intrinsic value. We sometimes express this by saying things like "virtue is its own reward."

Why does Kant say that having a good will, or as we might say today a good moral character, is the *only* thing that has intrinsic value? Kant's answer is that anything else can be turned to evil by an evil will. Think about the suggested list of nonmoral values discussed above. Each one of these can be turned into an evil by an evil will. Knowledge can be used for evil ends, for example. Pleasure can be gotten from an evil means, such as that acquired by a sadist torturing someone for sexual pleasure. Even a relationship with God can sometimes look like a pact with the devil. Many dastardly deeds have been performed in the name of God. Love may be twisted, freedom abused, and power corrupted by an evil will. Anything other than a good will that is thought of as good in itself, and anything thought of as merely extrinsically valuable, may be transformed to an evil by an evil will.

Acting from Duty

If having a good will, or being a morally good person, is the highest good, then it is important to know what this means. Kant says that someone who acts with a good will is someone who does the right thing for the right reason. By the right "reason" he means the right motive. To do the right thing is to follow acceptable moral rules. So to be a morally good person, a person of good moral character, you must follow correct moral rules and you must do so with the correct motive. A good moral person is someone who follows correct moral rules for only one reason—respect for the moral law itself. This respect amounts to what Kant calls *acting from duty*. Someone who acts with a good will does what is right because it is his or her duty to do so and for no other reason. I will have a good will only if my actions are motivated by my duty to do what is right, and by duty alone.

Obviously, if I do what is wrong I will not be a morally good person. But even if I do what is right, but do it with the wrong motive, I will not be a morally good person either. If I tell the truth, keep my promises, do not harm others, and so on, because I might get punished if I do not do so, or because I will be praised if I do, or because it will increase the amount of pleasure and freedom from pain in the world, then I have not acted from the proper moral motive. I have followed the rules, but I have done so for the wrong reasons.

Behind this notion of acting from duty lies a fundamental difference between utilitarianism and Kantian ethics. Acting from duty is radically different from acting to bring about consequences of one sort or another. For the utilitarian, following rules is good because it is a way to bring about intrinsic nonmoral goods, especially those of pleasure and freedom from pain. Morality is thus merely a means to some nonmoral goods, and not worthwhile in itself. Morality is a servant of desire. I follow rules because of the consequences, because doing so will satisfy my desire for what I think of as the ultimate good. Being moral is a way to achieve happiness for utilitarians, not something good in itself. It is merely a means to acquire what I and others want.

For Kant, however, acting morally is a good in itself. The goodness of morality is in acting rightly, not in the results of so acting, results that may or may not turn out as we had hoped. In following rules regardless of their consequences, simply because doing so is our duty, we are fostering what is finest and most noble in ourselves. We act in accordance with our *reason* when we act from duty, instead of acting from desire. In acting morally we act according to what we think, not what we feel. In doing what is right just because it is right, and not because it will get us something that we desire beyond acting rightly, we are not blown about by our desires. Instead, it is we who control our desires, not they us. In this way we freely govern ourselves by our reason, the nobler part of ourselves. In so doing we honor what is most human in us, that which is the source of our freedom and dignity. In the end, "acting morally" for Kant will turn out to mean "acting rationally," as we will soon see.

Kant's Theory of Obligation

Having seen something of Kant's value theory, let us turn now to his theory of obligation. If being a good person requires us to do what is right from a sense of duty, the question now is, How do we determine what is right? How do we tell which rules we ought to follow? Our duties cannot consist simply in following rules that promote pleasure and the avoidance of pain, as the utilitarians claim, since that would make right action depend upon consequences, on how well they satisfied our desires. So Kant cannot use the principle of utility as his guide.

Instead, the rules that we ought to follow for Kant are those that are right or wrong in themselves. Their rightness or wrongness is not determined by the outcomes of following them but by some property intrinsic to the type of action to which they refer. Lying is wrong, for example, not because it generally leads to more pain than pleasure, but because there is something about lying itself, regardless of its consequences, that makes it wrong. The same goes for breaking promises, killing, stealing, and the like. To help us discover what this intrinsic property might be, and thus what list of moral rules we ought to follow, Kant gives us a principle as our guide, a principle that he calls the categorical imperative.

The Categorical Imperative

So far we know what we ought to strive for in life—a good will, being a morally good person. We also know that a good will or a morally good person is one that chooses to follow morally correct rules out of respect for the moral law itself— simply because it is our duty to follow such rules, and not because of any consequences that may or may not follow from doing so. Kant calls these rules that describe our duties **maxims.** What we do not know yet is how to determine which maxims to follow. Kant's answer is to follow those rules allowed by the **categorical imperative.** As the principle of utility guides decisions about which rules to follow for utilitarians, the categorical imperative, what Kant calls the "supreme principle of morality," is the principle that provides this guidance for Kant. We will have a good idea of Kant's ethics once we understand what he means by the categorical imperative.

Imperatives are commands. Some commands are *hypothetical*. They have this form: "If you want this, do that." We tell our children to clean up their rooms, for example, if they want to watch television. Hypothetical imperatives describe actions that we may perform if we want to achieve certain goals or satisfy certain desires. *Categorical* commands have this form: "Do it!" They contain no reference to any consequences that may follow, or to any desires that such actions may satisfy. They are not presented as choices that we may take or leave according to our interests. They are presented as obligations that bind us absolutely and unconditionally. There are no exceptions, no excuses, and no conditions that release us from their force.

The categorical imperative is the principle that describes this sense of unconditional duty that lies within all of us. According to Kant, it is the source of "the moral law within," the source of our feeling that we *ought to* perform or refrain from performing certain types of actions, no matter what. According to Kant, the categorical imperative may be formulated in three different ways. These three different formulations each highlight a particular moral insight about the general properties that any maxim must possess if it is to become an acceptable moral rule.

The First Formulation: Rules Must Be Universal

Kant's first formulation of the categorical imperative is this: *"Act only on that maxim whereby thou canst at the same time will that it should become a universal law."*[4] What this says is that what is right cannot simply be what is right for me, but must be something that I could rationally choose to be right for anyone. It must be something that I could will to be a **universal** law, something that everyone ought to do, a rule that everyone ought to follow all of the time. This first formulation of the categorical imperative has some kinship with the Golden Rule, which says that we ought to "do unto others as we would want them to do unto us." It requires that acceptable moral maxims be the same for all. Anyone acting rationally, and not just in their own self-interest, will act in ways that he or she would want others to act who were in the same position.

The main reason that Kant thinks of following the categorical imperative as acting reasonably is that acting against it leads to a contradiction, and holding contradictory beliefs is the height of irrationality. Kant gives us an example of how this first formulation of the categorical imperative works to determine correct moral rules. Imagine someone who needs to borrow money, he says, but knows that he cannot repay it. Nevertheless, he promises to pay it back as a condition for receiving it. The maxim he is following is this:

> "When I need money I will borrow it and promise to repay it even though I know that I will never do so." Now I personally might be able to live according to this principle of self-interest. But the question is: Is it right? So I ask myself: What if my

maxim were to become a universal law? Then I see at once that it could never even become a universal law . . . since it would contradict itself. For suppose it became a general rule that everyone started making promises he never intended to keep. Then promises themselves would become impossible as well as the purposes one might want to achieve by promising. For no one would ever believe that anything was promised to him, but would mock all promises as empty deceptions.[5]

Briefly put, it is wrong to break promises because if we all did so when it suited our immediate interests, it would destroy the very notion of promise keeping. It is not because of the consequences of all of us breaking our promises that it is wrong to do so, as the rule utilitarian might say. Instead, it is because it violates reason itself to break promises. Because moral maxims must be universalizable, it is a contradiction to think both that it is morally acceptable for us to break promises and to think that there are such things as promises at all. If we all broke our promises when it suited us, there would be no such thing as promise-keeping any more.

Three things are important to note here about the first formulation of the categorical imperative. First, the categorical imperative principle does not provide us with a list of concrete rules, such as "don't lie," "keep your promises," and so on. Instead it provides us with a property that any rule must live up to. This property has to do with the *form* that any rule must take—it must be universalizable.

Second, in saying that rules must be universalizable, Kant points out that morality includes an element of impartiality. You are supposed to consider yourself no less bound by rules than anyone else. You are supposed to consider your duties equal to those of everyone else, and therefore to consider yourself just as obligated to obey moral maxims as everyone else. Everyone, yourself included, is to act without regard for self-interest, but only out of respect for the law. If it is a duty for others to follow a certain maxim, then it is a duty for you as well.

Third, there are no exceptions to rules. Since the way that the categorical imperative gets applied to particular cases is to see if your act leads to a contradiction, then since any act of promise-breaking would lead to the same sort of contradiction mentioned in the quote above, any act of promise-breaking is wrong regardless of the circumstances. No matter how much it may hurt you to do so, no matter what the consequences, universalizable moral maxims must be followed at all times, without exception. It is never right to break promises, or to lie, or to kill someone, for example, however difficult it sometimes may be to keep these rules. Such rules describe actions that are *intrinsically immoral* for Kant. They are wrong in themselves, not just because of their consequences.

This third consequence of holding the categorical imperative may have been avoided by Kant if he had recognized that sometimes rules conflict, and that we have to choose which has the highest priority. It would have allowed him to escape from all the problems that are going to follow from believing that it is never right to break moral rules under any circumstances. As we have seen, it is right to break promises sometimes, namely, when a higher rule demands it.

The Second Formulation: Respect for Persons

The second formulation of the categorical imperative is this: *"So act as to treat humanity, whether in your own person or in that of any other, in every case as an end withal, never as a means only."* This may be the most important insight of Kantian ethics. It says that no maxim may be accepted as a legitimate duty if it includes using people for the good of another. The familiar phrase, "The end doesn't justify the means," expresses this insight. It is not right, even if it produces lots of good, to use a person for the good of others. We use persons when we manipulate them, or force them to do things, or otherwise control their behavior. In this way we treat them as things, as objects, as beings whose only worth lies in what they are good for.

At the root of this second formulation of the categorical imperative is the idea that rational human beings are good in themselves, they are the "jewels" of creation, that they have intrinsic value. We are not important solely for how much we contribute to society, for our "social worth," but we are worthwhile in ourselves. What makes us worthwhile is our reason. By reason we mean both our ability to understand the world around us and our use of reason to guide our lives, especially to achieve a good moral character. Even those of us who do not act rationally, those of us who are weak-willed and act only from desire, are intrinsically valuable, because we *could* act rationally. To use someone as a thing, a mere means to the good of another, is to violate that person's inherent worth as a rational being.

For example, suppose a medical researcher designs an experiment that uses twelve very old, dying, senile nursing home patients. They are to be injected with a dangerous virus and studied for knowledge of disease transmission. Suppose also that these people are given painkillers, so that during the experiment they feel even better than they did before. Suppose even further that valuable knowledge was discovered, knowledge that prevented millions of people from contracting certain forms of disease in the future. Would such an experiment be morally acceptable?

I hope that your answer is a resounding, "NO"! It is immoral, because it uses people, even people of such low social worth, as a mere means to the good of others—as "guinea pigs," we say. This is the major insight in Kant's second formulation of the categorical imperative. Not only must morally acceptable maxims be universalizable, but they must also respect persons as intrinsically valuable. No maxim is acceptable if it allows us to use people exclusively as a means to the good of others.

This does not mean that we can never, under any conditions, use people as a means to our good. We can use people as a means to our good if they allow us to do so, if they freely choose to be so used. The mailman brings my mail, the waiter serves my food, the nurse bandages my wounds. This is permissible, according to Kant, because I am not using them as mere objects. I am not forcing them or manipulating them against their will, for example. To do that would be to use them *only* as a means to my good. This is what the second formulation of the categorical imperative forbids, treating people merely as a means. Instead, we must **respect persons** as valuable in themselves.

Because a rule that involved using someone as a means would not be universalizable, Kant believes that the two versions of the categorical imperative are two different formulations of the same principle. A maxim that allowed slavery, for example, would be rejected as an example of using some people as a means to the good of others. But it would also be rejected as a valid maxim because it is not universalizable. If it was morally acceptable for you to own slaves, then it would be morally acceptable for everyone to own slaves. This would mean that everyone could be a slave—someone who owns nothing—which would contradict the very notion of ownership.

The Third Formulation: Respect for Autonomy

The third formulation of the categorical imperative is this: *"So act as if you were always through your maxims a law-making member of a kingdom of ends."* This statement will take a comment or two to clarify. First, by "kingdom of ends" Kant envisions a web of all rational beings, held together by the threads of shared moral maxims. Think of it as a "moral universe" where every person is related to every other one by their shared duties and mutual respect. Clearly this part of the third formulation is compatible with the first two.

What about the "law-making" part of this statement, however? What new property does that add to our list of properties that all moral maxims must possess? In addition to universalizability and respect for persons, what else does it say that rules must possess in order to be acceptable moral maxims? Kant's answer, in a word, is **autonomy.** That is, such rules must be freely chosen by ourselves. We may be trained in our youth to refrain from lying and stealing, and to treat each other with respect and so on; but until we accept these rules freely, and act upon them because we accept them as our duties, we are not creating a good will. We are acting in *accordance* with the law, perhaps, but not from *respect* for the law.

For Kant, we must see moral maxims as our own rules. However they were acquired initially, they must become rules that we give to ourselves, not rules imposed on us by others. This does not mean that we can create and follow any rules that we may wish, however. On the contrary, the rules by which we freely govern ourselves must follow reason. To follow reason is to follow rules that are universalizable and that respect persons as intrinsically valuable. Moreover, since moral maxims must be universalizable, then every time you decide to act on one you should think of yourself as creating a new law for everyone, for every member of the "kingdom of ends," for every other rational being. To create a good moral character we must submit to such moral rules, rules that would be acceptable to any rational being, and do so of our own free will. This is the meaning of the third formulation of the categorical imperative.

But why is it important to choose such an ethical life freely? Would we not be as "good" if we were just trained to follow rules that were universalizable and treated persons with respect? To understand why Kant insists that a good will requires autonomy or freedom, we must look closer at the meaning that this notion has for him. To understand Kant's concept of freedom we must first distinguish between freedom of action and freedom of the will. I am free to act if nothing prevents me from getting what I want. I am not free to go to the Bahamas, for example, if I cannot afford it, or if someone has a gun to my head threatening to shoot me if I do, or if the U.S. government has placed a ban on travel to the Bahamas. Absent these sorts of constraints, however, I am free to go. I can do what I want, I have freedom of action.

For Kant, however, freedom from external constraint is not true freedom. Being free to do what you want to, freedom of action, is not freedom of the will. Someone who does what he wants is someone who is still controlled by his "wants," by his desires. True freedom requires more than this; it requires freedom from internal constraint as well; it requires that we control desire itself; it requires that we can act contrary to our desires, just by willing to do so. To be truly free or autonomous is to be fully in control of ourselves, fully self-governing. True freedom requires reason to be in charge of our decisions, not desire. For reason to control behavior it is not enough to act *in accordance* with moral maxims. This is just another way to act from desire, the desire to do what others want you to do. Only by freely choosing to submit to moral rules are we truly free, truly autonomous beings.

What we submit to is reason as it is expressed in practical matters. These are the moral maxims that conform to the categorical imperative. Why we need to submit freely is because this form of self-legislation is the only way to rise above desire, to be truly rational beings. Reason is what is best in us; reason is what we most truly are. So to choose freely to submit to universalizable moral maxims is to live according to our true selves, not according to the wishes of others, not according to our own desires. It is to be truly autonomous.

Such an autonomous, self-governing life is the source of our dignity and deserves the highest respect. We are to respect and nurture our own autonomy as well as that of others, as a full expression of our rational selves. In practice this means that we are to see others as the center of their own life plans, and to respect their decisions even when we may disagree with them. In an autonomous person, such decisions are an expression of reason and thus are an expression of a good will, that most noble part of us all.

For Kant, the reason that a good will has intrinsic value is because it is the expression in action of our reason itself. Reason is followed when we follow rules that are rational, that any rational being would choose to follow, because to go against them would be irrational, would be contradictory. This is the first formulation of the categorical imperative, which tells us to follow universalizable rules. The second formulation tells us to respect persons as valuable in themselves. They are valuable because of their reason; that is what shines so brightly in them. That is why we must not treat them as things, as merely a means to the good of another. They are not mere things that may be prized as commodities are prized. People are not for sale—they are "beyond all price," as Kant says.

The third formulation of the categorical imperative recognizes that true moral behavior must be freely chosen behavior, and that any moral maxim must respect the autonomy of persons. If the goal of life is developing a good will, and if doing so amounts to acting according to reason, then the goal of life is to become as fully rational, and thus as fully autonomous, as possible. Reason allows us to rise above a merely animal existence; it allows us to escape the chains of desire; it allows us to govern ourselves, as do the gods.

Exercise C

Once again, use the same case study as you did in Exercises A and B, only this time decide what Kant would say is the right thing to do. As usual, give reasons for your answer.

Evaluating the Ethics of Kant

One of the major objections to Kant's theory of obligation is that it requires all moral rules to be *absolute*, to hold in all circumstances, regardless of the outcome of following them. Kant would be in trouble with our "luncheon date" case discussed earlier, because he holds that it is never right to break promises. His theory thus violates the criterion of **universality,** since it fails to account for cases in which a rule may be overridden by a "higher" rule. While this is a serious objection, it appears that it may be avoided by simply updating Kant's views to include the notion of one rule overriding another.

The idea that one obligation may override another, however, is not easily incorporated into Kant's theory because Kant's moral principle, the categorical imperative, gives us no way to rank competing rules. A utilitarian might say that helping the accident victim has the highest priority because following the rule "help others if you can do so without harming yourself" promotes more good than following the "keep your promises" rule. Would Kant say that the "help others" rule has the highest priority because it is universalizable? Promise-keeping is also universalizable. What makes one more universalizable than another? This is an important criticism because any adequate moral theory must be able to explain how to resolve conflicts between rules.

Another objection is that his theory of obligation violates the criterion of **external consistency** because his view of motivation is incorrect. The only worthwhile motive for moral action according to Kant is duty. If I choose to do something because I want to, or because I am afraid not to, or because it will bring me fame or fortune, then I have acted expediently perhaps, but not morally. For Kant, only if I act out of a sense of duty am I a good person, for only then does reason govern desire. The objection to Kant is that duty is not the best motive.

Instead, choices made out of love are often considered to be morally superior to those that are motivated solely by duty. For example, a mother who sacrifices for her children simply because it is her duty to do so is not nearly as admired as one who acts out of love for them. Instead, she is seen as cold and uncaring. For Kant to allow love as a motive would require him to admit desire into the arena of morality, and that he will never do. The whole point of morality is to rise above desire, to be guided by reason alone.

To disconnect our desires to do good for others (love) from morality is to remove feelings of kindness, compassion, and empathy from playing important roles in our moral lives. These are noble motives, ones that direct us to bring out what is best in us. We are not "pure" reason; we also consist of feelings and desires. Kant's theory fails to allow this side of us to have any role in morality. It violates the criterion of external consistency because it flies in the face of our conviction that the best people among us are those who do what is right out of love and compassion, not from their sense of duty. A more adequate moral theory than Kant's would be one that incorporated this fuller, richer, more humane idea of motivation.

The strengths of Kant's ethics are many. Though formulated around the time of the American Revolution, Kant's moral ideas continue to exert a great deal of influence on contemporary moral philosophy. One idea is especially important, the idea that we ought to **respect persons** and always treat them as ends in themselves. While we may differ with respect to our talents, and while some may contribute more to the welfare of mankind than others, we are all just as worthwhile as anyone else. Our value does not stem from our social worth; we are not simply beings who are good for something; but we are beings who have intrinsic value. To treat people with respect is to recognize this value inherent in each one of us, and to refrain from using people as mere things.

The second important idea that any adequate theory of morality should borrow from Kant is that of **autonomy.** People are autonomous insofar as they have the capacity to direct their lives by their own choices. As long as we do not infringe on the freedom of others, our choices and the behavior they produce ought to be respected. People's autonomy ought to be respected even if we do not agree with their choices, even if we think they are unwise or even harmful to themselves. As long as they are rational beings, people should be viewed as the center of their own life plans, as having the ultimate say about how their lives should go. Any ethical theory today that fails to include these two notions of respect for persons and their autonomy will surely be inadequate.

Virtue Ethics

We have seen that ethics studies how to determine which actions are morally right by constructing theories of obligation. Theories of obligation present a general definition of right action, usually formulated as a principle or a set of principles, and a set of instructions about how to apply the principle or principles to particular cases. We also have seen that ethics studies the good. It does this in two ways. First, it tries to identify what we called "nonmoral" goods, those intrinsic values that we believe will make us happy. In so doing it constructs theories of value, some of which are monistic while others are pluralistic. Second, ethics studies moral goods, those properties of persons that make them morally good, such as their moral character, their intentions, and their motives.

Most modern consequentialists and deontologists have focused less on what is good and more on what is right. When they have discussed the good at all, they have especially been concerned with nonmoral goods, such as pleasure. Often they are concerned with nonmoral goods only as a way to determine right from wrong, as is the case with consequentialism. They have spent very little time discussing moral goods, the sorts of things that make one a morally good or virtuous person. They are much more interested in identifying the moral principles that guide the formation of the rules that define right and wrong than they are in discussing what constitutes a morally good person. They are more interested in what makes actions right than in what makes a person good. Although Kant had much to say about moral goods, he focused mainly on the rules that one had to follow to achieve a good moral character, and especially on the basic moral principle to which all such rules had to conform, the categorical imperative.

Virtues and Obligations

The modern emphasis on principles and rules has not always been the focus of ethics. Many ancient Greek and Roman philosophers, Aristotle being the main example, believed that rules and principles are of secondary importance in our moral lives. What really counts in ethics is not knowledge of a set of rules and the principles that guide their formation but the development of good persons. Like Aristotle, modern day **virtue ethics** focuses on the kinds of persons we ought to be, not on knowing which rules and principles we ought to follow. It focuses on what is morally good, not on what is right. Doing what is right may be a part of what makes a person good. After all, you cannot be morally good while at the same time performing immoral actions. But being a good moral person is more than doing what is right.

A morally good or morally virtuous person is one who possesses a good moral character. A good moral character is one that consists of virtuous moral habits, or **virtues.** Virtues may be thought of as dispositions, or tendencies to behave in certain morally acceptable ways. Honesty, for example, is a moral virtue. It is the tendency to tell the truth. Dishonesty, on the other hand, is a **vice.** It is the tendency or habit of lying. There are other sorts of virtues besides moral virtues. Patience is a virtue, we are told, though not a moral virtue. We may also talk about intellectual virtues, such as good study habits and the desire to find the truth. A virtue may be thought of as any habit or skill required to achieve a certain goal. Because we are interested in what makes us good persons, we will discuss only moral virtues in what follows.

At first glance, talking about virtues seems to be just another way to talk about rules. The virtue of honesty, for example, seems to be nothing but living your life according to the rule, "Do not lie." So what's the big difference between virtue ethics and an ethics based on principles? There are many fundamental differences between these two approaches to ethics. It will be helpful for your understanding of virtue ethics to see just how it differs from an ethics that is based on principles and stresses obligations. Though on the surface they appear to be quite similar, they are really two very different ways to think about morality. We will begin by noting three major ways in which they differ.

The first difference is that virtue ethics has a lot to say about our **motives** for acting. Virtue ethics is especially concerned with what makes us good, and this is where the "goodness" of our actions lie, in our reasons or motives for acting. This is not to say that those who emphasize theories of obligation have nothing to say about motives, but in virtue ethics such discussions take center stage. In virtue ethics, it is generally considered that concern for my well-being and for the well-being of others is the best motive for action. This is very different from Kant's conception of motivation. For Kant, the only appropriate motive for moral action is duty. In acting from duty I act according to reason, whatever my feelings or desires happen to be.

The differences between these two ideas of the proper motivation for moral action is striking. To repeat an example from above, how cold would be a mother who fed, clothed, sheltered, and educated her children simply because it was her duty to do so. Instead, she is more admirable to us if she does so from concern for the well-being of her children—from love, in other words. In recognizing that the good of myself and others is a motive for action that is superior to duty, virtue ethics allows feelings and desires back into the moral life, though always under the control of reason. Unlike Kant, virtue ethics allows us to see moral choices as those of persons, not just abstract reason.

A second major difference between "obligation" and "virtue" approaches to ethics lies with their **goals.** The goal of theories of obligation is to teach us how to determine the difference between right and wrong. It achieves this goal by identifying rules and principles that we are obliged to follow, even if we do not want to. The goal of virtue ethics, on the other hand, is to show us how to be happy, how to live good lives, lives of "human flourishing," as Aristotle says. Part of a good life may include living up to your moral obligations, but virtue ethics has a much broader conception of the moral life than an ethics of obligation. It places the emphasis on achieving what is good for ourselves and for others, and not simply on identifying the obligations that we have to others. In virtue ethics, living up to our obligations is important only to the degree that doing so contributes to the grander scheme of living a rich and fulfilling life.

A third way in which virtue ethics differs from an ethics of obligation is in its approach to values. If the goal of virtue ethics is to show us how to live good and happy lives, then it must contain a conception of such a life, a **moral ideal.** Only in the light of such an ideal can we identify the particular virtues that we wish to develop. A moral ideal in this case is a general conception of the good life, a general idea of what sorts of persons we think we ought to be if we are to be truly happy.

Whereas theories of obligation talk about something that appears to be quite similar to a moral ideal when they talk nonmoral values, the two concepts function quite differently within their own moral theories. For example, for a consequentialist, such as Mill, the ideal of pleasure is used to determine right from wrong. If actions achieve it, they are right; if not, they are wrong. Our obligations and the rules and principles that guide them are seen as merely a means to bring about an ideal life, a life of happiness, one that maximizes pleasure while minimizing pain.

In virtue ethics, however, the virtues are not merely a means to bring about the life of happiness. Rather, the collection of virtues *is* the moral ideal itself. Living a good, or happy life *is* living virtuously. Virtuous character traits, the behavior that springs from them, and the appropriate feelings and attitudes that accompany them are all understood as good in themselves because they themselves constitute the good life. The good life is not anything over and above the virtues, any more than playing a good game of baseball is anything over and above hitting well, fielding well, running fast, and so on.

The conclusion is that virtues should not be thought of as obligations that have become habits, but rather as ways to contribute to the good life. The best way to think of virtue ethics is as not even using the concept of obligation at all. If ethics is about becoming happy persons, and if this is something that we all want for ourselves and others anyway, then it hardly makes sense to say that we are "obliged" to do what is ethical. Instead of identifying our obligations, the goal of ethics is to produce good and happy people, people living lives of human flourishing. The virtues are simply particular ways to contribute to such a life. If "right" means anything in virtue ethics, it means something like "behavior that contributes to the good life," while "wrong" means "behavior that is not good for us."

Aristotle: The Good Life

If living the good life is the goal of ethics, then it is crucial to know what we mean by the good life. One of the most famous conceptions of the good life that was developed in the context of virtue ethics is that of Aristotle (384–322 BCE).[6] According to Aristotle, what is good for any particular type of living thing is that which fulfills its nature. All living things of the same type share a common structure that results in common, natural behavior. Tomato plants all have the same sorts of leaves and roots and fruit, for example, which grow and develop in roughly the same way for each successful plant. Their good in general is the full development of the plant. That is how they realize themselves. That is how a tomato plant should be.

For human beings as well, the good life is the life of the full development of all of our natural ways of being. These include all of our various dimensions—biological, psychological, and intellectual. Special emphasis is placed by Aristotle on the development of what is distinctively human, however, our *rational* abilities, especially knowledge and virtue. While we are animals, and thus must satisfy our biological and emotional desires to be happy, we are also rational, and thus must satisfy the desires of reason as well, especially the desire to know.

A full, rich, happy life includes having wisdom, what Aristotle calls intellectual virtues. It also requires that we use this wisdom to direct our lives. The use of reason to direct our lives is called moral virtue. Each particular moral virtue is just another way to act rationally. We are fully developed as human beings, and thus have achieved our goal in life, and thus are happy, only when we have acquired the intellectual and moral virtues that the full development of our natures requires. So one thing that happiness requires is that we be morally good persons. But how do we tell which habits are moral virtues and which are vices, and thus what counts as a good moral character? What "set of instructions" does Aristotle give us for determining what is good for us in particular situations?

We can tell what is good for us in several ways. The way most of us develop our moral character is through moral *training*. Our parents, teachers, peers, and so on tell us what is morally good behavior. They also tell us what counts as appropriate feelings and attitudes and motives for acting. So we can learn what is good for us by training, by others telling us. We can also learn from our own *personal experience* which sorts of behaviors are good and which are not good for us. Most of us do not need to experience too many nights of drunkenness, followed by the inevitable morning hangover, for example, to learn quickly that drinking to excess is not good for us.

We can also tell what a good life is by observing the lives of those we admire, says Aristotle. We learn *by example* what is a virtue and a vice. We have examples of moral heroes and ordinary good people whom we admire and wish to be like. These examples are used as a template by society and by individuals to shape the moral ideals they wish to emulate. Christ may be a model for some societies and individuals, while the life of Socrates, or Confucius, or Buddha, or Mohammed, or any number of inspirational people may provide models of a good life for others.

Finally, we can also learn what is virtuous behavior by *figuring it out for ourselves,* by a process of reasoning Aristotle calls "phronesis." This term is best translated as prudence, or prudential reasoning. Aristotle gives us perhaps the most famous example of such reasoning in his discussion of what he calls the golden mean.

The Golden Mean

Prudential reasoning is a way of figuring out what is good for me in particular situations. In general, it begins with the assumption that morally good persons, persons who lead good lives, are those who live a life of moderation in all things. They choose the "mean" between extreme types of actions. For example, **courage** is a virtue, because it is the mean between the extremes of cowardice, on the one hand, and recklessness, on the other. A coward has too little courage, whereas a reckless person, someone who takes excessive risks, may have too much for his own good.

Another example of a virtue for Aristotle is **temperance.** To be temperate is to regulate your actions in matters of pleasure—avoiding the excesses of self-indulgence, on the one hand, and the deficiencies of abstinence, on the other. The happy life should contain pleasure but not be driven by its pursuit. **Generosity** is another virtue because it lies between the extremes of stinginess, on the one hand, and being overly generous, on the other.

For Aristotle, choosing the mean between extremes is the way for reason to control the excesses of the emotions and passions. Each extreme is either a deficiency of character or an excess of it—a vice, in other words. Extreme types of behavior are motivated by desire or feeling without the benefit of thinking through the consequences of such action. A life of moderation is not a life of safety or boredom but is a life where reason is in control. Such a life enables one to live fully, to live as closely to the ideal of a good life as possible. A life of moderation does not ignore our feelings and desires but channels them to their proper function, and thus controls them for the well-being of the person. The life of moderation, one that avoids the excesses and the deficiencies of behavior, is a life governed by reason, not a life directed by uncontrollable passions and desires.

According to Aristotle, it is not so much your duty to live a life of moderation as it is in your interest to do so. Without a life of choosing the mean, desires will rule your life, and you will be cut off from fulfilling many of your natural functions. You will not realize your full potential as a human being. You will not lead a good life. You will not be happy. In the end, what is important in Aristotle's version of virtue ethics is that one live as fully humanly as possible, that one live as he or she was meant to live, that one live a life that is directed by reason toward the well-being of the individual. Such a life is a truly good life.

Evaluating Virtue Ethics

The strength of virtue ethics lies in its insistence that there is more to ethics than using rules and principles to assess right and wrong behavior. In addition to doing what is right, our moral lives also involve becoming morally good persons. It is not enough to follow rules in order to become a morally good person. Just as following the rules of baseball will not make you a good baseball player, so following moral rules alone will not make you a good moral person. Having the hitting, running, and fielding skills required by the game, as well as a love for the game itself, is what makes a good baseball player. Following the rules of the game flows from those skills and the love of the game. The game is part of you.

In the same way, morally good persons are those who have acquired habits of doing what is right, not just knowledge of a set of rules. They exhibit morally good behavior as a way of being, not simply as an act of duty. They act according to these habits and with the feelings of sympathy, benevolence, and compassion that accompany them, not simply because they have been brought up to do so, or because they fear the consequences of society if they do not, but also because they see that doing so is good for them. They understand that living a morally good life is a large part of living a full, rich life. The basic insight of virtue ethics is that any moral theory that is going to be universal must include more than the identification of the rules and principles that determine right action. It must also include a thorough discussion of the persons who perform right actions, and provide an account of what it is that makes persons morally good.

Another strength of virtue ethics, one that also adds to its universality, is that it encourages us to go beyond the call of duty and to become the best persons that we can. It does this by presenting us with a moral ideal for which we are to strive. This moral ideal provides us with a conception of the good life, the sort of life that is the best life we can lead, the sort of life that is the most likely to make us happy. Virtue ethics is not so much interested in encouraging us merely to live up to the minimal duties we have to each other, but is also interested in encouraging us to develop ourselves as fully as possible. It does this by identifying the moral ideal for which we should strive, and showing us how to live up to it for our own good. These are elements that must be included in any moral theory that purports to explain all of our moral experience.

If the major strength of virtue ethics lies in its emphasis on good and evil, its major weakness lies in its minimizing the importance of right and wrong. Surely, a major part of our moral lives includes telling right from wrong, figuring out what our obligations or duties are, what rules we ought to follow. Any moral theory that does not give us a way to determine right from wrong would leave out a great deal of what is central to ethics. For virtue ethics to be **universal,** it must provide a way to determine right from wrong. How does it do this?

The easy answer provided by virtue ethics is that what is right is that sort of behavior that helps me to achieve the moral ideal, whereas what is wrong does the opposite. Right behavior is what produces a virtuous character, or virtue, while wrong behavior takes me away from my well-being and produces vice. Right actions are those that flow from virtuous people. They are what virtuous persons do. Wrong actions are those that flow from vices; they are what evil people do. So far so good. The problem arises when we try to use this general guideline to figure out right from wrong in particular situations. What we find, and what we will identify as the central objection to virtue ethics, is that virtue ethics provides us with no way to tell the difference between right and wrong. It gives us no theory of obligation.

To see this, note that right action cannot simply be what virtuous persons do, as it is possible to exhibit virtuous action but still do something wrong. For example, I may be loyal and brave in the service of a wicked cause, or I may give generously to help an evil man. Virtues may be placed in the service of evil. In addition, being a virtuous person alone is often insufficient for distinguishing between right and wrong. This is especially true when new moral problems arise, problems for which past moral training has provided little guidance. It is not crystal clear, for example, how having a virtuous character helps you know how to decide whether human cloning is morally acceptable. For such problems, it would seem that additional guidelines are required to determine which course of action is morally correct.

The method offered by virtue ethics, prudential reasoning, is not up to the task. In searching for the virtuous course of action, it looks for the mean between extremes. This mean is to be found in examples of virtuous people; it is what they do. But we have to know what is right before we can identify someone as a virtuous person. Only if I already know that cloning human beings is immoral, for example, can I identify those who speak out against it as exhibiting virtuous behavior. To say that what is right is what virtuous people do, especially when it involves new moral problems, is circular reasoning at its worst. This is an important objection, because if virtue ethics focuses only on the good and ignores how we determine our moral obligations, then it clearly leaves much of our moral experience unexplained.

One way for an adherent of virtue ethics to respond to this objection is to say that identifying obligations is not the business of ethics. The only obligations that we have are legal obligations. It is wrong to kill, break contracts, steal, and the like because it is against the law. Morality is simply not about obligations at all. It is about living full, rich lives. There is no need for a moral theory of obligation because we have no moral obligations, only moral ideals to pursue.

The trouble with this approach is that we clearly do have moral obligations not defined by the law. Think of abortion, for example, where the law in the United States allows us to use our own moral lights in deciding right from wrong. Are there not obligations discussed around this issue, often phrased as rights, such as the "right to life of the fetus," and "the right to privacy (choice) of the pregnant woman"? Moreover, do we not sometimes say that laws are immoral, such as those that allow capital punishment and prevent physician-assisted suicide? Clearly, one way that we judge legal obligations is by whether they conform to moral obligations. This is seen most clearly when we discuss our moral obligations prior to the formulation of legal obligations. At the time of this writing, there are no laws against human cloning, for example, but there certainly are strong beliefs about its moral appropriateness.

Another way that a proponent of virtue ethics might respond to the criticism that it has no way to tell right from wrong is to show us how it figures out right from wrong independently of appeals to how virtuous persons act. Prudential reasoning, we are told, focuses on the moral ideal and assesses behavior with respect to how well it helps us to achieve this ideal. Virtues may be identified as those character traits that help to achieve the ideal, whereas vices take us further away. Such a method thus allows us to determine right from wrong by referring to the consequences of our actions.

In defining right actions by reference to their consequences, virtue ethics borrows a theory of obligation from consequentialism. To determine right from wrong, it examines how the results of acting in one way or another will lead to harms and benefits for yourself and others. Sometimes virtue ethics may use deontological criteria as well, such as Kant's idea of treating persons with respect. What is clear is that it does not use its own criteria in deciding right from wrong. In a world where we already have agreement on right and wrong, it may be sufficient to say that right actions are those performed by good people, but this will not do in a world that continually cries out for new decisions about which morally acceptable courses of action to take.

Despite its weaknesses, the insights of virtue ethics about grounding rules and principles in the habits, motives, and feelings of people will have to be incorporated into any adequate ethical theory. What we do is important in our moral lives, but so too is what sorts of persons we become. Any adequate ethical theory will have to be heavily supplemented by the insights of virtue ethics if it is to have any chance at all of being successful.

Other Ethical Theories

There are many other types of ethical theories, all of which are staunchly defended by their proponents. We will briefly describe a few of these before developing our final theory.

Do No Harm

One approach to ethics that grows out of a reaction to utilitarianism, claims that we have no general moral obligation to do good for others, only to avoid harming them.[7] If we were really obliged to act for the good of everyone, and to do so without regard for how we were related to them, then we would have to lead very different sorts of lives than most of us do. For example, it is estimated that there are some 30,000 to 40,000 people who die each day around the world from the effects of malnutrition. Most of these people live in developing nations. They are strangers to us. We have no connection with them. Are we immoral because we do not save them from such a fate?

It is easy to see how one could answer "yes" to this question, and thereby seem to confirm the view of the utilitarian that we do have a general obligation to help others. If we did, however, we would have to spend our lives in pursuit of doing good and reducing evil whenever possible. A moral saint may take on such a mission perhaps, but it clearly strikes many as beyond the call of duty.

Instead, according to the "do no harm" theory, our only general moral obligation is not to harm others. The guiding principle of morality should be simply **do no harm.** If we choose to live on a mountaintop, spending our days in fasting and prayerful meditation, trying our best to get closer to God, are we leading immoral lives? On the contrary, such people have often been thought of as leading exemplary lives. Even if they were concerned only with their own lives and were not praying for the good of others, we certainly would not think of them as morally bankrupt persons.

A quick glance at the moral rules accepted by most of us will confirm that we have no general obligation to help others. Most rules are of this form: "Do not _____," where the blank is filled in with the description of a prohibited type of action—usually an action harmful to others. Most general moral rules simply oblige us not to harm others in specific ways. We are admonished not to kill, or lie, or steal, or break our promises, and so on.

If we have no *general* obligation to do good for others, it does not mean that we have no obligations whatsoever to help others. What we do have are obligations to help *specific* others. We must not only avoid evil, but also do good for those with whom we have special relationships. If we have children, for example, we must care for them. If we are members of a family, we are obliged to help family members in their time of need. If my brother is hungry, I am more obliged to feed him than to feed a stranger living in another country. Doctors must do good for their patients, teachers must do good for their students, friends must help each other, and so on.

Most of us find ourselves in special relationships with others, so we all have some duties to do good for some others. We might argue about whether a hungry stranger in another land is really my "brother." If he is, if we are all related as brothers and sisters in the human species, then there is no doubt that I am obliged to help him, too. If not, then my helping him or not is a matter of charity, not obligation. It is what ethicists call a **supererogatory** act. It is a praiseworthy act, but it is an act that goes beyond the call of duty.

The point for now, however, is that we do not have a general obligation to increase human happiness and decrease human misery whenever and wherever we can. According to "do no harm" ethics, I am only obliged not to harm anyone. I am not obliged to do good for anyone with whom I am not related in a special way.

The Ethics of Rights

The next ethical theory that we will consider is called an **ethics of rights.** Many moral problems are formulated in terms of rights. The abortion issue, for example, usually pits the "right to life" of the fetus against the pregnant woman's "right to privacy." The physician-assisted suicide issue is argued from the perspective of the dying patient's "right to self-determination" and his "right to avoid needless suffering" on the one hand, and the rights of society on the other. Many of the contemporary moral problems that divide society may be seen as conflicts of rights, with each side proclaiming that its rights should override the other's. An *ethics* of rights arose initially from attempts by political philosophers to determine criteria for acceptable *legal* rights. So to explain what is meant by the ethics of rights will require us first to say a few words about legal rights.

People often claim that they should have legal rights to things that strike others as downright silly. Do I have the right to be fed, clothed, and housed by others even if I choose not to work? Do I have the right to drive an expensive sports car even if I cannot afford to buy one? Do I have the right to cosmetic surgery to reduce my obesity? To a yearly vacation? To attend the opera? Because rights usually have correlative duties associated with them, to say that I have a right to something usually means that someone else has a duty toward me to do something or to refrain from doing something.[8] Because of this, it is important to be able to distinguish legitimate legal rights from the mere expression of desire.

Some rights are called "negative rights" because they require only that we leave people alone in the manner that the right protects. The right to free speech, the right to worship, and the right to own property are negative rights as they protect these freedoms in all of us and require of us only the duty to refrain from interfering with their exercise by others. "Positive rights," on the other hand, impose a duty on others to provide something to whoever has that right. For example, the right to life may be seen either as a positive right or a negative right. As a negative right it grants its bearer the freedom from being killed by others and imposes on others the duty not to kill. As a positive right, however, it grants its bearer those things required for life—food, shelter, health care, and so on. If the right to life is a positive right, as defenders of welfare programs have argued, then society has a duty to provide these goods to those who cannot provide them for themselves.

Legal rights are thought of as claims against someone else that the law is willing to support. If I have a winning lottery ticket, for example, I have a legally protected claim to the money that I won. If I own a house, I have property rights, the legally protected claim to keep others out of my house. Having a legal right also imposes upon others specific duties. My right to life, for example, imposes on you the duty not to kill me. My property rights give you the duty to stay out of my house unless invited in.

What makes these legal rights and their correlative duties legitimate for some political philosophers is that they rest on a foundation of moral rights that are called natural rights, or human rights. A **natural right** is a right that belongs to you apart from any legal system. If we have such rights, then they would have to be respected by others, even the government. Any government that tries to rob us of such rights is seen as morally corrupt, as the very purpose of government is to protect these rights. Any fellow citizen who violates these rights of ours is subject to punishment.

It is not uncommon to base the legitimacy of political systems on a foundation of natural rights. This seems to be the case in the United States, where we claim in our Constitution that we all possess the "unalienable" rights to life, liberty, and the pursuit of happiness. These are rights that no one can take from us because they are ours by nature. A legitimate government is supposed to uphold these rights. It is not supposed to allow one citizen to violate the natural rights of others, and it is not supposed to do so itself. Perhaps the best expression of natural rights is that of the United Nations, in its Universal Declaration of Human Rights, adopted in 1948. All human beings are supposed to have the rights listed therein, including what is required to meet their basic needs.

Such natural rights form the basis of an ethics of rights. Those who hold an ethics of rights determine moral right from wrong by identifying our natural rights and any other moral rights that may be derived from them. If I have a natural right to "liberty," for example, then I have a right to exercise this liberty in various ways. I have the right to think and speak and express myself in other ways, as long as doing so does no harm to others. Legal rights may then be seen as more specific ways to protect these moral rights, as the First Amendment to the Constitution protects free speech.

There is a long tradition of natural rights approaches to ethics that has much to offer in our search for an adequate ethical theory. Especially important is its insistence that any legitimate government must rest on a moral foundation. It may not follow just "any" laws of its choosing but must respect the basic moral rights possessed by all of its citizens. This tradition has also been important in picking out which of these moral rights are truly essential, such as the rights to life, liberty, and the pursuit of happiness. It is only by protecting such rights that any society may survive and flourish.

However, an ethics of rights does not provide the best guidance for determining right from wrong. Identifying moral rights is not merely a matter of identifying basic natural rights and the more specific moral rights that follow from them. An ethics of rights has it backward. For something to be identified as a "right" in the first place, the actions it requires or permits must be determined to be morally right actions. We would reject a claim that there is a natural right to take anything we please from anyone we please, for example, because doing so is morally wrong. We know this because such actions violate basic moral principles and rules. We must know which actions are right and wrong before we can identify something as a natural right.

Although the matter is not this simple, it is best for us at this point to think of rights as a shorthand way for talking about which actions are right. 'Right' used as an adjective is the most basic moral concept. 'Right' used as a noun is simply a way to refer to a related collection of obligations. To talk about the right to life is simply a way to refer to the moral rule that it is wrong to kill. Killing is wrong because it violates basic moral principles. If this is so, then it is best to understand rights as correlated with obligations or duties, and to understand obligations as determined by reference to principles. Because obligations, phrased as rules, define which actions are morally acceptable and which are not, we shall understand talk about rights as simply a shorthand way for talking about what is right and wrong to do. We will have little to say about an ethics of rights in what follows, both because natural rights presuppose principles, and because most of things that are important about rights can be understood by using the language of rules and principles.

The Ethics of Care

As the "do no harm" principle may be seen as a reaction to the excessive demands of utilitarianism, the **ethics of care** may be seen as a reaction to the narrowness of the male-dominated approach to ethics found in an ethics of rights. The basic claim made by one of its early proponents, Carol Gilligan,[9] is that men and women, whether by training or by natural inclination, have fundamentally different notions about the nature of moral decision making. According to this view, the ethical thinking of most men is legalistic. When faced with a moral problem, men determine which course of action is right by determining which rule (or which right) has the highest priority. They see moral problems as conflicts to be solved by appealing to abstract rules. One side triumphs over the other by using principles as their weapons.

According to Gilligan, however, most women solve moral problems quite differently. They attempt to resolve moral problems in ways that satisfy the personal concerns of all the individuals involved. This different orientation to moral decision making springs from a different set of values that many women hold dear. What is important to them is caring for others—being sensitive to their feelings, their points of view, their needs, and especially their relationships. Abstract rules ride roughshod over these values. The virtues prized by males—those of justice, with its special stress on impartiality, and duty, which places law over personal concerns—seem to ignore them completely. Neither provides much guidance for negotiating a moral settlement in which the interests of all parties involved are met to the degree that this is possible.

Gilligan's research findings have been hotly disputed. In particular, it is not at all clear any longer that the moral "voice" of women and men is really that different. Some women appeal to justice and duty as their primary moral guides; some men appeal primarily to the virtue of care. So instead of seeing an ethics of care as describing a woman's approach to morality, it is more helpful to understand it as a type of virtue ethics that may or may not be adopted by men or women. Caring for others is the central virtue in the ethics of care, and the moral ideal is the caring person. According to this view of morality, as a father cares for his children, as a doctor cares for her patients, so too should all of us care for each other and for ourselves. We live up to this ideal by empathizing with different points of view and by focusing on the personal, individual outcomes of our decisions.

An ethics of care has much to offer any ethical theory. Perhaps if we placed caring as high on our list of virtues as justice and duty, the world would not be such an impersonal place. Perhaps our communities, our families, and even our business institutions would be kinder, gentler, more human places to grow and develop. We will later draw on the strengths of an ethics of care in our attempt to find the best possible ethical theory.

Chapter 3

Our Ethical Theory

Having examined some of the strengths and weaknesses of leading ethical theories, it is now time to attempt to construct an ethical theory that is universal, consistent, and as simple as possible. This theory will serve as our guide in Part 2 as we attempt to solve particular moral problems. In its construction we will include both a theory of obligation and a theory of value. In constructing such a theory we will build on the strengths of the various ethical theories examined thus far. A good place to begin is with a theory of obligation.

A Theory of Obligation

A theory of obligation gives us a method for determining right from wrong. It does this by providing us with a **general definition** of right action, and with a **set of instructions** for how to apply this definition to make particular moral decisions.

The Nature of Right Action

Thus far we have examined two kinds of theories of obligation: consequentialist theories—including ethical egoism, act utilitarianism, and rule utilitarianism; and nonconsequentialist theories—including the deontological theory of Kant and virtue ethics. Our theory will be a **deontological** theory. In particular, it will consider the consequences of our actions as important in determining right from wrong, but it will also consider other factors as well.

This deontological theory of ours will be a **rule-centered theory,** like rule utilitarianism and Kant's theory. Unlike Kant, however, we will not consider the moral rules of our theory as absolute rules. If there is a conflict between rules, then the rule with the highest priority, the rule that best promotes our moral principles under the circumstances, will override a competing rule. The rules themselves are also justified by the principles our theory accepts as basic moral principles. So not only will such principles tell us why we have the rules that we do, but they will also provide us with the means for introducing new rules and for resolving conflicts between rules.

There are three **principles** in our rule-centered, deontological theory of obligation. In addition to playing the three roles mentioned above, they provide us with a general definition of right action. The three principles are beneficence, justice, and autonomy. Beneficence is similar to the utilitarian principle that requires us to do good and avoid evil. The principle of justice contains several related elements, but in the end it is closely related to Kant's "respect for persons" principle. The third principle, autonomy, is also similar to Kant's idea of autonomy. It is important to define each principle in some detail.

Beneficence

While the term **beneficence** sounds a lot like the more familiar term, "benevolence," the two have different meanings. "Benevolence" refers to a motive. A benevolent person is someone who wants to, or intends to, do good for others. He or she is motivated to act in their interest. Sometimes, however, well-intentioned, benevolent people end up doing harm as well as good. "Beneficence" means actually doing good. Let us define beneficence as the principle that requires us to **do good and avoid evil.** This is similar in meaning to "love," at least in its most general meaning. We will use beneficence instead of love, however, since love has too many other connotations to express our meaning clearly.

The principle of beneficence requires us to do two things: "do good" and "avoid evil." Some have even said that there are two separate principles operating here—the principle of beneficence and the principle of nonmalificence.[10] Although a case may be made for this interpretation, it is best to view "do good" and "avoid evil" as together forming one principle. Many moral choices are not clear-cut choices between good and evil. The very difficult ones especially require us to balance good and evil, and to perform the action that leads to a greater balance of good over evil than its alternatives. So doing good and avoiding evil are inextricably bound together and our principle of beneficence reflects that fact.

The way that this principle works in our theory is similar to the role of the principle of utility in rule utilitarianism. In its role as a *justification for rules,* for example, the principle of beneficence says that we must follow only those rules that produce more good or less evil than their alternatives. It is wrong to lie, for example, because a general practice of lying would lead to many negative consequences, many harms, for society. The way that it works in *introducing new rules* is also similar. Any new moral rule is acceptable only if following it would produce a greater balance of benefits over harms. Finally, beneficence is also used to resolve *conflicts between rules.* When rules conflict, the one with the highest priority will be the one that, if followed, will lead to the greatest balance of good over evil for the particular circumstances in question.

As it stands, beneficence is thus far an "empty" principle. It simply tells us to follow rules that promote a greater balance of good over evil. It needs to be filled in with a definition of "good" and "evil" in order to make it a concrete principle. This is a job for the second part of an ethical theory, providing us with a list of intrinsic moral values, the kinds of consequences that we want our actions to bring about or avoid. We will turn to the task of constructing such a list after we have completed our discussion of principles.

Justice

Most people think of justice as some form of equality. There are many forms of equality, however, and thus many varieties of justice. **Retributive justice** is concerned with the principles of punishment. It tells us how much is required to pay back for a specific crime, which punishments "fit" or are "equal to" which crimes. **Social justice,** on the other hand, often called "distributive justice," is concerned with how the goods of society should be distributed. We question, for example, whether a "just" society should let the rich get richer, even as the poor get poorer. We sometimes argue that we should share more, so that there is more equality among the rich and poor. These two meanings of justice flow from even more fundamental meanings that collectively appear as the principle of justice in our theory of obligation.

In our moral theory the principle of justice has three meanings, all related to one another. The most basic meaning of justice is that **all human beings are of equal intrinsic value.** Our talents, ambitions, and good fortune make us very different from each other in our "extrinsic," or social, value. We contribute at different levels to the good of others; thus we have different social worth. The scientist who finds a cure for cancer of a certain type contributes more than the drug addict who contributes little to society. The scientist thus has more social value than the drug addict. According to the principle of justice, however, both people are worthwhile in themselves, and worth just the same as each other. We are all intrinsically valuable, and all equal with respect to our intrinsic worth.

A second meaning of justice follows from the first. Because we all have the same intrinsic value, then **all human beings ought to have the same moral and legal rights.** This second meaning of justice says that moral rights should be the same for all. No one should have more of a right to life, for example, or less of a right to choose how his life goes, than another. In the same way, everyone ought to be equal under the law. We know all too well that a person who can afford the best lawyers has a much better chance of avoiding legal penalties than someone who has no money. However, while it may be true that money buys more "justice," we do not think that it should. Instead, as a moral ideal, the principle of justice says that everyone should be treated equally under the law.

The third meaning of justice follows from the first two. It is especially concerned with how people must be treated. In particular, it says that because people are equal in their intrinsic worth and in their moral and legal rights, they must be treated with respect. What this means in practice is that **people may not be used exclusively for the good of others.** This third meaning of justice in our moral theory is the way that the first two meanings get translated into an action-guiding principle. It is the meaning of justice that we will most often use in solving moral problems. It is very much like the principle expressed by Kant's second formulation of the categorical imperative, which requires that we treat no one exclusively as a means to the good of another.

Recognizing the principle of justice as a fundamental moral principle allows us to solve the problem of "justice" that plagues utilitarianism. If the principle of beneficence requires us to do good and avoid evil, the principle of justice forbids us to use an immoral means to do so. It especially forbids us to use people exclusively as a means to another's good. We have words that express this lack of respect for persons. We say that we are "discriminating against" them, or "using" them, or "taking advantage" of them, or "manipulating" them, or even "forcing" them to do something for the interests of another. Such people are used as "objects," as "things." The moral principle of justice requires that we not use people in this manner, and that we respect all people as equally valuable in themselves.

Because we implicitly hold this principle we recognize why many actions which produce good results in general are nevertheless immoral. For example, we know it is wrong to do such things as use incompetent human subjects in dangerous medical research. If we followed only the principle of beneficence, then it would be morally acceptable to do so, since great benefits might result for innumerable people. If, for example, we used dying patients with serious forms of dementia as subjects of exploratory brain research, it could lead to much greater understanding of the structure and function of the brain, producing many benefits for others. Despite its benefits, however, such an action would be as immoral as anything could be.

Nevertheless, this type of action would be allowed by utilitarianism, since utilitarians rely solely on something like our principle of beneficence to determine right from wrong. Without the principle of justice to prevent it, any immoral means would be allowed as long as it produced a greater balance of good over evil. Now we have a reason for why such practices are immoral, why the end does not justify the means—the principle of justice. Because "justice" has so many related meanings, we will name this third meaning, which requires us to respect all human beings and not to use them merely as a means to the good of others, **respect for persons.** From now on, when we talk about the "respect for persons" principle, we simply mean the principle of justice as understood in this third sense.

Autonomy

The third moral principle is called **autonomy.** This, too, follows from Kant's ethics, especially from what we have called his third formulation of the categorical imperative.[11] For Kant, what makes us intrinsically valuable is our ability to act rationally. At the core of this ability lies our freedom to choose reason over desire. This is the source of our dignity. This is what separates us from other animals and from computers that act according to their programmed instructions. We act on our own; we are self-governed. We decide what is right and wrong, and what is good for us and what is evil. We do this most nobly when we submit our decisions to the judgment of reason, to a consideration of what our behavior ought to be like, not just what we want it to be like. Our capacity to lead rational lives is the source of our worth and dignity, whether we use that capacity very frequently or not.

We shall define the principle of autonomy as follows: **rational beings may do what they want to, as long as their actions harm no one else.** People are rational if two conditions are met. First, they must understand the nature and consequences of acting on the options available. Second, they must be free to act. Babies and people who are heavily sedated are not rational because they do not understand what they are doing. Drug addicts are not rational, even if they understand the consequences of taking drugs, because their actions may not really be free.

Notice the important qualifying phrase in the definition of autonomy, "as long as their actions harm no one else." This principle says that we are free to act as we wish, but we are not absolutely free. Instead, our freedom must be compatible with the freedom of others. Because of this, it is always morally acceptable to interfere with the freedom of others when their actions threaten someone else, when their actions may produce harmful consequences to others. We do not allow people to kill and steal and otherwise exercise their freedom in ways that are harmful to others. We may also interfere with the choices of others if we suspect that they are not competent (rational) to decide for themselves. Someone who attempts suicide may be stopped without violating his or her autonomy, for example, because there is reason to suspect the person's competence. In the absence of such suspicions, however, we must back off and let such individuals behave as they choose.

Most of us have little problem with this principle, as long as we agree that the choice made by others is in their best interest and harms no one else. We do have a problem allowing people to act as they wish, however, when they choose to do something that we think is foolish or harmful to themselves. We may want to prevent them from acting in such a manner, but autonomy forbids it as long as they are rational and harming no one else. We may reason with them and try to educate them about the potential harms of their actions; we may plead with them and refuse to help them do what we think is wrong. However, the principle of autonomy requires us not to impose our will on theirs, and especially not to force them to act as we wish. People must be respected as the center of their own life plans, whether we agree with what they do or not. In a free and open society, we are required to allow rational people to make even what we consider to be poor decisions. We cannot force people to do what we think is good for them. As long as they are rational and their actions threaten to harm only themselves, we have to stay out of their affairs.

The Definition of Right Action

We may now present our general definition of right action.

> An action is right if it follows a rule that conforms to the principles of beneficence, justice, and autonomy.

This is the general definition of right action that we will follow in our attempts to determine which actions are morally acceptable and which are not. It claims that doing the right thing requires us to follow rules. It also claims that the rules to be followed are those allowed by the principles of beneficence, justice, and autonomy. To complete the development of our theory of obligation it now remains for us to discuss the **set of instructions** that will show us how to apply this abstract definition to concrete cases.

Moral Reasoning

This "set of instructions" will be called **moral reasoning.** Knowing right from wrong requires a very different type of process than knowing facts about the material world. Much of my knowledge about the things that exist in my world comes from observing them through my senses. I can see apples, I can hear someone singing, I can smell the freshly baked apple pie. Instead of being based on perception, moral knowledge is based on a process of reasoning. Moral knowledge is more like mathematical knowledge, at least in this one respect. It is not an exact science, as is mathematics, because very often more than one solution to a moral problem may appear to be acceptable. But it is like mathematics insofar as its knowledge is acquired by reasoning. As we reason to the solutions of mathematical problems, so we reason to the solutions of moral problems as well. We do not see or hear or touch the rightness of actions, as we see the color red or hear the song of a bird or touch the silky soft petals of a rose. Instead, we have to "figure out" right from wrong.

The various sorts of "figuring out" that we are about to discuss are collectively called moral reasoning. We say "various" because there is more than one type of moral reasoning. The claim that we will make is that all decisions about right and wrong may be seen as one of the following four types of reasoning. This is how we get to "know" right from wrong, by reasoning in one of these four ways.

1. *Habitual*

Sometimes knowing right from wrong requires very little reasoning. In fact, this is true for most of our moral decisions, when we know what is right simply by knowing the rule that applies to the given situation. How do I know that it is wrong for me to lie to my wife about the money I lost gambling? It is wrong to lie to her simply because it is wrong to lie. In a case such as this, *doing* the right thing may be difficult. It may be much easier to lie and hope that I do not get found out, especially if there is much to gain by breaking the rule against lying. What is not difficult, however, at least with moral decisions of these kinds, is *knowing* what is right.

Let us refer to this form of decision making as **habitual,** because it amounts to little more than conforming our behavior to the rules that are now present in us as habits. With habitual decision making, knowing what is right amounts to classifying behavior according to the moral rules that have been accepted by society and passed on to us by those who shaped our moral character. These rules have been internalized by us and are now present within us as a set of habits. Knowing these rules is usually enough to allow us to distinguish right from wrong in most particular cases of moral decision making. When we make moral decisions of the habitual type, we do not have to do much "figuring out." Instead, we simply act as creatures of habit, as we have been trained to do.

2. *Factual*

Some moral decisions, on the other hand, do require us to think quite a bit in order to figure out right from wrong. Let us call such decisions **moral problems.** Sometimes we are faced with a moral problem that requires us not so much to struggle to do the right thing, but to discover what course of action itself is right or wrong. One type of such a moral problem we will call **factual** moral problems. Although deciding what I "ought" to do is never simply a matter of gathering facts, facts do play an important role in determining right from wrong. The facts that are especially important for determining right from wrong when we are faced with factual moral problems are the consequences of our actions. With factual moral problems, the problem is that we usually do not know what is the right thing to do because we do not know enough about what the consequences of acting in certain ways will be.

Usually factual moral problems arise when a new technology is introduced, one with great potential for good or evil. Think of the various types of reproductive technology, for example, such as human cloning, donor eggs and sperm, surrogate mothers, embryo testing, and many more. Is it right for someone to clone a son or daughter? Like any action, this action is morally right if it follows a rule that conforms to the requirements of beneficence, justice, and autonomy. Unfortunately, the technology is too new for a rule to have been developed and accepted by society and merely passed on to you as part of your moral training. Without such a rule, we do not know whether particular acts of human cloning are right or wrong. Before establishing such a rule there will be many debates in classrooms, courtrooms, legislative assemblies, religious gatherings, and elsewhere. Eventually a rule will be accepted and perhaps even written into law. But how do you know what form such a rule should take?

The moral reasoning involved in constructing a new rule begins with an estimation of the *harms and benefits* of the new technology in question. Is this not what you do in discussing something like human cloning, for example? Do you not say such things as, "We should never allow cloning; the cloned child will be merely a copy of someone else; it will not have its own individuality." Or some of you may point to the possible benefits of cloning, such as having a child that is biologically that of one of the parents, while avoiding the transmission to the child of a genetic defect possessed by the other parent.

At least at the time of this writing, the cloning of human beings has not been achieved, let alone become an accepted practice; therefore, there are no *actual* consequences of cloning humans to examine. There is no way to discover what the actual consequences of a practice allowing cloning will be. The way we figure out right from wrong in the absence of such facts is to conduct thought experiments. We try to imagine what the *possible* consequences of such a practice might be. Thinking ahead in this way allows us to draw up restrictions to govern any new technology, restrictions that allow for its benefits while suppressing its harms.

All the while the attempt to construct a new moral rule is guided by principles. So far we have especially seen how a new practice may be guided by the principle of beneficence, the principle that tells us to follow those rules that promote a greater balance of good over evil. To follow this principle is to identify the possible harms and benefits of the new technology in question, and to think of ways to restrict these harms by regulations of various sorts, while allowing for its beneficial use. The other two principles must be consulted as well, however, if we are to end up with an acceptable moral rule. No rule would be acceptable, for example, if following it produced good consequences for some people at the expense of others. The process of developing successful human clones, for example, most certainly would require several hundred failures before we got it right. If this is so, it may be argued that cloning is wrong because it involves using some (the failed cloned embryos) for the sake of others (the later successful clones).

On the other hand, people should have the right to choose the reproductive technologies they wish to use, should they not? At least they do if such choices harm no one else. Here we appeal to the principle of autonomy. Now you can see how the process of formulating a new rule takes place. The principle of beneficence should be used first. We should first think of all the potential harms and benefits of a particular new technology and then devise guidelines that allow maximum benefits and minimum harms. Then the principle of justice should be used to disallow any benefits procured by immoral means. Finally, the principle of autonomy says that we can take advantage of any of the benefits not produced by an immoral means, as long as doing so does not harm anyone else.

3. *Conflict of Rules*

The most common type of moral problem arises when acceptable moral rules, rules that already conform to our three basic moral principles, happen to conflict with each other. If factual moral problems are solved by using our three principles to formulate a new rule, **conflict of rules** problems are solved by using our three principles to decide which of the already existing rules that are in conflict has the highest priority. Because these problems are often described as a conflict of "rights," we might say that they are solved by deciding which right overrides the other. For example, the abortion problem has been framed as a clash between the right to life of the unborn and the right of the pregnant woman to choose how her body will be used. The euthanasia issue may be seen as a clash between the right of terminal patients to determine the way they die and the right of society to be free from the harmful consequences of such a practice.[12]

For these types of problems, moral reasoning involves applying our principles one at a time. We first weigh the harms and benefits of following one rule or another. For example, earlier in Part I we decided that it was right to break your luncheon date to help the victim of an automobile accident. This was an easy decision because the life and health of the victim was much more important than a luncheon date. There was much more good to be gained and harm to be avoided by letting the rule "avoid harm if possible" override the rule to "keep your promises." To solve this moral problem you weighed the importance of one rule over another by implicitly applying the principle of beneficence.

In a similar fashion we also use the principles of justice in making such determinations about which rules have the greatest priority. Very often our obligation to treat people with respect forces us to choose one rule over another even when it is not more beneficial to do so. For example, for those who think of an embryo as a person, the right to life of such an embryo takes precedence over the mother's right to choose even an early abortion. If the embryo is a person, then it has the same intrinsic worth as all persons, and thus killing it would be wrong—even if the benefits of terminating the pregnancy outweighed the harms of doing so. This is how the principle of justice may be used to weigh the importance of one rule over another. Of course, those who believe that the issue of abortion should be settled by the mother's choice deny that the embryo is a person and that it has any rights in the first place.

The principle of autonomy also may be used in weighing the priority of one rule over another. In fact, all three principles sometimes are used to weigh the priority of one rule over another. Suppose, for example, that someone with a terminal illness wishes to kill himself. He knows that his future contains either constant pain or a semiconscious state brought on by painkillers. He wishes neither of these options; he no longer values his future if this is what it is to be. Suppose the person is rational. He is quite capable of making his own decisions. He orders all treatments stopped, says good-bye to his loved ones, and then administers a lethal overdose of a narcotic to himself. Is such an action wrong?

Another way to phrase the question is this: Which rule has priority here, "do not kill" or "the right to die"? Some say that killing yourself is wrong. They may appeal to the principle of justice, asserting that life of any sort has intrinsic value. On the other hand, do you not have the right to do as you wish, unless your actions harm others? It would appear so, especially since you no longer value your life, you no longer see it as valuable. The issue then becomes one of employing the principle of beneficence to examine the harms that may or may not result from such an action. If there are harms to others, then your autonomy may be suppressed. If not, then your life plans, including your plans about dying, ought to have priority.

As you can see, solving problems that require us to weigh the priority of one rule over another can sometimes be quite difficult. Sometimes it seems anything but clear to determine which rule it would be right to follow under the circumstances. I think you will find, with a little digging, that most of the problems that tear society apart today are problems for which both sides claim to have "right" on their side, and where there seems to be no clear winner among conflicting rules. Alas, ethics is not mathematics; it often contains many gray areas. However, I believe that we can make progress toward solving many of these problems by thinking hard about them. Many of them do have reasonable answers. Sometimes, however, our weighing of rules seems to result in no clear priority being established. Here, all we can do is to decide as best we can on the basis of the facts and the rules and principles that we currently live by. After that, we can only live with our decisions, knowing that we have done our best to figure out right from wrong.

4. *Conflict of Principles*

The most difficult moral problems arise not so much from a conflict between rules as from a conflict between principles themselves. Here is an example to illustrate how a conflict between basic moral principles presents us with problems that seem to have no good solution whatsoever. Whatever action is chosen, it seems that one of the principles must be violated in order to recognize the other. The example concerns survivors crowded into a lifeboat too small to hold them all.

Suppose that you are the captain of a ship that sinks in the ocean two hundred miles from the nearest land. There are nine survivors and one lifeboat that is equipped with a sail. The survivors represent a cross section of society—men and women, young and old, rich and poor, sick and healthy. There is enough room and enough supplies on board for *only* eight people to make it to shore. As the captain, you are the only one who knows how to navigate the little boat. Without your skill, all will be lost.

A serious decision has to made quickly. Sharks have found you and many are swimming around the boat. With all nine people aboard, the boat is beginning to sink lower and lower into the water. One of you has to go over the side to certain death or everyone will go down with the ship. Understandably, no one volunteers. You, the captain, have a gun and must now either force someone overboard or allow everyone to die. You happen to be a morally good person and will not perform an immoral act. You need to know very quickly what is the morally right thing to do.

This is a truly agonizing decision. Many of you may attempt to solve it by altering the case. Are you tempted to say, for example, that as captain you would sacrifice yourself? Then, of course, everyone would be lost, since only you know how to sail and to navigate. Do you want to say "shoot the sharks and let someone swim alongside"? Sorry, there are too many sharks. If you said the right thing to do is to throw someone overboard, did you add that we should throw the oldest, the sickest, or the most useless person overboard? If you did, you were following the principle of beneficence. The action producing the most overall good and least evil will be saving eight lives and killing the person with the least social value—the sickest, the oldest, or the person with the least social worth. Surely this decision has much to commend it. After all, imagine how horrible it would be to read a newspaper report that everyone went down with the ship when eight could have been saved.

No doubt many of you will be bothered by this solution, however, and choose another direction. After all, why is one life worth any more than another? If you were not the skipper, but instead you were the one who was the oldest, or the sickest, or the one who did not contribute much to society, would you feel unfairly treated by being forced into the shark-infested waters? Would you feel as though you were being used for the sake of others? I think so. The decision to throw the person with the least social worth overboard feels wrong because it violates the principle of justice. If someone had volunteered, then such a sacrifice would be acceptable. In the absence of such heroism, however, it is clearly a case of using someone merely as a means for the good of others, a clear violation of our general obligation to respect persons.

But what is a person to do when the principle of justice seems to condemn all nine people to their deaths? To treat everyone as an end in themselves requires that everyone go down with the ship, does it not? So it seems that whatever we do is wrong. Forcing someone over the side violates justice; letting everyone go down with the ship violates beneficence. Each option seems wrong because it violates a basic moral principle. When principles conflict, the moral problem seems to elude any satisfactory solution.

Someone among you may have figured out by now that there is a third option, one that acknowledges both principles. The passengers may be allowed to draw straws, or in some other way randomly choose who goes overboard. In this way, everyone gets an equal chance (justice) to be one of the eight survivors (beneficence). If the group agrees to this (autonomy) then all three principles are satisfied. The main point for now, however, is that our theory of obligation at least explains why such problems are so difficult to solve—because they arise from a conflict of our most basic principles. If these were not the principles that we follow, then such a decision would not be so difficult.

"Good Reasons" Arguments

When we engage in moral reasoning, especially in trying to solve moral problems of the last three sorts, we especially search for the harms and benefits that will follow from the adoption of a particular solution and try to discover whether it has any conformities with, or violations of, the principles of justice and autonomy. We should think of statements that express such benefits and conformities as "reasons for" a particular solution to a moral problem, and those that express harms or violations of the principles of justice and autonomy as "reasons against" it. Typically we collect such reasons for and against one solution or another and organize them into an argument. So to understand and organize our moral reasoning, it is helpful to think of these reasons for and against a particular solution to the problem as premises in an argument. But what is an argument, and what is a premise?

Think of an argument as a group of statements, one of which—called the conclusion, follows from the rest—called the premises. Think of the premises as evidence for the truth of the conclusion. This is not the place to discuss the many forms of arguments that exist, but it is important to draw the distinction between inductive and deductive arguments.

In a deductive argument, the conclusion is presented as necessarily true. An example of a deductive argument is this:

1. Socrates is a person.

2. All persons are going to die.

Therefore, 3. Socrates is going to die.

(1) and (2) are premises, and (3) is the conclusion. (3) is presented as necessarily true. That is, if (1) and (2) are true, (3) must be true.

By contrast, inductive arguments present their conclusions as probably true, the degree of probability depending upon the strength of the premises. In ethics we argue for what we believe to be the best solutions to moral problems. Our arguments will always be inductive, and therefore our conclusions will be presented as probably true.

Of the many types of inductive arguments that exist, the most helpful for moral reasoning is called a **good reasons** argument. This is an inductive argument in which the conclusion is a solution to a moral problem and the premises are all the reasons that support this solution. In such an argument, we first list the reasons that support the conclusion, and then we list refutations of any "reasons against," or objections. Because such an argument is an attempt to defend a particular solution to a moral problem, and since such problems will always have more than one possible solution, there will always be plenty of objections to any possible solution. Here is an example of how such an argument might be constructed for the "factual" moral problem we mentioned above, human cloning.

If I wanted to defend the rule "Cloning human beings should be allowed," I might argue that

1. Clones will be a good source of organ transplants.

2. Clones will help us to produce genetically superior children.

3. Clones will not contain the genetic defects of one of the parents.

4. I have the right to choose cloning if I wish.

The first three "reasons for" cloning list some of its benefits, and thus follow from the principle of beneficence. Premise (4) follows from the principle of autonomy. In the case of moral arguments, or moral reasoning, the premises will always be statements about harms or benefits or expressions of violations or conformities to the principles of justice or autonomy.

The sorts of moral problems to be discussed in Part 2 are not problems because they have no answers, but rather they are problems because they have more than one answer. It is important to know the "other side" as well as your own favorite solution to these problems. One reason for this is that only by knowing opposing views well can you know what their objections are to your view. Another reason is that knowing what others who do not agree with you believe and why they believe it may very well enlighten you, and at the very least make you more tolerant, more open to discussion, even more able to understand your own view by contrast with that of another. In any case, you must identify and reply to objections from the other side before your case is complete, before you have presented an adequate good reasons argument.

Those who oppose cloning, for example, will give reasons for their stance as well. These objections amount to pointing out the harms of cloning but also include pointing out how human cloning violates other principles, as described in the following "reasons against" cloning:

5. Cloning will shrink the gene pool, making us less genetically diverse.

6. Cloning robs a person of his or her uniqueness.

7. Clones are perceived as commodities for their parents.

8. Using clones for organ donors is treating them as a means.

Premises (5) and (6) express harms, while (7) and (8) show how cloning humans violates the principle of justice. Making an adequate case for cloning requires a response to these objections, especially by showing how the harms or the injustices mentioned may be avoided. So for example, premise (6) may be rewritten as

6. Cloning does not rob a person of his or her uniqueness because_____

The blank is to be filled in by your response to the objection. The same holds for all the other "reasons against" or objections, as well. They must all be refuted, and these refutations must be expressed as premises in an adequate good reasons argument. Responding to objections is a very important part of arguing for or against controversial moral positions. A defense lawyer would not win many cases if she simply presented evidence "for" her client, never attempting to refute the prosecutor's evidence against him. And so it is with moral reasoning; a case is only as strong as its ability to respond to the "other side."

We will have much more to say about moral reasoning a little later, and a great deal of moral reasoning to perform in Part 2. For now, however, it is time to say a few words about the other main branch on the tree of ethics—value theory.

Theory of Value

Identifying our obligations is only part of ethics, though it is the part that will be most important for us in this book, especially in Part 2. It is important to note, however, that we also make judgments about good and evil, as well as right and wrong. We call these **value** judgments. No ethical theory would be complete without discussing such judgments, however briefly.

In ethics, we make two types of value judgments. One type of judgment is concerned with **nonmoral values.** These are the things that we consider to be good, the things that we desire. They can be either good for something else—*extrinsically* valuable, or worthwhile in themselves—*intrinsically* valuable. Things that are worthwhile in themselves are the ultimate goals of life, the things that we ought to strive for if we are to be happy. They are the goods or benefits that our morally right actions are supposed to produce, according to the principle of beneficence. Possession of these goods, such as pleasure, love, knowledge, virtue, God, freedom, and so on, constitutes the "good life." Nonmoral values were discussed briefly above and we shall have little to add to that discussion, except to say that our theory of obligation will incorporate a pluralistic theory of value.

Moral Values

In ethics we also make decisions about **moral values.** Virtue ethics is especially focused on these sorts of judgments. For our theory of value to be adequate we will have to incorporate some of the insights of virtue ethics into our discussion of moral values. The main lessons that our theory has learned from virtue ethics are highlighted in what follows.

The first thing to note is that it is always persons who have moral value, not things or actions. A morally good person is someone who routinely *does what is right for the right reason.* The "right reason" means "with the proper motive, intention, attitude, and feeling." For example, in giving a lethal overdose of a narcotic to a suffering, terminally ill patient, a physician acts from mercy (motive) to kill the patient (intention). He may empathize with the patient's suffering (feeling) and consider his act an act of kindness (attitude).

If a morally good person routinely performs right actions for the right reason, then a morally bad person is someone who routinely *performs immoral actions for the wrong reasons.* The right motives for acting morally include such things as duty and kindness, whereas the right intention is always beneficence, increasing good or decreasing evil. Wrong motives include selfishness at the expense of others, and wickedness—the desire to do evil. Wrong intentions are always some form of malevolence, the deliberate setting about to do evil.

What about someone who performs *right actions for the wrong reasons?* Someone who tells the truth because he is afraid of getting caught if he lies, or someone who helps the needy because it makes her look good are not morally good persons. We do not admire such persons. We do not trust them. Their actions spring from a character that may lead to immoral actions any time it is in their interest. They may not deserve to be called morally bad persons either, since they do what is right.

Instead, we have other names for them, such as selfish, sleazy, untrustworthy, and the like. In a similar way, someone who *does what is wrong for the right reason* is also not referred to as a morally bad person. Such a person may have a kind heart but simply be misinformed or ineffective or foolish. We all know people who try hard to do good for others and often end up making matters worse. We may shake our heads at the outcome of their actions, but we admire their intentions nonetheless.

One lesson to be learned from this is that judging someone to be a morally bad person requires us to make two judgments. First, we must know whether the action the person performed is immoral. Such a judgment is made by applying the rules and principles of our theory of obligation. Second, we must know something about the motives, intentions, feelings, and attitudes of the person. Unless we know a great deal about a person, judgments about goodness or badness are notoriously difficult to make. Even those close to someone often do not know the individual's real motives or intentions. We can even fool ourselves sometimes about why we do certain things. Unless you can walk in another person's shoes, judging him or her to be morally bad is tricky at best. We can judge the actions as right or wrong, but we must often refrain from judging them to be good or bad.

Obligation, Excellence, and Aspiration

Something else that we learn from virtue ethics is that there is more to ethics than meeting our obligations to ourselves and others. Our principles and rules and theory of nonmoral value allow us to determine what these **obligations** are, what is the difference between right and wrong actions. Although this is an extremely important part of our moral lives, and the part upon which this book will focus, it is not the only important part of morality. In addition to fulfilling our obligations to others it is also important for each of us to strive for **excellence.** To strive for excellence means to push ourselves to become the best persons we can be. We are not obliged to strive for excellence, it is not our duty to do so, but only by doing so will we attain the fullness of life that we value so dearly. This is why we are often encouraged by our families, peers, and others to live as fully as we possibly can.

Being the best that we can be includes being morally good, but it also includes striving for nonmoral goods as well, striving for the happy life. Living a life of excellence includes having an idea of what counts as the good life. It requires us to have a moral ideal and develop a sense of judgment about how this ideal is to be realized in day-to-day affairs. Virtue ethics offers much to guide us here, not so much as a theory of obligation but as a supplement to such a theory.

Values and Obligations

One of the central questions in normative ethics today is how best to understand the relationship between virtue ethics, with its emphasis on value, and an ethics of rules and principles, with its emphasis on duties or obligations. Those who favor the approach of **virtue ethics** say that determining what we are obliged to do is an important part of ethics, but it is secondary to what sorts of persons we are to become. If we are good persons, then we will do what is right. What someone *does* follows from what someone *is*. On the other hand, those who think of ethics as a matter of discovering the principles and rules that ought to guide behavior see the determination of right action as the fundamental job of ethics. After all, a habit is a virtue only if it is the right thing to do. Let us refer to this latter approach, the rule-centered approach to ethics developed in Part 1, as an **ethics of principles.**

The Primacy of an Ethics of Principles

It seems to many that everything important that may be said in virtue ethics can be incorporated into an ethics of principles. All the important points of virtue ethics may be seen as part of an ethics of principles. For example, the *ideal of the good life* is an important part of virtue ethics, as it guides the selection of particular virtues. A particular virtue is simply one way to achieve the goal of happiness expressed in such an ideal. Such goals also appear in an ethics of principles, however. In any consequentialist theory, for example, right action is defined in terms of the good it is to bring about. In our theory, the principle of beneficence plays this role. If we define the good as a life of rational activity, as Aristotle does, then his version of virtue ethics appears to differ little from a consequentialist theory that defines morally right actions as whatever promotes rational activity.

Another important part of virtue ethics is its insistence that virtues have primacy over rules. That is, in determining proper moral behavior, a person's *character is more important than a set of rules.* There is some truth to this, of course. If someone has a very bad moral character, she can be expected to follow rules only when doing so serves her purposes. You have to be a good person to do the right thing, even when doing so denies you some selfish benefits. But virtues themselves may be understood as internalized rules, as habits of following rules. As such, they are more basic than virtues. We could do away with the term "virtue" altogether, and replace it with the phrase, "the habit of following a particular moral rule." The virtue of honesty then becomes the habit of telling the truth, while the virtue of beneficence becomes the habit of doing good for others. The benefit of understanding rules to be primary in ethics is that it allows us to explain better how something gets to be a virtue in the first place. A virtue is simply the regular habit of following a rule that conforms to principles. Virtue ethics, you will remember, has a difficult time with such explanations.[13]

The third area of importance to virtue ethics has to do with *judgments about moral values.* It claims that an ethics of principles ignores this area, focusing as it does on right actions. In doing so it leaves out the very heart of ethics, the creation of good persons. Following rules may produce right actions, but if it is not done with the right reason it will not produce a good person. Even when an ethics of principles, such as that of Kant, for example, has considered the motives for following rules, it has not identified the correct motives. For Kant, the proper motive is duty and duty alone. I am a good person when I do the right thing from a sense of duty or obligation. But it surely is not in keeping with our idea of a good person that he or she act only out of duty. This seems cold and uncaring, at best. Instead, virtue ethics claims that bringing about happiness for oneself and others is what should motivate our behavior.

Although this is an important insight, it is nevertheless one that may be easily incorporated into an ethics of principles. In fact, most ethics of principles do have ideas about what it takes to be a good person. They identify the requirements for having a good moral character in terms of internalized rules and principles, along with having the proper motives, intentions, and attitudes for acting. In training the young to do what is right, in forming within them the habits of right behavior, we also instill in them the proper intentions, motives, attitudes, and even feelings that should accompany such actions. As we said above, while conformity to rules and principles is the criterion for judging actions to be right or wrong, habitually acting with the right reason is the criterion for judging persons as morally good or bad.

From this discussion it would appear that a universal ethics requires only an ethics of principles, since everything important in an ethics of virtue may be incorporated into its framework. But such appearances are deceiving because an ethics of virtue has more to say that cannot be reduced to an ethics of principles. It is important that we get at what this is because ignoring it will not allow us to fully explain our moral lives.

Virtue Ethics Supplements an Ethics of Principles

One of the complaints of virtue ethics is that an ethics of principles does not recognize that ethics is more than identifying obligations. A great deal of ethics, perhaps the very heart of it, has nothing to do with obligations at all. Instead, it has to do with figuring out how to be happy. It has to do with identifying the important things in life, those that will make us happy, and developing the habits and attitudes (virtues) that will direct our lives to the achievement of such goals. If this is the goal of ethics, to describe the good life and how to get it, and not that of identifying which principles and rules to follow, then it hardly makes sense to say that ethics is about living up to our obligations. Why in the world would we ever talk about being "obliged" to do what is good for us?

Let me suggest a way that this important insight of virtue ethics may be seen as supplementing our ethics of principles. An ethics of principles asks, What obligations do we owe to each other? The answer is developed by identifying the basic principle or principles to be followed in the establishment of rules that everyone ought to follow. These are our minimum duties or obligations. These are things all of us are obliged to do or refrain from doing in order to get along with each other. Most of these duties take the form of prohibiting certain sorts of actions such as killing, stealing, breaking promises, and the like. In addition to these we also have obligations to do good for those with whom we have special relationships, such as our children, our family, our patients, our students, and so on. Finally, we may rise above the call of duty and perform heroic actions, actions that require great sacrifice and courage. We are not obliged to perform such supererogatory actions, but we surely admire our heroes who do.

Virtue ethics steers a different course from that of duty, one that sees the goal of ethics as producing people who desire to rise above the mere performance of their minimum duties. It does not ask, What must we do to live together successfully? Rather, it asks, *How do I lead an excellent life?* Although Aristotle thought of human beings as existing in communities and thought of communities as the force that shaped the character of individuals, he was not so much interested in what we "owe" to these others but in what is good for "me," for my life. While what is good for me includes doing good for others, because it is in my interest to promote the well-being of the community that supports me, the focus of ethics is on what is good for me.

So the goal of virtue ethics is to discover the ideal that I ought to strive for and the sort of person I must be in order to be happy. This is not the goal of an ethics of principles, which leaves open the question of how we are to lead our lives beyond the level of living up to our duties to others. Because virtue ethics does address this question, it clearly has a role to play in supplementing an ethics of principles. It shows what must be added to an ethics of principles in order for our ethical theory to provide as complete an explanation for our moral lives as possible.

The Role of Aspiration

In addition to fulfilling our obligations and striving for excellence, the moral life may also include a person's **aspirations** to go beyond the call of duty and even beyond concern for his or her own personal happiness. Fortunately for most of us, there are some few among us who choose to lead their lives in this manner. They are our saints and heroes, those who find merely performing their minimum duties and striving for personal excellence to be an inadequate life. Instead, they sacrifice their personal happiness for the sake of others. Such lives are exemplary; they are the stuff of stories and legends. They instill admiration in us and inspire us to be much more noble than we might be otherwise. It is the business of your moral educators, your parents, clergy, and others to encourage you to live such lives. Though it is not the primary job of philosophy to promote such lives, with any luck your deliberations about moral philosophy will contribute to such worthy ends.

Final Remarks on Ethical Theories

Our final words about ethical theory are these. To be a **morally good person** you must live up to the following ideals:

1. Do what is right and avoid doing what is wrong. That is, you must follow rules that conform to the principles of beneficence, justice, and autonomy—the principles that determine right from wrong.

2. Perform these obligations with the proper motive (beneficence, duty), and the proper intention (to bring about beneficence, justice, and autonomy), and with the proper attitude and feelings. In particular, you must not do what is right merely to look good, or to achieve some personal gain, or to escape from some fear.

To be a **morally excellent person** you must

3. Strive to lead a life that will produce an excellent person, a happy person, a person who gets the most out of life for himself or herself.

Beyond this, we may also aspire to live our lives beyond the call of duty and personal excellence. We may choose to sacrifice our happiness and even our lives for the well-being of others. Those who do are our saints and heroes, and for them we reserve our highest admiration.

Chapter 4

The Method of Ethics: Critical Thinking

If ethics is the study of right and wrong, good and evil—if that is its subject matter—then its method is **critical thinking.** We have already examined part of this method in our discussion of moral reasoning. But moral reasoning is only one part of critical thinking, and it remains for us in this section to spell out the nature of its other parts. Critical thinking as discussed here is a method of problem solving. As the purpose of Part 2 is to solve moral problems, it is important to become clear about all the elements of critical thinking so that we may use them in a deliberate way in our attempt to solve the moral problems that await us.

The Elements of Critical Thinking

Some people equate critical thinking with logic or reasoning skills, here, we will use the term in a broader sense. Although reasoning may very well be the heart of thinking critically, especially in philosophy, there is much more to it than just reasoning. For the sake of clarity, let us begin to illustrate its basic features with an example from everyday life.[14]

The first thing to note is the obvious one that not all of our behavior, or even much of it, requires thinking. For most of our lives we behave as creatures of habit. This is a good thing. If we had to think about everything we did there would be little time for action. If every morning we had to think through every step of driving our cars to work, for example, we would be late more often than not. When we first learn to drive we have to think because driving behavior is not yet habitual, not yet routine. But after we have developed driving skills through sufficient practice, we no longer have to think about what we are doing when we turn the key and start the engine, when we pull out of the driveway and head for work. In fact, we usually find ourselves thinking about something else at such times—unless, of course, something goes wrong.

What if the usual road we take to work is closed for repairs, for example? Now we have a problem, now we have to think about finding another route. Or worse, what if the car will not start? After addressing our beloved vehicle with unkind words we then have to start thinking, start figuring out how to solve the problem before us. The car will not start. We have already mentioned two ingredients of critical thinking:

1. There is a **purpose** for our thinking, a goal (we need to get to work).

2. There is a **problem** to be thought about (the car will not start). The objective of our thinking is to solve this problem so that we can achieve our goal (get to work).

The next thing we do is to think about what might be the cause of the car's failure to start. We think of possible solutions. There is no gas in the car, the battery is dead, the starter motor no longer works, and so on. To discover which of these is correct we start making observations. We look at the gas gauge and the battery charging gauge; we open the hood and check for corrosion on the battery terminals. We blow the horn, turn on the lights, the radio; we turn the ignition key again and listen to the starter motor. Of course, if we know nothing about cars we may be better off calling the local garage and having someone else figure out what is wrong, but in either case, we can now identify two more elements of the thinking process:

3. There are **possible solutions** (hypotheses) to our problem.

4. There is **information** that must be gathered.

Of course, the more we know about cars the less explicit all these steps will be. For someone who is a mechanic this sort of problem is routine and does not generate much thinking. But let us assume that we are automotive novices and need to include all the steps of thinking. This will allow our natural pattern of thinking to become explicit.

Note that the observations made are relevant only because I have assumptions that I believe to be true. Gas gauges measure accurately the amount of gas that is in the car; the battery is not dead if the lights work; the starter is okay if I hear a whirring noise when I turn the key, and so on. I may also have considered the temperature (if it's cold out it affects the battery), the moisture in the air (it is dry, so the ignition wires are not wet), and the age of the battery (I just bought the darn thing!). So we can add to our list that

5. There are **assumptions** that we make when we think.

Now it is time to move on to the next step, testing which hypothesis is true. This is often something that we cannot do directly. We cannot look into the gas tank or do a chemical analysis of the battery, or see inside the starter motor. We must reason or infer from what we can observe (facts) to what therefore must be true if these facts are true. We must reason, that is, from premises to conclusions, as we do when we say, "If the gauge reads 'empty' the car is out of gas." If we were to fill in all the steps of this inference it would read something like this:

a. Anytime a gas gauge reads "empty" the car is out of gas.

b. This gauge reads "empty."

c. Therefore, the car is out of gas.

Of course, we are making an assumption that the gauge is working properly, but that aside, our explicit inference would now allow us to test one of our hypotheses—that the car will not start because it is out of gas. This test will amount to a simple observation—looking at the gas gauge. If it reads "empty" we pour some gas into the tank and try to start the car again. If it starts we have solved the problem. If not, we go on to the next hypothesis. This is how we solve the problems of daily life when we are thinking well.

Science also uses this basic problem-solving strategy when it indirectly tests a hypothesis by verifying or falsifying the truth of what follows from, or what is "deduced" from, the hypothesis. The scientific method is often called the **hypothetico-deductive method** because it involves formulating hypotheses, making inferences as to what follows from the truth of such hypotheses, and then attempting to confirm by observation the truth of what has been inferred. For example, Darwin could not directly observe the processes of evolution that preceded him by millions of years. He could, however, infer that *if* such a process had occurred, *then* fossil records would have been left behind. These records, once uncovered, would go a long way toward confirming the hypothesis of natural selection.

Inferences are extremely important as well when we attempt to solve problems in philosophy. However, there is a major difference between the way they function in science and their role in philosophy. This difference especially has to do with the role that facts play in philosophy. In science and daily life, once you have inferred what is true, if your hypothesis is true, you can often settle the matter by appealing to facts. If you are out of gas, then the gas gauge will read "empty." Just a quick look at the gas gauge is often enough to confirm the original hypothesis. In science, designing an experiment to test a hypothesis is often extremely complicated, sometimes requiring expensive equipment, lots of time, and many inferences that require knowledge of complex theories. In the end, however, facts are usually the final court of appeal.

In philosophical problem solving, however, examining facts to test hypotheses is always insufficient. We need facts to solve philosophical problems, but facts alone will not do. This is because philosophical problems are concerned with how to interpret facts, or how to think about something in the absence of sufficient facts. Such problems arise when all the known facts are in and still there are further questions to answer, further problems to solve. Philosophical problems go beyond facts to a consideration of how to understand or interpret them. Later we will have more to say about how philosophers test their hypotheses, their proposed solutions to problems. For now, we may add to our list of thinking elements that

6. There are **inferences** involved. We draw conclusions from premises.

7. There is **hypothesis testing,** the verification of our proposed solution to the problem.

Finally, we have to consider the consequences of our hypothesis being true. If the car is out of gas I have to get some if I want to get to work by driving my car. If the battery is dead, and if that was caused by a wornout alternator, then I have to call the garage and spend quite a bit of money to repair the car. This means that I also have to find another way to get to work that day, and that the new expensive running shoes I had my eye on are now out of the question. So a final element of thinking is that

8. There are **consequences** that follow if my hypothesis is true.

These various aspects of thinking amount to a general definition of what it means to think, at least in the sense that thinking is a matter of solving problems.

The Structure of Part 2

This general definition of critical thinking may now be used to provide a **structure** that will be followed in discussing the moral problems of Part 2. This structure will reflect the pattern of thinking outlined above and will constitute for us the method of ethics. In addition to clarifying the nature of this method, we will also discuss the **standards** to which each element of critical thinking ought to conform. It is one thing to think, and quite another to think well. If the "thinking" part of critical thinking refers to the eight elements identified above, the "critical" part of critical thinking refers to the standards that good thinking ought to follow.

The Problem

Part 2 will be divided into chapters, with each chapter devoted to a single moral problem. Within each chapter will be several sections, reflecting the general pattern of critical thinking. The first section of each chapter will be called "The Problem." It will apply the first three steps of critical thinking to the problem at hand—identifying the purpose of our thinking, formulating the problem to be solved, and discovering possible solutions to the problem. The purpose of our thinking in Part 2 will always be to determine right from wrong. We will spend little time restating this goal for each chapter and instead focus on the other two steps.

The first step of the first section will be to **formulate the problem** to be discussed. This will especially require us to identify the problem before us, to distinguish it from related problems, and to define key terms. This last task is especially important. When the meaning of terms are unclear or confused with the meaning of other terms, a great deal of energy may be wasted arguing back and forth about what may amount to very different problems. Imagine all the energy that has been wasted in the abortion debate, for example, because of the different meanings attributed by people to the concept "person." A good definition must be **clear** and **distinct;** these are the standards of critical thinking that especially apply to this first section. It is often challenging to define terms clearly and distinctly. For example, could you give a clear definition of "person" right now, and distinguish it from a related concept such as "human being"? Though providing such definitions is often a difficult task, it is nevertheless a task that is required in order for us to be able to solve moral problems.

The next job of this first section will be to **identify possible solutions** to the problem before us. For some problems this task will be relatively straightforward. Often we will have only two possible solutions, namely, that actions of the type in question are right or they are wrong. Even here, however, we usually have to qualify possible solutions to distinguish them from others. For example, if the problem is whether capital punishment is immoral, one possible solution is simply that always and everywhere the use of capital punishment is wrong. Another possible solution is that it is not immoral. This possible solution must be qualified, however, especially by listing the sorts of crimes for which it may be morally acceptable.

In sum, the first section will define key terms, formulate the problem to be discussed, and identify its possible solutions.

Facts and Assumptions

The first task of the second section of each chapter, called "Facts and Assumptions," will be to **gather information.** This especially means that we will examine any **facts** that may be relevant to the problem. Because Part 2 requires that we apply moral principles to specific situations, there will always be facts that are relevant. Applied ethics requires us to understand the facts that define the situation, both scientific and commonsense facts. We cannot reasonably discuss the morality of abortion, for example, unless we know something about the scientific facts of fetal development.

It will often be important for us to know some **descriptive ethics** as well, some facts about the rules and attitudes that currently exist in society. The rules and attitudes about euthanasia in the United States, for example, will be found in the law, in medicine, in various religions, and in public opinion. These rules and attitudes do not determine what is morally right, but they are often helpful guides. What ought to be the case (normative ethics) may not follow from what is the case (descriptive ethics), but sometimes the two are quite closely related.

When gathering information we must make sure that it is **reliable.** This is the main standard to keep in mind when searching for facts. The reliability of information is often an issue in this day of talk shows, mass media, and the Internet. Anyone can say whatever she wishes and get someone to believe it. To know whether the information you have discovered is reliable, it is important to check your sources. There are many groups and individuals dispensing information that is slanted to their cause. Make sure that your sources are credible. One way to do this is to check the credentials of the source. If the person is a recognized expert in his or her field, that is a good reason to accept what he or she says as true. You may judge such people's level of expertise for yourself by examining such things as the degrees which they hold, the institutions with which they are affiliated, their accomplishments, and so on. If, on the other hand, an article appears with nothing but a name above it, and especially if it is an article on the Internet with no name above it, do not be quick to accept its contents as reliable.

Examining assumptions is also often crucial in solving moral problems. An assumption is simply a belief for which no evidence has been provided. It is a belief whose truth we take for granted. Assumptions often lie at the base of our thinking and control the sorts of evidence we are more or less likely to accept. For example, in debating the issue of government censorship, if I assume that the job of the government is simply to protect me from *others,* then I will be less likely to accept a law designed to protect *me* from the psychological and moral harms of pornography. If, on the other hand, I assume that the government should do more than police its citizens, that its laws should also help us to bring out what is best in us, I may be more open to censorship laws. Uncovering and examining assumptions such as these is an important part of critical thinking and will play an important role in this second section.

Another way that we will examine our assumptions is to become aware of the particular perspective or **point of view** that we bring to the problem. The idea that we can approach a subject in a purely objective manner, weighing conflicting evidence and evaluating arguments pro and con with no regard for our own needs, desires, and interests, is simply false. We are all finite creatures, living in a particular time and place, influenced by our culture and driven by our own needs and desires. Everyone brings to a discussion of controversial issues "prephilosophical" beliefs about the best possible solution. You, too, will naturally favor defending one possible solution over another, even before examining the available evidence. What solution you happen to favor will depend on your point of view, which itself is determined by your upbringing and your life experiences. Such a readiness to accept one view over another even before examining its reasonableness may exclude a fair hearing of competing views.

All of us tend to favor opinions that agree with our own, even if the evidence for our pet beliefs is inferior to the evidence for its competitors. Our point of view tends to steer us toward evidence that supports our view and away from evidence that does not. The more we can be aware of the role that our point of view plays in the acceptance of our beliefs, the freer we are from its influence and the more open we become to new ideas. Being aware of your point of view, the set of ideas or beliefs that color how you weigh certain facts and conclusions, is one way to lessen its influence, one way to allow yourself to take seriously possible solutions that do not agree with your own.

Here is my advice about the point of view you bring to the search for solutions to moral problems. First, be *aware* that you have one and, to the degree possible, be aware of how it might influence your thinking. With any luck you are in a class with students who have divergent points of view. By contrasting what they have to say with your own opinion, it may become easier to bring your own point of view to the surface.

Next, *accept* your point of view as a legitimate part of yourself. No one should criticize another for the point of view that he or she brings to the discussion. For the most part, you had little control over what experiences shaped your perspectives. Finally, try to see your point of view from a *distance*. Separate yourself from it as much as you can, holding it at arm's length, if you will. In this way you can examine it, challenge it, widen it, and thus come to own it or not. Above all else, stay as tolerant about the facts and arguments as you can, and struggle to give each possible solution a fair hearing.

In sum, in the second section of each chapter, our thinking will focus on gathering reliable information and on considering honestly and thoroughly any assumptions and points of view that may influence which possible solution we are most likely to accept.

Moral Reasoning

The third section of each chapter will be called "Moral Reasoning." By the time we get to this section we will have clarified key concepts, formulated the problem and identified its possible solutions, gathered information, and examined any relevant assumptions and points of view that may affect which solutions we may accept. Now it is time to argue for the various possible solutions we have identified. We will argue as hard as we can for each of them, whatever our personal preferences. In arguing hard for each possible solution, not just our favorite one, the strengths and weaknesses of each position will be revealed most fully, and the best solution will emerge.

As we have seen previously, moral reasoning involves two basic steps. First, the type of moral problem must be identified. Knowing whether it is a factual, conflict of rules, or conflict of principles type of problem is necessary to guide our reasoning. Next, we must formulate a good reasons argument for each possible solution. In such arguments possible solutions are defended by finding as many reasons as possible to support them, and then by replying to all the serious objections against them. Arguing for and against possible solutions will often be the most time-consuming part of each section. It is also the most important.

Having to argue for possible solutions that you may disagree with and may even detest will at first seem strange to most of you. Many of us are more comfortable in not arguing at all but instead simply stating our opinion and ending the conversation. Others may be comfortable in giving reasons *for* their views but not in answering the objections to them that others may present. The moral problems to be discussed in Part 2 are all controversial issues; they all have more than one reasonable solution. Usually, if one of these solutions is correct, it means that the others are not. Because of this, the possible solution that you favor is only as strong as its ability to withstand the objections of the "other side." As a good lawyer must consider the objections of the other side in building his or her case, so you must learn to identify and respond to objections from competing possible solutions.

Evaluation

If the third section is concerned with constructing arguments, the job of the fourth section, called "Evaluation," is to assess them. It is to decide which argument is best and therefore which possible solution is the most reasonable. The question now is, what makes one good reasons argument better than another? More precisely, what are the standards by which good reasons arguments ought to be evaluated?

The general **standards** or rules for evaluating inductive arguments require its premises to be relevant, reliable, and sufficient. To say that premises must be **relevant** means that their truth or falsity must matter to the truth or falsity of the conclusion. They are not relevant if their truth or falsity makes little or no difference to the truth or falsity of the conclusion. For example, suppose you are a defense attorney arguing in a courtroom that your client did not commit the rape for which he has been indicted. You point out that he has blonde hair and blue eyes. The judge quickly tells you that such matters are not relevant. You point out that the allegedly raped woman has a suspect sexual history. The judge throws that fact out as irrelevant as well. All that matters, the only facts that are relevant, are the facts that show that your client did or did not perform the act of rape.

The relevance of premises used to support moral conclusions will usually be a matter of their expressing what our principles require. That is, if the premises describe a harm or benefit, or if they express a concern of justice or injustice, or if they mention a matter of autonomy or its denial, then they are relevant. They are relevant because it is precisely these sorts of things that matter in determining right from wrong.

Premises must also be **reliable.** That is, they must be true. In inductive arguments, this does not mean that a premise must be known to be true with absolute certainty. Very little, if anything, is known with absolute certainty. Instead, to say that a promise is reliable means that there is good evidence to believe that it is true. You may claim that your client was somewhere else at the time of the rape, for example, but in the absence of any evidence that he was elsewhere, this premise does little to support your argument. If there were several eyewitnesses placing him at another location, however, that would make all the difference.

Finally, premises must be **sufficient.** That is, there must be enough of them to support the conclusion. Generally speaking, the more evidence there is, the stronger the conclusion. Sometimes the conclusion has to be adjusted to reflect the amount of evidence, or lack thereof. We will say more about this as we evaluate specific arguments in Part 2. For now we may summarize the tasks of fourth section. In this section we will examine the strengths and weaknesses of the arguments presented for various possible solutions by examining the relevance, reliability, and sufficiency of their premises. Our goal here is to reach a reasoned judgment, a judgment that one argument is stronger than the others. Always this will be difficult; sometimes it will be very difficult. This should not be surprising, since we will be discussing moral problems that have resisted solution for quite some time.

It is important to say what we mean by a **reasoned judgment,** and especially to distinguish reasoned judgments from statements of fact and opinion. Many people believe that statements may express only facts or opinions. If a statement expresses a fact, it is objective and can be proven; if it expresses an opinion, it is subjective and there is no sense in arguing about it. However, statements may also express reasoned judgments. These are beliefs that are neither facts nor mere opinions, but lie somewhere in between. They are opinions that have been supported by reasons, reasons that appear as premises in arguments. Taken together, such premises provide support for a possible solution, removing it from the ranks of *mere* opinion, to the category of justified moral belief.

In this fourth section the critical thinking skill of **testing** our possible solutions will require us to weigh the strengths and weakness of good reasons arguments. We will use our three rules of relevance, reliability, and sufficiency in this process, with the goal of forming a reasoned judgment. In forming a reasoned judgment we decide that the reasons given for one possible solution are superior to the rest, and that the solution expresses the most reasonable way to think and act.

In addition to forming a reasoned judgment that one case is superior to the others, in the Evaluation section we will also engage in our final critical thinking skill, exploring the **consequences** of this being the case. For example, if we decide that physician-assisted suicide is morally acceptable, does that mean we should support its legalization? Or, to take another example, if it is wrong to experiment on some animals, does that mean it is wrong to eat them as well? And if it is wrong to eat some animals, is it therefore wrong to eat all animals? Exploring consequences is an important task, one that relates our thinking closely to our actions.

Another Perspective

The final section of each chapter will be called "Another Perspective." In this section we will examine an approach to the issue under discussion that either differs from or supplements the one taken in the chapter. This will usually be a point of view that challenges or expands your pet solution to the problem at hand. Sometimes, for example, we will examine the different ways in which people from other cultures deal with the problem in question. At other times, we will focus on those within our own culture who have dramatically different beliefs from those accepted by the majority of people. At still other times, we will focus on personal accounts, on how the moral problem in question affects the lives and hopes of those who wrestle with it directly. Understanding an issue from another perspective very often allows you to understand better the one you have adopted all along.

Part 2

Moral Problems

SECTION A

Moral Problems Concerned with Life and Death

We have seen that not every moral decision with which we are faced is a problem. Some moral decisions are quite simple, requiring little or no thought. Others, however, are not so simple and require much thought. This is especially true for the problems that divide society deeply and painfully, many of which are of the "factual" and "conflict of rules" types. Our discussion of ethical theories in Part 1 has left us with clear guidelines for solving such moral problems. In Part 2, we will apply what we have learned there to think critically about twelve different moral problems. Part 2 has been divided into four areas, reflecting some common themes.

For each problem to be examined we will follow the format of critical thinking outlined in Part 1. We will first formulate the problem, clarify key terms, and present possible solutions. Next we will examine any facts, assumptions, and points of view that may be important for its solution. We will then construct arguments in support of each possible solution, and finally we will evaluate the strengths and weaknesses of these arguments to form a reasoned judgment as to which possible solution is best. Once having determined the morally acceptable course of action, we will end the discussion with a consideration of perspectives that may differ from the ones examined in the chapter. We will begin by discussing some controversial moral issues concerned with matters of life and death.

Chapter 5

Capital Punishment

Capital punishment, or the death penalty, is one of the many moral issues that divide society very deeply. It seems that every day some heinous crime is committed somewhere in this country, a crime for which many of us cry out for the death penalty. You probably are familiar with several examples of such crimes and remember how you felt when you first heard of them. For many among us, the feeling that vicious murderers should suffer the same fate as their victims is very strong. We become very angry when such crimes are punished with anything short of the death penalty and believe that in such cases justice surely has not been served.

Others among us are just as strongly opposed to the death penalty. We believe that life is too important ever to be taken intentionally—even when the life is that of a murderer. We believe that life in prison will serve society just as well. Such punishment surely is enough to satisfy the demands of justice. It also does just as good a job as capital punishment does of persuading would-be murderers to reconsider their deeds. Those who oppose the death penalty believe that it is time for the United States to end this barbaric and vengeful practice, just as almost all other developed nations of the world have done. We have enough violence in our society without the government itself taking on such a role.

The Problem

There are, of course, many forms of punishment. A mother may punish her daughter for being mean to her brother. A gang leader may punish one of the gang members for disloyalty. A teacher may punish a student for disrupting the classroom. The punishment of criminals by the government is the only form of punishment that will be of interest to us, however.

Clarifying Concepts

Such **punishment**[1] may be defined as the *justified, deliberate infliction of pain, by authorities, according to rules.* Each part of this definition is important, but we will focus on the first part—that punishment must be justified.

Punishment must be justified in two senses. A particular act of punishment must be legally justified. The criminal must be shown to have committed a crime for which he or she is liable to punishment. The general activity of authorities punishing people for their crimes must also be morally justified. After all, when the state punishes criminals, it is inflicting pain and suffering on them, especially the loss of their freedom. Such an action seems to violate the principle of benefi-cence, which requires us to do good and avoid evil. If punishment is morally acceptable, there must evidence that some greater good is to be gained by it, or that some greater evil is to be avoided, or that the punishment has a higher moral priority. This sort of justification is especially required when the punishment in question is the death penalty.

There are many types of crime for which the death penalty has been consid-ered morally acceptable. Chief among these is the crime of first-degree murder. Murder is referred to as "first degree" when it is performed intentionally and deliberately and freely. The murderer is usually in a sufficiently calm and rational state for a long enough period of time before the crime to have a clear choice in the matter, and thus to be able to stop himself or herself from murder-ing the victim. Sometimes we refer to such a murder as "premeditated." The contract killer who stalks and kills his victim for money, the terrorist who ignites explosives in a crowded area, and the rapist who deliberately kills his victim to avoid being identified later on—all these types of murderers could have stopped themselves from acting. Because of this we think of them as thoroughly respon-sible for their actions.

In addition to first-degree murder, other capital offenses have included such crimes as rape, armed robbery, kidnapping, treason, skyjacking, train-wrecking, drug-trafficking, perjury leading to the execution of an innocent person, and aggravated assault by a prisoner serving a life sentence. With the possible excep-tion of rape, these crimes are seen as capital offenses because they involve the like-lihood that someone will die. In planning any of these crimes, criminals are aware of this likelihood and accept it. They may thus be viewed as fully responsible if their crime results in someone's death. In addition to the above crimes that vari-ous states in the United States have listed as capital crimes, the federal govern-ment has added to the list of capital offenses many other types of murders of this sort. These include murders that occur during the process of smuggling aliens into the country or murders as a result of a drive-by shooting, or a civil rights offense resulting in death, or the murder of a police officer, a congressman, a Supreme Court justice, or a foreign official—to name just a few.

Killings that are not capital offenses are those that may result from an accident—an automobile accident, for example. Or they may result from negligence, as when a parent fails to seek medical care for her ailing child, who subsequently dies. Some people are killed as a result of anger and some as the result of a serious men-tal illness of the killer. These are all forms of killing; the victim is just as dead as the victims of first-degree murder; but these crimes are not considered by the law to be as wicked as capital offenses. They are lesser crimes because they were not committed by the criminal with the same premeditated state of mind as that of a capital offender.

Formulating the Problem

Because many crimes are punishable by the death penalty in this country, it is important in assessing the morality of capital punishment to specify for which of these crimes, if any, the death penalty should be viewed as morally acceptable. The death penalty has been ruled unconstitutional for rape alone, and because most of the crimes listed above have to do with murder or its likelihood, let us *formulate the problem* before us in this way:

Is capital punishment morally acceptable for the crime of first degree murder?

There are other problems about capital punishment that are related to this one, especially questions about whether it should be legally abolished or retained. Presumably, if it is immoral, capital punishment should be abolished. Likewise, if it is morally acceptable, it should be retained and used. However, even if capital punishment is found to be a morally acceptable form of punishment for first-degree murder, we might still wish to make it illegal. We may think that administering it is too costly, for example. Because of the lengthy and expensive appeals allowed to those convicted of capital offenses, the cost of administering the death penalty is at least twice that required to incarcerate a murderer for life.

We may also wish to make capital punishment illegal because we think the justice system as it currently exists is quite capable of executing an innocent person. Methods of gathering evidence have especially come under attack recently. Police and prosecutors from various parts of the country have been criticized on numerous occasions for manufacturing evidence that led to capital convictions, or for concealing evidence helpful to defendants in capital cases. The courts have also been criticized for providing less than adequate legal representation for defendants. As we will see in the next section, a great number of those sentenced to death have had either their convictions or their sentences overturned on appeal.

Finally, even if capital punishment is morally acceptable, we may wish to abolish it legally, because we believe that for the government to execute someone as a way to solve a problem sets a bad example for the citizenry in general. As you can see, the legal question is different from the moral question of capital punishment. However important the legal question may be, it is not the problem before us now. We will address it later, when we talk about the consequences of adopting one possible solution over another. For now, we will focus entirely on the morality of capital punishment.

Possible Solutions

There are two leading *possible solutions* to our problem. One is to claim that capital punishment is morally acceptable for the crime of first-degree murder. The other is to say that it is not an acceptable form of punishment for any crime. The goal before us now is to formulate a reasoned judgment as to which of these possible solutions is best. To do this we must examine the evidence for and against each, and express this evidence as a list of premises in a good reasons argument. We will begin this task by looking for any facts or assumptions that may serve as such premises.

Facts and Assumptions

Facts

Many *facts* are relevant to the solution of our problem. We may begin with some facts about the extent of the use of capital punishment in the United States. During the past twenty-five years, about fifty-five hundred prisoners have been placed on death row. As of this writing, some five hundred sixty or so already have been executed. Roughly two thousand of these fifty-five hundred prisoners were removed from the list of those to be executed, either by natural death, reversal of conviction, or resentencing. In 1997, for example, of the 256 prisoners who entered death row, seventy-six later had their death sentences overturned. Most of these are serving lesser sentences, some received new trials, and at least one was found to be not guilty as the result of a new trial. Currently, about thirty-three hundred inmates are awaiting execution in American prisons.

The average time between sentencing and execution is close to ten years, due mainly to the lengthy appeals process granted to each convicted capital offender. Many inmates appeal all the way through the state courts, and then continue to appeal their convictions and sentences through the federal justice system. The point of allowing such a lengthy appeals process is to guard against the possibility of executing an innocent person. This is always a frightening possibility. In fact, more and more capital convictions have been overturned recently, especially because of the new methods of DNA testing that have been used during new trails granted as a result of the appeals process.

Other relevant facts include the following. Most states today execute their capital offenders by lethal injection, though some use electrocution or gas. In a few states it is still legal to use firing squads and even hanging as the means of execution. About a third of the states allow capital punishment for those sixteen years of age or younger; for another third, eighteen is the minimum age. Some states execute the mentally retarded. About 40 percent of those on death row are to be found in three states—Texas, California, and Florida. There are almost as many minorities on death row—especially African-American and Hispanic males—as there are white males. Currently there are very few women capital offenders, well under fifty.

This is a good place to notice the difference between facts of the sort just mentioned and what may be inferred from them. For example, we just said that there are almost as many minorities on death row as white individuals. If you couple this with the fact that minorities are minorities—that there are roughly three times the number of white people in this country as minorities—more than one inference may be drawn. Some, for example, say it shows that minorities commit three times as many murders as their white counterparts. Others infer that capital punishment discriminates against minorities, as proportionally so many more minorities are given the death sentence than those in the white majority. There are ways to check the soundness of these inferences, of course, but the important point for now is that they are inferences. They go beyond the facts. Be careful about confusing facts with inferences or interpretations of facts.

Descriptive Ethics

Becoming familiar with society's current rules is a way for us to see what people *do* believe about the rightness or wrongness of capital punishment. Even though we are ultimately interested in what the rules *ought to be*, it is always good to start with an understanding of what they are. This is a job for **descriptive ethics.** It is especially important to examine the **legal rules** governing capital punishment. These rules are constructed by the federal government, by each state, and by the United States Supreme Court.

The federal government allows capital punishment for nearly fifty types of crimes, most of the sorts that we have mentioned above. In addition, thirty-eight states currently allow the death penalty, mostly for first-degree murder. As of this writing, the death penalty is illegal only in Alaska, Hawaii, Iowa, Maine, Massachusetts, Michigan, Minnesota, North Dakota, Rhode Island, Vermont, West Virginia, Wisconsin, and the District of Columbia.

State and federal legislative bodies may not pass and consider valid just any laws about punishment that they wish. Their statutes must pass the test of constitutionality imposed by the United States Supreme Court's interpretation of the Constitution. The Eighth Amendment to the Constitution of the United States specifically forbids punishments that are "cruel and unusual," for example. A state cannot punish its criminals in ways that violate this requirement. Many who wish to abolish the death penalty have pinned their hopes on the Supreme Court's ruling it to be a form of cruel and unusual punishment. However, the Court has made no such statement. It has, in fact, found capital punishment statutes to be constitutional as long as they comply with certain guidelines.

Some of these guidelines concern the types of crimes allowed to be classified as capital offenses. Other guidelines concern the process required to convict and sentence a person to be executed in a justifiable manner. A defendant must be properly defended by a competent attorney, for example, and have the right to appeal his or her conviction in both the state and federal courts. In sentencing a criminal to death, the jury must consider the circumstances of the crime, and especially what are called "mitigating circumstances." These are conditions that may lessen the responsibility of the murderer, such as his age or a psychological impairment of one sort or another. The general point is that capital punishment is legal in this country as long as convictions and sentencings follow such general guidelines.

Public opinion and religion also have much to say about the appropriateness of capital punishment, and what they say is also considered part of descriptive ethics. The majority of the American public, roughly two-thirds of us, believe that capital punishment is appropriate for some murders. This is the number of people who agree with the use of the death penalty when polls have been conducted after well-publicized and especially heinous murders.

In theory, many **religions** also agree with the death penalty. At least, they have in the past, often arguing that the biblical phrase, an "eye for an eye," applies also to a "life for a life." However, in more recent times many major religions have become strongly opposed to the death penalty. To allow it is one thing when there is no feasible option for dealing with murderers. With secure prisons, however, criminals may now safely be put away for life. There is no longer any need for them to be executed. Many religions thus argue that the value of life, even the life of a murderer, should take precedence over the needs of society for its retribution or its safety.

Assumptions

In addition to facts such as these and others that will be mentioned later, there are some important *assumptions* that underlie our beliefs about the moral acceptability of capital punishment, especially assumptions about the moral acceptability of any form of punishment. What we believe about why it is right for the state to punish in general will significantly determine our beliefs about what makes capital punishment in particular morally acceptable or not. As this text is supposed to encourage you to think for yourself, this is a good place for you to try to identify and clarify these assumptions.

Exercise 5.1

Begin the exercise by attempting to answer this question: *Why is it morally acceptable to punish criminals?* Why, for example, do we not simply scold them and tell them to go home and commit no more crimes? Do we not often punish our children in this manner? Or why do we not simply publish their names in the local newspaper and describe their offense? Would not the shame of this be sufficient to prevent crime? Or why do we not send criminals off for several sessions of psychotherapy? After all, are they not simply maladjusted human beings? Remember, the question asks you to say why it is "morally acceptable" to punish those who commit crimes.

Think of as many answers as you can to the above question, not just the first thing that comes to mind. For your second task, you should attempt to rank these answers in order of importance. Say why you ranked highest the reasons that you did. As your third and final task, see if you can explain how each of your first two answers to the question of why any form of punishment is morally right may be used to show how capital punishment is morally right.

Moral Reasoning

The problem of this chapter is to determine whether capital punishment is morally acceptable for the crime of first-degree murder. This may be classified as a **conflict of rules** problem. Because capital punishment involves killing someone, one rule that will be in conflict with others is "Do not kill." This is the rule that opponents of capital punishment appeal to in claiming that it is an immoral form of punishment. On the other hand, the state has an obligation to prevent murder and to administer a just punishment to those who commit such awful crimes. Those in favor of capital punishment often appeal to these obligations, which may be expressed as the following rules: "Prevent murder," and "Punish in proportion to the severity of the crime." There are other rules that play a role in the capital punishment issue, but these are the main ones.

For now, it will be helpful for you to think of the problem before us as one of determining which rule has the highest priority. Is "Do not kill" our highest obligation, or is it the combination of the other two rules? To answer this question and to determine whether capital punishment is morally acceptable, we must appeal to our three moral principles. Guided by the principle of beneficence, we must weigh the harms and benefits of following one or another rule; guided by the principle of justice, we must consider the fairness of doing so; and guided by the principle of autonomy, we must consider whether following one rule or another violates or supports freedom.

This is the framework to keep in mind as we construct good reasons arguments for and against capital punishment. This is what our arguments will be attempting to do, to show the priority of one rule or set of rules over another. How well they accomplish this task will be decided in the "Evaluation" section to follow.

The Case for Capital Punishment

To **make a case** for a moral belief means the same thing as to construct an argument for it. We will begin to make a case that capital punishment is morally acceptable by referring back to Exercise 5.1. The central question you had to answer there was, *Why is it morally acceptable to punish criminals?* There are several "official" answers to this question, two of which we shall discuss here. You may find it interesting to compare them with your own answers. Simply put, one answer is that punishing criminals is right because they deserve to be punished. The second answer is that it is right because doing so prevents or deters crime. Punishment prevents the criminal from committing the crime again. It teaches him a lesson. It also deters others who may be thinking of committing such a crime. As a threat to their freedom, it motivates them to refrain from committing the crime in the first place.

There is a second question about punishment that is often coupled with this one: *How much punishment is morally acceptable?* One answer is that the punishment received should fit the crime committed. Another answer is that we should punish just enough to deter the crime in question. A moral justification of punishment includes answers to both questions. One such justification is called **retributivism.** It accepts the first answer to each of the two questions. It thus claims the following as its moral justification of punishment: Criminals deserve to be punished, and they deserve to be punished in proportion to their crimes. A second justification for punishment is called **deterrence.** It accepts the second answer to each of the two questions, claiming that criminals should be punished in order to deter crime, and they should be punished just enough to do so.

Retributivism relies mainly on the principle of justice, especially the idea of justice as equality. Sometimes equality may refer to how goods are to be distributed. If there are four cookies and four children, "each gets one" would be a just rule to follow in dividing them up equally. A child who eats two-and-a-half cookies and gives one-half to each sibling may rightly be scolded by his parents for not being just or fair. This simple example is at the heart of our concept of social justice, which will be discussed in later chapters.

Sometimes equality may refer to paying a debt. If I borrow ten dollars from Jack, I must pay back to Jack an equal amount to settle the debt. Anything short of this is not just. It is too little. I will still owe Jack more money if I only pay him nine dollars. This simple example governs the principles of punishment for the retributivist and may be used to define what it means to punish someone in a fair or just manner. It claims that the punishment must fit the crime. It says that too little or too much punishment is not morally right because it violates the principle of justice.

The deterrence justification of punishment, on the other hand, relies especially on the principle of beneficence. Punishment produces harm, a violation of the principle of beneficence. But some harms are justified because they avoid greater harms. For many, exercising is painful, but is worth the pain because it produces a healthier body. This avoids a lot more pain in the long run. In the same way, the pain experienced by criminals is a lot less than the pain that would exist in society if they were not punished. If there were no punishment, there would be much more crime, and thus much more suffering on the part of all. Law and order is required in a civilized state, and law and order requires the threat of punishment to deter people from committing crimes. So punishment is justified by the principle of beneficence as a lesser of two evils.

Whereas the punishment of criminals may be justified by the principle of beneficence, it justifies only enough punishment to deter the crime. Any more punishment is excessive and therefore violates the principle of beneficence. We could send car thieves away for life, I suppose. But if six months of jail time is enough to teach them a lesson and to show others that "crime does not pay," then life in prison is excessive and therefore causes immoral pain and suffering. This last point is important for all forms of punishment, but especially for our discussion of capital punishment. The issue for us is not whether we should use capital punishment or no punishment for murder. It is whether capital punishment or life in prison ought to be used, when "life" means either life in prison with no parole or long-term imprisonment. As the death penalty is usually considered to be a greater punishment than life in prison, using it will require demonstrating that it works better than a life sentence to deter murder. If it does not, then it is excessive punishment.

It may strike you as somewhat strange that there are two general moral justifications for punishment. For the most part, those within the criminal justice system accept deterrence as the leading justification. It is deterrence that provides the important guidelines for determining proper sentences. In saying that punishment must fit the crime, however, retributivism seems to be more in line with our ordinary beliefs. In our everyday lives, most of us think that to punish too much or too little is unfair. We carry these beliefs over to the justice system, as well, objecting especially when it is "too soft" on crime. To be fair to the arguments on both sides, we will argue for capital punishment from each of the perspectives created by these underlying assumptions.

We are now in a position to construct an argument for capital punishment. The first premise is based on retributivism, especially on its answer to the second question of how much to punish.

1. The death penalty is the only punishment equal to the crime of first-degree murder. (J)

Any other punishment, even life in prison, is too little. Only losing your own life pays back adequately for the crime of taking another's. We commonly express this belief with the phrase, "a life for a life." Deep down, where our surging passions have their own language, we feel that justice has not been served unless the crime of murder has been paid for with the life of the murderer. Sometimes, especially when the murder has been especially heinous or close to home, we want the murderer to suffer even more than the death penalty allows. For the retributivist, at least the death penalty is required by justice. We will place a (J) after (1) to show that its claim follows from the principle of justice.

The second premise comes from the deterrence justification of punishment.

2. The death penalty is a more effective deterrent to the crime of murder than is life in prison. (B)

The claim here is that the threat of the death penalty will prevent more people from committing murder than the threat of life in prison. The murder rate will drop in a state that adopts the death penalty. States without it will have murders committed that might have been prevented if only they had had the death penalty. In the presence of the death penalty, criminals will think twice before carrying weapons, and especially before killing police officers and other government officials. The more widespread the death penalty, and the more we use it, the more the message will be sent to would-be murders and the fewer of them there will be. We place a (B) after (2) to show that it follows from the principle of beneficence. With fewer murders, there will be less pain and suffering in the world.

The rest of the argument for capital punishment consists of responding to objections. As might be expected, these objections will be presented by those who argue the other side—that capital punishment is immoral. In fact, because the cases for and against capital punishment argue for opposite conclusions, the reasons offered to support one will often be objections to the other. Because this is true, it will be helpful for us first to see the "reasons for" the claims from both sides. Then we can return to each case to reply to objections. This is the format that we shall adopt throughout Part 2 and that we will follow as we construct arguments for and against various claims. First we will hear the reasons for each case; then we will return to complete the arguments by responding to the reasons against their claim that are presented by the other side.

The Case against Capital Punishment

The first premise in the argument against capital punishment concerns the discriminatory manner with which the death penalty is used in the United States. We will use (') after each premise in this argument to distinguish it from the premises of the previous argument. Premise (1)' states:

1.' The death penalty discriminates against the poor and minorities. (J)

One of the ways we know this to be true is from the numbers of minorities and poor people on death row. As we said in the "Facts and Assumptions" section, there are almost as many minorities as there are white males awaiting execution. Now some may infer from this fact that minorities commit far more murders than their fair share. Perhaps this is correct. But the main point is that far more poor and minority individual are sentenced to death *for the same type of crime* than are their white and wealthier counterparts. If you are white and wealthy in the United States, your chances of being convicted of first-degree murder and receiving a death sentence are far less than if you are either poor or a minority. The federal justice system recently began to reexamine its administration of the death penalty for precisely this reason. Minorities were the defendants in 75 percent of the capital cases prosecuted by the federal government from 1995 to 2000. The death penalty, in short, is used in an inherently unfair, discriminatory manner. It places greater value on the lives of some than others. This is why there is a (J) after premise (1)'.

The second premise says:

2.' Innocent people may be wrongly executed. (B,J,A)

The killing of any innocent person violates all three moral principles. It causes great harm and it robs those killed of their value and their freedom. It would seem at first glance that no innocent person would be executed, as there are so many appeals allowed to those sentenced to die. However, we know that the threat of executing an innocent man or woman, however slim, is quite real. Many sentenced to death have had their sentences changed to life in prison as a result of the appeals process. Some few have even had their convictions overturned. This does not definitely mean that they are innocent of their alleged crime, but it may mean just that. After all, many who have been convicted of first-degree murder and sentenced to life in prison have been found later to have been innocent. Since the introduction of DNA testing these findings have been more and more frequent. The lesson here is that it is quite possible for an innocent person to be executed.

Finally, those opposed to the death penalty point to its cost and assert:

3.' The death penalty costs nearly twice as much to administer as a life sentence. (B)

At first glance this seems wildly improbable. Keeping a man or woman in prison for life seems much more costly. However, for the state to prosecute capital offenses costs a great deal, especially high-profile cases. In addition, the process of appeals is very costly. The funds used for appeals could be put to much better use in the criminal justice system, especially to support the hiring of more police officers, judges, and other officials, as well as to fund crime prevention programs. Because much greater good can be produced for society as a whole without the death penalty, we place a (B) after premise (3)'.

The argument against capital punishment needs two more things to be complete. It must answer objections from the opposition, and it must formulate a conclusion. We will return to these tasks soon. For now, however, after seeing some of the objections to capital punishment raised in premises (1)'–(3)', it is time to return to the argument in support of capital punishment to see how it will deal with them.

Replies to Objections

There is a rhythm to our arguments developing here, and we need to notice it. First we see what may be said in support of each view, whether that be positive evidence or simply objections to the opposing view. Then we will see how each possible solution responds to objections against it.

So far the argument for capital punishment looks like this:

1. The death penalty is the only punishment equal to the crime of first-degree murder. (J)

2. The death penalty is a more effective deterrent to the crime of murder than is life in prison. (B)

Now we must add premises that respond to the objections listed in premises (1)'–(3)'.

Premise (1)' claims that capital punishment discriminates against the poor and minorities. To this objection the proponents of capital punishment respond that the entire justice system does the same. It is not simply a problem for "capital" punishment, but for all forms of punishment. However, no one suggests doing away with all forms of punishment because they are discriminatory, so why do away with capital punishment? The problem is with the attitudes within the justice system itself, and perhaps even within the country as a whole. It is the racist and class discrimination that must be ended for punishment to be administered fairly, not the punishment itself. Besides, all who are executed deserve it. It is just that some who deserve the death penalty, especially the white and wealthy males who murder, manage to escape their just punishments. So we have the next premise:

3. The discriminatory use of the death penalty may be avoided by ending discrimination in the justice system. (J)

Premise (2)' states that innocent people may be executed. If this is so, if there is a constant danger of a wrongful execution, we should abolish the death penalty. However, proponents argue that the chances of executing the wrong person are extremely slim. Besides, there is even more chance that someone who is innocent will serve time in prison, yet we do not abolish all forms of punishment for that reason. Granted, if you are innocent and serving time in prison you may be found to be innocent and released, whereas if your punishment is the death penalty there is no reversing the sentence. Again, however, the extremely slim chance of executing an innocent person is simply one of the necessary evils of crime and punishment itself. It would be a far greater evil to abandon capital punishment, because then there would be more murders, and thus even more innocent people would die. So we say the following:

4. For an innocent person to be executed is unlikely, and if it happens it is a lesser evil than having no capital punishment. (B,J,A)

Premise (3)' asserts that capital punishment is too costly to use. It takes away from more productive uses of criminal justice funds. To this the supporter of capital punishment replies:

5. Cost should not be a factor in the distribution of justice. (J)

Just as we think it unfair to release prisoners earlier than scheduled for such reasons as overcrowded prisons, we should also think that giving a convicted first-degree murderer less than he deserves is wrong. It is an insult to justice. The problem is to raise more funds for the criminal justice system, not to abandon just punishments.

The argument is now complete except for its conclusion, which, of course, is one of our two possible solutions:

6. Therefore, capital punishment is morally acceptable.

As with all inductive arguments, this conclusion should be understood as expressing a probability, even if such a probability is not explicitly stated.

It is now the turn of those who oppose capital punishment to reply to objections. The first objection is found in premise (1), which claims that capital punishment is the only punishment that is equal to the crime of first-degree murder. It comes from someone taking the retributivist perspective—that the amount of punishment must be equal to the crime. It says that justice demands "a life for a life," as the only fitting punishment for first-degree murder. Justice demands the death penalty for such crimes. Anything else, such as life in prison, is too little. Only the murderer's own life is adequate payment for the life of his victim; only the death penalty "fits" the crime of first-degree murder.

In response to this objection, the opponent of capital punishment begins by questioning retributivism itself, especially its claim that the amount of punishment appropriate to a crime is determined by making punishments equal to their associated crimes. This must be true if "a life for a life" is to be accepted as a reason for capital punishment. However, such a "fitting" of punishments with crimes appears to be used nowhere else in the criminal justice system other than for the death penalty. We certainly do not take it *literally* for any other crime. For example, we do not rape rapists, steal cars from car thieves, or embezzle money from embezzlers. So why do we accept the idea that punishment must fit the crime literally when it comes to the death penalty? Why do we say that justice demands a life for a life? Clearly, there is no good reason to make a special case for the literal interpretation of this principle for just one form of punishment.

Even if we interpret this supposed requirement of justice less literally, it still has its problems. Some have suggested, for example, that "the punishment must fit the crime" is to be interpreted as meaning that the amount of pain received from punishment must be equal to the amount of pain the victim experienced. There is to be a proportion, not an identity, between a crime and its punishment. However, who can judge how much pain and suffering has been experienced by the victim and his or her family and friends, let alone by many in the wider society affected by the crime? And who can judge how much pain and suffering the criminal will experience by his punishment? For some criminals a period of incarceration may not be nearly as painful as even a short period is for others. Clearly, we do not determine the amount of punishment that is just by trying to make it equal to the harm caused by the crime.

Even if punishments were determined by fitting them to the crime, the belief that only the loss of the murderer's life fits his crime still has serious problems. "A life for a life" seems to be intuitively clear, but its sense quickly disappears when we examine it more closely. For example, suppose someone kills several people? How can the loss of his one life pay back for that? Suppose he tortures his victim mentally and physically before killing her. Should we not do the same to him before his execution? Is not the death penalty too little payment in such a case? Clearly, there is no literal equality between a murder and an execution to pay for it. Nor is there any proportional equality either. Some murderers do not experience the loss of their lives as an evil that equals the pain and suffering experienced by their victims and their loved ones. Some convicted murders have even requested the death penalty over life in prison.

The meaning of "the punishment must equal the crime," as a general theory of punishment, is something like this: "the greater the crime, the greater the punishment." This is all that justice requires, that we not use minor punishments for serious crimes and major punishments for minor crimes. If there were only ten different types of crime with ten different levels of punishment, for example, this principle would require that the highest crime receive the highest punishment, while the lowest crime receive the lowest, and so on. With capital punishment, although the death penalty would be allowed by this principle as the highest type of punishment, it is not required. A society may select life in prison as its highest form of punishment, as most developed nations have done. Justice does not demand that a murderer be executed, only that he or she receive whatever happens to be the highest punishment.

This idea that justice does not demand the death penalty is discussed by Steve Nathanson in the following passage. After dismissing the view that punishments must literally fit the crime, what he calls "equality retributivism," he discusses the view that he calls "proportional retributivism," the view that punishment must be at least proportional to the crime.[2]

> In implementing a punishment system based on the proportionality view, one would first make a list of crimes, ranking them in order of seriousness. At one end would be quite trivial offenses like parking meter violations, while very serious crimes such as murder would occupy the other. In between, other crimes would be ranked according to their relative gravity. Then a corresponding scale of punishments would be constructed, and the two would be correlated. Punishments would be proportionate to crimes so long as we could say that the more serious the crime was, the higher on the punishment scale was the punishment administered.
>
> This system does not have the defects of equality retributivism. It does not require that we treat those guilty of barbaric crimes barbarically. This is because we can set the upper limit of the punishment scale so as to exclude truly barbaric punishments. Second, unlike the equality principle, the proportionality view is genuinely general, providing a way of handling all crimes. Finally, it does justice to our ordinary belief that certain punishments are unjust because they are too severe or too lenient for the crime committed.
>
> The proportionality principle does, I think, play a legitimate role in our thinking about punishments. Nonetheless, it is no help to death penalty advocates, because it does not require that murderers be executed. All that it requires is that if murder is the most serious crime, then murder should be punished by the most severe punishment on the scale. The principle does not tell us what this punishment should be, however, and it is quite compatible with the view that the most severe punishment should be a long prison term.

So the fourth premise in the argument against the death penalty may now be written as a response to the "life for a life" objection:

4.' Justice does not require the death penalty. (J)

The fifth premise in support of the claim that the death penalty is immoral is a response to the objection found in premise (2), which states, in effect, that the death penalty works. It lowers the murder rate. People fear death more than imprisonment, so in states where there is a death penalty statute there will be fewer murders. To this objection the reply is simply a denial of its truth:

5.' The death penalty is no more effective a deterrent for the crime of murder than is life in prison. (B)

Notice that (5)' does not say that capital punishment is not a deterrent at all. Instead, it asserts that whatever the deterrent value of the death penalty, it is no greater than life in prison. Apparently, would-be murders are not more frightened by the threat of execution than by the threat of life in prison. The results of many comparison studies have been fairly consistent in this matter. These studies might compare the murder rate in a state when it did not have the death penalty with its murder rate when it did. Or they might compare murder rates in states that are demographically and economically similar, one of which has no death penalty whereas the other does. In all such studies there seems to be no proof that the death penalty is a more effective deterrent than life in prison—perhaps because neither is a very effective deterrent most of the time. Most murderers do not think ahead before they commit their awful crimes and judge the likelihood of being caught. If they do consider the consequences of their actions, most assume that they will not get caught.

Whatever the reason, states that have the death penalty clearly do not have lower murder rates than similar states that do not. In fact, some of the states with the highest murder rates, such as Texas, California, and Florida, do have the death penalty and use it frequently. Perhaps the most significant comparison can be drawn between the United States and other developed nations of the world. Whereas the United States retains the death penalty, most other developed nations have abolished it, or use it very infrequently. However, the United States has a much higher murder rate by far than the countries of Western Europe and Japan. Obviously other factors besides the presence or absence of the death penalty determine the number of murders committed within national borders. The important point for us to focus on for now is that if it provides no greater deterrence than the lesser penalty of life in prison, the death penalty may not be justifiably used as a deterrent to the crime of first-degree murder. It is excessive.

Two particular objections may be raised at this point, both concerned with the deterrent effect of capital punishment. One says that it would work better than life imprisonment if it were used more frequently and sooner than the ten or more years now required for a capital sentence to be carried out. To this objection the defender of capital punishment replies that there is little evidence that this is so, and also that it would surely lead to the execution of more innocent people. So we have this:

6.' If capital punishment were used more rapidly and more frequently, more innocent people would be executed. (B,J,A)

The next objection is more serious. It claims that although studies have not proven that the death penalty is a more effective deterrent than life in prison, common sense tells us that it must be—at least for some people. We can be pretty sure that the behavior of at least some would-be murderers will be altered by their fear of the death penalty. Perhaps it keeps them from carrying firearms during a burglary attempt, or from killing a woman they have just raped, or from shooting at a police officer. If, as is likely, even a few murders are prevented by the threat of the death penalty, then its effectiveness as a greater deterrent than life in prison has been demonstrated. What studies show is that we simply do not know whether the death penalty works; what common sense does tell us is that reasonable belief is that at least in some instances it is a deterrent. When faced with uncertainty about its deterrent value, we should err on the side of protecting possible innocent victims. Here is a much discussed statement of this position by Ernest van den Haag.[3]

> If we do not know whether the death penalty will deter others [more than life in prison] we are confronted with two uncertainties. If we impose the death penalty, and achieve no deterrent effect thereby, the life of a convicted murderer has been expended in vain (from a deterrent viewpoint). There is a net loss. If we impose the death sentence and thereby deter some future murderers, we spared the lives of some future victims (the prospective murderers gain too; they are spared punishment because they were deterred). In this case, the death penalty has led to a net gain, unless the life of a convicted murderer is valued more highly than that of the unknown victim, or victims (and the non-imprisonment of the deterred non-murderer).
>
> The calculation can be turned around, of course. The absence of the death penalty may harm no one and therefore produce a gain—the life of the convicted murderer. Or it may kill future victims of murderers who could have been deterred, and thus produce a loss—their life.
>
> To be sure, we must risk something certain—the death (or life) of the convicted man, for something uncertain—the death (or life), of the victims of murderers who may be deterred. This is in the nature of uncertainty—when we invest, or gamble, we risk the money we have for an uncertain gain. Many human actions, most commitments—including marriage and crime—share this characteristic with the deterrent purpose of any penalization, and with its rehabilitative purpose (and even with the protective). . . . But the uncertainty which confronts us favors the death penalty as long as by imposing it we might save future victims of murder. This effect is as plausible as the general idea that penalties have deterrent effects which increase with their severity. Though we have no proof of the positive deterrence of the penalty, we also have no proof of zero, or negative effectiveness. I believe we have no right to risk additional future victims of murder for the sake of sparing convicted murderers; on the contrary, our moral obligation is to risk the possible ineffectiveness of executions.

According to van den Haag, because the death penalty might work for at least a few would-be murderers, we ought to use it. We ought to execute all 3,300 inmates on death row. This will send a message to those few who will fear the death penalty enough to refrain from the act of murder that they may have otherwise committed. It is reasonable to believe that such a message will save a few innocent lives, and these few innocent lives are worth the price of the 3,300 who deserve to die for their atrocities.

Those who oppose the death penalty may respond to this objection in the following way. What the objection amounts to is the belief that thousands should be executed because doing so *might* save a few lives. However, there is no good evidence for this at all. Although a few inmates serving time for other crimes have claimed that they did not murder because of their fear of the death penalty, there is little evidence that their after-the-fact explanations of their behavior match its reality. There is, in particular, no evidence that those who do think about the consequences of their actions at all are not just as frightened by the prospects of life in prison.

Those who raise this objection claim that if executing 3,300 capital offenders "might" work to save a few innocent victims, this is good enough. Even if we do not know whether it works, if it might work, we should use it. But part of the deterrence justification of punishments that using a greater punishment when a lesser one will do just as well is immoral. Using a greater punishment violates the principle of beneficence. Besides, can you imagine what the reaction in society would be if all 3,300 inmates were to be executed over the next five or so years? That would amount to almost two executions per day. What kind of message would this send to an already violent nation, as it watches its government routinely handle problems of crime and punishment in a violent fashion? The last premise in our argument against capital punishment may now be stated.

7.' To use capital punishment simply because it might be a deterrent for a few would be immoral. (B)

The conclusion to the argument against capital punishment is this:

8.' Capital punishment is immoral.

Evaluation

The goal of this section is to arrive at a ***reasoned judgment*** that one of the possible solutions defended above is more reasonable than the other. To do this we must evaluate the arguments that support each solution and select the conclusion is most reasonable. Before beginning our evaluation, however, it may be helpful for us to describe more fully the relationship between this problem and our ethical theory.

Ethical Theory

The various elements that compose the problem of capital punishment may be sketched in the following manner.

B,J,A

RULES

1. Do not kill. (B,J,A)

2. Defend society against its capital offenders. (B)

3. Administer just punishment to capital offenders. (J)

4. Do not kill the innocent. (B,J,A)

5. Do not discriminate. (J)

6. Spend criminal justice funds in the most effective manner. (B)

ACTION

The question before us is whether it is immoral to execute first-degree murderers. That is the action under consideration. According to our ethical theory, this action is right if it follows from an acceptable rule. Even though there are legal rules that allow capital punishment in some states, ours is a moral question. It is a question of whether there should be a moral rule that says "Execute first-degree murderers," or whether the rule should be "Do not execute first-degree murderers." In effect, we want to know whether capital punishment is a form of justified killing.

The way to decide this is to examine some of the acceptable rules we already have that are relevant to this question. These are acceptable because they follow from our three moral principles, especially from the ones abbreviated by the letters B, J, and A and placed in parentheses after each rule. Because capital punishment is a question of killing, rule (1) is of central importance. Capital punishment is a form of punishment, and the purpose of punishment by the state is to deter crime and to administer justice to criminals; therefore, rules (2) and (3) are important as well. Rules (4) through (6) are also important, because they speak to some of the possible consequences of allowing capital punishment.

The moral reasoning that engages us in our attempt to solve the problem of capital punishment follows the pattern of a **conflict of rules.** We will solve our problem by determining which rule or set of rules has priority over the other. The proponent of capital punishment will argue that rules (2) and (3) have priority over rule (1). That is, capital punishment is a justified form of killing because it is a form of self-defense (2) and because it is required by justice (3). He will then show that rules (4) through (6) are not relevant or not important in judging the morality of capital punishment. This, in fact, is the good reasons argument *for* capital punishment.

The opponent of capital punishment, on the other hand, will claim that rule (1) has priority over rules (2) and (3). Life in prison is just as effective as capital punishment in defending society against would-be murderers, so capital punishment is not necessary. It is excessive. Likewise, justice does not demand capital punishment, only that the highest punishment be used for first-degree murderers. Additionally, opponents of capital punishment argue that rules (4) through (6) are both relevant and important, as capital punishment leads to the very harms that they prohibit. Again, this is just what the good reasons argument *against* capital punishment claims. It is important for you to recognize this point, that the arguments for and against capital punishment are really arguments about which rule or set of rules has the highest priority.

Your Evaluation

Let us turn now to the task of evaluating the good reasons arguments for and against capital punishment. We will begin by briefly reviewing the rules for evaluating inductive arguments that were spelled out in Part 1. First, each of the premises must be checked for relevance and reliability. **Relevance** is not much of an issue for us at this point. What makes a premise relevant in a moral argument is that it follows from a principle. Because it follows from one or more principles, it either expresses a harm or a benefit, or it describes a violation or acceptance of justice or autonomy—precisely the considerations that we use to determine whether a rule is acceptable. Because each premise of each argument has already been marked with the principle that it follows, all premises have been determined to be relevant.

Therefore, the focus will be on checking the **reliability** of the premises. We must check each one to determine whether its assertion is true or false, or at least more or less probable. In the case of premises that are replies to objections, when we check for their reliability we check for how well they have responded to the objections in question. This process of checking the reliability of premises will constitute the heart of our evaluation and will be the focus of most of our discussion.

You must take yet another step after checking for reliability has been completed, however: judging the **sufficiency** of the evidence. That is, you must judge that the premises you have found to be reliable collectively add up to enough evidence to support the conclusion. Often the evidence described in the reliable premises of each argument will not be sufficient to show that one solution is clearly superior to the other. Instead of recognizing a clear winner, we will often find ourselves judging one case to be stronger than another. We will weigh the strengths and weaknesses of each case much as a jury weighs the strengths and weaknesses of the cases made by the prosecution and defense lawyers, always with our eye on judging which is the more likely to be true.

During the process of evaluating an argument we must be on guard for the influence of our personal points of view. Our points of view sometimes tend to influence how we weigh the reliability of premises. Our biases may even preclude some possible solutions altogether—even before a fair hearing of the evidence in their favor. Someone who has had a close friend or family member murdered, for example, may find it very difficult to oppose the death penalty; someone else's life experiences may prejudice that person in the opposite direction. Perhaps you should think of yourselves as members of a jury, as we suggested above. Now, however, think of this jury as charged with the task of setting policy for society and not determining the guilt or innocence of an individual. As jurors must keep an open mind and attend to the evidence in their attempts to find the truth, so should you do so in your attempt to discover right from wrong. With the exception of a few remarks below, it will now be left to you to perform the task of evaluating the cases for and against capital punishment.

Exercise 5.2

The goal of this exercise is for you to make a reasoned judgment that one of the arguments presented in the previous section is superior to the other, and that its conclusion is the reasonable one to accept. Following are the arguments for and against capital punishment. Evaluate these arguments by testing each premise for reliability and by judging which collection of premises most sufficiently supports its conclusion. You may have to do some research on your own to make some judgments about reliability. For example, you may have to dig deeper than we have done so far to decide about the likelihood of executing innocent people, or the degree to which the death penalty discriminates against the poor and minorities, or the costs associated with the process of conviction, sentencing, and execution.

Perform this task carefully and with an eye to detail. I suggest that it be performed as an out-of-class, written assignment. You may be tempted to convince yourself that all premises supporting your preferred conclusion are reliable and that those offered for the other side are not. However, your intellectual growth will be better served if you try to keep an open mind and to judge the reliabilty of each premise according to the evidence. As is the case with all the controversial issues discussed in this text, there are strong arguments for each side. In looking closely and as objectively as possible at each premise of each argument, you may learn something new and important about the issue at hand.

Here are the arguments:

The Case for Capital Punishment

1. The death penalty is the only punishment equal to the crime of first-degree murder. (J)

2. The death penalty is a more effective deterrent to the crime of murder than is life in prison. (B)

3. The discriminatory use of the death penalty may be avoided by ending discrimination in the justice system. (J)

4. For an innocent person to be executed is unlikely, and if it happens it is a lesser evil than having no capital punishment. (B,J,A)

5. Cost should not be factor in the distribution of justice. (J)

Therefore, 6. Capital punishment is morally acceptable.

The Case Against Capital Punishment

1.' The death penalty discriminates against the poor and minorities. (J)

2.' Innocent people may be wrongly executed. (B,J,A)

3.' The death penalty costs nearly twice as much to administer as a life sentence. (B)

4.' Justice does not require the death penalty. (J)

5.' The death penalty is no more effective a deterrent for the crime of murder than is life in prison. (B)

6.' If capital punishment were used more rapidly and more frequently, more innocent people would be executed. (B,J,A)

7.' To use capital punishment simply because it might be a deterrent for a few would be immoral. (B)

Therefore, 8.' Capital punishment is immoral.

A Few Comments

My contribution to the process of evaluation will focus on premise (1) and the cavalier fashion with which it is often dismissed by those who oppose the death penalty. True retributivists think that capital punishment is morally acceptable even if it does not work to lower the murder rate. Whether it works or not, people deserve to die if they take another's life—it is a demand of justice. If retributivism is correct, then capital punishment proponents have a solid leg to stand on when they claim that we must have a "life for a life."

Opponents of capital punishment, however, often say that retributivism is not so much a cry for justice as it is an expression of our deep-seated feelings of revenge. Perhaps it is a legacy from our evolutionary past to want to kill people who have killed some of our group members. Perhaps only those groups who did so survived. Whatever the origin of these ideas most of us have such vengeful feelings on occasion, especially when we read or hear about particularly brutal murders, and especially those brutal murders with whose victims we identify.

However, these vengeful feelings do not provide a sound basis for moral beliefs or social policy. Maybe we cannot help having such feelings, but we can choose not to act on them. We as a society have to get past these feelings and form wise policies on the basis of reason, on the basis of what will produce the greatest good for all. Acting vengefully will not lead to such policies. So it is often said by those opposed to the death penalty that capital punishment is nothing but striking out in revenge, and such motives are not worthy of those who live in a civilized society. Their slogan is "capital punishment is nothing but revenge." They utter it and walk away as though that were enough to end the discussion.

There is some truth to this attack on premise (1) and retributivism in general. However, there is also something right about retributivism. It is not only a disguised form of revenge. It may be that on some occasions, but it also expresses a principle of justice that most of us do in fact accept. Most of us believe that people ought to pay for the harms they cause to others, and many who accept this retributive principle see no reason not to use it as a justification for capital punishment. For them, "an eye for eye" is clearly a requirement of morality. It is important for us, then, to see what is correct about retributivism and to see if what is correct about it carries over to capital punishment.

The main area in which most of us use the retributive principle is in our everyday dealings with each other. The moral dimension of our personal relationships is dominated by this principle. For example, suppose your sister took your best cashmere sweater against your wishes, and then returned it to you a ruined mess. However you might express it, you would be upset with her. For her to square things with you she would have to buy you a new sweater, one just as good as the original. In addition, she would have to apologize and say that she will never do such a thing again. This amounts to equal material and psychological payback, and it is required to repair the broken fibers of your personal relationship with your sister.

In my view, this is the truth of retributivism, what is right about it. We are psychological beings whose close connections with other people are based on trust and honesty and a whole range of related feelings that draw us together. Because of this, when someone wounds a relationship with us, we need to be paid back before we are willing to resume it. Sometimes the damage is irreparable, as may be the case when a husband cheats on his wife. This is a deep wound to trust and honesty, and if it is to be forgiven a great deal must be paid back for a long time.

However well this model works in the realm of human relationships, it is not helpful as a way to understand how the state should deal with its offenders. Whenever a crime has been committed, it is technically always a crime against the state. Even when there is a human victim involved, any crime is still considered to be a crime against the state. The state can prosecute a crime even against the victim's wishes, though it usually will not do so as it needs the cooperation of the victim to win its case. The state is not a psychological being. The officials of the state may be, but the state itself is not a person with psychological properties. It does not have vengeful feelings or feelings that trust or honesty or other ties have been broken. In the realm of human relationships, people may need to be paid back equally for harms done against them in order for justice to be served, but this is not true for the relationship between the state and its criminals.

The point is that retributivism is not reducible simply to feelings of revenge, as some opponents of capital punishment are quick to do. It is also a good principle of justice to follow in our personal relationships. Our human psyches demand it. However, it is not a good principle to follow in the criminal justice system, itself an impersonal entity. Instead, we should there follow a deterrence principle, punishing criminals to prevent and deter crime, and only to the extent required to do so.

Consequences

Finally, we must consider the ***consequences*** of adopting our reasoned judgment. If you have decided that capital punishment is morally justified, that it should be a rule adopted by society, then what follows? Should we press the states that do not allow capital punishment to change their policies and make it legal? Should we use it more frequently and more swiftly in the United States? Should we encourage nations that do not use it to begin doing so?

If you are in favor of capital punishment on deterrence grounds, should you not also be in favor of televised executions? After all, how can execution deter crime, how can potential murderers see what lies in store for them, if we are spared the horrors of the execution itself? If you are in favor of capital punishment on retributivist grounds, why should we use lethal injections, perhaps the easiest way to die, instead of executing prisoners in a less humane manner, a manner more equal to the way their victims died?

If you are opposed to capital punishment, on the other hand, if you believe that it is immoral, do you agree that it should be made illegal? Or do you think that it should be retained, on "the books," at least, so that the possibility of its use could maintain its threat to would-be murderers? My hunch is that consistency demands that those who are opposed to capital punishment on moral grounds should also be opposed to it on legal grounds as well. What do you think? Is it time for the United States to join the rest of the civilized nations of the world and abolish the death penalty?

Another Perspective

The following selection is from *Dead Man Walking*, by Sister Helen Prejean. The author, a Roman Catholic nun, was spiritual adviser to men on death row. Her experience working with these men gave her **another perspective** on the moral acceptability of capital punishment.

Dead Man Walking: Chapter 7

SISTER HELEN PREJEAN

DRIVING BACK TO NEW ORLEANS after my visit with the Harveys, I stop and pay my dollar at the entrance of the twenty-six-mile causeway. Here at these toll booths is where Vernon Harvey said he spotted Robert Willie in a federal vehicle and began his high-speed chase. Night has taken hold of the sky and the lake. All I can see as I drive are the shafts of light from the headlights and red flicks of taillights in front of me. I can't get my mind off Faith Hathaway.

She had been celebrating. No doubt the liquor had lowered her defenses. At what point did the chilling realization seize her that she was in danger, *real danger,* there in the front seat of a truck, wedged between two strangers—men, maybe with guns, whose remarks were becoming more and more sinister and who were taking her farther and farther away from the safe moorings of home and parents and friends—and help. As panic mounted, had she tried shutting her eyes tight, fighting to throw off the sluggish effects of the alcohol? It was a time when a woman needed her sharpest wits about her, a time to think clearly and keenly about escape. Or perhaps it was better that her wits were not so sharp. Better, maybe, for the anesthesia of the alcohol to dull the pain and horror soon to be hers.

Poor Vernon and Elizabeth. No matter that Faith was killed four years ago. Every time the terror is told, she suffers and cries out and dies again. *She suffered alone and in great terror and no one was there to comfort her.* Who can blame them for wanting to see her murderer executed? Maybe they feel that not to demand death, the harshest punishment possible, would be a betrayal of their daughter's memory.

Great as the sea is thy sorrow.

I wonder what will ever be able to heal the Harveys' pain and bring them peace. No, there is no replacing the unique universe of Faith Hathaway. Even if Robert Willie is destroyed, the aching void can never be filled.

I understand the Harveys' desire for retribution. Their lives have been violated by Robert Willie and they want to see him punished. They want to see him made accountable for his actions. They want to see him pay for what he did. So do I. In an ideal world, there would be no need for retribution. But in real societies, punishing the guilty is as integral to

New York: Vintage Press, 1994. Reprinted by permission.

the function of law as exonerating the innocent and preventing crime.

Susan Jacoby, in her insightful book *Wild Justice: The Evolution of Revenge,* says:

> Establishment of . . . the restraint that enables people to live with one another and the ineradicable impulse to retaliate when harm is inflicted has always been one of the essential tasks of civilization. The attainment of such a balance depends in large measure on the confidence of the victimized that someone else will act on their behalf against the victimizers . . . Stripped of moralizing, law exists not only to restrain retribution but to mete it out . . . A society that is unable to convince individuals of its ability to exact atonement for injury is a society that runs a constant risk of having its members revert to the wilder forms of [vigilante] justice . . .

But Jacoby maintains, and I agree, that the retribution which society metes out should be *measured.* Her objection to capital punishment is that such "eye-for-an-eye" retribution is as excessive as the original crime it punishes. But she also finds it excessive that those convicted of so heinous and irrevocable a crime as murder should be made to serve only a few short years in prison. The Bureau of Justice Statistics reveals that in 1986 the average amount of time served on a life sentence in the United States was six years, nine months.

Jacoby holds that the public's desire to see serious punishment consistently meted out for serious crimes is legitimate and that to ignore it encourages "the boundless outrage that generates demands for boundless retribution." But she says that punishment should be tempered: "There is, or ought to be, a vast middle ground between belief in the death penalty and acceptance of a system that allows too many killers to 'pay' with only a few years of their own lives— or to escape retribution altogether through legal and psychiatric loopholes—for a life they have taken from another."

Such measured retribution is attained, I believe, by sentencing which requires *nonnego-*

tiable long-term imprisonment for first-degree murder (also termed *aggravated* or *capital* murder). At least forty states in recent years have revised criminal codes to require life without parole or lengthy mandatory minimum years served for convictions they deem most serious. In a growing number of states—twenty-five as of 1992, including Louisiana—life-without-parole sentences are *true* life sentences. The only way prisoners serving such sentences can be released is by commutation of sentence by the governor, and because of the unpopularity of such commutations, governors now grant them rarely.

Most other states have taken extra precautions to assure that felony-type murderers are not released from prison after a few years served. They do this by legislating a statutory minimum time which a convicted murderer must serve before being eligible for parole. The Arizona criminal sentencing code, for example, demands that convicted first-degree murderers serve twenty-five years before eligibility for parole. Colorado demands forty years; New Jersey, thirty; Ohio, twenty; Indiana, thirty. The Kansas legislature, which in 1987 balked at reinstituting the death penalty because of its costliness,* in 1990 enacted a "Hard 40" statute, which stipulates that a perpetrator more than eighteen years of age who is guilty of premeditated murder must serve forty years' imprisonment before becoming eligible for parole. A South Carolina statute specifies that if the governor commutes a death sentence, he or she must sentence the prisoner to life without eligibility for parole.

---

*For eight years the Kansas legislature passed death-penalty bills only to have them vetoed by an anti-death-penalty governor. With a new pro-death-penalty governor in the statehouse in 1987, the legislature had its green light. But at a time when the financially strapped state was cutting some services 10 percent, the senate balked at the death-penalty process, which would cost an estimated $10 million the first year alone and $50 million before the first execution could be carried out.

As indicated earlier, public opinion surveys in a number of states show that support for the death penalty drops significantly when the public is assured that murderers will remain behind bars for life. And support for the death penalty also drops dramatically—well below the majority—when the alternative is presented of long-term imprisonment (at least twenty-five years) for offenders plus restitution by the offender to the victim's family.

This evening's encounter with the Harveys has to count as one of the most painful of my life. Never have I met such unrequited grief. What, I wonder, can I possibly do to ease their pain? I am out of my depth. Driving across these dark waters of Lake Pontchartrain, I realize how vulnerable we all are. Faith Hathaway—dead. Loretta Bourque—dead. David LeBlanc—dead. Children snatched from their parents in the night. I think of my sister, Mary Ann. I think of Mama. I think of Mary Ann and Charlie's five children, especially Helen, my namesake. I think of Julie and Marcy, my brother Louie's little girls. When I get home I will telephone Mama. I want to hear that everyone is safe.

This Robert Willie, who is he? I recoil at the thought of him. How dare he calmly read law books and concoct arguments in his defense? He should fall on his knees, weeping, begging forgiveness from these parents. He should spend every moment of his life repenting his heinous deed. But, judging from my first visit, he seems to be in a world of his own, oblivious to the pain he has caused others. Remorse presupposes enough self-forgetfulness to feel the pain of others. Can Robert Willie do that? I doubt it and wonder whether his death sentence makes his own repentance even more difficult. *Someone is trying to kill him*, and this must rivet his energies on his own survival, not the pain of others.

The tragedy for the Harveys will be compounded because the murderer of their daughter, about to undergo a dramatic death at the hands of the state, is certain to draw media attention, which will carefully note what the condemned man eats at his last meal and his farewell words to the world—far more attention than his victim received. We remember the names of the executed—Gary Gilmore, John Spenkelink, Ted Bundy. Who remembers the names of their victims? Meanwhile, human rights advocates will protest the execution (in Louisiana before an execution, scores of protest letters from Canadian and European Amnesty International members pour into the governor's office)—another kind of attention for the murderer, which to a victim's family is almost certain to seem misguided and unfair.

My hope for the Harveys is that eventually they will be able to overcome their terrible grief and once again live positive lives. How I can help them I am not sure, but I want to try. And Robert Willie? What can I possibly do for him? I will do what Millard Farmer asked me to do—accompany him, treat him with dignity—but I will also challenge him to take responsibility for his crime and to ask forgiveness of the Harveys.

Emotionally it's confusing to think of the Harveys and their needs alongside Robert Willie and his. Hearing the details of Faith's vicious murder, I find myself sucked into the Harveys' rage. But then I think of the death the state has in store for Robert Willie.

A few days after visiting the Harveys I visit Robert for the second time. I have a notebook on the front seat of the car. I'm not allowed to take it into the prison (only attorneys and news reporters can bring writing materials inside), but afterward I'll jot down notes from our conversation. I'm much more alert now than I was with Pat Sonnier. When the Pardon Board hearing comes up, facts about Robert's family life and background will be important. I feel that there isn't much time.

Robert comes into the visiting room. He is wearing a black knitted hat. He walks with a little bounce, poising momentarily on the balls of his feet. I dispense with preliminaries.

"I went to visit the Harveys," I say. "They told me about Faith's death. Robert, you raped and stabbed that girl and left her to rot in the woods. Why?"

"All right," he says, and he lights a cigarette. "I'm telling you what, ma'am, I'm real, real sorry that girl got killed, but like I told the police when they was questioning me, I didn't stab and kill that girl. Joe went crazy and started stabbin' her. I told them that when I gave my statement, and I offered to take a lie detector test then and there on the spot, but they wouldn't let me. I told them I don't kill women. I don't. But when Joe started stabbin' her, her hands went up and he told me to hold her hands and I did. But it was more instinct than anything, and with him slashing with that knife, there was blood everywhere, I was scared. I just did what he said, and afterwards we was runnin' around in those woods lost, goin' through brambles and mud and couldn't find the truck and I was some scared."

I groan inside. The truth. What's the truth? Not another one of those situations where two perpetrators each accuse the other and it's so difficult to ferret out the facts. He admits that he held Faith's hands. He did not come to her defense. Even if he's telling the truth and did not stab her himself, he is responsible for her death. Does he know what he did? And if he does, how can he live with himself?

"Robert," I say, "Vernon Harvey tells me that you taunted him in the courtroom. You said you'd never fry, is that true?"

"He said he'd see me fry and I said, 'The hell you will,'" Robert says. "I'd never show my inner feelin's out there in the courtroom, in public like that. Ever since I was a little boy I ain't ever showed my real feelin's. See, my daddy went to Angola when I was a baby. People would point to me and say, 'That's John Willie's kid,' and wham, there I am in a fight. My mama had her hands full in her own life, much less trying to take care of me. I don't blame her none for what's happened. She separated from my daddy when I was real young and married again, and me and my stepfather never got on too good. I'd stay with my grandmother sometime, my aunt and uncle some-

time, my mother and stepfather sometime. By the time I was in seventh grade I was sniffin' glue, paint, gasoline, you name it. Me and Joe were loaded on Valium, acid, and booze when this happened with Faith Hathaway. I had this light airy feelin' inside. I hadn't slept in two nights."

I say, "Robert, drugs don't explain violence like this. Thousands of people take drugs and don't slash and rape and kill people. The Harveys told me about that young boy, Mark Brewster, and his girlfriend whom you and Joe kidnapped after you killed Faith. They say you raped the girl and stabbed the boy and shot him and tied him to a tree and left him to die. The boy's paralyzed now for the rest of his life and God knows about the emotional scars on the girl. Did you do that?"

I am keeping my voice low, but it's an effort. I am quivering inside.

He pauses. He always speaks in a measured way and softly. "Yeah," he says, "I let Joe Vaccaro call all the shots and I went along. I wasn't thinkin' straight.

"The only other time I was involved in hurting somebody bad, where they died, was when me and my cousin struggled in the woods with this drug dealer for a big hunk of money—$10,000. We was all three fighting in the river and me and my cousin held his head under the water and then dragged him out and left him on the bank. We thought he was just unconscious, but he ended up dead.

"But with that couple we kidnapped, Vaccaro told me to kill the boy and I took out my knife, which was pretty dull, and I cut him across the neck and punched it into his side, but not hard or deep 'cause I really didn't want to kill him, and I said to Joe, 'He won't die,' and then Joe came up and shot him in the head."

He shakes his head. "I was stupid to let myself get messed up with Joe Vaccaro. He was supposed to be such a tough dude. He had been to Angola and so I was saying, 'Hey, man, he's been to Angola.' All that week when we were doin' all this, I knew it was wrong.

This voice kept going off in my head, 'This is wrong. This is wrong.' I was a damn fool."

"Have you ever told the Harveys that you're sorry?" I ask him.

"Well, ma'am that's hard to do because Vernon Harvey keeps holding these press conferences, mouthin' off about how he can't wait to see me fry. Personally, I think the guy is his own worst enemy. He just needs to let it go, man. The girl's dead now, and there's nothin' he can do to bring her back. Even watchin' me fry ain't gonna bring her back, but he won't let it go and he's just makin himself miserable, in my opinion."

"Robert," I say, "you understand, don't you, that you are the *last* person in the world with the right to say that to Vernon Harvey?"

"I guess you're right," he says, but he doesn't seem terribly convinced.

"Hell," Robert says, "it's hard, ma'am, to be having much sympathy for *them* when, here, they're tryin' to kill *me.* When somebody's after your hide, it kind of tends to occupy your mind, if you know what I mean."

"But look what these parents are going through," I say. "Their daughter raped and stabbed and left to die in the woods. What if someone did that to your mother? What would you want to do to them?"

"Kill 'em," he says. "I sure as hell would want to kill 'em."

I'm quiet then for a while.

I'm hoping he can take in his own words so he can feel the Harveys' pain. The quiet does not last long. He says, "I'm gonna be honest with you, ma'am, I believe in the death penalty in some instances, like for people who rape and torture little children. Messin' over adults is one thing, but little innocent kids? I'd pull the switch on them myself."

I have heard that prisoners are hardest on child molesters. I guess everybody's got a code of evil, a line beyond which they consider redemption impossible. But the irony jolts me. Here's a man condemned to death by the state and here he is defending the death penalty—not for himself, of course, only for

truly heinous killers. And I think of what Camus said, that every murderer, when he kills, feels innocent, that he always feels excused by his particular circumstances (p. 191).

I tell him that I think the state shouldn't have the power to kill anybody and that if the state is allowed to kill those who torture children, then why not those who kill old people, the mentally retarded, teenagers (close to home, but he doesn't get it), public officials, policemen? Where would it stop, I ask him, and who would decide?

He says he'll think about it, but he doesn't cede the point.

"Have you ever been close to death before?" I ask.

"Had someone shooting at me once," he says. "I was hiding behind a tractor in a barn and ping, ping, ping the pellets were hitting the metal on the tractor. That was a close call. My heart was racin' in my chest."

"Why was somebody shooting at you?"

"Well," he says, "he was the husband whose wife I was in bed with. He was supposed to be at work, but he walked in on us in their house one day, straight into the bedroom, and there we were. Me, I jumped up, grabbin' my pants and boots in my hand, and ran like hell for the barn, and there I am behind that tractor pullin' on my pants with one boot on and struggling to get the other boot on and *bam, bam,* those pellets were comin'."

And Robert Willie moves into a warm stream of memories now, telling of a woman seven years his senior who was "mature" and how he could have a *real* conversation with her. "Those younger ones, they couldn't sit still, they were too active, you just couldn't sit and talk." He admits that in the beginning he was partly drawn to "the adventure of loving a married woman."

"We'd go to the woods with a bottle and a blanket. She liked what I offered her. I used to come and see her when her old man would be at work and she'd cook for me, you know, a romantic meal, and we'd sit there for hours and eat and talk. She had a lot of real good thoughts about things and she drew 'em out of me, plus my real feelin's about things, I could share them with her and she was the only one."

He tells me how one night she and her "old man" were at one of the lounges and he was there too. "I went up to their table casual-like, not even looking at her directly, talking to her brother-in-law, when I feel this foot under the table touchin' my leg and here she is askin' me if I want to dance. Well, I plumb liked to fell out. I was nervous. We danced. Her old man was mad as hell.

"I left town for a spell to work on some barges and when I got back my friends told me, 'Your woman moved out of state.' Well, I tracked her down. I got her address and me and my cousin drove two days and arrived at her house at 6:00 A.M. and there was her truck parked in front, but we didn't know if her old man was in there with her. My cousin, he was nervous, and he said we'd better *back* our car into the driveway so we could get the hell out of there if her old man showed up."

He chuckles and he is taking his time telling me all this, like someone who has some rare coins in a box and who opens the box and takes each coin and holds it in his hand and turns it over and looks at it and then clinks it back into the box. I don't rush him. I let him have his moment.

"So we checked out the scene and didn't see the guy and went in and she fed us, and my cousin fell asleep, and I was hoping she and I could have us a good, long hunk of time, and the phone rang and it was her old man and he was in jail, and I breathed easy and knew we had some time. Now that is one real good feeling, to know you've got a good-sized chunk of time with somebody you love. You're kind of like on this little island all by yourselves and nobody can get to you. I never experienced love with anyone like I did with her. It was when she moved away and I didn't have her to talk to anymore that I really started goin' heavy into drugs. I guess I was trying to fill

the gap she left. I phoned her collect when I was in the federal pen in Marion a couple of years ago and she accepted the charges and we talked. I just wanted to hear her voice again. I had heard she was living with another man. I told her I just wanted her to be happy."

When he finishes I tell him that I don't know how much time we will have together but I want to make the most of it and share my best with him and that I am going to do my level best to invite him past some lines he's drawn—like not apologizing to the Harveys.

"If you do die," I say, "as your friend, I want to help you to die with integrity, and you can't do that, the way I see it, if you don't squarely own up to the part you played in Faith's death."

He is looking straight into my eyes. He is no whiner, and I appreciate that. Not much time. Have to talk straight and true.

I ask him if he has a Bible and if he ever reads it.

He says *yes* he has one and *yes* he reads it.

"Like W. C. Fields read his Bible?" I ask.

"Who?"

I explain that Fields was a famous comedian who claimed he read his Bible every day. When a skeptical friend asked, "Every day, Bill?" Fields said, "Yep, looking for loopholes."

He gives a little smile and says, no, it's more than loopholes he's after and that he reads his Bible late at night "when things settle down." He admits he never "got much religion" when he was growing up, but says he believes that Jesus died for him on the cross and will "take care" of him when he appears before the judgment seat of God.

I recognize the theology of "atonement" he uses: Jesus, by suffering and dying on the cross, "appeased" an angry God's demand for "justice." I know the theology because it once shaped my own belief, but I shed it when I discovered that its driving force was fear that made love impossible. What kind of God demands "payment" in human suffering?

But I figure now's not the time. Later, Robert and I can sort out theology.

To be truthful. To accept responsibility. Is this possible for Robert Lee Willie? I see at least one promising sign: he is pressing for better conditions for death-row inmates even though he'll probably be dead by the time the changes come about. I don't doubt that his motives are mixed. It's not pure altruism at work in him here. He likes to defy authority and the suit gives him new turf to "take 'em on."

I say, "You may want to check out some words of Jesus that might have special meaning for you: 'You shall know the truth and the truth will make you free.' It's in the Gospel of John, chapter 8."

"I'll do that. I'll check it out," he says.

Then he says, "I have a whole lot of stuff about my case—transcripts of my trials and newspaper clippings and legal papers—and maybe they would help you get a hold of things about me and my case faster."

I tell him I appreciate the trust.

"I tell you what, ma'am, I sure as hell don't trust nobody around this place—and that includes the chaplains who get their paychecks from the state just like other employees—but I do trust you. You're a fighter. I can't stand people that act like victims. That's why I don't much like niggers. They're always actin' like somebody owes 'em somethin.' Not just niggers. Chinks and spics, too."

Niggers? Chinks? Spics? We've got a long way to go, Robert and I. But I file it away for another day, another time. Not now. I am standing up to leave. He stands, too. I see that he has tattoos: L-O-V-E on his fingers and a string of skulls across his wrist.

"Appreciate your visit, ma'am," he says.

I put my hand up to the mesh screen and he raises his handcuffed hands toward the screen but he can't quite reach. He's much smaller than Pat.

Several days later I get several hefty manila envelopes in the mail from Robert, and I start to sift and sort through trial transcripts and newspaper clippings. This man's organized, that's certain. File folders are neat and tagged. Newspaper articles are arranged chronologi-cally. Here is a whole set of papers on the inmate suit to improve conditions on death row. I wade in.

The complaint is carefully typed. The grammar and spelling aren't perfect, but decent. Plaintiffs in the "Complaint for Declaratory and Injunctive Relief" declare themselves—three death-row inmates, Robert Willie among them—versus the defendants—the secretary of the Department of Corrections and the warden. It's a class-action suit and lists, in part, these grievances:

- Confinement in a six-by-eight-foot cell twenty-three hours a day.

- Inadequate lighting; in each cell there are no light fixtures; all light must come from lights on the tier.

- Telephone calls limited to one five-minute personal phone call per month.

- Inadequate heating and ventilation (in summer, one fan is turned on at the end of a hundred-yard tier with no cross-ventilation; the heat index in Louisiana can reach 115 degrees in July and August).

Bill Quigley, as it turns out, will be the attorney to see the suit settled for the inmates, eight years or so after Willie's initial filing. By the time the suit is settled the original plaintiffs (Robert Willie among them) will have been executed and the improvements gained will be modest: contact visits with attorneys and increased used of the telephone, plus a few other minor changes.

Once, when talking to Millard on the telephone, I mention the lawsuit to improve death-row conditions, and he says, "The prison officials consider these guys dead meat, anyway, know what I mean? Why worry about someone going to the dentist or having fresh ventilation or adequate recreation when they're planning to kill him anyway?"

Robert has told me that in Marion, the federal penitentiary, he had an excellent law library and he was "always in there digging into those books." Looking at the work he did on the suit, I can see—maybe for the first time in his life—he is honing his mind and his organizational abilities. Freed of drugs, he can read books, reflect, articulate his thoughts and opinions. True, there's self-interest in it, but maybe something more. Maybe for the first time in his life he has acquired knowledge and gained some authority and, perhaps, the satisfaction of being of service to others. He tells me how other inmates, out on the tier for their "hour," wend their way to his cell, asking him about legal issues in their "case" or how to go about getting their trial transcripts or how to use the Freedom of Information Act.

Then I read the newspaper articles.

Enter Robert Lee Willie, who addresses the judge as "Cap," smirks when the jury finds him guilty of murder, tells his mother to "dry up" when she weeps during his sentencing trial, and draws his hand menacingly like a knife across his throat when Mark Brewster appears in the courtroom. When Brewster's girlfriend appears, a young woman Robert raped, he winks and blows her a kiss.

And here are photographs: Robert when first arrested, with wild, long tangled hair; Robert, head shaved, hands and feet cuffed, looking at Vaccaro and grinning as they walk into the courthouse; Robert with a bandana on his head, caught close up by the camera, sneering.

Some incidents draw my attention:

An officer had to write Vaccaro's confession because he could neither read nor write.

Vaccaro, after first claiming Robert had shot Brewster, admitted in a second confession to shooting Brewster himself because he "wanted to put him out of his misery."

One file marked "Juvenile Record" has a thick stack of papers in it. I leaf through and watch Robert Lee Willie go from boy to outlaw.

When he's fourteen he shoplifts a bottle of wine from a convenience store.

A few months later he and his cousin steal two horses. Then he's picked up for truancy,

and there is this account: "While on patrol Sergeant Chatellier found RLW on the Tchefuncte Bridge. He took him to his aunt's house but he got smart with Sgt. C. and he brought him to the station. While Robert was sitting in the office, he stated he wanted to go to jail and told me he didn't care where his mother was and didn't want to go back."

Then, at the Tasty Donut Shop at two o'clock in the morning, Robert, now sixteen years old, is picked up by police for threatening bodily harm with a broken Coke bottle to his uncle, who was telling him he ought to be home.

He serves five months in the Louisiana Training Institute, the juvenile correctional facility.

He returns and the offenses mount: theft of a checkbook; burglaries of Jim's Chickentown, United Utilities, a neighbor's summer home; unauthorized use of "moveables" (a neighbor's truck); carrying a concealed weapon; driving while intoxicated; aggravated assault on a police officer . . .

He's in and out of jail. When he's twenty years old, he gets a suspended sentence of three years' hard labor for burglary and serves six months in the St. Tammany Parish Jail. He escapes by jumping from a third-story window. Shortly afterward he turns himself in to authorities. The report reads:

Subject was in the woods behind Wymers Store. Subject came out to the store and called the sheriff's office and said he would like to give his self up, that he was at the store and would wait for the deputies. Deputies arrived and arrested the subject . . . subject was transported to Charity Hospital in New Orleans because he could not walk on his feet [he had jumped three stories] and had cuts and scratches on his feet and arms.

Between 1972 and 1979, when he was twenty-one years old, Robert Willie was arrested thirty times. His last year of schooling is ninth grade. A tattoo of "Pam" appears when he's sixteen, "Peggy" at seventeen, and at nineteen, a skull and crossbones. One of the reports gives his name as "Little John Willie."

During one of his stints in the St. Tammany Parish Jail he meets Joseph Vaccaro.

I review Robert's trial transcripts and other legal documents. I see that Robert had been awarded a new capital sentencing trial by the Louisiana Supreme Court on grounds of improper arguments by Assistant District Attorney, Herbert R. Alexander. Urging the jury away from a life sentence, Alexander had argued that later in time a governor, who would "not know the facts of this case," might release Robert from prison. He also argued that if the jury decided on death, the final responsibility, in fact, was not theirs because there would be numerous appeals and reviews of the case by state and federal courts. "So the buck really don't stop with you. The buck starts with you."

I read the appeal petition to the Federal Fifth Circuit Court, filed by Ronald J. Tabak, an attorney whose Wall Street firm has volunteered to collaborate with Millard on Robert's appeal. I am struck by the substance, the thoroughness of the arguments. It's a thick document, 170 pages, bound with a blue cardboard cover. On the front page in large black letters is stamped "Pauper Case."

In the brief Tabak puts forth fourteen arguments on Robert's behalf. I don't understand some of the fine-tuned legal points, but several of the claims seem startling and obvious.

One is that pretrial publicity before Robert's second sentencing trial was so prejudicial that it required a change of venue. (Robert's second sentencing trial was held in the same parish courthouse as the first.) Tabak recounts the intense media coverage surrounding the first trial. The media had referred to the case as "the worst crime in the history of Washington Parish . . . the trial of the decade." The district attorney was quoted as having referred to Willie and Vaccaro as "animals." Some newspaper articles reported that Willie had "confessed" to having raped and killed Faith Hathaway and included reports of prior arrests and the fact that his father, who had previously killed another

man, was in jail for attempted murder. After trial and sentencing, the media repeatedly referred to the fact that Vaccaro had received life and Willie death, "leaving the impression," Tabak points out, "that Willie was more culpable than Vaccaro."

At voir dire for the second sentencing trial forty-seven of the fifty-two prospective jurors admitted to hearing of the case. In an affidavit, a jury expert brought in by Tabak's firm to study the possibility of bias on Robert's jury testified that people, convinced of the defendant's guilt, might lie at the voir dire out of a feeling that they could "get justice" by getting on the jury. She then cited cases of two such jurors, who first admitted to having an opinion on the case but within a few hours denied they had an opinion. There was one pool of jurors for both Robert and Vaccaro; and jurors who had been struck from one trial presented themselves for the other.

Tabak argues that the Louisiana Supreme Court, which reviewed the case and agreed that no change of venue was warranted, did not have the benefit of the jury expert's findings about biased jurors because she had been hired only after Tabak's firm—with financial resources to hire experts—took on the case.

But perhaps the most telling instance of impropriety during jury selection was this: "At least four members (one third of the jury) that convicted Petitioner were present when the attorney for Joseph Vaccaro stated [during Vaccaro's jury-selection process] that Robert Willie had killed Faith Hathaway. These assertions were made in the upstairs courtroom in which Vaccaro was being tried, only minutes before these jurors were sent to the downstairs courtroom to participate as jurors in [Willie's] trial."

Tabak argues that this statement was "far more devastating than any evidence used against Willie at trial and completely inconsistent with his defense. But neither Willie, his trial attorney, nor the trial judge knew that these highly prejudicial statements had been heard by four of the jurors."

Again, Tabak says, the Louisiana Supreme Court had been unaware that these jurors were exposed to such prejudicial statements because the defense attorney had not himself known of them.

Tabak ends the petition by citing claims of ineffectiveness of counsel, especially the defense counsel's admitted lack of preparation for both the sentencing trials (several days before both trials the defense counsel had informed the judge that he was not prepared). In the petition Tabak argues:

> The only mitigation witness called at the first trial was Robert's mother and at the second, an aunt, and even she was not prepared for the testimony. Five close family members said that they would have been glad to testify but were not contacted. Each would have brought

out about Robert's unsettled childhood bereft of adult guidance, his long-standing drug habit, his troubled mental state.

By contrast, Tabak, points out, Vaccaro's attorney had amply documented his client's troubled childhood and drug-abuse history and his client had received a life sentence.

In August 1984, the Fifth Circuit Court of Appeals denied the petition and a request for rehearing, and on November 12, the U.S. Supreme Court refused to hear the case. Now it is mid-November, and all that stands between Robert Lee Willie and the electric chair is the Pardon Board and the governor.

I can hear the words San Quentin guards used to yell when a death-row inmate was let out of his cell: "Dead man walking."

Chapter 6

Abortion

The opposition to legalized abortion in the United States is widespread, well organized, and often very passionate. If you have ever read about people who have killed doctors who perform abortions, or witnessed an antiabortion protest that got out of hand, you already understand the zeal of some of those opposed to abortion. If you have wondered how some politicians with very little talent have been elected to office just because they oppose abortion, you understand how well organized is the movement in this country to end permissive abortion laws. In addition, many citizens who may not be involved in public protest or political action harbor great resentment and moral indignation toward those who would kill their unborn babies.

On the other hand, support for the reproductive freedom of women is just as widespread, just as well organized, and just as passionate. Abortion may not be viewed as a good by those who wish to maintain its legal status, but they see it as sometimes being the lesser of two evils and as a morally acceptable choice for pregnant women. Above all else, those who support permissive abortion laws believe that women should retain their freedom to choose abortion according to their own moral standards and not have others determine how their bodies are to be used. Abortion is understood by them as terminating a pregnancy, ridding the body of a something that might have become a person, but surely not killing an unborn baby.

Between the extreme viewpoints of those who are opposed to abortion and those who would allow it under any conditions lies the view of many others who believe that abortion is morally acceptable under some conditions but clearly immoral under others. While despising what they perceive as the irresponsible and uncaring use of abortion, they understand that sometimes it ought to be permitted to avoid greater harms. When a woman is raped, for example, or when tests show that the fetus is seriously defective, abortion seems to be a more morally acceptable alternative than the continuation of the pregnancy—especially if it is performed early in the pregnancy. It is not always easy to say just what conditions must obtain for an abortion to be morally acceptable, but there are many who believe that sometimes such conditions clearly exist.

The Problem

Many of the disagreements among friends and foes of abortion focus on real issues of life and death; others arise from a misunderstanding of basic concepts. It is important for us to be sure of what we mean by some central concepts if we are to avoid such misunderstandings.

Clarifying Concepts

Let us begin by defining **abortion** as the termination of a pregnancy. Sometimes pregnancies are terminated by natural processes. Such events are called "spontaneous abortions," or more commonly, "miscarriages." The sorts of abortions of interest to us are those brought about by the intentional actions of a person, usually a physician acting upon a request by a pregnant woman. These are called "induced abortions." Usually, an induced abortion results in the death of the life that is growing within the pregnant woman. This life, after all, depends for its sustenance on the use of her body. When it is detached, it dies. Exceptions to this are some very rare types of abortions performed in the last three months of pregnancy. At this time the fetus is viable, that is, capable of living on its own biological systems. If an abortion results in the birth of a live and viable fetus, killing it is legally forbidden. Such an act would be infanticide, not abortion. Whether infanticide may ever be morally acceptable is a question we will not discuss here.

Another idea that needs clarification is that of **pregnancy** itself, especially the idea of when a pregnancy begins. To help clarify this concept, we will introduce the scientific names of the various stages of a pregnancy. One of these is **zygote.** A zygote is the fertilized egg that travels down the fallopian tube and into the uterus, prior to implanting itself into the uterine wall—a process that usually takes two weeks. From the second to the eighth week, the entity is called an **embryo.** From the eighth week on, it is called a **fetus.** The word "fetus" is also commonly used in a more general way to refer to the unborn during the entire period of gestation. We will use it in its narrower, more scientific sense unless otherwise stated.

Although when a pregnancy begins is itself a controversial matter, let us think of a pregnancy as the implantation of a fertilized egg into the wall of the uterus. It is not correct to say that a woman is pregnant simply because she has a zygote within her body. The fertilized egg may split into two zygotes during its journey down the fallopian tube to the uterus. If it does, it may create twins. Saying that the woman was first pregnant with one child, and then two makes little sense; therefore, it is best to date the beginning of a pregnancy from the time of implantation, when the zygote becomes an embryo.

One of the consequences of thinking of a pregnancy as beginning at the embryonic stage is that intentionally killing a zygote is not to be thought of as an act of abortion. The usual manner of ending the life of a zygote is by taking certain drugs, sometimes called "morning after" pills. These are usually concentrated versions of contraceptive pills that inhibit implantation. We could argue that such an act is immoral, perhaps because the zygote is a person with a right to life. But we cannot sensibly argue that it is wrong because it is an act of abortion. An act of abortion, as we said above, is the termination of a pregnancy, and a pregnancy does not begin until the embryonic stage.

One of the most important concepts in the abortion debate is the concept of a **person.** Discussions about what it means to be a person could easily fill a very long book. What we say about it here will be brief, controversial, and revisited later in this chapter. It is important to say something now, however, and for two reasons. First, part of the problem of this chapter will be expressed as a difficulty with the concept of a person. Second, the use of the term "person" is required if we are to avoid the conceptual trap illustrated by the following argument. In this argument, and in the rest of this chapter, the term "unborn" will be used to refer the entity growing within the mother at any stage of development, from conception to birth.

1. The unborn is a live human being.

2. It is wrong to kill live human beings.

Therefore, 3. It is wrong to kill the unborn.

Because killing the unborn is performing an act of abortion, this argument seems to present a very strong case against abortion. In fact, it is an argument often used in one form or another by foes of abortion. Psychologically, you may simply dismiss this argument as unfriendly to your own views or embrace it as a simple but effective tool. If you are to think critically, however, you must examine its merits. This is not the place to describe the rules for evaluating syllogisms, a type of deductive argument of which this is an instance. Instead, you may take my word for it that the argument stands or falls on the truth of its premises. If (1) and (2) are true, then the conclusion must be accepted by any reasonable person.

It certainly appears that (1) is true. All sorts of scientific evidence may be mustered to show that the embryo and fetus are alive. After all, the sperm and egg are each alive, so their combining to form a zygote that is alive and continues to live through the pregnancy should come as no surprise. Moreover, if the unborn was created by human parents, it is surely a form of human life, a human being. An analysis of its DNA would clearly demonstrate this fact. It is quite apparent, then, that abortion, no matter how early it is performed, involves the killing of a live human being. Premise (2) appears to be true as well. With the possible exception of self-defense, we do indeed consider it immoral to kill human beings. It is certainly illegal to do so, even when done with a motive of mercy, as is the case with euthanasia. Little else needs to be said in support of (2), which is one of our most deeply and widely held moral and legal beliefs.

The argument seems unshakable, but a closer look shows that its "conceptual trap" is based on what is called the ***fallacy of equivocation.*** A fallacy is an unsound form of reasoning. In this case, the same terms—"live" and "human"—are used with different meanings in each premise. The result is that the premises are no longer connected in the required manner and thus produce an unsound argument. In (1) they are used in a merely biological sense. Here, "live" means something like "able to function biologically," while "human" means "having human genes." If these terms were used with the same meaning in (2) that they have in (1), it would not at all be clear that (2) is true. After all, do we really believe it is wrong to kill biologically functioning entities with human genes? Every cell in the human body fits this description of what it means to be a live human being. Do we really think that it is immoral to kill any human cell?

The second premise is true only if "live human being" now expresses a moral concept as well as a biological one. Only if it refers to beings with moral status, beings with rights, beings that are due the protection of both law and morality, is it true to say that killing them is wrong. However, if we must use the same meanings in each premise in order to avoid the fallacy of equivocation, now premise (1) seems suspect. The idea that anything that is biologically human is a person with the same rights as born persons may be correct, but this needs to be shown and not just asserted.

We will return to this argument later in the chapter. The point for now is that the terms "live" and "human" are ambiguous. Because they have more than one meaning, and because this fact often leads to the sort of confusion expressed in the above argument, we will not use them in both senses in our discussion of abortion. Instead, we will use the terms "human" and "live" only in their biological senses, and use the term "person" to convey their moral sense. A person is a being with moral status, a being with rights and sometimes with obligations to others.

Formulating the Problem

We may now **formulate the problem** to be discussed in this chapter, the *moral* problem of abortion, as the following two-part problem:

1. *When is the unborn a person?*

2. *When is abortion morally acceptable?*

The two questions appear to be intimately connected. If some being is a person who has a right to life, and to kill that person is wrong, then it would appear that abortions are immoral once the unborn is a person.

There are several other sorts of problems that are often associated with the moral problem of abortion, problems that ought to be distinguished from it. For example, abortion can be a *psychological* problem in the sense that many women feel a deep sense of guilt and grief as a result of having an abortion. It is a *social* problem as well, as evidenced by the large numbers of abortions performed in this country—over 1,300,000 each year. In addition, it is a *political* problem of vast proportions, dividing people into rigidly opposed camps that struggle to maintain or decrease the availability of abortions. "Right to Life," or "prolife" groups as they are often called, oppose "right to choose" or "prochoice" groups in courtrooms, in public demonstrations, and within the political process of electing candidates and lobbying for legislative reform. Finally, it is a *legal* problem of great magnitude, and it has been for the past thirty or so years. We will comment at length about the law and abortion in the next section.

Possible Solutions

Now it is time to consider the **possible solutions** to our problem.

There are many ways to answer the two questions posed above. The first to be considered is called the **extreme conservative** view. According to this view,

1. The unborn is a person from the moment of conception.

2. Abortion is always immoral.

The "moment" of conception is the time when the sperm fertilizes the egg, mixing their genes to create an entirely new and unique entity. This view is called "conservative" because it restricts a woman's choice to abortion. As the unborn is a person at any stage of its development, even before it is implanted in the mother's uterus, it has from the moment of conception the same rights as persons who are born. Because it cannot exercise too many of these rights in its current condition, the major right it possesses is the right to life. If it has the right to life, then everyone else, including the mother, has a duty not to kill it.

This version of the conservative view is called "extreme" because it does not allow abortions even to save the life of the mother. In this view, if the mother has a weak heart, for example, and her life is threatened by the developing pregnancy, or if the delivery is complicated and threatens her life, having an abortion to save her life is still not morally acceptable. If the unborn is as much of a person as she is, if it has the same intrinsic value and the same right to life, then her life is to be no more valued than its life. There does seem to be an exception to this rigid rule. An abortion would be allowed by an extreme conservative if the pregnant mother had uterine cancer, for example, and had to have her uterus removed as an essential part of her treatment. Even here, however, the extreme conservative would argue that the removal of the uterus is the action morally allowed, not the abortion. Terminating the pregnancy is not the intended action; curing the cancer is. The abortion is simply an unavoidable effect of the hysterectomy and so is allowed.

The next view is the **conservative view.** It claims that

1. The unborn is a person from the moment of conception.

2. Abortion is immoral except to save the life of the mother.

This view is less extreme because it allows abortions to save the mother's life. The conservative appeals to self-defense to justify this claim. Just as a born person may be killed if he or she threatens another's life, so the unborn person may be detached from the mother's body if doing so is the only way to save her life. The extreme conservative rejects this appeal to self-defense on the grounds that the unborn is not intentionally attempting to kill the mother, as a born person might intentionally attempt to kill another person. As you might imagine, this difference in the two conservative views has generated a great deal of discussion. In practice, however, because the number of times a pregnancy threatens a woman's life is relatively small, the two conservative views are very closely related in practice.

The **moderate** view on abortion says that

1. The unborn becomes a person at some point during the pregnancy.

2. Abortion after this point is immoral; before this point it is morally acceptable under certain conditions.

Both (1) and (2) require several additional remarks if the moderate view is to be clearly understood. As to (1), the question that needs to be answered is just when in the process of gestation does the unborn become a person. Unfortunately, there is no agreed-on answer to this question among moderates. Perhaps the most common place to draw the line between not being a person and being a person is at **viability.** To say that the unborn is viable is to say that it is now capable of surviving on its own biological systems. If it were born prematurely, it could survive. The viability of the unborn is measured both by its size and the duration of gestation.

Today a fetus is usually considered to be viable at about twenty-four weeks, although viability may fall anywhere between twenty and twenty-eight weeks. The large variation of times occurs because much of the ability of the fetus to survive depends on its weight and its lung development, which vary from fetus to fetus. The survival potential of a fetus also depends heavily on the state of medical technology where it is born. If you are born prematurely in a modern hospital with an advanced neonatal intensive care unit, you will have a much better chance of surviving than you would if the medical facilities were less adequate. For convenience, let us think of viability as occurring at around the end of the sixth month of gestation.

Other moderates locate the beginning of being a person, or the beginning of **personhood,** as we shall call it, at other points of development. Some say that the unborn becomes a person when the zygote implants itself into the uterine wall. They reason much as we did before in discussing the idea that the beginning of a pregnancy occurs at implantation. If a zygote could split and become two zygotes, then it makes little sense to say it is *a* person before implantation.

For other moderates, the possession of an adequately developed **brain** is what distinguishes persons from nonpersons. The brain begins to develop quite early in the process of development, even during the embryonic stage. Brain waves associated with the neocortex, however—that part of the brain associated with the higher human functions such as thinking—do not begin to appear until the third or fourth month of development. The reasoning often used to support the view that you are a person when you develop a neocortex is that we do, in fact, consider a human being to be no longer a person when he or she loses higher brain functioning. We refer to people who have permanently lost the ability to think, to perceive, and even to be conscious at any level as being in a "vegetative" state. If this is so, then consistency demands that we should not consider someone to be a person until he or she acquires these abilities.

Still other moderates have selected **quickening** as their candidate for personhood. "Quickening" refers to movements of the developing fetus that can be felt by the pregnant woman. This first happens somewhere around the end of the third month or into the fourth month, as did the "brain" view just discussed. People who hold this view would often support it in the following way. They believe that the presence of a soul makes one a person. Once the soul appears it brings the material components of the fetus to life. Once there is life, there is movement. Once there is movement, it is felt by the mother.

Unfortunately, this argument is based on outdated science. We now know that there is movement and life from the moment of conception. If having a soul is what makes someone a person, and if we know that a soul exists because of the motion it causes, then a soul, and thus personhood, is present from conception. So revised, the argument for the "quickening" view is best seen as an argument for the conservative view. Quickening may certainly have psychological value for determining personhood. The fetus feels real, feels alive, when its movements can be detected. Quickening as a sign of personhood, however, has no basis in fact.

Finally, some moderates claim that **sentience** marks the emergence of a person. Sentience is the ability to be conscious, especially to be conscious of pleasure and pain. The reasoning behind this view is that being a person means having rights, and rights are something that come when you acquire an interest in avoiding pain and gaining pleasure; therefore, you become a person when you are able to feel pleasure and pain. This happens sometime during the fifth month, when the central nervous system and the brain are complex enough to produce these feelings.

Although there are many ways to be a moderate, all moderates share common beliefs, especially about the meaning of (2). One of these is that once you are a person, nothing permits abortion unless it is necessary to save the life of the mother or perhaps to avoid having a seriously defective child. Past the point of personhood, the moderate is, for the most part, just like the conservative: he or she believes that abortion is immoral. What about before this point? A commonly held belief among moderates, one that has to do with the second part of (2), is that becoming a person is a gradual process. The unborn does not go from being a nonperson to a person in an hour or a day. Because the development of personhood is a gradual process, it makes sense to say that the fetus becomes more and more like a person each day. Another generally shared belief is that all life is valuable and deserves respect; the unborn at any stage of development has value. It is not just a ball of cells. It is a potential human person.

If we put these last two beliefs together we get to the heart of the moderate view on the moral acceptability of abortion before the unborn becomes a person. Abortion is acceptable during this time under the following general conditions. Because all life deserves respect, there must always be a reason for an abortion. There must always be some greater evil that it avoids, for example. As the fetus becomes more and more like a person as the pregnancy progresses, moreover, the reasons must be more and more serious the later in pregnancy an abortion is to be performed. If we assume for the moment that a fetus becomes a person at viability, then abortions performed in the fifth and sixth months are morally justifiable only if performed for reasons such as rape or serious medical problems, whereas early abortions (in the first few months) may be performed for less serious reasons, such as financial reasons or the young age of the mother. The moderate wants us to respect life, wants us to give rights to the unborn even before personhood, and wants these rights to increase in importance as the fetus becomes more and more like us. The unborn is not to be treated simply as part of the mother's body, and abortion is not to be used as a form of contraception for an irresponsible person.

The next possible solution to consider is that of the **extreme liberal.** According to this view,

1. The unborn is not a person before birth.

2. Abortion is always morally acceptable.

This view is called "liberal" because it grants the pregnant woman great liberty or freedom to deal with her pregnancy as she sees fit. If she wants a child she may continue with the pregnancy; if not, she may terminate the pregnancy at any time. This view is called "extreme" because it allows no rights whatsoever to the fetus even in the final days of pregnancy. The unborn is never a person. It becomes a person only when it is born. This view strikes many as *quite* extreme, especially as there is no physical difference whatsoever between a born baby and a fetus one day before being born. The only difference is that a born baby breathes air to acquire its oxygen and is now detached from the mother's body. The point of the extreme liberal's insistence on denying that the fetus is a person is not to encourage late abortions. These are quite invasive and can be dangerous procedures for the pregnant woman. Some forms of abortion can also produce a fetus that is born alive and viable. Most physicians are reluctant to perform last trimester abortions, and most states allow them legally only for therapeutic reasons.

Instead, the point of insisting that the unborn is never a person is to deny to it any rights, at any time. Another way to say this is that for the extreme liberal the pregnant woman's right to decide for herself about whether to have an abortion always takes precedence over any supposed rights of the unborn. This view places all the moral weight on the mother's choice, whereas the conservative places it all on the rights of the unborn. For the conservative, the mother's wishes are irrelevant. As wanting to kill her born children could not justify their deaths, her wanting to terminate her pregnancy cannot justify abortion. The unborn is every bit as much of a person as a born child, so if one action is wrong, the other is also. For the extreme liberal, on the other hand, the unborn has no rights, so it may be aborted at any time.

The **liberal** view claims that

1. The unborn is a person at viability.

2. Abortion is morally acceptable up to viability and immoral after viability.

At first glance the liberal solution to our problem appears to be identical with one version of the moderate view. A closer look, however, shows that this is not the case. The liberal does agree with the "viability" moderate about personhood and the wrongfulness of post-viable abortions, but liberals disagree sharply with moderates about pre-viable abortions. For the liberal, no reason is required for pre-viable abortions, because the unborn has no rights whatsoever. Though the pre-viable unborn may be on its way to becoming a human person, it is not a person. At best, it is a potential person, and potential persons are not persons. They have no rights, according to the liberal. The pregnant woman alone has rights until the fetus is viable. In particular, she has the right to terminate her pregnancy whenever she desires to do so.

All the possible solutions discussed so far share a common assumption. They all hold that the first part of our problem, discovering when the unborn becomes a person, is a question that can be answered and that there is one answer that is more reasonable than the others. At least one author denies this assumption, however, claiming that no unshakable defense of one view over another is possible. But if we have no answer to the question of personhood, how can we answer the second question, the question about the moral acceptability of abortion? Is it all just a matter of opinion, with everyone free to answer the second question as he or she wishes?

According to our final possible solution, the morality of abortion can be discussed without any definitive answer to the personhood question. We will call our final possible solution the **Thomson** view, after its author, Judith Jarvis Thomson.[1] According to Thomson, something like the moderate view is correct, but not because we know that the unborn is a person from viability. In fact, we know little about when the unborn becomes a person. It is a question that allows for no definitive answer. The abortion question may still be answered, however, even in the absence of such knowledge. In the Thomson view, what you believe about when the unborn becomes a person makes less difference than most people generally think in how you answer the question about the moral acceptability of abortion.

Suppose you are a moderate on the personhood question, for example, especially one who chooses viability as the criterion of personhood. Then you believe that all third trimester abortions are immoral, except perhaps those intended to save the life of the mother. You hold the same belief if you are a liberal. This final possible solution also holds that even if you are an extreme liberal you ought to believe that last trimester abortions are immoral. This is because the unborn during the third trimester is so much like a baby that abortions performed during this period are immoral unless they are required to save the life of the mother.

Even the conservative view on personhood leads to a view of abortion that closely resembles the moderate view. We will examine Thomson's argument in detail later, but here it is in a nutshell. If we assume that the conservative is right and that a person exists from the time of conception, and if we assume that such a being has the same full rights as born persons, it still does not mean that abortions are not allowable. Appealing to self-defense in a broader way than the conservative does, Thomson argues that any time a pregnancy is forced on a woman she may use abortion to defend herself against an unwanted use of her body. Not only is self-defense enough to justify abortions when a pregnancy threatens the *life* of the pregnant woman, but it is also enough to justify abortions when a pregnancy threatens her *freedom* as well. From this perspective, even though the unborn has a right to life, this does not give it the right to anything required to keep it alive. In particular, it does not give it the right to use the mother's body against her will.

From this Thomson claims that the termination of any pregnancy that threatens the life or health of a woman, and any pregnancy that resulted from rape, incest, or failed contraception is morally acceptable. So for all views, whatever their stand on the personhood question, abortions are sometimes morally acceptable in the first two trimesters, and not morally acceptable during the last trimester—with a few exceptions such as to save the life of the mother and possibly to avoid having a seriously defective child. Her view, then, ends up being something like a moderate view, with the important difference that she takes no particular stand on the personhood question.

Facts and Assumptions

Facts

There are many *facts* relevant to the abortion debate. For example, it is important to know the *number of abortions* performed in the United States each year to understand the scope of our problem. From a high of roughly 1.6 million in 1990, the numbers have fallen to about 1.3 million today. There are various conjectures for this reduction in numbers, including welfare reform and the fact the most baby boomers are beyond their reproductive prime. Despite the reduction, however, this is still a high number, with about 22 percent of all pregnancies ending in abortion. The number of abortion providers has declined in the past decade as well, mostly because fewer hospitals offer abortion services now. From a high of nearly three thousand providers in 1990, the number of providers has shrunk to about two thousand today. Only about 7 percent of all abortions occur in hospitals, and fewer than 3 percent in doctors' offices. The rest are performed at abortion clinics. There are some four hundred fifty such clinics in this country, mostly located in highly populated areas. Many women have trouble obtaining an abortion because an abortion clinic is not easily accessible.

Other relevant facts include the various *stages of fetal development.* There are three major ones, as we have previously seen. From fertilization to implantation, roughly two weeks, the unborn is called the **zygote.** The zygote begins as the single cell organism that results from the combination of the sperm cell with the egg cell in the fallopian tubes. The joining of these two cells, called conception, results in the combining of their genes into the unique set of genes that will appear in every cell of the unborn. As the zygote grows, it travels down the fallopian tube toward the uterus. For the last part of this stage, once it reaches the uterus, it is called a **blastocyst**—a ball of cells that now gradually implants itself into the wall of the uterus.

The next stage of development, from two to eight weeks, is called the **embryo** stage. During this time the unborn begins to develop the physical structure of a human being, including arms and the beginning of legs, and all the major organs. Even brain waves can be detected before the end of this period. During the final stage, from the end of week eight until birth, the unborn is called a **fetus.**

There are various types of *abortion procedures* that are medically appropriate for these various stages. Generally speaking, the earlier an abortion is performed, the safer is the procedure. Most abortions, about 90 percent of them, are performed during the first trimester, with half of these occurring in the first eight weeks. The most common procedure used during this time is the surgical technique of **vacuum aspiration,** a process of suctioning out the contents of the uterus. Still used, but less commonn, is *D&C* (dilation and curettage), a process of dilating the cervix and scraping out the contents of the uterus.

Several surgical procedures are used for later abortions. One that is used in the second trimester is **saline injection,** a process of injecting a saline solution into the uterus that causes premature labor and the delivery of a pre-viable fetus. In addition, there are the more rarely performed techniques of **D&E** (dilation and evacuation) and **D&X** (dilation and extraction). In D&E, the second trimester fetus is dismembered in the uterus and its parts suctioned out. D&X is sometimes referred to as "partial birth abortion." It is a controversial procedure that is used usually for late second trimester abortions and even for third trimester abortions when the mother's life or health may be endangered by using other techniques. It involves inducing a breech (legs first) delivery, delivering only the arms, legs, and torso, puncturing the skull, and then vacuuming out its contents. The skull is then collapsed and the delivery completed. The last of these surgical techniques is called **hysterotomy,** a mini-cesarean section that has been used for last trimester abortions. It is a risky and rarely used procedure.

In addition to surgical techniques, there are also *medical procedures* that use drugs either to prevent implantation or to induce abortions. One type, called a **"morning after"** pill, is taken within a day after having sex. By increasing the presence of specific hormones, it works to prevent implantation. Another drug, **prostaglandin,** works within the embryonic stage of pregnancy to cause early labor, which expels the embryo from the womb. The most widely known of these drugs is **mifepristone,** commonly known as RU-486. This drug was first developed and used in France, and is about 96 percent effective. It has been tested in the United States and was approved for general use in September, 2000. It must be used by women whose pregnancy has been confirmed by a doctor and taken within seven weeks of the last menstrual period. It causes the uterus to shed its lining, thereby dislodging the implanted embryo. Two days after taking mifepristone, the prenant woman takes **misoprostol,** which causes contractions that expel the embryo.

Many fear that the availability of RU-486 will increase the number of abortions in this country. In France and England, where it has been used for ten years, the number of abortions has actually decreased. It may very well be the case that they will increase slightly at first in this country. As the number of abortion providers has decreased significantly over the past ten years, this pill will make abortion much more accessible to many women. One possible result of the availability of RU-486 may be that the number of *early* abortions will increase; the number of *all* abortions, however, will probably remain stable.

Descriptive Ethics

When we examine the ***descriptive ethics*** of abortion, what people and institutions *do* believe about its moral acceptability, we find many strong opinions. **Public opinion** polls, for example, consistently show that roughly 80 percent of Americans support a woman's right to choose an abortion. About 30 percent think that it should be legal in all circumstances, 10 percent in most circumstances, and 40 percent in some circumstances. This support varies with the reason for an abortion, however. There is generally greater support for a woman's right to terminate pregnancies caused by rape or incest, or for abortions performed for therapeutic reasons, than for elective abortions that are performed for less serious reasons, such as financial ones. Also, there is much greater support for abortions performed at an early stage of pregnancy than those performed later. Support for legalized abortions in the first trimester is high, but it drops off to about 25 percent in the second trimester and to less than 10 percent in the last trimester. Curiously, although support for early abortions is high, only about 50 percent of Americans consider themselves to be "prochoice," fully 45 percent refer to themselves as "prolife." Even more curiously, about 50 percent of Americans think of abortion as murder, whereas less than 40 percent do not.

Religion also has a great deal to say about abortion. The Catholic Church, for example, has consistently held an extreme conservative view on the basis of both faith and reason. Fundamentalist Protestants, about one-third of American adults, also have been a strong force of opposition to abortion. They have fought especially hard in the political and legal arena against its legalization. For us, engaged as we are in philosophical thinking, it is only human wisdom in the form of facts and reason that *justifies* a moral belief. Religion, however, is often a *source* of moral beliefs, and thus an important part of descriptive ethics. Sometimes the official position of a religion varies significantly from a statistical report of what its adherents believe. About two-thirds of American Catholics, for example, believe that abortion is sometimes justifiable, although the official position of the Catholic Church is to condemn it as murder.

There is much to say about the **law** and abortion. Prior to 1973, laws regulating abortion were made by each state and generally allowed abortion only for therapeutic reasons. Some states allowed abortion only if the mother's life was in danger; other, more liberal states, allowed it to prevent psychological harm as well. Many people who could afford it would travel to countries with more liberal abortion policies, such as Sweden, to have abortions. The less affluent were either denied a choice or were subjects of risky illegal abortions, often performed by less than competent people. Many died from such so-called back-alley abortions.

That all changed in 1973 when the Supreme Court of the United States rendered its decision on the now famous *Roe v. Wade* case. In this decision the Court ruled as unconstitutional all state laws that banned abortion for the first two trimesters. From the end of the first trimester onward, states could regulate the facilities where abortions were performed and require those who performed abortions to be properly credentialed, and so on. This oversight was allowed to ensure the safety of the pregnant woman. States could not, however, prevent pregnant women from having abortions during the first six months of their pregnancies, the time during which the vast majority of abortions are performed. After *Roe* it was solely up to the woman to decide whether to continue or to terminate her pregnancy. Citing what it called the "right to privacy," the right to decide for yourself how your life is to go and, in particular, how your body is to be used, the Court claimed that a woman's right to use her body as she saw fit was to prevail over any rights that the state had in controlling her pregnancy. The Court did say, however, that the state could regulate abortion for post-viable fetuses, because they could live if born prematurely. Most states do just that today, allowing last trimester abortions only for therapeutic reasons, or for rape or incest.

The Court's decision in *Roe v. Wade* resulted in a very liberal abortion policy in this country. However, this decision was not intended to convey the impression that because abortion is now legally permitted during the first two trimesters it was thus morally acceptable as well. The Court's decision did not *favor* abortion as a method of dealing with a pregnancy, but rather it gave to women themselves the right to make this decision according to their own moral beliefs. The Court was especially concerned that abortion law should not be based on the legal system's opinion as to when the unborn becomes a person. Justice Harry Blackmun, writing the majority opinion, says about this issue:

> When those trained in the respective disciplines of medicine, philosophy, and theology are unable to arrive at any consensus, the judiciary, at this point in the development of man's knowledge, is not in a position to speculate as to the answer.[2]

Since *Roe v. Wade,* there have been many attempts by those opposed to abortion to introduce laws designed to make it more difficult for women to have them. In all cases, the Court has maintained its findings of 1973, though often by the narrowest of margins. More important, the Court has found that several restrictions to abortion are constitutional, such as requiring a twenty-four-hour waiting period, requiring tests for fetal viability, requiring a woman to notify her spouse or a minor to gain parental consent, banning the use of public facilities and employees for abortion procedures, and allowing states to prohibit the use of Medicaid funds to pay for the abortions of those on welfare. Even though the heart of *Roe v. Wade* has been maintained, states are now free to regulate abortion in these many ways, making it more difficult for women to have access to abortion. The legal right of a woman to choose for herself whether to terminate her pregnancy remains intact—at least for now—but opposition forces are constantly attempting to dismantle the *Roe v. Wade* decision at its roots.

Assumptions

There are several important **assumptions** that are often made by people engaged in the abortion debate. For example, some people merely assume an answer to the personhood question, accepting fully that the unborn is or is not a person or becomes a person at a particular time. We have already made these sorts of assumptions part of the problem of abortion, so that any possible solution must examine them. This will be one of the tasks for the next section. For now, however, it is important for you to see how this assumption about personhood colors the abortion issue.

Examining assumptions is an extremely important part of critical thinking, especially in philosophy, and especially in ethics, and especially in the abortion debate. Because there are assumptions involved, the abortion issue often seems to be the most difficult of all moral problems to solve. It sometimes seems as though anyone's opinion is as good or as bad as that of anyone else. This is because there are different opinions about when the unborn acquires the right to life. If everyone held the same views about personhood, abortion decisions would be relatively straightforward and, for the most part, easily agreed to. To see this role that assumptions about personhood play in the abortion debate, it will be helpful for you to complete the following exercise.

Exercise 6.1

This is a case study. It describes the particular circumstances facing a pregnant woman as she thinks about the moral acceptability of an abortion. Your task in this exercise is to make this decision for her. That is, you are to say whether the abortion under consideration is morally acceptable. Moreover, you are to make this decision from the perspective of each of the possible solutions described in the previous section. Take each in turn, accept its particular assumption about personhood as correct, and then decide whether the abortion is morally acceptable. I believe that you will find that if everyone held the same assumption on personhood there would be widespread agreement on how to decide this case. By the way, just do your best with the view of Thomson. We have not yet developed her ideas fully, so it may be a bit tricky to take her perspective.

Case Study

Heather Mason is a nineteen-year-old woman who has recently dropped out of college for a year or two to find some direction in her life. She lives alone and is often lonely and depressed. She is constantly in search of a meaningful relationship and usually seeks it with older men. The relationships usually do not last very long. She does not use birth control pills or any form of contraception. She never intends to have sex with the men that she dates, but invariably she ends up giving in to their wishes.

Heather misses a menstrual period. After she misses two of them, she visits her doctor who confirms that she is pregnant. She knows who the father is but she is no longer attracted to this man. Their brief relationship is over and she tells him nothing. She has a family who will help her to raise the child, but she has decided that she wants to return to school and get her degree. Her family cannot help her do both. She always thought that abortion was wrong, but she does not see how she can do anything but rid herself of this pregnancy. Suddenly abortion does not seem so wrong to her; it seems like the lesser of two evils. Still, wanting to do the right thing, she struggles to figure out what that is. What would you tell her is the right thing to do if she came to you for advice?

Points of View

The ***point of view*** that you bring to the discussion of abortion will play an extremely important role. We are not purely rational beings but tend to favor the possible solutions that are consistent with our personal points of view. Our points of view have been shaped by our individual histories and they vary from one person to another. Your point of view or perspective on abortion may have been shaped by your religious upbringing, by the history and current reality of women's rights, by whether you are a man or a woman, by your own personal experience or the experience of friends and peers, or by any number of other factors.

Assumptions may be brought out into the open and challenged, but points of view do their work of influencing our decisions in the background, out of reason's sight. Points of view do exist, and they should be acknowledged and accepted as part of yourself. However, they should not be allowed to present an insuperable obstacle to your fair consideration of the evidence for any possible solution. Try hard to give each view a fair hearing; be tolerant even of possible solutions that you personally despise. It is one of the characteristics of an educated person that she or he can take another's point of view and examine it critically. At the very least, you will need to know how those with whom you disagree defend their positions, if only to discover their objections to your beliefs.

Moral Reasoning

In this section we will argue for three of the possible solutions that have been outlined in the first section of this chapter—the conservative, the moderate who draws the personhood line at viability, and the extreme liberal. In addition, the position of Thomson will be discussed in the "Evaluation" section. Because she does not defend a position on the personhood of the unborn, and because her answers to the abortion question represent challenges to the other views, her possible solution is best addressed there.

The extreme conservative view is not without merit, to be sure. However, the arguments for it are the same as those for the conservative view, except for the debate about whether abortion should be forbidden even to save the life of the mother. Given limited time and space, we will ignore the details of that debate here. The liberal view also has merit. However, the only major difference between the liberal and the moderate concerns the rights of the unborn during the first two trimesters. The liberal's view that the unborn has no rights during this period may be addressed by the same arguments used to defend the extreme liberal view. As to the several additional moderate views outlined in the first section, similar, though not identical, arguments may be used in their support as are used to support the moderate view selected here for defense. Once again, time and space are of the essence.

Each possible solution examined in this section will have to answer both questions that compose the moral problem of abortion as formulated in the first section. Let us call the first question—When is the unborn a person?—the "personhood question." The second question—When is abortion morally acceptable?—We will call the "abortion question." In the three views to be examined here, the assumption is that the personhood question must be answered before the abortion question can be answered. After all, it certainly seems that we cannot decide when it is wrong to kill someone until we decide which we have a "someone," or a person. This assumption will be questioned later by Thomson.

Because the problem of this chapter has two parts to it, the arguments will be more complex than those of the previous chapter. The best way to think of what follows is that we are going to address the personhood question first, for all three possible solutions. We will examine the "reasons for" each view on personhood first. Then, after reasons for each possible solution have been presented, we will return to address the objections to each that arise from competing views. Then we construct arguments for each position on the second part of our problem, the abortion question. These arguments will build especially on the results of the personhood discussion.

The Personhood Question

The Case for the Conservative View of Personhood

Let us begin with the argument for the conservative's claim that there is a person from the moment of conception. As in the last chapter on capital punishment, we will first examine the "reasons for" the claim in question, and later return to complete the argument by replying to the "reasons against" or objections to each claim. This procedure may seem cumbersome at first, but it is the best way to proceed. We cannot know what the objections to a view are unless we first examine the evidence used to support competing views. This is because the most common source of objections to one view is the reasons used to support its competitors.

One way to think of the conservative's claim about personhood is to consider the unborn as having the same moral status as a born baby, even from the time of its conception when it is merely a single cell organism. In fact, conservatives often speak about unborn "babies," or aborting an unwanted "child." These terms should be avoided in arguing for the conservative's claim about personhood, however, as calling someone a child or a baby already presupposes that it is a person, the very thing we are trying to prove. Instead, to make a case for the conservative view on personhood, reasons must be provided.

The first reason to believe that the unborn is a person from conception is that it is alive and a human being from the time it is conceived. Clearly the zygote is alive as it carries on biological functions such as cell division. Clearly it is human, as it is the product of human parents and contains human genes. There is no scientific dispute about this, our first premise.

1. The unborn is a live human being from the moment of conception.

No moral principle will be placed after this premise, as was done for all premises in the previous chapter. This is because the claim that we are trying to support on the personhood question is not a claim about right and wrong, but rather a claim about the moral status of an entity. The relevant sorts of premises that support such a claim are usually statements about some feature or features of the unborn, either physical or psychological, not descriptions of how actions may lead to harms or benefits, or how they do or do not conform to our other moral principles—justice and autonomy. With the abortion question, however, a question of right or wrong, we must show how premises conform or fail to conform to moral principles.

The second premise points up that the development of the unborn from conception to birth is one, unbroken, continuous process. There is no sharp point in the process of development when some natural feature of the unborn appears that makes it a person. Even the beginnings of all the major organs are present at a very early stage in development. In a sense, everything that is present in the born baby is present at the moment of conception. Its genes have preprogrammed the unborn at conception to be just what he or she is going to be. Everything important is there in the genes, just waiting to unfold. Now that we know so much about life in the womb, we may even want to celebrate the "conception" day as the time when the born child first begins to exist, instead of its birthday. Let us write the second premise as this:

2. All the biological features of the born child are present at the moment of conception.

Third, the unborn is unique. It is not part of the mother's body, as are her arms and legs and kidneys. It has its own unique set of genes, a combination of those of the biological parents, but different from each of them. The unborn should be thought of as *using* the mother's body to grow, not simply as tissue that is a part of the mother.

3. The unborn is biologically unique from conception.

From these three premises we may may infer our conclusion that the unborn is a person from the moment of conception. We will not write this down formally at this time, however, as the argument will not be complete until we add the conservative's replies to the objections that will come from the other possible solutions. We will return to this task after examining those arguments.

The Case for the Moderate View of Personhood

The claim made by our version of the moderate view is that the unborn becomes a person at viability and that before this time it is a potential person. The significance of saying that the unborn is a potential person prior to viability is that potential persons have some rights, though not the full rights of persons. Moreover, these rights increase the closer the unborn gets to viability. The fact that the unborn is on its way to becoming a person warrants an ever-increasing respect for its life the closer it gets to its goal. Premise (1) addresses the issue of potential personhood; (2) provides evidence for viability as the criterion of full personhood.

1. From conception the unborn is a live human being with a unique set of genes.

The moderate borrows this evidence from the conservative but from it draws a different conclusion. Whereas the conservative thinks that (1) is enough to prove personhood, the moderate is content to infer only potential personhood. The evidence for him shows that, like a planted acorn sending off roots and buds and beginning its journey to becoming an oak tree, the unborn is also beginning its journey to its genetically determined destiny. As the young plant is not yet an oak tree, however, neither is the pre-viable unborn a full person.

2. Somewhere between twenty and twenty-eight weeks of gestation the unborn could live independently of its mother's biological systems.

Suppose the pregnant woman had an accident twenty-four weeks into her pregnancy that produced labor and the birth of a viable child. Legally and morally the child would be a person. It would have the same rights as any baby born at the normal time of delivery, about forty weeks. Because the unborn is capable of biological independence at roughly twenty-four weeks, the moderate wishes to infer from (2) that the unborn at viability is a person every bit as much as babies born at later times. It has all the structures and functions of born babies; these are just less developed. Premises (1) and (2), taken together, support the conclusion that the unborn is a person at viability and a potential person before that time. As usual, we will await replies to objections before formally adding this conclusion.

The Case for the Extreme Liberal View of Personhood

According to the extreme liberal, abortion is always morally acceptable, even in the last trimester. Moreover, no reason is required to justify abortions at any stage in the development of the unborn. This position is more extreme than the legal view, which allows abortions to be restricted in the last trimester. Many are content to accept the liberal view on abortion on the grounds of women's suffering. If abortions were not legal, they reason, then women would be forced either to endure unwanted pregnancies or to risk illegal abortions. Clearly this argument fails to carry much moral weight. If I no longer want my born children, if they make me suffer, I cannot simply rid myself of them by killing them. They are persons, after all. The extreme liberal holds a view that is reasonable only if she can show that the unborn is not a person at any time before it is born.

Mary Ann Warren presents an argument that attempts to show just that. She first wants to point out that we already know what persons are. If we walked into a room filled with people and various objects, such as chairs and tables, we could pick out the persons from the nonpersons. So what do persons possess that nonpersons do not? If we can discover these person-defining characteristics that born persons have, then we can examine the various stages of fetal development for signs of them. Here is what Warren says are the characteristics present in all persons.[3]

> I suggest that the traits which are most central to the concept of personhood, or humanity in the moral sense, are, very roughly, the following:
>
> 1. consciousness (of objects and events external and/or internal to the being), and in particular the capacity to feel pain;
> 2. reasoning (the *developed* capacity to solve new and relatively complex problems);
> 3. self-motivated activity (activity which is relatively independent of either genetic or direct external control);
> 4. the capacity to communicate, by whatever means, messages of an indefinite variety of types, that is, not just with an indefinite number of possible contents, but on indefinitely many possible topics;
> 5. the presence of self-concepts, and self-awareness, either individual or racial, or both.

Unfortunately, these five psychological characteristics that she claims to belong to all persons are mostly absent from the unborn at any stage of its development. So following Warren's lead, we may write our first premise as this:

1. Before birth the unborn possesses at most only one of the five characteristics of persons.

The unborn is sentient, it can be conscious of pain and perhaps pleasure, after or during the fifth month of development. That is the only characteristic of persons that it possesses. There is no evidence that it has any of the other five characteristics by which it might be identified as a person. For Warren, this one characteristic of sentience is not going to be enough to constitute the unborn as a person before birth. This is the very conclusion that the liberal will draw after replying to objections.

Replies to Objections

It is now time to return to the partially formulated arguments on the personhood question that we have constructed to this point, and to examine how each view might reply to the objections directed against each of its arguments. The

conservative has presented thus far the following argument for his solution to the *personhood* question:

1. The unborn is a live human being from the moment of conception.

2. All the biological features of the born child are present at the moment of conception.

3. The unborn is biologically unique from the moment of conception.

From this it is supposed to follow that the unborn is a person from the moment of conception. The *moderate,* of course, will object to this conclusion. For him, pointing to the biological humanness of the unborn, as the above argument does, supports instead his view that a person emerges only some time after a good deal of development has occurred. The unborn certainly does not physically or psychologically resemble a born person at its early stages of development, for example, when it is just a ball of cells. Even during the embryonic stage it has a tail and gills. Clearly, claims the moderate, it is much more like a human person at viability than it is at conception. At viability it has most, if not all, the features it will have at birth, when it is clearly a person.

One way the conservative may reply to this objection is to point to the unique set of genes the unborn possesses from conception. But this reply alone will not do. It is not having genes that is important in constituting the unborn as a person. After all, every cell in the human body has genes. Instead, the important fact is that the fertilized egg has a unique set of genes. This is so because this cell in particular can grow into something that is obviously a person. So being a *potential* person because of the presence of a unique set of genes is the characteristic that makes the unborn a person for the conservative. As premise (2) asserts, these genes give to the unborn from conception all the biological characteristics it will ever have.

Unfortunately, this reply to the moderate's objection is not a strong reply because being a potential person may be interpreted as not being a person at all—not now, at least. After all, no one ever got wet from a potential thunderstorm. Instead, the conservative may take another tack and reply by attacking the moderate's own choice for marking personhood—viability. If viability will not do to define a person, then perhaps conception is the best place to mark its beginnings. John Noonan presents such a strategy in the following quotation.[4]

> There are difficulties with this distinction. One is that the perfection of artificial incubation may make the fetus viable at any time: it may be removed and artificially sustained. Experiments with animals already show that such a procedure is possible. This hypothetical extreme case relates to an actual difficulty: there is considerable elasticity to the idea of viability. Mere length of life is not an exact measure. The viability of the fetus depends on the extent of its anatomical and functional development. The weight and length of the fetus are better guides to the state of its development than age, but weight and length vary. Moreover, different racial groups have different ages at which their fetuses are viable. Some evidence, for example, suggests that Negro fetuses mature more quickly than white fetuses. If viability is the norm, the standard would vary with race and with many individual circumstances.
>
> The most important objection to this approach is that dependence is not ended by viability. The fetus is still absolutely dependent on someone's care in order to continue existence; indeed a child of one or three or even five years of age is

absolutely dependent on another's care for existence; uncared for, the older fetus or the younger child will die as surely as the early fetus detached from the mother. The unsubstantial lessening in dependence at viability does not seem to signify any special acquisition of humanity.

When the unborn is viable depends on the state of the art of medicine. If you were to be born prematurely in a first-class hospital you might survive at twenty weeks; if you were born in a less than advanced medical area you might not survive until you were a few weeks older. In the future, moreover, artificial incubators might be developed, ones that allow the unborn to grow to birth from the time of conception, pushing the time of viability back to conception itself. Do we really want to think of being a person as something this "external" to a human entity? Do we want to say "a hundred years ago you would be a person at seven months, whereas next century you will be a person at two months, or at conception"? Besides, are we not dependent on our mothers for our existence long after biological viability? If she takes the lead of Noonan, the conservative will write as her next premise,

4. Viability is too relative a criterion to determine personhood.

The *extreme liberal* has a more serious objection, one that strikes at the very heart of the conservative's evidence for personhood. Warren, for example, says:[5]

> [The conservative] argues for the classification of fetuses with human beings by pointing to the presence of the full genetic code, and the potential capacity for rational thought. . . . It is clear that what he needs to show, for his version of the traditional argument to be valid, is that fetuses are human in the moral sense, the sense in which it is analytically true that all human beings have full moral rights. But, in the absence of any argument showing that whatever is genetically human is also morally human, and he gives none, nothing more than genetic humanity can be demonstrated by the presence of the human genetic code. And, as we will see, the *potential* capacity for rational thought can at most show that an entity has the potential for *becoming* human in the moral sense. . . .
>
> Now if (1)–(5) (as previously outlined) are indeed the primary criteria of personhood, then it is clear that genetic humanity is neither necessary nor sufficient for establishing that an entity is a person. Some human beings are not people, and there may well be people who are not human beings. A man or woman whose consciousness has been permanently obliterated but who remains alive is a human being which is no longer a person; defective human beings, with no appreciable mental capacity, are not and presumably never will be people; and a fetus is a human being which is not yet a person, and which therefore cannot coherently be said to have full moral rights. Citizens of the next century should be prepared to recognize highly advanced, self-aware robots or computers, should such be developed, and intelligent inhabitants of other worlds, should such be found, as people in the fullest sense, and to respect their moral rights. But to ascribe full moral rights to an entity which is not a person is as absurd as to ascribe moral obligations and responsibilities to such an entity.

For Warren, coming from human parents, being alive and having human genes, and possessing all the physical characteristics of a person in a potential manner is enough to make the unborn a member of the human species. It is not, however, enough to make the unborn a person, to make the unborn a member of the moral community. For that, it must possess the five psychological characteristics shared by all current members of the moral community—born persons. It is not enough to claim that being genetically human is the same as being human in the moral sense, because an entity can possess human genes without being a person. People who are brain dead, but kept alive artificially have human genes and are not persons. Every cell in the human body has genes. Is a cell a person? On the other hand, there can be persons who do not possess human genes, as Warren points out above. So having human genes is not sufficient to make one a person, nor is it necessary to have human genes in order to be a person.

What is a conservative to reply to this objection? He might say that his criterion of personhood is less arbitrary than that of the extreme liberal, and thus is a better choice for determining personhood. After all, *most* persons that we know possess human genes, and *most* of those with human genes are persons. The five characteristics of the extreme liberal may appear to be possessed by *all* persons only because the extreme liberal ignores the very class of beings under discussion—the unborn human being. The strategy of the extreme liberal seems to work only because he focuses on born persons, both the human and the nonhuman ones, and asks what they all have in common.

Instead, the extreme liberal should be asking a question such as this: When should we extend full moral status to the unborn? In looking for the common features of born persons only, of those beings far more advanced in their development, the extreme liberal rules out in advance any chance that the unborn will be included in the class of those with moral status. She says, in effect, that the unborn is not a person until it shares the psychological characteristics possessed by born persons. But focusing on the characteristics of born persons seems much more arbitrary and exclusive than focusing on being human in the biological sense. It never allows the question of the unborn's moral status to arise. So the conservative may reply in this way to the objection that the unborn possesses almost none of the five characteristics of personhood:

> 5. Warren's five characteristics of personhood are arbitrarily selected to support the view of the extreme liberal.

Now the conclusion of the argument may be stated.

Therefore 6. The unborn is a person from the moment of conception.

It is next the turn of the **moderate** to reply to objections to each of his or her arguments. The moderate's argument thus far for the *personhood* question is this:

> 1. From conception the unborn is a live human being with a unique set of genes.
>
> 2. Somewhere between twenty and twenty-eight weeks of gestation the unborn could live independently of its mother's biological systems.

The moderate first has to reply to the type of objection raised by the *conservative,* Noonan, that viability is too relative a criterion, and that dependence on the mother continues even after birth. The moderate has little problem with this objection. First, viability refers only to *biological* dependence on the mother. It is true that children remain dependent on their mothers for years, and some people remain emotionally dependent on their mothers for decades; however, this type of dependence has nothing to do with the personhood question. For the moderate, you are a person when you can survive on your own biological systems.

The moderate is also not bothered by the fact that viability may vary from place to place and time to time and according to the state of the art of medicine. Even if we could push viability all the way back to conception, perhaps by growing our offspring in artificial wombs, this would simply mean that viability itself now is understood differently. Besides, if we did develop such technology and used it as the exclusive method for reproduction, there would no longer be any need for terminating pregnancies, as there would be no pregnancies. Remember, abortion is the termination of a pregnancy, not necessarily the killing of the unborn. The only reason to kill the unborn growing outside the mother's body would be for its own sake—to avoid a horrible life that would follow from a serious defect, for example. The moderate may safely reply to Noonan, then, that

> 3. Viability may be located at an earlier time in the future.

The second objection comes from the *extreme liberal,* Warren, who will once again claim that it is her five traits alone, not viability, that determine personhood. The moderate may respond to this objection in a manner similar to his conservative counterpart. He may simply point out the arbitrariness of selecting the features of only born persons to determine personhood, and write this as his fourth premise:

> 4. Warren's five characteristics of personhood are arbitrarily selected to support the view of the extreme liberal.

The moderate may now conclude the following:

Therefore 5. The unborn becomes a person at viability, and before viability the unborn is a potential person.

As expected, the **extreme liberal** has objections to face from the conservative and the moderate to his stand on the *personhood* question. So far he has argued,

> 1. Before birth the unborn possesses at most only one of Warren's five characteristics of persons.

Because these are person-defining characteristics, and because the unborn does not possess them to any significant degree before birth, the extreme liberal will conclude that the unborn is not a person prior to birth. The *moderate* and the *conservative* will, of course, object that their conceptions of personhood are superior to that of the extreme liberal because they are less arbitrary. We will not rehash these previously discussed objections, except to say that the extreme liberal will counter with the claim that having genes or being viable only show that the unborn is, at best, a potential person. For the extreme liberal, potential persons are not persons. This reply is expressed in the following premise:

> 2. Having genes or being viable are at best characteristics of potential persons, not persons.

It then seems to follow that

Therefore 3. The unborn is not a person before birth.

The Abortion Question

Having examined the various cases for personhood, it is now time to turn to the second question, the *abortion question*. The arguments to be constructed in support of each possible solution to this part of our problem will all build on the answers to the personhood question we have just examined. Instead of presenting the reasons for each view and returning later to answer objections, we will present each case fully. We do this to avoid confusion and because most of the objections are already known to us.

The Case for the Conservative View of Abortion

The conservative claims that abortion is always wrong except to save the life of the mother. This claim is based on the conservative's claim that the unborn is a person from the moment of conception. For the conservative, if the unborn is a person, then it clearly has the right to life. So the first premise is this:

> 1.' The unborn has a right to life. (B,J,A)

We will use (') after each premise to distinguish arguments on abortion from those on the personhood question.

From (1)' alone it follows that abortion is always wrong, unless it is performed to save the life of the pregnant woman. If someone has a right to life, then at the very least it is wrong to kill that person unless he or she is threatening your own life. We place all three principles after (1)' because wrongful killing violates all three. It causes pain and suffering, violating the principle of beneficence; and taking someone's life takes their intrinsic value and their freedom, violating the principles of justice and autonomy. Later there will be those who will question the right to life of the unborn and thus the wrongfulness of abortion. So we will add a second premise, which does not depend on the unborn being a person, in order to strengthen the conservative's argument against abortion.

> 2.' Abortion robs the unborn of its future. (B,J,A)

Premise (2)' is a premise used in an antiabortion argument presented by Don Marquis. His argument is different from most arguments on the abortion question because it does not assume anything about the personhood of the unborn. Even if the conservative argument for personhood fails, even if we cannot establish that the unborn is a person from conception, the type of argument presented by Marquis still stands as a powerful reason that abortion is immoral. Here is the argument in its briefest form:[6]

> What primarily makes killing wrong is neither its effect on the murderer nor its effect on the victim's friends and relatives, but its effect on the victim. The loss of one's life is one of the greatest losses one can suffer. The loss of one's life deprives one of all the experiences, activities, projects, and enjoyments that would otherwise have constituted one's future. Therefore, killing someone is wrong, primarily because the killing inflicts (one of) the greatest possible losses on the victim. . . . it would seem that what makes killing *any* adult human being prima facie seriously wrong is the loss of his or her future. . . .
>
> The claim that the primary wrong-making feature of a killing is the loss to the victim of the value of its future has obvious consequences for the ethics of

abortion. The future of a standard fetus includes a set of experiences, projects, activities, and such which are identical with the futures of adult human beings and are identical with the futures of young children. Since the reason that is sufficient to explain why it is wrong to kill human beings after the time of birth is a reason that also applies to fetuses, it follows that abortion is prima facie seriously morally wrong.

Marquis allows some exceptions to the wrongfulness of abortion, so he is not a true conservative. Seriously deformed fetuses may be aborted, for example, because their futures would not be valued by them. These exceptions aside, however, as it is wrong to kill a born person because it robs him of his future and all the experiences of that future, and as the unborn has a future just like a born person does, it follows for Marquis that abortion is immoral unless it is to save the life of the mother or unless it destroys a being with an unwanted future. It should be obvious that this premise follows from all three principles, once again, and so we place them after (2)'.

Perhaps the most serious *objection* to the conservative view on abortion comes from Thomson, who claims that even if the unborn has the right to life from the moment of conception, it does not follow from that alone that abortion is immoral. If a pregnancy is wanted, that is, if it was intentional or if no steps were taken to avoid it, then abortion is indeed immoral except to save the life of the mother. Thomson agrees with the conservative on this point. It is as if the mother made a contract with the unborn to give it life, and now she must live up to her agreement even if she has a change of heart once the pregnancy occurred.

However, Thomson argues that the matter is quite different for unwanted pregnancies. In general, whenever a pregnancy causes a woman's body to be used against her will she may defend herself by terminating it. While agreeing that abortion is morally acceptable as a form of self-defense when it is used to save the life of the mother, Thomson also says that self defense may be used to justify abortions performed for other reasons as well. So, even if it is granted for the sake of argument that the unborn has a right to life from the moment of conception, Thomson says that this does not give to it the right to use just anything it requires to keep itself alive.[7]

> For we should now, at long last, ask what it comes to, to have a right to life. In some views having a right to life includes having a right to be given at least the bare minimum one needs for continued life. But suppose that what in fact *is* the bare minimum a man needs for continued life is something he has no right at all to be given? If I am sick unto death, and the only thing that will save my life is the touch of Henry Fonda's cool hand on my fevered brow, then all the same, I have no right to be given the touch of Henry Fonda's cool hand on my fevered brow. It would be frightfully nice of him to fly in from the West Coast to provide it. It would be less nice, though no doubt well meant, if my friends flew out to the West Coast and carried Henry Fonda back with them. But I have no right at all against anybody that he should do this for me. . . .
>
> I am arguing only that having a right to life does not guarantee having either a right to be given the use of or a right to be allowed continued use of another person's body—even if one needs it for life itself. So the right to life will not serve the opponents of abortion in the very simple and clear way in which they seem to have thought it would.

It would appear that pregnancies caused by rape, incest, or failed contraception—all unwanted pregnancies—may be terminated in a morally acceptable way, even if the unborn is a person. It is a matter of self-defense, a matter of a woman defending her body against an unwanted use of it. It is every bit as much a matter of self-defense as is terminating a pregnancy to save a woman's life.

For the conservative, however, abortion for anything but saving a life is not a matter of self-defense. The unborn produced by rape or incest is, after all, not deliberately using the mother's body. Also, the conservative argues that if contraception fails, it produces a *wanted* pregnancy. We all know that there is always a chance that even the most reliable contraception may fail. So any time a woman engages in sexual relations, even if she is using a reliable form of contraception, there is a risk of pregnancy. For the conservative, because we know this, having sex that results in a pregnancy is to have a *wanted* pregnancy, not an unwanted one as Thomson claims. So the final premise of the conservative is this:

> 3.' Abortions for rape, incest, and failed contraception cannot be justified by appeal to self-defense. (B,J,A)

Because they are not a matter of self-defense they are wrongful killings, and thus violate all three moral principles.

Therefore 4.' Abortion is immoral except to save the life of the mother.

The Case for the Moderate View of Abortion

On the abortion question the moderate wants to demonstrate that abortions after viability are immoral, except perhaps to save the life of the mother. Before viability they are morally acceptable as long as there is a reason that provides a justification for abortion. The reason provided has to be more serious the closer the unborn gets to viability. First trimester abortions are less problematic than second trimester abortions, and thus require less serious reasons. Admittedly this is quite vague, but the general idea should be clear. No abortions should be chosen without careful moral thought. Just because abortion is legal does not mean it is morally unproblematic. Because the unborn is a potential person, there always ought to be a moral struggle on the part of the pregnant woman and others involved in the decision. Harms and benefits on both sides of the decision should be weighed, as should the moral status of the unborn at its particular stage of development. Perhaps in the first couple of months, abortions are morally acceptable to rid a teenager of an unwanted pregnancy, or for financial reasons, or because the pregnancy is unwanted. In the fourth, fifth, and sixth months, however, abortions should be allowed only for serious therapeutic reasons. So we offer the following premises:

> 1.' The unborn has a right to life after it becomes viable. (B,J,A)

> 2.' The unborn has an increasingly greater partial right to life from conception to viability. (B,J,A)

The moderate bases her position on the abortion argument on her conclusion to the personhood argument. The moderate claims that abortions after viability are immoral, whereas those prior to viability may be acceptable but become less acceptable the closer they get to viability. The closer the unborn gets to viability, the stronger the reason must be to justify abortion. Both the conservative and the extreme liberal, of course, object to this conclusion.

The *conservative* objects that the unborn's right to life begins at conception. The moderate will add the following premise to refute the conservative's objection:

> 3.' Being biologically human alone does not convey a full right to life. (J)

The *extreme liberal,* on the other hand, believes that since the unborn is only a potential person it has no rights whatsoever. The following comments reflect the moderate's view that some rights are present from conception, even if not the full rights of a person. The term "conceptus" is used to refer to the first two weeks of development, and zygote to the first part of this two-week period.[8]

> At the very least, however, the genetic evidence for the uniqueness of zygotes and embryos (a uniqueness of a different kind than that of the uniqueness of sperm and ova), their potentiality for development into a human person, their early development of human characteristics, their genetic and organic distinctness from the organism of the mother, appear to rule out a treatment even of zygotes, much less the more developed stages of conceptus, as mere pieces of "tissue," of no human significance or value. The "tissue" theory of the significance of the conceptus can only be made plausible by a systematic disregard of the biological evidence. Moreover, though one may conclude that a conceptus is only potential human life, in the process of continually actualizing its potential through growth and development, a respect for the sanctity of life, with its bias in favor even of undeveloped life, is enough to make the taking of such life a moral problem. There is a choice to be made and it is a moral choice.

The final premise in support of the moderate's position on abortion reads:

> 4.' Being biologically human alone does convey some rights to the unborn. (J)

Both premise (3)' and (4)' follow from the principle of justice, as each talks about the moral status of the unborn. Now the complex conclusion of the moderate may be inferred from these premises:

> Therefore, 5.' Abortions after viability are immoral, except to save the life of the mother; abortions before viability are morally acceptable only if they are performed for a reason that is appropriate to the stage of development of the unborn.

The Case for the Extreme Liberal View of Abortion

From the conclusion to her argument on personhood, that the unborn is never a person before birth, it is easy for Warren to answer the abortion question. The main premise she requires is this:

> 1.' The unborn has no rights.

The conclusion is that abortion is always morally acceptable. Just as the answer of the conservative to the abortion question—that abortion is almost always wrong—follows readily from his answer to the personhood question—that the unborn is always a person—so, too, the answer of the liberal to the abortion question follows readily from her view that the unborn is never a person. Presumably, if it is never a person then it has no rights—ever. In particular, it does not have the right to life. Lacking this right means, for the extreme liberal, that killing it is always acceptable. Though this conclusion follows easily from the extreme liberal's view on personhood, the real problem for the extreme liberal will come in the form of objections to which he must reply.

The extreme liberal has two serious objections to face on the abortion question. The first serious objection comes from both the *conservative* and the *moderate*. It might be called the "day before" objection. If abortion is always morally acceptable then it is acceptable the day before birth. This strikes many, including the legislative bodies of nearly every state in the nation, as too extreme—to put it mildly. It is very difficult to believe that for no greater reason than she wants to, a woman may have a morally acceptable abortion a few days before the birth of her baby. And since the fetus changes very little in the last trimester, except in size and physical maturity, the same would hold for abortions during any point in the last trimester. Jane English phrases this objection more precisely when she claims that last trimester abortions are immoral, even if the extreme liberal is correct in believing that the unborn is not a person. This is because fetuses are so much like persons at this time that routinely killing them would have the effect of brutalizing us, and of diminishing our respect for life.[9]

> A fetus one week before birth is so much like a newborn baby in our psychological space that we cannot allow any cavalier treatment of the former while expecting full sympathy and nutritive support for the latter. Thus I think that antiabortion forces are indeed giving their strongest arguments when they point to the similarities between a fetus and a baby, and when they try to evoke our emotional attachment to and sympathy for the fetus. An early horror story from New York about nurses who were expected to alternate between caring for six week premature infants and disposing of viable 24-week aborted fetuses is just that—a horror story. These beings are so much alike that no one can be asked to draw a distinction and treat them so very differently.

The extreme liberal has little to say by way of reply, except that such abortions would not occur in large numbers, even if only because they are risky and dangerous procedures for the pregnant woman, and because the law forbids them except for serious reasons. Because there would be few performed, the extreme liberal could reject the objection that his or her view would lead to a diminished respect for life.

2.' Third trimester abortions would not lead to a diminished respect for life. (B,J,A)

Because a diminished respect for life would presumably result in the loss of more innocent lives, we place reference to all three principles after (2)'.

A more serious objection arises from the very logic of the extreme liberal's own position. If a being is not a person until it acquires all five psychological characteristics—or at least most of them—even a born baby is not a person. If an infant is not a person, it appears that the extreme liberal must allow the killing of infants, called infanticide, as morally acceptable! If this extreme conclusion follows from the liberal's definition of a person, then surely there is something wrong with such a definition. If anything in life is clear, it should be clear that killing a newborn is immoral—unless there is something seriously wrong with it that will cause it to lead a meaningless life filled with suffering.

The extreme liberal has no good response for the first part of this objection. Newborns show no more signs of some of Warren's five characteristics of persons than the unborn does. For example, one-week-old babies show no developed capacity to solve problems, or to communicate about a wide range of topics, or even to exercise self-motivated activity. Moreover, some developmental psychologists claim that the emergence of a self-concept takes months. If this is true, the infant is not a person for some months.

The extreme liberal, however, accepts this conclusion that newborns are not persons, while rejecting the belief that infanticide is morally acceptable.[10] Infanticide is wrong, but not because it violates the right to life of a person. Rather it is wrong because the infant is wanted by others, even if it is not wanted by its parents. It has value—even though it is not valued by the mother—and destroying valuable items is wrong. As a great work of art that may be owned by the mother still has value even if she no longer wants it, so her born baby has value even if she does not value it. Just as destroying any desired natural resource or any great work of art is wrong, so destroying babies is wrong.

The extreme liberal's rejection of the moral acceptability of infanticide is based on this assumption, that the unborn has no value in itself but receives value only from being wanted by others. While the unborn is connected to the mother it is hers to detach as she sees fit. Her rights always override the interests of either the unborn or those who might wish to adopt it. Once detached from the mother and before it becomes a person, however, it is to be viewed as a precious commodity to be preserved because it is desired by others. The final premise is this:

3.' Infanticide is immoral, even if the infant is not a person. (B)

Because killing infants would lead to great harm, a B is placed after (3)'. We do not place either J or A there because killing infants who are not persons would not violate either. For the extreme liberal, the infant has no intrinsic value and no autonomy. According to the extreme liberal it has only the extrinsic value that comes from being wanted by others.

This conclusion now follows:

Therefore, 4.' Abortion is always morally acceptable.

Evaluation

The goal of this section is to evaluate the arguments constructed in the previous section, and to arrive at a ***reasoned judgment*** that one of the possible solutions we have defended is more reasonable than the others. Because a solution to our problem seems to require an answer to two questions, our task will be more complex than usual. For us, the central question of the two is the abortion question. What we really want to know is what is most reasonable for us to believe about the conditions, if any, that make abortion morally acceptable. The personhood question may be very important to answer, but mostly because it will help us to answer the abortion question. A good place to begin is by identifying the type of moral problem that the abortion question is, and by showing how it relates to our ethical theory.

Ethical Theory

The many elements that constitute the problem of abortion may be diagrammed as follows. Note that under the "Rules" heading, rules are expressed as rights. This is in keeping with the usual language of the abortion debate. As long as you remember that talk of rights, such as "the right to life," may be translated into talk about rules, such as "do not kill," there should be no confusion in listing rights here.

B,J,A

RULES

1. The right to life of the unborn. (B,J,A)

2. The right to life of the mother. (B,J,A)

3. The right to health of the unborn. (B)

4. The right to health of the mother. (B)

5. The right to privacy of the mother. (A)

6. Family rights. (B)

7. Society's rights. (B)

ACTION

All these rights follow from our basic moral principles. For example, the first two follow from all the principles, whereas (3) and (4) follow especially from B, and (5) follows especially from A. The reference to "family" rights includes such items as already having too many children to support, being too young or too involved in a career to raise a child, or having a spouse who is opposed to more children. The last item on the list is meant to point out the condition in some severely overpopulated countries, such as China, where abortions have been used as a means of population control. Including it on the list does not imply agreement with this policy. Like any item on the list, however, it is simply one of the factors that may be involved in a particular abortion decision. Not all of these rights are involved in all abortion decisions. The mother's right to life is hardly ever involved, for example, and the unborn's right to health—whether it has a serious defect—is not routinely a factor, either. But this list does capture most of the relevant items that enter into most abortion decisions.

"Action," of course, refers to a particular abortion decision facing a person. Such a situation may be spelled out in a case study. If our theory says, and it does, that an action is right if it follows a rule that conforms to B, J, and A, then determining the rightness or wrongness of an abortion decision will involve the following steps. First, the various "rights" involved in a particular decision must be identified. Always (1) and (5) are involved. Abortion usually involves killing the unborn and the mother's wish to terminate her pregnancy. The circumstances of the particular decision may add other factors to these two, but they are usually the major rights involved in all abortion decisions. Abortion always involves a clash of these two central items—the right to life of the unborn and the mother's right to do with her pregnancy what she wishes. This is why abortion foes are often called, respectively, **prolife** and **prochoice.**

The abortion problem thus may be seen as a **conflict of rules** type of moral problem. Any particular abortion decision must determine whether the unborn's right to life, plus any other factors that may weigh against the abortion, has a higher priority than the mother's right to privacy, plus any other rights that may favor abortion. For example, a spouse may be opposed to an abortion that is desired by his wife. So on one side of this conflict would be (1) and (6). If the mother's health was a factor, then the other side would find (4) and (5). Abortion decisions cannot be made with the precision that these numbers suggest. Ethics is not a branch of mathematics, after all. The numbers are just shorthand for describing the relevant factors of a particular case and for clarifying the type of decision making involved. What must be decided in an abortion situation is which right or set of rights outweigh the opposing right or set of rights.

To make this sort of decision in a rational manner requires us to provide evidence in favor of weighing one side as more important than another. "More important" means, "more in conformity with moral principles." This is what the "good reasons" arguments of the previous section have attempted to do. Arguments in favor of one view or another of personhood have provided evidence, expressed in their premises, that the unborn has or does not have a full right to life, at one time or another. Arguments in favor of or opposed to abortion have provided evidence that abortion is or is not morally acceptable under certain conditions. All these arguments are really attempts to resolve the conflict of especially two rights—the right to life of the unborn, and the right to privacy of the mother. The moral problem of abortion may now be seen as an attempt to determine the most reasonable belief about which of these rights has priority. The following exercise is a first step in your process of making this decision.

Your Evaluation

Exercise 6.2

Answering the personhood question seems to be an important step in deciding about the moral acceptability of abortion. Weighing the priority of the right to life against that of the mother's right to privacy will surely be influenced heavily by how strong a right to life, if any, the unborn possesses. Below are the complete arguments for the various positions on personhood that were developed in this chapter. Your job in this exercise is to evaluate these arguments according to the three criteria that are used to determine the adequacy of good reasons arguments—relevance, reliability, and sufficiency. For each premise, first ask yourself if it is **relevant.** That is, ask if what it says supports the conclusion or is irrelevant to its truth or falsity. Next, ask about the **reliability** of each premise—whether it is true or likely to be true. Finally, question whether the premises, taken collectively, are **sufficient** to prove what the conclusion claims. Decide whether there are enough reliable premises to prove the claim in question, or at least to make it likely to be true. Finally, even if no case is conclusive, decide which of the three is the most reasonable. It is better for the development of your thinking skills that you do not read my own brief evaluation of these arguments before you complete this exercise.

The Conservative Argument for Personhood

1. The unborn is a live human being from the moment of conception.

2. All the biological features of the born child are present at the moment of conception.

3. The unborn is biologically unique from conception.

4. Viability is too relative a criterion to determine personhood.

5. Warren's five characteristics of personhood are arbitrarily selected to support the view of the extreme liberal.

Therefore, 6. The unborn is a person from the moment of conception.

The Moderate Argument for Personhood

1. From conception the unborn is a live human being with a unique set of genes.

2. Somewhere between twenty and twenty-eight weeks of gestation the unborn could live independently of its mother's biological systems.

3. Viability may be located at an earlier time in the future.

4. Warren's five characteristics of personhood are arbitrarily selected to support the view of the extreme liberal.

Therefore, 5. The unborn becomes a person at viability, and before viability the unborn is a potential person.

The Liberal Argument for Personhood

1. Before birth the unborn possesses at most only one of Warren's five characteristics of persons.

2. Having genes or being viable are at best characteristics of potential persons, not persons.

Therefore, 3. The unborn is not a person before birth.

A Few Comments

My contribution to the process of evaluating the various arguments for personhood will be limited to the following few remarks. A case may be made that many premises are not *relevant*. For example, we could argue that having genes or being viable or having Warren's five characteristics is not relevant, as none of these alone determine personhood. Let us not pursue this line of criticism, however. We will allow that these factual matters may be relevant, and turn instead to question the reliability of the premises. The premises that state replies to objections are the best candidates for being unreliable, especially premises (4) and (5) of the conservative's argument, and premise (2) of the extreme liberal's argument.

The real problem with all the above arguments, however, as well as with any of the arguments that could have been constructed for either the liberal view or the various moderate views that we skipped, lies with the criterion of *sufficiency.* In none of the arguments is the evidence sufficient to prove that the conclusion is even likely to be true. For the most part, the premises are about facts, physical or psychological characteristics, that are or are not supposed to show that the unborn is or is not a person. If we include the liberal view and all the moderate views mentioned in the first section of this chapter as possible solutions, we have many facts indeed. Facts could be mustered to support the view that the unborn is a person from conception, from implantation, from the appearance of the neocortex, from quickening, from sentience, from viability and from birth. In addition, there are many facts to explain why it is reasonable to believe (or not believe) that a potential person exists at various times, a potential person who deserves some rights.

What is happening here is that because each position on the abortion question must be supported by a complementary position on personhood, then just those facts have been selected that appear to offer such support. Each view on personhood has selected the facts as being most important that support this particular view, and has ignored the others. Why is having genes a more important "personmaking" trait than having a neocortex or being viable? Why is being able to communicate and solve problems now more important than being able to do this later? To be a person is to have rights. How is it that having any of the features so far mentioned by any of these views on personhood bestows rights on an entity?

The reason that facts alone do not settle the personhood question is not simply because they are arbitrarily selected to fit the demands of the chosen view on abortion, but rather because being a person is not primarily a factual matter but a moral matter. Being orange is a factual matter. We can determine by observation if a piece of fruit, for example, is orange. Being a person, however, is not a factual matter. It cannot be determined by examining facts, especially the observable physical and psychological features of the unborn. Facts most certainly will help us to decide personhood. It matters quite a bit for some entity to be called a person, for example, whether it can feel pain or think or whether it belongs biologically to a class of beings who are readily accepted as persons. But to be a person is to have moral status, not to have particular types of observable features.

The problem with all the views on personhood mentioned above is that they ask, as if it were a factual question to be settled by observation, When is the unborn a person? Instead, the question should be asked in this way: *When, if ever, should we begin to protect the life of the unborn as fully as we protect the lives of born persons?* When the question of personhood is asked in this way, we see clearly that will have to be answered by a decision, not by a discovery of facts. The decision is a moral one; it is a decision about how much and when to value unborn lives. Facts may help to answer this question, but they will always be insufficient in themselves to provide a definitive answer. Instead, as with all questions of value, an answer must come from the individual and collective hearts of those with the power to decide.

If the personhood question has no objective answer, if every view is tainted with arbitrariness, then of what value are the arguments constructed for and against abortion that seem to depend heavily on answers to the personhood question? Let us examine the arguments for and against abortion before we make any hasty decisions about their merits.

Evaluating the Abortion Arguments

The Conservative Argument for Abortion

> 1.' The unborn has a right to life. (B,J,A)
>
> 2.' Abortion robs the unborn of its future. (B,J,A)
>
> 3.' Abortions for rape, incest, and failed contraception cannot be justified by appeal to self-defense. (B,J,A)

Therefore, 4.' Abortion is immoral except to save the life of the mother.

The premises of this argument are all relevant. The conclusion makes a moral statement, and each premise makes a moral claim in support of the conclusion. This is evident from the reference in brackets to the moral principles they follow. They are also collectively sufficient. If there are no justifiable exceptions to abortion except to save the life of the mother, then the conclusion follows. So we will focus on the *reliability* of its premises.

One objection may be directed at premise (2)'. The truth of this premise is important, says Marquis, because it states the reason that any killing is wrong. But does it? Is it not just one factor in the wrongfulness of killing? Is killing not wrong also because it usually causes pain and suffering to the one killed and his or her loved ones and because it robs the victim of his or her intrinsic value and autonomy? Even if people had only a few minutes to live, surely not much of a future, killing them against their will would be wrong. If this is so, then, as most abortions do not cause pain and suffering they are not wrong for that reason.

Moreover, you can rob someone of his or her intrinsic value and autonomy only if the person already possesses these characteristics. If the unborn is not a person at least until viability, then it does not possess these traits. So the only remaining reason that it is wrong to kill the pre-viable unborn is that it robs it of its future. But do we not rob beings of their future all the time? We kill animals for food, for example, robbing them of their future. Some people may believe that such actions are wrong, but the vast majority of people do not. Marquis may say that only "futures like ours" count as important, but is this not simply a form of discrimination? If futures like ours are the only important ones, is it not because we have intrinsic value? Is it not because we are persons?

We can also argue with the truth of (1)', but because it follows directly from the conservative's personhood argument we will not revisit it here. The most serious objection will be directed at the reliability of premise (3)', the denial of Thomson's claim that self-defense justifies abortion for rape, incest, and failed contraception. If Thomson is right, then even if the unborn is a person from the moment of conception abortions are still morally acceptable in order to save the life of the mother, and for rape, incest, and failed contraception. That surely covers quite a few circumstances and makes the conservative answer to the abortion question much closer to that of the moderate. What is the right way to think about the moral acceptability of abortion, assuming that the unborn is a person from conception? Is it the "Thomson" way of thinking, or the "old" conservative way of thinking? It is worth telling Thomson's very famous "violinist" story to help you to decide for yourself.

Suppose, Thomson says, that the kidneys of a famous violinist have failed. While awaiting a suitable donor for a transplant he needs the kidneys of someone else to do the job of cleansing his blood of harmful toxins. He needs the use of these kidneys for nine months. A simple surgical procedure will make it possible to hook up his kidneys to those of another. Hoses leading from a shunt that protrudes from one body may be connected to a shunt in the other person's body. In both cases the shunt is connected to the kidneys. The hoses may be easily detached by either party.

Suppose now that you awaken one morning to find yourself attached to the violinist. You have been kidnapped by his friends and forced into letting him use your body. While it would be generous of you to remain attached, says Thomson, morality surely does not require it. It would be an act beyond the call of duty. Even if no one else was available for the job, you could rightfully detach and allow the violinist to die. He does have a right to life, it is true. However, that does not give him the right to anything he needs to keep himself alive. In particular, it does not give him the right to use your body against your will. You may defend yourself against this action, even though it results in his death.

In the same way, if a pregnancy is unwanted, if it is an unwanted use of your body, then it, too, may be "disconnected." And this is true even though the unborn has a right to life. "Unwanted" means that the pregnancy was forced on you, or that you took steps to avoid it, such as using reliable contraceptives. According to Thomson, we are all supposed to know the relationship between sex and pregnancy by the time we have sexual relations, so that to have sex without contraception that results in a pregnancy, is to have a wanted pregnancy. We are, after all, responsible for all the foreseeable consequences of our actions, whether we consciously intend them or not. The upshot is that it is morally acceptable to terminate pregnancies caused by rape, incest, or failed contraception—all unwanted pregnancies, even if the unborn has a right to life from the moment of conception. This is every bit as much a form of self-defense as is unplugging from the violinist.

The Moderate Argument for Abortion

> 1.' The unborn has a right to life after it becomes viable. (B,J,A)
>
> 2.' The unborn has an increasingly greater partial right to life from conception to viability. (B,J,A)
>
> 3.' Being biologically human alone does not convey a full right to life. (J)
>
> 4.' Being biologically human alone does convey some rights to the unborn. (J)

Therefore, 5.' Abortions after viability are immoral, except to save the life of the mother; abortions before viability are morally acceptable only if they are performed for a reason that is appropriate to the stage of development of the unborn.

We will let the moderate's argument stand. The premises are relevant, as shown by the moral principles that accompany each one. Moreover, we have sufficiently debated the reliability of its premises in the previous section for you to decide for yourself now about their reliability and sufficiency.

The Extreme Liberal Argument for Abortion

> 1.' The unborn has no rights. (J)
>
> 2.' Third trimester abortions would not lead to a diminished respect for life. (B,J,A)
>
> 3.' Infanticide is immoral, even if the infant is not a person. (B)

Therefore, 4.' Abortion is always morally acceptable.

For this last argument, the place to focus our critical attention is on the reliability of premise (2)'. As we have seen, English claims that third trimester abortions are immoral precisely because they would lead to a diminished respect for life. She appears to be right about this, as witnessed by the widespread public opposition to last trimester abortions—even when these abortions are performed for therapeutic reasons.

If Thomson and English are right in their criticism of the way that both the conservative and the extreme liberal answer the abortion question—and that is for you to decide—then progress has been made in solving our original problem. If all but serious last trimester abortions are immoral, whatever your position on personhood, and if some abortions are morally acceptable prior to viability, whatever your position on personhood, then it seems that something like a moderate view is the most reasonable possible solution to accept. Thomson is not a moderate in the usual sense, as she holds no particular position on personhood. However, her "moderation" of the conservative and extreme liberal views is close to the traditional moderate's position in practice. And in practice, this position is very similar to the current law on abortion in this country.

Consequences

It is now time to consider the **consequences** of our evaluation of the arguments for both the personhood question and the abortion question. First, if you think that Thomson has it right, then the current law on abortion should remain as it is. It should continue to allow women to choose for themselves in the first two trimesters, and continue to restrict abortion for all but very serious reasons in the last.

Next, if the moderate is right that abortions become more serious moral matters the closer the unborn approaches to being a person, then second trimester abortions should be thought of as very serious moral matters. They should be performed only to avoid great harm, such as danger to the mother's life or health, or because of the discovery that the unborn has a severe defect. Abortions for other reasons, such as rape, incest, career hopes, the youthful age of the pregnant woman, and so on, should be performed only during the first trimester, and as early during that time as is possible.

In my personal view, there should be a great deal more education about abortion than currently exists, including moral education, especially as nearly one quarter of the five million or so annual pregnancies in this country will end in an induced abortion. Abortion should always be thought of as a serious moral problem, and not simply as a medical problem. Perhaps we could learn a lesson from those Japanese who practice a Buddhist religious rite called *mizuko kuyo,* a form of ritual grieving by mothers for their aborted fetuses. It is their way of allowing abortion as the lesser of two evils, while at the same time recognizing that it *is* a sorrowful, if sometimes necessary choice.

Another Perspective

In the following selection, Chinese physicians argue for the moral acceptability of third trimester abortions. Their experience with the difficulties of population control have given them **another perspective** on the moral acceptability of late, nontherapeutic abortions.

Can Late Abortion Be Ethically Justified?

REN-ZONG QIU, CHUN-ZHI WANG, AND YUAN GU

THORNY CASES

Miss A is a 25-year-old unmarried woman working in a factory. She lived with her boyfriend and became pregnant. She was not aware of her condition in the early stage of her pregnancy, because she lacked education in reproduction. After she realized that she was pregnant, she was afraid to undergo an abortion. She used a cloth to bind her waist to hide her illegitimate pregnancy from others, and she was burdened with anxieties every day. Her pregnancy was revealed when the fetus was eight months old. Responsible men in her factory escorted her to the hospital and asked the physician to perform an abortion. The physician agreed, because the young woman did not want the child, and because she had no birth quota as an unmarried woman.[1] The physician performed the abortion using an intraamniotic injection of Huangyan Flower,[2] and a 2800 g. dead baby was expelled the next day.

Mrs. B is another story. She is a 30-year-old accountant, the wife of an army officer. She has been pregnant two times, but only gave birth once, to a girl, and was given a "One Child" certificate.[3] When she became aware of being pregnant the third time, she felt a physical difference, and she inferred that the fetus might possibly be a boy. Her husband was performing his duty outside Beijing at that time. She made every effort to hide the truth for seven months. During this period she economized on food and clothing, and she

Reprinted by permission of The Journal of Medicine and Philosophy, *1989. © Swets Zeitlinger 1989.*

worked very hard to save money for the penalty fine;[4] both courses of action jeopardized her health. When her husband came home to visit, he persuaded her to give up the fetus in the interests of their family and country. Mrs. B. agreed, and was escorted by her husband to the hospital to undergo an abortion. After examination, the physician found her malnourished, dropsical, Hgb 4g., heart rate 120/min., fetal heartbeat quite weak. She was given supportive treatment first, and then an intraamniotic injection of Rivanol several days later. A 1800 g. dead baby was born the next day.

The experience of Mrs. C. is somewhat different. She is a 40-year-old worker in a state-owned factory, with two daughters and one son from five pregnancies. She wanted more children. When she conceived the sixth time, she succeeded in covering the truth until seven months later, when the cadres of her factory discovered her condition. The cadres asked her to give up the fetus, but she refused, because she believed the Chinese maxim "More children, more happiness." She said she did not care if she were fined. One month later she was persuaded to undergo an abortion, but the physician refused to perform the operation. The cadres of her factory complained that if she gave birth to a fourth child, the rewards of all of the workers would be diminished, because they had broken the birth quota assigned to the factory.[5] Finally the physician was convinced, and he performed the abortion with an intraamniotic injection of Huangyan Flower. The next day a 3000 g. live baby was born, and later adopted by an infertile couple.

REASONS FOR LATE ABORTIONS

From the cases described above we know that there are two groups of pregnant women who undergo late abortion: the unmarried woman, and those who want more than one child but who are convinced at a late date to forgo the fetus.

The rate of pregnancy in unmarried women has increased in recent decades. With the wide application and free distribution of contraceptives, and the opening of the door to foreign cultures, China is undergoing its own form of the "sexual revolution." But sex education is still unavailable to young men, including knowledge on how to use contraceptives. According to one study in nine villages of Jiangbei County in the Sichuan Province, the average rate of illegitimate pregnancies was 50–82%. In one village it was as high as 90%; and in another village the rates in 1979, 1980, and 1981 were 44%, 53%, and 71% respectively (Hua, 1984). We think that the figures may not be representative, but only indicative. In a region of Shanghai city, among the pregnant women who underwent abortion, the rate of unmarried women was 8.4%; but in recent years it has been as high as 40% in some hospitals in Beijing and other cities.

In the early stages of pregnancy, these unmarried women made every effort to hide the truth from others. However, it is hardly possible for them to raise a child by themselves, for moral and economic reasons. The average income of a young woman is below 100 yuan ($27) per month. And changes in the moral environment lag behind the change in the sexual behavior of youth. In Chinese public opinion, premarital sexual relations are still considered unethical, an illegitimate pregnancy even more so. In some cities, abortion in hospitals was allowed only for married women, in an attempt to decrease or put an end to illegitimate pregnancies. As a result, however, there was an increase in the rate of late and illegal abortions which usually led to the death of both mother and fetus.

In our opinion, appropriate sex and reproductive education should be provided to young people, and there should be a change of attitude toward premarital sexual relations and illegitimate pregnancies. We believe that the attitude should be more lenient, in order to make it easier for pregnant girls to tell the truth and to have an abortion earlier and more safely, if they do not want to carry the pregnancy to term.

The case of pregnancy in a woman who already has a child is much more complicated. It is the Confucian cultural tradition which encourages the Chinese to have more children. Confucius said "Among the three vices that violate the principle of filial piety, the biggest is to be without offspring." The Chinese turned this negative warning into a positive maxim: "More children, more virtues." In the case of Mrs. B, she wanted a male child. Chinese tradition values male children more highly than females, because genealogy is continued through the male. But the desire to have more children, or a male child, often conflicts with the state policy of "one couple, one child." In Mrs. C's case, it also conflicted with the interests of her colleagues in the factory where she worked. However, Mrs. B and Mrs. C were finally persuaded to agree to undergo an abortion in the interest of their country and their colleagues. Can this be ethically justified?

CONFLICTS OF VALUES

There are conflicts of values around the ethical issue of late abortion which cannot be solved exclusively by deontological theory. The Chinese Ministry of Health has promulgated a regulation to prohibit late abortions after 28 weeks, with the purpose of protecting the health and life of the mother as well as of the fetus. But at the same time, since the beginning of the 1980s, the Chinese government has promulgated a regulation of birth control which permits a couple to have only one child. These two regulations are in conflict, but the latter is the more powerful. It is argued that this regulation ("one couple, one child") is in the maximum interest of the maximum number of people. Rewards in a factory are connected not only with one's work performance, but also with one's reproductive behavior.

If you give birth to a second child, you will be fined *and* the rewards of all of your colleagues will be deducted. This practice forces a fertile married woman to consider the consequences of her reproductive behavior for others before making a decision. Some married women, most of whom are professionals and intellectuals, do not want more than one child. A few of them do not even want to get married. Some want more than one child, but they are reluctant to be in a position to be fined, or they think they should put the interest of their country first by carrying out the birth control policy. But there are still a few women who insist on having another child. The outcome is usually that they are finally persuaded to undergo an abortion, or they give birth to the child in spite of the financial or psychological pressures from their colleagues or their employers.

In our opinion, it is difficult to say which conduct is moral or immoral. For a woman not to have any more children, for whatever reason, may be labeled praiseworthy conduct; but if a woman wants more than one child, it is not a vicious desire. "Moral" or "immoral" may be too strong a label to apply in such cases.

But value conflicts exist. In preceding years, when the technology for late abortion was underdeveloped and no third party intruded, the balance would usually incline towards rejecting late abortion in the interest of protecting the mother and the viable fetus. Now the scale is more evenly stacked. On the one side is the presumed interest of the viable fetus; on the other are the interests of a big third party: the country, the factory and colleagues, and the family. If the mother stands on the latter side, she tips the balance against the fetus. If she insists on giving birth, or if the late abortion would jeopardize the mother's life, the scale could be a match, or the interests of the fetus could even prevail.

PHYSICIAN'S DILEMMAS

In two of the three cases described above, the physician did not hesitate to perform a late abortion. In the third case the physician was persuaded to perform the abortion by cadres of the factory where the pregnant woman worked.

There is a schism between physicians, ethicists, and the public over late abortions.

The first to explicitly defend prohibiting abortions after seven months was an obstetrician, Dr. J. K. Liu, at the 2nd National Conference on Medical Ethics (*Liu*, 1983, pp. 213–218). We have asked our obstetrician friends their opinions on this issue. They always say, "I don't know what I should do." Some of them prefer not to perform late abortions except for women with particularly troubled pregnancies. Others take their responsibility to society into account first, and perform late abortions with less hesitation. The overwhelming majority of Chinese physicians are employed by state-owned hospitals; they are labeled "state cadres" and have the responsibility of carrying out state policy. But all of them are perplexed; either way they harm one side, either the mother and fetus or society. Especially thorny is the case in which the aborted fetus is alive. Although the fertility rate is increasing now in China, and infertile couples are willing to adopt such a baby, should the physician tell the truth to the mother who had expressed a desire to give up the fetus? In some cases physicians do not do so, because they are afraid that the mother might change her mind and keep the baby.

The author of *An Outline of Medical Moral Theory* claims that in some cases, because a woman was coerced into an abortion in order to keep the birth rate low, the physician was coerced to perform late abortions, thereby violating both policy and medical morality (p. 80). But the author of *Essential Medical Ethics* claims that, "when the perinatal care came into conflict with birth control and eugenics, it must be subordinated to the needs of the latter, because these are in the interest of the whole nation and the whole of mankind, as well as in accord with the greatest morality" (pp. 191–192).

A questionnaire showed that 16% of the respondents assented to performing late abortions on women with second pregnancies, in order to conform with the state policy, 7% supported respect for the woman's free will without any interference, and 77% believed the late abortion should not be performed, but that a fine should be imposed. As for the question of who should make the decision on late abortion, 32% supported the pregnant woman and her family as the primary decision makers, 32% the physician, 9% the responsible men of the unit (factory, school, institute, etc.) where the woman was working; and 27% an ethical committee (unpublished report).

When making the decision to undergo or perform a late abortion, should the responsible parties take into account the interests of the third party, or only the interest of the woman, or only the interest of the fetus?

SOCIAL GOOD

Even as a member of an individualist society, one should be concerned about the social good, although more attention might be paid to individual rights or interests. If you are a carrier of the AIDS virus, do you have the right to have sex freely and spread the disease to others? No. A socialist country operating under the guiding ideology of Marxism favors a holistic social philosophy which asserts that a society is not merely the sum of its members but a non-additive whole which is more than the sum. Every member should put the interest of society as a whole in the first position and subordinate his or her interest to that of society. The problem is, Who is the representative of society and its interest, and how is the interest of a society as a whole known? Usually, someone claims that he is the representative, and it later turns out that this is not the case. However, in China the "one couple, one child" policy has been accepted by the majority of the Chinese people as in the best interest of the society as a whole. Of course, birth control is not the only factor, but it is one of the most important factors in modernizing underdeveloped countries in Asia, Africa, and Latin

America. In a sense, the success or failure of development depends on the use of birth control. Everyone, including the married couple and the physician, should take this into account.

But we should practice birth control in a more human way. We should make every effort to avoid late abortions, i.e., to use effectively the contraceptives and to perform the abortions earlier. In the case of a late abortion, voluntary consent of the mother is indispensable. The physician should determine whether the late abortion would cause any harm to the mother's health or endanger her life, and he should refuse to perform it if there is a high risk.

In preceding years the second pregnancy was treated with more leniency and flexibility than at present. If a couple in a rural area had a child who was disabled, or if they live in a rural area that has a birth rate lower than the quota, they were permitted to give birth to a second child. But this flexibility in policy has raised the birth level, and an upsurge of second births amongst China's rural families is jeopardizing the attempt to limit the population to 1.2 billion by the year 2000. The State Statistics Bureau reports that 40% of rural women have given birth to three or more children over the past several years. Compared with 1985, the number of second births last year climbed by 1.37 million people to 6.92 million, and the number of third or more births topped 2.88 million, 240,000 more than the previous year (*China's Daily,* 1987).

CONCLUSION

Our conclusion is that the late abortion can be justified ethically in China: (1) if the "one couple, one child" policy is justifiable; (2) if the couple and the physician take the social good into account; (3) if the mother expresses her voluntary consent, no matter whether the decision is made on the basis of her own original desire or after persuasion by others that is not coercive; and (4) if the late abortion will entail only a low risk to the mother's health or life.

NOTES

1. Every married woman gets a birth quota before pregnancy; also see note 5.

2. The extraction from an herb used as an effective drug to induce abortion.

3. Whoever has such a certificate enjoys favored treatment such as additional rewards at the factory, enrollment in a kindergarten for their child, etc.

4. If you give birth to a second child, you will be fined about 1000 yuan ($270), which can be about one year's wages

5. Every factory, school, or institute has a birth quota set by the authorities. Female workers are allowed to give birth to only a certain number per year, and the quotas are assigned to the married women on the basis of consultation with them each year.

Chapter 7

Physician Assistance in Dying

In 1900, the average life span of Americans was about forty years. About 30 percent of the population died before adolescence then, usually from an infectious disease such as smallpox or diphtheria. Statistically, we will live well into our seventies today, with promise for even much longer lives in the foreseeable future. Many individuals born in the year 2000 will probably be around at the start of the twenty-second century. One of the consequences of this beneficial increase in the length of our lives, however, has been a general decline in the quality of our dying. Most of us will die slowly, from degenerative diseases associated with aging, such as heart disease, cancer, stroke, and renal failure.

As with our longer life expectancies, another blessing of the twenty-first century is that medicine can stave off the inevitable more successfully than ever. This too, however, is not without its costs. Our dying may be prolonged with the aid of new drugs, surgical techniques, radiation therapy, dialysis machines, organ transplants, and other wonders of modern medicine. The use of these treatments is usually a good thing, allowing many of us to enjoy longer lives than nature itself would allow. However, sometimes these and similar measures have been used pointlessly to sustain our lives, simply prolonging our pain and suffering well past the point when a more merciful nature would have stopped.

In the past three decades, battles to allow dying patients the right to remove or not to initiate treatments have been fought and, for the most part, won. Now patients, or those who speak for them, have the right to refuse or remove even life-sustaining treatments, should they judge them to be of no benefit. It is currently morally and legally acceptable for patients, even those who are no longer capable of making their own decisions, to forgo treatments that do not cure them or improve the quality of their dying. No one any longer has to receive treatments that merely prolong their painful deaths. All patients have the right to refuse such treatment and to allow nature to take its course, to die a natural death.

Unfortunately, nature's course can sometimes be long and painful. Today most medical personnel are able and usually willing to manage effectively the pain of most dying patients, 80 percent of whom die in health care facilities. Hospice care is usually available for most patients, as well. The focus of hospice care, whether it is provided in a hospital, a long-term care facility, or at the patient's home, is squarely on the physical and psychological comfort of the dying patient. For hospice patients, curative treatments are abandoned as futile and replaced with concern for the physical, psychological, and emotional pain and suffering associated with dying. It is the patient as a person who is treated, not the disease from which he or she is dying. Patients and families are encouraged to talk about the dying process and often find it an extremely positive, meaningful, and important part of their lives. About 40 percent of cancer and AIDS patients die from the illnesses while under hospice care.

Although there has been much progress in the management of pain, in some cases pain cannot be managed effectively without large doses of narcotics. This may diminish significantly the patient's consciousness and cognitive capacity. People dying under these conditions are often faced with the options either of being in significant pain or being unconscious or nearly unconscious. For many, neither of these options is acceptable. Instead, they want not to take this trip that nature has planned for them; they want the right to end their lives prematurely if they so desire. They want the right not only to terminate treatment and to let nature take its course, but also the right to kill themselves or to have their doctors do that for them.

But having a moral or legal right to kill yourself or to be killed by others is risky business, to say the least. It is one thing to remove treatment and let a patient die a natural death, and quite another to hasten that dying. "Do not kill" is a moral and legal rule for which the only exception seems to be self-defense. It seems plain wrong to kill yourself—an act of suicide—or to have someone else do it for you— an act of killing. For many, even if such actions could be thought of as forms of self-defense, it would be better not to allow them. It would be better to keep administering painkillers as needed and let the natural process work. What they especially fear is that a rule allowing killing, even if the motive is to end pain and suffering, would surely be abused and in the end cause more harm than good.

For example, how could we ever be sure that patients mean what they say when they request to be killed? How do we know that they were not too depressed or too concerned with being a burden on others to make a rational decision? Further, what effect would such actions have on the medical profession, bent as they are on saving our lives and easing our pain? Would this not make doctors give up too early on some of us, if they thought that we were going to end up killing ourselves anyway? How would we control family members with questionable motives from encouraging their dying relatives to speed up the process? Further, if we accept the practice of allowing patients to kill themselves or allowing them to be killed by their doctors, would we not next be tempted to kill any dying patients who could no longer speak for themselves? Think of all the cancer patients who fit this profile. Would we next be tempted to kill patients who were not in danger of dying soon, but suffered from dementia of one sort or another? Think of all the old folks in nursing homes who fit this profile. What about seriously defective newborns; would it not be more merciful to end their lives with a lethal overdose of narcotics than to allow them to lead substandard lives?

The current fiery debate in society about killing dying patients focuses especially on what is called physician-assisted suicide and active voluntary euthanasia, terms that will be defined below. The goal of this chapter is to decide whether a rule allowing patients to kill themselves with the aid of their doctors (assisted suicide), or to have their doctors kill them if they request it (active voluntary euthanasia), should or should not be thought of as morally acceptable. Those in favor of such killings argue that it should be the right of anyone to decide for himself how much suffering he is willing to accept in his dying days. Those opposed will point out the wrongfulness of killing, and note the significant harm that most certainly will follow if such a rule is adopted by society.

The Problem

There is a great deal of confusion among many people about the various types of assistance that are available to aid people to die better deaths than nature itself might allow. Commonly these types of assistance are referred to as various forms of euthanasia. It is important to spend some time trying to sort out the various meanings of this term if we are to avoid misunderstanding the problem to be solved in this chapter.

Clarifying Concepts

The first order of business is to *clarify concepts.* This will take a little time, as there are many concepts to consider and many distinctions to be drawn among them. The word **euthanasia** comes from the Greek and literally means "a good death." Today, the term has come to mean the intentional killing of someone in order to avoid the pain and suffering associated with the person's dying. Sometimes euthanasia is called mercy killing. Although this is how the term will be used in this chapter, as a name for a type of killing, it has been given a wider meaning by some. According to this wider meaning, there are five different types of euthanasia. Listing and defining them requires that we first introduce several concepts— the concepts of active, passive, voluntary, and nonvoluntary euthanasia.

Active euthanasia refers to the direct killing of a person. Even though active euthanasia may occur apart from a medical facility, let us think of it as something that occurs in a health care facility and refer to the person who is killed as a "patient." With active euthanasia, for example, a patient may be killed by an overdose of a drug in order to escape from pain and suffering. **Passive euthanasia,** on the other hand, is not killing at all, but refers to removing or not initiating treatments, and allowing nature to take its course. In a typical passive euthanasia situation, a dying patient, or someone who speaks for the patient, refuses treatment that may prolong her life. This is most often done because she does not think the extension of life that such a treatment may provide is a benefit to her. And so a dying cancer patient may, for example, refuse another round of chemotherapy and let the cancer progress naturally. In her judgment, the extra few days or weeks of life would simply be more time to suffer.

Euthanasia of either sort is **voluntary** when it is requested by a competent patient. A patient is competent when he is able to understand both the nature and the consequences of his decision, and to choose it freely. Euthanasia is **nonvoluntary** when one or both of these conditions are absent. In the case of babies, people with dementia, or patients who are highly medicated, if there is to be euthanasia, someone else must make the decision for the patient. It should be added here that euthanasia is **involuntary** when it is performed *against* the will of the patient. Such an act is clearly wrong and will not be discussed in this chapter. We may now list and define four types of euthanasia:

1. **passive voluntary euthanasia**—removing or not initiating treatment at the request of the patient.

2. **passive nonvoluntary euthanasia**—removing or not initiating treatment at the request of someone other than the patient.

3. **active voluntary euthanasia**—intentionally killing the patient at the request of the patient.

4. **active nonvoluntary euthanasia**—intentionally killing the patient at the request of someone other than the patient.

We will say very little about passive euthanasia in this chapter, as it is already widely accepted both legally and morally. When we do speak of it, we will sometimes refer to it by its more common name these days, **letting die.** The important point is that (1) and (2) are to be understood as actions in which patients are allowed to die a natural death, free from unwanted medical treatments. Their deaths are caused by their diseases or conditions, not by the actions of human beings. They are caused by nature.

On the other hand, (3) and (4) are cases of *killing* patients. They die before their diseases or conditions would have killed them. They die because of a deliberate act of a human being. It is the moral acceptability of such acts of killing, not the moral acceptability of acts of *letting die,* that will be our chief concern in this chapter. Of the two types of active euthanasia defined above, our main concern will be active *voluntary* euthanasia—which we will simply call **voluntary euthanasia** from now on. Though a few remarks will be made later about active *nonvoluntary* euthanasia, our focus will be on the issue of competent patients who decide for themselves that they wish to be killed to avoid the pain and suffering that fills their dying days.

In addition to voluntary euthanasia, there is a second type of killing for the sake of mercy that will concern us here, called **physician-assisted suicide.** Physician-assisted suicide is a type of suicide in which the patient kills himself or herself. The "assisted" part of the name refers to the assistance provided by a physician, which usually consists of information about effective methods of suicide and the actual providing of drugs. Typically, the patient himself then administers an overdose of these drugs, which results in his death by his own hand.

Physician-assisted suicide is like voluntary euthanasia in many ways. Both have the same intention—the killing of the patient. Both have the same motive—mercy. Both have the same result—the death of the patient. Most important, both originate from the same source—the decision of the patient. It is this decision of a competent patient to be killed that initiates all the events that lead to her being killed, whether by her own hand or that of her doctor.

Physician-assisted suicide and voluntary euthanasia are also different in two ways that have significance for us. First, the cause of the patient's death is different. This has important legal significance, as the courts need to fix the immediate cause of death to determine liability. Although the cause of death in either assisted suicide or voluntary euthanasia is ultimately the patient's decision, the immediate cause in voluntary euthanasia is the physician's act, whereas in assisted suicide it is the act of the patient. In both cases the patient receives an overdose of a drug that kills her and she receives it because of her own decision to do so. But the person directly responsible for its administration, and the one legally responsible for the patient's death, is the doctor in voluntary euthanasia and the patient in assisted suicide. Another significant difference has to do with the effective regulation of assisted suicide and voluntary euthanasia. Many believe that involving a physician in the death of his or her patients has a much greater potential for abuse than simply allowing patients to kill themselves. The thinking is that if a patient has to perform the act, it is much more likely to occur freely and intentionally than if a second person is involved.

Although the idea is controversial, we will group physician-assisted suicide and voluntary euthanasia together under the general category of **physician assistance in dying.** The two may have significant *legal* differences, but in my opinion they are *morally* the same, and it is the moral problem of euthanasia that we wish to address in this chapter. Whether it is the patient or the physician who gives the overdose, neither act would occur were it not for the patient's own wishes. It is his or her decision that initiates the process. The doctor's role, should the doctor decide to comply with the patient's wishes, is determined by this decision and not the physician's own choice. In either assisted suicide or voluntary euthanasia, the doctor does what the patient wants.

Suppose, for example, the patient is receiving narcotics intravenously and a lethal dose of these narcotics could be administered by turning the valve that regulates the speed of the drug entering the bloodstream. Legally it matters, but does it make a moral difference—any difference in the harms or benefits, or in the patient's intrinsic value or autonomy—if the patient himself or the physician turns up the drip? In both cases it is the patient's free choice that initiates the action (autonomy), because she does not value her future (justice). In both cases the benefits associated with a more merciful death are the same to the patient (beneficence). This is why we will see assisted suicide and voluntary euthanasia as morally the same. It may be helpful for you to think of physician assistance in dying as essentially a choice on the part of the patient either to kill herself with the help of the doctor, or to have the doctor kill her. It may also be helpful to think of the method of killing in each case to be an overdose of narcotics. Although this method is not the only one available, it is the most common one, and thinking of it as the means of death will allow us to have a clear image of physician assistance in dying.

There is also a practical benefit to classifying physician-assisted suicide and voluntary euthanasia together. Because the arguments for and against each are very much the same, we may avoid a great deal of the duplication that would inevitably occur if we saw them as essentially different types of moral problems. In the discussion to follow we will sometimes speak of physician assistance in dying and sometimes of assisted suicide and sometimes of voluntary euthanasia, as is appropriate in the context. When the time comes to present a case for and against their moral acceptability, we will view them as essentially the same type of act—killing the patient at the patient's request. Any differences that might matter between the moral acceptability of assisted suicide and that of active voluntary euthanasia will be considered.

Formulating the Problem

We may *formulate the problem* of this chapter in the following way:

Is physician assistance in dying morally acceptable?

This problem may be seen as a **factual** moral problem. You will remember from Part I that these types of problems require us to envisage the possible outcomes of a particular type of action that have moral significance. We are interested in what sorts of harms and benefits to both individuals and society will follow if we allow or refuse to allow physician assistance in dying. We are also interested in examining whether physician assistance in dying will conform to or violate our other moral principles: respect for persons and their autonomy. Our problem should not be thought of as a problem whose solution is a simple "yes" or "no" answer, but rather as a request for a morally acceptable policy on physician assistance in dying. We are looking for a moral rule—a moral right, if you prefer—that ought to govern our behavior on physician assistance in dying. Such a rule will be the one most compatible with our three moral principles.

As we will see in the next section, the rules about physician assistance in dying are evolving at this time in our society, and an intense debate is occurring that will determine the nature of these rules in the future. Although some of the rules that will emerge will be legal ones, the problem for us is a moral problem. We are asking about the moral acceptability of physician assistance in dying and not about its legal acceptability—at least not until much later in the chapter. The moral and legal problems of voluntary euthanasia are different problems and should be seen as separate matters. It may be that we will find some form of physician assistance in dying to be morally acceptable but be unwilling to legalize it. It may be too difficult to regulate, for example, or we may think that legalizing it will encourage a greater use of it than appropriate. Perhaps we will find it immoral and decide to keep it illegal, or we may find it morally acceptable and decide to legalize it as well. We will return to discuss the relationship between the legal and moral acceptability of voluntary euthanasia in the "Evaluation" section. For now, we will focus on whether it is morally right or wrong, and not on whether it would be a wise and effective social policy.

Possible Solutions

Exercise 7.1

One possible solution is that physician assistance in dying is *never* morally acceptable; another is that it is *always* a morally acceptable choice for patients. A third is that it is acceptable under certain conditions. The point of this exercise is for you to list what these conditions should be. Think of your task as devising a rule that will be used to regulate physician assistance in dying. Should all patients be able to receive it, no matter what their type of illness, their degree of competence, or their level of suffering? Or should only some patients be eligible? If only some, list the criteria they must meet for eligibility. You will learn more if you do not read on before completing this exercise.

There are three *possible solutions* that come to mind immediately. One is that physician assistance in dying is never morally acceptable; another is that it is always morally acceptable; a third is that it is acceptable under certain conditions. Someone arguing for the first solution would undoubtedly claim that physician assistance in dying is killing, and killing is wrong. They would probably also point to all the abuses that would follow from allowing physician assistance in dying in society. Those who champion the second possible solution would appeal to the principle of autonomy, claiming that people have a right to decide for themselves how they want their lives to end—as long as their actions harm no one else. Those arguing for the third possible solution would appeal to autonomy as well, but also point to all the needless pain and suffering that physician assistance in dying would allow people to avoid. The first and third possible solutions will be defended in this chapter. The appeal to autonomy stressed by the second possible solution will be included in a defense of the third possible solution.

Because the third possible solution is in favor of physician assistance in dying under certain conditions, identifying the nature of these conditions is important. One of these conditions is that the patient must be **competent.** Although patient competence is assumed by the very definition of physician assistance in dying, it should be restated here as a requirement. Although we will talk briefly later about *nonvoluntary* euthanasia, we should keep in mind that we are only going to consider possible solutions to the problem of *voluntary* euthanasia and assisted suicide in this chapter.

A second condition is that the patient must be **terminally ill.** Generally speaking, this means that the patient has a condition from which he or she will die within six months. There is nothing that medicine can do to prevent this from happening. There are no treatments that will cure the person (curative treatments). Medicine at best can offer only treatments that will make the patient more comfortable (palliative treatments). This condition is fairly controversial and not acceptable to everyone who favors physician assistance in dying. Certainly there are many cases in which physician assistance in dying might be appropriate for patients who may suffer significantly from diseases or conditions from which they would prefer to escape, but whose natural deaths may not occur for a number of years. For now, however, let us consider physician assistance in dying only for patients whose deaths are expected to occur within six months. We will then see whether such a case may be extended credibly to nonterminal patients.

A third condition is that the patient is **suffering.** Most of us die from degenerative diseases these days, diseases that kill us slowly over a protracted period of time and have associated with them a great deal of pain. Pain management has improved so much today that most of this pain can be eliminated if a sufficient amount of narcotics is given, especially if it is given before the onset of pain. Unfortunately, to eliminate the feeling of pain for some patients requires such heavy medication that intermittent periods of near or full unconsciousness result. This does not present terribly cheerful options to some patients—to be in pain or to be totally sedated.

Even for patients whose pain can be successfully managed, the vast majority of dying patients fear the process of dying itself, especially their own gradual disintegration. Here the concept of suffering arises. Suffering refers to the patient's psychological and emotional states as well as to his or her physical pain. Many patients who have watched or heard about the horrible deaths of others that were caused by the very condition from which they now suffer abhor the prospect of taking such a trip themselves. They do not want to suffer the indignity of it all, just as much as they do not want to suffer its pain.

Facts and Assumptions

Facts

Important *facts* to consider in our attempt to solve our problem are those that concern pain and suffering. According to Kathleen Foley, M.D., one of the pioneers in effective pain management, 70 percent to 90 percent of advanced cancer patients have severe, unrelenting pain that requires the use of opioid drugs.[1] There is a great deal of dispute about whether the pain and suffering associated with dying can be eliminated by medicine. If pain and suffering can be eliminated, there will be less need for physician assistance in dying. There are also those who would argue that dying patients are unlikely to be sufficiently competent to make a rational decision about physician assistance in dying. If this is true, then physician assistance in dying is not even possible. Facts about pain and suffering, as well as facts about competence, are very important for us to investigate, as they lie at the very heart of the physician assistance in dying debate. We will discuss the issue of patient competence in the "Assumption" section. Here we will talk especially about pain and suffering.

We will begin by considering the extent to which the pain associated with dying may be controlled. **Pain** is a sensory state associated with physical damage to the body. It is usually accompanied by emotional distress as well, such as fear, anger, and depression. Ironically, one of the more notable outcomes of the push to legalize physician assistance in dying in this country has been improvement in pain management on the part of the medical profession. One motivation for such improvement was the desire to undercut the need for physician assistance in dying. If dying patients want to kill themselves or be killed by their physicians because of the uncontrollable pain that they experience, then better pain management might mitigate this need for physician assistance in dying.

Hospice workers are especially successful in managing pain, as are many physicians in large, modern teaching hospitals. Unfortunately, pain does not always get managed so well in other health care facilities, such as smaller, less modern hospitals and in long-term care facilities. Even though pain management has improved in recent years, many physicians—even those in modern teaching hospitals, continue to manage the pain of dying patients poorly. There are many reasons for this, most of which may be reduced to the limited training of physicians about proper pain management. These include poor assessment of patient pain, the use of wrong medications, and the underuse of medications because of excessive concern among physicians about addiction, tolerance, and toxicities.

Despite this practice of poor pain management, however, the pain of most dying patients *could* be managed successfully. With the possible exception of perhaps 10 percent of dying cancer patients suffering from persistent and severe pain, dying patients could be relatively pain free or suffer from only lower levels of pain most of the time. Still, the reality of pain management has not yet caught up to this ideal. The fact that about half of the oncologists in this country want physician assistance in dying available to them attests to this fact. In addition, over half the physicians in the Netherlands, where pain management is close to the ideal, believe that pain is significant enough in some dying patients to warrant physician assistance in dying. This finding is significant, as these are the people who are on the front lines in the battle against painful dying, the people who are in the best position to know what actually happens to patients as they die.

Studies performed on the elderly find that what they fear especially is the process of dying rather death itself. And it is not simply pain they fear. In addition to pain, they fear suffering. **Suffering** includes pain, but refers to more than pain. It includes psychological pain and emotional pain, but it is especially concerned with the *severe distress* that is associated with events that threaten the intactness of a person.[2] "Intactness" refers to loss of autonomy and dignity and to the gradual disintegration of a dying person. Where they once were vigorous directors of their own lives, living as they saw fit, filling their days with as much of whatever the good life was for them, they now are afraid of a burdensome life, a life over which they have little control, a life containing little pleasure and little meaning.

Reports from many of the people who have used assisted suicide, for example, show that they have not suffered terribly from unmanageable pain. Often they killed themselves not only because of the pain, but especially because they wished to avoid the other symptoms of dying that dramatically interfere with the quality of their lives, symptoms such as fatigue, general weakness, dyspnea, delirium, nausea and vomiting—the symptoms suffered by advanced cancer patients. In addition, they wished to escape the psychological pain often associated with dying, such as depression and anxiety, feelings of hopelessness, and impaired cognitive abilities. Finally, these patients especially did not want to experience their own disintegration; they did not want to experience themselves losing their autonomy, losing any meaning to their lives and their worlds, and being a burden to others.[3] These people committed suicide not only because they were in pain, but also because they wished not to suffer.

Physician assistance in dying has been practiced in the Netherlands since 1984. Though not legalized until 2001, acts of assisted suicide and voluntary euthanasia were not prosecuted prior to this time if they met certain conditions that the current law also requires. Among these conditions are that the patient must request such action, that the request must be made repeatedly, that a second physician must agree that physician assistance in dying is the correct course of action for the patient, and that the suffering experienced by the patient must be unbearable and without any prospect of improvement. The Dutch have an excellent health care system with almost universal insurance coverage. Moreover, they provide excellent palliative care to their patients. Yet about four thousand patients each year, most of them cancer patients, receive physician assistance in dying. If the patient must be in "unbearable" suffering as a condition for acts of physician assistance in dying that will be immune from prosecution, then it is reasonable to infer that there is a significant amount of suffering associated with many deaths. Clearly, dying patients suffer, and when it is available to them some of them choose physician assistance in dying because they wish to avoid this suffering.

Descriptive Ethics

Results of **public opinion** polls on the acceptability of physician assistance in dying have not always been easy to interpret. Some polls show that as many as 75 percent are in favor of physician-assisted suicide, for example, whereas others show significantly less support. The results of such polls depend on what questions have been asked and how well they are understood by those polled. For example, if the question is, "Would you support a law that helps physicians assist terminal patients to die?" a much more favorable response will result than if the question is, "Do you favor a law that allows doctors to kill their patients?" As stated, the first question may include removing treatment and letting patients die—actions that claim widespread support; the second question sounds like it is describing an act of murder.

In the polls that count most, those that have occurred in voting booths when legalizing assisted suicide has been a ballot initiative in the general elections of some states, some of the typical results have been as follows: California (1992), 46 percent in favor; Washington State (1991), 46 percent in favor; Oregon (1994), 51 percent in favor, and again in 1997, with 60 percent in favor, and Maine (2000), 46 percent in favor. In some other countries, such as Switzerland, Belgium, and Colombia, there is widespread popular support for physician assistance in dying. In addition, more than three-quarters of those polled in Canada, Britain, and Australia are in favor of it. In the Netherlands, where it is widely practiced, over 90 percent of the people believe it to be morally acceptable.

Medicine, and especially the powerful and influential American Medical Association, is officially opposed to physician assistance in dying. According to the association, it is acceptable for doctors to terminate treatment and let patients die, but it is never acceptable to kill patients or even to assist in their suicides. Polls of physicians, however, tell a different story. About half of all doctors in the United States support the right of patients to receive suicide assistance from their physicians. Moreover, perhaps 15 percent of doctors have already helped their patients to kill themselves by writing prescriptions for narcotics they knew were to be used for such purposes.

With the possible exception of some few very liberal Protestant denominations, such as Unitarian Universalists and the United Church of Christ, most **religions** are at least officially opposed to physician assistance in dying as well. A widely held view is that it is morally acceptable to terminate treatments that are no longer beneficial to the patient and to let nature take its course, but it is never acceptable to intentionally kill. God gives life, and only God should decide when it is to end. Pain at the end of life may be controlled by medication, and the suffering that cannot be mitigated by medical treatments is to be endured. Many religions teach that such suffering may even be a good way to reconcile the dying patient to his or her God and to loved ones here on earth.

The Catholic Church has been particularly outspoken for centuries in its opposition to physician assistance in dying, even in the face of great suffering on the part of the patient. It has held that sufficient amounts of painkillers may be administered to eliminate pain, however, even with the knowledge that sometimes sufficient amounts of painkillers can also be "person-killers." As pain progresses and more painkillers are required to bring it under control, the risk rises that the increasingly larger amounts of narcotics needed may lead to the failure of the patient's respiratory system, resulting in death. For the many who fail to see the difference between physician assistance in dying and administering painkillers in sufficient quantity to kill both the patient's pain and the patient, the Catholic Church and those in medicine and the law who have been influenced by its teaching, have appealed to the **principle of double effect.**

The principle of double effect is a moral claim that plays a significant role for many in the debate over physician assistance in dying. It states that an action that is otherwise immoral—in this case, killing the patient—may be allowed if it is the unintended and unavoidable consequence of a morally acceptable act—in this case, killing the pain. Administering painkillers has two effects in cases of this sort. It kills the pain and in sufficient quantities it may kill the patient. But if the patient, especially a terminal patient, dies because of too much pain medication, the death is not to be seen as a case of killing. If the amount of medication administered was no more than that required to kill the pain, then it was clearly the intention of those administering it simply to kill the pain, not the patient. The patient is not being deliberately killed but is being allowed to die as an unintended and unavoidable consequence of an otherwise merciful act.

According to this principle, if you are a doctor or nurse who increases a morphine drip at the request of a patient for more pain medication, and if as a result of this action the patient suffers respiratory failure and dies, you are not to think of yourself as someone who killed the patient. You are not a murderer, or even a merciful killer. If the patient herself is in control of the amount of pain medication received, as is often the case with dying, competent patients, then she as well is not to think of herself as committing suicide if she administers a lethal dose in the process of combatting her ever-worsening pain. She did not intend to kill herself, after all, only to end her pain.

There are many who find this distinction between "intentionally" killing a patient and "unintentionally" doing so not strong enough to support the distinction between the wrongfulness of taking an overdose, on the one hand, and the acceptability of doing so, on the other. This is especially true when the person administering the painkiller knows that it may lead to the patient's death. The law usually holds us responsible for all of the foreseeable consequences of our actions, even if we do not specifically intend them to occur. So why should someone who gives painkillers to a patient, knowing that they will eventually lead to her death, not be responsible for that death?

Instead, many prefer to scrap the principle of double effect and simply to talk about wrongful and rightful killings. In particular, those who support physician assistance in dying prefer to talk about the rightfulness of killing yourself to avoid pain and suffering, whether that killing be intended or simply an unavoidable consequence of adequate pain control. One of the benefits of doing so, they argue, would be greater public control over the practice of physician assistance in dying.

It would be out in the open, not hidden in the private world of the intentions of patients and physicians. Once out in the open it may be regulated more easily.

If in medicine and religion the official view seems to be that "letting die" is acceptable but that "intentional killing" is wrong, until recently this also had been the case as well for the **law.** Much of the law in the United States has been made in the courts, not in legislative bodies. Currently, the law allows any competent patient to refuse any treatment whatsoever. Health care providers can be sued for battery if they treat a competent patient without her consent. The only exception to this is emergency care, for which patient consent may reasonably be assumed.

The law about refusing treatments for patients who cannot speak for themselves has been worked out case by case in various states especially in the 1970s and 1980s. As a result of legislative action and especially as a result of various decisions by state supreme courts, it is now legally acceptable under some conditions to remove or not to initiate treatment even for those patients who cannot currently speak for themselves. One of the conditions that allows such actions is the existence of **advanced directives.** If the patient, while competent, has formulated instructions about which types of treatments are to be used or not, especially once that patient becomes terminal, then such instructions may carry the force of law. Just as a will is to be understood as a deceased person's instructions on how to divide his or her estate, so **living wills,** as some advanced directives are called, are instructions about which types of treatment the currently incompetent patient wishes to receive or refuse.

Not all states have adopted living will statutes, however. Recognizing that the conditions of dying are not always easy to envisage, they prefer instead a **health care proxy** model of decision making. Such a model is based on the "power of attorney" model. Just as someone who has the power of attorney has the legal right to make financial decisions for another person who is alive but no longer competent, so someone who has been appointed by a person to be her health care proxy, sometimes called a health care agent, may speak for the treatment options of that person, when she can no longer speak for herself. It is important to formulate advanced directives or to appoint a health care agent to protect your legal rights should you become unable to speak for yourself. If you do not do so, health care providers will usually consult with your next of kin about treatment options. Whereas this is often satisfactory, it sometimes may lead to the implementation of that person's wishes, not your own. Sometimes families just cannot let go and insist on treatments that offer little benefit to their dying loved ones.

Until the 1990s, physician assistance in dying had been illegal in the United States and in most of the rest of the world as well. During the 1990s, however, several states introduced ballot initiatives to legalize assisted suicide. Such initiatives would have the force of law if voted on favorably in general elections, but have been defeated in Washington (1991) and in California (1992). In 1994, however, such a measure, called the **Death with Dignity Act** passed in Oregon with 51 percent of the vote. It was challenged in the courts and put on the ballot again in 1997, when it passed with 60 percent of the vote. Other states are mounting such initiatives as well, but currently Oregon is the only state where assisted suicide is legal. In no state is voluntary euthanasia legal. All that is legally accepted, and this only in Oregon, is for physicians to help their patients to kill themselves—by providing drugs and information about how to use them properly.

To date, there is no federal legislation either accepting or prohibiting assisted suicide or voluntary euthanasia. In one important decision the United States Supreme Court has ruled that states may continue to consider such actions to be illegal, as most of them do, as there is no constitutionally protected **right to die.** On the other hand, states may legalize physician assistance in dying if they so desire. It is to be expected, then, that the evolving legal policy in the United States on physician assistance in dying will be worked out state by state during this and the next decade. It is likely that this will take the form of ballot initiatives, driven more by people who have organized to extend the right of assisted suicide and voluntary euthanasia to others, than by legislative bodies. It is not an easy thing for a legislator who has to run for office to take a positive stand on the acceptability of killing.

Assumptions

This section addresses three important *assumptions* made within the context of the debate on physician assistance in dying. The *first* is that the suffering associated with dying is always an evil to be avoided. Many religions reject this assumption; it is also widely rejected on nonreligious grounds. Those precious final days and hours spent with loved ones would be lost if physician assistance in dying was the preferred method of dying. The opportunity to care for dying family members, to express our love and thanks to them, to heal neglected wounds, all would be lost if their lives ended prematurely. If this is so, if in their suffering lie great blessings, then physician assistance in dying must be seen as an evil, as it robs us of these opportunities.

Relatively peaceful dyings often are very meaningful, very enriching times, both for dying persons and their families. This is especially true for patients and their families who have hospice care available to them. However, for those dyings contain much suffering, especially those relatively few that carry pain, ending the pain and suffering is the blessing. Such suffering surely is an evil. For family members or other loved ones to desire such a dying to be prolonged, or to object to its being hastened because *they* have unfinished business with the dying person, is to use the dying patient for their own good. Doing so violates one of our most basic moral principles, the principle of justice, the principle of respect for persons. In calculating the harms and benefits associated with dying, the competent dying patient should determine the limits of his suffering and be allowed to decide for himself when he has had enough.

But can a dying patient really be competent? That dying patients can be competent to understand the consequences of choosing physician assistance in dying, and can be free from psychological pressures to do so is a *second* important assumption of the physician assistance in dying debate. Opponents of physician assistance in dying often reject this assumption in favor of the belief that the depression, anxiety, anger, and other emotional states associated with suffering and the process of dying in general, as well as the presence of pain and pain medications, impair reason and render any judgment of the dying patient less than free and rational. They point out that we usually consider it merciful to intervene when depressed persons who are not dying try to kill themselves because they are not competent. Why should we not treat depressed persons who are dying in the same way? If a patient has to be competent to make physician-assisted suicide and *voluntary* euthanasia possible, and if such competence is always suspect, there is no basis for considering physician assistance in dying to be a morally acceptable practice.

Those in favor of physician assistance in dying admit that a dying patient's competence sometimes may be in doubt. This is not a reason to reject physician assistance in dying, however, but rather is a reason to regulate it so that competence may be verified. There are two main ways to do this. First, a dying patient's request for assisted suicide or voluntary euthanasia must be repeated over a period of time. This will ensure that it is not based on a feeling or emotion that may be fleeting. Second, all patients who request assistance in dying should receive counseling. Such counseling should help the patient explore in depth the nature of her real motives and wishes and goals. It should especially be concerned with discovering whether the patient has received adequate information about her diagnosis, prognosis, and treatment options, including available palliative care. It should also make certain that the patient understands this information thoroughly and accurately. Perhaps most important, it should explore the possibility that the patient has chosen physician assistance in dying because of pressure from others, such as doctors or family members. For physician assistance in dying to be rational, it must be based on patients' understanding and free choice. Counseling will help to ensure that these elements are present.

A *third* assumption is that there is a significant moral difference between the sort of assistance in dying that comes from killing—whether that involves the patient's killing himself or the physician's killing a competent patient—and removing life-sustaining treatment. We have seen that this latter type of intervention, sometimes called passive euthanasia, has been found whereas legally and morally acceptable physician assistance in dying generally has not. If one is acceptable and the other is not, presumably there's an important difference between them.

This assumption has been rejected by many. For them, removing someone from a respirator, for example, when that piece of equipment is keeping the person alive, has the same moral status as killing someone to hasten his death. Both actions have the same motive (mercy), the same intention (hastening death), and the same result (the death of the patient). In fact, killing may be even more moral, as it allows a painful dying process to come to a speedier end. In a well-known article, James Rachels discusses whether killing someone for the sake of mercy is any more or less reprehensible than allowing the person to die. In the following quotation he gives an example in which he claims to show that these two types of action are morally the same.[4]

> One reason why so many people think that there is an important moral difference between active and passive euthanasia is that they think killing someone is morally worse than letting someone die. But is it? Is killing, in itself, worse than letting die? To investigate this issue two cases may be considered that are exactly alike except that one involves killing whereas the other involves letting someone die. Then, it

can be asked whether this difference makes any difference to the moral assessments. It is important that the cases be exactly alike, except for this one difference, since otherwise one cannot be confident that it is this difference and not some other that accounts for any variation in the assessments of the two cases. So, let us consider this pair of cases:

In the first, Smith stands to gain a large inheritance if anything should happen to his six-year-old cousin. One evening while the child is taking his bath, Smith sneaks into the bathroom and drowns the child, and then arranges things so that it will look like an accident.

In the second, Jones also stands to gain if any thing should happen to his six-year-old cousin. Like Smith, Jones sneaks in planning to drown the child in his bath. However, just as he enters the bathroom Jones sees the child slip and hit his head, and fall face down in the water. Jones is delighted; he stands by, ready to push the child's head back under if it is necessary, but it is not necessary. With only a little thrashing about the child drowns all by himself, "accidentally," as Jones watches and does nothing.

Now Smith killed the child, whereas Jones "merely" let the child die. That is the only difference between them. Did either man behave better, from a moral point of view? If the difference between killing and letting die were in itself a morally important matter, one should say that Jones's behavior was less reprehensible than Smith's. But does one really want to say that? I think not. In the first place, both men acted from the same motive, personal gain, and both had exactly the same end in view when they acted. It may be inferred from Smith's conduct that he is a bad man, although that judgment may be withdrawn or modified if certain further facts are learned about him—for example, that he is mentally deranged. But would not the very same thing be inferred about Jones from his conduct? And would not the same further considerations also be relevant to any modification of this judgment? Moreover, suppose Jones pleaded, in his own defense, "After all, I didn't do anything except just stand there and watch the child drown. I didn't kill him; I only let him die." Again, if letting die were in itself less bad than killing, this defense should have at least some weight. But it does not. Such a "defense" can only be regarded as a grotesque perversion of moral reasoning. Morally speaking, it is no defense at all.

Legal scholars have also argued against the reasonableness of the passive/active distinction, as does Judge Roger J. Miner in the following passage.[5]

[T]here is nothing "natural" about causing death by means other than the original illness or its complications. The withdrawal of nutrition brings on death by starvation, the withdrawal of hydration brings on death by dehydration; and the withdrawal of ventilation brings on respiratory failure. By ordering the discontinuance of these artificial life-sustaining processes or refusing to accept them in the first place, a patient hastens his death by means that are not natural in any sense. It certainly cannot be said that the death that immediately ensues is the natural result of the progression of the disease or condition from which the patient suffers.

Moreover, the writing of a prescription to hasten death, after consultation with a patient, involves a far less active role for the physician than is required in bringing about death through asphyxiation, starvation, and/or dehydration.

Withdrawal of life support requires physicians or those acting at their direction physically to remove equipment and, often to administer palliative drugs which may themselves contribute to death. The ending of life by these means is nothing more or less than assisted suicide.

Even those on the forefront of medicine find the distinction between passive and active euthanasia to be less than helpful. For example, the former editor of the *New England Journal of Medicine,* Marcia Angell, writes:[6]

> Both withdrawing treatment and euthanasia do not require the participation of the patient. Either could be done without the patient's cooperation. In contrast, assisted suicide—the morally "intermediate" act—does require the patient's participation. To die, the patient must swallow the pills—a voluntary act of a necessarily aware patient. Thus, the traditional moral distinctions are entirely based on what the doctor does, not on the consequences of the doctor's action for the patient. The question asked is the nature of the doctor's act: Is it passive or active or intermediate? The moral judgment is discovered from the patient's perspective. We do not usually ask how the patient is affected. Because the patient seems left out of the moral equation, the distinctions seem to me somewhat artificial and ultimately unpersuasive.

Despite these reasonable claims to the contrary, for the time being it is important to maintain the distinction between killing and letting die. One reason is so the ongoing debate in this and other countries can clearly focus on the new types of assistance in dying that are being proposed by advocates of assisted suicide and voluntary euthanasia. If physician assistance in dying is ultimately rejected by most states, the distinction between killing and letting die will be an important one to maintain. If physician assistance is accepted, the wiser course may be to reject the distinction between killing and letting die, and simply speak about various ways in which patients may be assisted in their dying.

Points of View

For many of us, our personal histories shape our beliefs as much as does the evidence that may be used to support them. For example, if you have witnessed the death of a loved one, a death that was protracted and difficult, one that was racked with pain and suffering, you may be more likely to support physician assistance in dying than if you had not had that experience. On the other hand, you may have had experiences that weakened your sympathies for physician assistance in dying, such as watching people on TV ending their lives. This might especially be true if the suicide victims were not obviously suffering or terminally ill, if the means used to terminate life were cumbersome and mechanical, and if the attitude reflected by both patient and physician was clinical and matter-of-fact. If you watched the televised suicide presided over by Dr. Jack Kevorkian in the late 1990s you will know what I mean.

One obstacle to allowing a fair hearing to physician assistance in dying is the belief that it is wrong to kill under any circumstances. If you hold this belief, and if you especially hold it on religious grounds—it will prevent you from considering physician assistance in dying as morally acceptable. Typically, people say such things as "It's killing, and killing is wrong, period!" This prevents thoughtful consideration of the issues involved. Assistance in dying may be immoral, but it will not be so simply because it is a type of killing. Many types of killings are considered acceptable by most of us and by most religions as well. Usually these are classified as various forms of self-defense. In fact, the correct translation of the commandment that says "Thou shall not kill" is "Thou shall not murder," when murder is wrongful killing.

My advice is that you leave open the question of whether physician assistance in dying is to be thought of as a type of wrongful killing or a type of rightful killing. Let the arguments decide the issue for you; let the evidence have its day in the court of your reason. Whatever your personal experience has been, and whatever your religious persuasion may be, do not close your mind to any option at this point. Remember, we are talking about social policy when we talk about physician assistance in dying—what is good for us all collectively.

Moral Reasoning

The problem before us in this chapter is best thought of as a **factual** moral problem. It could be thought of as a **conflict of rules** problem, pitting the "do not kill" rule against some sort of "right to die." However, the struggle in society today about physician assistance in dying, while surely containing conflicting rules or rights, is essentially a struggle to discover a morally acceptable rule that will govern how we die. So let us think of our task in that way, as one of formulating a general moral rule. This rule will define the degree to which it is morally acceptable for individuals and their physicians to intervene in the natural processes of dying. We already have a rule that says it is morally acceptable to withhold or not initiate medical treatments when they are not beneficial to a person. To that degree, people have both a moral and legal "right to die." The issue now is whether we should extend that moral right to die to include physician assistance in dying, whether we should have a new rule in society that allows physician-assisted suicide and voluntary euthanasia, or whether we should reject either or both of them.

The process of constructing a new moral rule plays itself out in courtrooms, legislative bodies, and the pronouncements of religion and medicine. It also, and perhaps most important, churns on in the hearts and minds of all of us, who think and talk about it in our homes, in our classrooms, and in the privacy of our own minds. Public opinion is a powerfully persuasive force for moral change. It is listened to and heeded, especially when it is well informed. What *you* think about this matter counts for a great deal as society struggles toward a clearer understanding of what we all ought to be able to do when it comes to our own dying.

If a new moral rule is to be arrived at through countless debates among citizens, the criteria used to formulate such a rule ought to be our three moral principles—those of beneficence, autonomy, and justice. The best rule will be one that promotes the most good or eliminates the most evil; one that recognizes that people have the right to do as they wish as long as it harms no one else; and the one that accepts the intrinsic value of individuals and never uses them solely as a means to the good of another. On the basis of the evidence presented in the good reasons arguments to follow, we will attempt to construct a moral rule that conforms to these three principles.

The Case for Physician Assistance in Dying

If voluntary euthanasia is a form of *mercy* killing, we can expect one main reason in its favor to be mercy. That is, one central reason for physician assistance in dying is that it eliminates needless pain and suffering. We have already talked about the pain, and especially the suffering, associated with dying and will say little else about it at this time. Perhaps a particularly gruesome story or two about pain-filled dyings, would be effective here. These would be stories designed to make you *feel* the pain and suffering associated with some dyings. I will resist the temptation of appealing to your feelings, however, and instead appeal to your reason. The plain fact is that even though the pain associated with dying could be managed effectively in the vast majority of cases, it often is not. In addition, much of the suffering associated with many dyings cannot be eliminated. The depression, anger, anxiety, fear, loss of control, and pain associated with the awareness of our own gradual deterioration is quite often beyond the power of any person to manage.

One of the central tasks of medicine is to relieve pain and suffering. We think doing so is a good thing. We thank God when someone dies quickly from a condition that has the potential for causing a long, drawn-out, painful death. We think it is morally and legally acceptable to terminate or not initiate treatment when such treatment will do nothing but extend the painful dying of a person. We think that such an act is merciful. There is no point to dragging out a painful death by medical intervention that nature would have ended sooner by itself.

So, if we think that pain and suffering is an evil that medicine is justified in eliminating, why allow patients only "passive" euthanasia? Why not allow physician assistance in dying instead of forcing terminal patients to endure the slow, agonizing process of some particularly horrible natural deaths? Once a diagnosis has been made that the patient is terminally ill, and once the decision has been made to terminate all but palliative treatments, surely it is more merciful to allow those patients who wish not to suffer through nature's slow and agonizing death to have access to physician assistance in dying. Marcia Angell makes this point clearly.[7]

> Even when there is life-sustaining treatment to be withheld, doing so can entail a period of agony for someone who is conscious. Removing a respirator produces suffocation; terminating dialysis produces the symptoms of uremia; refusing feedings produces the symptoms of dehydration or starvation. What is passive for the doctor may not be so passive for the patient. For many years, of course, we have relied on caregivers to ease the last hours or days of suffering by giving large doses of morphine or barbiturates, but this is often done parsimoniously and erratically, by the grace of the doctors and nurses.
>
> Relying on our right to refuse treatment also does not speak to the needs of people who would like the option of choosing death not just near the end of a terminal illness but at the beginning, before they have undergone a long deterioration and become helpless. This was true of Janet Adkins, the first person Dr. Jack Kevorkian helped to commit suicide. She had early Alzheimer's disease and wanted to act while she was still able to.
>
> Because of these problems, which are appreciated by most people intuitively if not explicitly, our attention has turned increasingly toward physician-assisted

suicide or euthanasia as a means to hasten death. After all, the thinking goes, if the intent in withholding life-sustaining treatment is to cause a merciful death, why not accomplish the purpose faster and more humanely and at the time of our choosing, without relying on chance?

So we write our first premise in the argument for physician assistance in dying:

1. Physician assistance in dying is merciful. (B)

Because physician assistance in dying eliminates pain and suffering, and because these clearly are evils, we write (B) after (1) to show that it follows from the principle of beneficence. Beneficence requires us to do good and avoid evil.

The second reason in favor of physician assistance in dying follows from the principle of autonomy. In the context of the physician assistance in dying debate, this principle is often referred to as patient "self-determination." The basic idea is that all people, and dying, competent patients in particular, have the right to decide for themselves what sorts of dyings they want—as long as their actions harm no one else. We have already discussed the issue of terminal patient competence and will simply assume here that it is possible for some dying patients to make rational decisions. What our second premise will assert, then, is that such patients have the right to determine for themselves the conditions of their dyings, including physician assistance in dying.

Sometime this right is referred to as the **right to die.** This phrase is loaded with ambiguity, however. Sometime the right to die refers to the right to terminate treatment, sometime to the right to physician assisted suicide, sometime to the right to voluntary euthanasia and even sometime to the right to nonvoluntary euthanasia. Because of its ambiguity we will not talk about the right to die in our discussions, but instead continue to use the phrase "patient self-determination." The important point is to keep the idea underlying these phrases clear. All individuals who are competent have the right to decide for themselves how their lives will go, with the proviso that their actions harm no one else. This includes the right to decide how the end of their lives will go as well.[8]

> The moral argument in favor of permitting physician assistance in suicide is grounded in the conjunction of two principles: self-determination (or, as bioethicists put it, autonomy) and mercy (or the avoidance of suffering). The moral right of self-determination is the right to live one's life as one sees fit, subject only to the constraint that this not involve harm to others. Because living one's life as one chooses must also include living the very end of one's life as one chooses, the matter of how to die is as fully protected by the principle of self-determination as any other part of one's life. Choosing how to die is part of choosing how to live.

Those in favor of physician assistance in dying wish to protect this principle against others who claim to know best how a person's life should be led. Those in favor of physician assistance in dying want to ensure that people have the choice to use it. People may wish to reject the physician assistance in dying option, as most dying patients would, but they ought to have the choice and be able to exercise it if they so desire. Autonomy is an important principle to acknowledge and defend, especially when decisions are of major importance both to individuals and society. Those opposed to physician assistance in dying should simply not choose it for themselves; but they should not try to take this option away from those who may wish to exercise it. The freedom to decide for yourself is what is at stake here, and allowing physician assistance in dying in society is the only way to guarantee that freedom for dying patients. For those dying patients who believe that their continued existence is far worse than death, physician assistance in dying should be an option. After all, whose life is it, anyway? So our second premise, justified by the principle of autonomy, is this:

2. Physician assistance in dying allows patient self-determination. (A)

A third premise could be that there is no moral difference between many forms of passive euthanasia—which we find morally acceptable—and physician assistance in dying. We discussed this issue in the previous section and decided to assume that there is often an important moral difference between them. However, even if there were not, it is important to defend physician assistance in dying on its own, and not simply as a version of letting die. The reason for this distinction is that many people see an important moral difference between killing and letting die. So premises (1) and (2) will stand as the case for physician assistance in dying. We will add the conclusion when we return to reply to objections.

The argument for physician assistance in dying is a good reasons argument. In such arguments it is not necessary for the premises to be "connected" to offer support for the conclusion. They are supposed to support the conclusion individually, with each premise able to stand alone as evidence. The strength of the argument comes from the collective support of its premises. This is true of our argument for physician assistance in dying so far, but it is important to notice that these two premises are much stronger when seen as a unit than viewed as the sum of their individual strengths.

> It is important to recognize that in serving as the basis for the rights of dying patients, self-determination and mercy do not function as independent principles, each sufficient in itself. A mere request for physician-assisted suicide by a perfectly healthy person does not justify a physician's assistance. Similarly, the mere fact of pain or suffering in a terminal patient does not license a physician to end that persons life, if the person does not seek physician-assisted suicide. Fears that legalization would license assisted suicide for a healthy person without pain or suffering, or involuntary or nonvoluntary mercy-killing, are often expressed by those who oppose it, but this is to misunderstand what the basis of a patient's right would be under any of the current proposals. *Both* principles, self-determination and mercy, must be applicable for the patient to have any substantial claim on the physician's help.[9]

The Case against Physician Assistance in Dying

If either form of physician assistance in dying is a form of *killing,* then we can expect that the case against physician assistance in dying will rely heavily on the wrongfulness of killing. Both the suicide performed by a patient who dies by means of physician-assisted suicide and the killing performed in voluntary euthanasia are forms of killing—and killing is wrong. Killing someone or yourself has always been seen as wrong by the law, by religion, and by society in general. For many opponents of physician assistance in dying, merely pointing this out is a sufficient deterrent. Killing is immoral in itself, so physician assistance in dying is immoral as well. For those who think a bit more deeply, however, much more needs to be said about the wrongfulness of the killing involved in physician assistance in dying. To be sure, there are exceptions to the rule "Do not kill." In war, in personal acts of self-defense, and in cases of capital punishment, killing has been seen by many to be morally acceptable. These may all be considered self-defense of one form or another. Killing in self-defense, then, is a form of morally acceptable killing, whereas most cases of killing are morally unacceptable. Let us call morally unacceptable killing *murder.*

With the exception of Oregon's Death with Dignity Act, the law does not recognize physician assistance in dying as a form of justified killing. Even though the motive that drives the killing is mercy—unlike most killings, the **intention** behind the act is to end the life of the patient. In the law, it is a person's intention, not his motive, that carries the most weight. A killing done accidentally, for example, or through negligence, or because of an uncontrollable emotional state, is not as grave a crime as a killing performed with a cool, calm deliberate intention to kill. Of course, the law may change in various states, especially if enough people come to believe that physician assistance in dying is a necessary form of self-defense in today's impersonal world of medicine.

The necessity claim, however, is precisely what opponents of physician assistance in dying deny. For them, the main reason that physician assistance in dying should be seen as a type of murder is because it is not necessary. The pain and suffering associated with dying can be managed. That is the problem, to manage pain and suffering, not to allow people to kill themselves or to perform the act for them. With better pain management, with better treatment of the conditions associated with dying that cause people to suffer, and with better understanding and response to the psychological needs of dying patients, there will be no need for physician assistance in dying. So our first premise is this:

1.' Physician assistance in dying is a form of murder. (B, J, A)

Because killing people wrongfully harms them and takes away their intrinsic value and their autonomy, we place all three moral principles after (1').

Proponents of physician assistance in dying deny that it harms patients and insist that it helps them to avoid horrible deaths, that it is merciful. But if pain and suffering can be managed, then allowing physician assistance in dying may produce more harm than good to those individuals who choose to elect it. They will not live as long, for one thing. For another, they will miss the opportunity to experience and understand the significance of their natural deaths, an experience that can be filled with meaning for themselves and their families. In addition, there might have been an incorrect diagnosis of their illness or an error in predicting the amount of time that remains to them. Such errors are not uncommon in medicine. Also, there is the possibility that a new treatment may turn up, a "miracle cure," that may rescue a patient from the clutches of death—if only he or she had not bowed out of life early by using one or another form of physician assistance in dying.

Perhaps the most likely form of harm will come to those individuals who choose physician assistance in dying because they feel pressured either by circumstances or by others to do so. Some patients may choose physician assistance in dying to escape the mounting hospital bills that may wipe out a family's assets, or to eliminate the suffering endured by others as they watch their loved one die. More frightening, perhaps, is the social pressure that will be felt by patients to use physician assistance in dying if it ever becomes widely accepted in society. If it becomes the "normal" way to deal with death, then patients will be expected to choose it. Those who do not will be looked on as less than normal. This subtle pressure may force some to choose physician assistance in dying, even when they do not personally think it is in their interest to do so. So we write our second premise:

2.' Physician assistance in dying will harm individuals. (B)

In addition to the harms it may cause patients who use it, physician assistance in dying will also cause harms to the medical profession. There will be terrible conflicts created among and between members of medical teams. Doctors and nurses are trained to cure and comfort their patients, not to kill them. One might argue that they can refuse their patients' requests for physician assistance in dying, that the right of the patient to physician assistance in dying does not give the medical team a corresponding duty to perform it, does not require them to comply with their patients' wishes. However, it would be very difficult for physicians in general to not help their patients if physician assistance in dying were widely accepted. The medical profession, and doctors in particular, would then be viewed as killers, not healers. They would not be able to claim the same sort of trust from their patients that they have always received in the past.

Physician assistance in dying would harm the medical profession in another way as it would reduce efforts to search for new treatments. If patients routinely used physician assistance in dying when death was imminent, there would be no incentive to push medicine forward, to search for new treatments. If they are not going to be utilized by dying patients, what is the point of such research? The third premise, then, is this:

3.' Physician assistance in dying will harm the medical profession. (B)

Finally, physician assistance in dying will harm society in general. The social harms that are likely to follow from the acceptance of it take many forms, but at root they all spring from the same source—an erosion of our collective respect for life. If we see the lives of competent terminal patients as not worth living, it will become easier for us to see other lives in that way as well. Before we know it, we will be suggesting and approving social policies that terminate the lives of patients who cannot speak for themselves. In fact, there is evidence that many acts of nonvoluntary euthanasia have been performed in the Netherlands, despite prohibitions that strictly forbid it. Next we will be performing acts of involuntary euthanasia on older folks in long-term care facilities, especially if they suffer from serious cases of dementia. After that it will be defective newborns whose lives will not be worth living, and maybe even handicapped adults. Who knows where it will stop, once we start down the long slippery slope of ending lives judged to be not worth living?

This argument is usually referred to as the **slippery slope** argument. Just as taking the first few steps on an icy slope will lead inevitably to a slide all the way to the bottom, so, too, allowing any form of killing to be seen as morally acceptable in society will lead to the acceptance of other, more questionable forms. One well-known expression of it goes as follows:

> Euthanasia as a policy is a slippery slope. A person apparently hopelessly ill may be allowed to take his own life. Then he may be permitted to deputize others to do it for him should he no longer be able to act. The judgment of others then becomes the ruling factor. Already at this point euthanasia is not personal and voluntary, for others are acting "on behalf of" the patient as they see fit. This may well incline them to act on behalf of other patients who have not authorized them to exercise their judgment. It is only a short step, then, from voluntary euthanasia (self-inflicted or authorized), to directed euthanasia administered to a patient who has given no authorization, to involuntary euthanasia conducted as part of a social policy. Recently many psychiatrists and sociologists have argued that we define as "mental illness" those forms of behavior that we disapprove of. This gives us license then to lock up those who display the behavior. The category of the "hopelessly ill" provides the possibility of even worse abuse.
>
> Embedded in a social policy, it would give society or its representatives the authority to eliminate all those who might be considered too "ill" to function normally any longer. The dangers of euthanasia are too great to all to run the risk of approving it in any form. The first slippery step may well lead to a serious and harmful fall.[10]

Other social harms may follow as well, especially in this age of cost-conscious medicine and personal medical care. The temptation to utilize physician assistance in dying, or even nonvoluntary euthanasia, near the end of a patient's life when medical care is often very expensive, will be very great if killing is seen as allowable. The poor and uneducated will be quite vulnerable to the pressures of accepting such deaths once these deaths are considered socially "normal." Even if it might be morally acceptable for a few, especially those whose pain cannot be managed without total sedation, a better course is to allow it for none. The social harms that will result are too high a price to pay. And so our final premise in support of the case against physician assistance in dying is this:

4.' Physician assistance in dying will harm society. (B)

Replies to Objections

The claims presented here are contradictory statements. If one is true, then the other is false. Because of this, the reasons for one claim are also objections to the other. Although things do not always work out so neatly in building cases for and against controversial issues, they do in this case. The objections to those in favor of physician assistance in dying are just the "reasons for" those who oppose it, and vice versa. Let us begin by considering replies to the objections against physician assistance in dying.

The first objection, expressed in premise (1)', is that physician assistance in dying is a type of wrongful killing, or murder. Surely physician assistance in dying, be it assisted suicide or voluntary euthanasia, are types of killing, but are they wrongful killings?

Exercise 7.2

This exercise is to be performed in class by each of you. On a piece of paper write down all the reasons you can think of that show physician assistance in dying to be a type of wrongful killing, then write down all the reasons that show it is not. Exchange papers with another student. Now make written comments on his or her paper explaining why you agree or disagree with what that person said. Your instructor may wish to have some of you read these comments to the entire class and use them to begin a class discussion. To get the maximum benefit from this exercise, do not read on before you complete it.

According to some, the very act of killing is itself intrinsically wrong, and nothing can make it right. The Sixth Commandment, after all, says "Do not kill." Even if we allow religious evidence into our debate, however, the appeal to the Sixth Commandment is insufficient to settle the question. The proper translation of the Sixth Commandment is "Do not murder," not "Do not kill." The act of killing itself is morally neutral; only *wrongful* killing is immoral. True, killing is wrong in the vast majority of cases when human beings kill each other, but we do recognize morally acceptable killings—especially in cases of self-defense, as we said above. The question before us now is whether physician assistance in dying involves killings that are also morally acceptable. The way we determine whether a type of action is morally acceptable is to apply our three moral principles.

Killing is usually wrong because it generally violates our three moral principles. It is usually against the victim's will, so it violates the principle of autonomy. In taking someone's life, killing takes away his value, so it violates the principle of justice. And finally, killing violates the principle of beneficence, because it is painful, it robs the victim of his future, and it produces suffering in the family and friends of the victim. But these principles do not seem to be violated by physician assistance in dying. First, the killing is wanted by the patient, so it respects her autonomy. Next, because the dying, suffering patient does not value her life as it is, because she sees it now as an evil and no longer as a good, physician assistance in dying does not violate the principle of justice. Finally, it does not violate the principle of beneficence, because it will not produce a painful death. Rather, it will avoid one. Next, it does not rob the patient of a *wanted* future but rather avoids one that is unwanted. Finally, if properly planned and discussed, it should cause less suffering among family and friends than a natural death would. All things considered, watching someone die a peaceful death, surrounded by loved ones, with time to say good-bye, is less agonizing than watching someone die by nature's sometimes long and cruel path. We may now write the third premise in the argument for physician assistance in dying.

3. Physician assistance in dying is not wrongful killing. (B,J,A)

The next set of objections facing the proponents of physician assistance in dying point to its harmful consequences for the patient, the medical profession, and society at large. To refute these objections requires showing that these harms are unlikely to occur or that they can be controlled by properly regulating the practice of physician assistance in dying. The first of these objections, expressed in premise (2)', is that it will cause harm to patients, especially the harm of dying prematurely. First, this objection claims that there is no pain and suffering that cannot be managed, so there is no need for physician assistance in dying. For those who support physician assistance in dying, however, such a claim is simply false. Moreover, even if it were true, even if all pain and suffering *could* be managed, it is not managed well in so many cases. In the face of this reality, physician assistance in dying ought to be an option.

Next, (2)' claims that patients will miss the enriching experience of a natural death if they exit early through physician assistance in dying. But they can have the experiences of saying their good-byes, of healing family wounds, and of appreciating their lives before choosing physician assistance in dying. Once they have stopped treatments and said their good-byes, suffering, terminal patients think that avoiding a natural death is precisely what is most beneficial to themselves.

What about the possibility of a misdiagnosis? Will patients who are not really dying kill themselves unnecessarily? Clearly a second or third opinion is warranted to confirm the diagnosis, and thus to avoid this possibility. What about a just-discovered miracle cure? Should we worry that dying patients will kill themselves too early to benefit from these cures? Because new treatments are continuously in the medical research pipeline and may appear at any time, this objection is a valid concern. However, it is extremely unlikely that cures so dramatic as to save an otherwise terminal patient's life would not be known about in time. For example, while studies testing the efficacy of new cancer drugs are ongoing, they are generally known about well before the time that they become available to patients in general. If anything, the announcement of so-called miracle drugs is usually premature, often raising patient hopes well in advance of their final testing.

Finally, there is the very real danger that patients will choose physician assistance in dying solely because of the pressure placed on them by loved ones and society in general. None of us want to be a burden to our caregivers. None of us want to use our savings to pay end-of-life medical bills instead of being able to leave our assets as a legacy to our families. Will not the very existence of the physician assistance in dying option lead to its abuse, to its being used prematurely and in an involuntary manner by patients who might consider it an act of love for their families? Will it really end up being a way to undermine genuine autonomy rather than a vehicle to express it?

Several responses may be made to this objection. First, it is a real and serious objection and must be seen as a very likely result of accepting physician assistance in dying. Some few dying patients may choose to use physician assistance in dying to spare their families from the suffering that comes from watching them die. Despite the feeling that this should not be so, we have difficulty arguing that someone who wishes to use physician assistance in dying for the sake of his family is wrong in doing so. We make sacrifices for our loved ones throughout our lives, after all, and this may be seen as one among many. Remember, we are talking about patients who are dying and suffering and who want to hasten their final release, not patients who have many years of good life left to them.

The crucial point here is to ensure that such decisions are truly autonomous and are really seen by the patient as in his interest as well. To ensure that this is the case, the attending physician should counsel patients about such matters, and even require further counseling for patients whose motives are suspect. We have referred to the goals of such counseling previously in this chapter, in the "Assumptions" section. We can add that many patients would die later than they otherwise might if physician assistance in dying were available. If they choose to kill themselves without the assistance of a physician, they must do so while they have the physical and mental strength to do so instead of waiting until the last possible moment, when such strength may have dissipated. If physician assistance in dying were available, they could wait until their lives were closer to completion. Now our fourth premise may be written as this:

4. Physician assistance in dying will not harm individuals. (B)

Next we consider the objection that physician assistance in dying will harm the medical profession. Generally speaking, this objection says that involving doctors and nurses in the killing of their patients has the potential both to undermine some of the positive attitudes of medicine and to damage the doctor-patient relationship. As a result, much more harm will be produced than will be eliminated by physician assistance in dying. For example, because members of the medical staff are trained to save lives, physician assistance in dying will undermine this attitude. If patients are willing to kill themselves, then the motivation to use all available resources to save them from dying and to find new cures for their diseases and conditions will be undermined. Less care will be given to the dying, not more. The weakening of this heroic attitude of medical professionals, the attitude of rescuing patients from the grip of disease, may then spread to other patients, especially to those who are not terminally ill. In short, physician assistance in dying may very well cause medicine to treat us all less effectively. Perhaps we should follow the model used in Germany, allowing the dying to receive lethal doses of drugs, but only at the hands of their loved ones, not the medical profession. Whichever model we choose to govern how we care for dying patients, however, it should not include the recruitment of physicians as agents in killing.

There is some truth to this objection. Conflicts will certainly arise among members of medical teams about the appropriateness of physician assistance in dying in general, and for certain patients in particular. Some nurses and doctors will choose not to participate at all in physician assistance in dying; others will do so on a limited basis. Many, on the other hand, will see physician assistance in dying as part of their mission to ease the suffering of their patients. Many practice it already—about 15 percent to 20 percent do so, even though it is illegal. The way to deal with such conflicts is not to deny patients their rights, however, but to allow members of the medical staff to transfer patients to the care of others when the medical personnel cannot in good conscience honor their patients' requests for physician assistance in dying. This is the way we treat requests for abortion, and it will be an acceptable model for resolving conflicts about physician assistance in dying.

It is very unlikely that research physicians will stop looking for cures if society accepts physician assistance in dying. They are motivated by the desire to increase medical knowledge. Whether some few dying patients kill themselves will not deter that quest. It is also unlikely that physician assistance in dying will cause doctors and nurses to be less interested and less aggressive in the care of patients who may be cured. It is also unlikely that they will turn away from dying patients because some of these patients do not choose to die a natural death. In fact, there is evidence that allowing physician assistance in dying as acceptable medical practice will actually increase efforts by medical staff to control better the pain and suffering of their dying and distressed patients. If symptom management improves, the need for physician assistance in dying will decrease, at least for many patients. Most patients, after all, do not want to die. They want to live every day, every hour, every minute that they can do so. But they do not want to live lives of pain, suffering, and indignity.

There is some evidence that the doctor-patient relationship will be affected by the acceptance of physician assistance in dying. In an age when we are often treated by specialists who are strangers to us, we may reasonably be fearful if they have the authority to kill. However, remember that requests for physician assistance in dying come from the patient, not the doctor. They will usually involve the patient's primary care physician, a person better known to those patients who have one. This being the case, the doctor-patient relationship may actually improve with the acceptance of physician assistance in dying. It will mean that patients can trust their physicians to provide them with all the options they seek during their dying days. Now physicians have to say no to patients who request assistance in dying. They may terminate treatment and keep dying patients as comfortable as they know how, but they cannot—without risk to themselves— assist their patients to die speedier deaths.

Patients want assistance from their doctors because doctors know what to do, what drugs to prescribe, and what instructions to give. For those patients who cannot administer drugs to themselves, paralyzed patients for example, and who do not want to pressure a family member to do so, the doctor is the best candidate to act as the patient's agent. As in the Netherlands, the willingness of physicians to provide such help to dying patients is seen as a blessing by patients and produces a strengthening of the doctor-patient relationship.

For other patients, however, the acceptance of physician assistance in dying may very well strike fear into their hearts. The cultural beliefs and experiences of different racial and ethnic groups have produced different beliefs about the role to be played by the medical profession in their dyings. For example, there is some evidence that African Americans would have a great deal of difficulty in trusting their doctors if physician assistance in dying was an acceptable part of their care-giving. For many African Americans, even removing futile treatment is often viewed as a sign of indifference, disrespect, and even racism. They are more likely to demand treatments that provide no benefit to them as a way to ensure equal treatment. If a doctor has the power to kill patients, this will surely produce a great deal of anxiety in these patients. If a dying patient, because of his life experiences and cultural beliefs, perceives that others view his life as less than valuable, the acceptance of physician assistance in dying may very well weaken the trust between him and his physician, a trust that is required for successfully managing his pain and suffering.

This is a serious objection and one for which there is no easy answer. As a reflection of the larger issue of racism in society as a whole, it needs to be addressed through a long process of educating everyone about the purposes of physician assistance in dying, by recruiting more members of minority groups into the medical care system, and by fostering greater understanding among medical personnel and society in general of the various notions of death and dying accepted by various cultures. With the understanding that this particular problem of trust will not soon pass, we write the fifth premise in the argument for physician assistance in dying:

5. Physician assistance in dying will not harm the medical profession. (B)

The final objection is that physician assistance in dying will lead to social harms, that it will undermine our respect for life and lead us down the slippery slope to killings that are clearly wrong and terrible. For many who oppose physician assistance in dying, this is its most serious flaw—its potential for abuse. The objection is not so much that physician assistance in dying is itself immoral, especially for some few terminal patients whose pain and suffering cannot be relieved by anything but total sedation. Rather, the fear is what physician assistance in dying will lead to beyond itself that makes it immoral. Because the consequences of our actions are important factors in judging their moral acceptability, those who believe that physician assistance in dying is morally acceptable must examine the likelihood that such assistance will lead to immoral actions.

One form of the objection may be ruled out immediately, the version claiming that physician assistance in dying will lead down the slippery slope despite all efforts to halt it. According to this interpretation, the slippery slope objection claims that we will soon be practicing nonvoluntary euthanasia, infanticide, and murder of the elderly even though we think such actions are immoral. This is nonsense and is not what the more serious form of the objection means. Instead, the serious version of the slippery slope objection claims that physician assistance in dying will change our attitudes about life. If we accept physician assistance in dying in society, it will weaken our respect for life in all its forms, replacing that attitude with one that respects only lives of sufficiently high quality. Once this attitude has taken root, it will grow into a consensus among citizens to make other forms of killing morally and legally acceptable.

For many, physician assistance in dying is a way to respect life, not to undervalue it. It is not life itself, biological life, that contains value. People who are brain dead but hooked up to life-sustaining equipment, or people who are in a persistent vegetative state are biologically alive, yet few of us would value such an existence. Instead, biological life is valuable because it is a necessary condition for sustaining truly human qualities, such as consciousness, freedom, knowledge, love, pleasure, and virtue. Because it is difficult or impossible for people who are undergoing a painful death to experience these human qualities, physician assistance in dying may be seen as a way to respect life, not to undermine that respect. What is respectful about keeping someone biologically alive for years when that person can never again even be conscious of her surroundings?

We may argue that accepting physician assistance in dying, especially accepting it as a legal right, would make it less likely to be abused. This is because it is already in use now, though hidden from regulation. Moreover, allowing patients to control their pain with large amounts of morphine is also practiced with little regulation, even though such pain management often leads to the death of patients before nature's time. If physician assistance in dying were accepted, if it were out in the open, regulations that would ensure its proper use would be easier to enact.

Despite these remarks, the slippery slope objection is a serious and important one. For example, if physician assistance in dying for terminally ill patients were to have widespread legal acceptance, an attempt would soon be made to extend this right to those who were not terminal, but suffered great distress from a disease or medical condition. This is an allowable use of physician assistance in dying in the Netherlands, the place where physician assistance in dying is most widely and openly practiced. Because "terminal" means "expected to die within six months," and because such predictions are notoriously difficult to make, it would not be easy to allow terminal patients access to physician assistance in dying while denying it to those patients who are nonterminal but may be suffering just as much.

Next, there would be a call for extending physician assistance in dying to patients who had requested it while competent, but who had since lapsed into an incompetent state. In fact, there is some evidence that granting physician assistance in dying to such patients has occurred in the Netherlands, even though it is seen as a form of active nonvoluntary euthanasia and expressly forbidden under Dutch law. It would not be easy to argue against such a practice, as we already allow incompetent patients to decide for themselves which treatments to terminate and when to terminate them. These decisions are now made through their advanced directives, or through their health care agents. It would seem quite reasonable to extend this process to physician assistance in dying as well, a way to ensure patient self-determination.

It would also be quite tempting for many to extend physician assistance in dying to patients who were not competent and had not expressed their wishes to anyone. For severely handicapped infants who were not expected to live very long and who were suffering, physician assistance in dying would be much more humane than simply terminating treatment and letting nature take its course. Dying, suffering, noncompetent cancer patients, those who had not left any instructions about their wishes for dying, could also benefit from physician assistance in dying. Try to imagine for a moment one of your loved ones having to endure the slow deterioration of such a death and see how you feel about the mercy of ending it sooner rather than later.

You can see how easy it would be to generate the attitudes required to support the use of physician assistance in dying for classes of patients beyond those who were terminally ill. So there is a point to the slippery slope objection. Once assistance in dying was accepted for terminally ill patients, we probably would try to extend its acceptance for others. Does this mean that we should not accept it at all? Those who favor physician assistance in dying say no. Instead, two other paths may be taken. The first one is to accept it for terminally ill patients only, as has been done in Oregon, and to refuse ever to extend it beyond that point. The second is to accept it for terminally ill patients at first, and see how it goes. It may be that such acceptance will lead to improvements in the management of pain and suffering, and thus that physician assistance in dying will be used very seldom.

On the other hand, if physician assistance in dying becomes a successful option for dying patients, if there is widespread agreement that it ought to be present as one option among many to those who face death within six months, then discussions should take place about extending it to others. It may very well be that physician assistance in dying does have a legitimate role to play for nonterminal patients, as well as for terminal, noncompetent patients. That decision, just as the one that faces us now about the use of physician assistance in dying for terminal competent patients, should be made as a result of much soul-searching by all of us. It may very well be the case that physician assistance in dying for the terminally ill competent patient will lead to a desire to extend it to others. The slippery slope objection may be right about that. But this may not in itself be a bad thing, if the "others" for whom it is accepted are restricted to those for whom it ought to be accepted on the grounds of mercy, autonomy, and justice. The acceptance of physician assistance in dying for the competent dying patient will not lead us down the slippery slope to the callous acceptance of horrible and obviously immoral killings, but instead it will lead us to explore other areas where suffering patients may be treated more mercifully. So our final premise is this:

6. Physician assistance in dying will not harm society. (B)

Now we turn to the objections leveled against those who claim that physician assistance in dying is immoral. Once again, these objections are the "reasons for" the claim that it is not. The first one, found in premise (1), is that physician assistance in dying is merciful, thus conforming to the principle of beneficence. The second is that it allows patient self-determination, thus conforming to the principle of autonomy.

In response to the claim that physician assistance in dying is morally acceptable because it reduces pain and suffering, and thus is more merciful than simply letting patients die, opponents of physician assistance in dying simply point out that there are other, less dangerous ways to show mercy. Pain can be controlled through medication, and suffering can be controlled through hospice care. The fact that these are often not controlled should produce a cry for programs to better manage pain and suffering, not a cry for physician assistance in dying. There should be greater access to hospice care, for example. Less than 20 percent of dying patients currently use hospice services. In addition, there should be thorough training for physicians in pain management. Currently they receive almost no such training in most medical schools. Improvements in both areas are already under way in this country and should be pursued aggressively in the future. It is in the management of pain and suffering that true mercy lies, not in the dangerous precedent that will be set by accepting assisted suicide and voluntary euthanasia. The acceptance of these will be less merciful in the long run. As easier options for treating the dying, they may very well undermine efforts to improve palliative care.

> The combined and integrated relief of pain and suffering shaped to suit the peculiarities of their manifestation in each person is the aim of comprehensive palliative care and the more sophisticated hospice regimens. Patients treated this way

usually do not ask for termination of their lives; when they do ask for it, they tend to change their minds later. It is an injustice to offer these patients assisted suicide or euthanasia as options when so much more can be offered in the way of sophisticated treatment. Euthanasia and assisted suicide are easier options for the caregiver, since genuine palliative care demands much more on the caregiver's part. This is not to impute ill intent to those who conscientiously believe in the moral probity of assisted suicide but simply to recognize the emotional demands, the reality of fatigue and frustration, involved in the care of the terminally ill. Even the most beneficent among us must recognize these realities and the way they might alter our own approach to care if euthanasia or assisted suicide becomes a legal or moral option.[11]

So the next premise in the argument against physician assistance in dying is this:

5.' Adequate palliative care is more merciful than physician assistance in dying. (B)

Finally, opponents of physician assistance in dying must reply to the objection that patients ought to have a right to such assistance if they choose. To forbid its acceptance is to deny patient self-determination and thus to violate the principle of autonomy. One reply is that the decision to use assisted suicide or voluntary euthanasia can never be truly voluntary. Dying patients, according to this claim, are not capable of making rational decisions. This way of dealing with the objection has already been rejected in the "Assumptions" section, and we will not revisit it here. Instead, we will simply assume that some dying patients are capable of understanding their situation and their treatment options, and they are sufficiently free from depression and other emotional states to make a free choice in the matter of physician assistance in dying.

The best response to the objection that refusing to accept physician assistance in dying robs patients of their autonomy is that such autonomy is granted in the first place only to the degree that our actions harm no one else. This is what the principle of autonomy states: that rational persons have the right to do as they wish, as long as their actions harm no one else. In fact, however, a great deal of harm will result from the acceptance of physician assistance in dying—all the individual and social harms mentioned in the argument against physician assistance in dying, as well as the harms that will be visited on the medical profession. Physician assistance in dying is not a private act, appearances to the contrary. It has great potential for harming others. Because of this, individual choice may be prohibited for the sake of others, just as it is for stealing, lying, and assault. So our final premise says this:

6.' Patient self-determination in physician assistance in dying may be prohibited to avoid harm to others. (A)

Evaluation

The goal of this section is for you to arrive at a ***reasoned judgment*** that one of our possible solutions better solves the problem of this chapter, *Is physician assistance in dying morally acceptable?* This task will be accomplished especially by your evaluation of the arguments presented so far. You will examine each premise for relevancy and especially for reliability, and then judge whether they are collectively sufficient to support the conclusion. Before turning to that task, however, it is important to understand the role that has been played by our ethical theory in shaping the arguments to this point.

Ethical Theory

It is best to see this problem as a **factual** moral problem. It is a search for a moral rule, a rule that will serve as the basis for social policy in matters of physician assistance in dying. We already have a rule in this country that forbids physician assistance in dying. According to this rule, it is not legal (except for physician-assisted suicide in Oregon), is not accepted by most religions, and is not officially accepted in medicine. The question before us now is whether this official policy should change. The law seems to be poised to accept changes, as is evidenced by the willingness of more and more states to consider following the example of Oregon. In medicine, the occasional need for physician assistance in dying has been recognized by the many physicians who have complied with their patients requests. By some estimates, 15 percent to 20 percent of physicians have helped patients die, especially through assisted suicide, even though such an illegal act has been risky for them. Individual members of various religions do not always toe the official line, either. Instead they reflect the general opinion of the public at large, which seems to be split on the matter of physician assistance in dying.

So the "official" policy regarding physician assistance in dying is being challenged. How do we determine whether the morally acceptable course is to retain the current ban on physician assistance in dying or to allow it as our new rule, a rule that grants new rights to patients who are dying? The answer is that the most morally acceptable rule is the one that best conforms to our three moral principles—beneficence, autonomy, and justice. The rule that should govern our care for dying patients is the one which, if followed, will produce the most benefits and least harms, will recognize the autonomy of patients and the intrinsic value of their lives. This is how the arguments of the previous section may be viewed, as attempts to convince you that one proposed rule or another best satisfies the demands of these three principles. Will allowing physician assistance in dying reduce evil (pain and suffering), allow patients to choose for themselves, and value their lives more than forbidding physician assistance in dying? Or is the reverse true? That is the question for you to answer in this section. Here is how we might diagram the role of ethical theory in framing our question.

B,J,A

RULES

Rule 1: Physician assistance in dying is morally acceptable.

Rule 2: Physician assistance in dying is immoral.

ACTION

According to this scheme, individual acts of physician assistance in dying are morally acceptable if Rule 1 best measures up to our three moral principles; are they immoral if Rule 2 does the job best.

Your Evaluation

One of the problems with any book written about current moral problems is that sometimes change comes so rapidly that what is written at any given time may be subject to revision a year or two later. This is especially true about facts, which are such an important aspect of applied ethics. In performing the following exercise, then, you may wish to brush up on the latest facts about physician assistance in dying. A quick search of the Internet may be helpful. Search especially for facts about physician-assisted suicide and voluntary euthanasia.

Exercise 7.3

Here are the arguments for and against physician assistance in dying. Each premise has already been tested for relevancy as it was introduced. All the premises are **relevant** to the conclusion, because they all follow from one or more of the moral principles, as indicated by the letters in the parentheses that follow each one. So your job is to judge the premises especially for their **reliability.** You should decide how likely each one is to be true or false. Then you should decide for each argument which set of reliable premises most **sufficiently** supports its conclusion. This is the strongest argument, the one whose conclusion ought to be accepted as expression of a **reasoned judgment** about the moral acceptability of physician assistance in dying.

The Argument for Physician Assistance in Dying

1. Physician assistance in dying is merciful. (B)

2. Physician assistance in dying allows patient self-determination. (A)

3. Physician assistance in dying is not wrongful killing. (B,J,A)

4. Physician assistance in dying will not harm individuals. (B)

5. Physician assistance in dying will not harm the medical profession. (B)

6. Physician assistance in dying will not harm society. (B)

7. Therefore, physician assistance in dying is morally acceptable.

The Argument Against Physician Assistance in Dying

1.' Physician assistance in dying is a form of murder. (B,J,A)

2.' Physician assistance in dying will harm individuals. (B)

3.' Physician assistance in dying will harm the medical profession. (B)

4.' Physician assistance in dying will harm society. (B)

5.' Adequate palliative care is more merciful than physician assistance in dying. (B)

6.' Patient self-determination in physician assistance in dying may be prohibited to avoid harm to others. (A)

7.' Therefore, physician assistance in dying is immoral.

A Few Comments

A major reason to oppose physician assistance in dying is its potential for abuse, especially the sorts of abuses outlined in premises (2)' through (4)'. Some of these possible abuses could be mitigated by a combination of education and regulation. There is, for example, a need to change the current culture of dying that exists in some parts of the medical profession, a culture that allows people to die with the intense pain and suffering that many still endure. Eliminating this suffering will be accomplished especially by educating physicians more thoroughly than is the current practice about the proper methods of pain control. It will also require physicians to begin to think of their patients, not themselves, as the ones who should control the time, place, and method of their dyings.

The potential abuses that may be committed by patients against themselves may be dealt with through regulation. Whether a particular patient who requests physician assistance in dying is too depressed to understand the consequences of his action or is under too much pressure from himself or others to make a free choice are conditions that may be discovered. One way to do this, following the lead of the Netherlands and of Oregon, is to require patients to request physician assistance in dying repeatedly, over a period of time. This repetition will ensure that their request is not the result of a momentary state of mind that will change later. Another important condition that may be placed on patients requesting physician assistance in dying is that they be counseled by professionals who are trained to discover whether the request for physician assistance in dying is a truly autonomous decision.

The possible abuse that most people believe to be the most serious, and the one least able to be managed by regulations, is the possibility that its acceptance will start us down the slippery slope to obviously wrongful killings. Once we begin to allow killing for those people who have themselves judged that their lives are no longer worth living, we could then become desensitized to the value of lives that are similar. So physician-assisted suicide will lead to voluntary euthanasia, and this to nonvoluntary euthanasia, and all of this allowable killing will lead us to the acceptance of involuntary euthanasia. In this day of rising health care costs there will be a great temptation to end the lives of the aged and infirm among us who spend their remaining days in long-term care facilities. The temptation will also be great to end the lives of the handicapped and defective newborns, even those who believe that their lives are worth living.

The role played by this objection to physician assistance in dying is enormous. It is the reason, for example, that opponents of physician assistance in dying say that to deny patient autonomy is acceptable—because assisted suicide and voluntary euthanasia will harm others, and autonomy may be curbed whenever our choices result in harm to others. Notice that this reasoning leaves open the possibility that if such harms could be regulated, there would be nothing wrong with physician assistance in dying in itself. If only the slippery slope consequences of physician assistance in dying make it immoral, and if these can ' trolled, then physician assistance in dying would be morally acceptable basis of autonomy (self-determination) and beneficence (mercy).

Instead of trying to estimate the likelihood that physician assistance in dying will inevitably lead to involuntary euthanasia, the real horror to avoid, it might be interesting to explore very briefly the assumption that voluntary euthanasia and nonvoluntary euthanasia are always to be thought of as wrongful in themselves. If they are not, at least under some conditions, then they are not to be thought of as "abuses" to be avoided at all costs. Let us assume then, that the slippery slope objection says that assisted suicide is wrong because it will lead to the immoral actions of voluntary euthanasia, nonvoluntary euthanasia, and involuntary euthanasia—and not because it is intrinsically immoral in itself. But are acts of voluntary and nonvoluntary euthanasia always immoral?

For myself, I can see very little moral difference between assisted suicide and voluntary euthanasia. Should someone, for example, who is physically unable to administer lethal doses of pain killers lose his or her right to a painless death for that reason alone? Suppose someone was paralyzed, for example, and could not carry out the act of assisted suicide. What is the moral difference between that person killing herself by taking pain medication provided by the doctor, and the doctor assisting her by injecting the medication at her request? There is a legal difference, to be sure. The doctor's action was the immediate cause of death. But this action and the death that followed were initiated by the patient's choice, just as in assisted suicide.

Suppose, further, that a competent patient had repeatedly requested assisted suicide and then became incompetent just before the act was to be carried out. Suppose that he was dying at home, for example, and the doctor arrived with the requested medication too late. He arrived just in time to be informed by the patient's family that the patient's condition had progressed to a point that he was no longer able to speak for himself. They further informed the physician that before this occurred, he made one final clear and convincing request to them to have the doctor end his life with an overdose as soon as he arrived. If the doctor now complies with this wish he will be performing an act of nonvoluntary euthanasia. In this case, however, it is still an act directed by the (previous) wishes of the patient. We allow such actions to occur in cases of passive euthanasia. We allow treatments to be removed and total sedation to be administered even when a patient can no longer speak for herself, especially if we know through advanced directives or the patient's health care agent that these were her wishes. Why not here, in cases of nonvoluntary euthanasia, when the patient's wishes are clearly known to all involved?

The above line of reasoning will surely give ammunition to those who support the legitimacy of the slippery slope argument. They will claim that it proves their point, because someone is already arguing that if assisted suicide is morally acceptable, then so is voluntary and even nonvoluntary euthanasia. So how far behind can involuntary euthanasia be? How soon will it be until the argument is made by someone that the handicapped and the old and infirm should be killed *against* their will? But this reaction misses the point. The point is that some forms of voluntary euthanasia, and even some forms of nonvoluntary euthanasia, ought to be allowed because they arise from the wishes of the patient. Once we are sure that these wishes are genuine, there is little moral difference between actions of assisted suicide, voluntary euthanasia, and nonvoluntary euthanasia, at least in cases that are motivated by clearly expressed patient desires. If such actions are not to be thought of as "abuses," then it is clearly the threat of the potential wrongful killings of *involuntary* euthanasia that gives credence to the slippery slope argument. It remains to be shown by someone who knows much more than I do, that such killings are likely to occur simply because we honor the wishes of those who choose to avoid dyings filled with suffering and misery.

One final comment: We have spoken about "total sedation" above as an answer to those few dying patients whose pain and suffering cannot be managed. Such patients are doomed either to painful conscious states or pain-free unconsciousness. If physician assistance in dying is not available to these patients, and if they do not wish to remain in pain, their only choice is to be given large doses of painkillers and then to have their nutrition and hydration terminated. Such patients typically die within a few days or less. One author has called total sedation "terminal sedation"[12] because it is what kills the patient. The patient dies not from the terminal illness from which she suffers, but from the medication and from the effects of removing all food and water. Such an act of total sedation is performed with the full knowledge that death will be hastened. Such an act is motivated by mercy. We may argue, as most do, that the intention of such an action is to kill the pain and not the patient, and thus is not really killing. But if killing the patient is a known consequence of this act, it is difficult to maintain that the killing, too, was not intended. If it was intended, what is the difference between it and euthanasia? Should what goes on in the mysterious caverns of a person's mind be the criterion for distinguishing between rightful and wrongful killings?

The point is not to praise or blame total sedation, but to show how hard we struggle to construct moral rationalizations for actions such as total sedation, actions that are morally indistinguishable from euthanasia as now defined. We do this because we believe that something must be done for suffering patients, on the one hand, and that allowing them to kill themselves or allowing their doctors to kill them at their request are actions that should be shunned, on the other. Perhaps it is best to focus on this common element shared by both sides of the physician assistance in dying debate—that more needs to be done to ensure that the process of dying is as "good" as it can be. With this thought in mind, let us examine the consequences of accepting or rejecting physician assistance in dying.

Consequences

What follows is a list of actions that might be taken to improve the quality of a dying patient's life. Some of these are already widely accepted; the acceptance of others is currently the focus of debate. For patients with a terminal illness, then, we may do the following:

1. Remove or fail to initiate curative treatments at the request of the patient.

2. Remove or fail to initiate curative treatments at the request of someone who speaks for the patient.

3. Manage patient pain through adequate palliative care, even total sedation if necessary.

4. Manage patient suffering through hospice care.

5. Allow competent suffering patients who request it to kill themselves with the aid of a physician.

6. Allow competent suffering patients who request it to be killed by their physicians.

7. Allow suffering patients who are no longer competent to be killed by their physicians if they had previously requested it while competent.

8. Allow suffering patients who are no longer competent, or never were competent, to be killed by their physicians even if they had not previously requested it.

We already practice (1) through (4), and we find such practices morally and legally acceptable. If you believe that physician assistance in dying is immoral, and you are consistent, then you must stop with (4); you cannot allow (5) through (8)—either legally or morally. If you believe that some of the items from (5) to (8) are morally acceptable, on the other hand, you must still deal with the question of whether they should be legalized or simply accepted as customary practice in medicine. You must also consider the possibility that some of the practices described in (5) through (8) should remain illegal.

It may be wise, for example, to legally prohibit (7) because it will be too difficult to restrict it to just those cases which it may be morally justifiable. In addition, I believe that it would be a disaster to legalize (8). Not only would doing so be unwise, as with (7), but also the use of (8) would often be immoral itself. Killing someone who did not request it because you believe that the person may be suffering too much may often be a type of wrongful killing. Pain management, even to the point of total sedation in such cases, is a much safer and equally humane method for dealing with terminal, incompetent patients whose views on mercy killing remain unknown. The one possible exception to this is severely defective newborns who are suffering. Some have argued that killing them for their benefit, even though their wishes will never be known, is a morally acceptable action. This is a controversial and complex issue and will not be discussed here.

The main questions concern (5) and (6). If you believe that they are morally acceptable, should they be legalized? Both possibilities have their own potential harms and benefits. Oregon has legalized (5), while in the Netherlands (5) and (6), now legal, were widely practiced for over fifteen years before becoming legalized. They existed as practices of medicine that the Dutch courts allowed if physicians practiced them according to strict guidelines. Physicians who ignored these guidelines could be prosecuted by the justice system. One cautious approach may be to legalize (5) and experiment with its use for a while. If it does not lead to the sorts of abuses that people fear most, then (6) may be legalized thereafter. The benefit of legalizing both is that their practice will be open to scrutiny and regulation much more readily than if it were a private matter between physician and patient. In fact, since quite a bit of (5) is already practiced privately in this country, legalizing (5) would make it more subject to regulation and thus less likely to be abused than it is at the moment.

There is some reason to believe that one of the consequences of legalizing (5), and even (6), is that it will motivate the medical profession to become better able to manage pain, and that it will motivate the general public to demand greater access to hospice care. If the pain and suffering associated with many dyings is better managed, then there will be less need for physician assistance in dying. Paradoxically, then, legalizing physician assistance in dying should decrease the demand for its use. Remember, physician assistance in dying is to be a right of patients, not an obligation. It should be thought of as a choice that may be exercised or not, according to the patient's own wishes. This is an important matter for you to consider, as some day each of us may very well be faced with such a decision.

Another Perspective

Two groups especially opposed to physician-assisted suicide are hospice workers and the disabled. In the four brief selections included below, first a physician compares the hospice model to the assisted-suicide model and finds the former far superior. Next is a letter from a disabled person to a legislator addressing some of the reasons that persons with disabilities fear assisted suicide. The third selection is an editorial from a public policy analyst, who worries about the abuse of assisted suicide by managed care health providers. Finally, there is an editorial from two physicians, one an ethicist as well, which offers advice to physicians who must deal with requests from patients for assisted suicide.

This first selection is by Joanne Angelo, M.D., *Ethics and Medics* (July, 1995) v. 20, no. 7. The references have been omitted.

The second selection is a letter addressed to the local assemblypersons of Berkeley, California, who were considering an assisted suicide bill. This and other letters from disabled persons may be found at *http://www.independentliving.org*

The third selection is an editorial from the *Los Angeles Times,* February 2, 1998.

The final selection appeared as an editorial in *American Family Physician* (May 15, 1997), vol. 55, no. 7.

The Hospice Model of Care vs. Physician-Assisted Suicide

E. JOANNE ANGELO, M.D.

FEAR OF ABANDONMENT, fear of unbearable suffering, depression and despair are the root causes of suicide in the terminally ill. Hospice care demonstrates that terminally ill patients need not be left to die alone or in unfamiliar, sterile environments, and that pain and other symptoms can be prevented or adequately treated. Hospice care brings a specially trained team of nurses, physicians and home health aides into the home of terminally ill patients to provide the finest medical care exquisitely adapted to their changing needs in the last six months of their lives. The patient and the family are offered additional supportive services by social workers and volunteers and pastoral care workers. In a competent, caring hospice environment the patient is never abandoned, symptoms are controlled, and depression and despair can often be prevented. If depression occurs, it can be diagnosed quickly, and treated effectively.

THREE CRUCIAL FEARS OF THE TERMINALLY ILL

Fear of unbearable pain and anxiety about pain are among the most common concerns of the terminally ill. Pain and its consequent anxiety can be alleviated by adequate dosages of appropriate medications administered at regular intervals. The route of administration need not be by injection. Pills or liquids can be taken by mouth or alternatively medication may be administered by means of skin patches, suppositories, or intravenous or subcutaneous infusions. When pain is controlled, anxiety about pain diminishes, and the patient can remain alert, with the capacity to enjoy each day and to participate actively in decisions about his or her care.

Fear of excessively burdensome, futile treatments may cause patients to request lethal drugs. The hospice model of care assures them that in the final stage of their illness they will not be subjected to heroic attempts to prolong life at any cost which only serve to lengthen the dying process and make it unnecessarily burdensome.

Fear of loss of autonomy and personal dignity often is present in a hospital setting where the staff makes the rules and the menus, establishes the plan of care, and decides when family may visit and for how long. In sharp contrast, hospice patients and their families remain in control of all the aspects of their care. Hospice workers are invited into the patient's home and allowed to stay only as long as their presence is judged to be helpful. Each decision in the plan of care is made jointly by the patient, family, and staff.

THE BURDEN OF SUICIDE FOR THE FAMILY

Fear of becoming a burden on one's family may move some frail elderly or terminally ill patients to consider suicide. Suicide is a terribly burdensome legacy for the family and friends of the deceased. Rather than alleviating the burden on loved ones, by arranging for an early death the suicidal patient bequeaths a heavy burden to survivors. In my psychiatric practice I have encountered and cared for many relatives and friends who have lost loved ones through suicide. The survivors typically struggle with overwhelming feelings of betrayal, rejection, guilt, shame and anger. Bereavement after suicide is often prolonged and difficult, and the issues it raises can last a lifetime.

DEPRESSION AND DESPAIR

Depression and despair may be the consequence of loneliness or suffering which is more than the patient can bear. If competent, compassionate care is offered along with loving companionship this need not occur. Depressive symptoms may be due to a preexisting affective disorder, or to the terminal illness itself, or they may be the consequence of recent treatments or the result of multiple personal losses in old age.

Depression in the terminally ill is amenable to treatment with medication and psychotherapy. If the patient expresses suicidal ideation, one can sit with him or her and ask "What is the hardest thing for you about your situation today? What is it that seems unbearable?" The hospice team can then set about solving the present problem together with the patient and family by targeting the most troubling symptoms, assuring that the patient does not feel rejected or abandoned, and assisting him or her to live each day as fully and meaningfully as possible.

THE FAILURE OF OUR HEALTH CARE SYSTEM

Requests for assisted suicide in the terminally ill are symptomatic of a serious failure in the health care system—failure to address patients' fears and alleviate their suffering, and/or failure to diagnose and treat depressive illness effectively. A solution to a patient's distress is not to be found in the ultimate rejection and abandonment of the dying person through the final and perhaps most meaningful chapter of life, nor is it to be found in prolonging the dying process by the use of all available modern technology. The hospice model of care offers patients and their families all the medical and supportive services necessary to enable them to live meaningfully until natural death occurs. This model need not be confined to specialized hospice programs but has wide applicability to the care of frail elderly as well as chronically ill and severely handicapped persons.

It is absolutely imperative to defeat legislation allowing physician-assisted suicide. If physician and next of kin become accomplices in the suicide of their frail and vulnerable patients and family members, for whom they have an obligation to care, then we will in fact have "reverted to the state of barbarism which one had hoped had been left behind forever" as Pope John Paul II characterized our present culture of death.

CONCLUSION

The choice is ours. To enact legislation allowing physician-assisted suicide is to plunge our society more deeply into the culture of death. It is imperative to defeat such legislation, and in its placed to enact legislation which would increase the resources available to bring competent, compassionate health care to patients and families in their homes—not only in the last six months of their lives as is presently done in hospice programs, but also long term for the chronically ill, the severely disabled and the frail elderly. In doing so we would have to our credit a major step toward transforming our culture of violence and death into a civilization of love and life.

Letter to Assemblypersons

LUCY J. FIELDS

Tuesday 13 April 1999

Assemblywoman Kuehl, and other members:

I am writing to please implore you to vote against AB 1592 (Aroner), the so-called "Death with Dignity Act", scheduled to be heard by the Assembly Judicial Committee on April 20, 1999. This bill is not only unnecessary, but poses a great potential danger to the safety and well-being of the disability community.

One truly dangerous aspect of AB 1592, for persons with disabilities is, it delegates far too much authority for deciding who may use this law to the medical establishment. It is a known fact, especially within the disability community, doctors harbor a deep-seated bias against anything they regard as medically imperfect or diseased. Unfortunately, they usually always view us in the same clinical manner. When it comes to understanding the lives, needs, and concerns of persons with disabilities, the medical establishment is probably the greatest collective pool of ignorance and prejudice against us that exists. Despite everything we do to assert our equality and independence, the medical community persists in viewing disabled people as dependent. I've learned to see dependency not as insurmountable, but as one of the many challenges of life. For society to legitimize prescribing lethal drugs to people because they fear the unknown is unconscionable.

In the Oregon study, the *New England Journal* reported that, compared to a control group, the people who committed suicide had "shorter" relationships with the doctors who prescribed lethal doses. While the exact time difference is not given, media reports often show that the patient/doctor relationship was quite short. The first woman to commit suicide sought out a different doctor after her own physician refused to write a lethal dose prescription. She then went to an advocacy group which connected her to a doctor who, after a 2½ week relationship, assisted her in committing suicide.

What about the things the New England study did not include? The professionals who declined to assist their patients were not interviewed. They could have provided insight into the health of the people who died. Family members were not contacted. No attempt was made to determine if the prescribing doctors were affiliated with assisted-suicide groups. Were the drugs prescribed for medical reasons or for ideological reasons? None of the patients were autopsied to determine if they had been terminally ill.

The report admits the investigators do not know if there were other unreported deaths. Because there is no penalty for failing to report an assisted suicide, most likely more deaths did occur. A Dutch report showed 59% of doctors do not report euthanasia or assisted suicide.

In the Netherlands assisted suicide occurs routinely for people who are not terminally ill. Depressed people can be killed upon request. And most chilling of all, in one out of five cases the patient did not ask to be killed. In one year alone, 1050 people died from "involuntary euthanasia."

I plan to contact all members of the Assembly Judiciary Committee and urge them to: KILL THE BILL, NOT THE ILL.

Sincerely,

Lucy J. Fields

Red Flag on the Slippery Slope

LAURA REMSON MITCHELL

HMO's resistance to expensive treatments for chronic diseases puts them in good form to support assisted suicide.

IF PHYSICIAN-ASSISTED SUICIDE ever is legalized, your access to high-quality health care is likely to be significantly reduced, even though taking your own life may be the farthest thing from your mind. And if you happen to have a disability or serious chronic illness, you will be particularly at risk.

That's not just because of abuses, although I believe there would be many.

It's not just because of fears and stereotypes about disability that are so deeply rooted in our society, although such prejudice increases the danger.

The basic problem is that legalized physician assisted suicide would inevitably become the ultimate financial escape hatch in a health care system that increasingly is dominated by cost considerations, even at the risk of patient well-being.

Consider this: In the last few years, the Federal Drug Administration has approved three new drugs that, for the first time in history, have an impact not just on the symptoms but

Reprinted by permission of the author.

on the actual disease process in multiple sclerosis, a disease that has driven a significant number of people into the arms of Jack Kevorkian. Unfortunately, these drugs are expensive—about $10,000—$12,000 a year per patient.

Now think about the bean counters at Big-Bucks HMO. Under current law, if the HMO refuses to cover one of these drugs for an MS patient who needs it, and if the disease gets worse, the plan is on the hook to provide care that may turn out to be even more expensive than the treatment that was rejected. If the HMO refuses to provide care at that point and the patient's condition continues to decline, family members and friends are likely to start calling government regulators, elected officials and lawyers. Bad press about cases like this also could mean the loss of multimillion-dollar employer contracts for the HMO. So, all things considered, BigBucks HMO has good reasons to think twice about denying coverage.

But in a world where physician-assisted suicide is legal, the HMO would have other options. It could simply drop expensive treatments and services from the plan's benefit package, provide minimal care and, when the patient finds that life no longer is tolerable, offer "compassionate" assistance in dying.

Family and political outrage are unlikely to be much of a problem once the idea of physician-assisted suicide becomes routine. Suicide would end the patient's "suffering" (and the stress that suffering puts on the family) and the patient would be dead. Would anyone then even think to challenge the pattern of decisions that pushed the patient to the point of asking for help in dying?

Recent reports suggest that with managed care dominating more and more of the industry, health plans are less able to avoid high-risk patients than in the past. That's probably one reason why more plans are finding their profit margins shrinking or disappearing. I believe many also are now paying the price for failing to meet the earlier needs of the high-risk patients they couldn't avoid.

Yet the first response of the health care industry (and many business purchasers of health benefits) to reforms like those recommended by the President's Advisory Commission on Consumer Protection and Quality in the Health Care Industry and the California Managed Health Care Improvement Task Force has been to reject such proposals as "too expensive."

Legalizing physician-assisted suicide would allow health plans, insurance companies and public programs like Medicare and Medicaid to appear "compassionate" while they cut back or eliminate coverage for the health and support services that can make for a good quality of life even in the face of significant disability and illness. For that reason, legalization is likely to reduce access to the very things that might give a seriously ill or disabled person a desire to continue living.

But the ramifications of legalization go even further. If health plans begin cutting back on coverage of expensive new treatments for serious diseases like MS, Alzheimer's and AIDS, it would significantly weaken or even destroy the market for such treatments. And without a market large enough to at least recover their costs, the pharmaceutical companies and other investors who turn scientific research into usable health care products aren't very likely to spend the money necessary to develop those treatments. As a result, we may never see cures for many serious, currently incurable conditions, or improvements in the quality of life for people with severe disabilities and chronic health problems—even though such developments may be well within our reach.

As a public policy analyst, I've watched HMO problems that I anticipated five or six years ago become pronounced enough to create a consumer backlash and demands for change—even though most people ignored what I was saying years ago or dismissed it as "catastrophizing." Unfortunately, the effects of legalized physician-assisted suicide on the health care system would be subtle and insidious. By time they are recognized (if ever), it may be too late to change course. That's why we should avoid the mistake of moving down that road in the first place.

Physician-Assisted Suicide: A Very Personal Issue

HOWARD BRODY, M.D., PH.D.
AND GREGG K. VANDEKIEFT, M.D.
Michigan State University
East Lansing, Michigan

AN ELDERLY PATIENT in the late stage of decline from multiple chronic conditions recently inquired, "If I become so incapacitated that I no longer see any reason to go on, would you help me if I choose to end my life?"

A recently retired maintenance man came to the office because of somatic complaints, but his main concern was the care of his wife, who had become bedridden as a result of diabetes and renal failure. All efforts to obtain social services assistance had failed, and he faced the dilemma of either managing her total care by himself or losing all of his retirement savings to qualify for public assistance. He expressed both anger and hopelessness. At the end of one visit, he said over his shoulder as he was leaving the room, "You wouldn't by any chance have Dr. Kevorkian's phone number, would you?"

The two cases illustrate the "helpless hopelessness" many patients—and many physicians—feel when faced with terminal or debilitating illness. Even physicians who engage abstractly in debates about the ethics of physician-assisted suicide may be ill-prepared for encounters with patients such as these. Yet it is how we handle these encounters, not whether we can provide elegant answers in the policy debate, that tests our skill and character as family physicians.

At the level of law, ethics and public policy, the battle lines have been drawn and the barricades erected. Seven years of often acrimonious debate and analysis have changed the mindset of very few committed partisans. But the polarized and contentious nature of this debate has tended to obscure a more important reality: no matter whether the individual physician is morally opposed or in favor of physician-assisted suicide, the basic approach to a patient who requests suicide assistance should be very similar no matter what the physician's beliefs are.[1]

Even the strongest advocates of physician-assisted suicide acknowledge that in the majority of cases, something else short of death might relieve the patient's suffering.[2] Thus, physicians on both sides of the debate can approach the patient with the same basic agenda—hear the patient out nonjudgmentally, be sure lines of communication remain open, find out in the greatest of detail what led to the decision that death is preferable to life and start exploring alternatives to death as a means of relieving the patient's suffering.[3]

The physician must obtain from the patient an explanation of what it is about the patient's current health status that led to the request for physician-assisted suicide and what are the patient's unmet needs—physically, emotionally, socially and spiritually. A somewhat harder question to ask may be what are the underlying values that form the basis of the patient's present stance on suicide. The question that should dominate, at least at first, in the physician's mind is: What would it take for this patient to reconsider or rescind the request for assisted death? In the name of both

Reprinted by permission of American Family Physician.

honest disclosure and enhanced communication, it is probably best that this question be stated candidly to the patient.

One of the most difficult questions to ask the patient, and one that likely is unanswerable for the patient, is: What attitude, either for or against suicide assistance, would reassure the patient the most? At least two possibilities must be kept in mind. Some patients might raise suicide as a trial balloon, wondering whether their caregivers are sufficiently committed to try to talk them out of suicide. Physician acquiescence in the suicide request would simply reconfirm and deepen that patient's sense of depression and abandonment.[4] But one must also be alert for what could be called "Quill's paradox"—that a promise to assist suicide at a later time, if things become really extreme, is the "security blanket" the patient needs to better face present adversity and, in all likelihood, to go on to die naturally as the disease takes its course, without ever reopening the request.[2]

To engage in this sort of searching and forthright exploration, the physician must have self-confidence based on a thorough self-examination of one's own values, commitments and fears. An analysis of suicides assisted by Dr. Jack Kevorkian shows that, in many of the cases, individual physicians or the medical care system in general obviously failed in the care of the patient. A careful analysis of the reasons a patient is requesting suicide assistance is therefore likely to reveal, at the least, some ways in which the patient's physician or other physicians have let the patient down. If one is not prepared to accept this possibility, one can hardly ask the right questions or listen carefully for the answers.

Physicians with ambivalent feelings about suicide assistance might be reluctant to engage in a searching dialogue with the patient for fear of having to reveal their own doubts or of being challenged in new and uncomfortable ways. Advocates of suicide assistance are obviously in danger of being so eager to declare an ideologic alliance with the patient that they do an inadequate job of searching for practical alternatives to suicide. And devout opponents are in danger of hating both the sin and the sinner, of allowing their distaste for the practice to turn into judgmentalism or abandonment of this highly needy and vulnerable patient. It may be difficult for a physician opposed to assisted suicide to say, "I am as a matter of conscience unable to provide the specific sort of assistance you are asking, but I promise you that I will stand at your side as long as you are alive and always try as hard as I can to bring you greater comfort."

Two groups in our society that are most steadfastly against physician-assisted suicide are hospice workers and advocates for persons with disabilities. Their opposition should prompt all physicians facing a request for suicide assistance to re-examine their basic attitudes and skills. Far too many of us know too little about the latest hospice techniques, and we need to be watchful to never tell a patient that a symptom cannot be relieved simply because we personally do not have the skills to treat it.

Because hospice represents an interdisciplinary-team model for care, we must also guard against the illusion that we, by ourselves, can supply the same quality and breadth of care as a skilled hospice team. Further, we must accept that we have been brought up in a society that signals in all sorts of ways the devaluation of persons with disabilities. We must be alert for any prejudices that would lead us to agree prematurely that a request for death is "rational" simply because a person is handicapped. And we must be alert to the possibility that a request for death arises more from a lack of adequate social services and support than from the inexorability of the disease itself.

Ira Byock, a national spokesperson for hospice medicine and the author of the book *Dying Well: The Prospect of Growth at the End of Life*,[5] describes a series of moving vignettes of patients allowed to "die well" with excellent palliative care and emotional support. Some of the patients started out looking like ideal candidates for suicide assistance, certain to suffer miserable and painful deaths if the disease were allowed to unfold. Byock seems to suggest that the best hospice care is the answer for everyone—that no patient would continue to ask for assisted suicide if a hospice team were providing quality care.

While we do not agree with the generalization that hospice care can ever achieve a 100 percent success rate, we share Byock's optimism that something very special can occur when a patient and a physician come together in an open dialogue about impending death. By requesting assistance with suicide, the patient, ironically, has handed the physician a special privilege and gift. The patient has bared his soul in a way that few others will, even in the intimacy of the medical encounter, and has shown the highest possible level of trust in his physician. The physician may now repay that trust by joining the patient in a journey to look squarely in the face of things that frighten away most onlookers—death, dependency and medical "failure."[6] Along that journey may come enhanced comfort, spiritual peace and a better sense of how death can be a sad but fitting final chapter in one's life story.

For this patient-physician journey to have a reasonably happy ending, we must become much more comfortable engaging with our patients in conversation about the deep and ultimate meaning of life and death. Currently, very little in our medical training prepares us to address these issues. There can be few harder tasks in family practice and few tasks as potentially rewarding.

NOTES

1. Supanich B, Brody H, Ogle KS. Palliative care and physician-assisted death. In: Berger A, Levy MH, Portnoy RK, Weissman DE, eds. *Principles and practice of supportive oncology*. Philadelphia: Lippincott (in press).

2. Quill TE. Doctor, I want to die. Will you help me? *JAMA* 1993;270:870–3.

3. Block SD, Billings JA. Patient requests to hasten death: evaluation and management in terminal care. *Arch Intern Med* 1994;154:2039–47.

4. Miles SH. Physicians and their patients' suicides. *JAMA* 1994; 271:1786–8.

5. Byock I. *Dying well: the prospect of growth at the end of life*. New York: Putnam, 1997.

6. Brody H. Assisted death—a compassionate response to a medical failure. *N Engl J Med* 1992;327:1384–8.

SECTION B

Moral Problems Concerned with Social Justice

In Part 1 the moral principle of "justice" was defined as the claim that every person has the *same* intrinsic value and thus the *same* moral and legal rights as every other person. One of our central moral ideals is that people are all of equal value in themselves and that they all possess equal rights, whatever their social status may be. Low-income workers, handicapped individuals, and even criminals are no less valuable and possess no fewer rights than kings and presidents, doctors and poets, computer experts and wealthy businessmen. As Kant reminds us, the life of every human being, even the poorest and most miserable among us, is priceless.

If people all have equal intrinsic value and equal rights, it follows that they ought to be treated fairly. To be treated fairly means that people should not be taken advantage of, discriminated against, or used merely for the good of others. To do so would be to treat them as less valuable than others. It would be to treat them as things. But our principle of justice tells us that people are not things. They are not commodities to be valued solely by their social status, by their worth to others. According to our principle of justice, all people, whatever their social status, must be treated fairly.

One way to treat people fairly is for society to refrain from using them merely for the good of others. Very often in the chapters to follow, this concept will especially mean to refrain from unfairly discriminating against them. One of the requirements of "social" justice, then, is for social policies to *avoid unfair discrimination.* Another requirement of social justice is to ensure that every person has his or her fair share of the goods produced by society. What constitutes a "fair share" and what are the allowable means to acquire it are both controversial issues. For the moment, let us assume that a fair or just society would allow everyone to have an *equal opportunity* to live a full, rich life.

To have equal opportunity, to have just as good a chance as everyone else to achieve material success, we assume that people have available to them the means to do so. But some people have little chance of living full, rich lives because they lack precisely these means. Some people lack even the goods necessary to meet their basic subsistence needs. Without adequate food, shelter, education, health care, and decent employment opportunities, people are denied full participation in life. In a country such as ours, where there is an abundance of wealth, should anyone lack such goods? In a country such as ours, where the wealthy and even the middle class enjoy countless luxuries, is there any justification for abandoning the "priceless" lives of the poor to suffering and misery? Is allowing this to occur a violation of our treasured principle of justice?

For other countries, especially for those developing nations where poverty is more democratic, where most of the citizens are poor, a similar moral question may be asked. If the wealthy nations of the world possess a sufficient amount of wealth to meet the basic subsistence needs of those in poorer countries, is there any justification for not sharing some of that wealth to do so? If we have the power to prevent the misery and suffering that is a daily companion for many of the poor of the world, are we not immoral if we ignore this obligation? Does it not violate the principle of justice to ignore the priceless lives of the world's poor? Are we not, after all, our brothers' and sisters' keepers?

What constitutes the fair treatment of others is a question about **social justice.** The questions about fair treatment that will concern us in the following three chapters are especially questions about unfair discrimination and equal opportunity. In the three chapters of this section, we will discuss matters of social justice for people in our own country (Chapter 8) and for those across the globe (Chapter 9). In addition, we will also discuss widening the circle of those whose lives are to be thought of as "priceless," especially the lives of some animals. If it is right to think of some animals as having rights, then we must examine just what our obligations are toward them. We must especially investigate the social *injustices* we have routinely allowed ourselves at their expense, and to reassess what now ought to constitute their fair treatment.

Chapter 8

Justice at Home

There are many ways in which social justice is denied to some people, many ways in which some people are not treated fairly. Certain of these are prevalent enough for us to give them names, such as poverty, racism, and sexism. The central topics of Chapter 8 concern racism and sexism in this country, as well as our efforts at eliminating them. Racism and sexism are to be understood as attitudes that lead to forms of unfair treatment of people simply because of their race or gender. They cause people to be treated unfairly by placing obstacles in their paths toward achieving meaningful lives. They are immoral because they treat some people less well than others simply because of their race or gender. As such, racism and sexism are instances of unfair discrimination, and they are violations of social justice. There is little disagreement about this, but there is much disagreement about the moral acceptability of the policies in place in the United States for eliminating these practices. In addition to unfair discrimination, there is another leading question of social justice in our country, one that especially concerns matters of equal opportunity. This is the question of government-supported welfare programs. We will discuss this issue briefly here before moving on to the central question of this chapter: unfair discrimination.

Welfare—**Welfare** programs are designed to help the poor in the United States to meet their subsistence needs. Surely such needs must be met if the poor are to have an equal chance to acquire the goods of society. Thus welfare programs appear to be morally acceptable as a means of achieving social justice. However, such programs require the redistribution of income from the rich and middle class to meet the subsistence needs of the poor. Wealth must be taken from some and given to others. Is a just society obligated to meet the needs of those who are unable to do so for themselves, even at the cost of forcing people who have enough to share their wealth? Or should everyone, even those who cannot work, be left to their own resources, hoping at best for the charitable impulses of others to pull them through? This is one of the leading questions of social justice in our country, the question of the moral acceptability of government welfare programs.

The central moral question about welfare is not how to reform it to make it more effective and more equitable, but rather whether it should exist in the first place. Welfare is, after all, the redistribution of wealth by the government to meet the subsistence needs of the poor. Money is taken in the form of taxes from the rich and middle class and given to the poor in the form of cash payments, housing subsidies, food stamps, health care, and so on. For some, taking money from those who have earned it through the sweat of their brow to help others is a form of robbery. It is one thing to tax people to support programs that they agree to support. For example, taxes for defense, education, health care, and municipal services are acceptable to most people. However, to tax people to support social welfare programs is to *force* some people to provide for the subsistence needs of other people. It is one thing to help others voluntarily, through charitable contributions; it is quite another to be coerced by the government into doing so. For some, in taking money from the rich and middle class to support the poor, the government is acting like a thief.

Others, however, see welfare as a form of social justice that does not go far enough. They believe that capitalism is an inherently unfair economic system because it distributes incredible wealth to some while condemning others to a substandard existence. Even in the presence of our great wealth, for example, there are still about twenty million people, many of them children, who live far below the poverty line. Each day they struggle to meet their basic needs, even with the assistance of welfare. In the presence of great wealth, is it not immoral to allow this misery? Is this the sign of a just society, that it allows its weakest members to suffer? Indeed it is not!

In a truly just society—at least, in an affluent one—there would be adequate food, shelter, clothing, health care, and education for all people, regardless of their social status. In addition, there would be opportunities for everyone to participate even more fully in life, through additional government subsidized programs, such as programs in the arts, sciences, technology, and recreation. All too often these goods produced by society are available only to the wealthy. As they, too, are important for personal development and fulfillment, then they, too, should be available to all. In a truly just society, the rich and middle class would be taxed much more than they are at present to ensure that everyone has an equal opportunity to achieve his own version of the good life.

A welfare program such as the one in place in the United States is seen as immoral by some because it is a form of theft, and as immoral by others because it insufficiently redistributes the goods of society; it is perceived by still others to be morally acceptable as it stands. According to this third view, government welfare programs are a morally acceptable form of social justice because they do ensure that the basic needs of all are met. These programs allow everyone an equal opportunity to participate fully in life, while at the same time not taxing people any more than is necessary. Such an approach represents a balance between the "everyone for himself" and the "everyone gets a more equal share" approaches to social justice, because it addresses both the needs of the poor and the rights of the rich and middle class. For now, at least, this is the prevailing view in the United States. Although they may be in need of continual reform to make them more effective and less subject to abuse, welfare programs are widely perceived as a morally acceptable way to promote equal opportunity and thus to help build a just society.

Affirmative Action—Another way that people are excluded from full access to the goods of society is through unfair discriminatory practices. **Racism** is the practice of unfair discrimination against people simply because of their race, whereas **sexism** is the practice of unfair discrimination against people simply because of their gender. Such discrimination may take many forms, but it usually includes at its heart some type of economic discrimination. This especially means excluding people from jobs and educational opportunities, the main roads to economic success. Such discriminatory practices are no longer legal in this country, but nonetheless they continue, often in subtle ways, ways that are sometimes invisible even to people who practice them. Most people understand that such discriminatory practices are immoral, but they often disagree on how to eliminate them. One very controversial way to end such practices, called **affirmative action,** has been widely used in the United States since 1965.

The aim of government-sponsored affirmative action programs is to ensure fair treatment for those who have been unfairly discriminated against in the past, and who may otherwise continue to be treated unfairly in the present. Its goal of equal opportunity for all is a noble one, but some of the methods that affirmative action programs employ in their effort to achieve this goal have been very controversial. Among the more controversial means that have been used by the government is the use of goals and quotas to force businesses and educational institutions to increase their representation of minorities and women. To fill these quotas and to achieve these goals often requires selecting less-qualified candidates over more-qualified ones, simply because of their race or gender. These practices are a form of **preferential treatment,** the most controversial aspect of affirmative action programs.

Those who oppose preferential treatment often refer to it as a form of **reverse discrimination.** This name describes for them what is immoral about preferential treatment: it is every bit as much a form of unfair discrimination as are the discriminatory practices it attempts to eliminate. Those who favor such programs, on the other hand, see them as the only way to ensure equal access to the goods of society by those who have been systematically shut out in the past. For them, affirmative action programs allow minorities and women access to the same jobs, the same schools, and the same levels of achievement that were once the sole possessions of their white male counterparts. They do not see affirmative action programs as a form of wrongful discrimination but rather as a means to achieve a society in which discriminatory practices are eliminated and equal opportunity is a reality for all.

The Problem

The best jobs and the educational opportunities that lead to them are finite in number. Not everyone can be a physician, a lawyer, the CEO of a large corporation, a tenured law professor, or whatever else you may think of as the "best" job. So how do we decide who gets these highly desired positions? The immediate answer that comes to mind is "the most qualified persons gets them." Is this not what our parents taught us through our formative years, to work hard in school so that we can get ahead in life? Is this not how we plan to run our careers, to work hard and to get ahead? The economic goods of society are acquired as a result of competition, like a race. Everyone starts at the same line. Those who have the most talent, train the hardest, and run the fastest win. This is the American way, to work hard and become as qualified as possible to get into the best schools that you can. Once there, more hard work will lead you to more qualifications so that you can compete for the best jobs that are out there. Along with the best jobs come satisfaction and material success, essential ingredients for a full, rich, and happy life.

Most of us agree that the criteria to be used for distributing the limited number of the best jobs and the best educational opportunities should be the qualifications required for success in that area. Those with the highest SAT scores and best academic records should get into the best colleges. Those with the best scores on professional tests and the best academic records in college should get into the best professional schools. Those who have the best training, the best ideas, the best experience, and who work the hardest should become the CEOs of corporations. Most of us believe that competition is the rule that should be followed in the race for society's most powerful, influential, and rewarding positions. As long as the race is fair, as long as anyone with the talent who wants to put in the effort has an equal opportunity to win, then "to the victor, the spoils."

In the past, not everyone did have an equal chance of winning, or even participating in the race at all. Some people were not allowed to run because of their gender. Until recently, women who were just as qualified as men were systematically excluded from many types of jobs and from desired educational opportunities, such as law school and medical school. Other people were not allowed to compete because of their race. African Americans were excluded from trade unions, municipal employment, and many educational opportunities simply because of their race.

There is little serious disagreement that the racism and sexism that excluded women and minorities from competing for the best jobs and admission to the best educational institutions are immoral practices. There is, nevertheless, a great deal of controversy about how to eliminate these practices in society. Most agree that a good first step in this direction was the passage of the Civil Rights Act of 1964. Among other things, this sweeping legislation made it illegal to discriminate in employment and education on the basis of race, religion, gender, or national origin. From that point on, racism and sexism in hiring and the selection of students for admission to educational institutions was formally banned in this country. The idea was to guarantee equal economic opportunity for all, allowing everyone to compete on an equal basis for jobs and educational opportunities. From that moment on, the race was supposed to be open to all comers.

Unfortunately, little changed immediately for women and minorities. They continued to be underrepresented in many of the same areas of employment and education as before. There were still very few women and African Americans in law schools, medical schools and business schools, for example. African Americans were still largely excluded from trade unions, fire departments, and police departments, and both women and minorities had difficulty securing employment in large corporations. Some of this was caused by continuing practices of unfair discrimination, but much of it was the result of the very fairness introduced by the Civil Rights Act. Many African Americans were not able to compete successfully, for example, because the long legacy that slavery had bequeathed to them consisted mainly of poverty and inadequate education.

Because of the ineffectiveness of the Civil Rights Act alone to guarantee equal participation in the economic life of the country, then-president Lyndon Johnson signed Executive Order 11246. Arguing that past discrimination had left women and minorities at an unfair disadvantage to compete equally with white males for jobs and educational opportunities, Johnson introduced affirmative action programs to ensure their equal representation across the employment and educational spectrum. In his speech that launched the program in 1965, he referred to a now-famous version of the "race" analogy:[1]

> Imagine a hundred yard dash in which one of the two runners has his legs shackled together. He has progressed ten yards while the unshackled runner has gone fifty yards. How do they rectify the situation? Do they merely remove the shackles and allow the race to proceed? Then they could say that "equal opportunity" now prevailed. But one of the runners would still be forty yards ahead of the other. Would it not be the better part of justice to allow the previously shackled runner to make up the forty-yard gap; or to start the race all over again? That would be affirmative action toward equality.

Because we cannot turn back history and start the race over again, Johnson argued that we must give the shackled runners, especially women and those African Americans who have inherited the legacy of two hundred fifty years of slavery, the opportunity to catch up to the white males who are now far ahead in the race. For Johnson, who was determined to open economic opportunities to all, affirmative action was to be the means to guarantee that the race was really fair from then on.

Clarifying Concepts

There is a great deal of misunderstanding about several of the central concepts used in the affirmative action debate, especially the concepts of equal opportunity, discrimination, and preferential treatment. **Equal opportunity** for all means that everyone has a fair chance to acquire the goods of society. By "goods of society" we especially mean its material goods, all of which may be translated into money or wealth. Because the means to acquire these goods for most of us is our labor, and because the occupations at which we labor are largely determined by our educational opportunities, the gateways to the goods of society become its jobs and educational opportunities. It is important to note that equal opportunity does not necessarily mean that people are to possess the goods of society in equal amounts. It does not require the equal distribution of wealth. It does allow for inequalities of wealth, even great inequalities. Instead, equal opportunity for all means only that the competition for the goods of society will be fair.

In a society where there is equal opportunity, there is a *fair* chance for everyone to acquire the best jobs and the best educational opportunities. This is different from saying that there is an *equal* chance, especially if "equal" means "the same." As in a race in which there are people with various levels of ability, so in life some of us are born with various advantages or disadvantages that make success more or less likely. In addition to talent, other factors increase the likelihood that some will have a better chance of success than others, such as the state of their health, their prior educational advantages, and especially the level of their family's wealth and influence. Because it is unlikely that a person's talent and other advantages can be eliminated in the "race" for society's limited goods, to have an equal opportunity to achieve them means at most to have no obstacles placed in your path that others do not have to overcome. It means that no "shackles" should be placed on your legs, shackles that others do not have.

One type of obstacle to fair competition is unfair **discrimination.** Discrimination is not always unfair. Sometimes it is good to discriminate. People ought to have discriminating tastes when they purchase works of art, for example, or dine at fine restaurants. You should be able by now to discriminate between strong and weak cases for various moral claims. We all practice discrimination in entertainment when we purchase tickets or turn on the TV set to watch our favorite opera stars or sporting events. We often rank people and things as having more or less talent or beauty or intelligence or interesting lives, and treat them differently because of it. We do the same things with our friends, our lovers, and our colleagues, selecting them on the basis of their various physical, psychological, intellectual, and other characteristics. We do not treat all human beings equally in matters of taste and friendship and love. When it comes to matters such as these, we are and we ought to be discriminating in our choices. We should not treat all people equally.

When it comes to jobs it is also morally acceptable to treat some people better than others, but only when the characteristics on which such discriminations are based are relevant. When I pay to see a famous opera star because he has a wonderful voice, I treat him better than another opera singer whose concert I refuse to attend because he has a mediocre voice. Having a good voice matters for an opera star. It is a relevant characteristic on which to discriminate between him and other singers. It is an essential qualification for the job, and thus treating him better because he possesses this qualification, is not a case of unfair discrimination.

Some forms of discrimination in employment and education, however, are clearly unfair, and thus immoral. In particular, it is usually wrong to treat people better or worse when we are considering them for jobs or educational opportunities because of their race, religion, national origin, or gender. It is not always true that doing so is immoral, but usually a person's gender or race makes no difference or little difference to their ability to perform a particular job or to succeed in a particular program of study.

Racial and sexual discrimination are immoral because they treat people differently on the basis of *irrelevant* characteristics. Having a good voice is a relevant characteristic for opera singers; it is not for systems analysts. I could not fairly select one systems analyst over another because of the quality of her voice, unless it mattered for the performance of her job. Unless the job calls for singing analysts, the only things that matter are her training, ability, experience, and computer-related skills. The quality of her voice is surely irrelevant, as is her gender and her race. To refuse to hire someone who is best qualified for such a job because she is a woman or a racial minority is immoral because it discriminates unfairly. It treats people differently on the basis of characteristics that are irrelevant. By doing so, it places obstacles in the way of some people that are not burdens to others who do not possess those characteristics. It makes the race unfair from the very start.

If we can agree that unfair discrimination must be eliminated in order to have equal opportunity for all, the problem then becomes one of identifying the most effective means to accomplish this daunting task. The most obvious first step is to make such practices illegal. This has already been accomplished, as noted above, with the passage of the Civil Rights Act in 1964. But changing the law did not change the hearts and practices of society. The unfair discrimination shown to

African Americans and women continued, though in more subtle ways. In addition, even when the competition for jobs and educational opportunities was fair, the legacy of slavery, especially poverty and its companions, left many African Americans unable to compete successfully.

Something more was called for to ensure that African Americans and women, as well as Native Americans, the handicapped, and other minorities, were included among those who had true equal opportunity to acquire the goods of society. Something more was required to increase the number of women and minorities admitted to professional schools, something more was required to open employment opportunities to all in the trade unions, the municipal service sector, and large corporations. If women and minorities were going to move into the middle class and beyond in large numbers, if their achievements in life were going to be determined only by their talents and their efforts, then something more was required besides simply saying that from now on the goods of society are to be distributed fairly in this country. This something more was affirmative action.

Affirmative action is a government program that was begun in 1965 and was run by the Equal Employment Opportunity Commission (EEOC), located under the jurisdiction of the Department of Labor. It was initially introduced to benefit African Americans by requiring construction projects funded by the government to hire a certain percentage of minorities. It was extended to women in 1967, and to other disadvantaged minorities, including Hispanics, Native Americans, Asians (since removed from the list), and the handicapped in 1971. Starting in the late sixties the EEOC became much more aggressive in its attempt to include women and minorities in all occupations and educational institutions. It began to insist that any company receiving federal funds, including almost all educational institutions, increase their number of women and minorities. In some cases, especially when there was evidence of past discrimination, these companies were forced to hire women and minorities until the composition of their employees reflected the racial and gender balance of the wider community or the available labor pool.

Affirmative action programs have utilized various tactics to achieve their goal of equal opportunity. Sometimes affirmative action simply means greater efforts by companies and universities to recruit women and minorities. Most institutions have affirmative action officers who are charged with the duty of widely advertising available employment opportunities and increasing the number of women and minorities who apply. However, when such candidates are reviewed for the position, their qualifications are judged on the same basis as all others. Very few people have a problem with this sort of affirmative action, which simply encourages and enforces equal opportunity for all.

Affirmative action exists in other forms, however, that are quite problematic for many. What these forms share in common is that they grant **preferential treatment** to women and minorities simply because of their gender or race. These preferences may take many forms. Most notorious among the many ways to show preference is the *quota* system. Especially during the first decade of affirmative action, when it could be shown that a company or educational institution had been guilty of racial or gender discrimination in the past, the entity could be required by the government to establish a quota system of hiring or admission.

Such a system usually required the guilty party, whether it was a corporation, a trade union, a police or fire department, or a university, to select a set number of minorities and women before white male candidates, even if the women and minorities were less qualified for the position. The preferential selection system was designed to remain in place until the representation of minorities and women reached this quota, one that usually reflected their proportion in the wider society or available labor pool.

Because quotas are fixed numbers that had to be filled, meeting quotas would sometimes result in selecting people who were not only not as qualified for the position as their competitors, but who were plain and simply unqualified. In education, though not in business, quotas were eventually found illegal. Today, setting goals is the favored preferential selection system. *Goals* are not fixed numbers but rather percentages to be aimed at. The general idea of goals is to recruit and select qualified minorities and women. Like quotas, goals aim at selecting these candidates in numbers that reflect their general availability in society. However, unlike quotas, goals require the selection only of qualified candidates. They have no fixed number of places to fill. If not enough qualified candidates can be found to meet the goal set by a company's affirmative action plan, the government will not take any punitive action—as long as there was a sincere effort by the company or university to reach the goal. Goals may not have required the acceptance of unqualified people, but they still required preferential treatment. Many candidates who were accepted in order to reach a goal were still less qualified than some of their competitors who had been rejected.

Hiring people or granting them admission to educational institutions, even though they are less qualified than their rejected competitors, seems to fly in the face of what the Civil Rights Act stood for—equal opportunity for all. To treat some people better than others simply because of their race or gender seems to violate the principle of justice every bit as much as treating them worse because of these characteristics. On the other hand, it was quite clear in 1967 and beyond, that little progress would be made toward equal opportunity for all if such preferences were not allowed. This is the heart of the moral problem of those forms of affirmative action that include preferences. They seem to use one form of unfair discrimination to eliminate another. For this reason, many people refer to affirmative action as a type of reverse discrimination.

Formulating the Problem

Let us *formulate the problem* of affirmative action to be addressed in this chapter as follows:

> *Should less qualified candidates be selected for jobs and educational opportunities on the basis of their race or gender in order to promote equal opportunity for all?*

As we said above, the real problem is not with affirmative action, but with some of its forms—the ones that treat some candidates better than others on the basis of their sex or race. We will not address the innocuous forms of affirmative action that simply involve recruiting women and minorities or even hiring an equally qualified woman or a minority. It will simply be assumed that such actions are morally acceptable, especially when performed in the name of diversity. At the other extreme, we will also not consider whether someone who is *unqualifiable* ever should be selected over qualified candidates simply because of race or gender. Someone who is unqualifiable for a job or for admission to an educational institution is someone who could not meet the minimum qualifications no matter how much extra training or support he or she received. We will simply assume that such an action is immoral.

The above formulation of the problem does address two forms of preferential treatment that affirmative action programs have sometimes adopted—accepting for jobs or admission to educational institutions candidates who are *less qualified* than some of those who were not accepted, and accepting candidates who are *unqualified* but, who with some training and remedial work, may become qualified. Because the issue of qualifications is itself a complex one, we will focus especially on the first type of action—selecting candidates who are less qualified for the job or for admission to colleges or universities. We will, for practical purposes, consider those who are currently unqualified but may become qualified with some help as qualified to perform successfully.

This is a *conflict of rules* problem, as we will see more clearly in the "Moral Reasoning" section. The goal of affirmative action programs that allow the selection of less-qualified candidates on the basis of their race or gender is to achieve equal opportunity for all. It is especially to guarantee equal opportunity for those who have been denied it in the past and may very well continue to be denied it in the present, because of the racist and sexist attitudes and actions of society. But it achieves this goal at the expense of those candidates who are more qualified but not selected. Usually these candidates are white males, but this is not always the case. The main point is that now they seem to be discriminated against unfairly. They lose out simply because they are not of the right sex or race.

So the conflict here is between the rule "Do not practice unfair discrimination" (against the more qualified candidates), on the one hand, and something like "Achieve equal opportunity for all," on the other. It pits the noble goal of constructing an equal opportunity society, a society in which everyone has a fair shot at the good life, against what seems at first glance to be an immoral means to achieve it. Many believe that if we do not use some form of preferential treatment, the unfair discrimination against women and minorities that has existed in the past will surely continue. Passing the Civil Rights Act is in itself not sufficient to eradicate the practice. Many others see preferential treatment as simply replacing one form of unfair discrimination with another. As such, it is a serious violation of the principle of justice, one that ought not to be permitted, no matter how noble the social goal of equal opportunity for all. A truly fair society must be achieved, but another means must be found to bring it about.

Possible Solutions

Three **possible solutions** to our problem will be examined in the "Moral Reasoning" section. The *first* of these comes down on the side of the more qualified candidates who are rejected because they are not of the correct sex or race. It claims that preferential treatment programs are immoral because they themselves are forms of unfair discrimination. Although the goal of equal opportunity for all may be a noble one, it should not be brought about by an immoral means. Our concept of distributive justice has always favored competition as the fairest method for selecting those who will receive the best jobs and educational opportunities. The people who work the hardest and obtain the highest qualifications are the ones who "merit" these goods.

To change the rules, to allow preference to be given to those who are less qualified on the basis of the irrelevant characteristics of sex and race, is to practice the very forms of injustice that affirmative action programs were meant to eliminate. Preferential treatment in the name of a just society is itself an injustice. It is a form of unfair discrimination, only now discrimination "in reverse." It discriminates unfairly against the more qualified candidates, usually white males, who are being used as a means to achieve the goal of a truly equal opportunity society. As this first possible solution sees affirmative action as a form of unfair discrimination, only now in reverse, we will refer to it as the **reverse discrimination** view.

The *second* possible solution claims that preferential treatment is morally acceptable as a form of compensation for the past injustices borne by women and minorities. African Americans had to endure two hundred fifty years of slavery. Even after the end of slavery, African Americans and women were routinely excluded from most good jobs and educational opportunities. According to this possible solution, society is morally obligated to make up for these past injustices, to pay back the debt owed to the people who were systematically excluded from full participation in the economic life of this country. It must pay this debt in the form of preferential treatment now for members of those groups who were unfairly discriminated against in the past. Society must now distribute some of its goods, especially some of its jobs and educational opportunities, in a manner that gives preference to women and minorities. This is why types of affirmative action that employ preferential treatment are morally acceptable—because they are forms of **compensatory justice.**

The *third* possible solution will be called the **present injustice** view. According to this view, preferential treatment is morally acceptable, not as compensation for past acts of discrimination, but as the most effective way to eliminate present injustices. Even if everyone, regardless of race or sex, was to be judged from now on in this country solely by his or her qualifications, there would still not be true equal opportunity. According to this third view, the effects of past unfair discrimination continue to linger today. Many Native Americans and African Americans continue to suffer from poverty, poor education, crime, and other evils associated with life in a low socioeconomic class. Much of this is a legacy of their brutal treatment in the past from which they have not yet recovered. These disadvantages, as well as other sorts of disadvantages bequeathed to women and other minorities, have left them unable to compete equally. In addition, there is still a great deal of racism and sexism in society working in subtle ways to continue the exclusion of these groups.

To say that the Civil Rights Act fixed everything because now everyone has a fair chance is like saying that a baseball game between a Little League team and the Boston Red Sox is fair as long as they both play by the same rules. Even if the rules were the same for all, women and minorities would continue to be excluded from the goods of society because they are not currently equipped to compete equally. The only way to ensure inclusion is to distribute jobs and educational opportunities on a preferential basis. Once these groups have made it into the economic mainstream of this country, once they have come into the middle class in sufficient numbers, affirmative action programs that use preferential treatment for women and minorities may be terminated. For a time, however, they must be continued as the best way to ensure fair treatment for all.

Facts and Assumptions

Facts

Which of these possible solutions is the most adequate depends, to a large part, on the truth or falsity of many relevant *facts*. For example, if we knew that affirmative action programs that use preferences had achieved their goals, we might wish to eliminate them. If, that is, there is now in this country equal opportunity for all in employment and education, then it would not be morally acceptable to continue with preferences. The level of success of affirmative action may be known by examining the current level of representation of women and minorities in education and employment. If there is still evidence of underrepresentation, it would be helpful to examine facts that might explain why. For example, would an underutilization of African Americans and women on the highest executive levels of private corporations mean that they are not capable of doing the job? Facts about IQ levels or other related talents might be helpful to determine this. Or is their underrepresentation due to racist and sexist attitudes and actions? Perhaps psychological studies would shed some light on the continuing practices of racism and sexism, especially in its more subtle forms. It may be that minorities and women are just as talented as their competitors, but that societal and cultural obstacles prevent them from developing that talent. Perhaps sociological studies might shed some light on that issue.

Also, what about the fairness of some of the qualifications used to judge the relative merits of candidates? Do SAT scores really predict success in college, for example? Do written exams best predict the success of a person as a police officer? Do black police officers working in predominantly black neighborhoods serve more effectively than white officers who score higher on such tests? How well do minorities do in college or professional schools when they have been admitted with lower scores than their competitors? Do they graduate at the same rate? How do they perform later in their careers?

Exercise 4.1

In this exercise, you will practice the skill of gathering information. The facts that are relevant to the solution of our problem include those just mentioned as well as other common sense and scientific facts. List any additional factual questions you think are important, then search for answers to them and the questions presented earlier. This exercise is best performed as an out-of-class activity, though your results should be shared with the entire class.

Descriptive Ethics

The place to discover the current rules on affirmative action in this country is in the legal and political arenas. Since their inception, preferential treatment programs have been enforced by the government with various levels of intensity. Both the law on affirmative action and the government's willingness to enforce it have undergone many changes since passage of the Civil Rights Act and the proclamation of Lyndon Johnson's Executive Order 11246. Because affirmative action programs are only as effective as the willingness of the courts and political leaders to enforce them, we will examine the current rules of affirmative action by reviewing important legal cases. We will also examine the political climate surrounding the various presidents who have held office since 1965. Their willingness to enforce affirmative action policies has often been determined by political factors, such as public opinion, which waxes and wanes with such matters as the current state of the economy.

Beginning in the late sixties and early seventies, under the direction of then-President Richard Nixon, the Department of Labor began rigorously enforcing its requirement that all federal contractors establish an affirmative action plan as a condition for receiving federal contracts. Acceptable plans included an evaluation of any current "underutilization" of women and minorities in the contract or workforce. Such groups were considered underutilized if their numbers were fewer than might reasonably be expected by their availability. For example, a construction company building a highway through a major urban area where many minorities lived would be expected to hire a proportion of its workers from the community, even to the point of having its workforce reflect the racial profile of the geographical area.

Under the Nixon administration, minorities who had been for all practical purposes excluded from the construction trades were now allowed in by law. Construction companies were instructed to set goals for hiring, a policy that required them to show a good faith effort to recruit minorities and women. If it could be proven that a company had been guilty of deliberately unfair discrimination in the past, a specific hiring quota could be imposed on it, one that required the company to set aside a certain number of positions for women and minorities. In some cases, a specified number of minorities and women had to be hired for every white male employed by the company until the agreed-on quotas were met. Soon affirmative action plans were required of all companies doing more than $50,000 worth of business with the government each year. Because most educational institutions receive more than that in government funding, colleges and universities also were required to recruit more women and minority students, as well as hire and promote more women and minority professors.

Before long, affirmative action plans were in place everywhere. Nearly all corporations and educational institutions, as well as state and local governments and trade unions, whether by choice or by coercion, had affirmative action plans. For some, such plans were simply incentives to increase their recruitment efforts, to be sure to include highly qualified women and minorities as candidates for their available positions. Institutions were required, in other words, to take "affirmative action" to ensure that they practiced equal opportunity for all. In other cases, however, affirmative action programs necessitated preferential treatment. They required the acceptance of candidates who were not as well qualified as their competitors, at least according to the listed qualifications for the position. In the early to mid-seventies, when such preferential treatment programs were rigorously enforced, there was a great deal of race and gender consciousness in hiring and education, and a great sense of injustice among many of the rejected, "more-qualified" candidates.

People seeking positions in local fire and police departments were angry, for example, when they met the physical requirements and scored higher on the required tests than the applicants selected but were nevertheless not hired because they were not minorities or women. The same sense of injustice was felt by many who were refused admission to the college, university, or professional school of their choice, or refused a teaching position on the elementary, secondary, or college level, or refused a job in the local phone company, or refused a construction job, and so on—even though all these people were more qualified than the woman or minority applicant whose candidacy had been successful. The pressure exerted by the government on companies to comply with affirmative action plans made hiring extremely race conscious during this period. Some companies were especially interested in women who were minorities, for example, since such a person could count as two affirmative action hires.

The initial gains of affirmative action programs were considerable for women. Almost immediately the number of women accepted to law schools and medical schools increased dramatically. Other educational institutions and areas of employment from which women had previously been excluded also became available to them. For minorities as well, the initial gains were considerable. For African-American and Hispanic-American males, employment as teachers, firemen, police officers, and members of trade unions became a reality. In education, helped by generous financial aid packages, relaxed admission criteria, and aggressive retention programs, minorities flocked to colleges once closed to them, and did so at nearly the same rate as their white male counterparts.

In addition, the future of affirmative action looked rosy when the Supreme Court declared that various versions of preferential treatment programs were indeed constitutional. The first case it considered was *Regents of the University of California v. Bakke* in 1978. A white male, Alan Bakke, sued the University of California because it denied him admission to the medical school at Davis, even though he was more qualified than some of the minority candidates who were admitted. At the time, Davis set aside a certain number of places for minority candidates, who were judged by different standards from those used for the other candidates. As a result of *Bakke,* the Court struck down the use of quotas in educational institutions. No longer could a college or professional school set aside a certain number of seats for minority candidates, candidates who would be accepted according to separate, and usually lower standards of admission. However, schools were allowed to use goals in recruitment and they were allowed to use race as one qualification in the name of building a diverse student body.

Affirmative action programs in education from then on took the form of rigorously recruiting qualified minorities and women, and then judging them by the same standards as everyone else. Just as being from a different geographical area, or being an athlete, or having a variety of life experiences might count as a "qual-ification," so being a minority student also counted. In the name of building a diverse class, race and gender could be considered as part of an applicant's qual-ifications. The Court's decision to eliminate quotas in education was seen by many in the civil rights movement as a setback. However, as race could be con-sidered as a qualification, others saw little difference in practice between quotas and goals. If race counted as one qualification among others, then a candidate who was less qualified according to all previously used criteria might still be admitted because he or she had the added qualification of being a member of a certain race.

If *Bakke* defined the sorts of preferences that were legal in education, *United Steel Workers v. Weber* (1978) defined what was to be considered legal in business. Brian Weber worked in a chemical plant for the Kaiser Company in Louisiana. He sued when he was passed over for a promotion in favor of a less-qualified minor-ity candidate, who was promoted to fill a quota imposed on the company by the EEOC. The quota was in place because the EEOC had found a pattern of discrim-ination against minorities in Kaiser's hiring and promotion policies. As a result of *Weber,* the Court ruled that using quotas was acceptable if past deliberate dis-crimination by a company could be proven. Moreover, voluntary quota plans by a particular company to increase its minority workforce were also allowed, though not required in the absence of such proof.

In the late seventies, despite the deep entrenchment of the increasingly suc-cessful programs of affirmative action, a change in the political climate led to a turnabout by Nixon. Many thought that his administration rigorously imposed and enforced affirmative action plans to gain the black vote. However, the "white backlash" to these programs, the angry reaction of white males who perceived themselves to be losing jobs to less-qualified women and minorities, threatened to drive away more supporters than he might gain. During his last two years in office Nixon was hostile to the very preferential treatment programs he had helped to establish, as well as to many other initiatives associated with the civil rights movement.

When Ronald Reagan took office in 1981, he continued to undermine the effec-tiveness of affirmative action programs, especially those involving preferences. For example, he appointed Clarence Thomas to run the EEOC. Thomas, now a very conservative Supreme Court justice, was openly critical of preferential treat-ment. He also reduced its funding, thereby further reducing its availability. In addition, Reagan appointed several conservative justices to the Supreme Court. This led to an important ruling in *Wards Cove v. Atonio* (1989), in which the Court reversed the burden of proof requirement in discrimination cases. Formerly, an individual who believed that he or she had been discriminated against in employ-ment or education could bring suit and require the defendant to prove that such discrimination had not occurred. Now, the litigant had to prove discrimination against what was often a large organization with far greater resources than the individual had. Many litigants could simply not afford the legal fight, thus end-ing in practice their legal redress.

Although less openly hostile, Reagan's successor, George Bush, continued to oppose the aggressive implementation of preference programs. In particular, he vetoed the 1990 Civil Rights Act designed to mitigate the effect of the Court's ruling in *Wards Cove*. This time the political winds blew unfavorably, however, and public opinion forced Bush to change his stand and to support the new Civil Rights Act of 1991. This act restored some of the rights of those who sought punitive damages in the courts for acts of discrimination, thereby reversing at least part of the effect of *Wards Cove*.

With the election of Bill Clinton in 1992, supporters of affirmative action had reason to hope that its goals would once again be pursued rigorously. However, Clinton was opposed by a conservative Supreme Court as well as a Congress with a decidedly conservative Republican majority. The Court, in *Adarand Constructors, Inc. v. Pena*, further restricted the use of quotas in business. No longer would the Court simply accept statistics showing that minorities and women were underrepresented as proof of past discrimination. Now it required elaborate and expensive studies to prove that quotas were necessary to undo past discrimination. For all practical purposes, this decision eliminated the use of quotas as part of acceptable affirmative action plans. Only because of Clinton's courageous and clever defense of other preferential treatment programs, such as the acceptability of establishing goals in business, did Congress fail to eliminate preferential treatment programs altogether.

The next assault on affirmative action came not from the federal government but from individual states. California was first. In 1995 the massive University of California system ended racial preferences in admissions. Once implemented in education, this policy resulted in an immediate and very significant decline in the number of minority students at both the graduate and undergraduate levels. Berkeley, once a model of diversity, was especially hard hit. Then in 1996, under the leadership of Governor Pete Wilson, California passed by referendum Proposition 209. This measure ended affirmative action in government hiring practices. In the same year, Texas followed California in education, ending racial preferences in admissions at the University of Texas. Minority enrollments plummeted. Even though then-governor George W. Bush introduced a policy allowing the top 10 percent of high school graduates automatic admission to the University of Texas system, minority enrollments still remained low. Despite the negative impact on minority representation in higher education, some states such as Washington have already followed the lead of California and Texas, with many others expected to do so.

Assumptions

It is now time to recognize and question some of the ***assumptions*** about social justice that we and others have made to this point.

First, so far we have simply assumed that "equal opportunity" and not "equality of result" is important in a just society. However, a respectable argument might be made that a truly just society would not condone the great differences in wealth that mere equal opportunity allows. Instead, society's goods should be shared much more equitably. There should be no rich and poor; instead there should be economic equality. According to this model, the economy of a just society would be structured more as it is, for example, in a religious group. If you are a Trappist monk, you and your fellow monks all work hard and share equally in the fruits of your combined labors. Each person contributes what he can, and each person's needs are met. Any profits from the sale of goods that might be left over after meeting the basic needs of all are invested in things valued by the entire community.

To achieve this level of equality in the United States would require us to abandon our economic system, capitalism, and replace it with a socialist economy. In a capitalist economy there is private ownership of what Karl Marx called the "means of production." The factories, farms, and various sorts of businesses that produce goods and services may be privately owned. Successful businesses are those that meet the demands of their customers, and they often produce great wealth for their owners and managers. In a socialist economy, on the other hand, the government owns and manages the means of production, and the government plans and distributes the goods produced by them. In effect, everyone works for the government.

This level of control by a socialist government may ensure greater economic equality among its citizens, but the inevitable inefficiency that results from such a system has led to much lower standards of living in most socialist countries. Simply put, the argument against abandoning capitalism is that socialist economies have been dismal failures, as witnessed by the economic collapse of the former Soviet Union. A socialist society may have economic equality, but only because everyone's standard of living is low. Because of this we will continue to hold the assumption that equal opportunity, not equality of result is the goal of social justice. Capitalism may produce great inequalities of wealth, but it allows for a more affluent society overall; therefore even the poor are better off. Besides, in a society where there is true economic equality, everyone has an equal chance to be wealthy.

This brings us to our *second* assumption, that in fact everyone can have an equal opportunity to participate fully in the economic life of this country. It seems quite obvious that true equality of opportunity is not possible as things now stand. Those born with privilege have a much better chance of economic success than those born under various sorts of disadvantages. In a just society, we ought to do something to eliminate these disadvantages. We can do little about some of them, especially those caused by nature. For people born with significantly less cognitive ability than others, for example, little can be done to even out their chances for jobs that require a high intelligence. Other types of disadvantages, however, can and should be addressed in a just society. A single mother with three children and few marketable skills has less than an equal opportunity to succeed. This is why, in a just society, welfare assistance is required to meet her subsistence needs and those of her children. Once met, they all then have a chance to work hard and succeed.

Perhaps their chances are not equal to those born of privilege, those whose families are wealthy and influential. Perhaps welfare programs should do more to even out these differences by granting greater benefits to its recipients. To redistribute greater benefits to the poor, however, would weaken their desire to work, weaken the desire to do better than welfare assistance allows. More people would take advantage of welfare programs, requiring greater redistribution of income from the rich and middle class to the poor. This, in turn, would weaken the economy and in the long run everyone would be worse off, even the poor. So equal opportunity for all does not and should not mean the *same* opportunity for all. At best it means that everyone has a *fair* chance to achieve some level of economic success, when "fair" means that no obstacles, such as unfair discrimination, will be placed in the way. Perhaps for the disadvantaged of today, more than one generation will be needed for these disadvantaged individuals to have a chance to accomplish the same economic goals that those of privilege now enjoy.

Our *third* assumption is that in a just society, the disadvantages of *groups* of people, especially groups belonging to a particular race, ethnic group, or gender, are what affirmative action should eliminate. At first glance this seems right. After all, affirmative action was introduced originally to eliminate the legacy of two hundred fifty years of slavery. The cycle of poverty, poor education, crime, and hopelessness that had been passed on from African slaves to their African-American heirs, a cycle that had been encouraged by the exclusionary practices of a predominantly white society, had been a burden borne by a group. Similar remarks may be made about present day Native Americans, whose ancestors suffered greatly at the hands of those who opened this country to European immigrants. As a group, their legacy has also been poverty and its associated evils.

Hispanic Americans as a group also constitute a lower socioeconomic class, though their disadvantages are due more to the exclusionary policies of society than to their past mistreatment. The disadvantages bequeathed to women were also the result of being excluded from most of the powerful and influential jobs and educational opportunities. Even though their disadvantages were not always those associated with poverty, the subordination of women in general to the status of second-class citizens excluded them from full participation in the economic life of this country. Because it is groups such as these that have been discriminated against in the past, and because the results of this discrimination have continued into the present, it seems to be a warranted assumption that affirmative action programs ought to be directed to the undoing of injustices done to groups of people, especially those people who are classified as disadvantaged because of their race or sex.

Those who question this assumption, however, argue that the true disadvantages are those of *class,* not race or gender. Belonging to the lower socioeconomic class, not belonging to a particular race or gender, is what causes disadvantages. Those who are poor and not well educated, those who have not been taught a serious work ethic and who do not possess any marketable skills have less than an equal opportunity for economic success. Whereas many in the lower class may be those currently targeted for affirmative action, some are not. There are many poor and disadvantaged whites, for example, as well as many Asian and Latin American immigrants whose struggle out of poverty is enormously challenging. On the other hand, there are many members of current affirmative action groups who belong to the middle and upper classes, people who may still suffer some of the disadvantages that previously have been associated with their race or gender, but who seem to need little help from affirmative action programs to achieve economic success.

For those who question our third assumption, the target of affirmative action should be class, not race or gender. This is where the true disadvantages are to be found, this is where equal opportunity is scarce and must be given a boost. This is where the arrow of social justice should be aimed to ensure that those who really need extra help to participate fully in life get that help. According to this view, a truly just society would be blind to differences of gender and color and would instead help all those who were truly in need to raise themselves out of poverty, to prepare themselves to compete in the economic race, and finally to enjoy the fruits of their labors. Later in this chapter we will examine the considerable merits of this attack on our third assumption.

The *fourth* assumption is that qualifications, not preference, should determine who gets the jobs and educational opportunities. One of the persistent objections to preferential treatment programs is that they change the rules whereby the goods of society are distributed, especially its jobs and educational opportunities. The "old" rules gave out these goods on the basis of *merit*. Those with the highest qualifications deserved, or merited, these goods. According to our fourth assumption, preferential treatment programs are unfair because they distribute these goods at least partly on the basis of the irrelevant characteristics of gender or race. Even those who favor such programs agree that they are only temporary. Once they have done their job we will return as a nation to the use of merit.

Those who question the use of merit point out that it is neither the only method of distribution, nor is it necessarily the fairest. People born of privilege, for example, either because they have more talent or more wealth than others, have an easier time becoming qualified than those who are disadvantaged. What they achieve comes to them with less of a struggle. Perhaps we could use *effort* as a fairer rule of distribution—those who work the hardest get the jobs. However, hard work does not always produce good results. I, for one, do not want my brain surgeon to be a hard working but incompetent fellow. Perhaps we could use *need* as a rule—those who need the jobs most get them. Once again, however, the most needy are not always in the best position to perform the most effectively. Or maybe the fairest way is to use some sort of *random selection* procedure, a lottery of some sort. For example, we could have a nationwide lottery that matches Social Security numbers with available jobs and educational opportunities. This would surely be fair, but would it be efficient and effective? Would you want your lawyer or doctor to be selected by chance?

If we consider the efficiency and the effectiveness of a rule of distribution—as well as its fairness—then our fourth assumption, that merit should be the rule for distributing the goods of society, appears to be correct. However, to use this rule fairly at least two points need to be addressed. *First,* the disadvantages suffered by many, through no fault of their own, must be addressed if they are to have a fair chance to become competitive. Equal opportunity is possible under a merit system of distribution only if everyone has a chance to become qualified. At the very minimum, some form of special remediation may be required to eliminate the disadvantages faced by some to achieve such merit. Without making up for these disadvantages, merit will never succeed as an effective pathway to economic justice.

The *second* requirement for the fair use of merit is that the qualifications for various jobs and admission to educational institutions must themselves be fair. In particular, qualifications for various positions should not favor one group over another. Instead, they should be a measure of the likelihood of success in the position. People have argued, for example, that SAT tests should not be used as the major measure of merit for admission to college. They claim that these tests are not a neutral indicator of intelligence, but that they are culturally biased to favor white middle-class applicants. Just as important in predicting future success may be the degree to which an applicant has overcome disadvantages to achieve the level of success that he or she has already achieved.

The qualifications that have been established for many jobs may also be poor predictors of job performance. Written exams for positions in police or fire departments, for example, may not be the best measures of merit. Instead, physical strength, raw intelligence, and ability to interact successfully with the community may be better indicators of how a person will do. The general idea is that merit should be measured in ways that are relevant to the needs of the position under consideration. Without revised qualifications, a merit-based system of distribution will not be fair. In the face of an unfair system of merit, affirmative action and especially its preferential treatment versions seem to be the only alternative to ensure social justice.

The *fifth* and final assumption that will be considered is that the disadvantages suffered by minorities and women are indeed the result of unfair discrimination. Those who question this assumption argue that the underrepresentation of minorities and women, especially in the professions and in colleges and universities, is really the result of something else. They make such claims as "women just cannot learn mathematics," or "African Americans cannot think abstractly," or "Latinos are lazy," and so on. Such claims, that minorities and women are genetically or culturally inferior, are easily dismissed by anecdotal evidence. Brief discussions with female mathematicians, African-American philosophers, or Latino CEOs will quickly dispel these myths.

Some dismiss such anecdotal evidence and point out that some of these statements are statistically true, that they are true of "most" members of the group. For example, Richard Herrnstein and Charles Murray argue in their controversial book, *The Bell Curve: Intelligence and Class Structure in American Life*,[2] that African Americans are less intelligent than whites, as measured by standard IQ tests, and that this fact, not discrimination, is the primary reason for their economic underachievement. This book has met with harsh criticism from many who claim a cultural bias in the testing methods used by the authors. Such critics may point to the work done by former Harvard University president, Derek Bok and former Princeton University president William Bowen. They argue convincingly in *The Shape of the River: Long-Term Consequences of Considering Race in College and University Admissions*,[3] that when given the necessary support, African-American college graduates have careers that are as successful for themselves and society as do their white counterparts. Their poor academic preparation is what accounts primarily for their lack of success, not genetic differences. In the light of this evidence, and until proven otherwise, we will continue to assume that people of all races, ethnic groups, and genders can learn and can compete successfully, once the obstacles placed in their paths to success have been removed.

Points of View

The ***point of view*** that you bring to this discussion will depend, as always, on your own life experiences. You may have had no personal experience with affirmative action, but most of us have heard stories that affect our thinking. In the "Another Perspective" section at the end of this chapter are several stories about the personal experiences of various people, some of whom consider themselves victims of affirmative action whereas others think of themselves as beneficiaries. In addition, we present perspectives of people who manage affirmative action programs, people who are responsible for applying them in the real world.

Moral Reasoning

The problem before us in this chapter—*Should less qualified candidates be selected for jobs and educational opportunities on the basis of their race or gender in order to promote equal opportunity for all?*—is best thought of as a **conflict of rules** problem. The rule, "Promote equal opportunity for all" describes an obligation borne by the government of any society that champions social justice. To use preferential treatment programs as a means to this noble end, however, seems to clash with another rule that says "Do not practice unfair discrimination." Conflict of rules problems are solved by discovering which rule has the highest priority. This is to be determined by discovering which rule, if followed at the expense of the other, will promote more beneficence, justice, and autonomy.

Those who oppose preferential treatment in the arguments to follow will argue especially that such programs violate the second rule mentioned above, and thus violate the principle of justice. They will claim that while the goal of equal opportunity is a social good, and thus conforms to the principle of beneficence, it must be achieved in a way that does not create discrimination against more qualified candidates. Those who favor preferential treatment will stress the importance of the goal of equal opportunity and claim that preferential treatment is the only effective way to bring it about. Additionally, they will appeal to various ways to persuade you that the so-called injustices of affirmative action are either nonexistent or warranted as a means to eliminate much greater injustices. The minor injustices of preferential treatment programs are not so great as to constitute excessive sacrifices on behalf of the good of society in general.

The Case against Affirmative Action

We will begin with the case against affirmative action, remembering always that we are talking about its preferential treatment programs only. The claim of our first possible solution, called **reverse discrimination,** is that affirmative action is immoral. It is immoral because it is a form of unfair discrimination. Whereas discrimination against women and racial minorities is immoral, so also are the affirmative action programs that aim to bring it to an end. These programs are themselves forms of unfair discrimination, only now discrimination "in reverse." They discriminate (usually) against white males. The discrimination takes the form of bypassing candidates who are more qualified in favor of those who are less qualified, but who happen to be of a particular gender or race. Despite the fact that all this is done for a good cause—creating a society in which everyone has an equal opportunity—the more qualified candidates who are rejected are being used against their will as a means to this good.

We have seen in Part I that the principle of justice prohibits us from using people merely as a means to effect the good of others. Doing so violates the "respect for persons" meaning of justice, the meaning that prohibits us, for example, from using old, senile persons as research subjects without their consent, or from deliberately damaging the brains of death row inmates to see how such damage affects their behavior, or from examining how a fetus about to be aborted reacts to a dangerous drug. Although great good for others may come from these sorts of actions and millions of other people may benefit from them, they are nevertheless extremely immoral. They are immoral because they treat people as things; they use some people merely as a means to promote the good of others.

Deep at its core, affirmative action does the same thing—it uses people against their will to achieve social change. Even though the unfairness of affirmative action may not be as great as the past unfair discrimination practiced against women and minorities, and even though it may be minor compared to the types of actions mentioned in the previous paragraph, it is still a violation of one of our most fundamental moral principles. True, we may achieve a worthwhile goal through the use of affirmative action programs, the goal of a truly equal opportunity society, but to build a fairer society on the back of such unfair acts is just as immoral as using the old, the helpless, and the vulnerable to gain new scientific knowledge that will benefit millions of others.

To see the unfairness of affirmative action more clearly, imagine for a moment that the government announced that for at least the next twenty years it would be *dentists* who would be responsible for fighting our wars. Whatever their gender or age, dentists and dentists alone were going to be required to give up their careers and become the soldiers who stand on the front lines and risk their lives for the rest of us. Ignoring the fact that the number of applications to dental school would quickly become zero, the point is that such a suggestion is absurd. It is absurd not just because a military force of dentists might not be the most efficient, but also because it is so obviously unfair. What possible reason could there be to place the responsibility of defending our country solely on the backs of dentists? In the same vein, what possible reason could there be to make white males, especially younger, less wealthy white males, sacrifice their own plans to shoulder the responsibility of creating a just society? As Lisa Newton says:[4]

> All discrimination is wrong prima facie because it violates justice, and that goes for reverse discrimination too. No violation of justice among the citizens may be justified (may overcome the prima facie objection) by appeal to the ideal of equality, for that ideal is logically dependent upon the notion of justice. Reverse discrimination, then, which attempts no other justification than an appeal to equality, is wrong.

Echoing these beliefs, Justice Clarence Thomas wrote:[5]

Under our Constitution, the government may not make distinctions on the basis of race. As far as the Constitution is concerned, it is irrelevant whether a government's racial classifications are drawn by those who wish to oppress a race or by those who have a sincere desire to help those thought to be disadvantaged. There can be no doubt that the paternalism that appears to lie at the heart of this program is at war with the principle of inherent equality that underlies and infuses our Constitution.

And so we write the first premise in our good reasons argument against affirmative action:

1. Affirmative action is a form of unfair discrimination. (J)

If the first part of the case against affirmative action demonstrates that it violates the principle of justice, the second part attempts to show that it violates the principle of beneficence. It does this by failing to achieve the promised social good of equal opportunity for all. In fact, over three decades of affirmative action not only has not attained this goal, but it has actually made things much worse for society in general, as well as for various groups within society and for the many individuals who have become its victims.

For example, admissions and hiring policies based on preferences have made us more race conscious as a nation, not less, at least according to one writer.[6]

There is no "majority" in America who will not mind giving up just a bit of their rights to make room for a favored minority. There are only other minorities, each of which is discriminated against by the favoring. The initial injustice is then repeated dozens of times, and if each minority is granted the same right of restitution as the others, an entire area of rule governance is dissolved into a pushing and shoving match between self-interested groups. . . . Hardly an edifying spectacle, and in the long run no one can benefit: The pie is no larger—it's just that instead of setting up and enforcing rules for getting a piece, we've turned the contest into a free-for-all, requiring much more effort for no larger a reward. It would be in the interest of all the participants to reestablish an objective rule to govern the process, carefully enforced and the same for all.

For example, various ethnic groups are now protesting that the affirmative action groups currently recognized by U.S. medical schools—African Americans, Native Americans, Mexican Americans, and mainland Puerto Ricans—omit some other disadvantaged groups. Cambodians, Vietnamese, Filipinos, as well as Colombians, Haitians, Dominicans, among others, are even more underrepresented in medicine than the recognized groups. Because of this, the newer immigrant groups argue that they, too, should receive the benefits of affirmative action admission policies.

Preference programs have also harmed society by lowering the standards of performance in many jobs. This, of course, is to be expected if those with lower qualifications are hired over more qualified candidates. Louis Pojman says:[7]

Government programs of enforced preferential treatment tend to appeal to the lowest possible common denominator. Witness the 1974 HEW Revised Order

No. 14 on Affirmative Action expectations for preferential hiring: "Neither minorities nor female employees should be required to possess higher qualifications than those of the lowest possible incumbent." . . . Affirmative action with its twin idols Sufficiency and Diversity, is the enemy of excellence.

Similar remarks apply to educational institutions, claims Pojman.

> At several universities, the administration has forced departments to hire members of minorities even when far superior candidates were available. Shortly after obtaining my Ph.D. in the late 70s I was mistakenly identified as a black philosopher (I had a civil rights record and was once a black studies major) and was flown to a major university, only to be rejected for a more qualified candidate when it [was] discovered that I was white.

In addition to harming society in general, affirmative action harms the very groups within society that it intends to help. According to Justice Clarence Thomas,[8]

> There can be no doubt that racial paternalism and its unintended consequences can be as poisonous and pernicious as any other form of discrimination. So-called "benign" discrimination teaches many that because of chronic and apparently immutable handicaps, minorities cannot compete with them without their patronizing indulgence. Inevitably, such programs engender attitudes of superiority or, alternatively, provoke resentment among those who believe that they have been wronged by the government's use of race. These programs stamp minorities with a badge of inferiority and may cause them to develop dependencies or to adopt an attitude that they are entitled to preferences.

Very often minorities and women are the ones who oppose affirmative action for these very reasons. Many black professionals are opposed to affirmative action because others believe that their achievements have come only because of affirmative action. Minorities who have become successful don't want society to think they "made it" only because of their gender or race. To be stigmatized in this way promotes unjustified feelings of superiority in others, feelings that are often expressed in very subtle and painful ways. Young black and Hispanic college students also suffer from the negative attitudes created by preferential treatment. No matter how bright and industrious they happen to be, they still fear that others will think their success is the result of affirmative action alone.

Successful women are often opposed to affirmative action for similar reasons. Women as a group have benefited most from affirmative action, especially early on when they took advantage of their new access to jobs and educational institutions from which they previously had been all but excluded. Today, some in society still think affirmative action is necessary if women are to gain access to the top corporate and academic positions, as these positions are still predominantly controlled by men. However, many women do not believe that preference is required for them to achieve such success. Instead, they believe they can make it on their own.[9]

> A careful reading of the Glass Ceiling Commission's own statistics suggests that in almost every segment of the working world, the combination of equal opportunity and hard work have led to steady, impressive gains for women. In 1992, women held 23 percent of corporate senior vice-president positions versus 14 percent in 1982; the percentage of all female vice-presidents more than doubled in the same

period. From 1979 to 1993, women's wages increased by a whopping 119 percent. Meanwhile, the percentage of male managers fell from 65 percent to 51 percent. Yet . . . none of these positive employment trends can be definitively traced to affirmative action. . . . [W]omen's successes in the workplace are due not to social engineering, but to women's perseverance and merit which they demonstrate when given a fair chance to compete.

It is also interesting to note that the majority of women who voted in California voted *for* Proposition 209.

Many minorities and women believe that it would be far better to eliminate all forms of preferential treatment and to maintain only those affirmative action programs that focus both on the recruitment of qualified women and minorities and on the enforcement of the antidiscrimination laws already on the books. Shelby Steele, for example, says:[10]

> I think that much of the subtle discrimination that blacks talk about is often (not always) discrimination against the stigma of questionable competence that affirmative action delivers to blacks. In this sense, preferences scapegoat the very people they seek to help. . . . I would like to see affirmative action go back to its original purpose of enforcing equal opportunity—a purpose that in itself disallows racial preferences. . . . It can guard constitutional rather than racial rights, and help institutions evolve standards of merit and selection that are appropriate.

Finally, affirmative action harms those individuals who are more qualified but are rejected for jobs or admission to educational institutions because of affirmative action. Not everyone so rejected could easily find another position or another college or university that was as good as the one lost. In fact, especially in the seventies when the economy was poor and jobs were scarce, some of the candidates rejected for jobs had a hard time finding any suitable employment. Talented students who had worked hard and achieved success were refused admission to some colleges or refused financial aid because these goods were going to less-qualified minorities. People who worked hard to meet the qualifying standards for employment by police and fire departments were rejected because they were white, even though their qualifications were superior to those of some minorities who were accepted ahead of them. Unqualified minority teachers were hired in public school systems while eager and qualified white applicants were passed over. Corporations hired and promoted less-qualified people to fill quotas, blocking the career opportunities of many more-qualified white candidates. No wonder a white "backlash" to affirmative action programs grew very powerful in the late seventies and persisted through the eighties, heavily influencing government policies.[11]

> Thousands of whites have indeed been passed over for civil service jobs and university admissions because of outright quotas for racial minorities. [Also], a considerable number of private businesses have been denied government contracts because of minority set-asides. . . . The revolt against affirmative action has . . . been heavily influenced by the fact that, as preferential policies have extended throughout the economy, a critical mass of real or perceived victims of reverse discrimination has been reached—white males who have been denied jobs, rejected for promotion, or prevented from attending the college or professional school of their choice because slots were reserved for blacks(or other minorities or women).

Referring to the types of harms described in the previous two or three pages, our second and final premise in the argument against affirmative action says:

2. Affirmative action causes social and individual harms. (B)

As usual, we will continue this argument later in the chapter by replying to objections.

The "Compensatory Justice" Case for Affirmative Action

Among those who argue for the moral acceptability of the use of preferences, some claim that they are required as compensation for past injustices; others argue that they are necessary to achieve social justice today. The former type of argument is called the **compensatory justice** argument, and it will be examined first.

Although this argument was especially popular in the late sixties early seventies, a time when most of the controversial affirmative action efforts were directed toward improving the lot of African Americans, it may be applied to women and other minorities as well. As originally stated, its most important premise is that the great injustice of slavery has to be paid for. The injustice of slavery, of using people for the good of others, with all its attendant horrors, was an evil whose scope is barely imaginable today. If the wrongs of the past are to be righted, there must be compensation for the suffering, pain, misery, and death caused by whites and borne by slaves. The debt must be paid. But how is it to be paid, and by whom? Most important, to whom is it to be paid?

Some early proponents of this argument suggested that cash payments be made by the government to all living African Americans. As descendants of slaves, they are their rightful heirs. Although the cash payment notion was never taken very seriously, the idea was accepted by many that the past sins of whites against blacks could be compensated for now by whites as a group making some other sort of payment to blacks as a group. The payment of choice took the form of preferential treatment in jobs and educational opportunities. As the first premise of the "reverse discrimination" argument says, this compensation itself requires an injustice. After all, the brunt of such payments was to be borne by whites whose candidacies were rejected even though they were more qualified than the selected candidates.

Defenders of the compensation argument are not moved by the burden of this injustice, however. It is extremely minor by comparison to the great injustice of slavery. Moreover, it is temporary, as is the whole program of affirmative action. It needs to be in place only long enough to include groups previously excluded from the mainstream economic life of the country. Besides, most rejected white males can find other jobs and colleges. Their burden is so slight that it may be rightfully accepted as a requirement of compensatory justice. The first premise of the compensation argument for affirmative action says:

1.' Affirmative action compensates for past injustices. (J)

Usually there is a second premise added by those who defend affirmative action as a form of compensation. The second premise points to the benefits of affirmative action, especially the social benefits of equal opportunity for all. It asserts that affirmative action has benefited women and minorities since its inception, and that its continuation is necessary to achieve equal opportunity in all areas of economic life. Because this premise will also be used in the next argument, we will simply state it here, deferring its closer examination until we see it again.

2.' Affirmative action is necessary to achieve equal opportunity for all. (B)

The "Present Injustice" Case for Affirmative Action

The compensatory justice argument sees affirmative action primarily as a way to pay for past wrongs; the **present injustice** argument sees it as way to eliminate present injustices. The two arguments are not necessarily opposed to one another. They both defend affirmative action as morally acceptable, and they both see current injustices as largely a result of past injustices. However, those who defend affirmative action as a remedy for the continuing injustice of sexism and racism usually reject (1)' as misguided. Current injustices may have stemmed from those of the past, but there is no way to compensate now for the sins of the past. Their perpetrators are long gone and forever remain beyond human justice.

While rejecting (1)', however, they accept (2)' and focus on affirmative action as a necessary way to open the doors of educational and economic inclusion that are still shut to many. The argument first demonstrates that affirmative action has been effective in many areas, and then attempts to show that continuing affirmative action is the only effective means to eliminate those areas in which discrimination in jobs and education persists. Let us begin by examining the evidence for the success of affirmative action.

One thing is crystal clear. Affirmative action has helped *women,* and helped them perhaps more than any other affirmative action group. For example, thirty years ago women were effectively excluded from many colleges as well as from medical schools, law schools, and business schools. Today, women earn more than half the undergraduate degrees and half the master's degrees. In addition, the number of women graduates from professional schools is approaching equality with men. On every level of employment, when affirmative action plans were in place and enforced, women also made significant progress. In large corporations, financial institutions, police and fire departments, college and university faculties and administration, construction trades, and business ownership, the number of women participating in the workforce has increased dramatically. For the most part, this progress was accomplished without preferential treatment. Women were qualified; they just needed affirmative action to break down the barriers that had excluded them previously from full participation in the American economy. Affirmative action has worked so well for women that it is inconceivable to most college-age women today that they will be excluded from any position for which they are qualified. To cite just one example, businesses owned by women now employ more people than all the Fortune 500 companies combined and these are the nation's largest companies.

Affirmative action has also benefited minorities. African-American enrollment in college, for example, rose dramatically under its umbrella. In 1965 less than

5 percent of college students were African Americans. By 1980 it was over 9 percent, and by 1990 it was over 11 percent. Because African Americans as a group constitute a little over 12 percent of the population, their college enrollment numbers by percentage were close to those of white males. As with women, affirmative action opened up a wider choice of employment opportunities as well. From the early 1900s until the 1960s, wages earned by minorities in unskilled positions were about 60 percent of those earned by their white male counterparts. Poorer educational backgrounds and less relevant work experience may have accounted for about half this difference, but discrimination accounted for the other half. As a result of improved education and affirmative action hiring policies, by 1993 African Americans earned 75 percent of what white males earned. Professional positions also became available to educated African Americans through affirmative action initiatives. Many more members of minority groups became doctors, lawyers, college professors, and business owners, and a new African-American middle class was formed.

Similar remarks apply to other minorities. For example, as we have seen above, U.S. medical schools use affirmative action plans in the recruitment and retention of minorities. Such plans focus on four groups of minorities—African Americans, Native Americans, Mexican Americans, and mainland Puerto Ricans. Although some of the newer immigrant groups object to these limitations, the point is that affirmative action works. Collectively, minorities make up about 25 percent of the general population. As a result of affirmative action plans, the enrollment in some medical schools now reflects this proportion. In the year 2000, for example, the entering class of Harvard Medical School contained 25 percent minority students. It should now be clear that

1." Affirmative action has benefited women and minorities. (B)

The benefits of affirmative action have been considerable; however, much remains to be done to achieve the goal of equal opportunity for all. For example, although educational and employment opportunities have become widely available for women, there is still a great deal of disparity between men and women at the higher levels of education and employment. Less than 3 percent of the 2500 senior managers of Fortune 500 companies are women. Women run only three of these companies, as was the case more than twenty years ago. Only about 10 percent of the members of the U.S. Congress are women. Women still remain predominantly in traditional female jobs, as waitresses, administrative assistants, teachers, and nurses. They are less than 10 percent of all engineers and less than a quarter of all doctors and lawyers. Among those who are lawyers, less than 15 percent are partners in law firms. Women earn only a quarter of the doctoral degrees in math and science and hold dramatically fewer tenured faculty positions than men.

Women also earn less than men, even when they have similar qualifications and perform similar jobs. By some estimates women earn on average about 75 cents for every dollar earned by their male counterparts. In addition, the responsibilities of raising a family and maintaining a home still rest primarily in the hands of women, presenting them with obstacles for advancement not borne by most men. Minority women have an even worse lot. They are only about

15 percent of the undergraduate students in this country and less than 10 percent of the graduate students. They earn even less than white women, and much less than men.

> In survey after survey, a majority of women of all ages tell researchers they believe the country has not done enough to afford equality toward women. Asked if they think the workplace has changed dramatically, women are far more likely than men to say no, and that greater change is needed. Of course, they are right.[12]

If further efforts are required to ensure equal opportunity for women, even greater efforts are required to ensure it for minorities. The largest minority groups, African Americans and Latinos, together comprise 25 percent of the workforce, but they make up less than 10 percent of all the doctors, lawyers, and professors, less than 5 percent of all the scientists, engineers, and architects, and receive only 2 percent of all the doctorates in science. Unless you assume that nonwhite minorities are intellectually inferior to whites, or that there are cultural factors that prevent them from learning—assumptions that were previously rejected—the only way to understand the underrepresentation of minorities in the professions is to see it as a product of past and present discrimination. The Supreme Court may no longer see underrepresentation alone as a sign of discrimination, but surely it is currently the best hypothesis available.

As long as racism and gender bias are still with us, there is a need for affirmative action. Arguably, the most dangerous forms of discrimination come in subtle guises, often invisible even to those who practice them. Most people still prefer to work and to be educated with people like themselves. With the majority of the influential and powerful positions in society still firmly in the control of white males, this means that women and minorities will not be judged according to the same rules. Even among professionals there are often psychological obstacles to hiring minorities. For example, the respected University of Florida Law School has been accused by one of its associate deans of refusing to hire qualified black professors. He claimed that the "reason (not to hire black professors) is fear. . . . If we hire people who are like ourselves, that tells us we are good people and we deserve our jobs."[13] The associate dean resigned from his administrative position in protest. He is currently the only black professor among fifty teaching in the law school.

The effect of eliminating successful affirmative action programs has often been to decrease the representation of minorities. Perhaps the most well-known example of this is in education. Despite concerted efforts to recruit more minority students, the number of minority enrollments dropped dramatically at the University of Texas after the termination of its affirmative action plan. The same thing happened at the University of California, especially at Berkeley, once a model of diversity. These results show that it is too soon to end affirmative action in this country. Nor is it enough to retain only those parts of affirmative action concerned with enforcing the law. Until there is true equal opportunity for all, preference programs must remain in place. So our second premise is this:

2." Affirmative action is necessary to eliminate present injustice. (J)

Replies to Objections

The first objection to the **reverse discrimination** possible solution comes from the "compensation" view. It claims that affirmative action is required as compensation to minorities and women to pay for the unfair discrimination of the past. To this objection, those opposed to affirmative action reply that such payment is both immoral and impossible. It is immoral because it uses some people (the rejected white males who were more qualified) to pay this debt, and thus uses them against their will for the good of others. Moreover, it is impossible to make such payments because both those who owe the debt and those to whom it is owed no longer exist. Do we really believe that white males who are alive today, who may have never practiced unfair discrimination, should pay minorities and women who are alive today, who may never have been discriminated against, in order to make up for the sins of the past? And what about members of other groups, such as Asians, who are more qualified but are rejected? Are they to pay compensation for the sins of slavery? So the opponent of affirmative action replies to the compensation objection by saying,

3. Affirmative action is not fair compensation for past injustice. (J)

The second major objection comes from the "present injustice" view and claims that affirmative action is necessary to eliminate the ongoing discrimination of today. The opponent of preferential treatment programs may agree that enforcing the law and maybe even aggressively recruiting minorities is necessary to eliminate any vestiges of racism and sexism in employment and education. However, he strongly disagrees that preference programs are necessary. In addition to being immoral and ineffective, they are misguided. The real problem has little to do with race or sex; it lies with the disadvantages that accompany poverty. Those who are left out of the American Dream are primarily the members of the lower socioeconomic classes. They often suffer from inadequate education, poor housing, broken families, inadequate health care, crime, and other ills that prevent them from acquiring marketable skills.

The poor are the ones who need help in this country, whatever their race or gender. Although many women and members of minority groups fall into this class, many do not. On the other hand, many poor whites face the very same obstacles associated with poverty as do their minority counterparts. In the section on "Assumptions" we questioned the affirmative action assumption that race or gender ought to determine who is eligible for affirmative action. Here the opponent of affirmative action flatly denies it. It is class, not race, that matters. So, should affirmative action programs that employ preferential treatment be directed exclusively at those whose incomes fall below some norm?

No, according to opponents. Instead, there should be no preferential treatment at all. Other groups of poor immigrants have succeeded without special help, and so should the current poor. Others who oppose affirmative action, however, think that something should be done for the disadvantaged. However, if this class is to be singled out for special treatment, it ought to receive only various forms of **remediation.** Members of the economically disadvantaged classes ought to receive better educations, better living conditions, better health care, better job training, and so on—at least, better than at present. Only in this way will the poor be able to compete fairly. Instead of selecting less-qualified people for jobs and educational opportunities, the focus of government programs should be to ensure that anyone who wants to make the effort will be able to become qualified to compete. This is the way to ensure equal opportunity for all, and thus to benefit the whole society in the long run.

Pete Wilson was governor of California when Proposition 209 took effect. He holds this view of remediation as the pathway to diversity. After Proposition 209, minority enrollments in the University of California system declined sharply. In discussing what to do about this Wilson said:

> The fault lies with our public education system. This is why we have sought to remedy what is so wrong with it. It is penalizing poor children, those whose parents lack the income to provide them a better alternative. We cannot morally defend poor kids being trapped in bad schools. If we provide them with the health care and the kind of challenging education that every child of every ethnicity in every community in California deserves, we're going to achieve the diversity that is sought at the University of California and in every other way, but we will have done it on the natural, with high achievers of high intelligence having achieved their potential. That's how it ought to happen—not on the basis of unconstitutional and divisive explicit race-based preferences.[14]

For the final premise in his argument, the opponent of affirmative action will write:

4. Affirmative action is not necessary to eliminate present injustice. (J)

The first, and most damaging objection to the **compensation** view has already been discussed above, in response to premise (3). The objection claims that using affirmative action as compensation for past injustices is both immoral and impossible. The compensation view really has no good reply to this objection. In addition, it faces two other objections, both coming from the opponents of affirmative action. One states that affirmative action is an immoral means—a form of discrimination in reverse; the other claims that it does more harm than good. Because these objections will also be objections to the "present injustice" view, and because the compensation argument is the far weaker argument for affirmative action, we will abandon the argument at this point. It is safe to say that few, if any, people use it any more. There may be references to past injustices, but they are usually made to account for the origin of the present injustices—the real target of affirmative action.

The first objection to the **present injustice** view is that affirmative action is itself a form of injustice, a form of reverse discrimination. However, the defenders of affirmative action do not share this view. On the one hand, even if it is a form of unfair treatment, it pales by comparison to the unfair treatment that has been doled out to women and minorities. It is short-term, for one thing. Affirmative action is meant to be only temporary, meant to last only long enough to ensure equal opportunity for all. Second, its harms are relatively minor. Most of the more-qualified white candidates who were rejected can still find jobs and colleges to attend. There is no comparison between their suffering and the suffering endured by women and especially the suffering endured by minorities.

Besides, affirmative action is like a lot of injustices that are accepted for the greater social good. For example, young men (not women) between the ages of eighteen and twenty-four were always the ones in the past who were selected to die for their country in wartime. Were they not used for the good of others? Of course they were. We did not think of this as an injustice, however, but rather as the most effective means to the good of all. In the same way, the good of all is served by using some people today to ensure an equal opportunity society, a society in which they, too, will be better off.

In addition, even if affirmative action policies contain minor injustices, the degree to which they do so has been wildly exaggerated. For example, the number of reverse discrimination cases brought to the courts has been vastly overstated by many. Labor Department figures for the first half of the 1990s, for example, show that fewer than one hundred cases of alleged reverse discrimination were brought to the courts, and only six of these were found to have merit. In many judgments, the courts found that the minority candidate was actually more qualified than the white male. The white male had simply assumed that the job was denied to him because he was white, not because he was less qualified.

On the other hand, affirmative action may not be an injustice at all. Some would argue that it does not show favoritism but merely levels the playing field. What it does is not so much to give an unfair advantage to a minority or a woman but to *neutralize* the advantages of some of their white competitors. If merit is to be our guide, then we ought to consider that some white students, for example, may have had an easier time than their minority competitors in compiling their qualifications. Wealthy and influential families smooth the way for their children; the disadvantaged have many obstacles placed in their path to success. From this perspective, someone who appears to be less qualified may actually be more qualified than his or her competitors.

A disadvantaged minority student, for example, who scores lower on her SAT exams than her competitors may have had to overcome so many obstacles to achieve the score that she did that she may be seen as even more dedicated, more motivated, and more of an achiever than those whose higher scores reflect their advantages. Other examples illustrate the same point. The achievement of the disadvantaged may sometimes appear to be less, but the motivation, dedication, and skills required to produce it may reveal a person who will succeed even more than her more-privileged competitors. So the first objection is answered in the following way:

3." Affirmative action is not reverse discrimination. (J)

The next objection claims that affirmative action violates the principle of beneficence because it actually leads to more social harm than good. It is not an effective way to ensure equal opportunity for all, and it actually fosters more, not less, race and gender consciousness and conflict. We have seen the details of this claim already in the supporting evidence for premise (2), as it was presented in the argument against affirmative action. We have also seen the counterclaim in the supporting evidence for premise (2)" in the argument for affirmative action. However studies that might show clearly who is right about the harms and benefits of affirmative action have not yet been done in a thorough manner. There are many facts around, but they often cry out for interpretation, and the interpretations are usually slanted to meet the needs of the interpreters.

Clearly affirmative action has benefited women and minorities. Clearly it has caused a backlash, from some whites and from many successful minorities, each for their own reasons. Proponents of each side have made claims about the relative severity of these harms and benefits. Those opposed to affirmative action say that the harms have outweighed the gains; those in favor say the opposite. It would be helpful to have more objective knowledge about how much harm affirmative action has caused, and how much it has helped those for whose benefit the social engineering project was designed. We will return later to discuss this need for greater objectivity in the matter. However, as we are now defending affirmative action, we will write our fourth premise:

4." Affirmative action produces more benefits than harms. (B)

One final objection is that affirmative action is not a necessary way to produce equal opportunity for all. Instead, a combination of rigorously enforced laws against discrimination and greater efforts at remediation for those in disadvantaged socioeconomic classes will produce much better results. Because this approach does not appeal to race or gender, it escapes the criticism of reverse discrimination. Because it focuses on need instead of race and gender, it will more effectively eliminate disadvantages and lead to true equal opportunity. According to William Julius Wilson, the only minorities who benefit from affirmative action are the advantaged ones. Those with the advantages can get ahead when the racial barriers are removed. The truly disadvantaged minorities would benefit more from eliminating race-based programs and instead instituting class-based ones.[15]

> Long periods of racial oppression can result in a system of inequality that may persist for indefinite periods of time even after racial barriers are removed. This is because the most disadvantaged members of racial minority groups, who suffer the cumulative effects of both race and class subjugation (including those effects passed on from generation to generation), are disproportionately represented among the segment of the general population that has been denied the resources to compete effectively in a free and open market. . . . On the other hand, the competitive resources developed by the *advantaged minority members*—resources that flow directly from the family stability, schooling, income, and peer groups that their parents have been able to provide—results in their benefiting disportionately from the policies that promote the rights of minority individuals by removing artificial barriers to valued positions. . . . (and) they also reap disproportionate benefits from policies of affirmative action based solely on their group membership. This is because advantaged minority members are likely to be disproportionately represented among those of their racial group most qualified for valued positions, such as college admissions, higher paying jobs, and promotions. Thus, if policies of preferential treatment for such positions are developed in terms of racial group membership rather than the real disadvantages suffered by individuals, then these policies will further improve the opportunities of the advantaged without necessarily addressing the problems of the truly disadvantaged such as the ghetto underclass. The problems of the truly disadvantaged may require nonracial solutions such as full employment, balanced economic growth, and manpower training and education.

For those who favor affirmative action, however, class-based programs, as good as they sound, are both dangerous to needy groups and harmful to society in general. If we use poverty instead of race or gender as a measure for preferences, then many minorities who truly need preferences will not receive them. This is because poor white people vastly outnumber poor minorities. If the preferences were spread around evenly, minorities would receive less than they currently receive. This would be a disaster, because the poverty of whites has not held them back nearly as much as has the poverty suffered by minorities. Further, if enacted, preferential treatment for the poor would engender a culture of victimization in which even well-off people would struggle with each other to prove their entitlement to benefits.[16]

> Today, the overwhelming majority of people . . . identify themselves as middle class; political campaigns based on class warfare predictably crash. But, preferential policies that reward low-income status would encourage citizens to shed their middle-class "illusions" and adopt the language of oppression. The result would surely be a more polarized politics driven by a sense of grievance across the socioeconomic spectrum.

For these and other reasons, class is not the answer. What holds people back in this country is unfair discrimination, not poverty. Poverty by itself may be overcome by hard work, talent, and a bit of good fortune. Discrimination is persistent, however, driving down even the best, stigmatizing them when they succeed, and forever placing obstacles in their pathway to greater success. Affirmative action, and only affirmative action, can combat this evil; affirmative action, and only affirmative action, can lead men and women of all races to invent a truly equal opportunity society. So we write:

5." Affirmative action based on race and gender is the only way to eliminate unfair discrimination. (J)

Evaluation

It is now time to weigh the relative strengths and weaknesses of the cases for and against affirmative action, and to arrive at a *reasoned judgment* that one of our possible solutions is more reasonable than the other. As already stated, this is a *conflict of rules* problem. It pits the obligation of any government in a just society to provide equal opportunity for all against its obligation to make sure that the goods of society are not distributed unfairly. The central moral issues of preferential treatment are, first, whether the use of some people (the rejected white males with higher qualifications) for the good of society is justified. The second issue is whether programs of affirmative action that include preferences actually work to achieve their goal. If they do work, and if the apparent injustice of them can be explained away, then they are morally acceptable and should be retained. If they do not work we should get rid of them and seek a more effective means to solve the problem of providing equal opportunity for all. If they do work to create a fairer society, but do so only by using some people unfairly, then we should also terminate them and find another way to produce the kind of society that is fair to all.

We can begin our evaluation by showing how this problem relates to our ethical theory.

B,J,A

RULES

1. Promote equal opportunity for all.

2. Avoid unfair discrimination.

3. Use the most effective means to achieve equal opportunity.

ACTION

These rules follow from moral principles. The first two follow especially from the principle of justice; the third follows especially from the principle of beneficence. Those who argue for preferential treatment programs say that they are the most effective means to ensure that equal opportunity will be achieved, and that the injustices described by (2) are either nonexistent or minimal. In other words, they claim that (1) plus (3) have a higher priority than (2). Those who argue against affirmative action, on the other hand, claim both that it causes more harm than good, and that it is an immoral means to what is otherwise a good end. They claim, that is, that (2) has a higher priority than (1) plus (3).

Your Evaluation

Exercise 8.2

Here are the arguments for and against affirmative action. We will include only two, eliminating the "compensation" view as too weak for consideration. Because the premises all follow from basic moral principles, we already know that they are relevant to their respective moral conclusions. Your task is to examine the premises for **reliability** (are they true) and **sufficiency** (do they collectively provide enough evidence to support the conclusion). You may have to gather more information about the effectiveness of affirmative action, and you may have to judge whether the supposed injustices of it are significant enough for it to be seen as immoral. Be sure to be on your guard for your point of view. We will look at various points of view, as promised, in the "Another Perspective" section. It may be helpful to read that section before you continue.

The Argument Against Affirmative Action

1. Affirmative action is a form of unfair discrimination. (J)

2. Affirmative action causes social and individual harms. (B)

3. Affirmative action is not fair compensation for past injustice. (J)

4. Affirmative action is not necessary to eliminate present injustice. (J)

Therefore, 5. Affirmative action is immoral.

The Argument for Affirmative Action

1." Affirmative action has benefited women and minorities. (B)

2." Affirmative action is necessary to eliminate present injustice. (J)

3." Affirmative action is not reverse discrimination. (J)

4." Affirmative action produces more benefits than harms. (B)

5." Affirmative action based on race and gender is the only way to eliminate unfair discrimination. (J)

Therefore, 6." Affirmative action is morally acceptable.

A Few Comments

My brief evaluation will focus on *points of view*. There are two central questions before us:

1. Is affirmative action unfair?

2. Is affirmative action beneficial?

Even after more than three and a half decades of affirmative action, both questions are still extremely difficult to answer in any objective manner. It may seem strange that there is so much disagreement about the harms and benefits of affirmative action, as well as disagreement about its fairness or unfairness. After all, other new social policies were tried and either retained because they were beneficial or rejected because they were shown to have failed. Prohibition, for example, was abandoned when it was shown clearly to cause more harm than good. On the other hand, social security was retained because it clearly benefited society, despite its problems. Why can we not make the same sorts of confident judgments about affirmative action by now?

The basic answer is that whether affirmative action is perceived to be fair or unfair, beneficial or harmful, depends on your point of view. A minority who has struggled against all odds to reach a decent level of achievement only to be denied an opportunity that is open to others sees it as both fair and beneficial. Many women who struggle against obstacles not faced by men—sexual harassment, lower pay, child-rearing duties, the "old boy" network, and so on—also see it as fair and beneficial. They believe that there is so much prejudice, so much subtle racism and sexism, so much control by white males who favor their own kind that affirmative action at most neutralizes the advantage of white males and thus simply levels the playing field.

On the other hand, a more qualified but rejected white male sees affirmative action as both unfair and harmful. It changes the rules that he has lived by—the ethic of hard work and fair competition. To lose out to a more qualified candidate, someone who has more talent or who has worked harder or both, is one thing. Quite another is to be rejected after much hard work because someone less qualified is of the right race or gender and you are not. In addition, minorities and women who have "made it" often see affirmative action as immoral. It stigmatizes them, making them feel that others believe they are not good enough to have earned their way on their own. So whether affirmative action is immoral or not depends entirely on your point of view, does it not? If it does, there seems to be little point in gathering evidence and presenting arguments for and against its moral acceptability. If facts and arguments are to be interpreted very differently from different perspectives, there seems to be little hope that an objective evaluation of affirmative action is possible.

All is not lost, however. Some things are fairly clear. One is that minorities and women have made great strides under affirmative action. Jobs and educational opportunities from which they were once excluded are now open to them, at least much more open than before. Second, the degree to which white males have suffered because of affirmative action seems to be quite minimal. Most white males who were more qualified and lost out because of affirmative action have been able to find other employment or colleges to attend. Third, and perhaps most important, some of the goals of affirmative action have been met. There is now a black and Hispanic middle class with considerable power and influence. Asians, at least many groups of them, appear to be doing quite well without affirmative action. Women do not need it any more for entry-level positions, and they are progressing quite nicely on their own up the corporate ladder with little affirmative action help. The going appears to be painfully slow at some times, and obstacles are still being thrown in their paths, but armed with their talent and determination and protected by the law, the progress of women to the top of their fields seems inevitable.

So perhaps it is time for a reevaluation of affirmative action, a redirection of its efforts into areas where it is still needed. Affirmative action still has a role to play, but precisely because of its many successes it should have less of a role now than it did more than thirty-five years ago. Instead, preferences should be redirected more at those groups who need them most. Perhaps we need to focus now on the needs of the poor—on those in the economically disadvantaged class, and especially those who are minorities in this class. It is here, among those who are victims of both race and class, that the true need resides. We need all the brainpower we can get in this new global economy, and it is in our interest to spend our efforts to tap whatever resources we have. We cannot afford to lose bright, hardworking people, whatever their race, their gender, or their socioeconomic status.

We will all benefit by spending more time and money on improving schools and health care and the general living conditions of all Americans who need such help, especially those burdened by the legacy of racism. Those who are poor have little political power; they are easy to ignore; but we do so at our own peril. The minorities of today will be the majorities of tomorrow. We need everyone in our diverse society to be a full partner in the American experiment. The American experiment says that all people are created equal and have equal rights, whatever their race or gender. Very few, if any, countries have done a good job of counting people of different races and ethnic groups as equals. It is in the interest of all of us to do just that. Until our diverse society becomes one of true equal opportunity for all, in all areas of employment and education, the American experiment cannot be counted as truly successful.

Consequences

Finally, you must consider the *consequences* of accepting the reasoned judgment that you have formed as a result of your evaluation. If you find that affirmative action programs that use preferential treatment are immoral, then you probably also believe that they should be made illegal as well. You must still decide whether affirmative action programs that do not use preferences should remain in place as a way to enforce the laws against discrimination and to recruit qualified women and minorities more aggressively.

If, on the other hand, you have judged that affirmative action has been a successful and fair way to include women and minorities in the mainstream of the American economy, you must still decide whether it should be continued, and for how long. Do we want to keep it until the numbers show equal representation of all groups across all areas of education and employment? Would this be equal *opportunity* or equality of *result?* If we are to keep it for a while longer, should we redefine the groups who should receive its preferences?

Finally, if you judged affirmative action to be morally acceptable but no longer needed in many of the areas for which it was intended, then you must still decide whether any sort of preferences are necessary today. Specifically, you must decide whether various forms of remediation directed at the poor are warranted. Will this diverse, multicultural society of ours be one that exhibits a high level of social justice if it excludes from the poor, whatever their race or gender, the goods that this bountiful society of ours has to offer?

Another Perspective

In this section, through brief articles, letters to the editor, and e-mail responses to published opinions, we will hear some of the voices of those whose lives have been touched by affirmative action. Their experiences have shaped their point of view and largely determined their views about the moral acceptability of affirmative action. By examining many different points of view we may be able to overcome the force of any particular one of them, and to open ourselves to an examination of the facts and arguments in a more objective manner than might otherwise be possible.

Angry White Guys *For* Affirmative Action

PAUL ROCKWELL

The following article by *In Motion Magazine* columnist Paul Rockwell has appeared in several newspapers around the country, signed by groups of "angry white men for affirmative action" living in the communities served by those newspapers.

FOR OVER 25 YEARS opponents of affirmative action for women and people of color have overlooked a key American reality—the role of affirmative action in the lives of white men. Opposition to affirmative action is based on selective inattention to the social props on which white men themselves depend. It is not affirmative action itself, but affirmative action for women and people of color that is under constant attack.

Now is the time, before the 1996 elections, to redefine the terms, to expand the frame of reference in which affirmative action is discussed.

Most of us recall the first heated arguments over preferential programs that took place over 25 years ago in the teach-ins about the war in Vietnam. In the 1960s, the first big affirmative action debate was not about minority programs. It was about college students who were getting draft deferments during the hate wars in Indochina. It is easy to forget that minorities were over-represented on the involuntary battlefields of Asia. Black and brown kids from working class neighborhoods were being sent to die abroad, while primarily white college youth were building their own careers through one form of affirmative action, college draft deferment. Some professors, judges, and journalists who oppose affirmative action today took advantage of affirmative action (draft deferment) in college years ago.

Minority programs are only a small part of the spectrum of preferential policies in the U.S. It is time to consider the extent to which white males are intertwined with policies of preference. Tax breaks for corporations, subsidies for middle class home buyers, mass transit subsidies for white suburbs, bank bailouts for desperate bank executives, selective allotments for refugees, price supports for corporate farms—these are all shot through with considerations of need and preference. Special consideration may be valid or invalid, but preference for those perceived to be in need is a basic concept for American society.

In the past 50 years of social engineering, the vast majority of direct beneficiaries of affirmative action polices were not minorities; they were white males. Preferential social policies for those in need were not invented by civil rights leaders. Under Franklin Roosevelt, whom most white Americans still revere, the New Deal embarked upon a massive affirmative action approach to social crisis. With the critical exception of segregation, Americans approached their social problems—unemployment, poverty of senior citizens, re-entry needs of veterans and GIs, farmers needing price supports—through planned social engineering. The post-World War II Marshall Plan, a plan that provided billions of dollars for training and jobs, was a massive affirmative action plan for Europe. Former enemies got free training programs in Europe that were denied black GIs at home in America.

Paul Rockwell, Oakland, California ©1997. Reprinted by permission.

The New Deal concepts became unpopular only after they were applied to the crisis of segregation. It was not affirmative action itself, but the extension of affirmative action to minorities and women, that caused the backlash.

SOCIAL BENEFITS TODAY

We hear a lot about "angry white males" today. Well, we too are angry white males. But contrary to the caricature, we support affirmative action. As white men whose own families got free medical care, or unquestioned access to higher education through the GI Bill, who shared in the social uplift of the New Deal, we support affirmative action for those who are still left out. And we are not tear-jerk liberals, or millionaires who can afford to appear magnanimous. It is out of our own self-interest, as direct beneficiaries of social engineering, that we support programs of inclusion.

There is a normal tendency in most of us to overlook the social props, the network of special benefits on which we and our families depend. The late Mitch Snyder, advocate for the homeless, once gave an address to an affluent, white audience. He asked members in the auditoriurn: "Who lives in federally subsidized housing?" No one raised a hand. But then he asked homeowners to identify themselves. All hands went up, after which he pointed out that homeowners are subsidized. The U.S. Treasury gives up to $46 billion each year to homeowners' deductions in a system that predominately benefits people who earn more than $50,000 a year.

Tax breaks for home buyers may not be wrong. What is wrong is the smug psychology of the Governor Wilsons, the Pat Buchanans, who take advantage of all kinds of breaks for themselves while denying affirmative action for the most oppressed of society.

We hear a lot about the so-called stigma of affirmative action for minorities and women. We are told that affirmative action harms the psyches of African Americans, Latinos, and women. It is a strange argument. Veterans are not stigmatized by the GI Bill. Europeans are not stigmatized by the Marshall Plan. Corporate farmers are not stigmatized by huge water giveaways and million-dollar price supports. The citizens of Orange County, a Republican stronghold, seeking a bailout to cover their bankers' gambling losses, are not holding their heads in shame. The $500 billion federal bailout of the savings and loan industry, a fiasco of deregulation, is the biggest financial set-aside program in U.S. history. Its beneficiaries feel no stigma.

Only when the beneficiaries of affirmative action are women and people of color is there a stigma. Where there is a no racism, or sexism, there is no stigma.

Affirmative action is already part of the fabric of American life. We are all bound together in a vast network of affirmative action, of mutual support systems we take for granted. It is hypocritical and profoundly wrong to call affirmative action for minorities "racism in reverse," while treating affirmative action for bankers, farmers, and white men of power, as entitlements.

The four e-mail messages reproduced here were written in response to Paul Rockwell's article.

TELL ME WHY

tell me how denying a cambodian refugee—who has fled communist persecution and survived the hellish journey by small boat to America and then racism in America—admission to a program even though he has superior grades to a third generation mexican american is fair or just or anything less than reverse discrimination against asians. this is not some rare example. it happens all the time. the third gen woman in this case in 1/2 mexican and used her mexican name for the first time in her life just for admissions to University of California. she is a wonderful, bright, lovely, sincere person. but her test scores and all other relevant criteria were far below that of the asian applicant. this is unfair and unjust and racist toward the asian. this asian persons's life is changed forever due to reverse discrimination. i resigned from a board where i make these decisions because i could no longer participate in a system that fosters reverse discrimination. you can call it anything you want. . . . affirmative action etc. . . . but the aforementioned example is not some abstract example. tell the asian applicant they are an isolated example. tell them you are sorry. that they have to suffer their whole life to make up for some injustice done to the third gen mexican woman who is this case by the way came from a family with much greater financial resources than the asian family. but wait. . . . . the UC school had many asian and not many latinos and the latinos had inferior and I stress inferior grades/social activities etc. . . than the asian applicant. it is wrong.

two wrongs don't make a right

tell me why people of middle eastern background are not minorities according to most affirmative action programs. tell me why.

i am tired of affirmative action proponents calling me racist for raising these questions.

IF I WERE THE MINORITY . . .

AS A YOUNG WHITE MALE, I agree that discrimination is wrong but I deffinitely dont think Affirmative Action is the answer. I dont see how anyone could agree with it. Affirmative Action is not allowing minorities to accomplish goals themselves. It's also penilizing whites because of something their ancestors did. In a few years I will be appling for collages and I think it's extremly unfair that if my application and accomplishments are better than someone else's. I still may not be accepted because the collage must meet the governments quota system. If I were the minority in that case I wouldn't feel to wel-

comed either because I would know that I am not as well prepared than the rest of the students. Please allow my opion to be heard on your web page, I think that the American people have a right to

see someone else's opinon. Thanks a lot

ABOLISH AFFIRMATIVE ACTION

I AM AN AFRICAN AMERICAN female and I want to see an end to affirmative action "the exclusive, preferential treatment extending by white men to white men. I,m not just talking about the "good ole boy network. I want to see an end to white racial preferences that go beyond jobs and social organizations. There is a subtle, effective acceptance extended among white males who don,t even know each other, a kind of kindred connection that causes them to stick together, excluding those who don,t look like them. As a person who is least like a white male, I,ve clearly seen the back side of this affirmative action.

Current opposition to affirmative action for blacks and others comes from the same white men who have practiced affirmative action among themselves for centuries. From the inception of this country, the most privileged group has been white men, and they passed the legacy on so strongly that they are effective in defeating the slightest attempts by others seeking to gain opportunity.

People with true historical perspective understand the nefarious nature of white affirmative action "from slavery to Jim Crow to social and economic injustices of today. When I hear arguments against opportunity for the disenfranchised, I wonder at the audacity of heirs of slave owners who refuse to recognize the historical effects on our present conditions. White men will deny the ramifications of slavery on African Americans, but they won,t deny claim to any property, money, status or legacy inherited as a result of their ancestry.

In the discussion on affirmative action, everyone should have a clear understanding of slavery, segregation and the socio-economic system that moved the majority of African Americans from plantations to ghettos while keeping white men in power and on top.

AS THE DAUGHTER OF AN OFFICER IN THE AIR FORCE . . .

THANK YOU VERY MUCH for your positive articles on Affirmative Action.

As the daughter of an officer in the Air Force, I have moved around very much. I did not grow up in a Hispanic community. Being a minority did not make me any different from anyone else, really. I am now a freshman in college and in the middle of a culture shock. Suddenly, people are arguing with me and asking me if I feel guilty for receiving a schol-arship. I can only reply that I do not feel guilty for EARNING a scholarship, for working hard, for showing that I can be more than the Mexican maid that is present in many movies I have seen.

For the most part, I feel that many people's perceptions of affirmative action are grossly exaggerated. I am not a poor student who received a scholarship only because I am a Hispanic female. I am a very good student and an asset to my university. I do not appreciate the glares that I receive from other (white) students, who callously claim that I (and affirmative action) are the cause of all their problems. In reality, they feel very threatened by minority advancement. Given these current conditions, I am very grateful for your support.

-Dolores Montoya

Growing Up Racist and the Myth of Tolerance

ADAM GORDON

The last article is a column by Adam Gordon that appeared in the *Yale Daily News*, November 18, 1999.

NOBODY IS BORN RACIST. But by the time I reached first grade, my understanding of race was one that most Americans would find deeply troubling. That summer, I went to a day camp *near* my home. We had one black kid in our bunk. I tried to stay as far away from him as possible. I thought he was disgusting.

People often assume that these sentiments only exist in backwater towns of the rural South. But I am from the suburbs, the place where, as of the 1990 census, over half of all Americans live. I grew up in a household with two parents who had fought in the great liberal crusades of the 1960s. And somehow, by the time I was six years old, I did not want to have anything to do with this kid, who I had very strongly identified as being different from me without knowing anything about him.

I probably did not have any idea that such a reaction would be called "wrong" by my liberal family and community. Those lessons, though expressed in such staples of a liberal childhood as Sesame Street, are not explicitly taught until a little bit later on in life. I had surely learned by ninth grade in school that

Reprinted by permission of the Yale Daily News.

racism was wrong, and that the civil rights struggle had been one of the most heroic events in our nation's history. Yet that year, when I objected to my parents hiring someone to come clean our house every other week, it was because, deep down, I did not like the idea of a person who I assumed would be poor and black coming into my house.

Tolerance cannot be taught. It can only be learned through experience. As much as we hear over and over again that racism is wrong, we cannot conceive of the concept of a multi-racial society—where everyone is treated as equals—without actually living in diverse communities.

When I was little, I always somehow had the idea that America was half white and half black, with everyone who was not white being called black. My elementary school certainly was not even close to that ratio, or even to the actual racial composition of America as a whole (71 percent white, 29 percent non-white as of the latest census data). I guess I assumed that the black kids just went to school some-where else.

As I grew up, my town grew, too, more than doubling in population from the time of my birth to the time I graduated from high school. And it became more and more diverse. By the time I reached high school, my class was much closer to the national average in terms of racial composition. Encountering black people, Asian people and Hispanic peo-ple became a daily occurrence, and a few actu-ally showed up in my classes—despite a rigid tracking system starting in seventh grade that had the effect of keeping white kids from priv-ileged backgrounds away from the poorer, newer residents. And slowly but surely, from the cumulative effect of many daily interac-tions, my prejudice wore away.

For many suburban Americans, however, the black kids will always go to school some-where else. It always has been that way, and suburbanites hope it always will be that way. And so kids grow up in towns and school sys-tems that are practically all white. I have no

reason to believe that they are not severely prejudiced by this experience, given my own experience.

What first made me think about writing this column was the vehement debates over *affirmative action,* which have become com-monplace over the past few years. I could not believe that anyone would argue that our soci-ety has gotten past its prejudice. We still live in a nation polarized by race and class separation that is, in most metropolitan areas, even more segregated than in the time of the civil rights movement.

I cannot believe, though, that anyone sees *affirmative action* as the real solution to our prob-lems. *Affirmative action* was designed 30 years ago as a temporary measure to overcome past and current prejudices in society, with the assumption that—as our nation became more integrated and less prejudiced—we would phase it out. What we have done since then is use *affirmative action* as a crutch to justify prejudice and segregation. As Jim Sleeper, who is currently teaching a college seminar at Yale on race and national identity, argues in his book "Liberal Racism," "Some liberals support racial remedies [like *affirmative action*] as sops to their own consciences. They have no serious intention of redressing deeper inequities."

Similarly, current government initiatives to give more opportunities to the inner cities — such as empowerment zones and funding ren-ovations of inner-city schools—help poor minorities to some extent. But they send the message that "separate but equal" is an acceptable solution to problems. These initia-tives give the poor minority kids and families good teachers, good facilities and better hous-ing. But they still keep them away from true integration with the rest of society.

I would prefer *affirmative action* and increased funding for the inner cities to doing nothing at all to address prejudice and racial injustice. But the real solution must come through integration of our society, through building communities of people from different classes and races, which provide opportunity for true interaction. As Ty Hudson '01 pointed out to me, even metropolitan areas with heavy minority populations in the suburbs (such as Atlanta and Washington, D.C.) do not facilitate interactions between races and classes. Because the suburban lifestyle is in itself isolating, and makes it so easy for people to escape daily interaction with even their neighbors, it is possible for people to live in the same town without truly living together. We need to work towards a new conception of community that provides opportunity for real interaction between people from different backgrounds.

As a nation, we have a responsibility to provide equal opportunity and justice for all. This responsibility cannot be fulfilled without fundamentally changing society to truly integrate people across the barriers of race and class. Without integration, we will remain a nation divided. We will continue to pretend to teach tolerance, while our kids learn the true message of modern American society: prejudice.

Chapter 9

Global Justice

If justice hands us a moral obligation to treat all citizens of our country fairly, does it also require that we treat people from other parts of the world fairly as well? In particular, do wealthy nations, such as the United States, Japan, and some Western European countries, have moral obligations to be fair to citizens of poor countries, and at the very least require us to take steps to ensure that their basic subsistence needs are met? After all, we in this country have more than enough wealth to meet our own needs, and we have plenty left over to spend on luxury items as well. Is it a violation of the principle of justice for us to spend our excess wealth on things that we do not really need while so many people in the world are dying for want of a little food or medical attention?

On the one hand, it indeed does not seem fair that while we are awash in riches there are over a billion people worldwide, many of them children, whose subsistence needs are not being met. These people do not have enough to eat, and many of them do not have even basic health care. As a result more than 23,000 people die each day from the effects of malnutrition and poor health care. Each day! It has also been estimated that the crucial years in a child's physical development are those between ages two and six. This is when the scarcity of food usually has its most powerful negative impact. It costs about $200 to feed a child adequately during this period of time. In effect, for $200 a child's life could be saved. Does justice demand that we as individuals supply these goods to needy people, and that wealthy nations as whole do so as well?

On the other hand, it seems that our moral obligations to share our wealth do not extend to those in other countries. It is fine if we want to give away some of our money from the goodness of our hearts. But as we have a right to the fruits of our labors, we should not feel *obliged* to do so. Should we think it our duty to be our brother's keeper, when our "brother" is someone unknown to us, living in a far-off land? It seems instead that every country should be thought of as responsible solely for its own citizens. Besides, perhaps the reason that there is so much poverty and hunger in the world is that these countries are overpopulated, that their citizens have too many children whose needs far outstrip their country's resources. If this is so, it might be better, at least in the long run, not to share and to let their excess numbers die off until they have reached a responsible balance with nature.

Such questions and their possible answers concern matters of **social justice,** only now on a global scale. Typically such questions are about essential resources that are abundant in some countries and scarce in others. Because many of these resources—such as food, clothing, housing, health care, education, energy, and others—are required for a meaningful life, many believe that such an imbalance in their distribution as currently exists between rich and poor nations is simply unfair. If each person is intrinsically valuable, no matter what nation he or she may inhabit, then it seems to be wrong to let anybody die or live in misery, especially when such evils may be avoided. It seems to be a demand of social justice that resources essential for life be more evenly distributed throughout the world.

In this chapter we will restrict our discussion primarily to food and health care. We could have the same sort of discussion about other essential resources as well, but for practical purposes we will focus especially on the problems associated with malnutrition and its effects. We will ask whether we—have a moral obligation as individuals and as wealthy nations—to distribute essential resources more equitably throughout the world. We will call this moral question the problem of **world hunger.**

The Problem

The problem of world hunger depends heavily for its solution on a clear understanding of facts. Its best solution is largely determined by understanding both the causes of widespread malnutrition and the most effective means for its elimination. If it is caused by overpopulation, for example, the right course of action is to follow policies that most effectively reduce population growth. If, on the other hand, it is caused by unwise or immoral human decisions, these are the issues that must be addressed. We will examine facts of these sorts in the next section. For now we must clarify a few of the central concepts that have been used to frame the moral discussion.

Clarifying Concepts

As the central topic of this chapter is world hunger, we should begin our task of *clarifying concepts* by establishing the meaning of **hunger.**[1] We have all felt hungry at times, but persistent, chronic hunger is our concern here. Simply put, hunger is the inadequate consumption of food. A person suffering from hunger is someone who consumes an insufficient amount of the nutrients required for normal growth, good health, and ordinary daily activity. Hunger may be caused either by eating too little food—by having an inadequate caloric intake—or by eating too little of the proper types of food—such as foods containing protein and various essential vitamins. We will call this type of hunger **malnutrition.** Malnutrition may also be caused by diseases that rob the body of its nutrients, such as diarrhea and measles, or by the effects of parasites.

Children are especially vulnerable to the effects of malnutrition. Having too little food limits their growth and their cognitive development; it weakens their immune system, exposing them to many types of illnesses; and it inflicts on them conditions that range from anemia and dwarfism to blindness. When food intake is small enough for a long enough time, it ultimately leads to death by **starvation.** Starvation is usually associated with famine, when even the inadequate food supplies available to those in poor countries disappear. There is starvation in the world, to be sure. Rough estimates place the number of people who died from starvation during the 1990s at about 150,000 per year. But starvation is as much the result of armed conflict as it is a result of unfavorable weather conditions, and much of it will disappear when these conflicts are resolved. By far the larger problem is malnutrition. Estimates place the number of malnourished people at about 800 million worldwide. Each year about 10 million, the majority of whom are children, die from its effects.

Another important issue in addressing the problem of world hunger is understanding how population is measured, especially how projections of **population growth** or decline are estimated. Roughly, annual population growth is determined by subtracting the annual number of deaths from the annual number of births. Global life expectancy is on the increase, and projecting what it will be in the future is not always easy. Forecasting the annual number of births is even more difficult. The best way to estimate this number for the future is to know the current number of women of childbearing age and estimate the number of children each will produce. If we assume that, statistically at least, all women of childbearing age will have children, and that they will all have them as a couple, we can then say that each woman must have two children to replace the existing population. That is, the couple of childbearing age will be replaced by their two children. If the average couple has more than two children, the population will increase; if less, it will decrease. In this way, the population of the next generation may be estimated by current **fertility rates,** and the generation after that may be based on these initial projections. The measurement tools are more sophisticated than this simple model, and they have to be adjusted to allow for several variables, but the general idea should be clear. The number of people on this planet in the future will be determined by the number of births per woman of childbearing age today. In the section on "Facts" we will examine some of these projections. They are extremely important for deciding the best solution to our problem, because how we ought to deal with world hunger will depend largely on how big the problem is now and how big it is expected to become in the future.

Our final task in this section is to distinguish between **affluent nations** and **developing nations.** Here we will give an ostensive definition, simply identifying some of the countries that fall under each heading. This distinction is important because even though some hunger exists in wealthy countries, most of the world's malnourished people live in developing or poor countries. In fact, the problem of world hunger is considered by many to be a problem about poverty, not a problem about the scarcity of food. The world grows enough food to feed everyone; the dilemma is that some countries cannot grow enough or are too poor to import enough to meet the needs of their citizens. Moreover, if world hunger is to be eliminated, wealthy nations will have to share their abundance with the world's poor. So identifying which countries have the resources and which bear most of the burden of hunger will give us a better idea of the scope of the problem.

The affluent nations of the world are especially the United States, Japan, and several Western European countries, such as France, Germany, and the United Kingdom. Most of the world's poor, on the other hand, are found in Africa and Asia, especially South Asia. What **poverty** means for 300 million people who live in sub-Saharan Africa is that they exist on less than $1 a day. This is true for almost two-thirds of this population and for many who live in South Asian countries as well. In addition to Africa and South Asia, there is great and widespread poverty in East Asia, Central Asia, and many Latin American countries. Close to 3 billion people on this planet live on less than $2 a day, and most of them are located in these regions. This number currently represents nearly half the world's population.

Formulating the Problem

The misery and suffering that accompany starvation, malnutrition, and poverty surely call for some sort of a response, especially from people who live in the midst of plenty. This response may be thought of as a form of *charity,* a voluntary contribution of some of our wealth that springs from the goodness of our hearts. Indeed, there are many charitable organizations, such as Care and Oxfam America, that regularly request such contributions. Whether we give or not is up to us. If we choose not to, for whatever reason, we may feel a little guilty, a little less than proud of ourselves; but we do not think of ourselves as doing anything wrong, as committing an immoral act. If we do give, we rightly may think of ourselves as good persons, as persons who go beyond the call of duty to help others.

On the other hand, we may think of the response that such suffering calls for as an *obligation,* one that we owe to others, one that we have a duty to fulfill. Just as we are obliged to feed and care for our own children, so too we are obliged to help feed and care for the needy and helpless children (and adults) of the world. If we do have an obligation to help end the misery of the world's poor, then not contributing to this cause would be immoral. Failure to share would not just be stinginess, it would be downright wrong. If we have an obligation to help feed the poor of the world, then whether we ought to give is not our decision as individuals to make, any more than deciding whether to feed our own children is a decision to make. It is something that we must do. Failure to share would be simply immoral.

Because giving to charity is always an option, whether we are obliged to help becomes the interesting moral question. Indeed, this is to be the central problem of the chapter. We may ***formulate the problem*** as the following dual question:

a. *What obligations, if any, do individuals have to eliminate world hunger?*

b. *What obligations, if any, do affluent countries have to eliminate world hunger?*

The individuals mentioned in (a) are obviously those who can afford to contribute. Although there are many wealthy people in developing nations who fit this category, let us think of the individuals referred to in (a) primarily as citizens of wealthy countries—people like you and me. Next, although the two questions above are related, they are not the same. An individual may feel obliged to help, even though his or her country does not. On the other hand, an individual may not feel obliged to help, even though his or her nation might require such help from its citizens.

Having said this, however, we will emphasize the similarities between (a) and (b), not their differences. If, for example, enough people within a democratic country think that individuals have an obligation to help, then probably they will see that the collective power of their nation is brought to bear on the problem.

Conversely, a nation probably would not consider such helping to be an obligation unless a sufficient majority of its citizens believed it was. In what follows we will address both questions. However, as the collective will of a nation is required for really effective action, we will be concerned especially with answering (b).

Exercise 9.1

Most of the possible solutions discussed in previous chapters of this text have been provided for you. It is now your turn to come up with your own. This is a group exercise. Be sure to begin by assigning a group reporter who will present a summary of your group's recommendations to the entire class. For this exercise, focus first on yourself as you answer question (a). Then turn to question (b). Remember, you are not asking what would be nice, or kind, or charitable for you or your country to do, but you are asking what moral obligations, if any, the world's well-off people have to eliminate the misery of those in developing nations. I will present some possible solutions below, but you should construct your own ideas before you read on.

Possible Solutions

Three *possible solutions* to this problem will be considered in this chapter: the Neomalthusian view, the Humanitarian view, and the Developmentalist view.

The **Neomalthusian** view claims that for wealthy nations to come to the aid of developing nations is immoral. It is immoral to eliminate their chronic malnutrition, to care for their medical needs, and to save them from starvation in times of famine. Instead we should let nature take its course and allow them to die. This astonishingly harsh claim is presented by the Neomalthusian not simply as a description of the most expedient course of action, but as the morally correct thing to do.

Neomalthusians believe we should not help unsalvageable nations. An "unsalvageable" nation is one whose population has exceeded its "carrying capacity," the number of people whose subsistence needs that country can meet from its own resources. Just as a particular pasture can sustain the grazing of only so many cows, so each country can sustain only so many people. Wealthy nations may help poorer, overpopulated countries to control their population growth. By providing birth control, education, and funding for local government programs, we may encourage their citizens to have fewer children. But if they exceed their carrying capacity in spite of this help, we do them more harm than good in the long run if we bail them out with food and health care. If we do, there will be more of them to feed in the future, and thus many more of them to die as our finite resources become more and more depleted. The question is one of numbers: let some die now, or let many more die later.

The second possible solution is the **Humanitarian** view. Humanitarians claim that allowing people to die when their lives might be saved is immoral. It is not simply "kind" for individuals and wealthy nations to help the world's starving and malnourished; it is an obligation of everyone who can afford to do so. In matters of world hunger we ought to follow the general moral principle that we all seem to accept elsewhere in our lives, that it is wrong to allow something evil to happen when you could prevent it with little risk or harm to yourself. Rich countries can easily afford to help those in developing nations to avoid the evils of starvation, hunger, and disease. We can be our "brother's keeper" with little impact on our own standard of living. If everyone's life is intrinsically valuable, then we as individuals and as wealthy nations ought to share our abundance with others to prevent the evils of starvation, malnutrition, and disease.

The **Developmentalist** view, our third possible solution, agrees with the Humanitarians that rich countries ought to help eliminate world hunger. However, they claim that in addition to feeding people and caring for their ills, we ought to do much more to meet the demands of social justice. The riches of the world are in the hands of too few, at the expense of too many. Much more needs to be done to redistribute these riches more equitably. In many cases, the reason that developing nations are poor in the first place is because rich nations exploited them in the past and continue to exploit them now. In some respects, then, we owe developing nations a greater share of our wealth as compensation for past and present injustices.

Sharing the wealth also means helping developing nations to build their economies. To provide food and medical care in sufficient quantities to ward off today's miseries is not enough. Instead, we must invest in the economic growth and development of poor nations so they can provide for themselves in the future. One result of helping poor nations raise their standard of living is that their rate of population growth will decrease. It is simply a fact that as a country gets more prosperous its citizens have fewer children. Another result is that rich countries will have more trading partners. There will be more countries in the world that can afford to buy and sell goods, and thus even the rich countries will be better off if they share more now. By sharing significant amounts of our wealth, technology, and expertise now, everyone will be better off in the future.

Facts and Assumptions

Facts

Collecting accurate *facts* about a global population is difficult. Once gathered, the information often changes significantly within a few years. With that disclaimer, here is what we know now with a reasonably high level of probability. First, we know that we do not know very accurately the number of people who die from *starvation* each year. Starvation is usually the result of famine, and famine is often caused by political upheavals and wars. It may also be caused by drought or floods or other severe weather conditions—events that fluctuate dramatically from year to year. In addition, people who suffer the long process of starvation usually die from something else first, generally from illness. Given these qualifications, the numbers of those who starved to death in the 1990s range from 150,000 to 300,000 annually.

In terms of numbers, chronic *malnutrition* is the far more pressing problem. The good news is that the proportion of the world's hungry has fallen in the past ten years. In the 1980s and early 1990s between 20 percent and 25 percent of the global population was regularly estimated to be undernourished. Now the estimates are closer to 12 percent to 15 percent. The bad news is that the overall population has increased significantly, so although the percentages have shrunk, the actual number of people who are undernourished has not fallen.

Of the 50 million or so people who die each year from all causes, well over 8 million of them die from the effects of malnutrition. Perhaps a pause is called for here, just to let that number sink in. On average, around 23,000 people die each day, many of them children. Countries hit hardest by malnutrition in 2001 were the sub-Saharan African countries of Angola, Burundi, Sierra Leone, Guinea, Somalia, Sudan, Ethiopia, and Eritrea. In Asia the worst hunger exists in North Korea, Mongolia, Cambodia, and Bangladesh; in Latin America and the Caribbean, the worst conditions exist in Haiti, Nicaragua, Bolivia, and Honduras.

As with starvation, chronic malnutrition often leads to death by other causes, especially *disease* or illnesses such as diarrhea or measles or pneumonia. Diarrhea is treatable with inexpensive rehydration kits; measles may be prevented by immunization, and pneumonia may be treated by medication. For less than 3 billion dollars a year, all the children of the world could be immunized and treated for these preventable diseases. This fact is important, as these and related diseases account for at least three-quarters of the deaths of the chronically malnourished children under the age of five. This amounts to over 16,000 deaths each day.

The real cause of world hunger seems to be *poverty*. At least for now the world can produce enough food to provide everyone on the planet with sufficient amounts and varieties of food. However, not every country can provide enough food for its citizens. For wealthy countries, there is no problem—they simply import food from other countries. For those individuals within wealthy countries who cannot afford to meet their own subsistence needs, income is simply redistributed to them from other wealthy citizens in the form of welfare programs.

In poor countries, however, importing food and redistributing income are not possible. The level of poverty is concentrated heavily in developing nations, so that neither the individual citizens of these nations nor the nations themselves can afford to grow or to import sufficient amounts of food. Although many developing nations include very wealthy individuals, their wealth, even if massively redistributed, would be insufficient to meet the needs of all.

Many forecasters believe that world hunger will increase. The primary reason for this pessimism lies with projections of future *population growth*. Some believe that future population increases will mirror those of the past century—just under 2 percent per year worldwide. At 2 percent, population doubles every 35 years and triples every 55 years. In 1900 there were 1.5 billion people; in 1950 there were 3.5 billion. In 2000, there were roughly 6.1 billion. According to these projections, there will be some 9 billion people in 2025, 13 billion by 2050, and 25 billion by the end of the twenty-first century.

These figures are based on assumptions that the demographics of this century will develop in the same manner as those of the past century. A more accurate way to predict future population growth rates, however, is to identify the number of women worldwide who are currently in their reproductive years, and to examine their fertility rates—the number of children they are likely to have. The replacement fertility rate is slightly over two children per woman. Using this as a basis, the Population Division of the United Nations has issued its projections of population growth for the periods between 2000 and 2150.[2]

Their report makes three different assumptions about fertility rates and projects three different sets of numbers on the basis of these assumptions. According to the *medium* assumption, fertility rates will stabilize at replacement level by 2050, leading to something close to zero population growth. According to the *low* assumption, fertility rates will be at half a child less than the medium rate, leading eventually to negative population growth. Finally, according to the *high* assumption, fertility rates will be higher than the medium assumption by half a child, leading roughly to a doubling of the population every seventy-five years. These various population growth projections, based on three different assumptions about fertility rates, are shown in the following table (numbers are in millions):

Year	*Low*	*Medium*	*High*
2025	7275	7824	8379
2050	7343	8909	10674
2075	6402	9319	13149
2100	5153	9459	16178
2125	4074	9573	19986
2150	3236	9746	24834

You can see the great difference relatively minor changes in the fertility rate make in long-range projections of population growth. According to the low assumption, a fertility rate of just half a child less per woman gives us in 2050 a little more than half the population we currently have; a half child more than the medium assumption gives us four times as many people. Note that if fertility rates do not stabilize, if instead they grow gradually to 3.3 children, the report projects that there will be over 50 billion people by 2100, and over 250 billion by 2150!

Another important fact about population growth is that most of it occurs in developing nations. Rates of growth are already stable or even negative in most affluent nations; they are much higher in developing nations. Even though there has been much improvement in the past decade, the poor of the world reproduce at a much greater rate than the wealthy. Africa, for example, will increase its population from the 700 million of 1995, to 2.3 billion in 2150 if it continues to grow at its present rate. On the other hand, Europe will lower its population from 728 million to 517 million over the same period. This means that there will be far fewer citizens of rich countries in the future than now exist, and far greater numbers of the poor. Currently about a quarter of the global population lives in rich countries. If growth rates remain as they are today, this number will be down to 15 percent by 2050, and to around 10 percent by 2100. This wealthy group will have far too few resources to do much about world hunger if we wait for fifty years to act. In one hundred years the situation will be hopeless.

Descriptive Ethics

According to some, the very idea of nations having moral obligations to each other is absurd. Nations are amoral beings; they are not moral entities with rights and duties to other nations. Governments of rich countries have obligations only to their own citizens, not to the citizens of other nations. By law they may do only what is in the interest of their own citizens. From this perspective, talking about the obligations of rich countries to developing nations makes no sense, nor does talking about the obligations they do have, which is the task of **descriptive ethics.** On the other hand, nations are made up of people, who are moral beings. If enough of them in any democratic society insist that their governments adopt certain policies and perform certain actions, their governments must do so or risk being voted out of office. So whether in themselves nations are moral beings or not, they can and do act as moral agents on behalf of their citizens.

A sweeping set of moral principles accepted by all members of the United Nations is its *Universal Declaration of Human Rights* (1948). Among the forty or so rights this document claims are possessed by all human beings is everyone's right to have his or her basic subsistence needs met, especially to receive adequate food and health care. Those in developed nations can meet their own subsistence needs; those living on less than a dollar a day cannot. If all countries recognize every person's right to eat as a basic human right, there ought to be a corresponding duty on the part of wealthy nations to supply food for those who cannot do so for themselves.

Another way to examine the "obligations" rich nations have taken on themselves is to examine the goals and actions of the organizations they use to distribute some of their resources to the poor. Chief among these are the World Bank and the International Monetary Fund (IMF). The IMF is a collection of some 182 countries worldwide. It is like a big credit union. Each member country contributes its quota of funds according to its level of affluence. These funds are loaned to countries according to their need. The amount of money contributed by each country determines its level of influence over the funds. The United States is by far the heaviest contributor, providing about 18 percent of the total funds, with countries such as Germany, France, the United Kingdom, and Japan each contributing about 5 percent. The IMF regulates the value of various currencies and provides for the smooth flow of capital from one nation to another. More important, for our purposes at least, it provides loans to needy member nations.

The World Bank was founded in 1944 and consists of about 180 member nations. It is really a group of five organizations—the International Bank for Reconstruction and Development (IBRD), the International Development Association (IDA), the International Finance Corporation (IFC), the Multilateral Investment Guarantee Agency (MIGA), and the International Center for the Settlement of Investment Disputes (ICSID). These organizations are funded by contributions from wealthy nations and from private investment. Their mission is to aid the poorer nations of the world to develop their economies and especially to eliminate poverty. Together with the IMF, the World Bank has set a goal of reducing the 1990 levels of global poverty by 50 percent by the year 2015. To this end they assist developing nations and nations whose economies are becoming developed economies. This assistance takes the forms of loans, recently as much as $15 billion per year, as well as technical advice and support.

Organizations such as the World Bank and the IMF play an important role in redistributing money from wealthy nations to developing nations. However, for the wealthy nations, who control where the loans and other forms of support are to be directed, such redistribution is not seen as an obligation. Instead, it a practical and expedient mechanism which, in the long run, will prove beneficial for all, even wealthy nations. It is helpful for the economies of wealthy nations to have less global poverty because increasing the number of prosperous nations means more trading partners, more customers for the goods produced by wealthy nations.

The aid provided by wealthy nations through these organizations takes the form of loans. These loans have to be paid back, with interest. Although it is a noble goal to lend money and support to reduce poverty around the world, the heavy debt incurred by many poorer member nations as a result of these loans is often the burden that keeps them from making economic progress. If wealthy nations saw themselves as truly having obligations to developing nations, if they really believed what the UN Universal Declaration of Rights says, then the aid they provide to developing nations would take the form of grants, not loans. Wealthy countries would help poorer nations to feed themselves and to develop their economies—to raise their standard of living—with no strings attached. Currently however, such activities are viewed not so much as obligations but as wise and effective ways to maintain a stable global economy, an economy firmly in the hands of wealthy nations.

Assumptions

We have made several *assumptions* to this point. For example, the possible solutions claiming that rich countries have an obligation to eliminate world hunger assume that they can, that they have the resources to do so. At present this assumption is correct. Enough food can be grown and enough medicine can be supplied to eliminate the hunger and the many health care problems suffered by the world's poor. In addition, rich countries have enough wealth and know-how to help most developing nations build the infrastructure, institutions, and technologies required to develop their own economies, and thus to end the cycle of poverty in which so many of the world's poor are trapped. For the moment, then, the problem of world hunger can be solved—the resources are there.

In the future, however, matters may be quite different. If the "high" assumptions of population growth turn out to be true, if we add 2 billion to the overall population every twenty-five years, then soon the problems of hunger, illness, and poverty will be far beyond human solution. The belief that population will indeed increase that rapidly and that such increases will outstrip available resources is the assumption that drives the Neomalthusian to proclaim the immorality of sharing resources now. If we do, if we save lives today, there simply will be more people to die in the future.

The assumption that overpopulation is the cause of world hunger and poverty is not shared by all, however. The Developmentalists generally believe that overpopulation is a symptom rather than a cause of world hunger. The poverty and misery of developing countries is not caused by their citizens' thoughtless and uncontrollable desires to reproduce. Instead, it is the result of human decisions made by others. Wars, not overpopulation, cause most famines, for example. In addition, most poor nations of today were made poor by their past exploitation at the hands of currently wealthy nations.

In the past, many countries in Africa, Asia, and Latin America were colonized and stripped of much of their wealth by European nations, nations that were able to exceed their own carrying capacity because of this stolen wealth. Even today the exploitation continues. Local capitalists and government officials in poor countries form alliances with international businesses to produce goods for export, not for the benefit of their citizens. Even an extremely poor country such as Haiti, for example, could grow enough food to feed its own if so much of its land were not being used to produce citrus fruit, designed for the breakfast tables of wealthy nations.

According to the Developmentalist, then, it is politics, economics, and war that cause world hunger—not the existence of too many people. Poverty is the underlying cause both of hunger and illness, on the one hand, and of overpopulation, on the other. All who study the figures know that population growth is directly proportional to poverty. The poorer a nation, the greater is its rate of population growth. Many reasons are offered to explain this fact, and they will be examined later. The point for now, however, is that we have before us differing assumptions about the causes of world hunger, each with important implications for the correct solution of our problem.

If hunger is caused by overpopulation, the Neomalthusian recommendation not to share, as harsh as it appears, seems to make sense. If, on the other hand, hunger is caused by poverty, an entirely different tack is called for. More sharing, not less, is needed. If the poor of today become self-sufficient, they will find that having fewer children is in their interest, and "medium" or even "low" assumptions about population growth will be more accurate. Which of these assumptions about the causes of world hunger is true? Does overpopulation cause poverty, or does poverty cause overpopulation? We will examine this important question as we construct arguments for and against our various possible solutions in the next section.

Points of View

A safe bet is that most of you reading this book are well fed, you have adequate shelter, health care, and education. Even the poorer among you are well off relative to the sort of poverty felt by millions who live in parts of India, Bangladesh, and many countries in Africa and Latin America. Your degree of affluence shapes your point of view in one way or another. Perhaps if you are very wealthy and want for nothing you are less able to understand the true condition of the suffering poor. On the other hand, if because of poverty you have tasted hunger and illness, you may be better able to empathize with that half of the world's population that lives with these twin evils on a regular basis.

Your religious convictions may also influence which of the following arguments will capture your attention. Religion often calls us to a higher duty, to love our fellow human beings, not simply to avoid harming them. If you are to act as a "good Samaritan," if you are to consider your neighbor to be anyone in need, then you may be convinced by those arguments that we ought to do just that. Whatever your life experiences have been to this point, and however they move you to help others, in examining the follow arguments, recognize your feelings and motives but try to stay focused on the evidence that is presented to support each premise. If we are to arrive at a *reasoned* judgment, then we should follow reason. Emotion and desire, driven by our particular histories, may be the engines that motivate our search for answers, but if our answers are to be correct, reason must be our judge.

Moral Reasoning

The majority of the problems discussed so far in this text have been "conflict of rules" problems. They were solved by arguing that one rule had priority over another one, where "having priority" meant "promoting more beneficence, justice, and autonomy." The problem before us in this chapter also might be classified as a conflict of rules problem. We might, for example, see it as a clash between the right to keep what we earn and the right of those in poorer countries to have their subsistence needs met. However, the most helpful way to classify the moral problem of world hunger is as a **factual** moral problem.

A factual moral problem, discussed in Part 1, is solved by drawing up a new moral rule, one that treats people fairly (J), respects their autonomy (A), and especially allows the good consequences that may result from our actions to occur while preventing any of the evils that we can imagine (B). The problem of world hunger also cries for the creation of a new moral rule, a new idea of what our obligations in this matter ought to be, especially given the increasing enormity of this problem. As matters now stand, most of us consider helping those in developing nations to be acts of charity, acts we or our nation may or may not perform as we desire. According to this widely held view, we do nothing wrong if we do not contribute to the well-being of others. The Humanitarian and the Developmentalist, however, both claim that helping is a matter of obligation, not simply charity, while the Neomalthusian claims that *not* helping is a matter of obligation. These are all claims about the nature of a new moral rule.

Which moral view is correct will be determined largely by which "facts" or consequences will follow from their adoption. Because we do not know what these outcomes will be, we must form hypotheses about what they might be. In the next sections we will construct arguments for each view containing premises that make certain factual claims. Some these claims will be about the causes of population growth and its likely future growth rates. Other facts will be guesses about the consequences expected to follow from adopting one policy (moral rule) or another. The arguments will have this form: "If these facts are correct, then clearly our obligations are these." Of course, matters of justice and autonomy are also important. But for factual moral problems, the principle of beneficence, the principle that tells us to consider the harms and benefits of our actions, will be of primary importance.

The Case for the Neomalthusian View

Neomalthusians get their name from Thomas Malthus, who first argued at the very end of the eighteenth century that the primary cause of world hunger is overpopulation. No matter how much food we can grow per acre or how efficiently we can distribute it, persistent population growth will eventually burst beyond the limits of technology to feed the world's hungry. If continued population growth is allowed, then widespread malnutrition, illness, and even starvation are inevitable. These claims have been adopted by contemporary followers of Malthus, and especially by the most well-known Neomalthusian, Garrett Hardin.

In a couple of widely read articles,[3] Hardin lays out the reasons for his claim that it is immoral for affluent nations to help those in developing countries who cannot control their own population growth. Though much of what he published was written in the 1970s, his argument today would probably begin by accepting the United Nations' "high" assumptions about projected population growth. According to these figures, discussed in the previous section, this planet will contain over 8 billion people in 2025, over 10 billion by 2050, over 13 billion by 2075, and close to 20 billion by 2100. There is no way that food production can be increased sufficiently to feed such large numbers of people. There is no "technological fix" to the problem of world hunger.[4]

> It is fair to say that most people who anguish over the population problem are trying to find a way to avoid the evils of overpopulation without relinquishing any of the privileges they now enjoy. They think that farming the seas or developing new strains of wheat will solve the problem—technologically. We try to show here that the solution they seek cannot be found.

Food production cannot keep up with such dramatic growth in population. Even if food can be grown in more places and in more ways than are currently available, the best we can do is to grow enough food to feed about 14 billion people. At this point, which will probably occur in little more than fifty years, population growth will leave the technology of food production far behind. In addition, most of the population growth will be in developing nations. So even if we could grow enough food to feed more than 14 billion, countries that need the food would be both too overpopulated to grow enough for their own people and too poor to buy it from others. If population growth is not reduced, widespread starvation, malnutrition, and illness will be the inevitable result.

We have seen from the figures of the previous section that the greatest poverty, malnutrition, and deaths from preventable illnesses occur in those countries with the highest population growth rates. Clearly, overpopulation is the current cause of the evils of world hunger that affect three billion human beings today. It will also be the cause of the far greater misery that lies in store for many billions more if those in poor countries continue to reproduce at current rates. Those of us in wealthy countries, even though our populations are shrinking, will suffer greatly in the not too distant future, as the poor of the world storm our gates for their share of the world's resources. So the first premise in support of the Neomalthusian claim that it is immoral for wealthy countries to feed those in developing nations is this:

1. World hunger is caused by overpopulation.

We will not place a moral principle after this premise, as it makes a factual claim, not a moral one. The factual claim is highly relevant, however. If (1) is correct, then anything done to increase population growth will seem to be a great evil, whereas actions aimed at decreasing the rate of population growth will appear to be quite morally acceptable. It would seem, then, that wealthy nations should try to help developing nations reduce their population growth rates. Perhaps we can try education on matters of family planning. Perhaps we should supply birth control and even offer abortion services. Perhaps we should provide financial incentives to governments of developing nations who introduce programs that keep population down. Perhaps we should threaten them with negative financial incentives if they fail to do so.

Unfortunately, such measures have been tried and proven to have little effect on the rate of population growth. People have to want to have smaller families before they are ready to use family planning methods. In too many countries, however, the incentives to have larger families remain higher than those to have smaller ones. For reasons that will be explored later—reasons such as higher child mortality rates, the use of children as forms of cheap labor, and the use of children as a form of social security, people in many developing nations continue to have many more than replacement numbers of children. Some poorer countries have stabilized their populations, but many have not done so and seem very unlikely to do so in the future. Moreover, nothing that wealthy nations have done so far has decreased this trend to any significant degree. Consequently, the second premise is this:

2. Many developing nations cannot sufficiently control their population growth rates.

Again, (2) is not a moral but a factual claim. Like (1), it is highly relevant to later moral claims, however. If programs of education or financial incentives do not work, then the way is open to justify harsher measures of population control. Harsher measures are in fact just what the Neomalthusian advocates. Hardin claims, for example, that the governments of the world should restrict the reproductive rights of their citizens, by education, if possible, but by force if necessary.[5]

> The only way we can preserve and nurture other and more precious freedoms is by relinquishing the freedom to breed, and that very soon. "Freedom is the recognition of necessity"—and it is the role of education to reveal to all the necessity of abandoning the freedom to breed.

Such coercive measures, however, are likely to fail. Even China's policy of limiting urban couples to one child has met with only limited success. If such a powerful and repressive government cannot force its citizens to limit their "breeding," then other, less powerful, governments probably have no chance of success at all. If global population growth cannot be stabilized by education or coercion, then what can be done to avoid the inevitable misery that lies in wait for us all? Hardin's answer is that if people will not control their own rate of growth, nature will do the job for them. And we who could help the world's starving, malnourished, and disease-ridden peoples of developing nations had better cooperate with nature as it goes about its business. Briefly and harshly put, we should not help to feed the world's poor and should not try to cure their ills. Instead, we should simply let them die. In fact, because it is a lesser evil in the long run, letting them die as a way to control population growth is the morally acceptable thing to do.[6]

> If poor countries receive no food from the outside, the rate of their population growth will be checked by crop failures and famines. But if they can always draw on a . . . (worldwide system of sharing food) in time of need, their population can continue to grow unchecked, and so will their "need" for aid.

Hardin illustrates his straightforward argument with the help of several color-ful metaphors. Many people think of this planet as a "spaceship," with finite resources that must be cared for and shared by all. This is a dangerous way of thinking for Hardin, who replaces it with the metaphor of a "lifeboat." According to this metaphor we are to think of each rich nation as a lifeboat filled with peo-ple who have sufficient resources for themselves. The poor nations, 70 percent of the Earth's population, should be thought of as people swimming in the water around the lifeboats. What, if anything, are passengers in the lifeboats morally obliged to do about the awful fate that awaits their fellow human beings?

According to traditional ways of thinking, their moral obligation is to help those in the water, to take them into their lifeboats. Individuals may give up their seats if they wish, according to Hardin. Such acts of charity will produce no harm to the group, because the number of people in the lifeboat will not be changed. But if masses of people are allowed to climb on board, to join the current passengers, then everyone will go down with the ship. As Hardin says: "Complete justice, complete catastrophe."

For Hardin, the lifeboat metaphor is especially appropriate for describing the liberal immigration policy of many wealthy countries. Just as a lifeboat has a fixed "carrying capacity," so the resources of even wealthy nations are finite. We can afford to meet the subsistence needs of only so many. After that, we all go down with the ship. That is, we will all become increasingly poorer if we spread our resources too thinly. By allowing too many poor people into our country, our land will exceed its carrying capacity, and there will not be enough food, health care, education, and other resources for everyone. Our standard of living will decrease; we will become a poor nation. If our immigration policy becomes directed by an ethic of sharing, then tragedy will be the inevitable outcome.

Similar things may be said about our foreign aid programs. If they embrace an ethic of sharing, if they include humanitarian aid to developing nations, then tragedy will be just as inevitable. Whether we take the people to food through immigration, or take food to the people through foreign aid, being "kind" to our fellow human beings in the short run will produce disastrous consequences in the long run. Hardin refers to this as "the tragedy of the commons." Perhaps in your town there is a "commons," an open grassy space where everyone is free to walk about. In the past such areas were used as grazing lands that farmers could use in common. Because the space was limited, however, each farmer who used it could graze only so many cows or sheep. If it was overgrazed, if the grass could not grow back fast enough because the number of grazing animals exceeded its car-rying capacity, it would become a mudfield—a tragedy for all.

In the same way, if food and other resources become a "commons" by becom-ing available to all through international programs of sharing, then a similar tragedy will result. Just as individual farmers concerned only about their own self-interest might allow more than their share of cows to graze the commons, resulting in its ruin, so also supplying food to overpopulated nations allows them to exceed the carrying capacity of their nations. If their numbers go beyond their country's ability to supply them with resources, then they must rely on food from without. If they are poor, they must receive this food as a form of charity. Such charity is misplaced, however, as it merely postpones the inevitable.

As the poor are allowed to survive through grants of humanitarian foreign aid, they will continue to reproduce. Only now there will be more of them to reproduce. If we then continue to feed these greater numbers of people, they will continue to overpopulate their countries in ever higher numbers. Their demands on the resources of rich nations will increase proportionally. Because rich nations have finite resources themselves, eventually we will not be able to feed them. We will have to allow nature to take its cruel course of action. We will have to allow them to die off until their numbers fall back to where their own nations can sustain them. Only now there will be many more billions to die than there were before. This is why feeding the world's poor today is immoral, because it means that billions of people will pay the price in the future.

It is far better to let nature take its course today than to put off this inevitable tragedy until fifty years from now, when there will be a far smaller proportion of rich people than there is at present, and a total of four billion more poor people on this planet. Not only will there be more poor people to die then, but because the poor will not allow the rich to hoard their resources, the rich will also go down with them. The conclusion seems inescapable.

> For the foreseeable future, our survival demands that we govern our actions by the ethics of a lifeboat, harsh though they may be. Posterity will be satisfied with nothing less.[7]

So the third premise, following the principle of beneficence, says,

3. Feeding those in developing nations will produce great harm. (B)

The Case for the Humanitarian View

As Hardin has been the best-known advocate of the Neomalthusian view, Peter Singer has been the best-known advocate of the Humanitarian view. Especially in his widely anthologized "Famine, Affluence, and Morality,"[8] he makes the case for the Humanitarian's claim that individuals and wealthy nations are morally obligated to aid those in developing nations. The argument presented there is built on the principle of beneficence, especially the part that obliges us to avoid evil. He also makes some relevant factual claims, especially in more recent writings,[9] that lend support to his moral claim. As we did with Hardin, we will start with Singer's factual claims.

The first and most important fact is that rich countries *can* eliminate the hunger, poverty, and disease that especially afflict their poorer brothers and sisters around the globe. Sometimes the problem seems so enormous that people simply walk away from it or try to convince themselves, as Hardin has, that helping to save human lives and to prevent misery and suffering is a bad thing. The truth is, however, that the standard of living is so low in most developing nations that it takes very little in U.S. dollars to make a big difference. Most of the suffering and dying is borne by children, and most of this stems from malnutrition; the effects of malnutrition are felt by children mostly between the ages of two and six years, and it takes only about $200 to feed a child adequately during this period. Therefore, $200 will save the life of a child.

As I write this chapter it is the holiday season. People are crowding into malls and spending great sums of money on gifts that are usually in no way necessary for sustaining the basic needs of their recipients: $300 for a cashmere sweater; $1,000 for a diamond pin; a $500 bicycle for a five-year-old child. Then there is the second, perhaps even third home. Winter vacations? Of course, they are a must. A $25 dollar bottle of wine? Let's buy a case while we are at it! Perhaps we should save some; after all, we do want that thirty-foot sailboat and a sports car before we get too old. In the meantime, more than 23,000 people—18,000 of them children, die each day from the effects of malnutrition. These lives could be saved by some of the money that we and other citizens of wealthy nations spend on some of our luxury items.

The effects of malnutrition, especially some forms of illness and disease, can also be eliminated with relatively few resources. The six major killers of children worldwide are diphtheria, measles, pertussis (whooping cough), polio, tetanus, and tuberculosis. The United Nations had been making great progress in immunizing children around the world against these childhood diseases, but recently it has fallen far short of its goals because of funding cutbacks. Now about 130 million children born each year receive no immunizations. No huge sums are required to provide effective immunization programs. In the early 1990s, when 80 percent of the world's children had been immunized against these diseases, the annual annual UN budget for this program was around $180 million. How many billions do we spend on consumer items? How much do we spend on weapons systems that are unnecessary for the nation's defense? How much more important are the lives of millions of children, lives that could be saved if only a small portion of these funds were directed toward their welfare? So the Humanitarian's first premise is this:

1.' Affluent nations have the resources to eliminate world hunger.

If we *can* eliminate world hunger, the next question is whether we are *obliged to* do so. We all may contribute from the goodness of our hearts, of course. Charity is always an option for dealing with the evils of world hunger. However, the question that interests Singer is whether we have a moral obligation to help, not simply whether doing so would be nice, or kind, or humane. For Singer, individuals and wealthy nations clearly have an obligation to provide food and medical support to the people of developing nations. It is not an option, any more than feeding our own children is an option. It is an obligation.

The world is very small today. Information flows freely between nations. We know about the suffering out there. We no longer have any reason to believe that those suffering are not our moral brothers and sisters, our moral children, our moral families. Just as we are obliged in the United States to contribute through some of our taxes to the welfare of those who cannot meet their own subsistence needs, so, too, we ought to think of ourselves as obliged to supply the necessities of life to those who cannot provide for themselves. We should no longer believe that the elimination of world hunger is optional.

Singer's argument that individuals and wealthy nations have a duty to eliminate world hunger rests on the acceptance of one very fundamental moral principle.[10]

> I begin with the assumption that suffering and death from lack of food, shelter and medical care are bad. . . . My next point is this: if it is in our power to prevent

something bad from happening, without thereby sacrificing anything of comparable moral importance, we ought, morally, to do it.

This last sentence describes the moral principle that Singer believes should be universally accepted. The phrase "comparable moral importance" needs clarification. By this he means "something as bad as the evil that was avoided." For example, if I see a child drowning in a shallow pool, I ought to reach in and pull him to safety. I may get my new running shoes wet. Perhaps that is a bad thing. However, it pales in importance to the life of a child. Not to save the child would be immoral because we all believe in Singer's principle. On the other hand, if someone was drowning in a deep pool and we could not swim, then we are not obliged to dive in and save that person. Something of comparable moral importance, our own life, may be lost in trying to save the drowning person. We are required to get help and otherwise do all that we can, but not to do anything that require sacrificing something of comparable moral importance.

Singer's principle seems at first glance to be similar to at least one-half our principle of beneficence, a principle that requires us to "do good *and* avoid evil." Singer does not require us to do good in general. He requires us only to prevent evil if possible and if doing so is not dangerous. It seems to be an acceptable principle on the surface, but a closer look may make us hesitate before we adopt it. For Singer, it is a principle that will require us to change our lives dramatically. In particular, if accepted as the moral guide that will outline our obligations to eliminate the evils of world hunger, it will require us to reduce our standard of living dramatically. As it requires us to sacrifice to the level of comparable moral importance, it requires that we contribute our resources until we have ourselves reached the level at which only our subsistence needs are met. We do not have to go any further than that, as our own lives would then be in jeopardy. But we do have to go to that level, because anything we possess that is not essential to our basic needs is better used to prevent the death and suffering of others.

For several reasons Singer replaces this principle with another one, that expresses the same idea but in a much weaker fashion. He believes that following the stronger principle may harm the consumer economies of rich nations, and lower their standard of living. If they stopped spending money on *all* items that were not essential for their survival, their economies would crumble and they would soon be poor nations, and thus unable to help. Besides, such a great sacrifice on the part of all citizens is much more than is required to eliminate world hunger. Instead, he gives us a weaker version of the principle to serve as a sufficient moral guide.[11]

> If it is in our power to prevent something very bad from happening without thereby sacrificing anything morally significant, we ought, morally to do it.

This weaker version of the principle does not require us to give away everything that we do not need, reducing ourselves and our families to the same level as those in developing nations. Saying that we do not have to sacrifice "anything morally significant" means that we do not have to allow bad things to happen to us in order to save others. It means that we ought to refrain from purchasing frivolous items and instead contribute what we do not spend on them to save others.

We spend on average about a third of our income on luxury items. We do not have to give up all of these, and we do not have to give up our fine houses and cars and schools, either. These are items that are important for the happiness of ourselves and our families. We are obliged to contribute what we might have spent on *some* of our luxury items, items that are not essential to our happiness or well-being. Is there any conceivable reason that a person should buy three cashmere sweaters instead of just one, when others are dying for want of so little?

We may choose to contribute as individuals. We may also choose to contribute collectively as a nation, through some sort of national "luxury tax." Such a tax may be deducted from our earnings and distributed as humanitarian foreign aid by our government. How much of your present and future salary would you be willing to contribute? 1 percent? 5 percent? more? less? Singer's second premise is this:

2.' We are obliged to prevent evil whenever we can, and whenever doing so does not harm us. (B)

We will return later to the arguments of the Neomalthusian and the Humanitarian so they may reply to objections.

The Case for the Developmentalist View

Developmentalists agree with Humanitarians that world hunger ought to be eliminated, and that it should be eliminated primarily through the efforts of wealthy nations. However, they do not believe that supplying food and medical care alone will be sufficient to accomplish this task. There is some truth to the Neomalthusian claim that such efforts alone are doomed to failure if population continues to rise. Instead Developmentalists claim that wealthy nations must aid poor nations to develop their economic systems if the battle against world hunger is to be won. Developmentalists may be thought of as "enlightened" Humanitarians. They follow the famous Chinese proverb: "Give a man a fish and you feed him for a day; teach him to fish and he will be fed for life."

People are hungry primarily because they are poor. Poverty is at the root of the problem, not lack of food. There is plenty of food to feed the world's hungry, it simply is not being distributed to them. The criterion for distribution is wealth. Rich countries, like Japan and many Western European countries, have populations that have exceeded their carrying capacities. They are able to support their large numbers because they can buy food from other countries. Poor countries must follow suit and eliminate their poverty in order for any long-term solution to world hunger to be effective. In short, they must not rely on handouts from wealthy nations but must develop their own economic systems.

With the help of organizations such as the IMF and the World Bank, organizations supported primarily by wealthy nations, developing nations must learn how to attract investment; develop technologies; build factories, roads, and communication systems; and produce marketable goods. If they do this, their standard of living will increase and they will be able to support themselves. So enlightened aid calls for wealthy countries to encourage the economic development of poor nations and to assist them in establishing the political structures required to undergird a modern economic system. This means helping them to create democratic societies and capitalistic economic systems. This is what to "teach a man to fish" means today.

The claim of the Developmentalist is not that it would be wise or nice of wealthy nations to offer such aid. Indeed, it would charitable to end misery and suffering. It would also be wise. If poor nations became richer, we would have more trading partners and our own economies would grow. Helping other countries become economically independent is a wise investment. It is also wise to help them to establish democratic systems of government in which all citizens have rights and the government is "for" the people. This will encourage more stable governments, and fewer wars, and thus more favorable conditions for prosperity. The Developmentalist, however, presents a much stronger claim, a moral claim that wealthy nations have an *obligation* to share their resources generously to help developing countries pull themselves out of poverty. This is a huge task and will require the redistribution of great sums of money from rich to poor countries. Why should wealthy nations consider it a moral obligation to share so richly from their hard-earned resources?

One reason is that wealthy nations owe such help to poor nations. We owe it because we got rich in the first place largely by exploiting the resources of what we now call developing nations. Most of the poverty in the world is located in those countries in Latin America, Africa, and Asia that were colonized in the past primarily by European countries. The British, Dutch, Spanish, French, and other European countries all were able to exceed the carrying capacities of their nations because they essentially stole the wealth of now-developing nations to support their numbers. These colonized countries were supporting their populations quite well before they were invaded and controlled and reduced to poverty.

The United States has also exploited poor nations in Latin America and elsewhere in the world. One typical pattern was to provide support, financial and military, for local governments and armies. Then, with the general population under control, local capitalists would join forces with U.S. businesses to produce goods for export. So bananas, coffee, citrus fruit, rubber, sugar, tobacco and other crops became the primary agricultural products. These were grown mostly for export, using cheap peasant labor. There was less land available to grow food to feed these workers, who were now reduced to a state of servitude and poverty. Today, in many parts of the postcolonial world, such forms of exploitation still continue. Now, however the culprits are just as often multinational corporations as they are foreign governments or local capitalists.

Given the facts of past and present exploitation, we could write our first premise in the Developmentalist argument like this: "Past and present exploitation caused the current poverty of developing nations." We might then infer from it that if wealthy nations created the poverty that currently exists in poor countries, justice demands that they compensate these nations for their losses. This is the reasoning used by Fidel Castro in a recent address to the United Nations.[12]

> Current underdevelopment and poverty have resulted from conquest colonization, slavery and plundering in most countries of the planet by the colonial powers. . . . (Wealthy nations are morally obligated to) . . . compensate our nations for the damages caused throughout centuries.

Instead of taking this tack, however, Developmentalists use the facts of exploitation to make a broader and ultimately more effective point. They argue that overpopulation is not the cause of world hunger, as the Neomalthusians claim. Instead, the real cause is poverty, and poverty is the result of the political and economic decisions made by human beings.

Decisions made by human beings to exploit others economically, or to fight wars, or to form and maintain unjust governments, or to dominate in any number of ways the lives of their fellow human beings—decisions such as these create the misery of poverty and world hunger. They create hungry nations by creating poor nations. Ultimately, it is not because people have too many children that their children are malnourished and die from crippling illnesses; it is because they are poor that the misery of hunger has them in its grips. They are poor because they were made poor and kept poor by others. So we write our first premise as a statement of fact:

1." Political and economic decisions have caused the current poverty of developing nations.

But if they are poor, however unjustly such poverty was created, why do people continue to have so many children? Do they not see that doing so makes matters worse? Do they not see that these children will face lives of misery? Are the Neomalthusians not correct after all, that overpopulation is the real cause of world hunger? If they did not have so many children in the first place, then there would not be such an enormous problem of world hunger.

In a way, the Neomalthusians are right. Overpopulation does cause world hunger. However, the reason that people have lots of children is because they are poor. For the Developmentalist it is extremely important to point out that having lots of children is a *symptom* of poverty, not its cause. Just as spots are a symptom of measles, not its cause, having lots of children is a symptom of poverty, not its cause. People simply have lots of children when they are poor. The causal sequence thus runs this way: exploitation creates poverty, poverty leads people to have more children, and having more children leads to the misery of world hunger.

If the underlying "virus" that causes people to have lots of children is poverty, then we might ask why this should be so. You might think that the opposite should be the case, that people would understand that their prospective children would be miserable and thus not have them. What is the matter with people in poor countries? Are they so ignorant, are they so selfish to want to bring children into such a world? In fact, there are many reasons that people living in poverty have lots of children.[13]

> For the very poor, large families may appear an asset rather than a liability. Their children have a shorter period of economic dependence than children of richer families, and only children can provide for old age or illness or other contingencies which in richer countries can be handled by social or private insurance schemes.

Also, in poor nations the child mortality rates are very high, so more children than are necessary are required in order that some might survive. There are other reasons for having large families, including cultural and religious reasons that prevent women from controlling their own reproductive choices. Enough has been said, however, to make the point that because poverty causes overpopulation, poverty is the ultimate cause of world hunger. This will be our second premise.

2." Poverty causes world hunger.

These first two premises are important. They allow us to see the problem of world hunger as a problem with a solution. If overpopulation is the cause of world hunger, and if it is destined to march along its determined path, then nothing can be done by human beings to end world hunger. Nature will have to do the dirty work of "thinning" the human herd when finally there are more people than can be fed. However, if hunger is caused by poverty and poverty is caused by human choices, the problem of world hunger can be solved. If the rich nations of the world put an end to poverty by investing in the economies of poor nations, a project that will require massive redistribution of wealth from the rich to the poor, then world hunger can be eliminated. We will later discuss how likely rich countries are to undertake this challenge, but for now we write:

3." If rich nations contribute to the effort, poverty can be eliminated.

Once poverty is eliminated, once the standard of living increases in previously poor nations, population decreases will soon follow and world hunger will come to an end. So we may write this as our fourth premise:

4." The economic development of poor countries will eliminate world hunger. (B)

Once poverty is eliminated, not only will the evils of world hunger be eliminated, but the hope for a better life will now become possible. Once poverty is gone, the reasons for having large families will also disappear. Perhaps the "medium" or even the "low" assumptions about population growth will then be reasonable assumptions to make. In any case, as soon as their standard of living increases significantly, women in previously poor countries will begin to have fewer children. Just as hope for better lives for their children inspires women in rich countries to have fewer children, women in poor countries will have the same aspirations. They will have fewer children because benefits will be gained by their doing so. In a more prosperous country, having fewer children will produce better lives for all.

Along with prosperity, moreover, comes better health care. A result is lower child mortality rates and thus less need to have many children just to ensure that some survive. In a more prosperous and democratic society, children will not be required for cheap labor or social security, either. Better education is also a by-product of prosperity. Women will understand and desire effective birth control measures, for example, and will rebel against the cultural and religious obstacles to their freedom. They will develop marketable skills and thus be less dependent on their husbands for their existence. Along with this economic independence will come greater reproductive freedom for women and they will have much more voice in how many children, if any, they wish to have. It is well demonstrated that the emancipation of women from male domination leads directly to lower fertility rates.

Once poverty is eliminated and poor countries are better off, rich countries will be better off as well. They will have more trading partners, for example, an essential ingredient in a growing global economy.[14]

> The United States can maintain its own economic vitality only within a healthy international economy whose overall strength will increase as each of its component parts becomes more productive, more equitable and more internationally competitive. To sustain a healthy global economy, the purchasing power of today's poor people must rise substantially, in order to set in motion that mutually reinforcing exchange of goods, services and commodities which provides the foundation for viable economic partnership and growth.

In a prosperous global economy there will also be fewer unstable governments and thus fewer wars and greater national security. In addition to being the right thing to do, helping poor nations develop their economies is also the wise thing for rich nations to do.

5." The economic development of poor countries will benefit both rich and poor alike. (B)

Reply to Objections

We will begin with the argument of the **Neomalthusian.** The claim made by Hardin, that no food aid should be given to overpopulated countries, is plausible only if allowing people to die is the only way to control population. This, of course, is vehemently denied by the Developmentalist, as we have just seen. The Humanitarian also denies this, especially by questioning premise (2) of the Neomalthusian argument. If (2) is false, if there are other ways to control population, there is no reason for the harsh morality of the Neomalthusian. Premise (2) says that "many developing nations cannot sufficiently control their population growth rates." Instead, according to the current objection, it should say that many "have not" done so. A number of countries thought previously to be incapable of controlling their population have done so quite dramatically. Especially if governments act now and act decisively, the Neomalthusian's pessimistic predictions of the forthcoming population explosion may be altered, and with that the need for his type of drastic action will have no foundation.[15]

> A comparison of population trends in Bangladesh and Pakistan illustrates the importance of acting now. When Bangladesh was created in a split with Pakistan in 1971, its political leaders made a strong commitment to reduce fertility rates, while the leaders in Islamabad wavered over the need to do so. At that time, the population in each country was roughly 66 million. Today, however, Pakistan has roughly 140 million people, while Bangladesh has some 120 million. By putting family planning programs in place sooner rather than later, Bangladesh not only avoided the addition of nearly 20 million people during this 25-year period, it is projected to have 50 million people fewer than Pakistan does in 2050.

The Neomalthusian is not terribly bothered by this objection, however. After all, Bangladesh, an example of a country supposed to have been successful at controlling its population, still doubled it in thirty years. The Neomalthusian may admit that some countries have recently done an even better job than Bangladesh at encouraging their citizens to have smaller families. In China, for example, the average woman could be expected to have 6.5 children in 1965; today the figure is 1.4. Other countries have made great strides in reducing their rate of population growth as well, countries such as Mexico and Brazil in Latin America, Kenya and Zimbabwe in Africa, and Thailand and Indonesia in Asia. Nevertheless, population is still growing rapidly. Even if Bangladesh has 50 million fewer people than Pakistan in 2050, some project that it will still double its population to 240 million by that time.

Further, even if the Developmentalist is right that economic development will end overpopulation, something the Neomalthusian does not admit, achieving this sort of economic reform worldwide will take so long as to be ineffective. For the Neomalthusian, recent improvements in population control through encouragement of family planning and the future hope for population control through economic reform will not be enough by themselves to head off the inevitable disasters associated with world hunger that await us in the coming decades. So the Neomalthusian deflects this first objection, and as a result we will let premise (2) remain without modification.

The second objection may be called the "moral objection." It comes in many forms but all are essentially reducible to the following: Every human life is intrinsically valuable. Especially in the light of future unknowns, no life today should be treated with anything less than the full respect it deserves. We do not know whether the Neomalthusian population assumptions are accurate. Even if they are, there is no justification for letting people die today in order to save more from dying in the future. Because every life is precious, we must save everyone and then work hard at avoiding greater future tragedies.

Singer phrases this objection by means of his principle that requires us to prevent evil from occurring as long as it does us (not future generations) no moral harm. He uses a version of the principle of beneficence as his central moral principle and argues that letting people die when they could be saved—the Neomalthusian form of population control—will result in greater harm than benefit. The Neomalthusian, of course, denies this, citing the misery and death that will descend on many millions more in the future. Indeed, to refute the Neomalthusian claim is difficult.

At least one writer thinks we ought feed people and save lives today even if the dire predictions of the Neomalthusian turn out to be true. Appealing to the principle of justice and interpreting this principle to mean that "fair" treatment means "equal" treatment, Richard Watson says that just as all people on a lifeboat are expected to share food equally, even if all end up dying as a result, so it is the case with Lifeboat Earth:[16]

> We *should* share all food equally, at least until everyone is well-nourished. Besides food, all the necessities of life should be shared, at least until everyone is adequately supplied with a humane minimum. The hard conclusion remains that we should share all food equally even if this means that everyone starves and the human species becomes extinct.

Perhaps a more effective way to phrase the objection is neither to assume that fair treatment means equal treatment, nor that the extinction of the human species may be the result of sharing, and to appeal to the principles of both autonomy and justice. These are principles that most of us accept elsewhere in our moral lives, and using them as guides throws much light on the moral demands of world hunger. For example, Onora O'Neill, following Kantian notions of autonomy and justice, argues that morality requires not only that people must be fed but that they must also be given the opportunity to lead meaningful lives.[17]

> A fundamental Kantian commitment must be to preserve life in two senses. First, others must not be deprived of life. The dead (as well as the moribund, the gravely ill, and the famine-stricken) cannot act. Second, others' lives must be preserved in forms that offer them sufficient physical energy, psychological space, and social security for action. Partial autonomy is vulnerable autonomy, and in human life psychological and social as well as material needs must be met if any but the most meager possibility of autonomous action is to be preserved. Kantians are therefore committed to the preservation not only of biological but of biographical life. To act in the typical ways humans are capable of, we must not only be alive, but have a life to live.

Creating these opportunities for all on a global scale will require the sort of great redistribution of wealth envisioned by the Developmentalist. Such efforts are justified, claims O'Neill, by the everyday moral principles accepted by most of us—justice and autonomy.

The Neomalthusian has to agree that his ethic of not sharing violates commonly held moral principles. Nevertheless, he still believes that doing nothing in the face of world hunger, especially for countries who refuse to control their population growth, is the morally acceptable thing to do. The principle of justice, in particular, has no place in the moral debate for the Neomalthusian. Following it would create so much evil that it must be overridden by the principle of beneficence. "Avoid evil" at all costs is the moral clarion call of the Neomalthusian. To do this the principle of justice, that requires us to respect life and to treat all people fairly must play a secondary role to the principle of beneficence. To do what is right requires that we treat some people unfairly. There will simply be too much evil created if we allow justice to guide us. Those who are allowed to die today are clearly being used, and *should* be used, for the good of future generations. Otherwise millions more will die in the future. Just as the number of people in an overcrowded lifeboat should be reduced to avoid the evil of allowing everyone to drown, so too the number of people on the planet needs to be reduced so that the entire human race is not lost. Richard Watson may find the extinction of the human species to be morally acceptable, but the Neomalthusian clearly does not.[18]

> We cannot safely divide the wealth equitably among all peoples so long as people reproduce at different rates. To do so would guarantee that our grandchildren, and everyone else's grandchildren, would have only a ruined world to inhabit.

So we write our final premise in the Neomalthusian argument as this:

4. Our moral obligation is to avoid evil, even it requires us to violate the principle of justice. (B,J)

There are two objections against the **Humanitarian** view that we will discuss. The first comes from the Neomalthusian and claims that the sharing advocated by the Humanitarian will lead to more misery than good, at least in the long run. Here is how Singer responds to this objection:[19]

> This point . . . is an argument against relieving suffering that is happening now, because of a belief about what might happen in the future. . . . I accept that the earth cannot support indefinitely a population rising at the present rate. This certainly presents a problem for anyone who thinks it is important to prevent famine. (However), one could accept the argument without drawing the conclusion that it absolves one from any obligation to do anything to prevent famine. The conclusion that should be drawn is that the best means of preventing famine, in the long run, is population control. It would then follow . . . that one ought to be doing all one can to promote population control.

For Singer, even if Hardin is right, it simply means that we have two obligations. One is to feed the hungry now, and the other is to work for future population control. So premise 3', in which Singer replies to the first objection, says,

3.' Humanitarian aid will not create a greater problem in the future, as long as we also work for population control. (B)

The second objection against Singer also comes from the Neomalthusian view. It claims that the Humanitarian view would ruin the economy. Because we would stop purchasing luxury items, such items would no longer be produced. As our economy is based largely on the buying and selling of such products, it would shrink. We would become a poor country ourselves, and then become part of the problem of world hunger.

Indeed, accepting the strong version of Singer's principle seems to require us to reduce our standard of living to the level of those we wish to help, to the level that we have sacrificed all but what is of "comparable moral importance." However, Singer wants us to follow the weaker version of his principle, which does not require that we sacrifice things of "any moral significance." This will cause much less suffering for us and have a much less negative effect on the economy. Even this principle, however, will slow down the economy somewhat. This slowing does not appear to bother Singer very much from a moral standpoint as the lives that could be saved in the process are far more important than a healthy economy. However, for practical reasons he says that

> there must be a limit to the extent to which we should deliberately slow down our economy; for it might be the case that if we gave away, say, 40 percent of our Gross National Product, we would slow down the economy so much that in absolute terms we would be giving less than if we gave 25 percent of the much larger GNP that we would have if we limited our contribution to this smaller percentage. . . . Since Western societies generally consider one percent of the GNP an acceptable level for overseas aid, the matter is entirely academic.[20]

If in theory it is possible to weaken our economy by giving too much, in practice such an outcome is hardly likely to occur. So the last premise in the Humanitarian argument is this:

4.' Humanitarian aid will not ruin the economies of rich countries. (B)

The central objection directed at the **Developmentalist** view is that its noble ideal of worldwide prosperity can never be accomplished. It is simply too long and too difficult a task. It is also a task for which there is little enthusiasm on the part of rich countries, who will be asked to share significant portions of their wealth to eliminate the poverty borne by strangers. In effect, this objection is directed at the truth of premise (3)", which asserts that "poverty can be eliminated." It may be true that *if* poverty is eliminated world hunger will end, as (4)" asserts, nevertheless, this objection claims that poverty will in fact never be eliminated. If it cannot be eliminated, moreover, if all our efforts are bound to fail, then we have no obligation to work toward its elimination. After all, we are not obliged to do what cannot be done.

Developmentalists have responded to this objection from two different perspectives. Some claim that poverty can be eliminated, but only if we adopt a form of worldwide *socialism.*[21] Following Karl Marx, they claim that need, and need alone, should be the basis for distributing the resources within any country and throughout the world as a whole. Because everyone's subsistence needs are roughly the same, according to the socialist everyone should get an equal share of the world's food, shelter, energy, health care, and so on. If any wealth is left over, it too should be divided equally, for the good of all.

To create such a world, a massive redistribution of resources from rich countries to poor ones would be required. The only way that this could happen would be to change the political and especially the economic arrangements that currently exist. In particular, capitalist economic systems would have to be abolished, along with their central doctrine of private property. In particular, no longer would private ownership of businesses be allowed. Instead, governments would own the farms and factories and tools used to produce goods and services. Everyone would work hard and share equally in the goods produced by their labors. Within countries, there probably would have to be a centralization of power to run such an economy. Internationally there would also have to be a central power to ensure that currently rich nations redistribute much of their wealth to poorer ones so that global economic justice can be achieved. Only by switching from capitalism to socialism can we both create justice within each nation and ensure global justice as well. The socialist claims that only by eliminating private property can we eliminate poverty.

The establishment of worldwide socialism may be one way to eliminate poverty, but the chances of currently independent and wealthy capitalist nations voluntarily adopting worldwide socialism is remote, to put it mildly. Instituting such a change would take a bloody conflict, one that would introduce more suffering than the poverty it would attempt to eliminate. Besides, socialism has proven to be a rather inefficient economic system itself. If it were adopted worldwide we might have more equality, but only because everyone would be equally poor. Instead of eliminating hunger, socialism might have the effect of broadening its scope.

Others who defend the Developmentalist view claim that poverty can be eliminated by getting rich, *capitalist* countries to see that global justice is in their interest as well as in the interest of poor nations. In fact, this view already has been widely accepted. Rich nations do realize, for the most part, the economic and military benefits of global prosperity. They have formed international groups, such as the World Bank, to pool some of their wealth and direct it toward the economic development of poorer nations. But how well have these efforts fared thus far, and what results can we expect in the future? Will the voluntary efforts of wealthy capitalist nations alone be enough to create some semblance of global justice? In particular, will they be sufficient to eliminate poverty?

Poverty can be measured in many ways, depending upon what "poverty" means. For those affected by poverty it may be felt as a loss of freedom, an inability to control one's life. Or it may be felt as hunger, and as the frustrating feeling of having to watch members of your family go to bed hungry each night. Or it may be felt as a sense of hopelessness, a sense that every day will be a bad day. A more objective way to measure poverty, and the one we shall adopt here, is by income. The most extensive figures on global income especially focus on the measurement of extreme poverty. *Extreme poverty* may be defined as living on $1 or less each day, or $2 or less each day.

Although developmentalists wish to increase the prosperity of developing nations far beyond this point, they have set for themselves the more modest goal of reducing extreme poverty. In 1995 the World Bank adopted the goal of halving the 1990 levels of global poverty by 2015. By examining the results of their efforts thus far, we may form a rough idea of what the likely results might be by 2015. Unfortunately, although some progress has been made, the news in general is not good. According to the World Bank 2000–2001 report,

> Extreme poverty declined only slowly in developing countries during the 1990s: the share of the population living on less than $1 a day fell from 28 percent in 1987 to 23 percent in 1998, and the number of people remained roughly constant as the population increased. The share and number of people living on less than $2 per day—a more relevant threshold for more middle income economies such as those of East Asia and Latin America—showed roughly similar trends.[22]

Even though the percentage of the extremely poor has fallen by 5 percent, the total numbers of those living in extreme poverty has remained fairly constant because global population has increased rapidly. On the basis of this gloomy result, is there any reason for believing that success in reducing poverty by 50 percent is possible by 2015?

Projections are simply guesses based on certain assumptions. The World Bank projects three different scenarios for 2015, based on three different sets of assumptions about economic growth.[23] One set calls for significant economic growth in developing nations, another for little economic progress, and a third for retaining the economic status quo of the 1990s. If the first is true, the goals of eliminating 50 percent of the 1990 extreme poverty levels will be met by 2015. If the second or third is true, there will be little progress toward this goal. In fact, matters may even worsen. But which scenario is the most likely?

It is difficult to say, but what is not difficult to say, and what the report concludes, is that unless more aid is received by developing countries, the goal of reducing poverty is out of the question for all but perhaps a few East Asian countries. Sub-Saharan Africa, which will continue to be mired in poverty under even the most hopeful assumptions about global economic development, is especially in need of aid. Without a renewed effort by wealthy nations, nearly 200 million more people, about a 1.4 billion altogether, would be forced to live on less than $1 a day by 2015. Even in the most optimistic scenarios, which project that the World Bank goals will be met, about 2.3 billion people will still be forced to live on less than $2 a day in 2015.

So the objection to (3)″, that "poverty can be eliminated," is very serious. Poverty can be eliminated if rich nations contribute to the success of the economies of poor nations. But will they see the need and muster the political will to do so? Because the answer to this question is unknown at present, the Developmentalist must rewrite premise (3)″ to respond to the current objection:

3.″ If rich nations contribute to the effort, poverty can be eliminated.

Evaluation

The moral problem of this chapter was formulated previously as follows:

What obligations, if any, do individuals have to eliminate world hunger?
What obligations, if any, do affluent countries have to eliminate world hunger?

Now we evaluate the arguments for our three possible solutions—the Neomalthusian view, the Humanitarian view, and the Developmentalist view—and formulate a *reasoned judgment* that one of them is more reasonable than the others. This is a task you will be asked to perform on your own, as usual. Before you begin this assignment, however, examine just how our ethical theory may be used to as a guide through the maze of the factual and moral premises that have been laid out.

Ethical Theory

The problem of world hunger is best viewed as a **factual** moral problem, as we said earlier. These are usually problems in the first place because we lack information, or knowledge of the facts that might be used to solve them. If we could jump into the future and see whether increased food aid now would cause evil consequences later, as the Neomalthusian claims, or that sharing more now would actually lower population growth rates, as the Developmentalist claims, we would know the right thing to do. Lacking these facts, however, we must construct hypotheses about the consequences of acting or not acting, and then formulate a moral rule that conforms to our three principles and serves as a guide to individual and national action.

In competition for the best moral rule are the three claims made for our possible solutions.

Neomalthusian: Do not aid overpopulated countries.
Humanitarian: Provide humanitarian aid to all poor countries.
Developmentalist: Assist in the economic development of poor countries.

We may now see the arguments used to support these claims as attempts to show that the claim in question ought to be the moral rule adopted by individuals and rich countries because it best conforms to our three moral principles.

Your Evaluation

Exercise 9.2

The arguments for each of our possible solutions are written in full below for you to evaluate. In evaluating these arguments you are to examine the **relevance,** the **reliability,** and the **sufficiency** of each of the premises for each argument. If the statement of a premise is followed by a moral principle, then you already know that the premise is relevant, that it matters to the truth or falsity of the conclusion. The main problem in evaluating these arguments will come from attempting to judge whether their premises are reliable, and whether they contain a sufficient number of reliable premises to support their conclusions.

The Neomalthusian Argument

1. World hunger is caused by overpopulation.

2. Many developing nations cannot sufficiently control their population growth rates.

3. Feeding those in developing nations will produce great harm. (B)

4. Our moral obligation is to avoid evil, even if it requires us to violate the principle of justice. (B,J)

Therefore, 5. We are obliged not feed those suffering from hunger in developing countries.

The Humanitarian Argument

1.' Affluent nations have the resources to eliminate world hunger.

2.' We are obliged to prevent evil whenever we can, and whenever doing so does not harm us. (B)

3.' Humanitarian aid will not create a greater problem in the future, as long as we also work for population control. (B)

4.' Humanitarian aid will not ruin the economies of rich countries. (B)

Therefore, 5.' We are obliged to feed those suffering from hunger in developing countries.

The Developmentalist Argument

1." Political and economic decisions caused the current poverty of developing nations.

2." Poverty causes world hunger.

3." If rich nations contribute to the effort, poverty can be eliminated.

4." The economic development of poor countries will eliminate world hunger. (B)

5." The economic development of poor countries will benefit both rich and poor alike. (B)

Therefore, 6." We are obliged to contribute to the economic development of poor countries.

A Few Comments

Knowing the right thing to do involves knowing the consequences of our actions, and some of these very consequences are just what we do not know; how then are we to decide the right thing to do about the problem of world hunger at this point, and what is it that we are to decide? What should an individual do? Should you buy that expensive sweater, take that vacation, and go out dinner when the money spent on these things could help save the life of a child? Or would your contribution do more to harm the growing numbers of the poor, at least in the long run? And on a grander scale, what should rich countries do, if anything, to help? Should they send massive amounts of humanitarian aid to meet the chronic problems of poverty and malnutrition? Or would such international aid also harm everyone in the long run?

The Neomalthusian may be right that humanitarian aid will be harmful in the long run, especially if population growth remains unchecked. In the absence of any conclusive evidence that our efforts cannot reduce population growth, however, we should err on the safe side and assume that helping the poor to meet their subsistence needs will produce good consequences, as long as we also help poor nations develop their economies. So both the Humanitarian and the Developmentalist have it right. In the short run we should make contributions to humanitarian agencies in order to reduce the misery of our less fortunate neighbors on this planet. In the long run, we as individuals and as wealthy nations should also work for and contribute to their economic independence, improving their opportunities to live happy, meaningful lives. Until proven otherwise, we should continue to believe that the benefits of doing so will far outweigh the harms of our inaction.

If the reasoned judgment that we ought to share more may be made by appeal to the principle of *beneficence,* it may also be supported, perhaps even more strongly, by appeal to the principle of *justice.* Justice, in its primary meaning, tells us that all human beings—even wretchedly poor strangers—are intrinsically valuable, that all people are priceless ends in themselves. To allow people to die when they might be saved in order to spare greater numbers from the same fate in the future is to use these people as a means to the good of others. They are being used for the good of future generations, people who do not even exist yet, people who may never exist. By allowing them to die when they might be saved, even with the noble intention of avoiding many more deaths in the future, we are treating some people as less valuable than others. We are using them as things.

The Humanitarian/Developmentalist solution also can be supported by appeal to the principle of *autonomy.* Allowing people to suffer from hunger and poverty is robbing them of their autonomy. With stricken bodies and minds, the world's extremely poor cannot live lives that are guided by their own choices, and thus their lives are often empty of meaning. It is our autonomy, our ability to live as free and rational creatures, that lies at the root of our worth and dignity; it is our autonomy that makes us worthwhile in ourselves. This is why it is terribly wrong to allow people to go unfed, to suffer disease and illness. It reduces them to powerless and meaningless lives, lives of misery and suffering.

Unless we can show that humanitarian and economic aid is harmful, it not only should proceed, but should be increased dramatically. There is little reason to defer humanitarian aid, as some have suggested, and to wait for the achievement of economic development as the only solution to world hunger. Producing a world that is sufficiently prosperous would eliminate world hunger, to be sure, but eliminating worldwide poverty may never occur. Wealthy nations may have neither the resources nor the will to contribute sufficiently to that cause. It is a goal that should be maintained, but we should recognize that its realization may take many, many decades.

In the meantime supplying food and medical care to developing nations is not a waste. Hunger can be managed even in the absence of prosperity, even in the face of poverty. As long as *absolute* poverty is eliminated, people will have enough to eat. It appears, then, that supplying food and medical care is compatible with the principles of beneficence, justice, and autonomy, and thus that contributing to the well-being of those in developing nations is a moral obligation for individuals. Until we can be shown that doing otherwise is harmful, the moral rule that we should follow in the area of world hunger should be this: *People with more income than is necessary to meet their subsistence needs should provide humanitarian aid to, and assist in the economic development of, poor nations.* This is a rule that ought to be followed by all individuals who consider themselves to be morally good persons.

Consequences

Suppose you accept this solution to our problem. What then? What *consequences* would it have for how you live your life if you believed you had a moral obligation to contribute to the reduction of hunger and poverty in the world? Here is how Singer says it should change the lives of individuals if the strong version of his principle were to be followed:

> An American household with an income of $50,000 spends around $30,000 annually on necessities. . . . Therefore, for a household bringing in $50,000 a year, donations to help the world's poor should be as close as possible to $20,000. The $30,000 required for necessities holds for higher incomes as well. So a household making $100,000 could cut a yearly check for $70,000. Again, the formula is simple: whatever money you're spending on luxuries, not necessities, should be given away.[24]

Do you still think that the Humanitarian/Developmentalist solution is right? Do we "have to" contribute as much as Singer says, or else think of ourselves as immoral? Is contributing as much as he recommends an act of duty, and therefore not even to deciding a moral option, or is it an act of charity, and therefore at our discretion whether to contribute?

What about the consequences for wealthy nations? The preceding arguments claim that they must increase their humanitarian aid as well. Many wealthy countries pay dues to the United Nations that total far less than 1 percent of their gross national product. Far more than this is required to eliminate hunger, poverty, and disease. By one estimate, about $13 per hungry person a year would be required in foreign aid, over and above what poor nations contribute to their own hunger relief, to provide minimal nourishment to the world's poor.[25] If there are roughly 3 billion people who require such aid, those living on less than $2 a day, then rich countries would have to give $39 billion dollars a year to eliminate malnutrition. In its most generous year, 1988, the United States contributed $4 billion toward this effort. In 2000, the contribution for worldwide health care from all developed nations combined was only 5 billion dollars. Clearly, far more generous contributions are required from developed nations if we are to eliminate world hunger, let alone sickness and poverty.

The trouble is that nations do not have moral obligations to one another. Nations are supposed to refrain from harming each other, but governments have no right to spend a nation's resources to help other nations. If directed to, of course, they may increase their foreign aid budgets, but enough citizens must agree for this to be allowed. So once again the moral burden falls to the individual to agree to give up some of his or her wealth for others. Would you allow the government to tax you for humanitarian aid and for purposes of supporting the economic development of other nations? Pretend for a moment that a law was proposed to tax all citizen 1 percent of their income for such foreign aid. Would you be in favor of such a law? What about 2 percent, or 5 percent or, as Singer has just suggested, far more than that? Would you vote for a president who ran on such a platform of global justice?

Here is what former President Clinton said in an address in London, during his final trip in office as president, when he was still leader of the developed world:

> No generation has ever had the opportunity that all of us now have to build a global economy that leaves no one behind, and in the process, to create a new century of peace and prosperity in a world that is more constructively and truly independent. . . . The great question before us is not whether globalization will proceed, but how . . . and what is our responsibility in the developed world to try to shape this process so that it lifts people in all nations.[26]

Another Perspective

The following article is from *Drought and Hunger,* ed. Michael Glantz (Cambridge, MA: Cambridge University Press, 1987). The author takes the perspective of China's experience with hunger and famine and suggests that Africa might benefit from the lessons learned there.[27]

Famine and Famine Relief: Viewing Africa in the 1980s from China in the 1920s

LILLIAN M. LI, PROFESSOR OF HISTORY, SWARTHMORE COLLEGE

DURING 1984 AND 1985, as the tragedy of the Ethiopian famine has been played out in Africa, another human drama has unfolded in the United States and Europe. Although anticipated by experts for years, and in progress for months, the famine in Ethiopia did not reach the American public's attention until October 1984, when NBC evening news aired a BBC special about Ethiopia. As they ate dinner, Americans could watch with horror the specter of emaciated, fly-ridden bodies dying of starvation before their eyes. During the following winter and spring, millions of dollars poured into relief organizations such as Oxfam America and Catholic Relief Services, completely overwhelming their staffs. Rock stars, having already made a best-selling record, *We Are the World*, donated their talents to the ultimate transoceanic media event, "Live Aid"— grossing millions more for African relief.

A year later, the crisis in Ethiopia has peaked. Although several million remain "at risk," homeless and severely malnourished, summer rains in 1985 have brought the hope of a successful harvest in some areas. The flow of millions of dollars of international assistance has helped to limit the number of human fatalities. Yet, as Africans and African specialists know, the deep underlying causes of famine have not been addressed, and the deteriorating economic conditions in much of sub-Saharan Africa suggest that hunger and famine will continue to haunt Africa for the foreseeable future.

Just as Africa seems to be the "basket case" of the world today, half a century ago, it was China that was called "the land of famine." From the late nineteenth century, massive famines hit China like relentless waves, taking millions of lives. The 1876–79 drought-related famine in north China may have cost 9–13 million lives. Floods in the 1890s cost additional thousands. Each decade of the twentieth century brought major catastrophes. Nature seemed cruel and unforgiving, as droughts and floods alternated to create what seemed by the 1920s to be a chronic condition of famine in one part of China or another.

The American public was well aware of "the starving Chinese." Pictures of ragged and wide-eyed Chinese children filled the American newspapers. Unlike today, however, the real medium of fund-raising was neither journalists nor rock stars, but missionaries. In an era when thousands of young Americans went out to Asia to serve Christ, churches were the backbone of the relief effort. Collec-

tions were taken, sermons preached, relief stamps sold. The China Famine Fund of 1921 churned out slogan after slogan to nag the American conscience. "Famine relief is a sermon without words," the posters said, "Pick a Pal in China," "Give China a chance to live!" "15 million starving—Every minute counts." Articles explained, "How your dollar reaches a starving Chinese." "Self-Denial Week" was proclaimed. No contribution was too small. One could buy "Life-saving Stamps." "Each mercy stamp purchased for 3 cents provides food for one day for a Chinese" (Presbyterian Historical Society, 82/20/11).

In many respects the problems faced by Africa today resemble those experienced by China in the first half of this century. First, recurrent African famines take place in a physical environment whose natural instability and vulnerability have been exacerbated by human behavior. In the Sahel, the effect of drought has been greatly magnified by the spread of the desert southward, which, in turn has probably been caused by overgrazing of livestock, deforestation, and other land-use practices. In north China, similarly, since at least the mid-nineteenth century, the natural tendency of the Yellow River to overflow its banks had been greatly increased by neglect of dike repairs, and also by silting generated by continual deforestation of the upland areas.

Second, famine in Africa occurs in the context of a population explosion, which is sometime mistakenly taken to be the cause of the famine itself. Despite poverty and hunger— some would say because of them—Africa's population is growing faster than that of any other region of the world. Unlike Africa, China by the early twentieth century had already experienced centuries of high population density, but the rate of population growth seemed to many contemporary observers to have accelerated and to be creating Malthusian pressures on the land.

Third, the very low standard of living of large sectors of the population in Africa was also found in China in the 1920s and 1930s, and was frequently observed by foreigners. Chinese peasant life was characterized by malnutrition and poverty, high infant mortality, and low life expectancy.

Fourth, low productivity in agriculture is held largely responsible for Africa's increasing inability to feed itself, but the reasons for this low productivity are disputed. Similarly, both Chinese and foreigners in the 1920s and 1930s agreed that Chinese agriculture could be more productive but disagreed about the causes of agricultural stagnation.

Fifth, wide income inequalities in Africa are intensified by a growing urban-rural disparity in living standards and opportunities. In China before 1949, an ever-widening urban-rural gap seemed even more stark because most of the major cities were treaty ports where foreign privileges and the foreign presence were prominent.

Finally, Africa's serious economic problems are unfolding in a political context that is, in most African countries, quite unstable. In Ethiopia, of course, full-scale secessionist wars have greatly contributed to the severity of the famine. Likewise, China between 1911 and 1949 was in a state of political disorder, in which the major actors were militarists whose primary concern was their own survival.

Such apparent similarities—although on further examination they may be more apparent than real—strongly suggest that Africans may well wish to consider what lessons the Chinese experience with famine may contain for them. China has, after all, managed to avoid any major famine in the last 20 or more years. Although still a very poor country, China is proud of its self-sufficiency in food. With the recent economic reforms, there is every hope that the material life of the Chinese people will continue to improve. So far has China come from being "the land of famine" that last spring the Chinese Red Cross received donations from thousands of ordinary Chinese people, including school children, to aid famine victims in Africa (*China Daily*, 23 May 1985). . . .

"LESSONS" OF THE CHINESE EXPERIENCE

WHILE IT WOULD BE FOOLISH for an outsider to pass judgment on the relative merits of these African issues, the Chinese conquest of famine over the past decades does, I believe, contain some lessons for Africa today. The appropriate lessons, I shall argue, are not the obvious ones.

There are several key aspects of the Chinese developmental experience in the period since 1949 that should be considered. First, with the establishment of the People's Republic of China (PRC), virtually all forms of Western assistance and trade that had been so prominent during the earlier Republican period were curtailed and, after about 1959, all forms of technical and financial assistance from the Soviet Union were also terminated, leaving China to pursue an independent path, free of foreign interference. Second, through rapid steps, the organization of agriculture became collectivized into large-scale communes. In this it was the mobilization of labor rather than new technology that was emphasized. Third, the distribution of grain was strictly controlled by the state through a system of rationing in the urban areas and a minimum guarantee in the countryside. Fourth, both food production and food distribution were managed by a highly centralized and powerful state apparatus that placed high priority on eliminating famine.

While it is the first three aspects that comprise the distinctive characteristics of the "Maoist" model of development, in my view it is the fourth characteristic—state policy—that may have been the most critical to the Chinese experience and that may be the most relevant to the African crisis. Almost complete economic self-sufficiency, as the ultimate expression of Chinese nationalism, may have been indispensable in establishing the legitimacy of the new national government, but it can hardly be said to have contributed directly to the elimination of hunger and famine. Collectivization may also have had greater political benefits than economic. Although grain output in China increased 75% from 1952 to 1977, agricultural growth barely kept pace with population growth (Tang & Stone, 1980, 13), and per capita grain output in 1980 was probably no greater than in the 1930s (Li, 1982, 701). Although it is too soon to evaluate the commune system definitively, the spectacular increases in output since the beginning of de-collectivization in 1978, strongly suggest that the communes may have inhibited growth by stifling individual initiative and motivation.

The system of food rationing, backed by a state reserve system, was probably the most important factor in the elimination of famine in China. Although the average per capita caloric availability of food in 1980 was probably no better than that in the 1930s, the critical difference between the two periods was that strict controls under the PRC assured the most equitable distribution of extremely meager resources. In a very real sense, then, the Maoist model gave higher priority to the *social* goal of equitable distribution than to the purely *economic* goal of growth. This degree of control over the distribution of food resources has probably never been achieved by any other government in world history, and it could not have been achieved in China without a highly powerful state system. Our growing understanding of China's state-granary and grain-price reporting system in the eighteenth and nineteenth centuries, moreover, permits us to understand that the food-distribution policies under the PRC represent an intensification of state policies from previous eras of Chinese history rather than a completely new direction (Li, 1982, 702).

The Maoist model has, of course, had a broad appeal to radical movements all over the world. Policies of isolation, at least from Western trade and aid, have been adopted in Cuba, Burma and other socialist countries, while land reform at least, if not collectivization, has been on the agenda in countries as distant and different as Ethiopia and Nicaragua. It is becoming painfully clear,

however—at least to some observers—that such policies have often failed to raise the level of productivity. Even more painful should be the recognition that the Maoist model has now been repudiated by China, the very country that created it.

By contrast, the policy of strict rationing, which did work remarkably well in China to spread meager resources, is unlikely to be attempted on such an ambitious scale by any other country because it would be politically unpopular and, therefore, impossible to implement. The critical factor is not the type of ideology, political system or social policy, but a state policy that places the very highest priority on eliminating hunger and famine. It is state policy, together with the political capability to enforce it, that I believe are the transferable lessons of the Chinese experience.

Such a view is likely to meet serious objections. In Africa, many enlightened people regard the state and bureaucracy as the cause of the problem, not its solution. They see the clumsy manipulations of agricultural marketing boards and the corruption of their politicians as the very source of food distribution problems and, consequently, advocate a free market to eliminate the bottlenecks and disincentives that have occurred. To this, one can only respond that political control seems unavoidable in a situation crying for rapid solution. The relevant choice is between good government and bad, not between having political controls and not having them.

Second, there are those on the Chinese side who will surely object that in China, too, over-centralization of state power has had disastrous, indeed tragic, consequences. The Chinese government has now acknowledged that during the "three lean years" of the Great Leap Forward, 1959–61, a massive famine did occur in China. Some American demographers now calculate that as many as 30 million may have died of hunger and malnutrition during those years—making the Great Leap Forward the largest famine ever recorded in world history (Ashton *et al.*, 1984). Although bad weather certainly was a factor, this famine was primarily the result of overwhelming pressure put on communes to say they had fulfilled the unreasonable quotas of the Great Leap, when in fact they had not. It was, in short, truly a man-made famine (Bernstein, 1984).

State power can be a terrible force for evil, but whether it must necessarily be so, and whether the Great Leap famine was an inevitable consequence of overcentralization, or an aberration, is not yet clear. Here again, it seems that the choice must be between enlightened state policy and unenlightened policy, and not between policy or no policy.

Finally, some may object that the highly politicized model of famine prevention and control developed in China may be totally inappropriate for Africa and other areas of the world. China, after all, has had a unified state and culture for thousands of years, and bureaucratic centralization has not been difficult to achieve there. But African states lack the tradition of national unity and the political culture of bureaucratic rule.

Certainly, Africa has a great disadvantage in this respect, but it is not the Maoist model, or even a Chinese model, that I am advocating, but simply state policy that will place the highest priority on eliminating hunger and famine. Such policy must necessarily be appropriate for its culture. India may serve as an example of another populous and poor country that has eliminated famine through appropriate state policy, but a policy distinctly different from the Chinese model.

In the 1960s and earlier, it was India, not Africa, that was considered the most dangerously food-deficit area of the world, the "basket case" of its time, and among the largest recipients of grain from the United States under Public Law 480. Today, India is self-sufficient in food and even an exporter of rice. Although this happy turn of events has often been attributed to the recent successes of the Green Revolution, India has, in fact, succeeded in avoiding famine for a far longer period of time, virtually since its independence. The Bengal Famine of 1943 constituted

such a psychological trauma, as well as a human tragedy, for the Indian people that, in the view of many observers, no Indian government since then could afford to permit famine to recur. To this end, India possesses a Public Distribution System for food, a key element of which is a system of fair price shops in urban areas (Chopra, 1981, chapters 1 & 27). In addition, as Michelle McAlpin's chapter illustrates,[1] India has effective famine-warning and famine-relief systems. Despite devastating drought and severe crop shortages in Bihar in 1966–67, and again in Maharashtra in 1970–73, for example, no actual famine took place, if famine is measured by excess mortality.

Despite this commendable record in famine prevention, India is still tormented by widespread hunger, malnutrition and poverty. According to one estimate, perhaps one-third or more of India's population is malnourished (receiving fewer than 2100 calories a day; Sanderson & Roy, 1979, 107). As Amartya Sen has pointed out, there is a profound irony in the fact that India's life expectancy is much lower than China's (Sen, 1984, 501).[2] Measured by all standards of human welfare, life in China for the very poor is far more secure than life for India's poor. Yet, it is India that has completely avoided famines over at least the last 30 years, while China produced the Great Leap famine. In India, Sen asserts, a famine such as the Great Leap's could not have occurred because the more open political system would not have allowed it. Yet, from the African perspective today, what is most important is what the Indian and Chinese experiences share: a high priority assigned to the prevention of famine, and a state apparatus able to implement food control.

AFRICA'S PATH?

My emphasis on policy and politics has several implications. . . . First, it suggests that the emphasis given to economic development may be misplaced. Current economic development projects that stress local initiative and self-sufficiency assume a bottom-up type of development process, whereby economic development will be achieved gradually and political development will follow. The expectation that political democracy will necessarily emerge from economic development is based on Western liberal assumptions that may well prove to be disappointing. My stronger objection is that this model is too slow to address the immediate threat to millions of Africans of hunger, disease and starvation. To meet the African food crisis, strong and enlightened political leadership must take precedence over gradual economic planning.

Second, economic development models often bypass the very poor and ignore their immediate problems, a point stressed by Randall Baker.[3] Like him, I believe that the urgent questions posed by hunger and famine must be addressed as issues separate from, and prior to, long-term economic development projects. Both the examples of China and India show—albeit in strikingly different ways—that even very poor countries can do what Baker has suggested: move national food security, especially for the very poorest, up to the highest priority and solve successfully that problem even before agricultural production "takes off." While the economic development of poor countries will eventually solve the problem of widespread hunger and malnutrition, the elimination of famine need not wait for that higher stage of development.

Third, the priority assigned to policy and political development places the question of international assistance, the original focus of this chapter, in its proper context. Foreign aid need not be summarily rejected by African nations as a precondition to their true political independence, but it can be used effectively if closely controlled by a responsible host government. China's limited use of foreign assistance after 1928, and its selective use of World Bank and other international financing at present, are two examples of use of foreign aid conditional on domestic Chinese political control.

In conclusion, an international perspective, and particularly a Chinese one, suggests that there is both good news for Africa and bad

news. The good news is that famine in Africa *will* eventually end. In modern times each region of the world has, in turn, broken out of its famine cycle, and Africa will not be an exception. The experiences of China and India in particular should bring hope to Africa. The bad news, however, is that it may be much more difficult for Africa than for China or India, primarily because it lacks a tradition of political unity and bureaucratic experience. In addition, the militarization of politics and the superpower competition for influence in Africa greatly handicap the efforts of governments to implement a "food first" policy.[4] What is important for Africans is that their governments' political fortunes should be linked to their ability to put a stop to famine, not just for the urban middle class, but for the rural poor as well.

ACKNOWLEDGMENTS

I wish to thank the following people who generously shared their insights about various topics discussed in this chapter: Joel Charny, James Field, Shirley Holmes, Raymond Hopkins, John Kerr, James McCann, Michael Scott, Robert Snow, Subramanian Swamy, Deborah Toler and Homer Williams. None, however, should be held responsible for the views expressed. Swarthmore College and the National Endowment for the Humanities provided support during the period when I worked on this chapter.

NOTES

1. "Famine Relief Policy in India: six lessons for Africa" in Glantz, pp. 391–414.

2. Sen states that life expectancy in India is 52 years, while life expectancy in China is 66–9 years. According to the *1984 World Population Data Sheet* (Population Reference Bureau, Washington, DC), life expectancy in India was 50 years, and in China 65 years.

3. "Linking and Sinking: economic externalities and the persistence of destitution and famine in Africa" in Glantz, pp. 149–170.

4. This term is borrowed from the title *Food First* by Lappé & Collins (1977).

Chapter 10

The Moral Status of Animals

The issues examined thus far in this section on *social justice* have concerned groups of people who have been denied, to one degree or another, a full share of the goods of society. Attempts to solve these problems have usually begun with the recognition that all human beings are valuable in themselves. From this it follows that all people should have the opportunity to live their lives in full and meaningful ways. At the very least, all people should have their basic subsistence needs met and should be free from the various forms of unfair discrimination that may deny them the opportunity to live full and meaningful lives.

As the first two chapters of this section focused on the unfair distribution of the goods of society, the third chapter focuses on the unfair distribution of its evils. Some evils, such as those produced by storms, earthquakes, and disease, cannot be avoided; other forms are deliberately created by human beings. Sometimes this evil is directed toward other human beings in the forms of war, crime, and violence. At other times, however, evil is deliberately created to achieve good for human beings. Animals, nonhuman animals, bear most of the burden of this type of evil.

We raise animals in deplorable conditions, then slaughter them painfully and proceed to eat their flesh and use their skins. We cage them and use them in millions of scientific experiments each year, some of them quite painful. We test caustic chemicals on them. We hunt them for sport. We keep them pent up in small cages in zoos. We use them for entertainment in rodeos, circuses, horse races, polo matches, and other sporting events. We kill them to provide clothing for ourselves. We tolerate abusive pet owners. We gather homeless pets and euthanize them. If we treated human beings in this manner we would surely be the most cruel, immoral society that ever existed. In fact, for some who believe that animals have moral status, this is exactly the moral situation that exists. If animals have "moral status," they must be considered along with human beings when we consider the consequences of our actions on others. They must be counted as one of the "others" when we consider the harms and benefits of our actions on ourselves and others. In addition, any being with moral status may not be used simply as a means for the good of others. It may not be treated as a thing or merely as a piece of property.

Instead of talking about the moral status of animals, some talk about the "rights" of animals. For the moment we may use these terms interchangeably. Many claim that nonhuman animals have moral rights that are equal to those of human animals, especially the rights to be free from pain and suffering. To treat them in the evil ways mentioned previously is morally comparable to treating humans in this manner. We would deplore such treatment of humans and take firm steps to prevent it; some animal rights advocates who deplore such treatment of animals often take quite dramatic steps to prevent it. Medical researchers have been mailed letters warning them of harm if they continued their experiments, letters that were booby-trapped with razor blades to impress them with the threat. Animals have been "liberated" from farms and zoos. Hunters have been harassed as they stalked their game, as have whaling vessels and those who kill baby seals. Institutions that profit from animal "exploitation" have been subject to protests, boycotts, and acts of civil disobedience. There are numerous groups advocating the rights of animals, most of whom have established their own Web sites.

Some press for an outright ban on the use of animals solely for human benefit; others reject this extreme position in favor of their own extreme position. Arguing that only human beings have moral status, they believe that animals are simply a means to the good of human beings. Just as a chair is a piece of property and is good for sitting, so animals are just property that is good for food, sport, and medical experiments. According to this more conventional view, there is no moral problem with harming and killing animals for human purposes because animals are not moral beings. They have no moral status; they have no rights.

Somewhere between these two extremes lies the view that denies animals have full moral status but asserts that there is too much needless animal suffering and death. According to those who hold this view, we ought to be much more concerned with the welfare of animals. For example, they believe that it should be considered immoral to raise animals in the wretched conditions that we often do, and to kill so many of them for food. Many medical experiments are unnecessary as well and ought not to be performed. Zoos should provide better environments for animals, and hunters should hunt animals only to reduce their numbers in overpopulated areas, not for sport. Some animal studies, some hunting, and some raising of animals is important for human beings and is morally justified. But animals can suffer as a result of our actions, and we ought not let them do so if it is at all avoidable.

To what degree, if any, animals should be thought of as having moral status, especially the right not to suffer and die for the good of human beings, is usually not classified as a problem of social justice. Admittedly, it is a bit of a stretch to include it here. However, if animals are moral beings, then they can be the victims of unfair discrimination. If they have rights as humans do, then using them as a means to the good of humans not only violates the principle of beneficence but also violates the principle of justice. It violates the principle of beneficence because our treatment of animals often produces great pain and suffering for them. Even if we raised, killed, and experimented on animals in painless and humane ways, doing so would still violate the principle of justice. To use any being with moral status merely as a means to the good of others is to treat it unfairly. It is to practice unfair discrimination, in this case an unfair distribution of the burdens of society. Matters of unfair discrimination are matters of social justice.

The real moral question here is this: What should our moral ideals look like in the treatment of animals? The answer depends on whether animals are to be thought of as having moral status or moral rights. Should we widen the circle of those who have moral rights to include animals and thus treat them more as equals? Or should we keep them out of the moral universe inhabited by human beings and simply be less cruel to them than we have been in the past? Should we think of animals simply as our property, and thus not worry about how we treat them any more than we might worry about how we treat the plants in our garden? This is a very complicated issue, one that will require the examination of some of our most deeply held moral beliefs.

The Problem

What, if anything, we should change about our treatment of animals will depend significantly on how we treat them now. The facts that will be examined in the next section will be very important for solving the problem of this chapter. If some of the atrocious ways that we have treated animals have changed since they were first brought to the attention of a wide audience in the mid–1970s, if things have vastly improved since then, there may no longer be a need for drastic change. If, on the other hand, conditions have improved little, the problem may demand a dramatic response from all people who consider themselves morally good persons.

Of course, facts alone will not settle the issue. Facts can often be open to more than one interpretation. For example, a man spanking a child may be seen as a child abuser by some and as a parent teaching discipline by others. The treatment of animals may also be viewed in various ways, depending especially on how they are valued. Sometimes animals are given *extrinsic* value only. They are valued only for what they can do for others. For example, some people may view storing monkeys in small cages and using them in painful medical experiments as simply necessary for medical advancement. The monkey has no value in itself. It is just a monkey. It is replaceable by other monkeys.

On the other hand, sometimes we view animals as having *intrinsic* value. We see them as worthwhile in themselves. Beloved pets are vested with great value by many of their owners, for example. These owners often consider them more important than some humans, and treat them better because of it. Pets have value because their owners give them value. Like works of art or fancy sports cars, they have value because they are desired or wanted by their owners. To harm their pets deliberately would be as immoral for many pet owners as it would be for them to harm a child. How we value animals determines how we treat them, so it is important for us to revisit and even expand the notion of value discussed in Part 1.

Clarifying Concepts

Things may have value in more than one way. Objects desired as beautiful works of art have aesthetic value, good scientific research has cognitive value, and right actions performed with the proper motive have moral value. The two general categories of value that are of special interest to us are extrinsic and intrinsic values. **Extrinsic value,** sometimes called "instrumental value," is what things have that are *good for* something. Tools that are useful for building have extrinsic value, for example, as do animals that are useful for providing food for humans.

Intrinsic value, on the other hand, is a property possessed by things that are *good in themselves.* Some philosophers have claimed that most of the "things" that have intrinsic value are various states of mind—such as pleasure or knowledge.

Others have claimed that love or freedom or virtue also count among the intrinsically valuable, and still others, such as Kant, have claimed that rational beings are intrinsically valuable. Human persons are considered to be intrinsically valuable by most people. We think it is wrong to use them simply as instruments for another's good. Many animal rights activists think that at least some animals also have intrinsic value.

Inherent value is often thought of as identical with intrinsic value. The two terms are considered synonymous by most. However, one of our possible solutions to the problem of this chapter, the *animal rights* view, will make a distinction between these two types of value. Both are types of value that a being has in itself. Saying that a being has either intrinsic or inherent value means that it is worthwhile not just because it is valued by others for a certain purpose, but because there is something within it that is valuable, regardless of its usefulness to others.

According to the animal rights possible solution, and especially according to one of its staunchest defenders, Tom Regan, to say that a being has *intrinsic* value means that it has certain characteristics that make it valuable. As Kant had said before, if a being can think and reason and make free choices, it has characteristics that make it intrinsically valuable. On the other hand, a being is *inherently* valuable, or worthwhile in itself, not because it possesses such characteristics, but just because it is the being that it is. No matter how smart, or how free, or how creative we may or may not be, we are all worthwhile in ourselves and all *equally* worthwhile in ourselves. According to Regan, it is the individual being that is valuable in itself. It is the bare individual and not the characteristics it possesses that are valuable. If it loses some of those characteristics, it still retains its full value. A noted mathematician and a cognitively challenged child may have different extrinsic value and different intrinsic value, but they have the same inherent value.

The characteristics that make any being intrinsically valuable are called **value-conferring characteristics.** Any being that possesses them is intrinsically valuable. Included among these characteristics are rationality and autonomy, as well as the ability to perceive, to remember, to experience emotions and feelings, to desire, and to experience yourself as having a past and a future. Beings who have such characteristics experience themselves as **subjects of a life,** as individuals who are conscious of having a life that matters to them. Being a subject of a life, as opposed to a mere creature of instinct or a being with no consciousness at all, is what, for many, makes having a life so valuable.

Another important moral concept is that of **moral status.** To say that a being has moral status is to say that it must be counted among those who have moral relationships to all other beings with moral status. If we think of these relationships—especially the rights and duties that exist among and between those with moral status—as comprising a "moral universe," then having moral status means that a being is part of the moral universe. In the history of Western civilization this universe has gradually expanded over the centuries. Slaves, members of minority races, and women have gradually been given full moral status over many centuries—at least in principle. We still question whether fetuses have full moral status; in the future we may question whether certain types of alien beings that we may discover have it. Some say that even very sophisticated computers may be granted moral status some day.

Another way to say that a being has moral status is to say that it is a **person.** We used this term in the chapter on abortion, but we will avoid it here, preferring instead the phrase "moral status." Although the concept of a person may be used in its moral sense as a synonym for moral status, to confuse it with the concept of a human being is too easy. It just sounds too strange to most of us to ask, for example, if an animal is a person, especially as we often use the terms as mutually exclusive. So although may be technically correct to frame the question of this chapter as a question about the personhood of animals, we will use the term "moral status" instead.

In this chapter we will examine the sort of value that animals have in order to decide about their moral status. We do this to discover the morally acceptable ways to treat animals. Some of the possible solutions that will be examined in this chapter are based on decisions about moral acceptability using different theories of obligation from the one adopted in this text. Revisiting these theories, originally discussed in Part 1, will be helpful.

Two of our possible solutions, the *animal welfare* view and the *animal liberation* view, adopt a utilitarian theory of obligation. According to **utilitarianism,** an action is right if it results in a greater proportion of good over evil consequences than its alternative. Only the consequences count in determining right from wrong, the consequences for everyone with moral status who is affected by the action. In order to make moral decisions we must consider the harms and benefits that result from our actions and choose the action with the greatest amount of benefits or the least amount of harms. From the perspective of our ethical theory, utilitarians determine right from wrong in much the same way we would if we used only the principle of beneficence.

For a utilitarian who believes that animals have moral status, any moral decision concerning animals has to take into account the consequences of our actions on them as well as any consequences they might have for humans. The raising and killing of veal calves for food may produce good consequences for humans, but the pain and suffering of doing so for the young animals is considerable. Not raising veal calves for food may very well produce a greater balance of good over evil than doing so. To use another example, testing cosmetic products by placing caustic materials in the eyes of animals may avoid some possible harm to humans who may otherwise have eye injuries. However, whether such testing is morally acceptable depends on the amount of pain and suffering experienced by the animals. If their misery outweighs the pain of a few human beings who might otherwise experience pain, it is wrong to use animals for such tests.

Another ethical theory often appealed to by the animal rights possible solution, is called the **rights theory.** According to this view, to say that animals have moral status means that they have rights. All beings with moral status have rights. These rights should be seen as basic, as not depending on anything more basic, such as principles or rules. In addition, rights should be understood as equal in everyone who has them. If an animal has a right to life, for example, this right is as important as a human being's right to life.

From the perspective of our ethical theory, adopting a rights theory would be similar to adopting a set of rules such as "Don't kill," "Don't steal," and so on, with no reference to the moral principles that justify them. Instead, to have a right is to have a protected freedom. A right to worship, to protest, to vote, and so on, are protected freedoms in most democracies. These are sometimes called *negative* rights because they require only that a person be left alone to do as he or she wishes. Rights may also be thought of as claims to something that others have a duty to provide. Welfare rights are claims to have the subsistence needs of some met by others. These sorts of rights are *positive* rights, as they require that others not just refrain from interfering with your freedom but that they provide you with whatever you have a right to. Those who claim that animals have rights sometimes mean they have positive rights. Owners of animals, for example, have the duty to provide them with food and shelter. For the most part, however, the focus is on negative rights, the right to be left alone, the right to be free from confinement, pain, suffering, and death. Animal rights supporters believe it is immoral to use animals for food, clothing, scientific experiments, entertainment, and so on because it violates these moral rights. According to the animal rights view, it is just as wrong to use animals for food as it would be to use a human child for food.

Our final concept is that of **speciesism.** This concept was popularized by Peter Singer, the main advocate of the animal liberation view, in the 1970s. It is used as a way to classify our treatment of animals as a form of unfair discrimination, comparable to racism and sexism. Just as *racism* is a word for a form of unfair discrimination, a way to refer to the manner in which some people treat other people in an inferior way because they are of a different race, and *sexism* is a word that refers to treating some people unfairly because of their gender, so *speciesism* is also a name for a form of unfair discrimination—a way to refer to the treatment of non-human animals in an inferior manner just because they are not human animals.

Formulating the Problem

In many respects the problem of Chapter 10 resembles the abortion issue because determining what is morally acceptable treatment of animals is a two-part problem. The first part has to do with the moral status of animals. Once we know the moral status of animals, the second part of the problem addresses the moral acceptability of using animals for the benefit of human beings.

Let us *formulate the problem* addressed in this chapter as follows:

a. *What is the moral status of animals?*

b. *Under what conditions, if any, may animals be used for the benefit of human beings?*

We will see later that part (b) is best classified as a **conflict of rules** type of moral problem, where the conflict essentially is between animal interests and human interests. Part (a) is not a question about right and wrong, but is at root a question about the value of animals. As was said previously, there are many ways that animals may be used for the benefit of human beings. Although much could be said in what follows about the use of animals for entertainment and for sport, as well as hunting animals for profit, we will focus on two of the most controversial of uses of animals for the benefit of humans—factory farming and animal research.

Possible Solutions

Four *possible solutions* are defended in Chapter 10: the conventional view, the animal welfare view, the animal liberation view, and the animal rights view.

The first is called the **conventional** view because it has dominated thinking in the West at least until very recently. It claims that *animals have no moral status.* This is because they have no intrinsic value. They may be more or less valued by their owners, but in themselves they have only extrinsic value. Animals are the property of human beings and may be used by them to suit their purposes. It may not be morally acceptable to inflict needless pain and suffering on animals, however. Being needlessly cruel to animals is wrong, but only because of the effect that such cruelty could have on us. Many a wicked person started out by being cruel to animals. Although we are morally obligated to avoid being cruel to animals for trivial purposes, we may cause them pain and suffering when doing so serves important human interests. Animals are ours to use for our own benefit. If they are useful for food, entertainment, medicine, or the progress of science, they may be used for those purposes with no moral hesitation.

The **animal welfare** view claims that *animals have some moral status,* but a lesser moral status than that possessed by human beings. This is because they have some intrinsic value, though less of it than human beings. Human beings are always and everywhere more valuable than animals, and thus always and everywhere have more moral status than nonhuman animals. Because animals have some moral status, however, the animal welfare view claims that causing animals to suffer is usually immoral. We should avoid being cruel to animals ourselves as a moral obligation. We should also work to eliminate the needless suffering inflicted on animals by others. We should especially work to end the cruel practices of factory farming, as well as the painful and often useless experiments in which animals are used as subjects.

Nevertheless, although causing needless animal suffering is wrong, some animal suffering is permitted. According to the animal welfare view, when the use of animals for human purposes is important enough, even when that involves some suffering and even death on the animal's part, then using them may be morally acceptable. Sometimes animals are needed for food, and sometimes the experiments that use them as subjects save millions of human beings from suffering and death. We should always treat animals in the most humane ways possible when we do use them for our own good. But because their moral status is not on a par with that of human beings, it is sometimes morally acceptable to use them for our purposes.

The third view is called the **animal liberation** view. Its chief advocate has been Peter Singer, an ethicist whose ideas on world hunger were examined in the previous chapter. His book, *Animal Liberation,*[1] first published in 1975, has converted many to the various animal liberation and animal rights movements that are now alive and well in this and many other countries. Singer is a utilitarian, so he believes that the consequences of actions alone determine their morally acceptability. He also believes, as do all utilitarians, that the consequences of our actions must be counted equally for everyone with moral status who may be affected by them. We are not supposed to count ourselves or our family members, for example, as more important than others when we calculate the effects of our actions.

The important claim made by the animal liberation view is that *nonhuman animals have full moral status*. Just as in the past we have widened the moral status circle to include those formerly excluded—women, slaves, and humans of all races—those who hold the animal liberation view now propose that we widen the circle even further to include nonhuman animals as well. Moreover, unlike animal welfare advocates, they propose that the moral status of nonhuman animals be on a par with that of human animals. On their utilitarian view, using *nonhuman* animals in painful medical experiments or as sources of food is immoral, because it would cause a greater balance of evil over good for the total group of those with moral status—human and nonhuman animals. If animals have equal moral status with humans, then causing pain and suffering to animals is just as immoral as causing pain and suffering to human beings.

To defend his view Singer does not appeal to the intrinsic value of animals, but rather depends especially on the concept of "having interests." Having interests, for Singer and for most utilitarians, is the very basis of morality. If no one had interests, if there were no things a person wanted to possess or wanted to avoid, there would be no need for morality. Morality promotes the fulfillment of positive interests (benefits) and prohibits the causing of negative interests (harms). Because animals are conscious, because they are sentient beings, they can feel pain and can suffer in other ways as well. Because they can suffer, animals have interests—especially the negative interests not to feel pain, not to suffer, and not to die. Rocks are not conscious and thus cannot suffer, so they do not have such interests. This is why they are not moral beings, why they do not have moral status—because they cannot be harmed or cannot benefit from the actions of others. But animals can be harmed. This is why it is not immoral to step on a rock, but it is immoral deliberately to step on the head of a puppy. You cannot hurt a rock, but you can hurt a puppy.

If we grant for the moment that animals have interests and that having interests is the basis for having moral status, can we still not discriminate between the interests of humans and those of other animals? Are not human beings vastly superior and thus vastly more important than nonhuman animals? After all, human beings can reason, communicate, and create grand things much more fully than animals. Humans are superior beings, they have more intrinsic value, do they not? So why then should we think of animals as our moral equals? Why should we think of their suffering and their interest in avoiding it as equally important as human interests? After all, they are just animals, are they not?

To think and act this way is to practice what Singer calls "speciesism." Human beings may have more of the characteristics that we all consider valuable. They indeed are more intrinsically valuable than animals. However, when it comes to suffering, the most important of all interests for morality to protect, the suffering of human animals is no more important than the suffering of nonhuman animals. They can suffer just as much as we can, so to deny that their suffering is as important as ours and thus that they do not have equal moral status is simply a form of prejudice. For Singer, this is speciesism, and speciesism is as unfair a form of discrimination as racism or sexism. The animal liberation view rejects speciesism and argues for an equal consideration of the interests of all animals, human and nonhuman alike. For them, causing nonhuman animals to suffer is as immoral as causing human beings to suffer. In particular, using any sentient animal for sport, for food, and for research is almost always immoral.

The final view to consider is the **animal rights** view. There is an ambiguity in the phrase "animal rights" that should be clarified to avoid confusion. On the one hand, it refers to the general view that animals have moral status and ought to be treated as such. This is the common meaning that the phrase has for most "animal rights" advocates. On the other hand, it refers to a specific way of defending the view that animals have moral status. According to this view, animals have moral status because they have rights. Singer holds an animal rights view in the first sense of the phrase but not in the second sense. For him, animals have moral status because they can suffer, and thus they have an interest in avoiding suffering, and thus they must be considered equals among those for whom be harmful consequences of our actions must be considered.

The leading advocate of moral status for animals because they have rights has been Tom Regan. His book, *The Case for Animal Rights* (1983),[2] as well as numerous other writings has been extremely influential to many in the the animal rights movement. Because of the very radical view it has taken, it may have produced even more zealous converts than Singer's writings. In this book and elsewhere, Regan claims that *some nonhuman animals have rights.* To say that they have rights means essentially that they have moral status. They have especially the right to life and the right not to suffer. Not only do animals have such moral rights, moreover, but they possess them just as fully as human animals do.

Now anyone can claim rights for any entity. I may claim that pine trees have rights, especially the right not to be used as Christmas trees. This is hardly a convincing claim, however. Why should we find Regan's claim that animals have rights any more convincing? To justify his claim Regan begins with another claim—that some animals, especially mammals with properties similar to ours, have intrinsic value. Regan argues for this claim much as Kant argued for the intrinsic value of human beings. Just as Kant claimed intrinsic value for human beings because they are rational and autonomous, so Regan argues that some animals have intrinsic value because they have similar properties. In particular, some animals can be conscious of themselves as having a past and a future. Because of this they can experience themselves as the "subject of a life." This life includes their beliefs, emotions, desires, future expectations, and ability to reason and communicate. This is why they are intrinsically valuable—because they are not only biologically alive but because they also have value-conferring characteristics similar to our own.

His second bold claim is that not only are nonhuman animals to be valued in themselves, but their value is just as high as that of human animals. Even though human animals have value-conferring characteristics to a higher degree than most nonhuman animals, nonhuman animals are still just as valuable as human beings. We will have to wait for the section on "Moral Reasoning" for a fuller account of why animal rights proponents hold this position, but they do. They believe that all animals who are subjects of a life, human and nonhuman alike, have equal value, and thus have equal rights.

Because of animals' value and their rights, to use animals for human purposes is always wrong, even if we do so in humane ways. Just as it is not morally acceptable to raise and kill a child for food, or to use a human being in medical experiments designed to benefit others, it is immoral to use nonhuman animals for food or as subjects in such experiments, or in any number of other ways that we use animals for human purposes. As a child has moral status because it has rights, so also do animals have moral status because they have rights. Rights exist because both human and nonhuman animals have equal value as subjects of a life.

Facts and Assumptions

Facts

One *fact* of importance is that *many nonhuman animals have several of the same characteristics and abilities that we think of as important for human animals to have.* In particular, some animals can have a psychological life, an inner conscious life, that is similar in many respects to that of a typical human being. Some animals can be conscious of themselves as having a past and a future. They can form beliefs, have emotions and desires, understand general concepts, reason, communicate, form attachments to other animals, and so on. They may not possess all of these properties in the same way or to the same degree that human animals do, but many nonhuman animals are quite like us in a number of these ways. Anyone who has an intelligent pet, or has observed animals using sign language, or has read about the behavior of wolves or whales or dolphins knows this already.

Another relevant fact is that *animals can suffer.* Although this was not always an accepted fact, those who dispute this claim today usually use the word "suffer" with a different meaning from its ordinary use. If suffering includes knowing what misery lies ahead, understanding its probable intensity and duration, grieving one's loss, and so on, then maybe most animals do not suffer. If it means experiencing physical pain, on the other hand, then surely there is little doubt that most animals can suffer. They act as though they are suffering. Many of them have physiological structures that are similar to ours, structures that enable us to feel pain. It would strain belief beyond reasonable bounds to hold, for example, that a conscious animal feels no pain when it is severely burned and cries out in misery.

Animals can also suffer emotionally. They can feel loss, fear, anxiety, loneliness, and depression. We cannot get into the consciousness of animals to verify the presence of these psychological states, but neither can we get into the consciousness of other human beings. We simply take their behavior as an expression of these states. Moreover, several studies have been done to create these emotions in animals. When research animals exhibit fear behavior, depression behavior, and any other sorts of behavior the experiments were designed to produce, these behaviors are taken to be expressions of such emotional states, as they would be in human beings.

A third fact or set of facts is that *animals do suffer.* In fact, eliminating animal suffering is the goal of most animal rights activists, a goal that many pursue vigorously, sometimes even beyond the limits of the law. If we are to select the most reasonable possible solution to our problem, it is extremely important for us to understand the extent of animal suffering, especially the suffering caused by human beings.

There are many ways in which human beings cause pain and suffering to animals. We trap and hunt them for sport and profit, cage them in zoos and circuses, and abuse them in farm and domestic settings. The two most widespread and troublesome ways of causing animals to suffer, however, are factory farming and research. In *factory farming,* especially in raising chickens, pigs, and cattle, the focus is placed on human interests at the expense of animal interests. Animals and animal products are produced for food in the fastest and the most economical ways possible. This makes a steady and relatively inexpensive supply of meat, cheese, milk, and eggs available for human use, but it makes life for the animals raised for food truly horrific.

Most of the chickens raised for food in this country are raised on factory farms. Up to twenty chickens are crowded together per square meter in polluted conditions, with little light and almost no exercise. After eight to nine weeks they are slaughtered. About six billion chickens are raised for food in this manner each year. Most chickens used for egg production are also kept in crowded conditions, with five or six to each fourteen-inch-square wire mesh cage. These cages are stacked on top of each other in long rows, with as many as fifty thousand birds in each large shed. Because of these crowded conditions, and because they lack the freedom to engage in their natural behaviors such as nesting and foraging, they often become aggressive. To prevent injury to each other much of their upper and lower beaks are cut off with hot irons. This is a very painful procedure, since it cuts right through the nerves of their beaks with no anesthesia.

The most cruelly confined cattle are the male calves of dairy cows.[3] These are calves raised for veal. The tenderness of veal is achieved at the expense of these baby calves. They are taken from their mothers a few days after birth and confined in crates. These crates are less than two feet wide and have uncomfortable slatted floors that allow the feces and urine of the calves to fall down below the cages. They are fed a milk substitute from which the iron has been removed. This causes anemia, which makes their flesh light in color and makes them very weak. They can hardly stand, but stand they must with no exercise through their short sixteen-week lives. About 10 percent of them die from sickness before this time.

The manner in which pigs are raised and bred is perhaps the most sickening of all. It surprises many to learn that pigs are very intelligent, very social animals. Yet over 90 percent of factory-farmed pigs are raised in highly mechanized "hog houses," most of which are located in North Carolina. Ten million pigs are produced in that state each year. Each hog house is about the size of a football field and contains up to one thousand pigs. These animals live their entire lives packed tightly together in abominable conditions, where all aspects of their lives—feeding, lighting, reproduction, and even nursing their young—are managed with assembly line precision. Nursing sows are kept in what are called "battery cages," steel cages with bars that nearly immobilize them. Their young can just reach them to suckle but cannot otherwise come into contact with their mothers. This causes great distress for the mothers.

There are enormous problems of pollution associated with this type of farming. Each pig creates some three gallons of waste each day. Much of this waste lies in lagoons, untreated. It can can leak into streams and other bodies of water and create human health hazards. The animals themselves are victims of pollution and crowding and the other conditions in which they live as well, conditions that would cause widespread illness if left untreated. They are fed great quantities of antibiotics to avoid this. In fact, more than half the antibiotics produced in this country are fed to animals. Such use also causes a health hazard for humans, as the antibiotics are passed on to us when we eat the flesh of animals. The practice of using drugs for preventive purposes in animals and the subsequent ingestion of these drugs by people who eat animal flesh lead to an overuse of antibiotics for humans, creating strains of bacteria that will be resistant to antibiotics in the future.

In addition to the billions of animals that suffer and die each year as a result of factory farming, millions more suffer from their role as *research subjects.* There are several different types of research that use animals as subjects. Some 40 percent of animal experiments use animals as subjects in scientific research, seeking to discover the causes of disease, the effects of various forces on the body, methods of animal learning, and so on. The National Institutes of Health spend about $3 billion a year to support this type of research. Other types of research use animals as subjects in medical experiments. These are directed toward finding cures for disease, and focus especially on such items as testing for the effectiveness of various surgical techniques and the effectiveness and toxicity levels of various drugs, which are always tested on animals prior to their use on humans. Medical experiments account for about 25 percent of all animal experiments. Another 15 percent of the animals used in experiments are used in educational institutions. Here mostly dogs serve as instructional material for medical students, while frogs, mice, pigeons, and rats are used as instructional material by high school and college biology and psychology students.

The final 20 percent of animal experiments are for testing the safety of consumer products. Countless animals have been used to test various sorts of consumer goods for safety, such as cosmetics, pesticides, and various types of food additives. Perhaps the most famous of these experiments are the Draize tests. These tests are named after J. H. Draize, an employee of the Federal Department of Agriculture who invented them in the 1940s.[4] The tests measure how irritating a substance is to the eyes of a rabbit. After a rabbit is immobilized and its eyes forced open, drops of substances such as cosmetic products or household cleaning products are placed in each of its eyes. The eyes are then forced closed and observed over the course of several days for damage. Many sorts of caustic substances have been tested in this manner, including oven cleaner and bleach, causing severe damage and great pain to the animals. It has been one of the real triumphs of the animal rights movement in this country that Draize testing has all but ceased for cosmetics. Nevertheless, animals continue to be subject to consumer product testing on a grand scale.

Although accurate figures are difficult to come by, approximately twenty to twenty-four million animals are used as subjects of scientific and medical research each year in the United States.[5] Worldwide, the numbers are estimated to be around 100 million. About 85 percent of the current number of animals used in research in this country are rats, mice, or birds. Many medical and scientific experiments use nonhuman primates, dogs, and cats as subjects. Although these animals often receive analgesics or anesthesia to eliminate the physical pain that they would otherwise experience, there are still many animals who have no medication or who are undermedicated. Such experiments often cause considerable pain to these animals. Even if the animals are used in painless procedures, the requisite handling, confinement, and isolation causes them much stress-related suffering. In the end, most animals used in experiments are killed so that their tissue may be studied further.

Since the 1970s the number of primates used in experiments has remained about the same in this country, accounting for about 1 per cent of all animals used. Most of these are monkeys, but the number also includes chimpanzees, gorillas, and orangutans. Currently, some ninety to one hundred researchers in the United States are working with nonhuman primates. The number of dogs and cats that serve as research subjects has dropped nearly 50 percent over the same time period. Worldwide, the total number of animals used as research subjects has been halved since the 1970s. Much of this reduction in animal suffering is due to the political activity of animal rights groups. In addition, the discovery of alternative methods of research—methods that use human tissue and cell cultures or computer simulations, for example—has also contributed to the reduction of the number of animals used in medical and scientific research.

The recent trend toward using animals less often as research subjects is good for some, but it does little to reduce the pain and suffering endured by the millions of animals who continue to be used as research tools. For example, in a commonly used test, called LD80 (lethal dose 80 percent), researchers vaccinate animals against a particular disease such as diphtheria or tetanus. Then they expose them and a control group of animals (ones not vaccinated) to the disease. The vaccine is considered successful if 80 percent of the vaccinated animals stay healthy and 80 percent of the control group dies. Improvements in this test have led to a 50 percent reduction in the number of animals required as subjects.[6]

Fewer animals are required in another test as well, LD50 (lethal dose 50 percent). In this test about 200 animals are required as subjects to test for the toxicity of a substance—usually a household substance, a pesticide, or a food additive. The animals are force-fed the substance, often a very painful process itself, in order to determine the dose that would kill half the group. The good news for animals is that current protocols call for only one-tenth the number of animal subjects to determine the lethal level of the substance. Because LD50 is a fairly common test, used on approximately 5 million animals each year—including dogs, rabbits, rats, and monkeys—the improved version ought to use "only" about half a million animals.

Despite the downward trend in many areas of animal research in the 1990s, however, there has been a recent upward trend in the area of DNA research that uses animals. In some of the more promising yet frightening versions of this type of research, the egg of a female animal, usually a mouse or a monkey, is genetically altered, then fertilized, then implanted into a female of the species and grown to term. The genetic alteration involves splicing into its DNA the defective gene of a human being. Usually it is a gene known to be responsible for some type of human genetic disease or propensity to contract a disease. The genetically altered animal, called a "transgenic," then develops the disease. Because it now contains a more accurate model of human DNA, it may be studied more effectively for possible cures. The number of animals, especially mice, used for genetic engineering research has already increased tenfold since 1990.[7] Monkeys are often used in such tests and will probably be used much more extensively in the future.

Some of the more horrific animal experiments that have been documented by many animal rights activists, such as members of PETA (People for the Ethical Treatment of Animals), include studies of the effects of drugs and alcohol on the hearts and lungs of dogs, studies of cats with electrodes implanted in their brains to increase scientific understanding of sensation and neurological disorders, studies performed on chimpanzees to test new vaccines against hepatitis B, studies of brain-damaged monkeys whose skulls have deliberately been crushed, and others that are equally painful. Discussion of these sorts of especially cruel experiments has been kept to a minimum because the degree to which animals ought to be used as research subjects should be decided on rational grounds. Although the cruel treatment of the animal subjects counts as part of these grounds, focusing on the more dramatic cases of animal experimentation may reduce the issue solely to an emotional one. The benefits of using animals as research subjects must also be given a fair hearing before we form a reasoned judgment about the moral acceptability of animal experimentation.

Research using animals has led to the development of vaccines for smallpox, diphtheria, tetanus, polio, measles, chicken pox, Lyme disease, and other diseases. It has also produced insulin for the control of type 1 diabetes, chemotherapy for cancer patients, open-heart surgery and pacemakers for heart patients, various techniques for organ transplants, antibiotics, anesthesia, advances in the detection and treatment of various sorts of cancer, and the detection and beginnings of treatment for AIDS (acquired immunodeficiency syndrome). It has also been responsible for the development of treatments for kidney disease, eye ailments, stroke, arthritis, and spinal cord injuries—to name just some of its benefits.

Descriptive Ethics

Although the number of animals used in experiments has declined recently, and this decline may continue as more and more alternatives to animal research are found, most researchers hold little hope that animals may be replaced altogether as subjects of research. If this is so, it is important to formulate regulations about the proper conditions, if there are any, for conducting morally acceptable animal research. As usual, we will begin with the rules currently in place, with descriptive ethics. In the process we will also examine the laws and regulations governing factory farming.

We will begin by examining what the **law** has to say about acceptable animal research. The first point is that raising animals on factory farms and using them in experiments is legal in this and most other countries. There are, however, restrictions in the form of legislation and regulations. Generally, these restrictions are fairly strict in most European countries, where researchers must often be licensed by the government, receive approval for their experiments from a national committee, and even receive training designed to make them more sensitive to the pain, stress, and needs of their animal subjects.

In the United States, on the other hand, rules and regulations are generally less strict, and less strictly enforced. At one time in this country you could beat to death an animal that you owned with no legal repercussions. Now cruelty to all animals is forbidden by both state and federal laws. Owners must treat pets and farm animals humanely or pay the legal price. For purposes of raising animals for food, however, especially on factory farms, other than the requirement that animals must be fed and sheltered and not be the victims of intentional cruelty, there are very few laws or regulations to control just how they are housed, fed, caged, or otherwise handled.

The central piece of legislation governing the treatment of animals in this country, the Animal Welfare Act, is aimed especially at regulating animal research. Passed in 1966 and amended several times since then, this law establishes humane guidelines for the use and care of animal subjects of research and requires each institution that uses animals to form an institutional Animal Care and Use Committee that oversees these guidelines. These committees are composed of scientists, at least one member of the general public who is not affiliated with the institution, and at least one veterinarian. They are charged with inspecting the institution's laboratories and approving all research protocols. In addition to this type of oversight, inspectors of the U.S. Department of Agriculture (USDA) make surprise visits to these institutions each year to ensure that USDA guidelines are being followed.

Animal rights activists have criticized this law primarily on three grounds. First, it excludes from protection both rodents and birds, by far the most commonly used research animals. Second, the standards that define humane treatment are often left to researchers themselves to establish. For conscientious and caring institutions this may be quite acceptable. For other institutions, however, such standards seem like no standards at all. For example, the degree to which animals experience pain and suffering, something that must be reported to the USDA each year, is determined by the institutions themselves. According to these reports, more than half the animals used experience no pain or suffering, another third had pain that was relieved by anesthesia or analgesia, while less than 10 percent experienced pain. Since simply being confined induces distress, many believe that these figures vastly underrepresent the true facts of animal suffering.

Third, because of insufficient funding the USDA has far too few inspectors to enforce its guidelines effectively. In 2000, for example, it had a budget of only $10 million, and only seventy inspectors to visit some 1,300 laboratories as well as to inspect animal dealers and transporters. In response to animal rights activists, the USDA budget for enforcement was increased slightly (by $2 million) in 2001. In addition, the continuing legal efforts of animal rights activists to include birds and rodents under the umbrella of the Animal Welfare Act appear to be paying off, and it is likely that they will soon succeed.

In addition to legal restrictions, the spirit of the self-imposed rules being accepted more and more by animal researchers appears to be governed by what the **scientific community** refers to as the "three Rs"—reduction, refinement, and replacement. The number of animals used in experiments is being *reduced* by eliminating unimportant research or by using improved statistical techniques; it is also being *refined* to cause less suffering; and it is being *replaced* where possible by using alternative methods of research. The general idea that is gaining wider acceptance in the scientific community is not to use animals first, but only when necessary. And when it is necessary to use animals, the experiment should be conducted as humanely as possible.

Public opinion has become less supportive of animal research in the past two decades. In 1985 about two-thirds of Americans agreed that "scientists should be allowed to do research that causes pain and injury to animals, even to dogs and chimpanzees *if* it produces new information about human health problems."[8] In 1995, however, that number had fallen to 53 percent. In Europe there is even less support. The key factor in determining public opinion is the importance of the experiment for essential human health. Using animals to test consumer products is not favorably received; using them for cancer research is. Public opinion is less supportive of animal research now; indeed public pressure has been the main motivator for improving the ways that animals are treated.

In addition to the law, the scientific community, and public opinion, most of the major **religions** officially accept animal research that is humane and important for human health. This is surely true of the major Western religions—Judaism, Christianity, and Islam. Animal life may have value, but human life—created in the image of God—has considerably higher value. Moreover, according to most scriptural traditions, God has given human beings control, even dominion, over animals. This does not mean that we can do anything we wish to animals. Our control is governed by kindness. Instead, it means that we are the "stewards" of animals, we control their lives for their own well-being as well as for the well-being of ourselves. However, while religion says that we must be kind to animals, it also says that when animals are necessary for human well-being, when they can serve as a source of food, clothing, or beneficial scientific knowledge, they may be used to serve us—as long as we treat them as humanely as possible in the process.

Followers of Hinduism and Buddhism are less willing to accept harm to animals for human purposes. Hindus believe in human reincarnation, sometimes in the form of an animal, so they are are reluctant to harm animals. Although Buddhists believe that all life is sacred, they largely leave to an individual's conscience the decision of whether humane animal experiments are acceptable because they benefit mankind or unacceptable because they harm animal life. As there are Buddhist and Hindu scientists who conduct animal experiments, some have clearly chosen the path of revering human life and kindness more than animal life, at least on some occasions.

Assumptions

We have made many *assumptions* so far, some of them factual and some of them moral. Among the *factual assumptions* is the belief that animal experimentation really does lead to beneficial scientific knowledge and to the development of cures and treatments for human illnesses. Another assumption is that at least some animal experiments are irreplaceable, that no other methods of investigation will work or work nearly as well. Some dispute these assumptions, as we will see in the next section.

Other types of assumptions made thus far are *moral assumptions.* For example, some of the possible solutions that we have examined in the previous section rely heavily on particular theories of obligation. The animal liberation view usually is defended by appeal to the "principle of utility," which says that an action is right if it produces a greater balance of good over evil than its alternatives. This moral principle is assumed by them to be correct. Followers of the animal rights view, however, reject this theory of obligation in favor of the "rights" view. We will examine both these assumptions about what is the correct theory of obligation more carefully in the next section. It may be helpful at this time to note that each appears to possess only part of the truth.

Further assumptions are made by our various possible solutions about values, and especially about what sorts of beings have *intrinsic value* and why. The conventional view holds that only human beings have it, because only they are rational and autonomous. The animal welfare view says that nonhuman animals have some intrinsic value, as they have some of the value-conferring characteristics. The animal liberation and animal rights views hold that at least some nonhuman animals have value in themselves, and they have it to the same degree that human animals do. These assumptions about the types and degrees of value possessed by animals are important, and they will be carefully examined in the next section.

Exercise 10.1

For this exercise, reflect on what you already believe about the value of animals, especially their value relative to human beings. You might begin by asking yourself whether you believe that human beings have value in themselves and why. To help you with this, pretend that a group of alien beings, very different in appearance from us, visit this planet and gain control of our lives. They are decent, intelligent beings, but consider us to be of lesser value than themselves. They wish to perform medical experiments on us and promise to do so painlessly. You have the job of convincing them that this would be wrong. What would you say?

After you have made your case to them, imagine a nonhuman animal being able to speak and making a similar case to you. Would the same reasons apply in both cases? Explain why or why not.

Points of View

There are many *points of view* that may color how disposed a person might be to accept the belief that nonhuman animals have moral status. The question is liable to have many different sorts of answers when seen through the eyes of an animal researcher, a member of PETA, a hog farmer in North Carolina, a sport hunter, a whaler, a fisherman, a pet owner, a person dying from an illness for want of a cure, and so on. For now, before we begin to present the cases for our various possible solutions, follow up the exercise you just performed by asking yourself whether there is anything in your personal history that leads you to support the beliefs you just expressed in Exercise 10.1, especially something that may prevent you from being open to all the evidence. This is an important exercise because some of the views to be discussed will ask you to adopt a way of thinking that is very different from the way that most people currently think. To give these views a fair hearing we must be open-minded. Part of what opens our minds to new ways of thinking is an honest recognition of our own biases and perspectives that have been created by our personal histories.

Moral Reasoning

The problem of Chapter 10 has two parts. One part asks: *Under what conditions, if any, may animals be used for the benefit of human beings?* This is a moral problem about right and wrong actions. Let us call it the "animal treatment" question. It is best thought of as a **conflict of rules** problem. On the one hand, some of the ways we treat animals—such as factory farming and animal research—clearly cause them harm. On the other hand, this sort of treatment often produces great benefits for human beings. So there is a conflict between human welfare and animal welfare. Clearly doing good and avoiding evil for human beings is a moral obligation. It follows directly from the principle of beneficence. What is not so clear, however, is the degree to which this obligation takes priority over the welfare of animals. When doing good for ourselves and other human beings requires us to harm animals, we must judge whether this obligation toward human beings has priority over any other obligations.

To make this judgment we must answer the first question of our two-part problem, *What is the moral status of animals?* Let us call this the "moral status" question. If animals are not to be thought of as equally important or as valuable as human beings, and if because of this they are to be thought of as having little or no moral status, then clearly human welfare takes precedence over animal welfare. If, on the other hand, nonhuman animals are to be thought of as having moral status on a par with human beings, then in most cases their welfare would take priority. In particular, factory farming and most animal research clearly would be prohibited for beings whose moral status is the same as it is for human beings.

In what follows, a two-part case will be presented for each possible solution. We will first present and defend its position on the "moral status" question, and then see what follows about the "animal treatment" question. As usual, we will present all the reasons that support each claim first, and later return to consider the objections against each view.

The Case for the Conventional View

The conventional view claims that factory farming and animal research are morally acceptable actions. It begins its defense of this claim with the following premise:

1. Only rational, autonomous beings have intrinsic value.

Only beings that can understand, can think, and can direct their lives by their own free choices are truly valuable in themselves. Such beings occupy the top rungs of the ladder of creation. They are the most noble creatures of God or evolution. As Kant suggested over two centuries ago, beings who are free and rational are the rarest, the most priceless gems in the universe. As far as we know, everything else in this vast universe behaves as it does because of the inflexible laws of nature to which they must bend. Only autonomous beings can rise above these inexorable laws. Only intelligent beings can think for themselves; direct their own lives; create art, literature, and music; establish business, legal, and political institutions; and dream, plan, build, and appreciate new worlds.

Because of these value-conferring characteristics, human beings are in a special class in the animal world. They are the only beings with intrinsic value. Because human persons are so much more valuable than any other type of animal, their lives and interests must be protected. They must be kept from harm and allowed to have what is necessary to lead full, rich, meaningful lives. This is why morality exists, to protect beings with intrinsic value and to enhance their lives. This is why we grant people rights and impose duties on them, to make sure that they are protected from harm and granted the opportunity to use their rational minds, to make the choices that they think are best for themselves and for others, to create better worlds in which we all may live. Morality is of, for, and by the people with intrinsic value.

2. Only beings with intrinsic value have moral status.

Although animals may be conscious, even the "higher" ones have nothing like the rational consciousness of human beings. They are driven by instinct, not thought; they seek only to satisfy their biological urges, not to create, plan, and improve the conditions of life in a free and rational manner. Many religions express this belief by claiming that animals do not have souls. Some philosophers, especially the famous seventeenth-century French philosopher, René Descartes, went so far as to deny consciousness to animals. They were simply automatons to him.

We know today that animals are conscious on some level, but they are clearly not even remotely on the same level of importance as human beings. Any value-conferring characteristics they possess are vastly inferior to those of human beings. Animals may be of some value, even great value. Like a work of art, however, they are valued only insofar as they are wanted by human beings. Their importance lies only in what they can do for us. It does not reside in any characteristics they may possess in themselves. So our third premise is this;

3. Animals have no intrinsic value.

From these three premises we may infer the following conclusion:

Therefore, 4. Animals have no moral status.

This argument, as the answer of the conventional view to the "moral status" question, is not a "good reasons" argument. Instead, it is a deductive argument. To avoid distraction we will not bother to examine its logical structure right now. You should be able to see that it is a valid form of reasoning. Later when we evaluate it, we will need to pay attention only to the reliability of its premises.

If nonhuman animals have no moral status, they have no rights and no interests that we must take into consideration. Just as we do not have to consider trees and rocks during our moral deliberations, so also we may ignore the effects of our actions on animals. Because they have no moral status, they have no rights and no interests that must be protected. If this is so, then we may use them for our bene-fit, even if this causes them to suffer.

> 5. Using animals for the benefit of human beings is morally acceptable. (B)

We place a (B) after premise (5) to show that this moral claim about right action follows from the principle of beneficence. In this case beneficence allows us to do things that are in the interest of humans, who have moral status, at the expense of animals, who do not. Because our "moral circle" does not include animals, we do not have to consider the harmful effects our actions may have on them, only the good effects they may have for us. Factory farming is a practice that certainly has benefits for human beings. It provides us with a steady, safe, reliable, and eco-nomical source of food. Doing away with factory farms would make meat and animal products much more expensive and thus much less available. In addition, using animals as research subjects has also been beneficial for human beings, as we saw in the "Facts" section. So we may conclude;

> Therefore, 6. Factory farming and animal research are morally acceptable.

Premises (4) and (5), along with the conclusion (6), form a good reasons argu-ment that answers the "animal treatment" part of our problem.

The Case for the Animal Welfare View

According to the *animal welfare* view animals have "some" intrinsic value because they have some value-conferring characteristics. Rationality and autonomy are the only such characteristics that matter for the conventional view. In addition to these, however, there are other characteristics that animal welfare proponents believe to be quite important in determining the intrinsic value of a being. Among these are the capacity to form beliefs, to remember the past, to anticipate the future, to perceive, to experience emotions, to have feelings such as pleasure and pain, to have desires, and to have other psychological states. Beings with these characteristics are capable of experiencing their lives as having a past and a future, and thus are capable of experiencing themselves as self, and as having a life that matters to them. Combined, these characteristics form the inner life of an individual, its self. Most mammals are thought to have such an inner life, though to varying degrees. We will refer to beings who have these characteristics as **sub-jects of a life.**

The animal welfare view disagrees with the conventional view by claiming that all these value-conferring characteristics, not just reason and autonomy, count in bestowing value on the lives of a being. As this is so, any subject of a life has intrinsic value.

> 1.' All subjects of a life have intrinsic value.

The animal welfare view agrees with the conventional view on some points. In particular, they agree that having intrinsic value confers moral status on a being, and that the job of morality is to protect and to enhance the lives of all these very special sorts of beings that are valuable in themselves. In particular, the animal welfare view claims that

2.' All beings with intrinsic value have moral status.

Next, animal welfare advocates claim that many animals share many of the value-conferring characteristics possessed by humans. Animals can reason, can have beliefs and desires, can suffer, and so on, though to a lesser degree than humans. Humans have these characteristics most fully, while nonhuman animals, depending on the species they belong to, possess them in various degrees. If this is true, then they too are subjects of a life, though to varying degrees.

3.' Many nonhuman animals are subjects of a life to varying degrees.

As we learned from premise (1)' that all subjects of a life have intrinsic value, we may now assert the following:

4.' Many nonhuman animals have some intrinsic value.

The use of "some" in premise (4)' is extremely important. It defines the central way by which the argument of the animal welfare view differs most dramatically from the arguments to follow. Premise (4)' says two things: that all subjects of a life, because they have some value-conferring characteristics, have a value unto themselves; and they are not valuable simply because they are valued by us, but have lives of their own that are worthwhile in themselves. More important, premise (4)' says that nonhuman animals do not have as much intrinsic value as human beings have. They are less valuable, less important, than we are. This is because they do not possess value-conferring characteristics as fully as we do. Their lives are not as rich as ours. Such lives are not capable of achieving the level of quality that a human life can reach. As R. G. Frey states,

> What matters is not life but the quality of life. The value of a life is a function of its quality, its quality of its richness, and its richness of its capacities and scope for enrichment; it matters, then, what a creature's capacities for a rich life are.
>
> Here, the human and animal cases differ. The question is not, say, whether a chicken's life has value; I agree that it does. The chicken has an unfolding series of experiences and can suffer, and it is perfectly capable of living out a life appropriate to its species. The question is whether the chicken's life approaches normal adult human life in quality (and so value), given its capacities and the life that is appropriate to its species, and this is a matter of the comparative value of such lives. It is in this context that the claim that normal adult human life is more valuable than animal life occurs, and I defend it on the ground of the greater richness and potentialities for enrichment in the human case. . . .
>
> Of course, we share many activities with chickens; we eat, sleep, and reproduce. But such activities do not exhaust the richness of lives with music, art, literature, culture generally, love, science, and all the many joys and products of reflection. . . . No chicken has ever lived thus. . . .
>
> The man's life is more valuable than the chicken's because of its higher quality, greater enrichment, and greater scope for enrichment.
>
> This explanation allows that the chicken's life has some value; what it denies is that the chicken's life has the same value as the man's.[9]

If nonhuman animals have some intrinsic value, but have less of it than human animals, we may infer this from premises (1)' through (4)':

Therefore, 5.' Many nonhuman animals have some moral status.

Because animals have a lesser degree of moral status than human beings do, animals may be used for our purposes. The "higher" animals such as chimpanzees, those with more value-conferring characteristics, must be respected more than the "lower" animals, such as mice, those whose lives are not so richly endowed. Because all animals who are subjects of a life have some degree of moral status, however, their lives and interests must be respected. They may be used by us only for important purposes. As they do have some interests that must be considered by human beings, especially an interest in avoiding pain and suffering, their use always must be made as painless as possible. However, since animals have less moral status than humans, their lives and interests are not as important as human lives and interests. When necessary, important human interests may override whatever rights animals may have.

For example, using animals for food and research conveys many benefits on human beings, so it is in our interest to use animals for these purposes. However, we are morally obligated to respect their (lesser) interests, so if we do use them as a source of food and as research tools, we must do so in ways that minimize their suffering. Not to do so would be to treat nonhuman animals as mere things, as beings with no intrinsic value whatsoever, as beings with no moral status. So we may now supply the animal welfare answer to the "animal treatment" question:

Therefore, 6.' Using nonhuman animals for food and research is morally acceptable if done humanely. (B)

A (B) is placed after premise (6)' because the truth of premise (6)' is arrived at by weighing the harms and benefits of certain practices both for the humans and for the animals involved. Given the facts of factory farming, for example, especially the suffering it causes to animals, this conclusion rules it out as a type of "humane" method of producing food. Much less harm is caused when animals are raised in humane conditions, in ways that allow them to lead as full and happy a life as they can. If it is to be morally acceptable to eat the flesh of animals, they must be a source of food for humans only if this can be done with little or no suffering on their part. If they can be raised humanely and killed painlessly, then they may be used for food in a morally acceptable manner. It may cost more to raise animals humanely than it does to factory farm them, significantly more, in fact, but according to the animal welfare view, doing so correctly balances human and animal interests.

Animal research is also permitted by proponents of the animal welfare view, but only if the knowledge to be gained from it is really important, and only if there is no other way to gain this knowledge. Experiments that produce trivial results, such as experiments that test cosmetic products, are definitely immoral. They cause great pain to animals while producing little valuable knowledge. Experiments that produce important knowledge are also immoral if this knowledge can be acquired through alternative means. Sometimes research using human tissue, human cells, and computer simulation leads to knowledge that is just as valuable as that gained by using live animals. These sorts of experiments should replace animal research whenever possible. In all cases, animals should be housed and handled humanely, and they should receive adequate amounts of anesthesia and painkillers. We may use them as experimental subjects when the results promise to yield great benefits for human beings, but we must always do so with consideration for their interests.

The Case for the Animal Rights View

Before going directly to the argument for the animal rights view, we will compare its central claims and strategy to the other possible solutions discussed thus far. The animal rights view is the most radical of all of our possible solutions. It claims, in effect, that using nonhuman animals solely for the benefit of human animals is always immoral. More specifically, it claims that any use of animals for food or research is just as immoral as using humans for these purposes. The reason is that all nonhuman animals who are subjects of a life not only have value in themselves, but they have just as much of it as human animals do. All subjects of a life, human and nonhuman alike, have equal value in themselves and thus equal moral status. Because defenders of the animal rights view prefer to refer to a being's moral status as its *rights*, they claim that all animals who are subjects of a life have the same right to avoid suffering and the same right to life as human animals do.

In claiming that only human animals have intrinsic value, the conventional view focuses on the differences between humans and animals, claiming that only humans have the ability to think and to create their own lives by their choices, and that only these value-conferring characteristics matter in determining the worth and thus the moral status of a being. The animal welfare view claims that more than these value-conferring characteristics matter, and that anyone who is a subject of a life has value in himself and thus at least some degree of moral status. The animal rights view agrees with the animal welfare view that all animals who are subjects of a life have value in themselves, and thus possess moral status.[10]

> We are each of us the experiencing subjects of a life, a conscious creature having an individual welfare that has importance to us whatever our usefulness to others. We want and prefer things, believe and feel things, recall and expect things. And all these dimensions of our life, including our pleasure and our pain, our enjoyment and suffering, our satisfaction and frustration, our continued existence or our untimely death—all make a difference to the quality of life as lived, as experienced by us as individuals.

Their major disagreement with the animal welfare view is with its claim that various subjects of a life, especially nonhuman animals, have *degrees* of value, and thus degrees of moral status or rights. Instead, the animal rights view claims that any being who is the subject of a life has a life that is just as worthwhile in itself as any other subject of a life. If this is so, and if the possession of rights is determined by this value, any being that is valuable in itself has the same rights as any other being with such value. In particular, animals have the right not to be used solely for the purposes of human beings—no matter how beneficial that use may be to human beings. As a child or an adult human being cannot be used for research or food, animals cannot be so used.

To defend this extreme position, Regan makes a distinction between various types of value, one that is often overlooked by his followers and his critics alike. It is an important distinction, but one that is a bit tricky to grasp at first. Regan needs this distinction to avoid the following problem. On the one hand, his answer to the "moral status" question is that all nonhuman animals who are subjects of a life have the same moral status as human beings. This is because the lives of human beings and animals are worthwhile in themselves and worthwhile to the same degree. On the other hand, Regan also accepts the view that human lives are more valuable than the lives of mice, for example. This is because humans possess value-conferring characteristics to a higher degree than mice and most other nonhuman animals, and thus have more intrinsic value than mice. So how can he claim that human beings have more intrinsic value than animals while also claiming that human and nonhuman subjects of a life have equal value?

The way he does it is to distinguish between **intrinsic value** and **inherent value**—a distinction that most ethicists do not make. For most, these terms are used interchangeably. For Regan, however, there is a difference in their meanings that is crucial. By "intrinsic" value, he means what proponents of the conventional view and the animal welfare view mean—the value that a being has in itself, a value produced by its value-conferring characteristics. Regan agrees with the animal welfare view that animals of different species have different levels of intrinsic value, because they possess different degrees of value-conferring characteristics. This allows him to say that the life of a human is more valuable than the life of a mouse.

Because we vary in degrees of intrinsic value, and because a being's intrinsic value is used by conventionalists and animal welfare advocates to determine moral status, Regan has to find some other way to support his claim that human and nonhuman animals have *equal* moral status, or rights—even though we have different levels of intrinsic value. If he does not, it will be difficult for him to avoid sliding into the animal welfare view, which grants animals varying degrees of lesser moral status than human beings and thus allows them sometimes to be used for our purposes. The idea of *inherent* value, as something different from intrinsic value, allows him to make this move.

Inherent value is not based on the possession of value-conferring characteristics; rather it is a property of an individual. It is a property of any individual who is the subject of a life, no matter how lowly that life may be, no matter how little intrinsic value it may possess. The difference between intrinsic value and inherent value is explained by Regan using the analogy of a receptacle—in this case, a cup and what goes into the cup. The cup is the individual who has inherent value; what goes into the cup are the value-conferring characteristics, which have intrinsic value.[11]

> On the receptacle view of value, it is *what goes into the cup* (the pleasures or preference-satisfactions, for example) that has value: what does not have value is the cup itself (i.e., the individual himself or herself). The postulate of inherent value offers an alternative. The cup (that is, the individual) has value *and* a kind that is not reducible to, and is incommensurate with what goes into the cup (e.g., pleasure). The cup (the individual) does "contain" (experience) things that are valuable (e.g., pleasures), but the value of the cup (individual) is not the same as any one or any sum of the valuable things the cup contains. *Individual moral agents themselves have a distinctive kind of value,* according to the postulate of inherent value, but not according to the receptacle view to which utilitarians are committed. It's the cup, not just what goes into it, that is valuable.

To say that individuals have inherent value is not to make a claim about their value-conferring characteristics, but rather to make a claim about them as individuals, independent of these characteristics. The claim is not that their characteristics make them inherently valuable; rather, they are valuable in themselves. The distinction between intrinsic value and inherent value rests on this distinction between the characteristics of individuals and their "bare" selves. It is as though we could think of the self as a shell, devoid of content, on the one hand, and the value-conferring characteristics of that self, floating apart from the self that embodies them, on the other.

These characteristics may come and go, and thus the individual may become more or less intrinsically valuable. Regan's point, however, is that the individual remains valuable in himself or herself, even if he or she loses the ability to reason, or to perceive, or to feel pleasure and pain, and so on. If during his life Einstein had suddenly lost the ability to think, if he had suddenly lost this immense value-conferring characteristic, he would still have been an inherently valuable individual, and just as valuable as anyone else. We are not simply receptacles of experience or locations where value-conferring characteristics reside. Instead, any being who is the subject of a life possesses inherent value.

Moreover, anyone who is the subject of a life has inherent value that is equal to the inherent value possessed by all other such subjects. No matter how little intrinsic value a subject of a life may have, it has the same inherent value, the same value as an individual, as all other subjects of a life. Brain-damaged babies and mentally challenged adults certainly do not have the same rational capacities as other human beings, yet they have the same inherent value. Brilliant scientists do not have more inherent value than people of average intelligence, nor do people whose level of creativity, emotion, or even autonomy far surpasses that of their peers have more of it than these others. Each subject of a life has a full share, an equal share of inherent value. So we write this as our first premise:

> 1.# All subjects of a life have equal inherent value.

Because morality is for the purpose of protecting and enhancing the lives of all of those with inherent value, defenders of the animal rights view accept the next premise as well:

> 2.# All beings with inherent value have equal moral status (rights).

The third premise challenges the view that only human animals are subjects of a life. Rather, this view denies that humans are the sole possessors of a rich inner life. There is ample evidence today that the continuity between humans and animals is greater than our differences. This is to be expected if we are to believe that the characteristics we possess evolved from those of other animals. Animals can think, can reason, can use language to communicate, can perceive, can feel, can have emotions, can enter into social arrangements with other animals, can act intentionally, and so on. Not all animals have all these capacities and levels of conscious experience, and not all animals that do have them possess them to the same degree. Not all humans do either, however. That does not stop us from asserting that they are subjects of a life and possess equal inherent value with all other humans.

To deny the experience of animals such as dogs, cats, pigs, chimps, dolphins, whales, and so on, who may have a richer inner life than some human beings, is simply an unfair prejudice. At least the more psychologically developed animals, the animals most like us, are subjects of a life just as human animals are; and being the subject of a life is what bestows inherent value; and this is always equally possessed by all who have it; therefore, the third premise is this:

> 3.# Some nonhuman animals have inherent value equal to that possessed by human animals.

From premises (1)# through (3)# we may now infer the following:

Therefore, 4.# Some nonhuman animals have moral status (rights) equal to that possessed by human animals.

If animals are to be considered morally equal to humans, if they are to be thought of as having equal rights, we must change our thinking about animal treatment in quite dramatic ways. The way to tell what is morally acceptable treatment and what is not is to ask if such treatment would be morally acceptable for humans. Can we use human beings as a source of food? Can we use them in dangerous experiments for which they did not volunteer? Hardly. Since nonhuman animals have the same rights as human animals, neither can they be used for such purposes.

Note that because they have inherent value they cannot be used solely for human purposes. It is not just because such actions cause them pain and suffering that it is wrong, as animal welfare and animal liberation proponents claim. Even if we could use animals in painless ways for our benefit, it would still be wrong to use them. Even if we could raise them in ways that they enjoyed, and even if we killed them painlessly, it would be wrong to use them for food. Even if we used them only in important experiments, and even if we gave them enough painkillers when we experimented on them for them to be pain-free, it would be wrong to use them as research tools.

Regan's argument is similar to Kant's, when Kant said that it was immoral to use someone merely as a means to the good of others—whatever the benefit to be gained. Kant was thinking only of humans when he claimed that we were not to be treated as things, not to be valued solely in terms of our usefulness to others. Instead, because we are valuable in ourselves, because we are "priceless," we must be treated as "ends in ourselves." In short, Regan appeals to the "respect for persons" principle, one version of our moral principle of justice, to defend his claim stated here:

> 5.# Using nonhuman animals merely for the benefit of human animals is always immoral. (J)

A (J) appears after premise (5)# because if Regan is right that human and nonhuman animals have equal rights, then treating animals merely as a means, using them solely for our benefit, violates the principle of justice. Any use of animals in research is immoral, no matter how important the results may be, or how painlessly the experiments are conducted, or how low on the scale of importance we may consider the animal subjects to be. Animals may not be used even for the development of human life-saving drugs, or for finding cures for cancer or for AIDS. After all, would using human beings without their consent to test various AIDS vaccines be morally acceptable? Regan says,[12]

> In the case of the use of animals in science, the rights view is categorically abolitionist. Lab animals are not our tasters; we are not their kings. Because these animals are treated routinely, systematically as if their value were reducible to their usefulness to others, they are routinely, systematically treated with a lack of respect, and thus their rights routinely, systematically violated. This is just as true when they are used in trivial, duplicative, unnecessary or unwise research as it is when they are used in studies that hold out real promise of human benefits. We can't justify harming or killing a human being (my Aunt Bea, for example) just for these sorts of reasons. Neither can we do so even in the case of so lowly a creature as a laboratory rat. It is not just refinement or reduction that is called for, not just larger, cleaner cages, not just more generous use of anesthetic or the elimination of multiple surgery, not just tidying up the system. It is complete replacement. The best we can do when it comes to using animals in science is—not to use them. That is where our duty lies, according to the rights view.

For the animal rights view, factory farming is also immoral. As we said previously, even if animals are raised humanely and killed painlessly, it is immoral to use them for food. *Any* use of animals for food is immoral, just as eating the flesh of any human being is immoral. Regan continues:

> As for commercial animal agriculture, the rights view takes a similar abolitionist position. The fundamental wrong here is not that animals are kept in stressful close confinement or in isolation, or that their pain and suffering, their needs and preferences are ignored or discounted. All these *are* wrong, of course, but they are not the fundamental wrong. They are symptoms and effects of the deeper, systematic wrong that allows animals to be viewed and treated as lacking independent value, as resources for us—as indeed, a renewable resource. Giving farm animals more space, more natural environments, more companions does not right the fundamental wrong. . . . Nothing less than the total dissolution of commercial animal agriculture will do this.

Therefore, 6.# Using nonhuman animals for food or research is always immoral. (J)

The Case for the Animal Liberation View

The animal rights view and the animal liberation view agree on how the "animal treatment" question should be answered. Proponents of each view work tirelessly to eliminate the use of animals solely for the betterment of mankind. In fact, many animal rights activists appeal equally and sometimes indiscriminately to either view to defend their actions. Despite the similarities of their goals, however, there are important differences between these two views, especially on the "moral status" question. Their differences on this question have important practical consequences for the animal treatment question as well, although these consequences are seldom emphasized.

The major figure who defends the animal liberation view is Peter Singer. Singer agrees with the animal welfare position that human and nonhuman animals have different levels of value, depending on the degree to which they possess value-conferring characteristics. Human beings, for example, are certainly more valuable than nonhuman animals, as chimps are surely more valuable than mice. However, he does not infer from this, as Frey did, that different types of animals have different degrees of moral status. That is because, for Singer, moral status does not depend on having intrinsic value. Instead, it depends on having *interests.*

Like Frey, but unlike Regan, Singer is a utilitarian. You will remember from Part 1 that utilitarians are consequentialists. That is, they believe that what makes an action morally acceptable is solely the consequences it produces. If an action produces a greater balance of good over evil than its alternative, then it is morally acceptable. To determine the consequences of an action everyone affected by it must be taken into consideration. "Everyone" here refers to all those with moral status. But who has moral status?

Singer's answer is that *all sentient beings have moral status.* For Singer, the purpose of morality is to protect and enhance the lives of all sentient beings, not just humans. Sentient beings can have sensory experiences and can feel pain and pleasure. Beings who are not sentient, such as plants, rocks, and oceans, do not require the protection afforded by morality because they cannot experience the harms and benefits of the actions of others. They have no interest in acquiring benefits and being protected from harms, since they cannot experience them. Sentient beings, on the other hand, do have such interests. All sentient beings actively pursue their own good and attempt to escape from evil. In particular, all sentient beings can suffer, and they can suffer just as much as any other sentient being. Because of this, all sentient beings have roughly similar interests in avoiding such suffering. So we may begin the argument for the animal liberation view with this claim:

1.* All sentient beings have interests.

Because the purpose of morality is to protect and enhance the interests of sentient beings, and especially to protect sentient beings from suffering, then all sentient beings belong to the class of those for whom morality must apply. The purpose of morality is not just to protect the interests of rational beings, as the conventionalist holds. Being rational is not the test for having moral status. There are many mentally handicapped humans who are not rational, yet they are included in the circle of those who are protected by morality. We protect them because they can suffer, and so they have the same interest as everyone else in avoiding such suffering. All sentient beings have an interest in avoiding suffering, so all sentient beings have moral status. They deserve to be protected from suffering; they all belong under the umbrella of moral protection.

In addition to having moral status, all sentient beings have it equally. Utilitarians believe that everyone who has moral status must be considered just as important in calculating consequences as everyone else. I cannot favor those near and dear to me over others whom I may not care so much about. We cannot weigh the consequences of actions for myself, my family, members of my race or my gender, or any particular individual or group more favorably than we weigh them for others—even strangers. Everyone who has moral status is to be counted equally. The way that anyone who is affected by actions is just as important as the way anyone else is. In particular, the suffering of any sentient being is just as important to consider as the suffering of any other.

2.* All sentient beings have equal moral status.

Because most nonhuman animals are sentient beings, they also have moral status. Singer disagrees with Frey that their moral status is to be correlated with their level of value-conferring characteristics. He quotes his ethical mentor, Jeremy Bentham, about the importance of sentience as the feature that is most important in deciding who should receive the protection of the moral community:[13]

> What else is it that should trace the insuperable line? Is it the faculty of reason, or perhaps the faculty of discourse? But a full-grown horse or dog is beyond comparison a more rational, as well as a more conversible animal, than an infant of a day or a week or even a month, old. But suppose they were otherwise, what would it avail? The question is not, Can they *reason?* nor Can they *talk?* but, Can they *suffer?*

In commenting on this passage, Singer points out the fundamental importance of sentience—not reason, language, or any other value-conferring characteristic, as what determines moral status:

> In this passage Bentham points to the capacity for suffering as the vital characteristic that gives a being the right to equal consideration. The capacity for suffering—or more strictly for suffering and/or enjoyment or happiness—is not just another characteristic like the capacity for language or higher mathematics. Bentham is not saying that those who try to mark "the insuperable line" that determines whether the interests of a being should be considered happen to have chosen the wrong characteristic. By saying that we must consider the interests of all beings with the capacity for suffering or enjoyment Bentham does not arbitrarily exclude from consideration any interests at all—as those who draw the line with reference to the possession of reason or language do. The capacity for suffering and enjoyment is a *prerequisite for having any interests at all*, a condition that must be satisfied before we can speak of interests in a meaningful way.

Nonhuman animals may not have all the value-conferring characteristics that humans have. They may not be as valuable as humans are. But they can suffer every bit as much as human animals can. Because the main purpose of morality is to protect the interests of those who can suffer, nonhuman animals must be considered to have moral status as well and as fully as human animals. In their ability to suffer, all animals are equal; in their interests in avoiding suffering, all animals are equal; so in their moral status, all animals are equal.

To consider the interests of nonhuman animals in avoiding suffering to be less important than those of human animals is simply to express a prejudice for the human species. It is to practice what Singer calls "speciesism," a form of prejudice that favors members of your own species over those of other species, a form of prejudice that should be abandoned as most of us have abandoned racism and sexism. As women and minorities were finally given full moral status, at least in principle, so Singer believes that now it is time to widen the circle of those protected by moral sanctions and to include nonhuman animals within its scope. They can suffer as we can. To ignore their suffering as unimportant, as the conventionalist does, or to consider it to be not as important as the suffering of humans, as the animal welfare view does, is just to practice speciesism. So we write:

Therefore, 3.* nonhuman animals have moral status that is equal to the moral status of human animals.

Singer believes that this answer to the "moral status" question now leads to answers similar to Regan's, and not Frey's, on the "animal treatment" question. He agrees with Frey that there are different levels of importance among animals, but he does not follow Frey in claiming that this justifies different levels of moral status. On the one characteristic that counts the most in determining moral status—the capacity to suffer—all animals are equal, and thus they must be treated equally.

While agreeing with Regan that all animals have equal moral status, however, Singer does not justify this claim in the same way that Regan does. In particular, he does not believe that all sentient beings have either equal intrinsic value or equal inherent value. He has no concept of inherent value, and he believes that the intrinsic value of various beings differs from species to species. This prevents him from appealing to the "respect for persons" Kantian-inspired moral principle used by Regan to condemn *any* use of nonhuman animals for the benefit of human animals.

Instead, as a utilitarian Singer believes that morally acceptable actions are those that increase the *total* good and reduce the *total* evil in the world. We must calculate the aggregate results of our actions to decide whether they are morally acceptable. Singer wants us to allow animals into the circle of those who must be considered when we estimate the harms and benefits of our actions, so we must now consider the harmful and beneficial effects of our actions on all human animals and on all nonhuman sentient animals alike. Because it is the *total* consequences that matter most in determining right from wrong, the total number of pleasurable and painful states of the sentient beings affected by the action, Singer's more moderate position appears to allow actions that would be rejected by Regan.

For example, it seems as though Singer should allow animals to be used for food as long as doing so produces a greater balance of good over evil for all concerned. This would exclude factory farming, of course, as the practices employed there cause great pain and suffering for the billions of animals involved. Eliminating factory farming and substituting more humane ways of raising animals may cause more negative consequences for humans—as meat, eggs, milk, and so on would now cost more. But these are trivial harms compared to the harms suffered by animals on factory farms. If animals were raised and killed in humane conditions, however, it would be good for them and for us. We would have meat and animal products to eat, and they would lead relatively happy lives. So it seems that Singer should be *for* the use of animals for food if they are raised humanely. It seems that his position should be very much like the animal welfare view on this issue.

Singer does not see things this way, however. He does think that it would be morally justifiable to eat meat if necessary. To save a more valuable human life, an animal such as a chicken may be killed. However, it is almost always not necessary to eat the flesh of animals, because there are viable options. We can eat other things—plants in particular—and be just as healthy. By becoming vegetarians we can at once avoid harming animals while still producing the same benefits for our-selves. In fact, as the benefits of vegetarianism are considerable, all sentient beings—human and nonhuman animals alike—will be better off. The total good will increase if we stop using animals for food, and the total evil will decrease. It is not because they are valuable in themselves, and that they therefore may never be used solely for the good of others, that it is wrong to use animals. Instead, it is wrong because vegetarianism produces a greater ratio of good over evil conse-quences than using animals for food.

In a similar manner Singer argues that using animals as research subjects is almost always wrong. In the first place, many experiments that cause animals great suffering are silly or trivial and should be eliminated on these grounds alone. In the second place, much of what is important that has been discovered by using animal subjects, such as the development of many vaccines, could have been discovered in other ways. In fact, many research protocols may now be per-formed on animal or human tissue or even cells, and some can be performed through computer simulation. But what about important animal experiments for which there are no alternatives? What about experiments that use a few animals to test drugs or vaccines that could save hundreds of thousands of human lives? It would seem that such experiments should be allowed on utilitarian grounds, especially as the total good will be dramatically increased while only a few sen-tient beings will suffer.

Singer holds firm that almost all animal experiments are not acceptable because there are alternatives. But he does say that just as eating animals may in rare cir-cumstances be acceptable, some really important animal experiments may also be morally acceptable. He uses what seems to be a quite strange criterion to tell which experiments are important enough to be allowed as morally acceptable—the brain-damaged infant. This criterion says that if researchers think an experi-ment is important enough to use a brain-damaged infant as a research subject, then they may also use an animal.[14] Such an infant has very little mental capacity, far less than that of many experimental animals. If it is the presence of these capac-ities that make life valuable, then Singer is prepared to say that the lives of some animals are more valuable than the lives of some humans. To deny this is simply to practice speciesism once again.[15]

> We may legitimately hold that there are some features of certain beings that make
> their lives more valuable than those of other beings; but there will surely be some
> nonhuman animals whose lives, by any standards, are more valuable than the lives
> of some humans. A chimpanzee, dog, or pig, for instance, will have a higher degree
> of self-awareness and a greater capacity for meaningful relations with others than a
> severely retarded infant or someone in a state of advanced senility.

Presumably we would not use a brain-damaged infant in any experiment, no matter how important it was. Some animals have higher mental capacities than such a child will ever have, and for Singer this makes their lives more valuable than the infant's life; therefore we should not use animals in experiments either. There are options that will lead to a greater overall good for everyone concerned, human and nonhuman animals alike. So we may write this:

> 4.* Using nonhuman animals for food or research almost always produces a
> greater balance of evil over good. (B)

The animal liberation view may now answer the "animal treatment" question:

Therefore, 5.* Using animals for food or research is almost always wrong. (B)

We place a (B) after premise (4)* and this conclusion, because what makes using animals in these fashions wrong is that doing so causes a greater balance of evil over good. It is important to include the term "almost" in (5)*. Even though the answers to the "animal treatment" question of Singer and Regan are very similar in practice, they are quite different in principle. The main difference lies with the utilitarian reasons offered by Singer for the exceptions that he is willing to allow. These differences will be examined closely when we consider objections to all views.

Replies to Objections

This is the usual place to discuss objections to our various possible solutions and to see what replies might be made to them. However, we are going to break from our usual pattern and move right into the "Evaluation" section. We do this for two reasons. First, the arguments for each possible solution are complete. The objections to each argument will not add any new premises because they all take the form of questioning the reliability of one or more of the existing premises. Second, questioning the reliability of premises is the basic work of the evaluation process. So we will avoid duplication if we perform the task of replying to objections in the "Evaluation" section.

Evaluation

Ethical Theory

The issue of this chapter is a two-part problem:

a. *What is the moral status of animals?*

b. *Under what conditions, if any, may animals be used for the benefit of human beings?*

Question (a) is the "moral status" question, a question about the degree to which we ought to value and protect the rights and interests of nonhuman animals. Part (b) of our problem, the "animal treatment" question, is a question about the moral acceptability of some of the ways we treat animals. In particular, we have focused in this chapter on using animals for food and research. This question is best viewed as a **conflict of rules** problem, a conflict that pits the interests of nonhuman animals against those of human beings. We may adopt the language of rights theorists to describe this conflict and say that we have a conflict between the rights of human and nonhuman animals. The conflicting rules may be expressed as follows:

1. Do not harm or kill animals.

2. Use animals for the benefit of human beings.

It appears that if we do not harm or kill animals we cannot use them for our most important purposes (food and research); therefore there is a genuine conflict that requires us to decide which rule has the highest priority. The rule with the highest priority is the one that, if followed, leads to the most beneficence, justice, and autonomy. That is the rule we must follow.

Deciding which rule has priority is complicated by disagreements about how to answer question (a). The conventionalist, for example, says that rule (2) always wins, because it conforms to the principles of autonomy, beneficence, and justice. It conforms to autonomy because it allows us to what we wish with animals. Autonomy requires that in exercising our wishes we do not harm anyone, but because animals have no moral status they are not a "someone." It conforms to beneficence because it benefits us to use animals for food and research. If it does not benefit them it is fine, because as beings with no moral status, they do not have interests that must be considered. Finally, it does not violate the principle of justice to use animals for our benefit as we are not using "someone" for the good of another.

The animal rights view, on the other hand, argues that rule (1) always wins. Because animals have moral status equal to that of human beings, and because using them harms them significantly, using animals for food and research, as well as in any number of other painful ways, violates all three principles. It violates autonomy because autonomy allows us to do what we want to only if it harms no one else; it violates beneficence because using animals for human purposes harms them significantly; and it violates justice because it amounts to using someone solely as a means to the good of another.

Most of the arguments in the "Moral Reasoning" section focused primarily on the moral status question. If animals have no moral status, then rule (2) always has the highest priority. If they have moral status equal to human beings, then rule (1) always wins. If they have some moral status, then sometimes rule (1) wins, and sometimes rule (2) does. Let us think of the arguments already examined in the previous section, as well as the objections to them that we are about to consider, as so many attempts to persuade us rationally that one or another of these two rules has the highest priority.

A Few Comments

My contribution to the process of evaluation will precede yours in this chapter. This is because my comments will focus on clarifying several serious and complex objections to our possible solutions. Discovering the degree to which it is morally acceptable to use animals for human benefits, the "animal treatment" question, is a complex issue for more than one reason. The most important of these is that it presupposes an answer to the "moral status" of animals question. This question itself is complex and forces us to question some of the very bases of morality itself. So it will perhaps be more efficient for me first to provide the objections to each view in question, and then have you attempt to respond to them later, as your contribution to the evaluation process.

Behind the solutions of each view to the problem of this chapter lie various assumptions about both factual and moral matters that vary from view to view. The *factual assumptions* concern beliefs about what sorts of characteristics animals do have, and to what degree they have them. Just how aware of themselves as selves are rats, for example? Just how rational are pigs? Just how able to communicate with language are chimps? Other factual assumptions include beliefs that using animals for food and research has been both necessary and beneficial for human beings and will continue to be necessary and beneficial in the future.

Other beliefs underlying the arguments for our various possible solutions are *moral assumptions.* Some philosophers, such as Singer and Frey, follow a utilitarian theory of obligation; others, such as Regan, champion a rights view. There are also differences of opinion about which, if any, of the value-conferring characteristics are required for moral status, and even assumptions about the purpose of morality itself. Some believe that morality exists only to protect and enhance the lives of free and rational beings; others believe that morality should also offer protection for the interests of all subjects of a life, and even for all sentient beings who may not be subjects of a life.

Objections to all possible solutions may be directed either at the reliability of their premises or at the many and varied assumptions their arguments presuppose. The complexity of these arguments leave them open to many objections, but we will focus on just a few of the more important ones. We begin with the two-part case for the *conventional* view.

1. Only rational, autonomous beings have intrinsic value.

2. Only beings with intrinsic value have moral status.

3. Animals have no intrinsic value.

Therefore, 4. Animals have no moral status.

5. Using animals for the benefit of human beings is morally acceptable. (B)

Therefore, 6. Factory farming and animal research are morally acceptable.

The most important objection to the conventional view is directed at the reliability of premise (1). Premise (1) states that only rational, autonomous beings have intrinsic value. From this it seems to be an easy step to deny intrinsic value, and thus moral status, to animals. From there it is an even easier step to say that the use of animals for human benefit is morally acceptable. So defenders of each of the other three possible solutions reject the claim of premise (1) that only reason and autonomy confer intrinsic value. They also point out that some nonhuman animals are more rational than some human animals. Clearly they have a point.

It is one thing to say that the life of a chimp, or a dolphin, or a wolf have less value than that of a normal human being, but it is quite another to deny that the lives of these animals have *any* intrinsic value whatsoever. To say that the extreme suffering of an animal should be a matter of moral indifference, something to be excluded from moral consideration as easily as we exclude the effects of our actions on rocks and trees, seems wildly implausible. In the light of what we now know about the great capacity of some animals to reason, to communicate, to have emotions and feelings, and to form social relationships, it seems quite barbaric to say that their lives have no value worth protecting within our moral systems. Even the law protects animals from abuse by their owners, breeders, and handlers. So the major objection against the conventional view is that it denies to animals any thread of intrinsic value.

The case for the *animal welfare* view is this:

1.' All subjects of a life have intrinsic value.

2.' All beings with intrinsic value have moral status.

3.' Many nonhuman animals are subjects of a life to varying degrees.

4.' Many nonhuman animals have some intrinsic value.

Therefore, 5.' Many nonhuman animals have some moral status.

Therefore, 6.' Using nonhuman animals for food and research is morally acceptable if done humanely. (B)

At first glance it would seem that the animal liberation view and the animal rights view would welcome the claims of the animal welfare view. Although not as fully vested in the protection of animals, allowing them to be used for the benefits of humans in some instances, at least animal welfare advocates champion the humane treatment of the many animals who are used for food and research. This seems, at the very least, to be a step in the right direction. However, both animal liberation and animal rights proponents see animal welfare advocates as among their chief threats. The blatant speciesism of the conventional view is easier to deal with because it is so obviously wrong. The appeal to "humane" treatment advocated by the animal welfare position, however, permits people to believe that using animals for food and research is acceptable as long as it is done painlessly.

Tom Regan especially objects to the reliability of premise (5)', which claims that nonhuman animals have some moral status. For animal welfare advocates, premise (5)' follows from premises (3)' and (4)', which together claim that nonhuman animals have only some intrinsic value because they possess only some of the value conferring characteristics. To say that they have "some" moral status is to deny that they have moral status equal to that of human beings. But Regan objects to premise (5)', appealing to his view that subjects of a life have equal moral status (rights) because they have equal *inherent* value.[16]

> Some will say that animals have some inherent value, only less than we have. Once again, however, attempts to defend this view can be shown to lack rational justification. What could be the basis of our having more inherent value than animals? Their lack of reason, or autonomy, or intellect? Only if we are willing to make the same judgment in the case of humans who are similarly deficient. But it is not true that such humans—the retarded child, for example, or the mentally deranged—have less inherent value than you or I. Neither, then, can we rationally sustain the view that animals like them in being the experiencing subjects of a life have less inherent value. *All* who have inherent value have it *equally*, whether they be human animals or not.

In saying that animals are valuable in themselves, but less valuable than human beings, the animal welfare advocate is trying to capture an intuitive "truth" that most of us accept—the belief that animals are important, but not as important as we are. The reason is that although they share some characteristics with us—such as reason, some forms of language, and especially sentience—they do not do possess these characteristics as fully as we do. Regan's point is that because we do not classify humans as having different degrees of value according to the different degrees with which they possess these characteristics, we should not classify animals as less valuable for the same reason. The least rational among humans is given the same protections of the moral system as the most rational. A brilliant scientist does not have more of a right to life and more of a right to avoid pain and suffering than the least intelligent and articulate human being. So animals, some of which are more intelligent than some humans, should also be granted full inherent value, and thus full moral status.

Singer attacks premise (5)' in a similar manner:

> Once we ask why is it should be that all human beings—including infants, the intellectually disabled, criminal psychopaths, Hitler, Stalin, and the rest—have some kind of dignity or worth that no elephant, pig, or chimpanzee can ever achieve, we see that this question is as difficult to answer as our original request for some relevant fact that justifies the inequality of humans and other animals. In fact, these two questions are really one: talk of intrinsic dignity or moral worth does not help, because any satisfactory defense of the claim that all and only human beings have intrinsic dignity would need to refer to some relevant capacities or characteristics that only human beings have, in virtue of which they have this unique dignity or worth.[17]

Singer's objection to the animal welfare view is that it cannot provide a criterion for distinguishing between the intrinsic value of human beings and the intrinsic value of at least some animals. If all humans have equal intrinsic value, and if some animals have more of the value-conferring characteristics that have been proposed as a basis for granting such value to human beings—intelligence, reasoning ability, communication skills, emotion, sentience, and so on—then some animals should have at least the same degree of intrinsic value as some humans. Saying that they should only have "some" intrinsic value seems to be nothing but another version of speciesism.

The argument for the *animal liberation* view, especially as defended by Peter Singer, is as follows:

1.* All sentient beings have interests.

2.* All sentient beings have equal moral status.

Therefore, 3.* Nonhuman animals have moral status that is equal to the moral status of human animals.

4.* Using nonhuman animals for food or research almost always produces a greater balance of evil over good. (B)

Therefore, 5.* Using animals for food or research is almost always wrong. (B)

Among the objections raised against this argument, two stand out as central. Both may be traced to Singer's assumption that utilitarianism is the correct ethical theory of obligation. The first objection is directed at the reliability of premise (4)*. The objection claims that using animals for food and research will actually lead to a greater balance of good over evil than not using them. If we were to use one hundred transgenic mice to find a drug that effectively controlled the symptoms of cerebral palsy, for example, it is quite difficult to believe that the harms caused to these mice would not be outweighed by the benefits experienced by thousands of humans. Even if nonhuman animals have the same moral status as human animals, even if we are to count their suffering equally with that of humans, still, on utilitarian grounds at least, such experiments would be morally acceptable. If all that matters are the consequences, then the use of animals as research subjects is justified whenever there is no alternative and the knowledge gained leads to a greater balance of good over evil for all involved.

Even the use of animals for food may be justified using Singer's own utilitarian principles. As long as they are raised humanely and killed painlessly, animals and animal products may be used for human consumption. Factory farming is immoral, of course, because it causes so much suffering to animals. But raising animals in humane conditions, where they have room to roam about and relate to other animals in a natural way, is actually an overall *benefit* to animals—even if they are later killed for human use. This is because these humanely raised animals lead natural lives that are relatively happy ones. If they were not raised to be used as food, they never would have existed in the first place. They never would be the recipients of the benefits of life. The world would have less good in it—even for these animals themselves—if everyone was a vegetarian.

Even killing animals, as long as it is done painlessly, does not remove any overall benefits. This is because once a particular animal is dead another will be raised to replace it, leaving the aggregate good the same as it was before. Now, if we add to the total good experienced by animals the benefits experienced by human beings who use animals for food, then on utilitarian grounds we should say that using animals humanely for food is our moral obligation, not the opposite. The total good produced by doing so, relative to the small harms experienced by humans and animals alike, seems to dictate this decision.

A second objection is also directed against Singer's acceptance of utilitarianism. It claims that his acceptance of a utilitarian theory of obligation actually commits him to the belief that it is morally acceptable to use human beings as research subjects! How can a view that rejects the use of animals for such purposes be seen as accepting the use of humans for the same purposes? For Singer, all that matters in determining the moral acceptability of an action is the total amount of harms and benefits produced, the harms and benefits for all concerned, the aggregate harms and benefits. So, if we could use human research subjects whose lives have little or no value, because they have few or no value-conferring characteristics, we could learn a great deal from them that would benefit many other human beings. Especially if we were careful not to cause them any pain in the process, the aggregate results would almost surely be beneficial. Using human subjects for research purposes, especially if their lives have little value, would undoubtedly increase the total amount of good over evil in the world, and thus should be seen as a moral obligation.

If you happen to be a strict utilitarian, what reason is there for not using patients in vegetative states as research subjects? They are not sentient beings any longer, so they would experience no pain or suffering as a result of the experiment. Even if the experiment caused them to die, their deaths would not count as a loss, because they have none of the value-conferring characteristics that make a life worthwhile. We may as well add senile and terminally ill residents of nursing homes to the list of experimental subjects also. If we select only those who have no family or friends (to avoid causing them to suffer) to serve as research subjects, and if we use them painlessly, administering generous amounts of painkillers, then great overall benefits may result for others. These patients will suffer no harm, as they will not be allowed to feel pain, and as their lives, soon to be over from their illnesses, are not worth living in the first place. There will be no increase in harm as a result of using them in experiments, and there will be a great increase in benefits for the rest of us. Imagine all we can learn about Alzheimer's disease, for example, if we can conduct experiments on the live human brains of people who have the disease.

Although Singer personally would not promote such experiments as morally acceptable, his utilitarian theory leads to this consequence. But if, according to utilitarianism, it is morally acceptable to use some human beings as research subjects for the benefit of other human beings, then perhaps there is something wrong with utilitarianism as an ethical theory of obligation. In fact, this "human subjects of experimentation" objection turns out to be an instance of the general objection we raised against utilitarianism in Part 1—the "justice" objection. According to the ethical theory adopted in this text, the principle of justice forbids us to use a person merely as a means to the good of another. Regardless of the benefits that may result, as each person is intrinsically valuable he or she may never be used merely as a means to the good of others.

Singer certainly seems to embrace this principle as well. His numerous writings on animals have always protested their use simply for human purposes. However, closer examination of his views shows that there is no place for it in his utilitarian view of ethics. This is why the logic of his ethical position commits him to the moral acceptability of using human beings for research. It requires that only the good for *all*, not the good for *individuals*, count in determining right from wrong. For the utilitarian, the good of the individual matters less than the good of the aggregate. This sort of thinking allows for the use of the individual for the common good, something strictly prohibited by the principle of justice. For the utilitarian, however, the end does justify the means.

The *animal rights* argument is this:

1.# All subjects of a life have equal inherent value.

2.# All beings with inherent value have equal moral status (rights).

3.# Some nonhuman animals have inherent value equal to that possessed by human animals.

Therefore, 4.# Some nonhuman animals have moral status (rights) equal to that possessed by human animals.

5.# Using nonhuman animals merely for the benefit of human animals is always immoral. (J)

Therefore, 6.# Using nonhuman animals for food or research is always immoral. (J)

There are some criticisms of the animal rights view that are common but not very powerful. Some attack the consequences of its conclusion, saying, for example, that it is too absolutist a view. Saying that animals that are subjects of a life should *never* be used for food or should *never* be used as experimental subjects seems to them to be too extreme. Are we to believe, for example, that using one hundred mice in experiments that eventually result in a cure for melanoma and save the lives of countless human beings is immoral? If the animal rights view is correct, the answer is "yes." Just as using human subjects in such experiments would be immoral, so too is using animal subjects.

Others attack the reliability of premise (4)#, saying that animals have no moral status, or rights, because only moral *agents* have moral status.[18] That is, only those beings who can make free moral choices have such status. Animals do not play the moral game. They do not make choices to do what is right or wrong, or to direct their lives toward something that they have determined is intrinsically valuable. They do not make judgments that they or others have done something that is morally praiseworthy or blameworthy. According to this objection, because they do not have the capacity to be moral "actors" or agents, they should not be be considered members of the moral community. They should not be given moral status.

However, babies and severely retarded children do not have this capacity either. Yet we consider them to be members of the moral community. They may be moral "patients" instead of "agents," but they have moral status nonetheless, especially the right to the protection of the moral community. In the same way, just because animals cannot be moral agents does not mean that they should not fall under the protection of the moral community.

More serious objections are directed at the assumptions of Regan's argument, especially his assumption that the rights view is the correct moral theory of obligation. Some of the difficulties of such a theory were discussed in Part 1 and will not be revisited here. The first problem that many have with it is that claiming someone has a right to something seems to require justification, and Regan offers precious little of that. In the absence of any good reason that we should grant rights to some particular being, it seems that our claim is nothing but the expression of a subjective preference. We might claim that animals have the right not to be used as food because doing so would increase the total amount of misery in the world. This would be an attempt to justify a right by appealing to the principle of utility. Regan does not take such an approach, however, but rather makes rights themselves fundamental. It is on them that all our other moral beliefs are supposed to rest, whereas they themselves have no foundation.

Instead, we are just supposed to "see" or "intuit" the truth of various claims that rights of certain sorts exist for certain types of beings. Regan's intuitions tell him that subjects of a life have rights. Suppose my intuition tells me that only human beings have rights. Suppose yours tells you that in addition humans and animals, rivers and trees all have rights as well. Rivers especially have the right not to be polluted, and trees have the right not to be used for fuel or lumber. Is that enough to give them the protection of the moral community? It would appear that the rights view is based on intuitions that allow some to grant rights only to humans, whereas others grant them to nonhuman animals, and still others grant them to trees and rivers. Without being anchored on a foundation of reasons that explain why a being of a certain sort should be granted rights of a certain sort, the very process of claiming that a being has rights seems to be nothing but a matter of opinion.

The second objection to Regan's use of the rights theory is that it denies rights to many sentient beings. Regan restricts rights to subjects of a life. If only subjects of a life can have rights, however, then some animals that do not have the requisite level of conscious experience to qualify as subjects of a life must be seen as not having rights. It is not always easy to tell what degree of consciousness an animal has, but some animals seem clearly unable to do such complex things as remember their past or anticipate their future—both requirements of being a subject of a life. Among this class of animals that are not subjects of a life are some that can suffer. Does this mean that the animal rights view denies rights to some animals that can suffer? The answer appears to be that it does. The second major objection to the animal rights view, then, is that it does not go far enough in granting rights to animals. It denies moral status to some animals that can suffer, just because they do not have the requisite value-conferring characteristics to make them subjects of a life. This itself sounds dangerously like speciesism.

The final objection denies the reliability of premise (1)#, that all subjects of a life have equal inherent value. More specifically, the objection claims that the entire case for the animal rights view rests on a misguided theory of value. On the one hand, Regan and others who hold the animal rights view think that the *intrinsic* value of beings is determined by the degree to which they possess the value-conferring characteristics that make them subjects of a life. According to this idea of value, however, one embraced by the animal welfare and the animal liberation views, human and nonhuman animals have different degrees of value, because they have different degrees of value-conferring characteristics. Valuing non-human animals less than human animals, however, allows us to use them under certain conditions for our purposes, as the animal welfare argument has shown. Regan will have none of this. For him, under no circumstances is it morally acceptable to use animals merely as a means to the good of humans, no matter how painlessly this is accomplished.

So he introduces the concept of *inherent* value, as distinct from intrinsic value, and claims that although all beings that are subjects of a life have unequal intrinsic value, they nevertheless have equal inherent value. Our inherent value is supposed to lie with just the bare "shell" of our individuality, devoid of any of its value-conferring characteristics. Despite the differences in the levels of intrinsic value possessed by human and nonhuman animals, all subjects of a life have equal moral rights because we all are equally important as individuals.

Most views on the moral status of animals, and most moral philosophers in general, believe that it is the possession of value conferring characteristics that gives a being its value, and thus its moral status. It is because they possess these characteristics—because they can reason, can form beliefs, can have memories, can perceive, can suffer, can be subjects of a life—that we think it important to allow them into the moral community and to offer them its protection. Regan also appeals to the link between these characteristics and a being's value, especially when he wants to avoid the absurd conclusion that there is no difference in value between humans and nonhuman animals of various sorts.

He abandons the connection between such traits and value, however, when he wants to claim that all subjects of a life have equal value. And so he needs two concepts of value—intrinsic value that varies from species to species, and inherent value that does not. Inherent value becomes the source of a being's moral status, so we can say that all subjects of a life have equal moral status or rights. So although he acknowledges different levels of value among species by appealing to different degrees of intrinsic value, he ignores these differences in value when it comes to granting moral status by his appeal to inherent value, which we all are supposed to share equally.

By establishing moral status on the basis of inherent value, Regan may ignore the variations in degrees of value-conferring characteristics possessed by various human and nonhuman animals and thus avoid grading the moral status of beings according to the degree to which they possess such characteristics. This enables him to escape the conclusions embraced by the animal welfare view. If all subjects of a life have *equal* moral status, even though they have different levels of intrinsic value, then all have the same right to life and the same right to avoid pain and suffering.

Appealing to inherent value, however, as distinct from intrinsic value, is a conceptual device with no foundation. What in the world does it mean to talk about the worth of individuals devoid of the very characteristics that give them this worth? It is not merely being an individual that gives worth. If this were so, individual trees and rocks would have inherent value. Instead, it is being an individual of a certain type that produces value. The type of an individual a being is, moreover, is determined by the characteristics possessed by that individual. Individuals cannot be separated from their characteristics when value is ascribed to them, because it is these very characteristics that determine that value.

This final objection, then, claims that there is no such thing as a being's inherent value, as distinct from its intrinsic value. True, it is the individual who has value, not his or her fleeting mental states, but the individual cannot be spoken of in any meaningful way apart from his or her value-conferring characteristics. We are not just beings; we are thinking, feeling, perceiving beings or we are not. The moral status of a being depends on its intrinsic value, and this is determined by its value-conferring characteristics. Any view that denies this, any view that requires us to believe that all subjects of a life have equal moral value, requires us to consider the right to life of a man, for example, to be of no more significance than the right to life of a mouse. In the end, such a position runs the risk of doing more harm than good to the interests of animals.

Exercise 10.2

For this exercise, make a **reasoned judgment** that one of the views discussed in this chapter is the most adequate solution to our problem. First, summarize its answer to the moral status question and to the animal treatment questions. Then show how, as a proponent of this view, you might respond to the objections that I have directed against it. Finally, list the moral consequences of this view. That is, list the additional moral obligations, if any, that ought to be accepted by anyone holding such a view. Some possible consequences are mentioned in the next section. It will be more beneficial for you to think of some on your own before reading on.

Consequences

Depending on which view you have selected, the moral *consequences* of doing so can be enormous. If you practice your moral beliefs, and if they are consistent with the position you have just selected in Exercise 10.2, then dramatic changes in your life may be necessary. If you believe that the conventional view is correct, this will require little or no change in your behavior. This is the traditional and currently prevailing view, one that has shaped the beliefs most of us have about the morally acceptable ways to treat animals. If, on the other hand, you have previously accepted the conventional view, but now believe that one of the others is correct, there are significant consequences for you to recognize.

For example, if you believe that the animal liberation or the the animal rights view is correct, then your moral beliefs will have to change dramatically. These are revolutionary views that demand radical changes in thought and action. For example, if you hold the animal rights view, you are morally required to become a vegetarian, and probably even a "vegan." A vegan neither eats animals or animal products nor uses any animal product—such as leather or fur. It is also morally required that you be opposed to all instances of animal experimentation. Many animal rights advocates, in fact, conduct public protests against such uses of animals and work tirelessly to introduce legislation that does the same. Some even practice civil disobedience in the name of animal rights, and even more extreme groups, such as the Animal Liberation Front, have used violence to "liberate" animals and to intimidate researchers. These acts of violence have been disavowed by the intellectual leaders of the animal rights and animal liberation movements but are still practiced by a small segment of people, especially in European countries.

If you adopt the animal liberation view, your moral behavior must change in similar ways. In theory it may be acceptable to use animals for food and research, but in practice, because there are alternatives, doing so is almost never morally acceptable. Try to imagine how much your life would change if you became a vegetarian, or even a vegan. Perhaps you already refrain from eating animal flesh and other products, but most of us do not. For animal rights activists, such a lifestyle is not only healthy and morally correct but it is also the best strategy for closing down factory farms. If we all stop eating animals, there will no longer be a need to raise them for food.

If you believe that the animal liberation view is correct, you will probably also have to believe that the process for how medicine and science in general go about developing new products and procedures must be changed dramatically. With a general prohibition against using animal subjects, either cells or tissue studies will have to do. When these are insufficient, humans with the condition under investigation will have to serve as research subjects. In some cases, heroic humans without medical problems may serve the cause of medicine by volunteering as research subjects. Researchers are very nervous about the animal rights and animal liberation movements, which they perceive as serious threats to science and especially to medicine.

If you believe that the animal welfare view is correct, your life will still change quite dramatically. You do not have to be a vegetarian, but you cannot eat meat that comes from factory farms. You must also be opposed to any other inhumane way that animals are treated, such as using them in unnecessary and painful experiments, or confining them in small cages in zoos or circuses, or hunting them for sport. In short, any human use of animals for our benefit must be humane if it is to be morally acceptable.

In the end, the question is whether we are going to continue to use animals as we always have or start to treat them in kinder, gentler ways. For many, there will be no rest until we begin to see animals as fellow travelers through life, beings who have lives and interests of their own, lives and interests that are just as important to them as ours are to us.

Another Perspective

Exercise 10.3

The point of this exercise is for you to examine various points of view or perspectives on the moral acceptability of animal experimentation. To do this efficiently, each member of the class should bring in an article that he or she has found on the Internet or through a journal or newspaper search. The article should express clearly the author's opinion and reasons for his or her stance on animal experimentation and should clearly indicate the perspective from which it was written. For example, the author may be an animal rights activist, a researcher, a pet owner, a veterinarian, a member of the cosmetics industry, a hunter, a circus owner, a farmer, and so on. Each student should comment on how the perspective seems to slant the interpretation of information in one or another direction. If time allows, the results of individual assignments should be shared with the entire class so that the power of a point of view to influence the interpretation of facts might be appreciated fully.

Moral Problems Concerned with Sex and Reproduction

The moral problems discussed in this section have to do with one of the most basic of all human desires, sexual desire. One of these, the problem of *pornography*, concerns the exploitation of this desire. The moral issue for us will be how best to eliminate or at least to minimize this exploitation. Pornography is a rapidly growing business in this country. Not only is it easily available in film and print, but it is now widely disseminated through the Internet and soon will be even more widely available through the various forms of electronic communication that digital television will allow. Some theorists think that when men view violent and degrading pornography on a regular basis their beliefs about women often change, and not always for the best. Many also claim that perhaps even actions toward women can be affected, as is evidenced by the apparent association of pornography and sex crimes.

The moral question for us will not focus on the moral acceptability of various forms of pornography. Instead, it will be concerned with the best methods of eliminating especially the most pernicious forms of pornography, or at least of minimizing their impact. There are laws now against some forms of pornography, but they are often vague and difficult to enforce. Should we simply educate people about the harms of pornography and let them decide for themselves whether to refrain from viewing it? Or should we, by law, eliminate the production, sale, and possession of even common forms of pornography? In short, to what degree, if any, should we censor pornography? This is the moral problem of Chapter 12.

In Chapter 13 we turn to the question of reproduction. The "normal" way to reproduce requires sexual intercourse between members of the opposite sex but various forms of technology have been developed to aid those who cannot produce children in this manner, or who choose not to do so. Beginning in the early 1960s, a steady stream of reproductive technologies has been discovered and used to help people conceive and give birth to healthy children when they might not otherwise be able to do so. These technologies have great potential for good, but they also have great potential for evil. They need to be regulated to ensure that their use will benefit humankind and not result in harms. These are exciting times, and the recent breakthroughs in microbiology and especially in genetics guarantees that they will continue to be exciting. However, before we stray too far from nature's way of making babies we need to reflect on the wisdom of our choices. Because new technologies exist does not mean that we ought to use them. We ought to use them only if they are good for us and preserve our intrinsic value and autonomy. In Chapter 13 we address some of the harms and benefits of the new reproductive technologies, and attempt to construct regulations for their use in the form of moral rules.

The problems raised by reproductive technologies are relatively recent ones but we begin Section C with a problem as old as morality itself. The moral problem of Chapter 11 concerns the proper relationship between sex, love, and marriage. Should morally acceptable sexual behavior be confined to marriage, or is it enough to be in love to justify sex between two people? Do sexual relations need moral justification at all? Why not, in this age of reliable contraceptives and individual freedom, simply see sex like any other activity that people enjoy? Should it not be understood simply as a private matter, to be engaged in at a person's discretion? If it's enjoyable and if there is consent of all involved, why limit sex to those who are in love or to those who are married? With proper precautions to prevent unwanted pregnancies and disease, why not classify sex as morally acceptable whenever it occurs between consenting adults?

Those who believe that sex requires marriage to be morally acceptable often argue that this is so because sex is primarily for reproduction. If this view is accepted, then homosexuality seems to be morally unacceptable. If the requirements for morally acceptable sexual activity are consent or love, on the other hand, then there seems to be room for the acceptance of homosexuality as well as nonmarital sex. Or is there? Is sexual activity between two people of the same sex wrong in itself? Is there something perverse or unnatural about it that makes such behavior immoral even if people do consent to it, even if they are in love, and even if, as is now possible, they are legally married? It is to these questions about sex, love, and marriage that we first turn in thinking about the moral implications of sex and reproduction.

Chapter 11

Sex, Love, and Marriage

Before the development of reliable contraceptives in the 1960s, for two people of the opposite sex to have intercourse was risky business indeed. The primary risk was an unwanted pregnancy. For the most part, a pregnant, unmarried woman did not have the option of abortion at that time. She either had to marry the biological father, raise the child herself, or give it up for adoption. Very often none of these choices were happy ones, so it was both possible and desirable for society to condemn sex outside of marriage as immoral.

With the introduction of reliable contraceptives, especially the "pill," sexual intercourse became much less likely to result in an unwanted pregnancy. Liberated from this fear and buoyed by the sense of individual freedom produced by the 1960s counterculture, young people in this country and abroad began the so-called sexual revolution. The prohibitions of an older generation against the harms of extramarital sex were brushed aside as vestiges of an era gone by. Sexual taboos fell one by one until the revolution was complete, until a new set of moral beliefs that accompanied sexual liberation was firmly in place. Sex was no longer morally acceptable in marriage alone but now was thought of as morally acceptable between people who were in a loving relationship, and even between people who just wanted to have fun. There was no more harm to be found in such behavior, so why not?

The sexual revolution has been slowed by the fear of sexually transmitted diseases (STDs), especially AIDS. People are more careful now about choosing their sex partners. But these cautions are not to be understood as a return to a conventional morality. Instead, the attitude is that now it simply is prudent to have sex with fewer partners. It is wiser to be in a monogamous relationship, for example, than to have multiple sex partners. These are just matters of safety, not matters of right and wrong. The sexual revolution has been won by the revolutionaries. The prevailing moral view today is that for single people at least, sex outside of marriage between people in love, and even nonmarital sex without love, is not immoral. In fact, even sex between two people of the same sex is widely held to be morally acceptable. The question before us in this chapter is whether this increasingly widely held moral view about nonmarital heterosexual behavior and homosexual behavior is correct. Apart from appealing to fears of unwanted pregnancies and STDs, what can someone say to convince people that the current liberal view of sexual activity is incorrect?

Some argue that marriage may not be required for morally acceptable sex but that love surely is. Sex without love may be pleasurable, but it is empty. The main purpose of sex is not simply to use each other's bodies for pleasure, but it is to express a deep love between two people. Sex is so close physically that if love is absent, if there is no friendship, no caring, no emotional bond between lovers, then the pleasure of sex quickly turns to emotional pain.

Others will argue that even love is not enough. They will point out that love, unrecognized by marriage, is fragile and fleeting. The closeness and commitment of two people in a good marriage far exceeds that found in a loving "relationship." Besides, the incidence of unwanted pregnancies, divorce, single-parent families, STDs, and a general breakdown of the family unit all cry out for a return to conventional morality. If sex is condoned only in marriage, there will be a dramatic decline in such social ills. Chief among the social ills spawned by separating sex from reproduction is the acceptance of homosexuality, a perversion of the true meaning and purpose of sex. Sex is supposed to be for reproduction, so to use it solely for pleasure or the expression of love, especially by people of the same sex, is a perversion of its proper function and thus is wrong in itself. Only a return to the conventional morality will save the family, the social unit on which society rests.

The Problem

The belief that various forms of sexual activity are private matters and thus beyond the scope of morality is rejected in this chapter. Although sexual behavior is ordinarily something that takes place in private, this does not mean that it cannot affect others and oneself for good or ill, or that it is beyond violating the principles of autonomy and justice. Society already criminalizes sexual behaviors the majority of its citizens oppose, such as rape, incest, adultery, and sodomy. In addition, parents, educators, and others who shape the moral values of children, wish to encourage some sexual behaviors and to discourage others. So there is a sense that some forms of sexual activity are wrong and others are morally acceptable. Sexual behavior is not thought of as simply a personal preference, as taste in clothes or cars or art may be. The shifting and changing moral ground on which such attitudes rest, however, requires a reexamination of the reasons that support the various beliefs about sexual morality found in society today. Such an examination can begin in no better place than with a clarification of basic concepts.

Clarifying Concepts

Because this chapter is about sexual morality we need to be clear on what we mean when we talk about sex. In its narrowest meaning, the concept of **sex** refers to the anatomical and physiological properties that distinguish males from females. To ask about someone's sex is to ask whether he or she is male or female. **Sexuality,** on the other hand, refers to psychological properties, especially the meaning that being male or female has for a person, the role that one's sex plays in life. Because judgments about right and wrong are always judgments about actions, the concept of **sexual behavior** is the one that will be most important to us in this chapter and is what most people refer to when they speak of "having sex." The problem of this chapter is which types of sexual behaviors are morally acceptable in which types of contexts.

Sexual behavior may include many types of behavior. It may include kissing and petting, which leads to sexual arousal, oral and anal sex, sexual stimulation of a person by himself or herself, sexual intercourse between members of the same sex or members of the opposite sex, group sex, sex with animals, and even sex with inanimate objects. We will focus especially on sexual intercourse between members of the opposite sex, sometimes called "straight sex," and on sexual behavior between members of the same sex, or **homosexual** behaviors. A homosexual is someone who is sexually attracted to members of the same sex. Female homosexuals are often called **lesbians;** male homosexuals are often referred to as **gay.** People who detest and attempt to repress and degrade homosexual behavior are often referred to as **homophobic.**

Some people refer to certain types of sexual behaviors as **perversions** and to those who perform such acts as "perverts." Someone is perverse if he or she deliberately acts contrary to what is considered normal. Sexual perversions, then, are deliberate sexual desires and the behaviors to which they lead that go against the norm, the way that most people behave. Actions may violate social norms, in which case they are called "abnormal," or they may be contrary to natural ways of behaving, in which case they are called "unnatural." Sex acts with animals and inanimate objects are considered perverse by many, both because they are abnormal and because they are unnatural acts. Others argue about whether homosexuality is unnatural and therefore perverse. Because perverse acts violate accepted norms, many consider them to be immoral. The link between being abnormal or unnatural, on the one hand, and being immoral, on the other, is an important link that will be examined carefully in this chapter.

Another important concept is that of **consent.** One of our possible solutions will claim that sexual behavior is morally acceptable whenever it occurs between consenting adults. True consent requires that the person consenting understand the nature and consequences of the act consented to and freely choose to perform the act. This rules out forced sexual behavior, such as rape, as it is not freely chosen. It also rules out more subtle forms of coerced sex, such as threats to be fired by one's boss or to be flunked by a professor if sexual favors are not granted. Sex based on deception is also considered immoral, as agreement to engage in sexual behavior might have been denied if the truth had been known. A married man who tells a woman that he is single, for example, deceives a woman so that she will agree to sex when she otherwise would not have done so. Because she is deceived, because she cannot understand the true nature and consequences of her behavior, she is not a consenting adult.

One of our possible solutions claims that sexual behavior is morally acceptable as long as the two people are in love, so it is important to understand the concept of **love.** In general, to love someone is to intend to do good for them, and to do your best to see that your intentions are realized. To say that a mother loves her child, for example, or that a boy loves his dog or that a friend loves another friend all incorporate this general idea of doing good for another. Romantic love includes the desire to do good for the other as well, but it also includes feelings of sexual desire, "infatuation" as it is sometimes called, and even downright lust. Some refer solely to these feelings when they talk about "being in love." For the possible solution claiming that love is enough to justify sex, however, love does not mean infatuation. Rather, it refers to a concern and caring for the lover as well as sexual desire. To be in love requires an emotional closeness as well as a physical attraction. To be lovers requires first that there be a friendship. Unlike infatuation, this emotional bond takes time to nurture, so this kind of love is possible only in a long-term relationship. Let us think of romantic love then as physical attraction plus a close emotional bond. It requires a couple to be friends first, and lovers only later.

The final concept for clarification concerns the **purposes of sex.** Clearly, there are at least three important ones. First, sex may be used for *pleasure.* Unless it is forced on someone, sexual behavior almost always results in some level of pleasure. Next, in addition to pleasure, sex may be used to express *love.* In the physical intimacy of sex lies an opportunity to show affection, caring, and emotional closeness—all expressions of love. Finally, sexual intercourse may be used for *reproduction.* This is its primary purpose throughout the animal world, and surely its main biological purpose for humans as well. Although reproductive technology has made reproduction without sex possible, sexual intercourse is still the method of choice for most. For many, the ideal use of sex occurs when all three of its purposes are combined, when it is used in a pleasurable and loving way to conceive children. Because sexual intercourse can occur without love, however, and with reliable contraception, it can also occur without reproduction, these three main purposes of sex can be separated.

Formulating the Problem

Many of the problems discussed in this text are formulated in a positive manner, asking us to examine the conditions under which some type of action is morally acceptable. Here we formulate the problem in a negative way and ask for the conditions under which sexual behavior is immoral. To do this is to place the burden of proof on those who would restrict sexual behavior. Because sexual desire is very strong and basic, like hunger or thirst, our freedom to express it should be restricted only for good reasons. Our sexual behavior significantly shapes the sort of person that each of us is. It ought to remain a matter of personal choice, a matter left to the exercise of our autonomy, unless we can be shown that some form of harm or some violation of the principle of justice will result from our choices. As is the case with any sort of behavior, the moral acceptability of our sexual behavior will be judged by appeal to our three moral principles. So we *formulate the problem* of this chapter in the following way:

> *Under what conditions is sexual behavior immoral?*

The law also asks a similar question as it seeks to restrict the sexual behavior of citizens. Our moral problem is different from its corresponding legal problem in several ways, however. The chief difference lies with the scope of morality and the law. Simply put, the law focuses on preventing public harms, harms to others, whereas the goal of morality includes avoiding private harms as well. The law usually permits most actions between consenting adults, for example. This is not always true, as there are laws in several states against some types of "private" sexual behavior, such as adultery and homosexuality. But such laws are difficult to enforce, so they are seldom used in practice. As we will soon see, however, the moral prohibitions discussed in this chapter include both public and private harms as reasons for restricting sexual behavior.

Possible Solutions

Three **possible solutions** to our problem are discussed in this chapter. The first is called the **liberal** view. Liberals claim that sexual behavior is morally acceptable when it occurs between *consenting* adults. Presumably, when accurately informed persons consent to an act freely (autonomy), they believe that it will cause them benefits, not harms (beneficence), and that it does not use them merely as a means to the good of another (justice). According to the liberal, sexual partners need not be married nor even be in love for their sexual behavior to conform to our three principles. Sexual behavior is immoral only when at least one of the participants is not consenting.

As true consent requires that a person understand the action and its likely consequences, it is not possible whenever there is a lack of accurate information, especially due to deliberate deception on the part of one of the partners. *Deception* may occur if someone withholds information that is expected or deliberately lies. If a married man believes that a woman will not have sex with him if she knows that he has a wife then he deceives her if he withholds that information or tells her that he is not married. Perhaps he removes his wedding band, or says that he is divorced, or lies about the stability of his marriage relationship. Whichever route is chosen, in not allowing for a free and informed decision, deception violates autonomy. Because its goal is to use the person, to take advantage of him or her for the sake of the other's pleasure, it also violates the principle of justice. Most likely, it will also violate beneficence, by leading to some form of harm.

Coercion is another way to eliminate consent. In its more overt forms, such as rape, coercion clearly violates all three moral principles. In its more subtle forms, it does so as well. For example, someone in a supervisory position may request sexual favors from his or her supervisee. If the person in the subordinate position takes this offer as a threat and considers that a refusal may mean loss of his or her job or loss of an expected and much needed raise, then agreeing to sex is not a free choice. As such, it violates the principle of autonomy. Moreover, it involves using a person and causing that person harm, so it violates our other two principles as well.

The "adults" requirement is included to restrict sexual behavior to those who can truly consent. The assumption is that children lack the knowledge or power to do so, thus sex with children is immoral. In the absence of consent, sexual activity with children violates the principles of autonomy and justice, and very likely the principle of beneficence as well. In sum, for the liberal, sexual behavior is immoral whenever it occurs between adults and children, and between adults when it is based on deception or coercion. Otherwise, sexual activity between consenting adults, even casual sex between strangers, is morally acceptable. In addition, sex with oneself, such as masturbation, is also allowed by the liberal. Homosexuality is allowed as well, as is oral sex, anal sex, and even various forms of sado-masochistic behavior. Even adultery is allowed if both marriage partners agree that sex with others is acceptable. For the liberal, as long as there is consent, there is moral acceptability. If people agree to it, and if no one gets hurt, then why not?

The next view claims that more than consent is required for morally acceptable sexual behavior. In addition to consent, *love* is required as well. This view is called the **moderate** view of sexual morality. It does not require that two people be married for sexual behavior to be morally acceptable, as does our next possible solution, but it does insist on more than the minimum "consent" requirement of the liberal. When people are not in love, what they consent to is merely the right to be used by another for pleasure, while they, in turn, use the other person as well. Such actions may be free, and thus conform to the principle of autonomy, but they violate the other two moral principles.

So-called one-night stands, for example, a paradigm case of sex without love, are permissible for the liberal. The moderate believes, however, that in mutually agreeing to use each other's bodies with no emotional connection, people violate the principle of justice. Even though the choice is free, they are still being used merely as a means for the good of another. Most important, such behavior inevitably leads to harm, thus violating the principle of beneficence also. It leads to harm because sex without love denies a basic need, a need that is expected to be satisfied with sexual behavior. In the absence of emotional intimacy, the physical intimacy of sexual intercourse leaves a person feeling empty and used. As love withheld by a parent is felt as a harm, as it leaves a person with an emotional scar, so too does sexual behavior harm a person when there is no love. For the moderate, then, sex is immoral when love is absent.

Moderates do allow sexual behavior without marriage. They also permit homosexuality, as people of the same sex can also be in love with each other. Love is the key. When it is present, and when sex is used to express it, then any number of sexual behaviors is allowed. When it is absent, however, sexual activity is harmfully using another person and is immoral on these grounds. The moderate also rejects various sorts of sexual perversion, such as sex with animals and sex with inanimate objects. Not only is consent absent in these cases, but love is absent as well. In short, the moderate solves our moral problem by agreeing with the liberal that consent must be present for sexual activity to be morally acceptable. In addition to consent, however, love must be present also.

Our third and final view is called by many the "conventional" view. However, although many still accept its claims, it no longer clearly represents the generally accepted view of society. Instead, we will label it the **conservative** view. The basic moral claim of the conservative is that sexual behavior, especially sexual intercourse, is morally acceptable only within the confines of marriage. The conservative is not opposed to the use of sex for pleasure or for demonstrating love but believes that the central and natural purpose of sex is reproduction. It is a good thing for pleasure and love to accompany sexual behavior, but only if that behavior is directed toward reproduction. If the possibility of reproduction is eliminated, if sexual pleasure or the expression of love is allowed to occur without the chance of reproduction, then such sexual behavior is immoral for the conservative. Sex for pleasure alone, or for pleasure and love alone, goes against nature. It perverts the natural purpose of sexual behavior—reproduction—and is therefore immoral.

But if sex is primarily for reproduction, then why insist on marriage? Why not simply reproduce with whomever one desires? The simple reason, claims the conservative, is that marriage is necessary because raising the children produced by sex requires a stable family. The best families, the ones most likely to produce the best sorts of children, are two-parent families, in which one parent is male, the other female. This provides the best type of environment for the child, the best chance for it to lead a happy, meaningful, and productive life. For the conservative, because sexual behavior is primarily for reproduction, it should be confined to marriage.

Sexual behavior outside of marriage is wrong for two reasons. First, as we have seen, nonmarital sex is immoral in itself because it is unnatural. Second, it is immoral because so-called free love—using sex for pleasure alone, or for love—leads to all sorts of social ills. Having sex simply for pleasure or to express love leads to unwanted pregnancies, divorce, the spread of sexually transmitted diseases, lack of respect for the family and family values, and so on. So any type of sexual behavior that is not between married people and open to the possibility of reproduction is immoral for both of these reasons. Masturbation, sex with contraception, oral sex, and anal sex are all immoral. Most of all, the conservative believes that homosexual behavior is especially immoral. Not only will such behavior lead to harm, but it is a clear form of unnatural and perverse behavior.

Facts and Assumptions

Facts

We will begin by examining the extent to which sexual behaviors have changed since the 1960s, when the so-called sexual revolution began, and the degree to which **public opinion** has found such changes to be morally acceptable. First it is important to note that the very concept of "having sex" itself is understood differently by different people. In a survey of college students, for example, virtually all students agreed that penile-vaginal intercourse counts as having sex.[1] Nearly 20 percent, however, did not think of penile-anal intercourse as having sex, and almost 60 percent did not consider oral genital contact as having sex. Finally, mutual masturbation was considered as having sex by only 20 percent of males and 12 percent of females. With this notion of what counts as having sex in the background, let us examine how some sexual behaviors, especially premarital sexual behaviors, have changed in the past four decades.[2]

First, in the 1960s, 25 percent of young men and 45 percent of young women were virgins at their nineteenth birthday. Today, about 20 percent of each sex are virgins at nineteen. In the 1960s, 90 percent of young women got married without first living with their partner. Today only 30 percent do. Forty percent of women were virgins when they married in the 1960s. Today that number is 14 percent. Today, by the time they turn eighteen, 30 percent of Americans have had one or no sex partners; 30 percent have had two to four partners; 20 percent have had five to ten partners; and 20 percent, ten partners or more.

Public opinion about the moral acceptability of nonmarital sex has changed as well. Three-quarters of adult Americans now believe that premarital sex for adults—though not teens—is morally acceptable. It has become seen as "normal" behavior. This is a vastly changed attitude from that held prior to the 1960s, when "living with someone" was considered by many to be shocking. If someone did have premarital sex before the 1960s, and many certainly did, it was most likely to be with someone to whom the person was engaged. If pregnancy occurred, marriage soon followed.

Nevertheless, despite the dramatic change in their attitudes about premarital sex, most Americans are far more conservative in both their sexual attitudes and behaviors than might be expected. Most married Americans, fully 80 percent, have never had an extramarital affair, for example. Most continue to hold the same moral beliefs about adultery and teenage sex that were prevalent decades ago—that they are immoral. In fact, perhaps because of the dangers of STDs, opposition to marital infidelity has actually increased since the mid-1980s. Tolerance for homosexuality has risen somewhat recently, especially among women. More people, as many as 30 percent, now believe that it is not learned behavior but has a strong genetic determinant. Still, two-thirds of Americans continue to believe that homosexual activity is immoral.[3]

Scientific facts are quite relevant to our discussion of sexual morality, especially scientific facts about the causes of *homosexuality.* If homosexual behavior is learned, for example, then it can be unlearned. Through strict moral and legal prohibitions, perhaps society can ensure that it is never learned to begin with. If homosexuality violates our moral principles, then to condemn it as immoral makes sense. If sexual desires for those of the same sex are genetically based, on the other hand, then there is little point in moral or legal condemnation of homosexual behavior. Whereas there is a difference between having a desire and acting on it, sexual desire is so strong that there is little hope of controlling its expression in behavior if it is "natural." If homosexual behavior is determined by genetic makeup, then people so disposed cannot help having their feelings and desires any more than heterosexuals can help having theirs. For homosexuals, such behavior is natural. If some people are genetically destined to be attracted to those of the same sex, saying that it is immoral is foolish. To say that people *ought to* refrain from homosexual behavior makes no sense if doing so is not possible for them. People cannot be obliged to do things that are impossible. If homosexuality is natural, it cannot be immoral.

Unfortunately, science is not yet clear on the causes of homosexuality. It would appear to have a biological basis, though no specific biological differences between homosexuals and heterosexuals have been definitively discovered to date. Homosexuals themselves do not experience their desires for those of the same sex as a choice, as something that they could change. In addition, so-called *reparative therapies,* treatments of various sorts designed to change a person's sexual orientation, have always failed. They fail, that is, to transform a person with sexual desires for members of the same sex into a person with heterosexual desires. At the very most, such therapies encourage people not to act on their homosexual desires, but they do nothing to eliminate them. The American Psychiatric Association removed homosexuality from its list of mental illnesses in 1973, as did the World Health Organization in 1981. Today, most major scientific organizations whose members may treat homosexuals state that homosexuality is not a choice, that it appears at a very early age, that it is not subject to voluntary change, and that treatment should be directed toward helping homosexuals become comfortable with their sexual orientation. In a 1994 statement on homosexuality, the American Psychological Association said:

> The research on homosexuality is very clear. Homosexuality is neither mental illness nor moral depravity. It is simply the way that a minority of our population expresses human love and sexuality. Study after study documents the mental health of gay men and lesbians. Studies of judgment, stability, reliability and social and vocational adaptiveness all show that gay men and lesbians function every bit as well as heterosexuals.
>
> Nor is homosexuality a matter of individual choice. Research suggests that the homosexual orientation is in place very early in the life cycle, possibly even before birth. It is found in about ten percent of the population, a figure which is surprisingly constant across cultures, irrespective of the different moral values and standards of a particular culture. Contrary to what some imply, the incidence of homosexuality in a population does not appear to change with new moral codes or social mores. Research findings suggest that efforts to repair homosexuals are nothing more than social prejudice garbed in psychological accouterments.[4]

Even in the light of such a strong statement by an organization of professionals who are in a good position to understand homosexuality, the scientific community is still undecided about whether homosexuality is the result of "nature" or "nurture." Part of the reason is that previous claims to have discovered the biological basis of homosexuality have all turned out to be less than convincing. One claim, for instance, is that homosexuals have different levels of hormones in their bodies than their heterosexual counterparts, or that parts of their brain are smaller, or that differences in chromosomes have been discovered. In addition, studies of identical twins separated at birth and raised in different environments have concluded that there is a biological basis for sexual orientation. Even animal studies have been performed that claimed a genetic basis for homosexuality. None of these studies, however, have been accepted without criticism. It is safe to say that a biological basis for homosexuality, though considered quite probable by many, has yet to be scientifically confirmed.

The *nature* view claims that our sexual orientation is preprogrammed by our genes, which create appropriate hormones and exhibit this orientation in our brain structure. However, others believe that even if a gene that "causes" homosexuality were identified, it would do so only by predisposing people to that sexual orientation. According to this view, environmental causes—*nurture*—play the leading role in determining sexual orientation. The nurture view claims that people must be taught to follow their sexual predispositions and that they can be taught otherwise. Suggested environmental causes of homosexuality have included the influence of society, the family, peer groups, and morality. In the family, for example, a dominant mother and a weak and remote father are likely causes for male homosexuality, whereas lesbians are produced by unmet mother love. Same-sex attraction is caused in both cases, it is claimed, by the desire to satisfy the need for unmet parental love. In a similar way, for adolescents who are confused about their sexual orientation and fear not being able to fit into a heterosexual peer group, identifying with and being accepted by a homosexual peer group may be the answer. Doing so meets the needs for acceptance and the avoidance of isolation. This view sees much of homosexuality as a matter of recruitment into a group and not something solidly determined by biological destiny.

Until a cause is proven, we would be wise to consider homosexuality the product of many factors. In the discussion to follow we will assume that the determinants of sexual orientation are a complex combination of biological, psychological, and social factors. Instead of deciding prematurely that homosexuality is beyond moral judgment because it is not subject to control, homosexual behavior will be judged as morally acceptable or not on the same grounds that are used to judge any action. If it violates our moral principles, it is immoral; otherwise, it is not.

Descriptive Ethics

The rules for regulating sexual behavior in society are to be found especially in religion and the law. Most **religions** distinguish between sexual orientation and sexual behavior. While accepting people of various sexual orientations, many religions do not find homosexual behavior to be morally acceptable. Some few liberal Christian religions, such as Unitarian Universalists and the United Church of Christ, allow homosexual members, ordain homosexual ministers, and even perform same-sex unions. Some Eastern religions accept homosexuality as well. For example, Hindus, affirming the spiritual side of ourselves, allow same-sex actions as long as they promote our spiritual advancement and are not simply based on satisfying our bodily desires. Reform Jews welcome members of any sexual orientation, and some rabbis who who are Reconstructionist Jews even perform same-sex commitment ceremonies. Some moderately liberal Christian denominations, such as the Episcopal Church find their membership split on matters of sexuality and especially on the moral acceptability of homosexuality. Whereas they accept homosexual members, and even ordain nonpracticing homosexuals, they do not ordain practicing homosexuals.

Most conservative denominations of Christian and Jewish religions, as well as all of Islam, believe that homosexuality in particular, and all sex outside of marriage in general, is immoral. The policies of the Church of Jesus Christ of Latter-Day Saints (the Mormon Church) and those of the Southern Baptists are aggressively antihomosexual, as are the policies of Orthodox Jews. The Roman Catholic Church has been quite outspoken on the matter of homosexuality and on other matters of sexual behavior for centuries. It condemns all human sexual behavior outside of marriage, and even some forms of sexual behavior within marriage. It does so on the basis of both faith, the revealed word of God found in scripture, and reason. To understand their argument from reason is important as it is so often referred to by those who defend the conservative view.

The appeal to reason rests on *natural law ethics.* This is an ethical theory of obligation claiming that there is such a thing as human nature, a nature shared by all human beings of all cultures and all historical periods. This does not mean simply that all humans have the same *biological* nature, something that most people could accept. Rather it means that we all have the same *moral* nature, something much more difficult to accept. In particular, natural law ethics claims that we all have natural desires that point us toward specific goals. The achievement of these goals constitutes the good life, the life of a fully developed human being, the life of someone living in full accordance with his or her nature. Any action that promotes the flourishing of human nature is morally acceptable; actions that go against the fulfillment of its goals are immoral.

The reason some forms of sexual behavior are immoral is that they lead us away from the true goals of our sexual human nature. Sex may be used for procreation, as an expression of love, or simply for pleasure. The main goal or purpose of sex, the one that helps our human nature to flourish, is reproduction. The other purposes of sex are acceptable, but only if achieved as a result of the use of sex for reproduction, not independently. Every morally acceptable act of sexual behavior has to be open to the possibility of reproduction or it is a violation of human nature. This is why masturbation, anal sex, oral sex, homosexual behavior in general, and even contraception are immoral—they are sexual actions that are not used for procreation. As such, they pervert the true purpose of sexual activity. Sex is not supposed to be *just* for pleasure, or *just* for love. If it is used that way it prevents the true flourishing of human beings. It prevents the development of sex into love and into a lasting, meaningful relationship within which the lives of both parents and children will flourish.

This view is outlined in the Vatican's (1975) *Declaration on Sexual Ethics*.[5] This document claims that premarital sex is wrong, that love is not enough to justify sex. In what follows, the term "finality" should be taken to mean "true purpose or goal."

> Experience teaches us that love must find its safeguard in the stability of marriage, if sexual intercourse is truly to respond to the requirements of its own finality and those of human dignity. These requirements call for a conjugal contract sanctioned and guaranteed by society—a contract which establishes a state of life of capital importance both for the exclusive union of the man and the woman and for the good of their family and of the human community. Most often, in fact, premarital relations exclude the possibility of children. What is represented to be conjugal love is not able, as it absolutely should be, to develop into paternal and maternal love. Or, if it happens to do so, this will be to the detriment of the children, who will be deprived of the stable environment in which they ought to develop in order to find in it the way and the means of their insertion into society as a whole.

In a similar way, homosexual acts are immoral because they "lack an essential and indispensable finality." Even if people cannot help their sexual orientation, even if they are not personally responsible for it, homosexual actions "are intrinsically disordered and can in no case be approved." Masturbation is also immoral, as it is

> the deliberate use of the sexual faculty outside normal conjugal relations (which) essentially contradicts the finality of the function. For it lacks the sexual relationship called for by the moral order, namely the relationship which realizes 'the full sense of mutual self-giving and human procreation in the context of true love.'

For the Catholic Church, many cultures place too much emphasis on individual sexual freedom. As a result, the higher good of society and the value of chastity outside of marriage are all but ignored. Only within marriage, a marriage witnessed, recognized, and sanctioned by society and the church, can love reach its fullness, its mature expression. Only here does sex express this love most fully as it is used for its proper purpose, to produce and raise children in a loving home.

The **law** regulates sexual behavior in several ways. All states prohibit sex with minors, for example, and many have laws against adultery. In addition, whereas most of the fifty states have repealed their sodomy laws, a few still have laws that criminalize oral and anal sex, especially when these are homosexual acts. The United States Supreme Court, in *Bowers vs. Hardwick* (1986), upheld the right of states to criminalize such behavior, even when it performed in private between consenting adults. In an action more favorable to the legal rights of homosexuals, however, the same court ruled against a Colorado constitutional amendment that struck down all previously passed state laws designed to prohibit discrimination based on sexual orientation.

In the past, the law has not always protected the rights of homosexuals as forcefully as it has protected those of heterosexuals. It has allowed gays and lesbians to be discriminated against in housing, employment, and even in child custody cases. It has allowed homosexuals to serve in the military only if they hid the nature of their sexual orientation. It has allowed the Boy Scouts of America to dismiss scoutmasters because of their sexual orientation. It has often turned its back on "gay bashing," refusing to consider such actions as hate crimes. Because of this the majority of assaults against homosexuals, just because they are homosexuals, go unreported.

Since the mid-1980s, homosexual groups have organized to fight such discrimination, and legal institutions have responded with varying degrees of acceptance to their demands for equal rights. Many states and municipalities have passed laws forbidding discrimination against homosexuals. Two states, Hawaii and Alaska, have even passed same-sex marriage laws. These laws, however, were overturned by state constitutional amendments. In a reaction to such initiatives, in 1996 the U. S. Congress passed the Defense of Marriage Act, which restricts legal marriages to those between a man a woman. Vermont has since legalized *civil unions* between homosexual couples. These are not marriages in the full sense of the term but do grant homosexual couples some of the rights of married couples. For example, in civil unions, family health care and insurance plans may be extended to partners of homosexuals. Also, civil unions allow partners to make medical treatment decisions for each and other to claim retirement benefits, death benefits, and jointly owned property of deceased partners. In short, civil unions allow homosexuals the financial, medical, and legal security previously denied to them because of their sexual orientation. Homosexual groups are well organized and will continue to use the legal and political process to expand their battle for equal civil rights in housing, employment, the military, and especially same-sex civil unions and even state-recognized marriages.

Assumptions

There are two ***assumptions*** that we have accepted to this point that are challenged in this section. The *first* assumption, made especially by the liberal, is that people *can* freely consent to casual sex. This assumption has been challenged by Onora O'Neill, who claims that they cannot. The *second* is that heterosexual intercourse is acceptable in marriage. This assumption, accepted by all three possible solutions, has been challenged by Andrea Dworkin, a radical feminist. Dworkin claims that heterosexual intercourse is usually immoral even within marriage.

According to O'Neill, the way people communicate in casual sexual relationships is similar on the surface to the way they communicate in committed romantic relationships. The terms of endearment are similar, as are the gestures of intimacy. However, in casual sex, such forms of communication do not mean what they ordinarily do in the sort of loving relationship they were fashioned to express. Instead of expressing affection, trust, and commitment, for example, they express merely a mechanical format empty of meaning. In the context of casual sex, miscommunication and thus deception are inevitable. Expectations of affection often arise with the language of intimacy and are just as often dashed by the emptiness of its absence. O'Neill comments further in the following two quotations.[6]

> Deception remains a possibility in any relationship, and more so where much is conveyed elliptically or by gesture. In brief sexual encounters. . . . the discrepancy of expression and underlying attitude offers many footholds for deception; (the) underlying attitudes and outlook can become, as it were, decoupled from the expression and gesture which convey them to the other, so that the language of intimacy is used deceptively.

In addition to deceit, casual encounters also are filled with the potential for subtle coercion. Although morality demands that we treat the other with respect, in casual sex it is all too easy to use the other merely as an object for personal pleasure. With sexual intimacy comes a deeper knowledge of the other person's character and desires. This knowledge may be used, intentionally or not, to manipulate the sexual partner, especially to define the needs of the sexual partner so as to fulfill the needs of the other. Instead, if we are not to be manipulative, we must understand our partners well enough to know what they want, what truly are their ends, and to respect these ends.

> Respect for others—the most basic aspect for sharing their ends—requires the greatest tact and insight when we are most aware of ways in which others' capacities to pursue ends autonomously are vulnerable. . . . In intimate relationships it is all too easy to make the other an offer he or she cannot refuse.

O'Neill shows that it is extremely easy to deceive and manipulate others in casual sexual encounters. In the language of moral principles, such encounters have considerable potential to violate the principle of justice—by treating people merely as a means to the good of others. However, she has not shown that it is *impossible* for adults to treat each other with respect in such situations. For now at least, the assumption of the liberal that there can be casual sex that treats people with respect—because they are consenting adults—will be accepted as true. We will we have occasion to revisit this assumption in the "Moral Reasoning" section. You might want to consider its truth or falsity at this point while the remarks of O'Neill are fresh in your minds.

Exercise 11.1

This is a small group exercise. The issue to be explored by discussion among members of the group is whether people who hardly know each other can truly consent to sex. One way to think of this exercise is to question whether O'Neill is correct in saying that they cannot because there is no way to avoid subtle deception, and thus no way for the person who is not dominating the activity to be used by the other.

Another way to explore the issue of true consent is to consider the situation that many college students find themselves in quite frequently. There is a party with lots of drinking, which is then followed by sex between two people who hardly know each other. Is this a situation where true consent is possible, even if verbal consent is given by both parties? Is true consent quite unlikely, or are people aware of the potential pitfalls of being used by another and accept them as part of the risk of casual sex, risks worth the pleasure that such activity promises? Give reasons for your response.

Andrea Dworkin questions the second assumption by claiming that heterosexual intercourse, even within marriage, is usually immoral. This is because intercourse itself—which Dworkin sees as penetration, as occupation, as domination—is always a violation of a woman's body. Though our male-dominated culture may believe that heterosexual intercourse in normal and natural, it is really an abusive action. She says: [7]

> A human being has a body that is inviolate; and when it is violated, it is abused. A woman has a body that is penetrated in intercourse: permeable, its corporeal solidness a lie. The discourse of male truth—literature, science, philosophy, pornography—calls that penetration *violation.* This it does with some consistency and some confidence. *Violation* is a synonym for intercourse. At the same time, the penetration is taken to be a use, not an abuse; a normal use; it is appropriate to enter her, to push into ("violate") the boundaries of her body. She is human, of course, but by a standard that does not include physical privacy. She is, in fact, human by a standard that precludes physical privacy, since to keep a man out altogether and for lifetime is deviant in the extreme, a psychopathology, a repudiation of the way in which she is expected to manifest her humanity.

Intercourse by nature is dominance for Dworkin. Nature and society have seen to that. Whereas rape is recognized as immoral as well as illegal, it is simply one end of the spectrum of immoral intercourse, a spectrum that has as its other end consensual sex. For a woman truly to be free, she must be free from all forms of such domination, from rape to marital intercourse. Even if women were in total control of intercourse—its initiation, direction, duration, and intensity—the act itself subordinates women by its very requirements of being penetrated.

For Dworkin, intercourse represents the deeper reality of male hatred for women. Women should rebel against such treatment, should stop allowing themselves to be objects of male sexual desire, should stop collaborating in their own dehumanization. Unless and until heterosexual intercourse can occur without objectification and domination, it should be resisted by women. Children can be produced through *in vitro* fertilization; love, even romantic love, can be gotten from other women; communities can be formed of women to meet the needs of each other. For Dworkin, there are many deep layers of meaning and control present in heterosexual intercourse as it is often practiced today, and what she has to say about it coercive nature is at once shocking and enlightening. For now, however, we will retain the assumption that heterosexual intercourse can be practiced in a morally acceptable way, though possibly it often is not.

Points of View

Just what sexual behavior is considered by a person to be morally acceptable varies greatly with that person's *point of view*. Points of view on sexual matters are often determined by age, family status, sexual orientation, and religious affiliation. There is an old saying that "a conservative is just a liberal with a teenage daughter." This highlights how family roles affect our thinking about sex. Sexual orientation clearly colors a person's view as well. If you are homosexual or bisexual you probably will find no merit whatsoever in some of the arguments that appeal to the abnormality and unnaturalness of same-sex relations, and you may find great merit in those that appeal to the freedom of the individual.

If you are in your late teens or early twenties, you may be more inclined to believe that love or even consent justifies sexual behavior, and that marriage is not required. If you are in your sixties or older and the veteran of a long and happy marriage, you may be more inclined to reject this point of view. If you belong to a conservative religion, or a liberal one, or none at all, your views about the moral acceptability of sexual behavior will also be colored by these contingencies. Try to clarify what point of view you carry with you as you prepare to analyze the arguments found in the next section. To be fair to the evidence, and thus to learn something new, we must be open to their merits. We must try to do our best not to allow our point of view to close us to any real consideration of possible solutions opposed to our own. At the very least, we must recognize that our own position is only as strong as our ability to refute, and thus first to understand, opposing viewpoints.

Moral Reasoning

The problem of this chapter—*Under what conditions is sexual behavior immoral?*—is best seen as a type two moral problem. These sorts of problems require the formulation of a moral rule, best thought of in this case as a rule that will set restrictions on sexual behavior and serve as a general social policy. The best moral rule will be the one that most fully conforms to our three moral principles—beneficence, justice, and autonomy. Restrictions on sexual behavior will be justified to the extent that they increase its good outcomes or reduce its harmful ones, that they best allow for respecting persons, and that they best allow for the maximum exercise of autonomy.

The Case for the Liberal View

The claim of the **liberal** is that sexual behavior is morally acceptable when it occurs between consenting adults. For the liberal, there should be no restrictions placed on individuals by society other than consent. True consent must be both free and informed. There is no true consent when there is coercion, as a coercive choice is not free. There is also no true consent when there is deception, as a choice based on a lie is not accurately informed. Sex is always immoral when true consent is absent cause of coercion or deception. Clearly, nonconsensual sex based on coercion violates all three moral principles. An act such as rape, for example, does harm to a person and is a violation of her autonomy and intrinsic value. More subtle forms of coercion, such as threats from a boss to be fired or not promoted, or bribes that appeal to deep wants violate these principles as well.

In addition to being free, true consent requires that a person must receive the correct information from the other party involved in order to make an informed choice. Deceiving another makes the sexual behavior that follows an immoral act. Lying about your marital status, for example, or saying that you truly love someone when you really do not, are common forms of deception. Most people would tell such lies, whether they are direct lies or lies of omission, because they believe that if the other person knew the truth he or she would choose not to have sex. At the very least, such lies violate the autonomy of the potential sexual partner and on these grounds alone may be judged as immoral actions.

If consent is present, however, the liberal believes that sexual behavior is morally acceptable. People do not have to be in love or be married to have morally acceptable sex. If it is a free and informed choice of each person involved, to restrict their behavior and thus to deny their wishes would be a violation of their autonomy. We may, of course, prevent people from acting as they desire when their behavior is likely to harm others, but what is the harm to *others* of consensual sex? As long as adults are involved and as long as they are honest and free, they may choose to use each other's bodies for their own purposes. Just as society should not interfere with the books people read, or with their hobbies, or with their preferences in sporting or cultural events—unless such activities cause harm to others—so also it should also stay out of the business of monitoring private sexual behaviors. Our sexual behavior is our own business and for others to attempt to control it is wrong. So we may write this as the first premise in the argument for the liberal view:

1. Consenting adults should be free to have sex as long as their sexual behavior harms no one else. (A)

In addition to its conformity to the principle of autonomy, the liberal view also satisfies the principle of beneficence. After all, even when sex is not at its best, it is usually pleasurable; and pleasure appears on almost anyone's list of things that are intrinsically valuable. Pleasure is a good and sex generally produces it. This is why most people choose to have consensual sex, to acquire this good. Pleasure may come in many forms. People may want sex for the pleasure that orgasm brings, or for the release from tension and anxiety that accompanies most sexual behavior, or for the excitement, the physical closeness, the sense of self-esteem it produces, or just to connect with another human being on some level.

In addition, sex is a way to avoid some of the evils of life that afflict many human beings. It may be used to escape from loneliness, or to satisfy the need to be desired by others, or to free oneself from the sexual repression that Sigmund Freud has argued causes various forms of neurosis. What is a person supposed to do who wants to put off marriage plans for a while, or who may have been married and is now divorced, or who has not found someone to really love, or who just wishes to travel through life in a single marital state? Are such persons, perhaps the great majority of us at some times of our lives, supposed to do without sex and suffer the harms of doing so because someone else says that they must be in love or be married before they can have sex? The liberal says that they are not. The liberal claims that sex—even in the absence of love or marriage—produces good and prevents evil for the individual, and thus conforms to the principle of beneficence. So we may write:

2. Casual sex promotes good consequences and avoids harmful ones. (B)

The rest of the argument for the liberal view consists of responding to objections from our other possible solutions. Before moving on to a consideration of the moderate and conservative views, however, we should note that the liberal argument justifies homosexual as well as heterosexual behavior. The liberal sees no moral difference if two people freely choose to have sex with members of the opposite sex or members of the same sex. In both cases, gender is not important in determining the moral acceptability of sexual behavior. Rather, autonomy and beneficence are the central concerns. As long as two people—of any gender—truly consent to it, and as long as the sexual behavior to which they consent harms no one else, then such sexual behavior is morally acceptable for the liberal. Homosexuals have the same needs and desires for sex as do heterosexuals. To deny them access to sex would be to deny them the benefits and the escape from harms that sexual behavior produces.

The Case for the Moderate View

The claim of the **moderate** is that sex is morally acceptable when two people are in love. The moderate believes that sex must be consensual, of course, as does the liberal. However, the moderate adds the restriction, not required by the liberal, that two people ought to be in love before engaging in sexual behavior. Sex without love is morally unacceptable for the moderate. It does not matter if the sexual behavior occurs within a heterosexual relationship or a homosexual one, but it does matter that there first be a relationship between two people—a loving relationship. This is precisely why the casual sex allowed by the liberal is immoral, because it is devoid of love. The moderate view will argue against the lovelessness found in casual sex, but it does not require the more stringent conditions required by the conservative—that people must be married for sex to be morally acceptable. It is not the formality of a legal marriage that is important. Instead it is the love in the hearts of lovers that makes their behavior morally acceptable. For the moderate, in addition to consent, love is the only condition required for sexual behavior to be morally acceptable. The argument begins with an acknowledgment of the liberal's insistence on freedom, coupled with the condition that love must be present:

1.' Consenting adults who are in love should be free to have sex as long as their actions harm no one else. (A)

The central point of the moderate is that sex with love is more beneficial than casual sex, and that sex without love may even be harmful. We will spend a little time making this point and begin by reminding ourselves of what we mean by "love." Love was defined in the "Clarifying Concepts" section as wanting to do good. You may do good for yourself (self-love) or for others. Romantic love includes this concern for the good of others, but it also includes sexual desire for the other. If restricted to this desire, love would be nothing but infatuation. Infatuation is that collection of feelings a person experiences when he or she is "falling" in love. It is like a drug, "the love drug," that makes a person feel almost obsessed with his or her beloved. Infatuation is a wonderful feeling, but it is fleeting. The true heart of "being" in love is the care and concern of each for the other, a concern especially evident in the emotional bond between them. In true romantic love the people involved care about each other, not just about themselves. They seek the good of their partners, not just their own good. Most important, they use sex to express this love and not solely for selfish pleasure.

But why is sex for love better than casual sex? Not because it is more pleasurable. Sometimes sex with someone you hardly know may be even more pleasurable than sex with someone you love. Instead, the reason is that sex between two people who love each other is both more meaningful and less harmful than sex between people who do not share love. It is more meaningful because of the very nature of sex and love. Love is a basic desire. A basic desire is a wanting, a longing that must be satisfied for a person to be happy. In fact, once our biological desires are met, once we have sufficient food, clothing, shelter, and so on, love may be our *most* basic desire. Philosophers and psychologists have often argued about which desires are the most basic. Some say that pleasure is our deepest desire, or that power is, or that greed is, or that knowledge is, or that freedom is, or even that a close relationship with God is most basic. Love must surely count among these very basic desires and thus must be thought of as necessary for happiness. If being happy is getting what you really want—and love is one of the things we really want—love is required for happiness. It is intrinsically valuable, one of the essential goods of a full human life.

Even love is required for happiness, not everyone has to love you for you to be happy. Some people play only functional roles in our lives. The letter carrier, the telephone operator, and the checkout person at the store do things for us. In some cases they may also be our friends; nevertheless, if they do not love us we will not be unhappy because of it. But love is required from at least some people, especially parents, if happiness is to be achieved. If a mother or father do not love their children it will be very difficult for those children to find happiness. They will always have a hole inside that no one else can fill up. They will search for love from others to compensate for this absent parental love.

In a similar fashion, if love is missing in sex, it too is felt as an absence, as an emptiness. Care, concern, and emotional closeness are essential parts of sex. This is not so for other forms of shared activities, such as playing golf. Two people are so physically close when they have sex that if they are not also emotionally close, sex seems to be a meaningless act. Without love, sex is just a mutual use of each other's bodies for selfish pleasure. There is no human meaning to it, no expression of anything between persons.

What sex is supposed to express, what the "language" of sex was designed to communicate, is a sharing of love, not just a sharing of bodies. When no love is shared, there is an awareness that something is missing that ought to be there. Unlike playing golf with a stranger, when a person does not feel unloved after the match is over, people feel unloved after casual sex. Love was supposed to have been there and it was not. Because there was no love that the sex expressed, the act is experienced as meaningless. To be loved by those who are supposed to love you is so important that casual sexual behavior, even very pleasurable casual sex, ends up harming an individual in the end. In this way, it violates the principle of beneficence. So whereas sex with love produces goods, sex without it leads to harms. We write as our second premise:

2.' Sex with love produces more good and less evil for individuals than sex without love. (B)

Finally, in addition to avoiding harm and promoting the good of individuals, sex with love produces good and reduces evil for society as well. For example, sex with love prior to marriage is a good way for people to learn whether they are compatible. Living together for a while, in a loving relationship, can show people how they will interact if they do decide to get married later. This will reduce the number of bad marriages and thus result in fewer divorces, sparing great personal and social harms. Sex with love will also cut down on the number of STDs, as there will be less sex with multiple partners whose sexual and medical histories are unknown. In short, sex with love will lead to better, more stable marriages and families, and result in less disease than casual sex. For these and similar reasons, it is good for society.

3.' Sex with love produces more good and less evil for society than sex without love. (B)

The Case for the Conservative View

The claim of the **conservative** is that sex is morally acceptable only within the confines of marriage. For the conservative, the moderate is correct that sex with love is more meaningful than casual sex, but the moderate does not go far enough. Only in a relationship recognized publicly by the community, only in a relationship in which people are joined together "until death," only in a relationship dedicated to having and raising children is the sexual bond between two people fully in the best interest of the individual and society. It is here, in marriage, that sex is most meaningful, because here it is used for its proper purposes. Pleasure and love are not the true purposes of sexual behavior. Instead, although pleasure and love are important accompaniments of sex, its true purpose is to create and foster families, the backbone of society. So although sex with love produces more good than casual sex, sex for the purpose of creating and nurturing children produces the most good. Because of this, claims the conservative, sexual behavior ought to be confined to marriage.

The conservative begins the defense of his claim by first pointing out that sex outside of marriage is intrinsically wrong. It is wrong in itself—whatever its consequences may be. Our approach to morality in this text has not labeled any actions as wrong in themselves. Instead, our theory of obligation judges actions as right or wrong by the degree to which they conform to or deviate from our three moral principles. Conservatives who claim an intrinsic wrongfulness of sexual behavior outside of marriage appeal to a different theory of obligation to justify their claim. Often this appeal is to natural law ethics.

Natural law ethics was developed especially by the theologian St. Thomas Aquinas in the twelfth century. As we have seen in the "Descriptive Ethics" section, it is often used as a moral norm by the Roman Catholic Church even today. Building on the teachings of Aristotle and later Roman philosophers, it claims that all human persons have a common human nature. Our human nature is not simply our biological nature—the structure and function of our bones, blood, internal organs, and so on—but is also our natural ways of behaving. A way of behaving is natural if it arises independently of learning, and thus culture. So natural ways of behaving are the same across all cultures and all historical periods. These ways of behaving arise initially as impulses or even desires to act in one way or another, and are later shaped and refined by the particular culture in which the person happens to reside.

For Aquinas, the most fundamental natural impulse is to *do good and avoid evil.* This is the first and most fundamental "natural law" we all know in our hearts, without ever having been told.

> This is the first precept of law, that *good is to be done and promoted, and evil is to be avoided.* All other precepts of the natural law are based upon this.[8]

To understand more concretely what doing good and avoiding evil means, however, there must be some good, some desired outcome that we may use to judge whether our actions are good or evil. For Aquinas, as for Aristotle before him, this desired outcome, this goal or purpose of our actions, is the full development of our human nature. The purpose of morality is to provide guidance and training to help us live according to our natures, to live according to what is in our interests as human beings. Only by doing so can we expect to live full and rich lives. So doing good means living in accordance with human nature; doing evil means living opposed to its true needs. Actions are morally acceptable according to this theory of obligation if they contribute to the flourishing of human nature; they are immoral if they violate it.

There are further natural laws mentioned by Aquinas. These arise from fundamental natural inclinations and serve as guides to determine what does and what does not serve human nature, and thus what belongs to the natural law. Among these are desires we share with all living beings, such as the desire to survive. We also share with animals natural impulses to reproduce and raise offspring. Another desire, a uniquely human one, is the desire to know—to understand the world, ourselves, and especially God. Aquinas puts it this way:

> For there is in man, first of all, an inclination to good in accordance with the nature which he has in common with all substances, inasmuch, namely, as every substance seeks the preservation of its own being, according to its own nature; and by reason of this inclination, whatever is a means of preserving human life, and of warding off its obstacles, belongs to the natural law. Secondly, there is in man an inclination to things that pertain to him more specially, according to that nature which he has in common with other animals, and in virtue of this inclination, those things are said to belong to the natural law, *which nature has taught to all animals,* such as sexual intercourse, the education of offspring and so forth. Thirdly, there is an inclination to good according to the nature of his reason, which nature is proper to him. Thus man has a natural inclination to know the truth about God, and to live

in society; and in this respect, whatever pertains to this inclination belongs to the natural law: e.g., to shun ignorance, to avoid offending those among whom one has to live, and other such things regarding the above inclination.[9]

As Aquinas states, these natural inclinations are best fulfilled within a society that supports such behaviors, so living in a society is also part of our nature. Whatever contributes to the health and well-being of society, and especially to its basic natural unit—the family—is also part of the natural law, as it is required for the flourishing of human nature. This point is often overlooked by liberals and even by moderates, as they stress individual happiness in isolation from society. However, there is no individual happiness apart from the societies that mold and support individuals. Societies create the conditions in which individuals can flourish. Without a strong and stable society, individual happiness is not possible. This is an important point because it requires us to see sexual behavior in the broader context of society and to consider the effect on society that such behavior has.

The basic point of natural law ethics is that because human nature does not change or vary from culture to culture, any action that violates it, that becomes an obstacle to its flourishing, can be labeled as intrinsically wrong for all times and places. Such actions are referred to as *perversions* of human nature as they are contrary to its goals. They are also referred to as *unnatural.* Because the point of living is to satisfy our most basic desires, to fulfill our human nature, anything that perverts human nature, anything that is unnatural, is most definitely immoral.

From here it is an easy step to the first premise in the good reasons argument for the conservative. Because sex is for reproduction, any sexual behavior that eliminates reproduction as a possibility is unnatural. It is a perversion of the natural moral order and thus is immoral. Sex merely for pleasure or simply to express love disconnects it from its primary purpose, procreation, and goes against the natural order of things known to us in our hearts and minds. Just as eating is for nourishment and health, and may be accompanied by pleasure, so also pleasure and love are important accompaniments of reproduction. But they are not the primary purposes of sex. If eating were used just for pleasure it would be harmful to us physically. We would eat too much and eat too many foods with little nutritional value. Soon, our bodies would suffer the consequences. In a similar way, if sex was used just for pleasure, it would soon be cut off from families and society and thus from its main purpose—and all would suffer the consequences.

As we said earlier, successfully raising children requires a long-term commitment between a man and a woman, so reproduction requires marriage. Children require a mother and a father if they are to be raised with the best chance of flourishing. Families, in turn, need a stable and supportive society if they are to be successful at their task. The proper use of sex, the use for which we were designed as human beings, is to have and raise children within a stable and supportive society. This is why marriage—a long-term union recognized, embraced, and supported by society—is required. Only sexual behavior within marriage is morally acceptable, as it alone conforms to the natural purpose of sexual behavior.

From this it follows that engaging in sexual behavior outside of marriage is immoral. Further, sexual behavior even within marriage that precludes the possibility of reproduction is also immoral. All nonmarital sex, usually undertaken with the express intention of avoiding pregnancy, is a perversion of nature; so too is masturbation, oral sex, anal sex, and even the use of contraceptives—whether there is a marriage or not—as all eliminate the possibility of conception. Especially immoral are all forms of homosexual behavior. This is the grandest perversion of all, as it most dramatically flies in the face of the natural moral order of things, the way things are supposed to be when they are done rightly. So the first premise say this:

1." All nonmarital and nonreproductive sexual behavior is unnatural and thus immoral. (B)

A (B) is placed after (1)" to show that being unnatural means perverting our natural good.

In addition to violating our natural good, nonmarital sex used simply for pleasure or even to express love, violates the principle of justice. Torn loose from its proper mooring, sex for pleasure ends up as simply using each other as sex objects. We make "things" of each other in such sexual behavior, and we forget the "priceless" value of each human being. Even when consent is truly informed and voluntary—a rare occasion indeed—the *respect for persons* meaning of justice is violated. In casual sex, people simply use each other solely as a means to their own good. In doing so they lose their respect for each other and for themselves.

Even in a loving relationship such a result is possible, though less likely. The entire relationship is designed to meet the needs of only the individuals involved. Although there may be concern for each other in the process of satisfying sexual desires, these desires themselves have been removed from their wider significance—their contribution to children and society as a whole. The sexual relationship itself has been cut off from its natural goals, and thus those within it are using each other, albeit lovingly, for their own private good. This itself disrespects their full humanness, their intrinsic value as human beings. So we may write this:

2." Nonmarital sex uses people solely as sex objects. (J)

The conservative argument now focuses on the individual and social harms that nonmarital sex produces. It begins by pointing out the considerable harms for the *individual* that result from nonmarital sex. First, as the moderate has already shown, casual sex leads to a denial of love and a feeling of emptiness, even a feeling of being used. In addition, even when love is present, individuals may suffer many harms not present within a marriage. For example, without the "cement" of marriage there will be more broken relationships, and more pain and suffering because of it. This is because nonmarital commitment is often weaker than marriage. People who are not married are less likely to stay together when troubles arise, depriving them of the opportunity to solve problems together and to grow even closer as a result. The give and take of marriage, especially of marriages blessed with children, the acceptance of the good with the bad, allow people to learn more about themselves and each other, and thus to become even more in love than most nonmarried couples will ever be. The third premise is this:

3." Nonmarital sex leads to individual harms. (B)

In addition, many social harms are the direct result of casual sex, premarital sexual relationships, and the growing tolerance of homosexuality. For example, the number of *unwanted pregnancies* has increased dramatically in this age of "free love," as have the number of *abortions,* more than a million a year. Since the introduction of reliable contraceptives and the resultant change in social attitudes about nonmarital sex, the number of *divorces* has also increased dramatically. Almost half the marriages in this country now end in divorce. When nonmarital sex was not socially sanctioned, the divorce rate was much lower. In addition, the spread of *diseases,* especially AIDS, is directly related to greater tolerance of nonmarital sex, especially homosexual sex.

Finally, and perhaps most important, in addition to increased numbers of unwanted pregnancies, divorces, and diseases of various sorts, the changing attitudes associated with the sexual revolution have threatened the very foundation of society. With the acceptance of sex outside of marriage, the *family* unit itself, the cornerstone of society, is now under siege. The ideal of the two-parent family, one male and one female, is fast disappearing. In fact, less than 25 percent of all U.S. households today are composed of nuclear families—a father, a mother, and children. In its place the single-parent family, or even the same-sex family, is becoming more and more accepted. Many single-parent families have come about through divorce or the death of one spouse and cannot be avoided. However, to accept single-parent families and even same-sex families as the equal of the traditional ideal is where the moral problem lies. To view these alternative family structures to be as good as, or even better than, traditional family structures is a grave error. It encourages people to have single-parent families because they see them as a good. With no longer any social disapproval attached to single-parent and same-sex families, nontraditional families have become threatened. Because many believe that traditional families do the best job of raising children, and that they are the basis for a strong and stable society, this threat to the traditional family is a threat to all of society.

In addition, *family values* are also under attack. The existence of sexual violence and pornography on television, film, and the Internet has resulted from the "free-love" culture of today and continues to support its growth. The tolerance of nonmarital relationships, openly homosexual relationships, and casual sex as a norm also undermines the acceptance of sex only for procreation within marriage. In short, the importance of the two-parent family, so crucial for the stability of society, is directly threatened by separating sex from its procreative function and condoning its use for love alone, for pleasure alone, or simply for the acceptance of a personal lifestyle. This personal freedom to live our sexual lives in any of a number of ways of our choosing may seem to be a blessing, but in the long run it will lead to the ruination of the family and thus to the decay of society itself. So we write the final premise for the conservative argument:

4." Nonmarital sex leads to social harms. (B)

Replies to Objection

The first set of objections is directed at the *liberal* view and comes from the arguments presented so far by both the moderate and the conservative. One objection is that true consent to casual sex is not possible. Because you already discussed this in Exercise 11.1, it will not be addressed here. Instead we will turn to the objection that casual sex is harmful to the individuals who engage in it. The moderate's version of this objection is the most important one and is found in her claim that casual sex denies a person the love that should be present in sexual behavior, and thus harms harming a person who is deprived of this basic good.

The liberal may respond to this objection in a couple of ways. First, she may simply deny the claim and assert that two people not looking for love may engage in sex simply for fun. As long as they freely choose such behavior, there is no reason that they should be harmed. Second, the liberal may agree with the moderate that sex without love is not as good as sex with love but still deny that sex without love is harmful. To say that sex in a loving relationship is better is not to deny that casual sex is good. The liberal is not claiming that consensual sex is the highest form of human sexual activity, only that it is not immoral. People who engage in casual sex may desire love, even marriage and children as higher goods. In the meantime, however, casual sex is better than no sex. So we may add a premise to the liberal's argument, a premise that responds to the liberal's objection:

3. Casual sex does not harm consenting adults. (B)

Another objection comes from the conservative, who claims that casual sex violates the respect for persons principle. In casual sex, people simply use each other as objects, sex objects, and deny the intrinsic value of each other. In response to this objection, the liberal may agree that there is a mutual using of each other but deny that this amounts to a violation of the principle of justice. After all, we use people all the time without consideration of their intrinsic value. Some people simply play functional roles in our lives, such as the plumber, the letter carrier, and the banker. But they volunteer for such roles; they accept these jobs willingly, usually for the monetary compensation that such jobs bring.

Moreover, because we do not recognize their intrinsic value in these does not mean that we deny it. Simply put, these people consent to be used by others to achieve their occupational goals. In the same way, people who engage in consensual sex freely choose to be used by others so they may use the others in turn to achieve their sexual goals. The respect for persons principle requires only that we do not use others merely or exclusively as a means. In casual sex, people recognize the intrinsic value in each other even while they temporarily use each other as sexual objects. Using someone against her will as a sex slave might be an instance of violating the respect for persons principle, but consensual sex surely is not. So the liberal says this:

4. Casual sex does not violate the respect for persons principle. (J)

Next, the liberal denies the objections of the moderate and the conservative that casual sex leads to social harms. Unwanted pregnancies and the resultant abortion of many of them may be avoided by taking proper precautions. The same is true for STDs. The problem is not that casual sex is immoral but that it is often engaged in unsafely. There is no threat to love or the family either, because having casual sex is often a temporary way of living one's life, often followed by love and even marriage. Moreover, family values may be threatened by violence and pornography, but these are not the result of casual sex. What people do in the privacy of their own lives, as long as they are careful to avoid its dangers, has no effect on the public lives of others. So the liberal may write this:

5. Casual sex does not cause social harms. (B)

Finally, the liberal must respond to the objection of the conservative that non-marital sex is immoral because it violates human nature. Because the moderate faces the same challenge, we will pass this task on to him, taking on faith for the moment that the liberal may borrow the same argument. On the basis of that promissory note the liberal may claim:

6. Casual sex is neither unnatural nor immoral. (B,J,A)

All three moral principles are placed after this premise to show that we are refer-ring to our own moral theory to determine right from wrong.

The *moderate* faces the same "social harms" objections from the conservative as those leveled against the liberal and may respond in similar ways. We will not repeat the details of the liberal response here but simply assume that the moder-ate may use the same reasoning. For the sake of completeness, we will write as part of the moderate's argument,

4.' Sex with love does not cause social harms. (B)

In addition, the liberal claims that the moderate's view denies sexual autonomy. In restricting sex to those in loving relationships it prevents people who are not in love from having the choice of sex without love. Moreover, by denying choice, the moderate violates the principle of beneficence, as casual sex produces many goods, not the least of which is pleasure. The moderate may respond by claiming that such choices are not truly free. They are merely a response to desire, not the expression of our higher autonomous selves. True freedom is exercised when we see the value of sex as an expression of love and restrain ourselves from the pleasure of casual sex. Such an approach places sex on a higher plane, where it is at once a more fulfilling activity, a more human activity, and thus a fuller expression of our autonomy.

5.' Sex with love allows more autonomy and beneficence than casual sex. (B, J)

Finally, the moderate must respond to the "natural law" objection of the con-servative. Here more than one approach is open to the moderate. First, he may simply dismiss natural law ethics as an incorrect theory of obligation, one based on the mistaken belief that there is a natural moral order common to all regardless of time or culture. Or he may agree that there is such a thing as a common moral order but insist that determining right from wrong is not a matter of deciding which acts are natural and which are not, but more a matter of appealing to some-thing like our theory of obligation. Or, he may accept the whole natural law pack-age and question just what "natural" means. Why, he might ask, is sex for pleas-ure any less natural than sex for reproduction? Surely our impulses tell us that sex is for pleasure. The same may be said about sex for love, and even for homosex-ual behavior. Homosexuals, after all, experience a strong desire for members of the same sex as their natural inclination.

If natural impulses must be channeled by reason into behavior that is truly in our interests, then surely with the discovery of reliable contraceptives and the strong biological determinants of sexual preferences, reason must finally agree that sex need no longer be tied to reproduction to be for our good. In fact, claims the moderate, the only reason for the dominance of the conservative view for all the previous centuries when it truly was the conventional view was that sex outside of marriage was risky business, not that it was opposed to human nature. If there are three main purposes of sex—pleasure, love, and reproduction—it seems hardly defensible in these days, when pleasure and love can be separated from reproduction by reliable contraception, to place reproduction at the top of the "natural" list.

After all, love is present in more instances of sexual behavior than reproduction is, and pleasure is almost always present. On this measure of frequency, sex for pleasure is more natural than sex for love; sex for reproduction seems rare and thus abnormal by comparison. It may be better to restrict sex to those in love; it may even be better to restrict it to marriage. But if this is done, the reason is because it produces more good and less evil, and because it best promotes autonomy and justice—not because doing so is more in keeping with the natural order of things. Sex for reproduction may be the norm in the animal world, but for humans there are many more purposes for sexual behavior than creating children. Surely one of the most important of these is to express our love for each other. So we may write:

6.' Sex with love is neither unnatural nor immoral. (B,J,A)

The *conservative's* argument is composed of claims that the other views are wrong. They are all objections to the other possible solutions. If these objections can be answered by the other views, the conservative argument has nothing, except perhaps appeal to tradition. We have just seen the other views attempt to answer the objections of the conservative to their possible solutions, so we will not repeat that process here. Instead, we will turn to the "Evaluation" section, where we will weigh the reasonableness of all three views by deciding which premises are reliable and which are not.

Evaluation

The task before us in this section is to weigh the relative strengths and weaknesses of the arguments for all three possible solutions and to arrive at a ***reasoned judgment*** that one is more reasonable than the others.

Ethical Theory

The problem before us—*Under what conditions is sexual behavior immoral?*—is a **factual** moral problem. Solving this problem requires formulation of a rule that will define morally acceptable sexual behavior. This rule will be the one that best conforms to the principle of *beneficence*—which requires that we do good and avoid evil; the principle of *justice*—especially as it requires us to have respect for persons; and the principle of *autonomy*—which allows us to do what we want to, as long as our actions harm no one else. The conservative has said that the best rule is the old one, the one that precedes the sexual revolution, the one that requires us to wait for marriage before we engage in sexual activity. The moderate has said that love is enough to justify sexual activity, the love present in a long-term relationship in which partners care about each other and are emotionally close as well as physically close. The liberal, on the other hand, has said that these restrictions of love and marriage are not acceptable. Although love and marriage may be better, more meaningful ways to be with someone sexually, there is nothing wrong with casual sex. It is fun, has lots of benefits, and harms no one, so the moral rule regulating sexual behavior should be "sex is morally acceptable whenever mature adults agree to it."

As with most factual moral problems, the central issue is often that our knowledge of facts is insufficient to determine what the harms and benefits of various actions actually will be. If we knew, for example, that casual sex would destroy the two-parent family, and that two-parent families with a male and female as parents are essential for raising healthy children, we might wish to discourage casual sex through moral sanction. Or to take another example, if we knew that waiting for marriage to have sex would drive people prematurely into ill-advised marriages, then we might wish to be more sympathetic either to the sex with love or even the casual sex possible solution. It will be your job, in judging the reliability of the premises of the various arguments to follow, to consider the likelihood that some of the harms or benefits claimed by our various possible solutions will actually occur. You may wish to refer to previous sections, especially the section on "Facts," to find evidence that supports or undermines your estimates. In addition to passing judgment on likely harms and benefits, you will be required by some premises to make judgments about how much some of the restrictions on sexual activity proposed by our possible solutions violate the autonomy of individuals. Finally, in judging the reliability of at least a couple of the following premises, you must consider whether any of the sexual behaviors allowed by our possible solutions permit people to be used by others in ways that violate the principle of respect for persons.

Your Evaluation

Exercise 11.2

The complete arguments for each possible solution are given below. Your task is to evaluate these arguments. In well-reasoned arguments such as these, evaluation consists of testing the premises for relevancy and reliability. Each premise has already been tested for **relevance** in the process of presenting it, as each premise follows from a moral principle. So focus, as usual, on the **reliability** or truth of the premises. Then, after you have judged the reliability of each premise of each argument, and eliminated those premises you consider to be false or at least unlikely, consider whether the premises left standing are **sufficient** to support the conclusion. Finally, judge which of the arguments of our three competing possible solutions is the most cogent. The conclusion of that argument should be accepted by you as the most reasonable. As usual, be on guard for the influence of your point of view. Try to be open and tolerant of the evidence for all possible solutions, rejecting or accepting premises on the basis of their merits, not on the basis of personal preference.

The Argument for the Liberal View

1. Consenting adults should be free to have sex as long as their sexual behavior harms no one else. (A)

2. Casual sex promotes good and avoids harmful consequences. (B)

3. Casual sex does not harm consenting adults. (B)

4. Casual sex does not violate the respect for persons principle. (J)

5. Casual sex does not cause social harms. (B)

6. Casual sex is neither unnatural nor immoral. (B,J,A)

Therefore, 7. Sexual behavior is morally acceptable between consenting adults.

The Argument for the Moderate View

1.' Consenting adults who are in love should be free to have sex as long as their actions harm no one else. (A)

2.' Sex with love produces more good and less evil for individuals than sex without love. (B)

3.' Sex with love produces more good and less evil for society than sex without love. (B)

4.' Sex with love does not cause social harms. (B)

5.' Sex with love allows more autonomy and beneficence than casual sex. (B, J)

6.' Sex with love is neither unnatural nor immoral. (B,J,A)

Therefore, 7.' Sexual behavior is morally acceptable between people who are in love.

The Argument for the Conservative View

1." All nonmarital and nonreproductive sexual behavior is unnatural and thus immoral. (B)

2." Nonmarital sex uses people solely as sex objects. (J)

3." Nonmarital sex leads to individual harms. (B)

4." Nonmarital sex leads to social harms. (B)

Therefore, 5." Sexual behavior is morally acceptable only for married heterosexual couples.

A Few Comments

A brief statement of my own view will begin by comparing sexual activity to running. Running may be for many things. A person may run for the sheer pleasure of it, or for reasons of health, or for competition. Competition may be nothing but a local road race, or it may be a national race or even an Olympic event. The act of running takes on different meaning in these various contexts, some more dramatic, more exciting, and more significant than others. In the same way, sexual activity may be performed in various contexts that bestow on it various levels of meaning and significance. It may occur between two people who hardly know each other and be engaged in for pleasure, esteem, relief of tension, and so on. It may occur between two people who are in love and who may even be planning to be married some day. Here it may be used for all the purposes just described, but also to express the love and affection so cherished by the lovers. Finally, sex may be used for all these things, and for the very grand role of creating and raising children within a relationship that two people have promised to nourish for life.

In the same way as running is just running, however, sex is just sex. Its meaning is determined by the context in which it is used and the intentions of the parties involved. There is nothing about "plain sex" in itself that ties it only with an expression of love, or with an intention to procreate. Pleasure may be a natural accompaniment to sex, as perspiring may be a natural accompaniment to running; evolution has seen to that. But love is not essential to sex, as many people in bad marriages, and as many people who engage in casual sex, may witness. Since the introduction of reliable contraceptives, procreation is no longer an inevitable accompaniment of sex either, except perhaps for the animal world. As one author states,[10]

> The most comprehensible attempt to build an extraneous purpose into the sex act identifies that purpose as reproduction, its primary biological function. While this may be "nature's" purpose, it certainly need not be ours. . . . While this identification may once have had a rational basis which also grounded the identification of the value and morality of sex with that applicable to reproduction and child rearing, the development of contraception rendered the connection weak.

The point is that the various uses of sex may be separated, and sex may now be used for a variety of reasons. Each of these uses of sex should be judged as morally appropriate or not on its own merits. If sex is to be used for pleasure alone, for example, then there should be no deception or coercion between parties. If it is to be used within a loving relationship, then in addition to "consent" rules, there will be other restrictions as well, such as the need to show affection, concern for the other's needs, and perhaps even fidelity. In marriage, of course, the moral rules are even more strict, including not only consent, love, and fidelity, but also a lifelong commitment to nurturing each other and the family, which grows from this nurturing. On this account of things, casual sex between consenting adults is not immoral. It may not be as rich and rewarding as sex with love, which itself may be less fulfilling than marriage and raising children, but none of these choices for how to use sex is immoral unless it violates the moral rules within its context.

Within a "morality of aspiration," a view of morality requiring us to aspire to higher ways of living if we are to live a morally acceptable life, a case may be made that sex with love is more morally acceptable than casual sex, and that sex within marriage is more morally acceptable than sex with love.[11] I am sympathetic with the view that says we ought to live our lives as fully and richly as possible. I believe that people should be encouraged to aspire to higher ways of living, both for their own good and the good of others. I believe that a life that contains only casual sex, for example, is not as rich as a life that knows love.

But morality does not require that we go beyond the call of duty. It does not require us to aspire to a higher calling on the pain of being immoral. We do, for example, require that people continue to learn for their entire lives, even though such a life would be more rewarding; we do not require that people sacrifice most of their worldly possessions to help others, even though such actions are kind and noble; we do not require people to be saints and heroes, even though such is the stuff of admiration. To fall short of these aspirations is not to be immoral, only less heroic than some of our fellow human beings.

In my opinion, saying that nonmarital sex is immoral can only be justified by assuming a morality of aspiration, a morality that requires us to aspire to a higher purpose for our sexual behavior. Unless you accept a morality of aspiration as what determines right from wrong, a view that has been discussed and rejected in Part I, it is difficult to conclude that casual sex or sex with love are immoral actions. It may be *better* to have sex in a loving relationship; it may even be *best* to use sex within marriage; but it is not immoral to use it for pleasure alone.

Consequences

Of course there are many consequences that follow from the acceptance of each of the possible solutions described in this chapter. Some of them are obvious. For example, if you adopt the conservative view, you are morally obliged to remain a virgin until marriage. If you adopt the sex with love view, on the other hand, you must wait for sexual activity only until you get to know and care about a person.

The consequences of adopting a particular view that I wish to focus on, at least briefly, concern especially the moral acceptability of sexual behavior between *homosexuals.* I have assumed throughout that the arguments for each possible solution apply equally to heterosexual and homosexual sexual activity. If consent is all that is necessary to make sex morally acceptable, for example, then there is no good reason to reject homosexual sex between consenting adults as immoral. Similar remarks may be made for the moderate view. Homosexuals may love each other just as fully and honestly and thoroughly as heterosexuals. If you accept either of these views, then it appears that you must also accept homosexual sexual activity as morally acceptable.

However, there is another avenue open to you for rejecting homosexual activity as immoral, even if you are a moderate or a liberal. You may reject it on the grounds that homosexuality is a type of perversion, and that all perversions are immoral. If you are a conservative, of course, and if you defend your conservative position by appealing to the natural purposes of sex, then no matter how sympathetic you are to the growing evidence that sexual *orientation* is primarily determined by biology, you must also condemn homosexual *behavior* as immoral, because you believe it is a perversion of the natural moral order. As all views may reject homosexual behavior as a type of perversion, an additional word about sexual perversion may be in order here.

If a perversion is an act that is unnatural, then surely some sexual acts are perversions. At a minimum, natural sexual behavior is between persons. It may be between two (or more) persons, or between a person and herself or himself and not be perverse. Sex with an animal or a material object of some sort, however, is perverse. Sex with an animal is not only perverse but it is also immoral, though not because it is perverse. Rather, it is immoral because it is harmful and disrespectful to the nonconsenting animal in question. On the other hand, sex with a shoe, while perverse, is not immoral. It may be pathological and require some sort of treatment for the good of the person involved, but it does not violate any of our moral principles.

In the same way, even if homosexual behavior is a perversion, whether it is immoral is still an open question. To establish its immorality, we would have to show that it led to harm to others, or that it violated one or more of our other moral principles. In the absence of evidence that homosexual behavior causes harm to others, such as homosexual teachers turning first graders into homosexuals, there is little reason to consider it immoral. Besides, in what sense is homosexuality to be thought of as a perversion? If perverse simply means abnormal, and if abnormal means more or less what most of us do not do, then homosexuality is indeed a perversion. But so is playing first violin for the Boston Symphony Orchestra, or playing shortstop for the New York Yankees. "Abnormal" in these instances does not mean "immoral." Instead, it means "better than normal." So saying that homosexuality is abnormal does not mean that it is immoral. If, on the other hand, being sexually perverse means not using sex for procreation, then homosexuals surely are perverse. But then, of course, so is anyone who has sex outside of marriage, and so is anyone who uses sex even within marriage when that sexual behavior is not open to the possibility of procreation. Any husband and wife using contraceptives, for example, engage in perverse sexual behavior by this account.

To single out homosexual behavior as immoral, when the very same reasons used to justify heterosexual behavior may be used to justify it, is to be guilty of unfair discrimination. This discrimination is widespread in society and often protected by law and the underlying homophobia that supports the law. The real battle for homosexual equality today lies in this area of civil rights; with the attempt of gays and lesbians to gain rights equal to those of heterosexuals—especially in the areas of housing, employment, family benefits, and the like. Underlying this battle for legal recognition, however, are the sorts of moral positions and arguments we have addressed in this chapter. In my opinion, although there may be strong feelings in many cultures that homosexual behavior is wrong, there is no good reason or set of reasons why this is so. Usually we cannot help but the feelings we have, often we can change them over time, and almost always we can choose not to act on them. The growing tolerance of homosexuality in the public arena attests to this ability of human beings to base their beliefs on evidence, not prejudice.

Another Perspective

The following article by Jeff Jordan, "Is It Wrong to Discriminate on the Basis of Homosexuality," first appeared in the *Journal of Social Philosophy*, v. 30, no. 1 (1995). Jordan argues that discriminating against homosexuals may be acceptable, especially in terms of same-sex marriages.

Is It Wrong to Discriminate on the Basis of Homosexuality?

JEFF JORDAN

MUCH LIKE THE ISSUE of abortion in the early 1970s, the issue of homosexuality has exploded to the forefront of social discussion. Is homosexual sex on a moral par with heterosexual sex? Or is homosexuality in some way morally inferior? Is it wrong to discriminate against homosexuals—to treat homosexuals in less favorable ways than one does heterosexuals? Or is some discrimination against homosexuals morally justified? These questions are the focus of this essay.

In what follows, I argue that there are situations in which it is morally permissible to discriminate against homosexuals because of their homosexuality. That is, there are some morally relevant differences between heterosexuality and homosexuality which, in some instances, permit a difference in treatment. The issue of marriage provides a good example. While it is clear that heterosexual unions merit the state recognition known as marriage, along with all the attendant advantages—spousal insurance coverage, inheritance rights, ready eligibility of adoption—it is far from clear that homosexual couples ought to be accorded that state recognition.

The argument of this essay makes no claim about the moral status of homosexuality per se. Briefly put, it is the argument of this essay that the moral impasse generated by conflicting views concerning homosexuality, and the public policy ramifications of those conflicting views, justify the claim that it is morally permissible, in certain circumstances, to discriminate against homosexuals.

1. THE ISSUE

The relevant issue is this: does homosexuality have the same moral status as heterosexuality? Put differently, since there are no occasions in which it is morally permissible to treat heterosexuals unfavorably, whether because they are heterosexual or because of heterosexual acts, are there occasions in which it is morally permissible to treat homosexuals unfavorably, whether because they are homosexuals or because of homosexual acts?

A negative answer to the above can be termed the "parity thesis." The parity thesis contends that *homosexuality has the same moral status as heterosexuality*. If the parity thesis is correct, then it would be immoral to discriminate against homosexuals because of their homosexuality. An affirmative answer can be termed the "difference thesis" and contends that there are morally relevant differences between heterosexuality and homosexuality which justify a difference in moral status and treatment between homosexuals and heterosexuals. The difference thesis entails that *there are situations in which it is morally permissible to discriminate against homosexuals.*

It is perhaps needless to point out that the difference thesis follows as long as there is at least one occasion in which it is morally permissible to discriminate against homosexuals. If the parity thesis were true, then on no occasion would a difference in treatment between heterosexuals and homosexuals ever be justified. The difference thesis does not, even if true, justify discriminatory actions on every occasion. Nonetheless, even though the scope of the difference thesis is relatively modest, it is, if true, a significant principle which has not only theoretical import but important practical consequences as well.

A word should be said about the notion of discrimination. To discriminate against X means treating X in an unfavorable way. The word "discrimination" is not a synonym for "morally unjustifiable treatment." Some discrimination is morally unjustifiable; some is not. For example, we discriminate against convicted felons in that they are disenfranchised. This legal discrimination is morally permissible even though it involves treating one person unfavorably different from how other persons are treated. The difference thesis entails that there are circumstances in which it is morally permissible to discriminate against homosexuals.

2. AN ARGUMENT FOR THE PARITY THESIS

Perhaps the strongest reason to hold that the parity thesis is true is something like the following:

1. Homosexual acts between consenting adults harm no one. And,

2. respecting persons' privacy and choices in harmless sexual matters maximizes individual freedom. And,

3. individual freedom should be maximized. But,

4. discrimination against homosexuals, because of their homosexuality, diminishes individual freedom since it ignores personal choice and privacy. So,

5. the toleration of homosexuality rather than discriminating against homosexuals is the preferable option since it would maximize individual freedom. Therefore,

6. the parity thesis is more plausible than the difference thesis.

Premise (2) is unimpeachable: if an act is harmless and if there are persons who want to do it and who choose to do it, then it seems clear that respecting the choices of those people would tend to maximize their freedom. Step (3) is also beyond reproach: since freedom is arguably a great good and since there does not appear to be any ceiling on the amount of individual freedom—no "too much of a good thing"—(3) appears to be true.

At first glance, premise (1) seems true enough as long as we recognize that if there is any harm involved in the homosexual acts of consenting adults, it would be harm absorbed by the freely consenting participants. This is true, however, only if the acts in question are done in private. Public acts may involve more than just the willing participants. Persons who have no desire to participate, even if only as spectators, may have no choice if the acts are done in public. A real probability of there being unwilling participants is indicative of the public realm and not the private. However, where one draws the line between private acts and public acts is not always easy to discern, it is clear that different moral standards apply to public acts than to private acts.[1]

If premise (1) is understood to apply only to acts done in private, then it would appear to be true. The same goes for (4): discrimination against homosexuals for acts done in private would result in a diminishing of freedom. So (1)–(4) would lend support to (5) only if we understand (1)–(4) to refer to acts done in private. Hence, (5) must be understood as referring to private acts; and, as a consequence, (6) also must be read as referring only to acts done in private.

With regard to acts which involve only willing adult participants, there may be no morally relevant difference between homosexuality and heterosexuality. In other words, acts done in private. However, acts done in public add a new ingredient to the mix; an ingredient which has moral consequence. Consequently, the argument (1)–(6) fails in supporting the parity thesis. The argument (1)–(6) may show that there are some circumstances in which the moral status of homosexuality and heterosexuality are the same, but it gives us no reason for thinking that this result holds for all circumstances.[2]

3. MORAL IMPASSES AND PUBLIC DILEMMAS

Suppose one person believes that X is morally wrong, while another believes that X is morally permissible. The two people, let's stipulate, are not involved in a semantical quibble; they hold genuinely conflicting beliefs regarding the moral status of X. If the first person is correct, then the second person is wrong; and, of course, if the second person is right, then the first must be wrong. This situation of conflicting claims is what we will call an "impasse." Impasses arise out of moral disputes. Since the conflicting parties in an impasse take contrary views, the conflicting views cannot all be true, nor can they all be false.[3] Moral impasses may concern matters only of a personal nature, but moral impasses can involve public policy. An impasse is likely to have public policy ramifications if large numbers of people hold the conflicting views, and the conflict involves matters which are fundamental to a person's moral identity (and, hence, from a practical point of view, are probably irresolvable) and it involves acts done in public. Since not every impasse has public policy ramifications, one can mark off

"public dilemma" as a special case of moral impasses: those moral impasses that have public policy consequences. Public dilemmas, then, are impasses located in the public square. Since they have public policy ramifications and since they arise from impasses, one side or another of the dispute will have its views implemented as public policy. Because of the public policy ramifications, and also because social order is sometimes threatened by the volatile parties involved in the impasse, the state has a role to play in resolving a public dilemma.

A public dilemma can be actively resolved in two ways.[4] The first is when the government allies itself with one side of the impasse and, by state coercion and sanction, declares that side of the impasse the correct side. The American Civil War was an example of this: the federal government forcibly ended slavery by aligning itself with the Abolitionist side of the impasse. Prohibition is another example. The 18th Amendment and the Volstead Act allied the state with the Temperance side of the impasse. State mandated affirmative action programs provide a modern example of this. This kind of resolution of a public dilemma we can call a "resolution by declaration." The first of the examples cited above indicates that declarations can be morally proper, the right thing to do. The second example, however, indicates that declarations are not always morally proper. The state does not always take the side of the morally correct; nor is it always clear which side is the correct one.

The second way of actively resolving a public dilemma is that of accommodation. An accommodation in this context means resolving the public dilemma in a way that gives as much as possible to all sides of the impasse. A resolution by accommodation involves staking out some middle ground in a dispute and placing public policy in that location. The middle ground location of a resolution via accommodation is a virtue since it entails that there are no absolute victors and no absolute losers. The middle ground is reached in order to resolve the public dilemma in a way which respects the relevant views of the conflicting parties and which maintains social order. The Federal Fair Housing Act and, perhaps, the current status of abortion (legal but with restrictions) provide examples of actual resolutions via accommodation.[5]

In general, governments should be, at least as far as possible, neutral with regard to the disputing parties in a public dilemma. Unless there is some overriding reason why the state should take sides in a public dilemma—the protection of innocent life, or abolishing slavery, for instance—the state should be neutral, because no matter which side of the public dilemma the state takes, the other side will be the recipient of unequal treatment by the state. A state which is partial and takes sides in moral disputes via declaration, when there is no overriding reason why it should, is tyrannical. Overriding reasons involve, typically, the protection of generally recognized rights.[6] In the case of slavery, the right to liberty; in the case of protecting innocent life, the right involved is the negative right to life. If a public dilemma must be actively resolved, the state should do so (in the absence of an overriding reason) via accommodation and not declaration since the latter entails that a sizable number of people would be forced to live under a government which "legitimizes" and does not just tolerate activities which they find immoral. Resolution via declaration is appropriate only if there is an overriding reason for the state to throw its weight behind one side in a public dilemma.

Is moral rightness an overriding reason for a resolution via declaration? What better reason might there be for a resolution by declaration than that it is the right thing to do? Unless one is prepared to endorse a view that is called "legal moralism"—that immorality alone is a sufficient reason for the state to curtail individual liberty—then one had best hold that moral rightness alone is not an overriding reason. Since some immoral acts neither harm nor offend nor violate another's rights, it

seems clear enough that too much liberty would be lost if legal moralism were adopted as public policy.

Though we do not have a definite rule for determining *a priori* which moral impasses genuinely constitute public dilemmas, we can proceed via a case by case method. For example, many people hold that cigarette smoking is harmful and, on that basis, is properly suppressible. Others disagree. Is this a public dilemma? Probably not. Whether someone engages in an imprudent action is, as long as it involves no unwilling participants, a private matter and does not, on that account, constitute a public dilemma. What about abortion? Is abortion a public dilemma? Unlike cigarette smoking, abortion is a public dilemma. This is clear from the adamant and even violent contrary positions involved in the impasse. Abortion is an issue which forces itself into the public square. So, it is clear that, even though we lack a rule which filters through moral impasses designating some as public dilemmas, not every impasse constitutes a public dilemma.

4. CONFLICTING CLAIMS ON HOMOSEXUALITY

The theistic tradition, Judaism and Christianity and Islam, has a clear and deeply entrenched position on homosexual acts: they are prohibited. . . . As a consequence, many contemporary theistic adherents of the theistic tradition . . . hold that homosexual behavior is sinful. Though God loves the homosexual, these folk say, God hates the sinful behavior. To say that act X is a sin entails that X is morally wrong, not necessarily because it is harmful or offensive, but because X violates God's will. So, the claim that homosexuality is sinful entails the claim that it is also morally wrong. And, it is clear, many people adopt the difference thesis just because of their religious views: because the Bible or the Koran holds that homosexuality is wrong, they too hold that view.

Well, what should we make of these observations? We do not, for one thing, have to base our moral conclusions on those views, if for no other reason than not every one is a theist. If one does not adopt the religion-based moral view, one must still respect those who do; they cannot just be dismissed out of hand. And, significantly, this situation yields a reason for thinking that the difference thesis is probably true. Because many religious people sincerely believe homosexual acts to be morally wrong and many others believe that homosexual acts are not morally wrong, there results a public dilemma.[7]

The existence of this public dilemma gives us reason for thinking that the difference thesis is true. It is only via the difference thesis and not the parity thesis, that an accommodation can be reached. Here again, the private/public distinction will come into play.

To see this, take as an example the issue of homosexual marriages. A same-sex marriage would be a public matter. For the government to sanction same-sex marriages—to grant the recognition and reciprocal benefits which attach to marriage—would ally the government with one side of the public dilemma and against the adherents of religion-based moralities. This is especially true given that, historically, no government has sanctioned same-sex marriages. The status quo has been no same-sex marriages. If the state were to change its practice now, it would be clear that the state has taken sides in the impasse. Given the history, for a state to sanction a same-sex marriage now would not be a neutral act.

Of course, some would respond here that by not sanctioning same-sex marriages the state is, and historically has been, taking sides to the detriment of homosexuals. There is some truth in this claim. But one must be careful here. The respective resolutions of this issue—whether the state should recognize and sanction same-sex marriages—do not have symmetrical implications. The asymmetry of this issue is a function of the private/public distinction and the fact that marriage is a public matter. If the state sanctions same-sex marriages, then there is no accommodation available. In that event, the religion-based morality proponents are faced with a public, state sanctioned matter which they find seriously immoral. This would be an example of a resolution via declaration. On the other hand, if the state does not sanction same-sex marriages, there is an accommodation available: in the public realm the state sides with the religion-based moral view, but the state can tolerate private homosexual acts. That is, since homosexual acts are not essentially public acts, they can be, and historically have been, performed in private. The state, by not sanctioning same-sex marriages is acting in the public realm, but it can leave the private realm to personal choice.

5. THE ARGUMENT FROM CONFLICTING CLAIMS

It was suggested in the previous section that the public dilemma concerning homosexuality, and in particular whether states should sanction same-sex marriages, generates an argument in support of the difference thesis. The argument, again using same-sex marriages as the particular case, is as follows:

7. There are conflicting claims regarding whether the state should sanction same-sex marriages. And,

8. this controversy constitutes a public dilemma. And,

9. there is an accommodation possible if the state does not recognize same-sex marriages. And,

10. there is no accommodation possible if the state does sanction same-sex marriages. And,

11. there is no overriding reason for a resolution via declaration. Hence,

12. the state ought not sanction same-sex marriages. And,

13. the state ought to sanction heterosexual marriages. So,

14. there is at least one morally relevant case in which discrimination against homosexuals, because of their homosexuality, is morally permissible. Therefore,

15. the difference thesis is true.

Since proposition (14) is logically equivalent to the difference thesis, then, if (7)–(14) are sound, proposition (15) certainly follows.

Premises (7) and (8) are uncontroversial. Premises (9) and (10) are based on the asymmetry that results from the public nature of marriage. Proposition (11) is based on our earlier analysis of the argument (1)–(6). Since the strongest argument in support of the parity thesis fails, we have reason to think that there is no overriding reason why the state ought to resolve the public dilemma via declaration in favor of same-sex marriages. We have reason, in other words, to think that (11) is true.

Proposition (12) is based on the conjunction of (7)—(11) and the principle that, in the absence of an overriding reason for state intervention via declaration, resolution by accommodation is the preferable route. Proposition (13) is just trivially true. So, given the moral difference mentioned in (12) and (13), proposition (14) logically follows.

6. TWO OBJECTIONS CONSIDERED

The first objection to the argument from conflicting claims would contend that it is unsound because a similar sort of argument would permit discrimination against some practice which, though perhaps controversial at some earlier time, is now widely thought to be morally permissible. Take mixed-race marriages, for example. The opponent of the argument from conflicting claims could argue that a similar argument would warrant prohibition against mixed-race marriages. If it does, we would have good reason to reject (7)–(14) as unsound.

There are three responses to this objection. The first response denies that the issue of mixed-race marriages is in fact a public dilemma. It may have been so at one time, but it does not seem to generate much, if any, controversy today. Hence, the objection is based upon a faulty analogy.

The second response grants for the sake of the argument that the issue of mixed-race marriages generates a public dilemma. But the second response points out that there is a relevant difference between mixed-race marriages and same-sex marriages that allows for a resolution by declaration in the one case but not the other. As evident from the earlier analysis of the argument in support of (1)–(6), there is reason to think that there is no overriding reason for a resolution by declaration in support of the parity thesis. On the other hand, it is a settled matter that state protection from racial discrimination is a reason sufficient for a resolution via declaration. Hence, the two cases are only apparently similar, and, in reality, they are crucially different. They are quite different because, clearly enough, if mixed-race marriages do generate a public dilemma, the state should use resolution by declaration in support of such marriages. The same cannot be said for same-sex marriages.

One should note that the second response to the objection does not beg the question against the proponent of the parity thesis. Though the second response denies that race and sexuality are strict analogues, it does so for a defensible and independent reason: it is a settled matter that race is not a sufficient reason for disparate treatment; but, as we have seen from the analysis of (1)–(6), there is no overriding reason to think the same about sexuality.

The third response to the first objection is that the grounds of objection differ in the respective cases: one concerns racial identity; the other concerns behavior thought to be morally problematic. A same-sex marriage would involve behavior which many people find morally objectionable; a mixed-race marriage is objectionable to some, not because of the participants' behavior, but because of the racial identity of the participants. It is the race of the marriage partners which some find of primary complaint concerning mixed-race marriages. With same-sex marriages, however, it is the behavior which is primarily objectionable. To see this latter point, one should note that . . . the kind of sexual acts that are likely involved in a same-sex marriage are objectionable to some, regardless of whether done by homosexuals or heterosexuals. So again, there is reason to reject the analogy between same-sex marriages and mixed-race marriages. Racial identity is an immutable trait and a complaint about mixed-race marriages necessarily involves, then, a complaint about an immutable trait. Sexual behavior is not an immutable trait and it is possible to object to same-sex marriages based on the behavior which would be involved in such marriages. Put succinctly, the third response could be formulated as follows: objections to mixed-race marriages necessarily involve objections over status, while objections to same-sex marriages could involve objections over behavior. Therefore, the two cases are not analogues since there is a significant modal difference in the ground of the objection.

The second objection to the argument from conflicting claims can be stated so: if homosexuality is biologically based—if it is inborn[8]—then how can discrimination ever be justified? If it is not a matter of choice, homosexuality is an immutable trait which is, as a consequence, morally permissible. Just as it would be absurd to hold someone morally culpable for being of a certain race, likewise it would be absurd to hold someone morally culpable for being a homosexual. Consequently, according to this objection, the argument from conflicting claims "legitimizes" unjustifiable discrimination.

But this second objection is not cogent, primarily because it ignores an important distinction. No one could plausibly hold that homosexuals act by some sort of biological compulsion. If there is a biological component involved in sexual identity, it would incline but it would not compel. Just because one naturally (without any choice) has certain dispositions, is not in itself a morally cogent reason for acting upon that disposition. Most people are naturally selfish, but it clearly does not follow that selfishness is in any way permissible on that account. Even if it is true that one has a predisposition to do X as a matter of biology and not as a matter of choice, it does not follow tht doing X is morally permissible. . . . The reason that the appeal to biology is specious is that it ignores the important distinction between being a homosexual and homosexual acts. One is status; the other is behavior. Even if one has the status naturally, it does not follow that the behavior is morally permissible, nor that others have a duty to tolerate the behavior.

But, while moral permissibility does not necessarily follow if homosexuality should turn out to be biologically based, what does follow is this: in the absence of a good reason to discriminate between homosexuals and heterosexuals, then, assuming that homosexuality is inborn, one ought not discriminate between them. If a certain phenomenon X is natural in the sense of being involuntary and nonpathological, and if there is no good reason to hold that X is morally problematic, then that is reason enough to think that X is morally permissible. In the absence of a good reason to repress X, one should tolerate it since, as per supposition, it is largely nonvoluntary. The argument from conflicting claims, however, provides a good reason which overrides this presumption.

7. A SECOND ARGUMENT FOR THE DIFFERENCE THESIS

A second argument for the difference thesis, similar to the argument from conflicting claims, is what might be called the "no-exit argument." This argument is based on the principle that:

(A): No just government can coerce a citizen into violating a deeply held moral belief or religious belief.

Is (A) plausible? It seems to be since the prospect of a citizen being coerced by the state into a practice which she finds profoundly immoral appears to be a clear example of an injustice. Principle (A), conjoined with there being a public dilemma arising over the issue of same-sex marriages, leads to the observation that if the state were to sanction same-sex marriages, then persons who have profound religious or moral objections to such unions would be legally mandated to violate their beliefs since there does not appear to be any feasible "exit right" possible with regard to state sanctioned marriage. An exit right is an exemption from some legally mandated practice, granted to a person or group, the purpose of which is to protect the religious or moral integrity of that person or group. Prominent examples of exit rights include conscientious objection and military service, home-schooling of the young because of some religious concern, and property used for religious purposes being free from taxation.

It is important to note that marriage is a public matter in the sense that, for instance, if one is an employer who provides health care benefits to the spouses of employees, one must provide those benefits to any employee who is married. Since there is not exit right possible in this case, one would be coerced, by force of law, into subsidizing a practice one finds morally or religiously objectionable.

In the absence of an exit right, and if (A) is plausible, then the state cannot morally force persons to violate deeply held beliefs that are moral or religious in nature. In particular, the state morally could not sanction same-sex marriages since this would result in coercing some into violating a deeply held religious conviction.

8. A CONCLUSION

It is important to note that neither the argument from conflicting claims nor the no-exit argument licenses wholesale discrimination against homosexuals. What they do show is that some discrimination against homosexuals, in this case refusal to sanction same-sex marriages, is not only legally permissible but also morally permissible. The discrimination is a way of resolving a public policy dilemma that accommodates, to an extent, each side of the impasse and, further, protects the religious and moral integrity of a good number of people. In short, the arguments show us that there are occasions in which it is morally permissible to discriminate on the basis of homosexuality.

NOTES

1. The standard answer is, of course, that the line between public and private is based on the notion of harm. Acts which carry a real probability of harming third parties are public acts.

2. For other arguments supporting the moral parity of homosexuality and heterosexuality, see Richard Mohr, *Gays/Justice: A Study of Ethics, Society and Law* (NY: Columbia, 1988); and see Michael Ruse, "The Morality of Homosexuality" in *Philosophy and Sex* eds. R. Baker & F. Elliston, (Buffalo, NY: Prometheus Books, 1984), pp. 370–390.

3. Perhaps it would be better to term the disputing positions "contradictory" views rather than "contrary" views.

4. Resolutions can also be passive in the sense of the state doing nothing. If the state does nothing to resolve the public dilemma, it stands pat with the status quo, and the public dilemma is resolved gradually by sociological changes (changes in mores and in beliefs).

5. The Federal Fair Housing Act prohibits discrimination in housing on the basis of race, religion, and sex. But it does not apply to the rental of rooms in single-family houses, or to a building of five units or less if the owner lives in one of the units. See 42 U.S.C. Section 3603.

6. Note that overriding reasons involve *generally recognized* rights. If a right is not widely recognized

and the state nonetheless uses coercion to enforce it, there is a considerable risk that the state will be seen by many or even most people as tyrannical.

7. Two assumptions are these: that the prohibitions against homosexual activity are part of the religious doctrine and not just an extraneous addition; second, that if X is part of one's religious belief or religious doctrine, then it is morally permissible to hold X. Though this latter principle is vague, it is, I think, clear enough for our purposes here (I ignore here any points concerning the rationality of religious belief in general, or in particular cases).

8. There is some interesting recent research which, though still tentative, strongly suggests that homosexuality is, at least in part, biologically based. See Simon LeVay, *The Sexual Brain* (Cambridge, MA: MIT Press, 1993), pp. 120–122; and J. M. Bailey & R. C. Pillard, "A Genetic Study of Male Sexual Orientation," *Archives of General Psychiatry* 48 (1991): 1089—1096; and C. Burr, "Homosexuality and Biology," *The Atlantic* 271/3 (March, 1993): 64; and D. Hamer, S. Hu, V. Magnuson, N. Hu, A. Pattatucci, "A Linkage Between DNA Markers on the X Chromosome and Male Sexual Orientation," *Science* 261 (16 July 1993): 321–327; and see the summary of this article by Robert Pool, "Evidence for Homosexuality Gene," *Science* 261 (16 July 1993): 291–292.

Chapter 12

The Censorship of Pornography

A line from a 1940s Cole Porter song says: "In olden days a glimpse of stocking was looked on as something shocking, now—heaven knows—anything goes!" Compared to the relative tameness of the 1940s, it is today that anything seems to go in the adult entertainment business. *Business* is the correct term, too, as the pornography market in this country has grow from a $10 million per year industry in the 1970s to a $10 *billion* industry today. Depictions and descriptions of sex are sold in magazines, videos, CDs and DVDs, nightclubs, bookstores, television, on the Internet, and even in video games. Phone sex is also a big business, with close to half a million calls made each day to dial-a-porn numbers. With the arrival of the interactive features of digital television, people will be able to send pornographic material from one television set to another.

The proliferation of pornographic material has serious consequences that call for moral scrutiny. Many worry about the effect that viewing pornography has on minors, for example. When sex scenes are commonplace on afternoon television, when the Internet is full of easily accessible pornographic material, when even the local drugstore displays adult magazines next to the toothpaste, it is not easy to screen pornography out of the lives of our youth. Others worry about the negative effects of pornography on the community. If porn shops can be located near grocery stores, and nightclubs next to the local church, and if pornographic videos are rented across the street from the elementary school, the quality and decency of community life are threatened. Many people are concerned with the moral message sent by displays of pornography to all citizens, young and old alike, as well as the psychological impact of viewing men and women—but especially women—as simply sex objects.

Most important, however, are the harms produced by pornography. These harms are suffered mostly by women, and not just the women who appear in pornographic material—*all* women. Some people who view pornography come to think of women as they are portrayed. Even if pornography could be kept off the streets and airways so that it was available only to those adults who wished to view it, it would be a source of great harm. It gives men a distorted picture of women and what women really want and need. Some men come to believe that the fictions depicted in pornographic material, especially the treatment of women as things who exist solely for the pleasure of men, really do portray the way that women deep down want to be treated. If such an image of women is accepted, it not only prevents men from having real relationships with women, but it also leads some men to cause them serious harm. Serial killers and rapists attest time after time to their reliance on pornography, especially violent pornography, to provide the stimulation and the motivation for their crimes. Many citizens believe

the time has come to take a stand against pornography and its evils, to end its proliferation, and for the law to eliminate it altogether.

If we grant for now that at least some forms of pornography are immoral
because of the harms they produce, the focus becomes one of identifying the best
method to eliminate them. Many see the only effective method as censorship—
government censorship in this context. They want legal penalties imposed on
those who produce, display, sell, and view such material. Currently some forms
of pornography are legally censored in this country. There are legal criteria for
judging between pornographic works that are illegal and those that are not. The
question of this chapter is whether such laws should be expanded to include additional types of pornographic material, or whether they should stay as they are, or
whether they should be eliminated altogether. The central moral problem of this
chapter will focus on the morality of *censorship*, not on the moral acceptability of
pornography itself. Whether pornography is morally acceptable may count as
evidence for whether censorship ought to be allowed, but the moral acceptability
of government censorship itself is our major concern.

The Problem

Censorship poses a moral problem because it represents an expansion of the
power of government over the individual. It curbs individual freedom in the
name of the common good, in the name of protecting us from each other. The government does this all the time, of course, and the instrument it uses is the law. In
fact, laws may be thought of as restrictions imposed on individual freedom. There
are various sorts of laws that restrict our freedom in various ways. Laws against
killing and theft are examples of criminal laws. They exist to deter would-be criminals from committing murder and larceny. Other laws, such as contract laws, protect us from less violent harms by allowing us to litigate our grievances against
others in a court of law. Still other laws, those that regulate aviation, communication, and the sale of food and drugs, for example, protect us from some of the
harms of large, complex systems of which most of us have little knowledge.

For the most part, we accept these sorts of laws readily. We gladly give up our
freedom to kill others in return for the government's protection of our own lives;
we gladly sacrifice our freedom to break valid contracts for the protection offered
by the courts to defend our own contract rights; and we gladly allow the government to tell us we cannot eat certain sorts of food or take certain medications
when these may be harmful to us. The government protects us through its laws,
and we are usually glad of it. Although we are grateful for the protection the government gives us from each other, we bitterly protest government interference
with our private lives. We want to live our lives as we see fit, not as the government decides we should live them. The very power required for the government
to provide protection to all of its citizens may also be used to abuse individual
rights. In a free and open society such as ours, we are always on guard for such
abuses of power and scream mightily when the least hint of them appears.

This delicate balance of government authority and individual freedom is the
context in which the moral problem of censorship arises. By censoring pornogra-

phy the government is interfering in our private lives. Why should adults who wish to view pornographic material in the privacy of their homes not be allowed to do so? From a moral perspective, it seems clearly to be a violation of the principle of autonomy. If we are not harming anyone else, why should we not be allowed to do as we please? On the other hand, the proliferation of pornography, especially some of its more extreme forms, seems to be harmful to individual and public life. But is it harmful enough to be subject to government control, and are there other methods of dealing with its harms? Much of what we have to say for and against censorship in this chapter will deal with such questions, questions about its possible harms and how best to deal with them. Before we begin this discussion, however, we must spend some time clarifying central concepts.

Clarifying Concepts

Everyone agrees that defining pornography clearly is not easy. Roughly, pornographic works contain depictions or descriptions of sexuality designed to produce sexual arousal; many find these depictions obscene or offensive. Beyond this, capturing the essence of **pornography** is hard because there is a strong subjective element in what different people find pornographic. "A glimpse of stocking" might have been shocking to some in the past, but for many today, watching totally nude, simulated, consensual sex seems simply routine. Instead of trying to define pornography, we will give examples of its various types. The study of pornography conducted by the Meese Commission (1986),[1] an important study that will be discussed later in this chapter, divides various sorts of pornography into three main categories. The following quotes are from that study.

First is the category of "sexually violent material." This sort of material includes

> actually or unmistakenly simulated or unmistakenly threatened violence presented in sexually explicit fashion with a predominant focus on the sexually explicit violence. . . . Some of this material involves sado-masochistic themes, with . . . whips, chains, devices of torture, and so on. Another [recurrent theme involves] a man making some sort of sexual advance to a woman, being rebuffed, and then raping the woman or in some other way violently forcing himself on the woman. In almost all of this material . . . the woman eventually becomes aroused and ecstatic about the initially forced sexual activity, and usually is portrayed as begging for more. There is also a large body of material, more "mainstream" in its availability, that portrays sexual activity or sexually suggestive nudity coupled with extreme violence, such as disfigurement or murder. The so-called "slasher" films fit this description.

The *second* category is called "nonviolent degrading materials." Such materials may not depict violence against women, but they do include men dominating, humiliating, and degrading women. This category include material that especially depicts or describes women as

> existing solely for the sexual satisfaction of others . . . or in decidedly subordinate roles in their sexual relations with others, or that depicts people engaged in sexual practices that would to most people be considered humiliating. Indeed, forms of degradation represent the largely predominant proportion of commercially available pornography.

The *third* category contains "nonviolent and nondegrading materials." These are materials

> in which the participants appear to be fully willing participants occupying substantially equal roles in a setting devoid of actual or apparent violence or pain.

This last category is sometimes called **soft-core pornography,** or "erotica." According to the Commission, the last category contains material that is not without its social harms, often depicting scenes of nudity and simulated sex as well as extramarital sex and loveless sex. Because the sex in the third category occurs between consenting adults who are portrayed as equals, it is the items in the first two categories that are considered to have the greatest potential for harm. We will refer to the sexually violent and/or degrading material contained in these first two categories as "hard-core" pornography. Although there is some discussion in what follows of soft-core pornography, this chapter is especially concerned with the moral acceptability of censoring hard-core pornography. This point is important for the discussions to follow.

The essential properties of hard-core porn are not just its depictions of sex but the use of sex as an instrument of violence and degradation. Some want to include another element in its definition as well, an element that is equally essential, namely, the condoning or endorsing of the depicted violence and degradation. Hard-core porn sends the message that real women like being treated in ways that hurt and humiliate them, and that real men ought to oblige them. It is one thing to show a rape scene and the horror and suffering that follows; such a film or video could be instructive and helpful. It is quite another to show the same scene and have people, even the victim, praise the rapist as a real man. As one writer puts it,[2]

> What makes a work a work of pornography, then, is not simply its representation of degrading and abusive sexual encounters, but its implicit, if not explicit, approval and recommendation of such behavior that is immoral, i.e., that physically or psychologically violates the personhood of one of the participants. Pornography, then, is verbal or pictorial material which represents or describes sexual behavior that is degrading or abusive to one or more of the participants *in such a way as to endorse the degradation.*

If we combine the definition of pornography contained in the last sentence of this passage with what we have said about pornography so far, we may now define **hard-core pornography** as *depictions or descriptions of endorsed violent and/or degrading sexual behavior that are designed to produce sexual arousal.* This definition will serve well enough to guide the discussions of this chapter.

Exercise 12.1

For this exercise, answer the following two questions:

1. If it is morally acceptable to censor violent and degrading pornography, is it also morally acceptable to censor any violent and degrading material, even if it contains no depictions or descriptions of sex?

2. Is there any type of pornography that is not harmful, that may even be beneficial?

The next concept for clarification is that of **censorship** itself. To censor something is to suppress all or part of it because it violates some standard. Parents may censor the reading material of their children to screen out violence. Repressive governments may censor the media and ban books that are critical of its policies. Democratic governments may censor military information during wartime for the protection of their national interests. The mechanism of the government's censorship of pornography could take any number of forms, depending on whether the censoring government in question is local, state, or federal.

Local officials may remove material from circulation when they believe it represents illegal pornography. Often antipornography groups bring such material to their attention. In large cities, officials may establish censorship boards to review questionable works, as did the mayor of New York City in 2001, when he formed what was called a "decency standards" board. The committee was asked to make recommendations about which works could or could not be displayed in publicly funded institutions in New York City. The state of Utah became the first state to appoint what has been called a "porn czar." This job especially concerns educating community leaders about the extent of pornography and the nature of community standards so they may better police their own communities. On the federal level, the government may act as a censor by passing legislation, by regulating the criteria for funding the arts, by placing political pressure on the various media, or in any number of other ways.

If government censorship becomes more widespread than it is currently, it would probably require that censors or censor boards be established to screen various types of media for the presence of pornographic material. Much of this screening is currently the function of the particular industry itself, such as the television or the film industries. Each publishes a rating schedule to alert people to the degree of pornography and violence that may be present in a work. Self-imposed standards are not very effective, however, and public frustration with the growth of pornography within these industries may lead to external censorship. Undoubtedly, external recommendations for censorship would be challenged by those who manage the media in question, and the matter would end up in the courts. It is the courts, and especially the U.S. Supreme Court, that have the final say about what may or may not be censored. The courts currently do censor some forms of pornography. The rules for this form of censorship will be discussed in the "Descriptive Ethics" section.

Formulating the Problem

The problem of this chapter is not whether some forms of pornography are immoral, although this will be an important consideration. Instead, the problem is about the moral acceptability of government censorship of pornography, especially hard-core pornography. It is a **conflict of rules** problem. On the one hand, there is the rule that says "people ought to be able to say whatever they want to, as long as doing so harms no one else." This is a specific instance of the general moral principle of autonomy and may be phrased as the right to free expression. This right includes not only linguistic expression, but also literary, artistic, political, and religious expression as well as the right of others to hear and view such expressions. This is the moral right given legal standing by the First Amendment to the U.S. Constitution, which guarantees free speech, or freedom of expression.

In conflict with the right to free expression is the rule that says "prevent the individual and social harms of pornography." This is a specific instance of the general moral principle of beneficence, which requires us to do good and avoid evil. It may be phrased as the right to protection from the harms of pornography. When the government is doing the protecting, this right finds its legal expression in the current laws that allow the government to practice censorship. So the problem of Chapter 12 represents a conflict between individual freedom of expression and the duty of the government to protect its citizens from harm. We *formulate the problem* as follows:

> *Under what conditions, if any, is it morally acceptable for the government to censor pornography for consenting adults?*

The inclusion of the phrase "consenting adults" is meant to focus on our problem as a question that concerns the very *existence* of pornography, not so much its display. Perfectly acceptable laws are in place that restrict the display of pornography, laws whose purpose is to keep it away from minors and nonconsenting adults. In theory, at least, adults who do not want to view pornographic works and children will not be exposed to it. Pornographic videos are supposed to be kept in a separate room in the video rental stores, for example, and "adult" nightclub acts are supposed to be off limits to minors. Such laws are discussed below in the "Descriptive Ethics" section. The question here is whether adults who choose to view pornographic material in the privacy of their homes, or in nightclubs, or on the Internet, and so on, should be prevented from doing so by the government.

Possible Solutions

One *possible solution* claims that government censorship of pornography is always immoral. This anticensorship position appeals to the principle of autonomy and its legal expression in this context, the First Amendment, to justify its claims. Those who support this view claim that pornography, even its hard-core versions, cause no public harm and may even be beneficial to some individuals. According to this possible solution, which is called the **anticensorship** view, not only should there not be any broadening of government censorship, but even the minimum current censorship laws should be eliminated. Even if some private harms are associated with pornography, the method for avoiding them should be education, not government coercion. Nor is it the job of government to protect public morality through censorship. Widespread government censorship, even if it reduces private harms and upholds a common morality, will cause more harm than the good it produces.

Another possible solution appeals to the principle of beneficence and claims that government censorship is morally acceptable because it reduces the harm caused by pornography to both individuals and society. The intensity and extent of pornography today threatens both individuals and society and must be reigned in if we are to remain free from its harms. This solution supports this claim by providing evidence of the harms of pornography, especially evidence that it causes public harms, and by trying to show that government censorship, even more of it than currently exists, is the only effective way to avoid these harms. It does not claim that all forms of pornography ought to be censored, only the hard-core versions of it. We will call this the **censorship** view.

Facts and Assumptions

Facts

Some of the important *facts* about pornography concern its proliferation over the last three decades. Access to pornography is growing at a rapidly increasing rate and shows little sign of diminishing. No longer is pornography something that a fringe element of society seeks out in restricted movie theaters and hard-to-get magazines. Since the introduction of videocassettes and VCRs in the 1980s and the proliferation of video rental stores, masses of people can now watch pornographic films in the privacy of their own homes. Some eight to ten thousand hard-core videos are produced each year, compared to somewhere around one hundred per year in the mid-1970s. The majority of these videos are produced in southern California, where "porn stars," usually women, can earn as much as $100,000 a year for their talents.

The porn business, or "sex industry," as it is called, has become a large and profitable business, growing from about $10 million in annual revenues in the mid-1970s to close to $10 billion today. Large reputable companies are now in the porn business, especially companies that carry porn videos over cable lines, such as AT&T, Time Warner, and hotel chains such as the Marriott, the Hyatt, and the Holiday Inn chains.[3] The growing presence of pornography on television, in film, in nightclubs, in magazines, and especially on the Internet shows no sign of diminishing. On the Internet alone a search under "pornography" yields over a million responses. Of course, not all of these are Web sites devoted to graphic displays of pornography. Some are sites devoted to antipornography themes. Still there is a very large and ever-growing number of pornographic Web sites. The Internet sites are not nearly as profitable as porn videos, at least not yet, but they are nevertheless quite popular. The *Playboy* site alone gets about five million hits a day. Telephone sex is very profitable as well, with over a quarter of a million callers each day to various sites, costing anywhere from $1 to $4 a minute, and totaling about a billion dollars a year in revenues. Some estimates are that nearly two-thirds of such calls are from minors.

The **scientific facts** of greatest relevance for solving our problem are those that concern the harms produced by various sorts of pornography. Harms may be of many sorts. Philosophers often divide them into private harms—harms done by an individual to himself or herself—and public harms—harms suffered by someone else as a result of a person's action. The sorts of *private harms* that pornography has been accused of producing include psychological harms and moral harms. *Psychological harms* might include such things as forming distorted beliefs about the opposite sex and a false image of the nature of sexuality. Men who view hard-core pornography, for example, may form unrealistic expectations about sexual relationships with women. They may be more willing to be more aggressive, less thoughtful and caring, and less concerned with a woman as a person. They may become desensitized to the humanity of women and come to see women merely as objects for their own sexual satisfaction. Such beliefs, if reenforced frequently enough, produce a warped character and make it difficult for a man to have a full, rich relationship with a woman.

There is some scientific evidence that habitual viewing of hard-core pornography can cause these sorts of psychological harms. When men are subjected to repeated exposure to hard-core pornography and their reactions studied, their psychological states are not the same as those of a control group, a group not subject to the same exposure. Summarizing some of these studies, the Meese Commission concluded:[4]

> The evidence [shows] significant attitudinal changes on the part of those with substantial exposure to violent pornography. These attitudinal changes are numerous. Victims of rape and other forms of sexual violence are likely to be perceived by people so exposed as more responsible for the assault, as having suffered less injury, and as having been less degraded as a result of the experience. . . . We have little trouble concluding that this attitude is both pervasive and profoundly harmful, and that any stimulus reinforcing or increasing the incidence of this attitude is for that reason alone properly designated as harmful.

Private harms may also include *moral harms.* By moral harms we mean a decrease in interest in conforming to the moral rules of the community, especially in sexual matters. People who view hard-core pornography, and even soft-core pornography, are less willing to believe that sex belongs only in marriage, for example, or that various sorts of sex, such as homosexual sex and sadomasochistic sex, are perversions. Further, these beliefs are translated into action, into how they conduct their own sexual behaviors. Again, the Meese Commission report says

> it is far from implausible to hypothesize that materials depicting sexual activity without marriage, love, commitment, or affection, bear some causal relationship to sexual activity without marriage, love, commitment, or affection.

The moral convictions of individuals are shaped by pornography and, for many, not at all for the good.

Public harms are of several types. One type is *moral harm.* In addition to affecting the moral beliefs of individuals, pornography may weaken the moral beliefs of society as a whole. If enough individuals are sufficiently exposed even to soft-core pornography, let alone to its hard-core versions, the moral convictions of society will probably be weakened. The Meese Commission continues:

> There are undoubtedly many causes for what used to be called the "sexual revolution," but it is absurd to suppose that depictions and descriptions of uncommitted sexuality were not among them.

Another way pornography harms society may be called *neighborhood decay.* This refers to the negative effect that displays of pornography have on the level of decency present in a community. Porn shops, strip joints, and X-rated movie theaters are bad enough in themselves, but they also attract drug dealers, prostitutes, and higher levels of crime. Pornography may easily and rapidly lead to the decay of neighborhoods, destroying safe and decent environments and making them unfit for raising children. Most of the time, but not always, these social harms may be prevented by suitable zoning laws that forbid the existence of such establishments within residential and commercial neighborhoods.

A third way pornography harms society as a whole, and especially one-half of it most directly, is by *degrading women*. Women are portrayed as mere objects, not full persons. They are depicted in roles that are subordinate to men, roles that show them as objects of sexual violence or, in the absence of violence, in roles that are often degrading and humiliating. Moreover, they are portrayed as enjoying such roles. In addition to the obviously negative portrayal of women present in hard-core pornography, there is a more subtle way that even the consensual sex of soft-core pornography works to harm women—it serves to sanction male dominance over women as the natural way of things. Pornography

> eroticizes hierarchy, it sexualizes inequality. It makes dominance and submission into sex. Inequality is its central dynamic; the illusion of freedom coming together with the reality of force is central to its working. Perhaps because this is a bourgeois culture, the victims must look free, appear to be acting freely. Choice is how she got there. Willing is what she is when she is being equal. It seems equally important that then and there she actually be forced and that forcing be communicated on some level, even if only through still photos of her in postures of receptivity and access, available for penetration. Pornography in this view is a form of forced sex, a practice of sexual politics, an institution of gender inequality.[5]

The most serious sorts of public harms are *sex crimes*. It seems fairly clear that long-term exposure especially to hard-core pornography does have a negative effect on an individual's psychological and moral well-being. It also seems fairly clear that such exposure, when sufficiently widespread, can have negative effects on the moral convictions of society, on the level of decency and safety to be found in its neighborhoods, and on the degree to which men are willing to treat women as second-class citizens. However, there is some dispute over whether a direct causal link exists between pornography, especially hard-core pornography, and sex crimes, such as rape. Finding such a direct link would add a great deal of ammunition to the case for government censorship, as the government has the right to restrict individual freedom whenever such freedom leads to harm to others. The many studies performed for the Meese Commission led its members to conclude that there is such a link, but other studies have failed to demonstrate this direct causal connection. This is such a central issue in the censorship of pornography debate that we will simply say for now the matter is undetermined. We discuss it further in some detail in the "Moral Reasoning" section.

Descriptive Ethics

Most **religions** are opposed to pornography primarily because it undermines the views of sex, marriage, and family they support. By depicting homosexual and nonmarital sex, to say nothing of violent and degrading sex, pornography attacks the very roots of the family and exclusive use of sex within that institution. The official position of the Catholic Church echoes the beliefs of most major religions:[6]

> Pornography consists in removing real or simulated acts from the intimacy of the partners, in order to display them deliberately to third parties. It offends against chastity because it *perverts the conjugal act*, the intimate giving of spouses to each other. It does grave injury to the dignity of its participants (actors, vendors, the public), since one becomes an object of base pleasure and illicit profit for others. It immerses all who are involved in the illusion of a fantasy world. It is a grave offense.

Although most religions believe that pornography is immoral, most of our current rules on the *censorship* of pornography are to be found in the law. Several types of **laws** are used to regulate pornography. Some, such as zoning laws, regulate its *location*. Local governments may decide where the places that house otherwise legally acceptable pornographic materials may be located. Theaters, porn book shops, nightclubs, and so on all fall within the purview of such laws. Laws also regulate the *display* of pornography. The objective of such laws is to make sure that those who do not wish to view pornography may avoid doing so. Pornographic magazines, X-rated videos, and the like must be kept in restricted areas within the stores that sell or rent them to ensure that they are kept away from minors and adults who have no interest in such materials. You cannot display *Playboy,* for example, next to the chewing gum in the local drugstore. Laws also prevent the *sale* of some forms of pornographic material through the U.S. Postal Service. There is very little mainstream opposition to any of these laws, as they are aimed toward preventing children and nonconsenting adults from being exposed to pornographic material.

The attempt to shield children from pornography on the Internet, however, has met with a great deal of opposition. The main problem is that if pornography is eliminated on the Internet for children, it is also eliminated for everyone else, even those adults who wish to view it. The U.S. Congress passed a law in 1996, the Common Decency Act, which attempted to censor Internet pornography. The Supreme Court ruled in *Reno v. ACLU* (1997), however, that such a law was an unconstitutional infringement on the First Amendment right to freedom of expression. They found that software used to block or "filter" pornography on the Web could not distinguish between the forms of pornography that are illegal and not protected by the First Amendment, and other forms of pornography that are legal. Congress tried again in 1998, with its Child Online Protection Act. This bill met the same fate in the courts in 2000.

Censoring the Internet for the benefit of children remains a very large and complex problem. Its solution will probably lie outside the domain of law. Some have proposed that the public at large become the censors of the Internet. This could happen if consumer groups put pressure on large Internet service providers to place blocking software on their servers. Or pressure may be exerted on such institutions as schools and libraries, where children spend much of their time on the Internet, to install such filters. However, censorship by the masses may be less desirable than government censorship. It may turn out to be quite harmful as it is often quite narrowly informed and often excludes the interests of many citizens.

Even if censorship by the majority is beneficial to society, filtering software is too unrefined at this time to censor effectively. Most of it simply recognizes key words and blocks any documents containing them. The problem with this is that much of what may be educational or artistically uplifting will be thrown out with the pornography. In addition, porn sites can be constructed to circumvent these blocking devices. As filtering software becomes more refined, other legal attempts may be made to censor the Internet. For now, however, short of installing blocking software on their home computers and educating their children about the pernicious nature of pornography, parents can do little to eliminate the access of their children to pornographic Internet sites.

If some laws are directed at the display of pornography, others are aimed at its very existence. Some of these are laws about *child pornography* and are widely accepted. Because children cannot truly consent to participate in the creation of such material, its very existence is understood to be evidence of child sexual abuse. In *New York v. Ferber* (1982) the Supreme Court ruled that the creation, sale, and possession of any material showing children under the age of eighteen in pornographic poses is illegal for this very reason. To avoid the prosecution that follows from using live actors, some inventive child pornographers have begun to use computer simulated faces on their actors, creating "virtual" actors. The Supreme Court is considering the legality of such material as of this writing and probably will continue to censor pornography that uses either real or virtual actors who look like they are younger than eighteen years of age.

Most people agree that laws against child pornography are appropriate, but there is quite a bit of resistance against laws that prohibit adult pornographic works intended for consenting adult audiences. One of our possible solutions, the anticensorship view, objects to government censorship because such laws place restrictions on individual freedom. Should the government tell *consenting* adults what they can or cannot view in the privacy of a nightclub, or even in the privacy of their own homes? Should it be the government that says what artists and writers and moviemakers can or cannot produce? It seems not, as this appears to violate at least one of the freedoms guaranteed by the First Amendment—freedom of expression. The First Amendment to the Constitution of the United States says: "Congress shall make no law respecting an establishment of a religion, or prohibiting the free exercise thereof; or abridging the freedom of speech, or of the press; or the right of the people peaceably to assemble, and to petition the Government for a redress of grievances." So is it not unconstitutional for such laws to exist?

In fact, many laws abridge free expression and they are not unconstitutional. Time and again the U.S. Supreme Court has upheld the right of state and local governments to censor sexual obscenity. No rights are absolute rights. Any right may be overridden by a competing right that has a higher priority under the circumstances. So even free expression may be suppressed when its exercise would be likely to lead to harm. "You cannot yell fire in a crowded theater" (when there is no fire), said Chief Justice Oliver Wendell Holmes, as a way to make this point. If the courts find that any form of expression may cause harm, what it refers to as a "clear and present danger," it may prohibit such expression. Early in the twentieth century such harms included simply being offensive or threatening to what was perceived as a publicly shared morality. On this basis, such books as James

Joyce's *Ulysses* was banned in this country, as was D. H. Lawrence's *Lady Chatterley's Lover* and two of Henry Miller's works, *The Tropic of Cancer* and *The Tropic of Capricorn*. The courts even went so far as to ban Aristophanes' *Lysistrata*, Ovid's *The Art of Love*, and *The Arabian Nights*.

Times have changed, of course. Today these works would never be banned. However, the principles for restricting freedom of expression remain the same. These principles were formulated in several cases that came before the Supreme Court. In *Roth v. United States* (1957), for example, the Court states that obscenity is not protected by the First Amendment. In *Miller v. California* (1973), the Court spelled out the standard for judging which pornographic works are obscene. In *Paris Adult Theatre v. Slaton* (1973) it ruled that even if pornographic films were shown only to consenting adults they could be banned because they constituted an affront to the moral decency of the community. More recently, the Courts have placed their emphasis less on the potential of a work to be offensive to public morals and more on its potential to produce sex crimes or other forms of antisocial behavior, such as the degradation of women. Because of this, the Courts now are especially interested in censoring the hard-core sort of material referred to earlier as "sexually violent" material, as well as various forms of "nonviolent degrading" material. The main point for now is that government censorship currently is clearly legal in this country, especially when it is applied to hard-core pornography.

Even though we are concerned in this chapter with what ought to be the case, with what sorts of pornography, if any, ought to be censored by the government, we need to know what currently counts as censorable pornographic material under the law. Just saying that "hard-core" pornography may be censored is inadequate; the concept is too vague to provide legal guidance. Instead, the courts have defined a particular sort of pornography that is illegal. It is not protected by the First Amendment and thus may be censored. It calls such pornography **sexual obscenity;** for the courts, most obscenity has to do with sex, so sometimes it is just called obscenity. One of the ways the law places restrictions on our First Amendment right to free expression is to prohibit the creation, display, sale, and possession of obscene materials. Obscene materials are not protected by the First Amendment and may be declared by the law to be illegal forms of expression.

There are various forms of pornography which the court does not define as obscene and are thus protected forms of expression under the First Amendment. But some forms of pornography are considered obscene and are subject to legal restriction—to government censorship. For the most part this pornographic material is the worst of the hard-core pornographic material. So legally, at least, pornography is subject to government censorship only if it is obscene, that is, disgusting, repulsive, lewd, or indecent. Unfortunately, saying that pornography is sexual obscenity often leads to confusion in the courtroom and to obscenity cases that are difficult to prosecute. This is because the concept of obscenity, like the broader concept of pornography itself, is somewhat subjective. Something is supposed to be obscene if it is disgusting, repulsive, lewd, or indecent. However, what one person finds disgusting, lewd, repulsive, and so on, another may find humorous, or curious, or even boring.

To make matters less subjective, in the U.S. Supreme Court case of *Miller v. California* (1973), the courts established a set of guidelines for determining whether something is pornographic. It is called the **Miller test.** Although this serves as the legal definition of pornography, it is less a definition than a test a supposedly pornographic work must pass to be considered obscene and thus subject to censorship. The Miller test says that a pornographic work is obscene, and therefore may be banned from public consumption, if it meets all three of the following conditions:

1. The average person, applying contemporary community standards, would find that the work appeals to a prurient interest in sex.

2. The work must depict or describe sexual conduct in a clearly offensive manner.

3. The work, taken as a whole, lacks serious literary, artistic, political, or scientific value.

This definition gives some guidance to the courts, but it is often difficult for them and for others to apply in practice. For example, condition (1) is extremely subjective. A work may arouse sexual feelings in some, but it may not in others. And who represents the "average person" and what are the "community standards" in a large city such as Los Angeles? Similar problems arise for the other conditions as well. The point to emphasize for now is that the vagueness of the concept of sexual obscenity creates great difficulty in proving in court that a work is an instance of sexual obscenity; thus, enforcing obscenity laws is not easy.

Some who wish to expand government censorship beyond its current limited scope have taken a different approach to pornography in hopes of accomplishing their goal. Catherine MacKinnon, a lawyer, and Andrea Dworkin, whose views on sexual morality we have examined briefly in the previous chapter, view pornography not so much a legally unprotected expression as a type of discrimination against women. They see it as a form of hate literature that encourages violence against women. Pornography is not just words or depictions that may or may not lead to harmful behavior, but is itself a type of action that is harmful to women. It is a way of constructing a social reality that subordinates women to men, and thus discriminates against them unfairly. Their hope is that if pornography can be viewed as a form of unfair discrimination against women simply because they are women, current laws against any forms of unfair treatment, civil rights laws, may be applicable both to the hard-core and soft-core versions of pornography. This would mean that anyone who created or distributed pornography could be sued on civil rights grounds.

If current civil rights laws did apply to pornography, they would not simply allow the already permissible elimination of pornographic material that is obscene, but also the elimination of all forms of pornography, even soft-core porn. Under this conception of pornography, the courts would have to view pornography through the lens of the Fourteenth Amendment, with its guarantee of "equal protection" under the law, and not the First Amendment, with its guarantee of "free expression." If this argument were accepted by the courts, if they agreed that even pornography that was not classifiable as obscene was a form of unfair treatment of women, then any woman who felt threatened or denigrated by it could sue the manufacturer of the material for damages.

To this end MacKinnon and Dworkin have introduced legislation in several states, often in the form of local ordinances. Their first successful attempt was in Indianapolis in 1983. Soon after its passage, however, the ordinance was challenged on constitutional grounds. In *American Booksellers v. Hudnutt,* the U.S. Seventh Circuit Court of Appeals struck down the ordinance because it represented the censorship of pornographic and artistic material that is protected by the First Amendment and falls outside the Miller test. Defendants argued that the Miller test is too narrow and allows expressions harmful to women to be protected when they should be censored. In its opinion, however, the court replied that unless clear and present danger can be shown—unless, that is, the pornography in question can be shown to cause immediate danger—censoring it is not permissible. Pornography that is not obscene presents no generally agreed-on clear and present danger. Further, the court argued, if it were to uphold the ordinance, it would encourage laws against all forms of expression that someone might deem discriminatory, such as racist materials, or ethnic slurs or words, or pictures that make fun of handicapped persons. Such words and depictions may discriminate against various groups, but education, not legislation, is the best road to their elimination. Legislating against free speech, even in the name of the public good, will produce much worse harm in the long run. As the Court wrote,[7]

> It ought to be remembered by defendants and all others who would support such a legislative initiative that, in terms of altering sociological patterns, much as alteration may be necessary and desirable, free speech, rather than being the enemy, is a long-tested and worthy ally. To deny free speech in order to engineer social change in the name of accomplishing a greater good for one sector of our society erodes the freedoms of all and, as such, threatens tyranny and injustice for those subjected to the rule of such laws. The First Amendment protections presuppose the evil of such tyranny and prevent a finding by this Court upholding the Ordinance.

On review, the U.S. Supreme Court let this ruling stand. Currently, it is legal to practice government censorship in this country, but only on sexually obscene materials. Even this is too much for the anticensorship view whereas it is indeed too little for those who hold the censorship view and want all forms of hard-core porn eliminated from society. Some, like MacKinnon and Dworkin, want soft-core porn censored as well.

Assumptions

Because government censorship places restrictions on what people may do, we need to examine our general **assumptions** about the conditions under which a government may legitimately impose such restrictions in the form of laws. The question, then, is this: Why should any laws exist?

Exercise 12.2

This is a small group exercise. Your task is to answer the question just posed, Why should any laws exist? Remember that laws are restrictions on our freedom. Why should we willingly agree to such losses of freedom? Why should we willingly relinquish control over some of our behavior to government authority? Think of all the reasons you can in response to these sorts of questions and write them down on a list. To help you think, imagine what things would be like without certain sorts of laws.

Next, consider some examples of laws that a government could not legitimately impose on its citizens. Write them on a list as well. Can you discover a pattern and perhaps state in a general way the sorts of laws that are and are not permitted by the government? Share the results of your discussions with the rest of the class.

One of the foundational works of Western civilization is Plato's *Republic.* Among the many themes included in this dialogue is a discussion of the purpose of governmental authority in the form of its laws. Plato was opposed to democracy because he believed that rule by the masses meant rule by baser, less human desires. Only well-educated people, wise men and women, could govern a state, because only they know what is truly good, what is truly in the interests of all, what will truly make us happy. Such rulers, "philosopher-kings," as Plato called them, had the right to impose laws on others for their own good. The state, in effect, had the right to act as a parent to its citizens, not only protecting them from each other but also governing their private lives—especially their moral lives—always toward the end of making them better people.

In this classic statement of the purpose of government, Plato pleads for the recognition of the state as more than just a group of individuals who are free to pursue their own ends as they desire. Such a society, he claims, leads to selfish and base behavior and will surely collapse under its own moral corruption and incompetence. Instead, the state should be viewed more like a parent. As a father and mother shape the character and lives of their children, the state's job is to shape the character and lives of its citizens, to make them better and therefore happier people. A strong society needs people of strong moral and intellectual character. If they exist, the society that grooms them remains strong. If they do not, the society will collapse in a heap of moral corruption. In the name of building this character, society has the right to act parentally toward its citizens. Censorship would surely exist in such a state. For Plato, it is necessary to eliminate material that appeals to the lower, baser desires of human beings and thus undermines this character.

In a famous essay, John Stuart Mill rejects this view that the law may be used to govern our private lives. Instead, he says there is only one reason for governmental authority in the form of laws, and that is to protect us from each other. In his essay "On Liberty," he says:[8]

> The object of this essay is to assert one very simple principle, as entitled to govern absolutely the dealings of society with the individual in the way of compulsion and control, whether the means used by physical force in the form of legal penalties, or the moral coercion of public opinion. That principle is, that the sole end for which mankind are warranted, either individually or collectively, in interfering with the liberty of action of any of their numbers, is self-protection. That the only purpose for which power can be rightfully exercised over any member of a civilized community, against his will, is to prevent harm to others. His own good, either physical or moral is not a sufficient warrant. He cannot rightfully be compelled to do or forbear because it will be better for him to do so, because it will make him happier, because, in the opinions of others, to do so would be wise, or even right.

These are good reasons for remonstrating with him, or reasoning with him, or persuading him, or entreating him, but not for compelling him, or visiting him with any evil in case he do otherwise. To justify that, the conduct from which it is desired to deter him, must be calculated to produce evil in some one else. The only part of the conduct of any one, for which he is amenable to society, is that which concerns others. In the part which merely concerns himself, his independence is, of right, absolute. Over himself, over his own body and mind, the individual is sovereign.

In addition to being a classic statement of the principle of autonomy, the preceding passage also presents a detailed answer to the question of Exercise 12.1. It says that laws are legitimate only when they are designed to prevent someone's actions from harming *others*. Everyone, except perhaps an anarchist who believes that government laws are never justifiable, thinks that laws created to avoid the sort of public harms we generally call crimes are legitimate uses of government authority. The general principle that states this belief is called the **public harm** principle. It says that laws are legitimate if they serve to prevent actions that are harmful to others. This, for Mill, is the only valid use of government power, to protect us from each other.

He totally rejects other reasons for laws, such as the government's attempt to protect us from ourselves, or to make us better people. He is worried about big government and its ability to interfere with our lives and to dramatically suppress individual freedom. For him, writing in the mid-nineteenth century, the harms that individuals may do to themselves in the exercise of their freedom are considerably less than the harms they are likely to suffer at the hands of an all- too-powerful government. For Mill, the government should never be allowed to decide for individuals what is morally acceptable or otherwise physically or psychologically good for them. Such a parentalistic view, even if well-intentioned, robs us of too much of our freedom. Better that we allow people to make their own mistakes in living their lives as they see fit, than have the government "protect" us from ourselves by deciding how we ought to live.

Most people accept the assumption that laws exist to prevent public harms, but they agree less about what should count as a public harm that is subject to legal restraint. Some want to expand the notion of public harm beyond crimes committed against individuals to include harms to society as well. For some, such harms that might be caused by pornography include *neighborhood decay,* or the negative effects of pornography on the quality of life of a community. The courts have always included this as a type of public harm that they had the power to regulate, so in discussing the public harms of pornography we will include it as well. If it is morally acceptable for the government to censor pornography to avoid public harms, these harms will include both crimes and neighborhood decay. When it comes to pornography, its primary public harms appear to be sex crimes, the degradation of women, and neighborhood decay.

In addition to preventing public harms of the sort just mentioned, others today believe, with Plato, that the power of government should also be used to maintain a decent level of *public morality.* They would include the corruption of this morality as another type of public harm. After all, society is more than a collection of individuals. It is also a system of institutions and shared systems of beliefs, such as political beliefs and moral beliefs. Threats to these can be just as real as physical and psychological threats to individuals. Moral corruption can bring ruin to a society just as surely as crime can. As we have seen, the Supreme Court seems to agree that public harms may include the moral effects of actions on society as a whole. In the 1973 U.S. Supreme Court case of *Paris Adult Theatre 1 v. Slaton*, the Court decided that even consenting adults could be prevented from seeing adult films in a local theater because the films were obscene and thus a threat to public decency. We as well will consider threats to the public morality as a public harm and include it on our list of censorable actions.

In addition to assuming that laws exist to prevent crimes, to protect the quality of life of citizens, and to uphold the public morality, another assumption that is accepted by some is that laws exist to prevent individuals from harming themselves. This is called the **private harm principle.** Among the harms we bring on ourselves are physical harms, psychological harms, and moral harms. According to the private harm principle, the government may legitimately require us to do things to prevent *physical harm* to ourselves, such as wearing motorcycle helmets and seat belts, and refraining from ingesting certain sorts of substances. It may also try to protect us from *psychological harms.* In the case of pornography, psychological harms might include harmful and distorted beliefs and attitudes about women, sex, and marriage. In addition, pornography may lead to moral harms as well, such as a greater willingness to use sex in violation of generally accepted moral norms. Censorship laws are the government's primary means of preventing the psychological and moral harms that we bring on ourselves from viewing pornography.

Generally speaking, those who oppose censorship have a perspective on individual freedom from government interference that is similar to that of Mill. They believe that no censorship of pornography should exist unless pornography can be shown to cause sex crimes. On the other hand, those in favor of greater government censorship often side with Plato on the extent of government authority over the individual, allowing censorship to prevent other sorts of public harms and private harms as well. These assumptions about the legitimate extent of law will have an important role to play in the section on "Moral Reasoning." There we argue for and against the moral acceptability of government censorship laws and present various reasons that such laws should or should not exist. These reasons will be particular instances of the reasons any laws should exist. They will appeal especially to the appropriateness of government censorship as a tool to prevent various sorts of public and private harms.

Points of View

A person may bring many ***points of view*** to the question of censorship. These points of view will influence significantly which arguments and types of evidence are weighed most favorably. For example, if you have been the victim of a sexual assault and the person who committed the assault admitted to the influence that pornography had on his action, you will probably have little sympathy for those who worry that government censorship is a threat to freedom of expression. Mothers and fathers with young children who are home alone for long periods of time also may be more sympathetic to government censorship, as they worry about what their children view on television or see on their home computers in their absence. Older people surfing the Internet may well wonder whatever became of moral decency and support greater censorship as well.

On the other hand, if you are an artist whose grant application was rejected by the National Endowment for the Arts because it was judged "indecent," you might worry more about freedom of expression than censoring pornography. Porn stars might wonder why all the fuss exists about something they see as just a business. Shy young men or women who are curious about sex may also resent censorship, as it may rob them of a safe way to satisfy their curiosity. Students who have not been exposed to much hard-core pornography may also wonder what the problem is and be resistant to the censorship of what their experience has told them is rather harmless material. Men and women who work with ideas, such as academicians and librarians, would be little inclined to favor censorship of any sort, even when the expressions in question are the often indecent and degrading ideas found in some of today's pornographic material. They may believe instead that a democracy should embrace a free and open exchange of ideas. Education, not coercion, should distinguish truth and art from trash.

Before approaching the arguments of the next section, examine your current beliefs on the moral acceptability of censorship and acknowledge the life experiences that may have produced it. Whatever your point of view happens to be, in addition to being aware of it, try to resist its power to turn you from a fair hearing of all the evidence before you decide which possible solution has the strongest case.

Moral Reasoning

The problem of Chapter 12 is this: Under what conditions, if any, is it morally acceptable for the government to censor pornography for consenting adults? This is a **conflict of rules** problem, which also may be phrased as a conflict of rights. On the one hand, there is the *right to free expression,* the right to create and view various sorts of depictions and descriptions of sexual behavior. This is part of a broader right that includes the right to linguistic, literary, artistic, political, and religious forms of expression. It is a right that is protected by the First Amendment and has its moral roots in the principle of autonomy—the right of each person to do what he or she chooses, as long as these actions harm no one else.

In conflict with the right to free expression is the right of individuals and society as a whole to be free from the harms of pornography. This right follows from the general moral principle of beneficence, which requires us to do good and avoid evil. When the protection comes from the government, it finds its legal expression in the current obscenity laws and the power of government to practice censorship. So the problem of Chapter 12 represents a conflict between individual freedom of expression and our right to have the government protect the individual and society from the harms of such expressions. The case for government censorship will focus on preventing harms; the case against censorship will focus on protecting individual freedom from the threat to it that government censorship represents.

The Case against Censorship

We will begin by defending the **anticensorship view.** Its claim is that all forms of government censorship are immoral. Such censorship is immoral because it violates the moral principles of beneficence, justice, and autonomy. The principle of *autonomy* allows consenting adults the right to free expression. As Mill says,

> This is . . . the appropriate region of human liberty. It comprises, first, the inward domain of consciousness; demanding liberty of conscience, in the most comprehensive sense; liberty of thought and feeling; absolute freedom of opinion and sentiment on all subjects, practical or speculative, scientific, moral, or theological. . . . [Human liberty also] requires liberty of tastes and pursuits; of framing the plan of our life to suit our own character; of doing as we like, subject to such consequences as may follow; without impediment from our fellow creatures, so long as what we do does not harm them, even though they should think our conduct foolish, perverse, or wrong. . . . No society in which these liberties are not, on the whole, respected, is free, whatever may be its form of government; and none is completely free in which they do not exist absolute and unqualified.[9]

At present, this category of free expression includes the right of consenting adults to create, to display, to sell, and to view pornographic material of all sorts. This includes both hard-core pornography, some of which is currently classified as sexual obscenity and prohibited by the law, and soft-core pornography, which currently is protected from government censorship by the First Amendment. So, following Mill's plea for the priority of individual freedom over government control, we may write this as the first premise:

1. Consenting adults have the right to free expression. (A)

The principle of autonomy, of course, does not permit actions that harm others. Anticensorship proponents claim that far from being harmful, however, pornography is actually beneficial to many. It appears to have an *educational* benefit for some who view it, especially those who are curious about sex but unwilling or unable to learn from firsthand experience. In addition, it appears to have a *cathartic* effect on people who might otherwise be tempted to commit sex crimes to satisfy their passions. Studies conducted in Denmark and Germany, for example, have shown fewer instances of rape since pornography became widely available. Far from inciting them to rape, many men who view pornographic material seem to have less of a need to act on their sexual desires. In some cases, viewing pornography even made people more *tolerant* of the opinions and lifestyles of others. It also made couples much more open and willing to talk about sex and sexual matters, producing a *therapeutic* effect which benefited their sex lives and their relationships in general. In addition, people *enjoy* viewing pornography. Women as well as men are huge consumers of pornography. In fact, half the rented porn videos are rented by women or couples.

That pornography is not harmful and actually has beneficial effects on various individuals was one of the findings of the President's Commission on Obscenity and Pornography, established by Congress in 1967. In its final report (1970) the Commission recommended the repeal of all laws prohibiting consenting adults from creating, displaying, selling, and viewing pornography. To censor pornography is to eliminate a source of pleasure, a source of catharsis, a source of therapy, and a source of education for many. Eliminating these goods through government censorship clearly violates the principle of beneficence.

2. Viewing pornography produces many benefits to individuals. (B)

In contrast to the benefits of pornography stand the harms of censorship. Even if pornography produces some harm, it is far less than the harms of censorship. Government censorship is harmful to the *arts,* for example. It even prevented people from reading Joyce's *Ulysses* and Lawrence's *Lady Chatterley's Lover* in the past. It will prevent consenting adults from free and open access to the Internet in the future. The necessarily subjective judgments about which sorts of depictions and descriptions are obscene and which are not make censorship an inherently dangerous mechanism for eliminating pornography. Along with the trash, too much of what is good is also subject to its power.

For example, materials on sex education, or discussions of the harms of rape, or works of art depicting nude bodies, and so on, may very well be subject to censorship as well. Shakespeare would certainly be in trouble with the censors, as would the Bible and other religious works. Artists, novelists, and poets would feel that their creative spirits were in chains, and they would wonder constantly whether their inspirations would be subject to legal challenge. The brush that sweeps away the sex associated with pornography is broad enough to sweep away valuable discussions and depictions of sexual matters as well as many universally admired works of art and literature and many widely accepted and admired forms of film and television entertainment.

Censorship is also harmful to *women.* Some feminists such as Andrea Dworkin and Catherine MacKinnon want to ban all forms of pornography—even soft-core porn. However, even though most feminists are strongly opposed to pornography as such, they are even more opposed to censorship. Censorship is harmful to women, they argue, because censorship itself has been the enemy of women's progress in the past and it will be their enemy in the future if given a chance. Women's progress has been progress against the male-dominated status quo, a status quo often defended by a male-dominated legal system. To use that system to stifle free expression is to threaten the recent freedoms gained by women over their own lives. It was not that long ago that Margaret Sanger, the founder of the modern-day birth control movement, was subject to prosecution under the Comstock obscenity laws of the 1870s for sending birth control information through the mails. Feminists especially fear becoming allies with right-wing politicians who campaign strongly in favor of expanded censorship because such "allies" have often been foes of women's rights in the past.

> The history of anti-porn campaigns in this country is partly a history of campaigns against reproductive choice and changing roles for men and women. . . . Recently the New Right campaign has focused on sex education in public schools. Antiporn activists on the right consider feminism and homosexuality [which they link] to be threats to the traditional family. . . . [Such threats] distract us from the harder, less popular work of reforming sexual stereotypes and roles, and addressing actual instead of metaphorical instruments of violence. The promise of the antiporn

movement is a world in which almost no one can buy pornography but almost anyone can buy a gun.[10]

Censorship also harms what is an essential part of any free society, the *free exchange of ideas*. Only by an open exchange of opinions, even opinions that some may believe to be foolish or nasty, can the truth be discovered. Censoring the expression of thought and opinion are among the most dangerous effects of censorship. As Mill says,

> The peculiar evil of silencing the expression of an opinion is, that it is robbing the human race; posterity as well as the existing generation, those who dissent from the opinion, still more than those who hold it. If the opinion is right, they are deprived of the opportunity of exchanging error for truth: if wrong, they lose, what is almost as great a benefit, the clearer perception and livelier impression of truth, produced by its collision with error. . . . If the cultivation of the understanding consists in one thing more than in another, it is surely in learning the grounds of one's own opinions. . . . He who knows only his own side of the case knows little of that. His reasons may be good, and no one may have been able to refute them. But if he is equally unable to refute the reasons on the opposite side; if he does not so much as know what they are, he has no ground for preferring either opinion.[11]

Associations of librarians are against censorship for this very reason. Libraries have long been the repository of ideas. In this electronic age, libraries may be more like "information centers" than repositories of books, but their function remains the same—to provide free and open access to ideas and information to all. Librarians continue to insist that the best way to reduce exposure to pornographic materials is through education and, in the case of children, parental guidance. Banning books, newspapers, and films and restricting what may appear in the electronic media is anathema to the ideals for which such organizations stand, ideals on which this free and open democracy of ours stands firmly planted.

In addition, the American Civil Liberties Union has often pointed to the harms of censorship. In a recent statement warning against the anti-pornography feminist movement it says:[12]

> History teaches that censorship is a dangerous weapon in the hands of government. Inevitably, it is used against those who want to change society, be they feminists, civil rights demonstrators or gay liberationists. Obscenity laws, especially, have been used to supress information and art dealing with female sexuality and reproduction. Thus, the growing influence of anti-pornography feminism threatens to undermine long-established principles of free speech.

So, because government censorship will eliminate valuable works of art along with the pornography it prohibits, because censorship is not truly in the interests of women, and because it runs contrary to the truly free exchange of ideas required for a liberal democracy, we may write this:

3. Government censorship is harmful. (B)

In addition to being harmful, government censorship is ineffective. Even though censorship laws that supposedly prevent sexual obscenity are currently in place, more and more such material is produced by the porn industry every year.

We are awash in pornography, despite existing censorship laws. On the Internet, censorship is particularly ineffective. Part of the reason is that blocking software is not precise enough to eliminate only sexual obscenity. It misses some obscene works and identifies works for elimination that do not fit the Miller standard. In addition, using the Miller test to define what is obscene in the first place is nearly impossible. If one of the criteria for judging which material this will include is that it is an affront to community standards, what community are we to refer to as we look for those standards? If a pornographic work is taken off the Internet because of an ordinance in Kansas City, it also disappears in San Francisco. Yet these two communities may have very different ideas about what sort of pornography is obscene. The "virtual communities" of the Internet are not geographical but are based on common interests. Members of such virtual communities may be located geographically all over the world. In such communities, the current Miller "community standards" concept has little meaning.

Moreover, much of the material on the Internet comes from foreign sources. If the Internet were to be purged of all its current pornographic Web sites that are created in the United States, there would simply be a larger market for foreign-based pornographic Web sites. In addition to the problems of policing the Internet, the technology now exists for homemade porn videos to be transmitted electronically from computer to computer, from one television set to another. Which strategy of censorship will be able to eliminate such traffic? A government would have to be enormously and frighteningly intrusive to prevent the transmission of homemade pornography. The existence of censorship laws that cannot be enforced, moreover, will simply lead to a disrespect for the law. This disrespect is ultimately more harmful for society than no law at all. Imagine how much respect for the law would diminish if searching the Internet at the local library became a crime. So the fourth premise states this:

4. Government censorship is ineffective. (B)

This is the evidence for the case *against* censorship. Later, replies to objections will be added to this current list of four premises. These objections will be found in the premises used to support the case *for* censorship. As these arguments defend opposing claims, the reasons for one can be expected to be objections to the other.

The Case for Censorship

The case for **censorship** focuses especially on the harms caused by pornography. Although it is true, according to the principle of autonomy, that people have the right to do what they want to, this does not mean that they are free to perform actions that harm others. The main contention of those who favor government censorship is that pornography does harm others. It is true that some harms are caused to those who participate in the production and distribution of pornography, but the sorts of harms most important for the censorship argument are harms caused by people who view pornography. Significant exposure, especially to hard-core pornography, causes viewers to harm others. It causes *public harms*. The point of the first premise is that the viewing of pornography by consenting adults leads to the worse sorts of public harms, *sex crimes*. Sex crimes include such acts as rape and child sexual assaults, as well as other forms of antisocial behavior, such as forcing people to perform degrading and humiliating acts.

If viewing pornography can be shown to cause such harms, then the case for censorship becomes very strong indeed. According to the *public harm principle,* an assumption accepted even by the staunchest defender of individual freedom, the government may always act to prevent us from harming each other. Such actions, when made illegal by the government, are called crimes. If viewing pornography can be shown to lead to criminal behavior, the case for censoring at least those forms of it that produce such behavior is won. So it is important to examine in some detail the evidence for this first premise in the case for censorship.

The evidence most often referred to for support is contained in the Meese Commission Report (1986). The earlier presidential commission (1970), the President's Commission on Obscenity and Pornography, had found no evidence to support such a claim. However, the Meese Commission, arguing that pornography had gotten much worse since 1970, did find that viewing pornography produced a criminal reaction in many people. Many of the studies it referred to in its report were studies performed on men whose physiological and psychological reactions were measured as they watched pornographic depictions of various sorts. The Commission presented its findings for each category of pornography in turn. To them, the case for claiming that *sexually violent material* caused sex crimes was the clearest and strongest.[13]

> When clinical and experimental research has focused primarily on sexually violent material, the conclusions have been virtually unanimous. In both clinical and experimental settings, exposure to sexually violent materials has indicated an increase in the likelihood of aggression. More specifically, the research . . . shows a causal relationship between exposure to material of this type and aggressive behavior towards women.

According to the Commission,

> it would be strange indeed if graphic representations of a form of behavior, especially in a form that almost exclusively portrays such behavior as desirable, did not have at least some effects on patterns of behavior.

As might be expected, pornographic displays of sexual violence produce behavioral changes by first changing the attitudes of its viewers. Even those who do not act on these psychological changes experience them. These changes include acceptance of the "rape myth," found in much sexually violent pornography. The rape myth involves a man making some sort of sexual advance to a woman, being rejected, and then raping the woman. Then the woman becomes aroused and is portrayed as liking the forced sexual activity and wanting even more. Viewing this lie over and over again in pornographic depictions causes men to believe it, and they begin to perceive victims of rape as partly responsible for the act and as suffering little damage from being raped. Because of this, many men in these studies came to view the rapist as deserving little punishment for his actions.

In addition to their findings about sexually violent material, the Commission found that even viewing *nonviolent degrading* materials produces harm.

> With respect to material of this variety, our conclusions are substantially similar to those with respect to sexually violent material. . . . [T]he evidence, scientific and otherwise, is more tentative but supports the conclusion that the material we describe as degrading bears some causal relationship to the attitudinal changes we have previously identified. . . . [T]he evidence supports the conclusion that substantial exposure to material of this type will increase acceptance of the proposition that women like to be forced into sexual practices, and, once again, that the woman who says "no" really means "yes". We believe that we are justified in drawing the following conclusions: Over a large enough sample of population that believes that many women like to be raped, that believes that sexual violence or sexual coercion is often desired and appropriate, and that believes that sex offenders are less responsible for their acts, will commit more acts of sexual violence or sexual coercion than would a population holding these beliefs to a lesser extent.

If viewing sexually violent and nonviolent degrading material produces harms, then these two categories, which we have earlier combined under the general heading of "hard-core" pornography, represent clear and present dangers to the public and do not deserve the protection of the First Amendment. Instead, they deserve to be censored. Indeed, the immediate reaction of the government to the Meese Commission Report was to step up the enforcement of its obscenity laws, at least for a few years.

Confirming the studies used by the Meese Commission, several other studies have also found a causal relationship between viewing hard-core pornography and attitudinal changes of the sort referred to by the Commission.[14] In addition, evidence gained from interviewing convicted criminals also lends support to the claim that pornography incites people to sexual violence. Gary Bishop, a man convicted of sexually abusing and then murdering five boys, said that

> pornography was a determining factor in my downfall. Somehow I became sexually attracted to young boys and I would fantasize about them naked. Certain bookstores offered sex education photographs or art books which occasionally contained pictures of nude boys. I purchased such books and used them to enhance my masturbatory fantasies. But it wasn't enough. I desired more sexually arousing pictures so I enticed boys to let me take pictures of them naked. From adult magazines, I located companies specializing in kiddie porn. Such material would temporarily satisfy my cravings, but soon I would need pictures more explicit and revealing. . . . Finding and procuring such sexually arousing materials became an obsession. For me, seeing pornography was like lighting a fire on a stick of dynamite. I became stimulated and had to gratify my urges or explode.[15]

Ted Bundy was a serial killer responsible for the sexual assault and death of at least twenty-eight young woman. In a prison interview one day before his execution he also blamed pornography for his crimes and warned of its pernicious and addictive properties.

> I think people need to recognize that that those of us who have been influenced by . . . pornographic violence are not some kind of inherent monsters. We are

your sons and we are your husbands. . . . Any pornography can reach out and snatch a kid out of any house today. . . . I've lived in prison a long time . . . and I've met a lot of men who were motivated to commit violence just like me. And without exception every one of them was deeply involved in pornography—deeply influenced by an addiction. There is no question about it. The FBI's own study shows that the most common interest among serial killers is pornography.[16]

With this evidence to support it, we may write the first premise:

1.' Pornography causes sex crimes. (B)

In addition to the harms of sex crimes, pornography also causes public harms of other sorts. Chief among these is the *degradation* of women. Scenes that show women having sex with animals, or in sadomasochistic poses, or in simulated scenes of being gang-raped or forced into oral or anal sex, or in other poses of sexual subordination and coercion—and all the while liking it—are humiliating and degrading to all women. Such degradation may lead to the sorts of public harms referred to by the first premise. These include especially the negative attitudinal changes caused in men who view such degradation, changes that may very well lead to harmful behavioral changes as well.

Even if such pornography did not lead to sex crimes, however, degrading pornography harms women in other ways. This sort of pornography pictures women as existing only as objects for the satisfaction of the sexual desires of others. It treats them merely as things, and thus violates that part of the principle of justice that requires us to respect persons, to refrain from treating them merely as a means to the good of another. It discriminates against women unfairly, treating them as second-class citizens in much the same way racism treats people as second-class citizens. For some, even soft-core pornography degrades women. Although in soft-core pornography women are portrayed as consenting to sex, they are still seen merely as sex objects, not as full persons equal in value to their male counterparts. Not only does pornography lead to violence against women, then, but it also is a lie about women, a sexist lie, a lie, moreover, that is believed by many men.[17]

> Pornography, by its very nature, requires that women be subordinate to men and mere instruments for the fulfillment of male fantasies. To accomplish this, pornography must lie. Pornography lies when it says that our sexual life is or ought to be subordinate to the service of men, that our pleasure consists in pleasing men and not ourselves, that we are depraved, that we are fit subjects for rape, bondage, torture, and murder. Pornography lies explicitly about women's sexuality, and through such lies fosters more lies about our humanity, our dignity, and our personhood.

Because such degrading pornography leads to harms and to disrespecting women, we write:

2.' Pornography degrades women. (B,J)

A third type of public harm is *neighborhood decay.* There are some 15,000 porn shops in this country, many thousands of video stores that carry pornographic material, adult movie theaters, strip joints, and other establishments that exist primarily for display and sale of pornographic material. Because they display pornographic material and attract people of questionable character, the quality of life in residential and commercial areas that contain them can suffer irreparable damage. Business and real estate properties decrease in value, resultant tax losses affect the quality of schools and the quality of recreational facilities and municipal services that depend on tax revenues for their support. Wealthy and middle-class residents move to other areas, and the neighborhood's downward spiral becomes inevitable.

   3.' Pornography causes neighborhood decay. (B)

Other public harms caused by pornography are *moral harms.* Moral harms that pornography may cause to individuals will be discussed under premise (5)', concerned with private harms. In addition to corrupting the morals of individuals, however, pornography also corrupts the morals of society. A democracy is more than just a group of individuals freely pursuing their own goals as they desire. Instead, in a democracy people also live according to shared sets of beliefs. These include political ideals, economic assumptions, and shared moral beliefs. If enough people cease to share such beliefs, society as a coherent group will cease to exist. In its place will be a collection of individuals who are governed by their baser instincts. Such a state will surely not flourish.

For its very survival, then, the government must maintain a public morality through its laws. It must attempt to shape the moral character of its citizens so that they will, in turn, influence the level of decency in a society. A strong society needs people of strong moral and intellectual character. If they exist, the society that grooms them will remain strong. If they do not, the society will collapse in a heap of moral corruption. In the matter of pornography, and in the name of building this character, society has the right to enforce a level of decent behavior through censorship.

The government may not be able to create virtuous people. For it to make the attempt may not even be desirable. Churches and parents may do the job better. However, it is surely permissible for the state to prevent the decay of virtue through its laws. It is surely acceptable for the state to avoid its own demise by preventing the widespread existence of the sort of pornography that exists today. This material appeals only to the lower, baser desires of human beings, and drags our noble side down into the muck and mire of sexual perversions. In doing so it breaks the moral fibers that hold us together, those tender threads of civilization that are threatened less by the enemy without and more by the enemy within.

Pornography is the enemy within. Viewing it leads to distorted views about sex, love, and marriage, causing people to think that nonmarital sex, homosexual sex, sadomasochistic sex, and divorce are perfectly acceptable. It drags the arts down to the lowest level as well, equating, for example, nude dancing and even live sex on the stage with artistic expression. Perhaps most dangerously, it leads to the view that such base behavior is no better or worse than other forms of behavior, just different. It leads to the view that there is to be no more shame among us about sexual matters. It leads to the view that anything goes. Pornography is a cancerous growth among us, a growth that causes not only crime, not only the degradation of women, not only neighborhood decay, but also the loss of a moral sense, an idea of what is virtuous and what is not, and thus it leads to the moral corruption of society. In the past we knew this better than we do now. Before the physical and psychological harms of pornography were thrust to the forefront of concern, the whole point of censorship was to uphold a shared sense of right and wrong, to maintain a decent, a civilized society. A staunch defender of censorship, Irving Kristol, says:

> Today democracy is seen as . . . nothing but a set of rules and procedures. Thus, the political system can be reduced to its mechanical arrangements. There is, however, an older idea of democracy, one fairly common until about the beginning of [the last] century, for which the conception of the quality of public life is absolutely crucial. The idea starts from the proposition that democracy is a form of self-government, and that you are entitled to it only if that "self" is worthy of governing. Because the desirability of self-government depends on the character of the people who govern, the older idea of government was very solicitous to the condition of this character. The older democracy had no problem in principle with pornography and obscenity; it censored them; it was not about to let people corrupt themselves.[18]

4.' Pornography causes harm to the public morality. (B)

Besides causing public harms, pornography also causes *private harms*. These harms especially include the *psychological* harms that viewing heavy doses of pornography can cause individuals. These harms were discussed in the "Facts" section and include forming distorted beliefs about the opposite sex and acquiring a false image of the nature of sexuality. Men who view hard-core pornography are more willing to be more aggressive, less thoughtful and caring, and less concerned with a woman as a person. They may come to see women merely as objects for their sexual satisfaction. Such beliefs produce a warped character and make it difficult for a man to have a full, rich relationship with a woman.

Other private harms are *moral* harms. People who regularly view pornographic material are less willing to believe that sex belongs only in marriage, for example, or that various sorts of sex, such as homosexual sex and sadomasochistic sex, are perversions. Further, these beliefs are translated into action, into how such men conduct their own sexual behaviors, which often means a decrease in interest in conforming to the moral rules of the community, especially in sexual matters.

5.' Pornography causes private harms. (B)

So far the argument for the moral acceptability of censorship has really been an argument for the immorality of pornography. At this point, an additional premise must be added to make it an argument for the moral acceptability of censorship. This premise says,

6.' Government censorship is the most effective way to eliminate pornography. (B)

The evidence for the truth of this premise will be discussed as we consider how each side replies to objections.

Replies to Objections

The two arguments presented so far defend opposing claims; therefore, the reasons that support one position will be objections to the other. We will begin with the *case against censorship* and its attempt to reply to the objections found in premises (1)' through (6)'.

The *first objection*, stated in premise (1)', says that viewing heavy doses of especially hard-core pornography causes people to commit sex crimes. If this is so, the freedom to view pornography may be suppressed by the government in order to avoid such harms. After all, the principle of autonomy, which lies at the root of premise (1)', allows us to do what we want to only *as long as our actions harm no one else.* If the creation, display, sale, and viewing of pornography increase the rate of rapes and other sexual assaults, even consenting adults may be prevented from viewing it. In short, the first objection says that government censorship is morally acceptable because pornography causes sex crimes.

The anticensorship view replies to this first objection by denying that there is any good evidence to show a causal relationship between pornography and sex crimes. The evidence of the Meese Commission Report and other studies have shown only that there is a correlation between pornography and sex crimes among a small part of the population. That is, they have shown only that viewing pornography is often associated with or correlated with sex crimes. They have shown, for example, that men who rape women quite often also view pornography. To say that these two actions go hand in hand, however, is not to show that one causes the other. Alcohol is just as commonly associated with sex crimes, for example. That is, people who rape also usually drink alcohol before setting out to do so. Does that mean that drinking alcohol causes sex crimes?

To show that two events are causally related is to show that if one of them (the cause) is present, the other (the effect) will surely follow. To show this requires not only demonstrating that these events are regularly associated, but also that no other events are likely to be causes. If viewing pornographic material is the cause of sex crimes and not just something that accompanies such acts, then all of those who participated in studies of the effects of pornography should have become rapists or other sorts of sexual offenders. They did not. The anticensorship view denies that pornography has been shown to cause sex crimes. Conceding that an association between these events may have been established, it claims that other possible causes of sex crimes have not been ruled out. In fact, many types of events other than viewing pornography seem much more likely to be the true causes of sex crimes.

For example, most sex crimes are committed by men who themselves have been victims of child sexual abuse. In addition, these men have often come from backgrounds of poverty and poor education. A much more reasonable assumption is that poverty, ignorance, and child sexual abuse produce people who are prone to commit sex crimes *and* view pornography, than to assume that pornography is the culprit. In other words, some underlying causes produce both the desire for viewing pornography and for sexually assaulting others. That is why pornography and sex crimes are regularly associated, because they both spring from the same personality, not because they are causally related themselves. On this account of things, people who view pornography will then commit sex crimes only if they have this underlying personality to begin with. Pornography does not cause sex crimes. As alcohol may give courage to sexual offenders, pornography may give them specific ideas of what sorts of illegal sexual acts to commit. But unless a person already has the sort of personality that incites them to sex crimes—a personality caused by such factors as childhood sexual abuse, poverty, and ignorance—pornography alone will not lead to such actions.

Even the Meese Commission Report admits that a causal relationship has not been established by the empirical evidence alone. The evidence only shows that people who watch sexually violent material for a long enough period of time will have certain attitudinal changes. They have more aggressive feelings about women, for example. Even though there is no evidence that they will act on these psychological changes, the Commission thought it reasonable to assume that some of them would. This assumption, however, goes beyond the facts, as the Report admits. In fact, if images of sexual violence were sufficient in themselves to cause sex crimes, the rate of rapes and other violent crimes should have sky-rocketed in this country as more and more people acquired access to these images. However, violent crime has actually dropped dramatically in the past decade, even as the number of television sets, VCRs, and computers with Internet access—all places where sexually violent material may be viewed—has grown dramatically. A particular sort of freedom should not be removed from society until and unless good evidence indicates that exercising it leads to public harms. Because pornography has not been linked causally to sex crimes, government censorship is not justifiable. So we add to the argument against censorship:

    5. Pornography does not cause sex crimes. (B)

The *second objection*, found in premise (2)', says that pornography degrades women. To this charge the anticensorship view has two responses. First, even if some forms of pornography do degrade women, this in itself is no reason for the law to curb First Amendment rights. If every time someone made disparaging or degrading remarks about a group of people the government's response was to put that person in jail, there would certainly be many overcrowded jails. This is not to say that negative depictions or descriptions of people because of their race, ethnicity, or gender are commendable. They should be resisted and protested at every turn. However, the battle should be waged through education and free speech, not through the denial of free expression.

Next, proponents of the anticensorship view may claim that pornography does not degrade women. It is not the sex found in pornography that degrades women, nor is it the objectification of women that is found in most pornography that is degrading. Many women, in fact, enjoy pornography as a type of sexual fantasy, a type of entertainment. Instead, it is sexism that degrades women, the attitude that women are inferior to men, and thus that they may be treated as unequals. It is this attitude of society that must be combated, not pornography. Just as describing a male as a sex object does not make him one, so the act of describing women as sex objects does not produce the corresponding reality either. True, some forms of pornography, perhaps most of it, express this sexist attitude, but they do not create it. Because pornography is often sexist, its lies should be resisted through education. The real enemy, however, is the more general sexist attitudes of society that affect women in the workplace, in the family setting, and in political and religious life. It is sexism in action that degrades women, not its expression in pornographic works.

6. Sexism, not pornography, degrades women. (B)

The *third objection,* found in premise (3)', is that pornography causes neighborhood decay. To this the anticensorship advocate answers quickly that such public harms may be removed by perfectly acceptable laws against the display and sale of pornography. Through selective zoning restrictions, for example, pornographic establishments may be forced to locate away from residential and commercial areas. Censorship is not necessary to protect the quality of life of a community, only relocation.

7. Neighborhood decay may be avoided through zoning laws. (B)

The *fourth objection* says that pornography corrupts the public morality. To this objection the replies are many. First, we may ask, "Whose morality"? It appears very doubtful that one set of moral beliefs, especially beliefs about sexual matters, is widely embraced by society. Is the Christian Right's notion of morality, for example, accepted by the majority of the "public"? Does anyone who thinks differently from this set of beliefs have a wrong idea of morality, or just a different one? This reply, in effect, says that there is no public morality to corrupt, just different moral visions that are often incompatible.

Even if society should have a shared set of fundamental moral beliefs around the issues of sexuality and pornography, even if such beliefs ought to maintain a certain level of public decency, these beliefs and the values they uphold should not be enforced by the law, but should be acquired through education and training. Boys and girls, men and women, families and communities should learn how to treat each other with respect through their families and religious institutions. It is there and in other places within society that values ought to be nourished; it is there that people should learn about the importance of character and integrity, especially in matters relating to marriage and equality between the sexes. Such values should not be enforced by law, but by education. It is not the job of the law to make us good people. That responsibility lies with our families, our friends, our religions, and our schools, and most of all with ourselves. We should strive to develop noble moral characters, but we should not be imprisoned because we fail to reach our goal. For a democratic government to impose a certain set of values on people is for the majority to force everyone to live according to its idea of what is best. Mill, for one, would shudder at such a loss of freedom, the freedom to determine for himself what is the best way to live his life. Because this premise states a matter of freedom, an "A" is placed after premise (8).

8. Public morality should be upheld by education, not legislation. (A)

As to *objection five,* that pornography causes private harms, the anticensorship advocate has this to say. Even if viewing pornography causes some negative attitudinal changes in some people, and even if it leads some people to have less than exemplary moral lives, and even if these two types of private harms outweigh the benefits of pornography pointed out in premise (2), preventing such harms is not a matter for the law. The answer is education and persuasion, not censorship. The government may provide such education and persuasion, as may our friends and family, and our schools and religious educators. To use the coercive power of the law to protect us from ourselves, however, is to give to the law the right to decide how we should live our lives. Consenting adults are not children and the law is not a parent. Part of the price of freedom is that people must be allowed to live their lives as they see fit, even if the majority of us do not agree with their decisions. To require them to live as the government sees fit, as the majority of citizens sees fit—even if the government is right—is to threaten the very core of freedom that we all cherish so dearly.

  9. Private harms should be avoided by education, not legislation. (A)

Finally, the *sixth objection* claims that government censorship is the most effective way to eliminate the growing harms of pornography. This is a direct denial of the truth of premise (4), which claims that government censorship is ineffective. The reasons for (4) will not be repeated here, and the sixth objection will simply be ignored until we revisit it in the "Evaluation" section. Instead, the conclusion of the argument against censorship may now be stated:

Therefore, 10. Government censorship is immoral.

  It is now time to turn to the objections that must be answered by *the case for censorship*. These objections are found in premises (1) through (3).

  The *first objection,* found in premise (1), is that censorship robs us of our autonomy. Those who argue for the moral acceptability of censorship have an easy answer to this objection. They simply point to the harms of pornography and remind us that there is no freedom to harm others.

  7.' There is no right to free expression that harms others. (A)

The *second objection* is that pornography is beneficial in many ways, so to censor it would violate the principle of beneficence. However, the harms of the contemporary $10 billion a year pornography industry far outweigh its benefits. Perhaps some soft-core pornography may be beneficial to some, but the sexual violence and degradation of women found in hard-core pornography, material that leads to numerous sorts of public harms, ought to be eliminated if the principle of beneficence is truly to be followed. The benefits of pornography are tiny by comparison to its harms and may be preserved in the soft-core material that was never intended for government censorship. Truly doing good means eliminating most forms of hard-core pornography, not embracing it.

  8.' Hard-core pornography is not beneficial. (B)

Finally, the *third objection* states that censorship itself is harmful—more harmful than any of the so-called harmful effects of pornography. It harms the arts, it harms women's rights, and it stifles the free flow of ideas. According to those who defend government censorship, however, the harms of censorship experienced by women in the past are a thing of the past. Censoring pornography is not the same as censoring sex education and family planning. Also, the search for the truth will not be harmed by government censorship of pornography, as pornographic materials have very little to do with the truth. The real problem comes from the potential for censorship to eliminate works of art along with the trash of pornography. This is a very real threat and may even be an inevitable by-product of censorship.

However, censorship may also enhance the arts. Without censorship to eliminate the trash from art, what passes for art often is trash. Without censorship, the valuable art will be lost and replaced with pornography. This can happen because people who know no better, people who are driven by their baser desires, will pay for pornographic entertainment. Where the money is, there the effort to entertain will be found. Censorship will give us more freedom rather than less. Currently a relatively few people in the media industries shape the tastes of the masses by producing whatever panders to their lowest desires for sex and violence. Sex and violence flood the media in a sea of trash. If this material did not exist, there would be more money and more room for true art, for inspiring works that lift our spirits and form our character on a higher plane. According to one lover of the arts and critic of the leniency found in today's courts,

> Censorship undertaken in the name of the public necessity to maintain the distinction between the non-obscene and the obscene, has the secondary effect of lending some support to the distinction between art and trash. At a minimum it requires a judgment of what is worthy of being enjoyed and what is unworthy, and this has the effect of at least supporting the idea that there is a distinction to be made and that the distinction is important. Our law as announced by the judges of our highest court now denies this . . . [and] has resigned in favor of the free mass market . . . because it attaches no significance to decisions the market will make. The popularization of the arts will not lead to their degradation because [according to the courts] there is no such thing as degradation. . . . What remains at large, unanswered, is whether "sophisticated critical judgment" can preserve artistic tastes . . . or whether there will be any sophisticated critical judgment. To ask this is to wonder whether the public taste . . . can be educated, and educated with no assistance from the law.[19]

Because censorship does not harm women, does not stifle the search for truth, and does not harm the arts, we may write this:

9.' Government censorship is not harmful. (B)

Finally, we may conclude:

Therefore, 10.' Government censorship is morally acceptable.

Evaluation

The arguments for and against censorship will be evaluated in this section so that a *reasoned judgment* may be formed as to which is the more cogent. The moral problem of this chapter is this:

Under what conditions, if any, is it morally acceptable for the government to censor pornography for consenting adults?

Those in favor of government censorship have argued that hard-core porn, materials that are sexually violent and/or degrading to women, ought to be censored. They are harmful and morally degrading and ought to be banished from society. If this possible solution is the correct one, and if the courts come to agree with it, then we will have a great deal more government censorship of pornography in the future than currently exists. Pornography is big business; it sells. It is growing rapidly year after year, both in quantity and in intensity. It saturates our society, panders to what is worst in us, and drags down the quality of our lives. If nothing is done to stem its tide, pretty soon anything will be allowed on television, or on the Internet, or in videos and nightclubs. Only the law has the power to rid society of pornography and its harmful effects, so the law should broaden its control over the porn industry. If increased censorship means giving up some of our freedom, so be it. We have already given up much of our freedom by allowing those who produce and distribute pornography to dictate the "artistic" tastes of society.

Those opposed to government censorship, on the other hand, have argued that the government should censor only materials that present a danger to the public. Because they believe there is little evidence of such dangers from viewing even hard-core pornography, there will indeed be little if any censorship in the future if the courts follow their lead. Even much of the material currently considered obscene and subject to censorship under existing laws would escape legal censorship. Some of it may be filth, but people who wish to seek it out have a right to see it. Those who choose not to view it may simply avoid pornography. A much greater threat to the quality of life would be to have a government so powerful that it can dictate what we read or view, and can determine what type and level of morality we must conform to, than to have pornography available to consenting adults. More education and persuasion is called for, perhaps, but not more censorship.

Ethical Theory

Before examining the strengths and weaknesses of these arguments we should refer to our ethical theory for guidance. The moral problem of Chapter 12 is a **conflict of rules** problem. On the one hand, there is the rule that says "people ought to be able to express themselves as they want to, as long as doing so harms no one else." This is a specific instance of the general moral principle of autonomy and may be phrased as the *right to free expression.* This right includes not only linguistic expression but also literary, artistic, political, and religious expression, as well as the right of others to hear and view such expressions. This is the moral right that is given legal standing by the First Amendment.

In conflict with the right to free expression is the rule that says "prevent the harms of pornography." This is a specific instance of the general moral principle of beneficence, which requires us to do good and avoid evil. It may be phrased as the right of individuals and society as a whole to be protected from the harms of pornography. When the protection comes from the government, this right to protection may be thought of as the corresponding duty of the government to provide it. This duty finds its legal expression in the current obscenity laws and the power of government to practice censorship in other ways as well.

Because protecting citizens from the harms of pornography may require the government to deny some instances of free expression, the right to free expression comes into conflict with the government's duty to protect us. So the problem of Chapter 12 represents a conflict between the right to free expression and the duty of the government to protect its citizens from the harms of such expression. Solving it requires discovering which of the conflicting sides has the highest priority. This will be the one that most fully conforms to the principles of beneficence, justice, and autonomy. Whichever right or duty has the highest priority is the one we must follow if we are to do the right thing.

Your Evaluation

Exercise 12.3

The good reasons arguments for each side contain premises that appeal to moral principles. Some of them refer to the harms of censorship or the harms of pornography (beneficence); others refer to various sorts of freedom to be preserved or lost by government censorship (autonomy); still others point out the ways in which pornography may or may not use people as mere objects (justice). In the process of evaluating these arguments you must apply the general criteria for judging the cogency of any argument such as these. The criteria tell us that each premise accepted must be relevant and reliable. Any which are not are to be thrown out. It also says those that are left must collectively add up to a sufficient amount of evidence to make the conclusion acceptable.

Because each premise is a concrete way to express some moral principle, we know the premises are **relevant.** You should begin your evaluation by first examining the **reliability** of each premise of each argument. You should ask yourself how likely it is to be true. Because each premise is denied in the opposing argument, you need to examine its reliability only once. If it is true, then its denial in the other argument is false. After checking the reliability of the premises, for all those that are relevant and reliable, judge whether they supply more **sufficient** amounts of evidence for their conclusion than the other side. The possible solution defended by the most sufficient reliable and relevant evidence (premises) is the one that is the most reasonable to accept. As always, be on guard for the influence of your point of view, trying to remain open to the evidence of both sides. Here are the arguments:

The Case Against Government Censorship

1. Consenting adults have the right to free expression. (A)

2. Viewing pornography produces many benefits to individuals. (B)

3. Government censorship is harmful. (B)

4. Government censorship is ineffective. (B)

5. Pornography does not cause sex crimes. (B)

6. Sexism, not pornography, degrades women. (B)

7. Neighborhood decay may be avoided through zoning laws. (B)

8. Public morality should be upheld by education, not legislation. (A)

9. Private harms should be avoided by education, not legislation. (A)

Therefore, 10. Government censorship is immoral.

The Case for Government Censorship

1.' Pornography causes sex crimes. (B)

2.' Pornography degrades women. (B,J)

3.' Pornography causes neighborhood decay. (B)

4.' Pornography causes harm to the public morality. (B)

5.' Pornography causes private harms. (B)

6.' Government censorship is the most effective way to eliminate pornography. (B)

7.' There is no right to free expression that harms others. (A)

8.' Hard-core pornography is not beneficial. (B)

9.' Government censorship is not harmful. (B)

Therefore, 10.' Government censorship is morally acceptable.

A Few Comments

In the 1970s and before, pornographic material was certainly available, some of it just as intense as what exists today. However, it was more difficult to create and acquire then, and thus pornography was only a $10 million a year business. Now, because of technological advances such as VCRs, digital television, and the Internet, pornography is widely available and has become a $10 billion a year industry. It is in our music, on our television sets (even in the afternoon), in films and videos, in plays and nightclubs, in novels and magazines, and especially on the Internet. The technology is there to deliver it to anyone, anywhere, and the huge profits reaped from doing so make it very unlikely that the pornography industry will soon disappear on its own. Because pornography is so widespread in our society, no one can any longer claim that it has no effect on those who choose not to view it. Whatever its other effects, it has a cultural effect on us all, and one very much for the worse, in my opinion.

The standard "liberal" response to this, with which I am quite sympathetic, is to say that education and political organization should be the tools that society should employ to reduce the amount of pornography in society—not censorship. The battle cry is this: educate people to its pervasiveness and its harms and they will just take steps to avoid it. Once that occurs, once the demand for pornography is dramatically reduced, market forces will also reduce its supply. Unfortunately, even if people joined together politically to fight institutions that create or display pornography, there is little hope for success. People may boycott Internet service providers, for example, until they eliminate or better conceal their pornographic Web sites. This has been done with some success. However, other providers will simply take up the slack and offer the eliminated services to those interested. People have been educating other people and fighting the movie industry and television for years, all in the hope of eliminating the sex and violence found there. The result has simply been more sex and violence than ever before.

The "conservative" response to the proliferation of pornography is, of course, more government censorship. Our society is so pluralistic, however, and there are so many different ideas about what is and what is not censorable material, that censorship, in addition to its other harms and its ineffectiveness, would be politically divisive as well. The specter of widespread censorship should not be allowed to raise its ugly head, at least until other methods to combat pornography have been tried, and tried in a serious way. These other methods primarily must be education and persuasion. This is the proper role of government, not censorship. That is, government resources should be directed at supporting programs of education and persuasion about the harms of pornography, just as they are directed at other forms of education intended to benefit society.

For example, we spend large sums of money trying to convince people not to use illegal drugs, not to drink and drive, and to use seat belts and motorcycle helmets. This is one way for the government to protect the health and safety of its citizens. Perhaps this model of government health and safety educational programs could be expanded to the arena of our "cultural health" as well. Perhaps the message could be that a culture whose entertainment vehicles are aimed at our baser, more infantile desires is not good for the development of our character, and thus is unhealthy for democracy. Even Mill, the staunchest supporter of the value of autonomy, says that autonomy is to be restricted to "human beings in the maturity of their faculties."

True freedom, the kind required for governing ourselves, is not simply the infantile freedom to follow our desires—which is the sort of freedom exploited by pornographers. It is rather the ability to choose what is truly in our interests as human beings living together in a political society. What an enlightened government ought to promote, through the funding of programs of education and persuasion—not through law—is a recognition of this distinction. These programs ought to supply guidance so that we may more wisely choose between those things we sometimes want but are not good for us, and those things that are truly good for us. The use of government funds to guide its citizens down the road of healthy human development may be parentalistic, but because it is educative and not coercive, it is not an abuse of power.

Consequences

Finally, a very brief word about the **consequences** of adopting one or the other of our possible solutions. If you think that the anticensorship view is the most adequate solution, then if you are consistent you must be opposed to all laws that censor pornography for consenting adults. Perhaps you also have to be opposed even to current laws against obscenity. Most forms of obscenity are forms of sexual obscenity, and most laws against them appeal to the same sorts of reasons for censorship that you have just rejected. You may accept laws that forbid the creation, sale, and possession of child pornography, of course, and of course you may accept laws designed to keep pornography away from nonconsenting adults.

If, on the other hand, you think that government censorship is the most reasonable way to deal with pornography, you must favor greater censorship than currently exists. The argument that you have accepted appeals to the harms of pornography. Surely, some of the hard-core pornography currently protected by the First Amendment is just as harmful, and just as obscene, as that currently censored. Are live sex acts, which may be censored, more harmful to view than "rape myth" videos, which are legal? If there is to be more censorship in response to growing amounts of pornography, then state and local officials must become more vigilant. Perhaps local censor boards need to be established and state officials appointed to provide guidance and education to such boards. Whatever the mechanism to be used, if you are for broader censorship you must also realize that in this free and open society, a proliferation of state, local, and federal government censorship would surely meet with great political opposition.

Another Perspective

The following selection is from Andrea Dworkin, *Pornography: Men Possessing Women*. New York: E.P. Dutton, 1989.

Pornography: Men Possessing Women

ANDREA DWORKIN

SHE WAS THIRTEEN. She was at a Girl Scout camp in northern Wisconsin. She went for a long walk in the woods alone during the day. She had long blond hair. She saw three hunters reading magazines, talking, joking. One looked up and said: "There's a live one." She thought they meant a deer. She ducked and started to run away. They meant her. They chased her, caught her, dragged her back to where they were camped. The magazines were pornography of women she physically resembled: blond, childlike. They called her names from the pornography: Little Godiva, Golden Girl, also bitch and slut. They threatened to kill her. They made her undress. It was November and cold. One held a rifle to her head; another beat her breasts with his rifle. All three raped her—penile penetration into the vagina. The third one couldn't get hard at first so he demanded a blow job. She didn't know what that was. The third man forced his penis into her mouth; one of the others cocked the trigger on his rifle. She was told she had better do it right. She tried. When they were done with her they kicked her: they kicked her naked body and they kicked leaves and pine needles on her. "[T]hey told me that if I wanted more, that I could come back the next day."

She was sexually abused when she was three by a boy who was fourteen—it was a "game" he had learned from pornography. "[I]t seems really bizarre to me to use the word 'boy' because the only memory I have of this person is as a three year old. And as a three year old he seemed like a really big man." When she was a young adult she was drugged by men who made and sold pornography. She remembers flashing lights, being forced onto a stage, being undressed by two men and sexually touched by a third. Men were waving money at her: "one of them shoved it in my stomach and essentially punched me. I kept wondering how it was possible that they couldn't see that I didn't want to be there, that I wasn't there willingly."

She had a boyfriend. She was twenty-one. One night he went to a stag party and watched pornography films. He called her up to ask if he could have sex with her. She felt obligated to make him happy. "I also felt that the refusal would be indicative of sexual quote unquote hang-ups on my part and that I was not quote unquote liberal enough. When he arrived, he informed me that the other men at the party were envious that he had a girlfriend to fuck. They wanted to fuck too after watching the pornography. He informed me of this as he was taking his coat off." He had her perform oral sex on him: "I did not do this of my own volition. He put his genitals in my face and he said 'take it all.' " He fucked her. The whole encounter took about five minutes. Then he dressed and went back to the party. "I felt ashamed and numb and I also felt very used."

She was seventeen, he was nineteen. He was an art student. He used her body for photography assignments by putting her body in contorted positions and telling her rape stories to get the expression he wanted on her face: fear. About a year later he had an assignment to do body casts in plaster. He couldn't get models because the plaster was heavy and caused fainting. She was a premed student. She tried to explain to him how deleterious the effects of the plaster were. "When you put

plaster on your body, it sets up, it draws the blood to the skin and the more area it covers on your body, the more blood is drawn to your skin. You become dizzy and nauseous and sick to your stomach and finally faint." He needed his work to be exhibited, so he needed her to model. She tried. She couldn't stand the heat and the weight of the plaster. "He wanted me to be in poses where I had to hold my hands up over my head, and they would be numb and they would fall. He eventually tied my hands over my head." They got married. During the course of their marriage he began to consume more and more pornography. He would read excerpts to her from the magazines about group sex, wife swapping, anal intercourse, and bondage. They would go to pornography films and wet T-shirt contests with friends. "I felt devastated and disgusted watching it. I was told by those men that if I wasn't as smart as I was and if I would be more sexually liberated and more sexy that I would get along a lot better in the world and that they and a lot of other men would like me more. About this time I started feeling very terrified. I realized that this wasn't a joke anymore." She asked her mother for help but was told that divorce was a disgrace and it was her responsibility to make the marriage work. He brought his friends home to act out the scenarios from the pornography. She found the group sex humiliating and disgusting, and to prevent it she agreed to act out the pornography in private with her husband. She began feeling suicidal. He was transferred to an Asian country in connection with his job. The pornography in the country where they now lived was more violent. He took her to live sex shows where women had sex with animals, especially snakes. Increasingly, when she was asleep he would force intercourse on her. Then he started traveling a lot, and she used his absence to learn karate. "One night when I was in one of those pornographic institutions, I was sitting with a couple of people that I had known, watching the women on stage and watching the different transactions and the sales of the women and the different acts going on, and I realized that my life wasn't any different than these women except that it was done in the name of marriage. I could see how I was being seasoned to the use of pornography and I could see what was coming next. I could see more violence and I could see more humiliation and I knew at that point I was either going to die from it, I was going to kill myself, or I was going to leave. And I was feeling strong enough that I left. . . . Pornography is not a fantasy, it was my life, reality."

At the time she made this statement, she couldn't have been older than twenty-two. She was terrified that the people would be identifiable, and so she spoke in only the most general terms, never specifying their relationship to her. She said she had lived in a house with a divorced woman, that woman's children, and the ex-husband, who refused to leave. She had lived there for eighteen years. During that time, "the woman was regularly raped by this man. He would bring pornographic magazines, books, and paraphernalia into the bedroom with him and tell her that if she did not perform the sexual acts that were being done in the 'dirty' books and magazines he would beat and kill her. I know about this because my bedroom was right next to hers. I could hear everything they said. I could hear her screams and cries. In addition, since I did most of the cleaning in the house, I would often come across the books, magazines, and paraphernalia that were in the bedroom and other rooms of the house. . . . Not only did I suffer through the torture of listening to the rapes and tortures of a woman, but I could see what grotesque acts this man was performing on her from the pictures in the pornographic materials. I was also able to see the systematic destruction of a human being taking place before my eyes. At the time I lived with the woman, I was completely helpless, powerless in regard to helping this woman and her children in getting away from this man." As a child, she was told by the man that if she ever

told or tried to run away he would break her arms and legs and cut up her face. He whipped her with belts and electrical cords. He made her pull her pants down to beat her. "I was touched and grabbed where I did not want him to touch me." She was also locked in dark closets and in the basement for long periods of time.

She was raped by two men. They were acting out the pornographic video game "Custer's Revenge." She was American Indian; they were white. "They held me down and as one was running the tip of his knife across my face and throat he said, 'Do you want to play Custer's Last Stand? It's great. You lose but you don't care, do you? You like a little pain, don't you, squaw.' They both laughed and then he said, 'There is a lot of cock in Custer's Last Stand. You should be grateful, squaw, that all-American boys like us want you. Maybe we will tie you to a tree and start a fire around you.' "

Her name is Jayne Stamen. She is currently in jail. In 1986, she hired three men to beat up her husband. She wanted him to know what a beating felt like. He died. She was charged with second-degree murder; convicted of first-degree manslaughter; sentenced to eight-and-a-half to twenty-five years. She was also convicted of criminal solicitation: in 1984 she asked some men to kill her husband for her, then reneged; she was sentenced on the criminal solicitation charge to two-and-a-third to seven years. The sentences are to run consecutively. She was tortured in her marriage by a man consumed by acting out pornography. He tied her up when he raped her; he broke bones; he forced anal intercourse; he beat her mercilessly; he penetrated her vagina with objects, "his rifle, or a long-necked wine decanter, or twelve-inch artificial rubber penises." He shaved the hair off her pubic area because he wanted, in his words, to "screw a baby's cunt." He slept with a rifle and kept a knife by the bed; he would threaten to cut her face with the knife if she didn't act out the pornography, and he would use the knife again if she wasn't showing pleasure. He called her all the names: whore, slut, cunt, bitch. "He used to jerk himself off on my chest while I was sleeping, or I would get woke up with him coming in my face and then he'd urinate on me." She tried to escape several times. He came after her armed with his rifle. She became addicted to alcohol and pills. "The papers stated that I didn't report [the violence] to the police. I did have the police at my home on several occasions. Twice on Long Island was for the gun threats, and once in Starrett City was also for the gun. The rest of the times were for the beatings and throwing me out of the house. A few times the police helped me get away from him with my clothes and the boys. I went home to my mom's. [He came after her with a rifle.] I went to the doctor's and hospitals on several occasions, too, but I could not tell the truth on how I 'hurt myself.' I always covered up for him, as I knew my life depended on that." The judge wouldn't admit testimony on the torture because he said the husband wasn't on trial. The defense lawyer said in private that he thought she probably enjoyed the abusive sex. Jayne's case will be appealed, but she may well have to stay in jail at Bedford Hills, a New York State prison for women, for the duration of the appeal because Women Against Pornography, a group that established the Defense Fund for Jayne Stamen, has not been able to raise bail money for her. Neither have I or others who care. It isn't chic to help such women; they aren't the Black Panthers. Ironically, there are many women—and recently a teenage girl, a victim of incest—who have hired others to kill the men—husbands, fathers—who were torturing them because they could not bear to do it themselves. Or the woman pours gasoline on the bed when he sleeps and lights the fire. Jayne didn't hire the men to kill her husband; the real question may be, why not? Why didn't she? Women don't understand self-defense the way men do—perhaps because sexual abuse destroys the self. We don't feel we have a right to kill

just because we are being beaten, raped, tortured, and terrorized. We are hurt for a long time before we fight back. Then, usually, we are punished: "I have lived in a prison for ten years, meaning my marriage," says Jayne Stamen, ". . . and now they have me in a real prison."

I've quoted from statements, all made in public forums, by women I know well (except for Jayne Stamen; I've talked with her but I haven't met her). I can vouch for them; I know the stories are true. The women who made these particular statements are only a few of the thousands of women I have met, talked with, questioned: women who have been hurt by pornography. The women are real to me. I know what they look like standing tall; I've seen the fear; I've watched them remember; I've talked with them about other things, all sorts of things: intellectual issues, the weather, politics, school, children, cooking. I have some idea of their aspirations as individuals, the ones they lost during the course of sexual abuse, the ones they cherish now. I know them. Each one, for me, has a face, a voice, a whole life behind her face and her voice. Each is more eloquent and more hurt than I know how to convey. Since 1974, when my book *Woman Hating* was first published, women have been seeking me out to tell me that they have been hurt by pornography; they have told me how they have been hurt in detail, how much, how long, by how many. They thought I might believe them, initially, I think, because I took pornography seriously in *Woman Hating.* I said it was cruel, violent, basic to the way our culture sees and treats women—and I said the hate in it was real. Well, they knew that the hate in it was real because they had been sexually assaulted by that hate. One does not make the first tentative efforts to communicate about this abuse to those who will almost certainly ridicule one. Some women took a chance on me; and it was a chance, because I often did not want to listen. I had my limits and my reasons, like everyone else. For many years, I heard the same stories I have tried to encapsulate here: the same stories, sometimes more complicated, sometimes more savage, from thousands of women, most of whom hadn't dared to tell anyone. No part of the country was exempt; no age group; no racial or ethnic group; no "life-style" however "normal" or "alternative." The statements I have paraphrased here are not special: not more sadistic, not chosen by me because they are particularly sickening or offensive. In fact, they are not particularly sickening or offensive. They simply are what happens to women who are brutalized by the use of pornography on them.

Such first-person stories from women are dismissed by defenders of pornography as "anecdotal"; they misuse the word to make it denote a story, probably fictive, that is small, trivial, inconsequential, proof only of some defect in the woman herself—the story tells us nothing about pornography but it tells us all we need to know about the woman. She's probably lying; maybe she really liked it; and if it did happen, how could anyone (sometimes referred to as "a smart girl like you") be stupid enough, simpleminded enough, to think that pornography had anything to do with it? Wasn't there, as one grinning adversary always asks, also coffee in the house? The coffee, he suggests, is more likely to be a factor in the abuse than the pornography—after all, the bad effects of coffee have been proven in the laboratory. What does one do when women's lives are worth so little—worth arrogant, self-satisfied ridicule and nothing else, not even the appearance, however false, of charity or concern? Alas, one answers: the man (the husband, the boyfriend, the rapist, the torturer—you or your colleague or your best friend or your buddy) wasn't reading the coffee label when he tied the knots; the directions he followed are found in pornography, and, frankly, they are not found anywhere else. The first-person stories are human expe-

rience, raw and true, not mediated by dogma or ideology *or* social convention; "human" is the trick word in the sentence. If one values women as human beings, one cannot turn away or refuse to hear so that one can refuse to care without bearing responsibility for the refusal. One cannot turn one's back on the women or on the burden of memory they carry. If one values women as human beings, one will not turn one's back on the women who are being hurt today and the women who will be hurt tomorrow.

Most of what we know about the experience of punishment, the experience of torture, the experience of socially sanctioned sadism, comes from the first-person testimony of individuals—"anecdotal" material. We have the first-person stories of Frederick Douglass and Sojourner Truth, of Primo Levy and Elie Wiesel, of Nadezhda Mandelstam and Aleksandr Solzhenitsyn. Others in the same or different circumstances of torture and terror have spoken out to bear witness. Often, they were not believed. They were shamed, not honored. We smelled the humiliation, the degradation, on them; we turned away. At the same time, their stories were too horrible, too impossible, too unpleasant; their stories indicted those who stood by and did nothing—most of us, most of the time. Respectfully, I suggest that the women who have experienced the sadism of pornography on their bodies—the women in the pornography and the women on whom the pornography is used—are also survivors; they bear witness, now, for themselves, on behalf of others. "Survivors," wrote Terrence Des Pres, "are not individuals in the bourgeois sense. They are living remnants of the general struggle, and certainly they know it." Of these women hurt by pornography, we must say that they know it now. Before, each was alone, unspeakably alone, isolated in terror and humiliated even by the will to live—it was the will to live, after all, that carried each woman from rape to rape, from beating to beating. Each had never heard another's voice saying the words of what had happened, telling the same story; because it is the same story, over and over— and none of those who escaped, survived, endured are individuals in the bourgeois sense. These women will not abandon the meaning of their own experience. That meaning is: pornography is the orchestrated destruction of women's bodies and souls; rape, battery, incest, and prostitution animate it; dehumanization and sadism characterize it; it is war on women, serial assaults on dignity, identity, and human worth; it is tyranny. Each woman who has survived knows from the experience of her own life that pornography is captivity—the woman trapped in the picture used on the woman trapped wherever he's got her.

Chapter 13

Reproductive Technology

For most couples who want children, the process of conception and pregnancy proceeds relatively smoothly and results in the birth of a healthy child. For others, however, nature is not so kind. Nature makes it impossible for some of them to have children at all. This may be because the couple is infertile. The man may not produce enough sperm, for example, and what he does produce may not be viable. Or the woman may not produce viable eggs or, if she does, she may have blocked fallopian tubes which prevents them from uniting with the male's sperm. Other couples may be able to become pregnant, but face the misery of enduring one painful miscarriage after another. Still other couples may be able to conceive and to achieve a successful pregnancy, but they cannot give birth to a healthy child. They may be carriers of a genetic defect their child inherits from them, a defect passed on through the reproductive material—the sperm or egg—of one or both of them. Each year some 150,000 children in the United States are born with birth defects. Some of these are caused by environmental factors, and some are due to inherited genetic defects. Though certain genetic disorders may have relatively mild symptoms, others result in lives that are filled with pain and suffering.

Whether the cause is infertility, miscarriage, or genetic defects, nature simply does not allow some couples to produce healthy children. Although nature may not allow it, human technology has discovered ways to overcome at least some of the failings of nature, permitting these couples to escape the misery and sadness caused by the absence of healthy children. These technologies, called **reproductive technologies,** are of several types. Some are aimed at preventing genetic defects, either by diagnosing such defects in advance or by eliminating them from the reproductive material to be used to create children. Others are ways to avoid the problems of miscarriages, and still others attack many types of fertility problems. As a result of the new reproductive technologies, millions of healthy babies have been born that nature alone would not have permitted.

A great deal of human suffering has been eliminated through the use of various reproductive technologies, but these human "corrections" of nature's failures often lead to problems of their own. For example, we may now be able to know whether a particular fetus suffers from a genetic disease before it is born. However, because there is no cure for such a disease, a couple pregnant with such a fetus is faced with the awful choice of aborting the fetus or allowing it to be born with the disease. With another technique, it is now possible to transfer an embryo created by a couple who has suffered repeated miscarriages to another woman's uterus. Such a "surrogate" mother carries the child through the period of gestation and then gives it to the biological parents. But what if she decides to keep it instead?

To take another example, we now understand the nature and function of various genes, especially some "defective" genes responsible for serious genetic diseases. We even have hopes of eliminating these defects in newly fertilized eggs prior to implanting them into the mother's uterus. In this way, the child born of such a procedure will be free of the otherwise inevitable genetic disease that nature would have produced. However, if we can replace defective genes with healthy ones, we might also some day be able to replace "normal" genes with "superior" ones, thereby creating children who are stronger, smarter, or more creative than nature alone would have produced. Gene enhancement, however, places us frighteningly in the middle of the creative process, one worked out by God or nature over millions of years. Comprehending the good and evil consequences of "playing God" in such a manner may be beyond the limits of our human understanding. In the long run, such power over the reproductive process may cause us more harm than good.

The **structure of Chapter 13,** the last chapter of this text, is significantly different from those that have preceded it. Chapters 5 through 12 have followed the structure that mirrors the process of critical thinking, a process outlined in Part 1. Here, however, that structure will not be followed for two reasons. The first has to do with *content*. There are many types of reproductive technologies. Some general moral issues are common to all, but each has its own unique set of problems. It would be much too cumbersome to attempt to solve a dozen or so moral problems in one chapter. We could focus only on one of them—human cloning, for example, or gene enhancement—but much would be lost if we did so.

The second reason has to do with *method*. If you have worked your way through all or most of the issues discussed in previous chapters, you now should be in a position to think critically through a moral problem on your own. You should be able to identify the problem and its possible solutions, clarify concepts, gather relevant and reliable information, construct arguments for various possible solutions, make a reasoned judgment as to which possible solution is best, and consider the consequences of adopting such a position. The material found in Chapter 13 will provide a starting point for your thinking. Its goal is to describe the nature of various reproductive technologies and to identify some of the moral problems to which they give rise. It contains many examples of moral problems for you to solve on your own. The first part of this chapter contains descriptions of various reproductive technologies. In the second part some of their associated moral problems are identified. The chapter concludes with an exercise that guides you through the process of thinking critically about a moral problem for yourself.

Types of Reproductive Technologies

Diagnostic Technologies

The first category of reproductive technologies is called **diagnostic technologies.** The various tools included in this category are used to diagnose the likelihood of a particular couple giving birth to a child with a genetic disease. To understand how these technologies work requires a word or two about genes. Genes are located in the nucleus of each cell of each living being. Genes, or genetic material, are what make up the DNA (deoxyribonucleic acid) molecule. This is a long, complex molecule that in human beings looks like a spiral staircase when it is unraveled. It comes in nature arranged into various clusters of genes called chromosomes. Human beings typically have forty-six chromosomes. Genes themselves are strings of chemicals long enough to give instructions to the cell, usually information about which proteins to make and how to use them. Because genes are constructed from only four chemicals, genes differ from one another only by how these chemicals are arranged, or sequenced. The main goal of the recently completed Human Genome Project was to discover the sequence of chemicals in the entire DNA molecule—some 100,000 or so genes.

Genes may be thought of as codes, analogous to computer programs. These determine how each cell will grow. Because we are composed of cells, genes determine what our physical and biological characteristics are. The color of our eyes and skin and hair, the size of our brain, our sex, our height—everything about us that is physical or biological is preprogrammed in our genes. Genes also provide a biological basis for many of our behavioral characteristics. Such characteristics are not as rigidly determined by our genes alone, however, as are our physical features. Just how we realize these behavioral traits depends in large part on the environment. Someone with the same genes as Michael Jordan, the great basketball star, will be very good at the game if he has the motive and opportunity to practice and play. In the absence of such environmental conditions, however, his genetically based physical skills may be directed elsewhere or not used at all.

Because our genes determine our biology and physical structure, when they are defective they may cause our bodies to function improperly; they may cause genetic diseases or disorders. There are some four thousand known types of genetic diseases. Many relatively common ones, such as cystic fibrosis, juvenile diabetes, Down's syndrome, Tay-Sachs, Huntington's disease, and sickle-cell anemia, have been linked to monogenic defects—one defective gene. Other genetic diseases, such as spina bifida and anencephaly, are caused by polygenic defects—more than one defective gene. In some cases, such as Huntington's, simply having the defective gene causes the disease. In other cases, the defective gene may be present without being expressed as a disease in the person who carries it. Only when such a "carrier" of a defective gene mates with another carrier is a child produced in whom the defect is expressed as a disease.

Diagnostic technologies allow people to know, with varying degrees of certainty, what their chances are of giving birth to a child with a particular genetic disease. These technologies are often sought out by people who are at risk for passing on such diseases. They may know that they are at risk because they may already have had a child with a genetic disease, or because there is a high incidence of a particular genetic disease in the families of one or both members of the couple. In addition, when the woman is over the age of thirty-five, any child she conceives is considered to be at a higher risk for some genetic defects, such as Down's syndrome.

Such a high-risk couple may begin with *genetic screening,* a variety of tests aimed at discovering whether they are carriers of defective genes. Such tests include extensive family histories and physical exams; they also involve DNA analysis and analysis of the chromosomes for abnormalities that may be signs of genetic defects. If a couple is found to be carriers of defective genes, their chances of passing on a particular genetic disease to their children may then be calculated according to various formulas. If such an at-risk couple decides that the odds of having a healthy child are favorable, additional tests may be performed to determine whether their roll of the dice was successful. Once the woman becomes pregnant, several well-known tests may be used to diagnose the fetus for signs of genetic disease.

The least invasive of these tests is *ultrasound.* Ultrasound is a form of imaging based on sound waves. It poses no medical risk for either mother or fetus. In the second trimester it can detect physical abnormalities that are associated with some genetic diseases, such as a malformed head or spine and abnormal structures of the internal organs. It can also detect the sex of the fetus late in the second trimester, a matter of importance for those genetic diseases that afflict members of only one sex. Unfortunately, a successful ultrasound is no guarantee of the absence of genetic disorders. Ultrasound can detect some gross abnormalities, but it often misses them. In addition, some genetic diseases have few signs of such abnormalities.

A more accurate test for the presence of a genetic disorder is *amniocentesis.* This procedure involves the insertion of a needle into the amniotic sac of the mother and the withdrawal of some amniotic fluid. This fluid contains fetal cells that may be examined directly for the presence of genetic defects, or for chromosomal abnormalities associated with such defects, or for the presence of certain enzymes also associated with genetic diseases of various sorts. There is some risk of miscarriage in this procedure, about 1 in 200, but the advantage is that it can detect many genetic diseases quite accurately. If the test results show a genetic defect associated with the presence of a genetic disorder, the couple is then faced with a choice of having the child or having an abortion. Because this procedure is typically performed early in the fifth month of pregnancy and the results are not known for two weeks, an abortion is not typically performed until late in the second trimester. Such abortions are complex and medically risky.

To avoid late abortions many couples prefer to use *chorionic villus sampling* (CVS). This technology may be used in the first trimester. The chorionic villus, fibrous tissue that lines the walls of the placenta, also contains fetal cells. The CVS test involves removing a small section of this tissue and examining the fetal cells it contains for the presence of genetic defects. The risk of miscarriage is slightly higher with CVS than with amniocentesis, and there is some evidence that CVS may cause limb defects in a very small percentage of children, defects such as the shortening of fingers or toes. Also, CVS is not able to detect all the genetic defects that amniocentesis can. In particular, CVS cannot detect neural tube defects such as anencephaly and spina bifida. However, for the diseases it can detect, CVS now rivals amniocentesis for accuracy. With the advantage of simpler and safer abortions as an option, and with its accuracy improving to the level of that of amniocentesis, CVS has become the test of choice for many seeking prenatal diagnosis.

In the future, as we learn more about which genes are responsible for which sorts of maladies, we will be able to screen for hundreds, even thousands, of genetically based disorders. In addition to amniocentesis and CVS, other forms of genetic testing will be developed, all with the purpose of eliminating defective genes from our potential offspring. For example, a technology that has recently been developed is called *preimplantation genetic diagnosis* (PGD). This very expensive and rarely used test depends on the technique of in vitro fertilization and implantation, which is discussed later. Roughly, sperm and egg cells from the couple are collected and united in a solution to create an embryo. After it grows to the four-cell stage, one cell is removed and its DNA is analyzed for the presence of a genetic defect. If such a defect is found, the embryo is destroyed. If a defective gene is not found, the embryo is transferred to the uterus of the woman with the hope that it will implant itself and develop normally. The advantage of this test is that it can detect the presence of genetic defects prior to pregnancy, thus avoiding abortion. Its disadvantages are that it is a very expensive, time-consuming, and often frustrating technology. On average, five tries are needed to achieve a successful pregnancy even after a suitable embryo is identified. Because of these considerations, this "high-tech" test is suitable only for couples with an extremely high risk of passing on a genetic disease.

Fertility Technologies

For some couples, the problem is not to avoid giving birth to children with genetic diseases but rather to achieve pregnancy in the first place. The normal method for becoming pregnant is to have sexual intercourse. If the timing is right, the woman has ovulated and her egg is fertilized by the man's sperm in the fallopian tubes. The fertilized egg then travels the rest of the way down the fallopian tube to the uterus. Here it becomes implanted in the uterine wall and the process of gestation begins. Many couples are not successful with one or more of these necessary steps, and require the intervention of **fertility technologies** if they are to achieve a successful pregnancy. Because many things can cause infertility, there are many types of fertility technologies. Although a woman can conceive a child with someone other than a man to whom she is married, for convenience, her partner is referred to as her husband in the discussions to follow.

The first technology to be discussed is *artificial insemination with the husband's sperm* (AIH). Artificial insemination had been used in animal husbandry for some time before it was introduced for human use in the 1950s. It is used to treat a form of male infertility in which the man cannot produce a sufficient amount of sperm in an ejaculation to fertilize his partner's egg. The sperm he produces may be otherwise healthy and viable, but through normal sexual intercourse it does not reach the egg for purposes of fertilization. In AIH, several samples of sperm are collected from the man through masturbation. These are placed together in a tube and centrifuged, creating a larger, condensed collection of sperm. This sample is then inserted with a syringe into the woman's vagina at her time of ovulation. AIH is the treatment of choice for this type of male infertility. Millions of children worldwide have been conceived using this method.

A variation of AIH is AID, *artificial insemination with donor sperm*. The procedure is the same as AIH, only now the source of the male reproductive material is someone other than the woman's husband. The reason for using the sperm of another can be that the husband's sperm is not fertile at all, or that using it would pass on a genetic defect to the child. In using donor sperm the biological father, the one who contributes the reproductive material, is not the nurturing father, the one who raises the child. The sperm donor may be a close family relative or friend; often he is anonymous. The source of such sperm in the past was often a medical student associated with the hospital providing the AID services. Now, however, because sperm can be frozen and preserved for long periods of time in a *sperm bank,* there are many sources of donated sperm. Many privately owned sperm banks store and sell this material to couples. It is usually classified by the characteristics of the donor, so that couples may select the type of biological father they desire.

One of the more dramatic of the fertility technologies is *in vitro fertilization* (IVF). "In vitro" is Latin for "under glass," so children concerned with this procedure are often referred to as "test-tube babies." A more accurate name for the technique is "external fertilization," as fertilization occurs outside the woman's body. This procedure is often used when the woman's egg cannot be fertilized in the natural way by the man's sperm because there is a blockage in her fallopian tubes. The sperm and egg cannot reach each other around this obstacle. Such blockages may be removed surgically, but this procedure is not always successful. Scar tissue forms quickly after such surgery, often closing off the passageway before a successful pregnancy can be achieved. IVF is a way to join the couple's reproductive material when surgical procedures are of no benefit.

In vitro fertilization requires that reproductive material be gathered from the man and the woman. In the man's case, sperm is collected through masturbation. In the woman's case, the procedure is more elaborate. First she takes a fertility drug, usually a powerful hormone, which makes her superovulate, that is, makes her produce several eggs at once. Then a scope is inserted through a small incision and used to suction the eggs from her ovaries. This procedure is called a laparoscopy. Once collected, the sperm and eggs are placed in a special solution where the sperm then fertilizes the eggs. The resultant embryos are now ready to be inserted into the woman's uterus, a procedure called "embryo transfer." At this stage the embryos are sometimes called "pre-embryos" as they are not yet implanted.

For even the best fertility clinics, IVF is successful on average in only one out of five attempts, primarily because of failure of the transferred embryo to implant itself. Very often in the past many embryos were transferred with the hope that at least some would implant themselves into the uterine wall and begin the process of gestation. However, this often led to dangerous multiple pregnancies, so only a couple of embryos are now implanted at a time. The rest are frozen and stored for use in case further attempts are necessary. The remarkable ability to freeze embryos and to thaw them in viable form makes further attempts to gather eggs from the woman unnecessary. This is important because most of the medical risks associated with IVF, relatively minor as they are, occur during the laparoscopy procedure.

To improve IVF success rates, variations on the process have been developed that mirror more closely the natural stages of fertilization. One is called *gamete intrafallopian transfer* (GIFT). Here the sperm and egg are placed in the fallopian tube, on the lower side of the blockage, and the egg is fertilized there, as it would be normally. It then proceeds to travel down the rest of the fallopian tube and, if all goes well, to implant itself in the uterus. Another variation is called *zygote intrafallopian transfer* (ZIFT). Here an egg is fertilized in vitro and then transferred to the fallopian tube, where it then continues its journey to the uterine wall. Both GIFT and ZIFT have resulted in slightly higher success rates than IVF. Because of the relatively low success rate, however, a pregnancy requiring IVF or its variations can cost as much as $30,000. For those thousands and thousands of couples who have used it successfully, however, the risks and costs are far outweighed by the otherwise unachievable miracle of birth.

Because IVF allows external fertilization, it is a gateway to many other reproductive technologies. Once reproductive material can be separated from the human beings who produce it, it can be manipulated, stored, and transferred in any number of ways. One recent technology, for example, involves injecting a single sperm into an egg, and transferring the resultant embryo into the uterus. This technology, called *intracytoplasmic sperm injection* (ICSI), is used for men whose sperm is infertile due to a variety of causes, such as being too weak to penetrate the outer shell of the egg. Although the sperm cannot fertilize the woman's egg naturally, it is still capable of fertilizing it if injected directly into the egg. Such couples could resort to AID but choose not to do so. Instead, they prefer to have children that are biologically their own. It involves IVF, so the procedure is expensive and not without its risks. In particular, many worry that such randomly chosen sperm will be weaker than nature would permit and thus produce a defective fetus. Despite its risks, sperm injection is used widely, especially in the United States and European countries.

Another technology, called *cryogenics,* involves freezing and storing reproductive material. Like any living cells, reproductive material lasts only so long on its own. If frozen, however, it may be preserved for long periods of time. Currently, sperm and embryos can be frozen and thawed successfully, but success has not been achieved with the freezing and thawing of female reproductive cells. Any eggs that are successfully fertilized must be fresh, not frozen. Since the development of IVF, sex is no longer required for producing children. With cryogenics, not only is nearness in space not necessary to produce embryos, but nearness in time is no longer required either. No one knows how long sperm will remain viable in a frozen state, but apparently it will do so for a long period of time. If this is true, then sperm gathered and frozen today could be used to fertilize the egg of a woman decades from now, and embryos created today could be implanted in some woman not yet born.

Another technology related to IVF, at least in one of its versions, is *surrogate motherhood.* Many women who have little trouble conceiving a child have problems with gestation, the process of growing the child within their body. Some women may have had hysterectomies, for example, and have no uterus; others may have clinical problems associated with their pregnancies. For these women, the problem of painful miscarriage after painful miscarriage may find its solution in the use of surrogate mothers. A surrogate in general is one who acts for or substitutes for another. Surrogate mothers are women who grow another woman's child in their bodies. After the baby is born, the surrogate mother gives it to the woman who will raise the child.

Sometimes a surrogate is a relative or friend. More commonly she is someone who is hired for the job. There are groups who arrange surrogacy relationships for a fee, though more and more commonly women willing to be surrogates connect through the Internet with women who desire their services. Typically surrogate mothers receive somewhere around $15,000 to $20,000 plus medical expenses for their efforts. In addition, there are legal fees and sometimes fees for agencies who help with the surrogacy arrangements. Usually a legal contract is signed by all parties that grant rights of payment to the surrogate and custody of the child to the nurturing parents. Though money is involved in the majority of surrogacy arrangements, most women who act as surrogates are motivated as much by altruism as they are by financial considerations and find great satisfaction in helping couples to have a child of their own.

There are two variations of this technology. The first uses the method of artificial insemination. In this procedure, sperm from the husband of the nurturing mother is used to artificially inseminate the surrogate mother. The child conceived is thus the biological product of the husband and the surrogate. The surrogate is both the biological mother and the gestational mother; the woman who will receive the child, called the intended mother, is the nurturing mother. Some medical groups involved with surrogacy reserve the name "surrogate motherhood" for this procedure. Another variation uses the technique of in vitro fertilization. Here the nurturing couple uses their own reproductive material to create an embryo in vitro. This embryo is then transferred to the surrogate. The nurturing parents in this case are also the biological parents; the surrogate is only the gestational mother. The name "gestational mother" is often used for this version of surrogacy. The once rare use of a surrogate solely as a gestational mother is now growing in popularity. Estimates are that it is used to create as many as one thousand babies each year in the United States, with that number expected to grow in the future.

There are other possible variations of surrogacy, most of which differ from the above two types only because they involve donated reproductive material. Either the sperm or the egg or both may be donated by a third party, for example, and the resultant embryo transferred to the gestational mother. In this case there are three "mothers": the biological mother, the one who donates the egg; the gestational mother, the one who carries the child; and the nurturing mother, the one who raises it. A further variation may be thought of as "surrogacy in reverse." For example, a woman who is capable of a successful pregnancy but who has non-functioning ovaries may receive a donated egg from another woman and use the IVF technique to carry and raise a child not biologically her own. Included among this class of women may be older women who are post-menopausal. Typically, the eggs of post-menopausal women are no longer viable, so the women cannot conceive naturally—even though they may be capable of successful pregnancies. By using donor eggs fertilized in vitro by sperm from their husbands or even by donated sperm, some women in their sixties have given birth to children. Even though such a woman is not the biological mother, she is the gestational and the nurturing mother. Another variation on this theme is for a woman to receive a donated embryo, one that was created and intended for use by another couple who have since changed their minds. With the existence of thousands of frozen embryos that will not be used by the couples who created them, this form of "embryo adoption" is becoming more and more popular.

One technology that has caused a high level of public reaction is *human cloning*. Plants, some animals, and even some forms of human tissue have been cloned successfully, but human beings—as of this writing at least—have not. One type of cloning is called *twinning*. In twinning a fertilized egg is divided after it grows to the eight-cell stage. Each four-cell embryo may then be transferred to the uterus of a female or frozen for later transfer. Twinning is how identical twins are created by nature, by a split in the early embryo resulting in two embryos, both of which implant and grow separately into two genetically identical offspring. Nonidentical or fraternal twins are created when the female releases two eggs in a given cycle, both of which are fertilized and both of which implant successfully. The technique of twinning is frequently used in animal husbandry. It is becoming more common in IVF procedures for human reproduction as well, as a way to create more embryos from a limited number of fertilized eggs.

Another type of cloning is called *somatic cell nuclear transfer* (SCNT). This is the type of cloning usually referred to in most discussions, and the type that we will refer to exclusively. It is different from twinning, even though the process of cloning a living being results in the production of another being genetically identical to it—a twin. Roughly, cloning involves removing the nucleus from a female reproductive cell and replacing it with the nucleus from another cell, a donor cell. The female reproductive cell is then stimulated with an electric current and begins to divide or grow as it would if it had been fertilized by sperm. Because the DNA contained in this egg comes from one cell and not from a combination of sperm and egg cells, the cells of the cloned embryo contain not a unique mixture of genes but the same genes found in all the cells of the donor. In human cloning, if the embryo is transferred to a uterus and a successful birth results, the baby born is genetically identical to the person who donated the cell. To be a clone of a person is thus to be that person's younger twin.

One use for human cloning might be to avoid passing on a genetic disease. A couple at risk for creating a child with a genetic disease and not interested in using donated biological material might clone one or the other of the couple to avoid such a result. In this way, they could be the parents of a healthy child who was not created from any biological source but their own. Others see cloning as a way to produce superior children. If the DNA of any donor cell can be copied, many will be tempted to use the DNA of "superior" persons as blueprints for their own children. Still others have expressed wishes to clone copies of former children or loved ones who have died, hoping no doubt that this new child could be a replacement. Still others, in search of immortality perhaps, have left instructions in their will to be cloned after their own deaths.

Even though cloning human beings in the future is possible, perhaps even likely, it is a technology that is currently filled with risks. The most famous case of cloning an animal to date has been the sheep, Dolly, who was born in 1996. Most animals cloned prior to Dolly, usually frogs or mice, had been copied from the DNA of young cells taken from embryos, or from undifferentiated cells found elsewhere in the body. Such cells are called "stem cells." To say that they are "undifferentiated" means that they have not yet begun to develop into specific kinds of cells, such as skin cells or blood cells. For a cell to develop into an adult cell of a specific type, called a "somatic" cell, some genes of the cell are turned off.

The most daunting technical problem of cloning had always been to clone from somatic cells, and thus find a way to turn back on all the genes present in the cell.

This is what Ian Wilmut and his team of researchers at the Roslin Institute in Scotland accomplished in 1996 with the birth of Dolly. Since that time many other types of animals have been cloned using their techniques, including pigs, cows, and goats. But Dolly was a success only after some 277 failed attempts, and most of the more recently cloned animals have developed serious abnormalities during gestation. Until our technical knowledge and skill is much more advanced than it is at present, such significant numbers of failures also would be the likely result of attempts to clone human beings.

Genetic Technologies

Cloning involves the transfer of genes from one cell to another; genetic technologies alter specific genes. Technologies that do this for therapeutic purposes are called *gene therapies.* Roughly, gene therapies aim at eliminating defective genes that cause genetic diseases and replacing them with healthy ones. The "knives" that cut out defective genes are viruses. Viruses infect the nucleus of a cell. Special viruses may be altered by splicing into their DNA copies of the gene in question. They then deliver this gene to the appropriate site, cut out its defective version, and replace it with the healthy gene. Under the direction of this healthy gene the cell then begins to manufacture the proteins it had failed to make before and to function normally.

At the present time such gene therapies are used solely to modify adult or somatic cells. For example, someone with juvenile or type-1 diabetes has a defective gene, the insulin-producing gene, in each cell. To treat this problem the person must take insulin for the rest of his or her life. In this way the symptoms of the disease are managed, but the disease still exists. To cure this problem permanently, a healthy human insulin-producing gene is spliced into a virus that is then injected into the pancreas of the person afflicted with this genetic disorder. If the virus splices the healthy gene into enough pancreatic cells, the pancreas can make enough insulin on its own. As the disease of type-1 diabetes is that the pancreas cannot make its own insulin, this amounts to a cure of this type of diabetes.

Unfortunately, genetic therapies designed to cure various genetic defects have met with limited success. Even if such therapies could successfully alter a sufficient number of cells initially, cells die off and are replaced with new cells that do not contain the healthy gene; therefore these therapies will be needed for life. Because of this, the goal someday is to use gene therapies directly on fertilized eggs. These are called germ-line therapies. Because a newly fertilized egg consists of only one cell, only one gene would have to be modified and only one time to eliminate a genetic disease. Once the defective gene is replaced by a healthy one, all cells that grow from the initial cell will copy the healthy gene. In this way, gene therapies may be used to cure all known genetic diseases caused by monogenic defects. This will probably involve preimplantation genetic diagnosis and will certainly require IVF and embryo transfer, but many believe that such costs are worth the result. The use of germ-line gene therapies is not a technology that is currently employed. If our knowledge and technological skills develop as rapidly in the future as they have in the past, however, the use of germ-line gene therapy in the near future seems inevitable.

In addition to curing genetic diseases, genetic technologies may also be used to enhance the genes of human beings, thereby creating superior children. *Gene enhancement* technologies are not currently used, and they do have a ring of "science fiction" about them, but they are surely in our future—at least as possibilities. One such technology might be closely related to germ-line therapies. Just as healthy genes may replace defective ones, "superior" genes may replace healthy but "inferior" ones. What counts as superior may be defined by society as a whole or may simply be what is considered desirable by the parents. If they want a child with hazel eyes, for example, the gene of their newly fertilized egg responsible for eye color could be replaced with a "hazel-color" gene. The same could be done for other traits. In theory at least, parents could design the traits of their children, creating through technology a child significantly different from what nature would have produced.

Unfortunately, most of the really interesting human characteristics, such as intelligence and creativity, are not based on one gene. Instead, they are polygenic traits. Some time will be needed to identify and modify such genes. In addition, how intelligent or creative a person becomes also depends heavily on the environment. How a child is raised determines much about how bright or creative he or she becomes. Nevertheless, such traits are largely determined by genes, genes that some day may be identified and prove amenable to modification. Until that time, just the very possibility of designing our offspring is sufficient to change our thinking dramatically in many ways. The fact that we could be co-creators of our children's characteristics, along with God or nature, surely leads to a change in thinking about the role of human beings in the universe.

An even more dramatic change in thinking results from the possibility of another gene enhancing technology: cross-species genetic alteration—sometimes called "hybridization." Here, genes from a nonhuman species may be spliced into the DNA of a fertilized human egg. In effect, this technology is used to create new forms of life, human beings with characteristics of animals, for example. For the most part, nature does not allow cross-species reproduction. The sperm from one type of mammal, for example, could not successfully produce a pregnancy in a female member of another species. The sperm would be seen as alien material and attacked by the body's immune system. On the genetic level, however, such mixing of species is possible. Many plants have been genetically modified, for example, to make them larger or more resistant to pests. Such genetically engineered plants produce more food per acre to feed the ever-increasing numbers of people on this planet. Such foods, often called "frankenfoods" by those who oppose genetically altered foods, have been the subject of much controversy.

Animals have also been genetically altered. Bacteria have been genetically altered, for example, to produce medicines. Almost all insulin is now produced synthetically. This is accomplished by splicing into bacteria an insulin-producing gene, allowing the bacteria to grow, and then separating the insulin from the other by-products. Other bacteria have been created for specific purposes such as dissolving oil slicks. Higher forms of animals, even mammals, have also been genetically modified. We discussed some of these "transgenic" animals in Chapter 10, animals that have been created for research purposes or for use as organ donors. In a similar way, human beings could be constructed in quite different ways by splicing genes from other species into newly fertilized human eggs. In theory at least, the entire pool of genes—plant as well as animal—and thus the entire list of characteristics in the whole of nature, may be intertwined to form new types of beings, even new types of human beings. This apocalyptic thought surely requires a change in thinking about what it means to be human.

Some Moral Implications

If the point of the previous section is to describe the nature of various reproductive technologies, the point of this section is to examine some of their moral implications. To discuss the **moral implications** of a reproductive technology is to discuss how it conforms or fails to conform to our three moral principles. As we are about to see, some technologies appear to violate the principle of *justice* by using some human beings solely for the good of others. Others produce harms, violating the principle of *beneficence.* Always in the background of our discussion of harms and benefits will be the principle of *autonomy,* warning us that people have the right to use these technologies unless society can show that doing so will cause harm to others. It is not the purpose of this section to argue for and against the moral acceptability of any particular reproductive technologies. That will be your task, later. It is simply to provide you with a starting point for thinking critically about the moral acceptability of one or more of these technologies on your own. It may be helpful first to list the ones we have mentioned thus far.

Reproductive Technologies

Diagnostic Technologies

- genetic screening

- ultrasound

- amniocentesis

- chorionic villus sampling (CVS)

- preimplantation genetic diagnosis (PGD)

Fertility Technologies

- artificial insemination with the husband's sperm (AIH)

- artificial insemination with donor sperm (AID)

- in vitro fertilization (IVF)

- intracytoplasmic sperm injection (ICSI)

- cryogenics

- surrogate and gestational mothers

- cloning

Genetic Technologies

- gene therapies

- gene enhancement

General Moral Issues

Each technology has its own specific moral implications; there are also **general moral issues** associated with them all collectively. For example, many complain that reproductive technologies are **unnatural.** There is only one natural way to make a baby. If nature or God has denied that to a couple, then they just ought to accept that fact. To use biology and medicine to "artificially" create a child is to go against natural processes and thus to violate morality. Even the language of reproductive technology is closely related to engineering terms. Diagnostic technologies, for example, may be seen as ways to "quality control" our offspring, whereas genetic technologies enhance or improve the "product." Fertility technologies upset the natural reproductive process most dramatically. They separate reproductive material from the persons doing the reproducing, for example, and the various functions of motherhood each from each other. In the end, children become commodities, specially designed by medical intervention to meet the wishes of the nurturing parents. Instead of violating the natural processes that define us as human beings, a childless couple ought to satisfy their desire for a child by adopting one or more of the thousands of unadopted children just waiting for loving homes. In short, reproductive technologies are immoral because they are unnatural.

A second general moral issue is closely related to the first. It claims that **being childless is not an "illness"** that requires a cure from medicine. Rather wanting a child is just a desire, like the desire to be several inches taller or many pounds lighter. The considerable efforts of medicine should not be used to satisfy such desires, especially when doing so is so costly and when there is so much more significant suffering for medicine to relieve. The basic medical needs of millions go unmet in this country while thousands and thousands of dollars are spent on one "high-tech" baby. Moreover, insurance covers the cost of many of these procedures—which means that we all pay for them—draining money away from areas where it would do much more good. Even if the "unnatural" argument is rejected, reproductive technology is still immoral because it is a wasteful use of medical resources. As such it violates the principle of beneficence.

A third general moral issue claims that using reproductive technologies is **playing God.** To accuse someone of "playing God" is usually to accuse the person of immoral actions. However, this phrase is often used so vaguely that it almost always requires further clarification. In the case of reproductive technologies, for example, it often amounts to the claim that these technologies are unnatural. Sometimes, however, it may mean that there is danger in their use. We have already considered the "unnatural" objection; the playing God objection will be understood here to mean that reproductive technologies have great potential for harm.

Some of these harms may be *biological harms.* For example, if in the future we reproduce most of our children using "superior" genetic material, we may inadvertently risk our genetic futures by narrowing our "gene pool." Think of a gene pool as all the genes that may be passed on through reproduction. If we select only genes of certain types for reproduction, we may eliminate some from our futures that may help us to survive should environmental circumstances change. If there are dramatic climactic changes in the next hundred years, for example, we may not be able to adapt sufficiently to survive them if we have narrowed our gene pool. The wisdom of nature behind human evolution, a wisdom that designed the processes of human reproduction and survival over millions of years, will surely stand in jeopardy from the extensive use of various reproductive technologies.

Other harms may be *social harms*. Even though many children are raised successfully in single-parent homes, the back bone of society is still the two-parent family. Such families are built on the relationship between sex, love, and marriage. Reproductive technologies make it possible for sex to be separated from reproduction. People are not required to make babies, only their reproductive material is required. If sex is no longer required for producing children, the institution of marriage itself is in danger of becoming obsolete. It is within our families, however, that we learn our values. Perhaps even more important, it is within our families and our families alone that we are loved for our own sake—the type of love required for our self-esteem and well-being. Reproductive technologies are thus immoral not only because they threaten our biological health as a species, but also because they threaten our psychological health as individuals.

Specific Moral Issues

Moral Problems Associated with Diagnostic Technologies

Even diagnostic technologies, which purport simply to provide information, have their share of moral implications. The results of **genetic screening,** for example, may be used for significant harms as well as benefits. First, genetic counselors are supposed to provide information, not advice. However, several studies have shown that such *neutral information is a myth,* especially in the context of counseling high-risk potential parents. In subtle ways, genetic counselors convey their own opinions about which course of action a couple should take. If this happens frequently enough, the opinions of genetic counselors, not their clients, will control decisions about whether a couple at risk for having a child with a genetic defect should take that risk.

Next, there are issues of *privacy* that are important. If the results of genetic tests were made known to insurance companies or prospective employers, they could be used to deny insurance or jobs to people. Medical information of various sorts is routinely requested by such companies of its applicants, and genetic testing may well be added to their list of required medical information. The results of genetic screening may be harmful to the client in other ways as well. In general, because there is no cure as yet for genetic diseases, simply *knowing ahead of time* that you have the associated gene may cause more harm than good. A man who discovers that he has the gene for Huntington's disease can do little but wait for its symptoms to appear in middle age. Or a woman with a family history for breast cancer may discover that she has the associated gene. With no cure for this genetic condition, she is faced with either long-term worrying about developing cancer or deciding to have her breasts removed just in case she might get breast cancer in the future. Knowing that you have a genetic "bullet" waiting for you can be a benefit sometimes; in other cases, it may create more problems than it solves.

The main moral issue usually associated with the medically harmless procedure of **ultrasound** is its use, along with abortion, for *sex selection*. One thing learned from most second trimester ultrasound tests is the sex of the fetus. A couple with three boys who desperately want a girl could use ultrasound to discover the sex of the fetus and have an abortion if the fetus was male. They could keep trying until a girl was conceived. Although many believe that no decent person would ever abort a healthy fetus merely because of its sex, there is some evidence to believe that such faith is naive. In the United States no reason is required even for second trimester abortions, when the results of an ultrasound test would show the sex of the fetus. Although such abortions are more risky than those that take place in the first trimester, there really is no way to prevent such actions from occurring, short of denying ultrasound tests to any but high-risk couples. As nearly 70 percent of pregnant women currently undergo ultrasound testing and the majority of these are not high-risk women, denying ultrasound to all but high-risk couples would require a dramatic change in testing policies.

Amniocentesis and **CVS** shared associated moral problems. One of these is *abortion*, which is very likely if a genetic or congenital defect is discovered in the fetus. Abortion is less of a problem with CVS, as it is performed earlier than amniocentesis. However, CVS involves more *medical risks* than amniocentesis, especially the risk of the procedure itself causing miscarriage. In addition, for both procedures, test results in a tiny percentage of cases can be "false positives." That is, they can show a defect that is not there. The result is often the abortion of a healthy fetus. Finally, there are similar *psychological harms* associated with both procedures. In most cases, recipients of these tests are high-risk couples. Often they already have a child with a genetic disease, and they are willing to abort the fetus if it has the same disease. The stress of loving one child with this disease while aborting another solely because the fetus has the desease can be very damaging to the mental health of the couple.

Along with its benefits **PGD** also has associated harms and some related issues of injustice. First, it *costs* a great deal. If this cost is borne by the individual, then only the wealthy will have access to the procedure's benefits. This seems to be a dramatic form of unfairness. If its cost is borne by society, on the other hand, and PGD made available to all, it diverts medical resources away from other needy health areas. Second, PGD may have *social harms*. It may be thought of as the start of a "slippery slope" down which society will inevitably slide. As an attempt to ensure that children are born free from genetic disease, it may inspire further technological inroads in producing children with genetically enhanced characteristics—superior children. The issue of genetic enhancement and superior children will be discussed later. For now, the thought of designing our children to be superior sends chills down the spines of many.

Moral Problems Associated with Fertility Technologies

In this section the moral problems associated with four of the fertility technologies are discussed. AIH has few moral problems, but **AID** has many. For example, most children born from this process have *unknown biological fathers*. Unlike adopted children, who may be able to acquire this information, with AID the anonymous sperm donor remains anonymous. Also, some people worry that many of the frozen sperm banks from which sperm is obtained for the AID procedure are *not carefully regulated* by outside sources. Many are simply self-regulated. This means that the standards in place for screening donors may vary from one institution to another. If this is so, there may be a chance that the donated sperm itself will pass on a genetic defect or create some other type of disorder such as AIDS.

AID also contributes to the decline in the traditional two-parent family, as *single women* may purchase and use donor sperm. Perhaps the most serious problem, however, is that the *nurturing father may not bond* as closely with the child born of AID as he might if it was his own biological child. If the saying "blood is thicker than water" is true, he may not love such a child sufficiently, and even reject the child in any number of subtle ways. It takes a man with a great deal of confidence in his own integrity as a man to have his wife carry a child conceived with another man's reproductive material. In fact, one reason some religions have rejected AID is that they consider it to be a form of adultery. From the other perspective, those who donate sperm must live with the thought that somewhere out there is a child who is biologically their own.

IVF and its related technologies, GIFT and ZIFT, do carry some *medical risks,* especially because of the drugs and the laparoscopy that are required. These possible harms to the hopeful parents, however, are minor in comparison to the benefits to be gained by them—a child of their own. The major moral problems of IVF have more to do with justice than beneficence. Most of these problems revolve around the general issue of the *moral status of the embryo.* The basic issue is this: If fertilized eggs have full moral status, then many of the procedures involved with IVF appear to be immoral. For example, five attempts are required on average for each successful pregnancy. This means that four attempts at implantation fail and that the embryos involved, usually more than one each time, all die. Also, many embryos are frozen after fertilization and kept in that state until they are needed. If the first or second attempt is successful, they may not be needed any longer. If there is no longer any intention to use them, they are kept in a frozen state and sometimes discarded.

If embryos have full moral status, if they are just as much persons as are little babies, then clearly killing, freezing, and disposing of them is immoral. Even if the intention behind their creation is a good one—to produce a healthy baby—the means used is not. They embryos that do not survive the IVF process are used solely as a means to achieve the goal of a healthy baby. This clearly violates the principle of justice, one of whose requirements is that we respect persons. However, if embryos are not persons, if they are merely balls of cells or bits of tissue with no moral status, the procedures involved in IVF are morally acceptable.

Again, if embryos are persons, the very process of developing IVF was itself extremely immoral. As with the cloning of Dolly, there were many failures, well over two hundred, before its first success in 1978. These failures—if the embryos involved were persons—were sacrificed immorally for the sake of the babies who were born later. These *first experimental subjects* gave no consent to a high-risk procedure that had little chance of success initially. If babies were experimented on in this manner the procedure would be about as immoral and illegal as might be imagined. Only by claiming that embryos do not have moral status, even partial moral status, can IVF be seen as morally acceptable.

Two central moral problems are created by **surrogate motherhood** technology. The first arises when and if the surrogate or gestational mother decides to change her mind and *keep the baby.* If the surrogacy uses the AIH method, the surrogate is the biological mother so she has a legal claim to the child. In some states, surrogacy is treated as a form of adoption. Just as a mother who has agreed to give up her child for adoption has a few days after its birth to change her mind, so it is with surrogates. Unless there is a law that says the contract in which she agreed to give up the child takes priority over her change of heart, she does have the right to change her mind.

Very seldom does this happen, but when it does, there is great heartache and misery all around, especially for the intended mother. The question for many legal and ethical scholars is whether contract law or adoption laws should have the highest priority in surrogate cases. When IVF is used as the method of surrogacy, the gestational mother has no legal rights to the child, at least as far as the courts have decided so far. Because the child is not related to her biologically, the gestational mother may be viewed simply as someone whose body is being used to grow it and not as the mother in any other sense.

Surrogacy also creates another, more general moral problem, the problem of identifying who is the *rightful mother.* Some very strange situations can arise with surrogacy and the use of gestational mothers. For example, if a mother is the gestational mother for her daughter's baby, the child may have a mother who is at the same time his or her grandmother. Or a sister who is a surrogate using AIH may be an aunt as well as a mother to the child. If in the gestational mother procedure the female reproductive material is contributed from some outside source, the child literally has three mothers. In the past, these three "mothers" were usually one and the same. The only woman who could give birth to a child was the one who contributed the reproductive material. With the exception of death, poor health, or adoption, this woman would almost always be the nurturing mother as well. One simple rule that has been suggested to determine the legal mother is that the woman who gives birth to the child is the mother unless there is a legally recognized contract or law saying otherwise.

Although the technology for **human cloning** is not yet fully developed, the arguments pro and con have been discussed for some time. One potential benefit of cloning is that it may be used to avoid passing on a *genetic disease* that might result if a husband and wife were both carriers of a recessive genetic defect and reproduced in the natural way. Cloning from the cell of one parent results instead in a child who is both free from the disease and biologically that of the couple. In the same way, if a husband's sperm were infertile, he could donate a cell and transfer its nucleus to his wife's egg. This would avoid using donated material and produce a child that is biologically their own.

Another benefit is that a clone could be a *tissue or organ donor* for a sibling if it was created from the sibling's cells. Clones are identical twins of the donor, although of a different age, so there would be no problem with the rejection of, for example, a bone marrow transplant to save the life of the first child. As a variation on this theme, some propose cloning themselves only to the embryo stage. Embryos are composed of *stem cells,* and stem cells are valuable for regenerating cells in the brain and central nervous system. These cells might be used for curative purposes and then the cloned embryos destroyed.

Another reason for cloning appeals to the principle of autonomy. People should be able to produce genetic *copies of themselves.* They should also be able to produce copies of others as well, perhaps famous or *"superior" people,* so that their child will have a chance to live life on a high level of excellence. The reproductive rights of people should include the use of any technology, according to the principle of autonomy, as long as its use produces no harm to others.

Those opposed to cloning believe that many harms will follow from its use. First, cloning is *medically unsafe.* Any attempt to clone a human being at this time would surely lead to numerous failures. Much more time must be spent on animal cloning before we turn to human beings. Without such extensive studies we are simply using some clones (those who fail to survive) for the sake of others (those who succeed in the future). Attempts to clone a human being now would clearly be a violation of the principle of justice. Even when the technical problems are solved and cloning becomes medically safe, other harms will result from its use.

Harms to the cloned children are among the most serious of these harms. Clones produced from the cells of superior people will be created for certain purposes. They will be expected to be like those people they supposedly copy. A child created from the cell of Michael Jordan, for example, will be expected to be a great basketball star. Other children may be cloned to replace children or parents or other loved ones who have died. Some will be cloned to be "just like dad." In all of these cases the child is seen as a product that has been copied from another for a certain goal. It has not been created for the unique, priceless original that each child ought to be. Such a child may be viewed a "commodity," not a being who is the object of unconditional love. Should the clone fail to be like its genetic twin, it risks not being valued at all by its creators.

Social harms are the other type of harm that cloning is likely to produce. There is already a trend in society to accept reproductive technologies with few questions and to demand them as a right when they could be helpful. Often accompanying this acceptance is a willingness to ignore some of their moral implications, especially their potential harms to children and society. In the rush to accept IVF, gestational mothers, donated reproductive material, and now cloning, the slippery slope is well greased for the slide to the use of genetic enhancement technologies. Accompanying this use will be the attitude that children are products intended to satisfy the desires of their parents. Those concerned about this cultural slide fear that the level of selfishness made possible by the new technologies will be very harmful indeed. Especially susceptible to attack are our deeply held cultural beliefs about the purpose and value of children. They are not to be thought of as a means to the good of their parents but rather as people of value in themselves. If reproductive technologies threaten to change the role of the family and to weaken the unconditional love found only there, many believe that the use of these technologies for reproduction should be prohibited.

Some believe that cloning will not be an important moral issue in the future because there will be much more refined methods of selecting the genes of our off-spring. With cloning, either by nuclear transfer or by twinning, the entire genetic package of someone else is copied. With various forms of genetic engineering, however, just parts of a DNA molecule can be changed. This is the technology behind gene therapy and gene enhancement.

Safety issues are the biggest moral concern for **gene therapies,** whether these involve somatic cell or germ-line therapies. Many of the experimental studies on the early uses of gene therapies in adults have shown little improvement in the genetic condition being treated and some negative reactions by patients. Gene therapies practiced on the fertilized egg, germ-line therapies, also involve all the safety issues present with any new reproductive technology that involves manip-ulating and transferring embryos. The process of removing defective genes and replacing them with healthy ones adds a level of technical complication that goes far beyond the manipulation involved in IVF or cloning. Perfecting germ-line gene therapy will require a great deal of study on animal embryos.

But for the safety issue, most people see germ-line genetic therapy as a blessing that far outweighs any associated moral problems. After all, this form of gene therapy will actually allow us to rid our children of the genetic diseases caused by monogenic defects. The amount of suffering that will be avoided because of this is incalculable. Some may object to the costs involved, but they pale next to the costs required to treat someone with a genetic disease over his or her lifetime. Oth-ers may object that it is a first step down the slippery slope of gene enhancement. Even if this is true, however, it is not an inevitable outcome of the use of gene ther-apies. Besides, the slippery slope objection is valuable only if there is something immoral about gene enhancement itself.

Gene enhancement technologies, often referred to as "designer gene" tech-nology, are the most troublesome of all for many who worry about the moral implications of reproductive technology. Splicing in genes to create healthy chil-dren is one thing; using this technology to create superior children and even human hybrids is quite another. According to the promise of this technology, human embryos may be genetically altered to create the sorts of characteristics desired by their parents. Their genetic code may be rewritten to improve the results that mere natural processes would produce. Our children will be smarter, taller, stronger, and more creative than they might otherwise be; they will possess the specific physical features that their parents want them to have. Traits of ani-mals may be spliced in as well. A child may be given the vision of a hawk, the sense of smell of a bloodhound, and the speed of a leopard.

Of course, this all depends on the development of the appropriate technology. The function of specific genes that compose the human DNA molecule will have to be understood much more fully than they are at present, as will the function of various animal genes. In addition, because most of the interesting human traits are polygenic, identifying and understanding sets of genes will also be required. This technology is a long way off, so there is time for careful reflection about its possible harms and benefits. Its main benefit will be to *create superior people.* For others, this so-called benefit is not a benefit at all. Instead, it is a serious social harm. *Eugenics* is the name given to the attempt to create superior people. The last large-scale attempt at a eugenics program resulted in Hitler's death camps. Eugenics programs are harmful because they always adopt a notion of superiority that favors those in power and attempts to eliminate those who are not. It assumes that some people are biologically superior to others and thus are morally more valuable as well. This means that some people, those who are genetically superior, have a right to better treatment than others.

Even if there was not one controlling idea of what is superior and what is not, even if individual parents made up their own minds about the characteristics that were good for their children, gene enhancement technologies would be immoral. The very idea of deciding a child's biological future—and thus the biological future of its children—all to fit the selfish desires of its parents, is even more frightening than cloning a child for the same reason. Gene enhancing technology possesses all the *general moral problems* mentioned previously. It is unnatural, it threatens to shrink the gene pool, it is playing God, it is a threat to the family, and so on. It also risks *harming embryos* in the process of developing the technology, as did cloning and IVF before it.

There are *individual and social harms* that are likely to result from gene enhancement as well. If only the wealthy can afford to use this technology, which seems likely, then two classes of people will exist. Even if gene enhancement is limited solely to the use of human genes, a new class structure will emerge based on whether, and the degree to which, genetic modification has taken place. Such a divide will surely discriminate unfairly against those who were born without gene enhancement. But even if everyone receives gene enhancement, eliminating the differences between the genetic haves and have-nots, a society filled with superior people will still create its own problems. If everyone's I.Q. is raised by 25 points, for example, will there be anyone interested in some fields of work that are essential to society but do not involve much use of intelligence? As has been said by many others, in such a society who will pick up the trash?

Perhaps the scariest thought of all is the use of genetic enhancement to create *hybrids*—human beings who have spliced into their DNA genes from other species. The creation of such hybrids is probably far in the future, but we would be unwise to ignore the moral implications of this potential technology. Some see this technology as beneficial because it can accelerate evolution. It may be used to *create the next species* of posthuman beings, whose future natures may only be imagined now in a sort of science fiction way. For others, however, this so-called benefit is once again really a great harm. Tinkering with life to prevent suffering is one thing; literally playing God is quite another.

Exercise 13.1

This exercise is the longest and most difficult in the book. It may be performed according to several formats—classroom presentations or discussions, or some form of group project. Whatever the format used, the goal is the same—to demonstrate that you are able to think critically about a specific moral problem on your own. I believe your thinking skills are best demonstrated in writing, so I will describe this exercise as one requiring an eight- to ten-page paper. One of the many moral problems discussed in this chapter may serve as the subject matter of your paper, or you may wish to select another topic with the advice of your instructor.

A major assumption of this text is that to think critically about a moral issue is to adopt the pattern of critical thinking outlined in Part 1 and followed in Chapters 5 through 12 of Part 2. Review the steps of critical thinking at this point and use this review to guide your writing. The *outline* of your paper should follow the steps below. My preference is that you construct a two- to three-page outline first, submit it to your instructor for approval, and then write a paper that follows your outline, but class size and time may not allow this.

Use the following steps as a guide:

1. *Identify the problem*—This will be the topic of your paper, the major question with which it will be concerned. Be sure to phrase it as a moral problem, especially a problem about right or wrong. Also be sure that it is a controversial topic, one with a good case for as well as against it. Moral problems sometimes involve a struggle to do the right thing. The type of moral problem you are to be concerned with in this paper, however, is to determine the right thing to do. So it is important that you address a controversial problem for which the right thing to do is itself in doubt.

2. *Clarify concepts*—Be sure to say what certain key concepts mean. As we described or defined various reproductive technologies earlier in this chapter, for example, or said what "assisted suicide" meant in Chapter 7, or what "moral status" meant in Chapter 10, you must decide what your central concepts are and clearly define or describe them.

3. *Identify possible solutions*—After you have clearly stated the problem you will address, think of all its possible solutions. Sometimes a type of action is always immoral or always morally acceptable. Often, possible solutions involve more than "black or white" solutions, however, and include acceptance of an action with certain restrictions. After having identified the possible solutions you will consider, select the one you are going to defend. You do not have to argue for all possible solutions, as we have done in the text, just the one that you will defend. You do have to be familiar with arguments that support opposing solutions, however, as they contain premises that are objections to your view.

4. *Gather information*—Collect information that supports your possible solutions. It may be based on scientific studies or common sense. Part of this information-gathering process should also be an examination of any rules already in place that may or may not be consistent with your possible solution. Be sure your sources are reliable. Most of these technologies are new and much of what is written about them is to be found in journals. Go to the library and do a journal search. Also, use the Internet to gather information, but only from reliable sources.

5. *Examine assumptions and points of view*—This is not always an easy task but it is an important one. It is important because your own biases are based on the things you accept as true uncritically, and this often depends on your own personal history. You do not have to include assumptions and points of view explicitly, but you should be aware of them. They exert an influence on the view that you have chosen to defend and the degree to which you accept some facts as more reliable than others.

6. *Moral reasoning*—This is the heart of your paper. It is here, probably in the longest section, that you will construct a good reasons argument for the possible solution you think is best. Again, you do not have to argue for all possible solutions, just the one you are defending. You do have to know the reasons that support opposing views, however, as these are the objections that you must reply to in your argument. Remember that part of your argument will include premises for your view (the pros), and part will include answering objections (the cons) to opposing views. A good strategy is to say which moral principle each premise follows. Recall that in a cogent argument, premises must be reliable *and* relevant. Because your conclusion is a moral statement, a statement about right and wrong actions, each premise will be relevant to the conclusion if it states something about a harm or a benefit, or a matter of justice or autonomy.

7. *Consider the consequences*—You should say what will happen if your possible solution is adopted. Show how it will change things in general and how it will make the lives of individuals better or worse if we adopt the view defended in your paper.

Be sure to begin your paper by sketching out the tension between opposing solutions. Get the reader to *feel* that there is a real problem that you are going to discuss, one that may affect him or her in important ways. Also include a conclusion in which you sum up your main points. Usually it is best if these sections are written last, once you know where your own thoughts are going. Good luck with this project. If you complete it successfully you should feel confident that you are now in an intellectual position to make your own thoughtful moral decisions.

The Morality of Human Cloning

The following readings address some of the moral implications of human cloning. They are included here for two reasons. First, if you decide to choose the topic of human cloning as part of Exercise 13.1, the readings may be used as a good source of reasons for and against it. Second, if you choose another topic, the quality of these articles will serve as a standard that your selected sources should match.

Human Cloning and the Challenge of Regulation

JOHN A. ROBERTSON, J.D.

THE BIRTH OF DOLLY, the sheep cloned from a mammary cell of an adult ewe, has initiated a public debate about human cloning. Although cloning of humans may never be clinically feasible, discussion of the ethical, legal, and social issues raised is important. Cloning is just one of several techniques potentially available to select, control, or alter the genome of offspring.[1-3] The

John A. Robertson, J. D., University of Texas School of Law, *Austin, TX 78705. Used by permission of the Massachusetts Medical Society.*

development of such technology poses an important social challenge: how to ensure that the technology is used to enhance, rather than limit, individual freedom and welfare.

A key ethical question is whether a responsible couple, interested in rearing healthy offspring biologically related to them, might ethically choose to use cloning (or other genetic-selection techniques) for that purpose. The answer should take into account the benefits sought through the use of the techniques and any potential harm to offspring or to other interests.

The most likely uses of cloning would be far removed from the bizarre or horrific scenarios that initially dominated media coverage.[4] Theoretically, cloning would enable rich or powerful persons to clone themselves several times over, and commercial entrepreneurs might hire women to bear clones of sports or entertainment celebrities to be sold to others to rear. But current reproductive techniques can also be abused, and existing laws against selling children would apply to those created by cloning.

There is no reason to think that the ability to clone humans will cause many people to turn to cloning when other methods of reproduction would enable them to have healthy children. Cloning a human being by somatic-cell nuclear transfer, for example, would require a consenting person as a source of DNA, eggs to be enucleated and then fused with the DNA, a woman who would carry and deliver the child, and a person or couple to raise the child. Given this reality, cloning is most likely to be sought by couples who, because of infertility, a high risk of severe genetic disease, or other factors, cannot or do not wish to conceive a child.

Several plausible scenarios can be imagined. Rather than use sperm, egg, or embryo from anonymous donors, couples who are infertile as a result of gametic insufficiency might choose to clone one of the partners. If the husband were the source of the DNA and the wife provided the egg that received the nuclear transfer and then gestated the fetus,

they would have a child biologically related to each of them and would not need to rely on anonymous gamete or embryo donation. Of course, many infertile couples might still prefer gamete or embryo donation or adoption. But there is nothing inherently wrong in wishing to be biologically related to one's children, even when this goal cannot be achieved through sexual reproduction.

A second plausible application would be for a couple at high risk of having offspring with a genetic disease.[5] Couples in this situation must now choose whether to risk the birth of an affected child, to undergo prenatal or preimplantation diagnosis and abortion or the discarding of embryos, to accept gamete donation, to seek adoption, or to remain childless. If cloning were available, however, some couples, in line with prevailing concepts of kinship, family, and parenting, might strongly prefer to clone one of themselves or another family member. Alternatively, if they already had a healthy child, they might choose to use cloning to create a later-born twin of that child. In the more distant future, it is even possible that the child whose DNA was replicated would not have been born healthy but would have been made healthy by gene therapy after birth.

A third application relates to obtaining tissue or organs for transplantation. A child who needed an organ or tissue transplant might lack a medically suitable donor. Couples in this situation have sometimes conceived a child coitally in the hope that he or she would have the correct tissue type to serve, for example, as a bone marrow donor for an older sibling.[6,7] If the child's disease was not genetic, a couple might prefer to clone the affected child to be sure that the tissue would match.

It might eventually be possible to procure suitable tissue or organs by cloning the source DNA only to the point at which stem cells or other material might be obtained for transplantation, thus avoiding the need to bring a child into the world for the sake of obtaining tissue.[8] Cloning a person's cells up to the embryo stage might provide a source of stem cells or tissue for the person cloned. Cloning might also be used to enable a couple to clone a dead or dying child so as to have that child live on in some closely related form, to obtain sufficient numbers of embryos for transfer and pregnancy, or to eliminate mitochondrial disease.[5]

Most, if not all, of the potential uses of cloning are controversial, usually because of the explicit copying of the genome. As the National Bioethics Advisory Commission noted, in addition to concern about physical safety and eugenics, somatic-cell cloning raises issues of the individuality, autonomy, objectification, and kinship of the resulting children.[5] In other instances, such as the production of embryos to serve as tissue banks, the ethical issue is the sacrifice of embryos created solely for that purpose.

Given the wide leeway now granted couples to use assisted reproduction and prenatal genetic selection in forming families, cloning should not be rejected in all circumstances as unethical or illegitimate. The manipulation of embryos and the use of gamete donors and surrogates are increasingly common. Most fetuses conceived in the United States and Western Europe are now screened for genetic or chromosomal anomalies. Before conception, screening to identify carriers of genetic diseases is widespread.[9] Such practices also deviate from conventional notions of reproduction, kinship, and medical treatment of infertility, yet they are widely accepted.

Despite the similarity of cloning to current practices, however, the dissimilarities should not be overlooked. The aim of most other forms of assisted reproduction is the birth of a child who is a descendant of at least one member of the couple, not an identical twin. Most genetic selection acts negatively to identify and screen out unwanted traits such as genetic disease, not positively to choose or replicate the genome as in somatic-cell cloning.[3] It is not clear, however, why a child's relation to his or her rearing parents must always be that of sexually reproduced descendant when such a relationship is not possible because of infertil-

ity or other factors. Indeed, in gamete donation and adoption, although sexual reproduction is involved, a full descendant relation between the child and both rearing parents is lacking. Nor should the difference between negative and positive means of selecting children determine the ethical or social acceptability of cloning or other techniques. In both situations, a deliberate choice is made so that a child is born with one genome rather than another or is not born at all.

Is cloning sufficiently similar to current assisted-reproduction and genetic-selection practices to be treated similarly as a presumptively protected exercise of family or reproductive liberty?[10] Couples who request cloning in the situations I have described are seeking to rear healthy children with whom they will have a genetic or biologic tie, just as couples who conceive their children sexually do. Whether described as "replication" or as "reproduction," the resort to cloning is similar enough in purpose and effects to other reproduction and genetic-selection practices that it should be treated similarly. Therefore, a couple should be free to choose cloning unless there are compelling reasons for thinking that this would create harm that the other procedures would not cause.[10]

The concern of the National Bioethics Advisory Commission about the welfare of the clone reflects two types of fear. The first is that a child with the same nuclear DNA as another person, who is thus that person's later-born identical twin, will be so severely harmed by the identity of nuclear DNA between them that it is morally preferable, if not obligatory, that the child not be born at all.[5] In this case the fear is that the later-born twin will lack individuality or the freedom to create his or her own identity because of confusion or expectations caused by having the same DNA as another person.[5,11]

This claim does not withstand the close scrutiny that should precede interference with a couple's freedom to bear and rear biologically related children.[10] Having the same genome as another person is not in itself harmful, as widespread experience with monozygotic twins shows. Being a twin does not deny either twin his or her individuality or freedom, and twins often have a special intimacy or closeness that few non-twin siblings can experience.[12] There is no reason to think that being a later-born identical twin resulting from cloning would change the overall assessment of being a twin.

Differences in mitochondria and the uterine and childhood environment will undercut problems of similarity and minimize the risk of overidentification with the first twin. A clone of Smith may look like Smith, but he or she will not be Smith and will lack many of Smith's phenotypic characteristics. The effects of having similar DNA will also depend on the length of time before the second twin is born, on whether the twins are raised together, on whether they are informed that they are genetic twins, on whether other people are so informed, on the beliefs that the rearing parents have about genetic influence on behavior, and on other factors. Having a previously born twin might in some circumstances also prove to be a source of support or intimacy for the later-born child.

The risk that parents or the child will overly identify the child with the DNA source also seems surmountable. Would the child invariably be expected to match the phenotypic characteristics of the DNA source, thus denying the second twin an "open future" and the freedom to develop his or her own identity?[5,11,13] In response to this question, one must ask whether couples who choose to clone offspring are more likely to want a child who is a mere replica of the DNA source or a child who is unique and valued for more than his or her genes. Couples may use cloning in order to ensure that the biologic child they rear is healthy, to maintain a family connection in the face of gametic infertility, or to obtain matched tissue for transplantation and yet still be responsibly committed to the welfare of their child, including his or her separate identity

and interests and right to develop as he or she chooses.

The second type of fear is that parents who choose their child's genome through somatic-cell cloning will view the child as a commodity or an object to serve their own ends.[5] We do not view children born through coital or assisted reproduction as "mere means" just because people reproduce in order to have company in old age, to fulfill what they see as God's will, to prove their virility, to have heirs, to save a relationship, or to serve other selfish purposes.[14] What counts is how a child is treated after birth. Self-interested motives for having children do not prevent parents from loving children for themselves once they are born.

The use of cloning to form families in the situations I have described, though closely related to current assisted-reproduction and genetic-selection practices, does offer unique variations. The novelty of the relation—cloning in lieu of sperm donation, for example, produces a later-born identical twin raised by the older twin and his spouse—will create special psychological and social challenges. Can these challenges be successfully met, so that cloning produces net good for families and society? Given the largely positive experience with assisted-reproduction techniques that initially appeared frightening, cautious optimism is justified. We should be able to develop procedures and guidelines for cloning that will allow us to obtain its benefits while minimizing its problems and dangers.

In the light of these considerations, I would argue that a ban on privately funded cloning research is unjustified and likely to hamper important types of research.[8] A permanent ban on the cloning of human beings, as advocated by the Council of Europe and proposed in Congress, is also unjustified.[15,16] A more limited ban—whether for 5 years, as proposed by the National Bioethics Advisory Commission and enacted in California, or for 10 years, as in the bill of Senator Dianne Feinstein (D-Calif.) and Senator Edward M. Kennedy (D-Mass.)

that is now before Congress—is also open to question.[5,17,18] Given the early state of cloning science and the widely shared view that the transfer of cloned embryos to the uterus before the safety and efficacy of the procedure has been established is unethical, few responsible physicians are likely to offer human cloning in the near future.[5] Nor are profit-motivated entrepreneurs, such as Richard Seed, likely to have many customers for their cloning services until the safety of the procedure is demonstrated.[19] A ban on human cloning for a limited period would thus serve largely symbolic purposes. Symbolic legislation, however, often has substantial costs.[20,21] A government-imposed prohibition on privately funded cloning, even for a limited period, should not be enacted unless there is a compelling need. Such a need has not been demonstrated.

Rather than seek to prohibit all uses of human cloning, we should focus our attention on ensuring that cloning is done well. No physician or couple should embark on cloning without careful thought about the novel relational issues and child-rearing responsibilities that will ensue. We need regulations or guidelines to ensure safety and efficacy, fully informed consent and counseling for the couple, the consent of any person who may provide DNA, guarantees of parental rights and duties, and a limit on the number of clones from any single source.[10] It may also be important to restrict cloning to situations where there is a strong likelihood that the couple or individual initiating the procedure will also rear the resulting child. This principle will encourage a stable parenting situation and minimize the chance that cloning entrepreneurs will create clones to be sold to others.[22] As our experience grows, some restrictions on who may serve as a source of DNA for cloning (for example, a ban on cloning one's parents) may also be defensible.[10]

Cloning is important because it is the first of several positive means of genetic selection that may be sought by families seeking to have and rear healthy, biologically related offspring. In the future, mitochondrial transplantation, germ-line gene therapy, genetic enhancement, and other forms of prenatal genetic alteration may be possible.[3,23,24] With each new technique, as with cloning, the key question will be whether it serves important health, reproductive, or family needs and whether its benefits outweigh any likely harm. Cloning illustrates the principle that when legitimate uses of a technique are likely, regulatory policy should avoid prohibition and focus on ensuring that the technique is used responsibly for the good of those directly involved. As genetic knowledge continues to grow, the challenge of regulation will occupy us for some time to come.

NOTES

1. Silver LM. Remaking Eden: cloning and beyond in a brave new world. New York: Avon Books, 1997.

2. Walters L, Palmer JG. The ethics of human gene therapy. New York: Oxford University Press, 1997.

3. Robertson JA. Genetic selection of offspring characteristics. Boston Univ Law Rev 1996; 76:421–82.

4. Begley S. Can we clone humans? Newsweek. March 10, 1997:53–60.

5. Cloning human beings: report and recommendations of the National Bioethics Advisory Commission. Rockville, Md.: National Bioethics Advisory Commission, June 1997.

6. Robertson JA. Children of choice: freedom and the new reproductive technologies. Princeton, N.J.: Princeton University Press, 1994.

7. Kearney W, Caplan AL. Parity for the donation of bone marrow: ethical and policy considerations. In: Blank RH, Bonnicksen AL, eds. Emerging issues in biomedical policy: an annual review. Vol. 1. New York: Columbia University Press, 1992:262–85.

8. Kassirer JP, Rosenthal NA. Should human cloning research be off limits? N Engl J Med 1998;338:905–6.

9. Holtzman NA. Proceed with caution: predicting genetic risks in the recombinant DNA era. Baltimore: Johns Hopkins University Press, 1989.

10. Robertson JA. Liberty, identity, and human cloning. Texas Law Rev 1998;77:1371–456.

11. Davis DS. What's wrong with cloning? Jurimetrics 1997;38:83–9.

12. Segal NL. Behavioral aspects of intergenerational human cloning: what twins tell us. Jurimetrics 1997;38:57–68.

13. Jonas H. Philosophical essays: from ancient creed to technological man. Englewood Cliffs, N.J.: Prentice-Hall, 1974:161.

14. Heyd D. Genethics: moral issues in the creation of people. Berkeley: University of California Press, 1992.

15. Council of Europe. Draft additional protocol to the Convention on Human Rights and Biomedicine on the prohibition of cloning human beings with explanatory report and Parliamentary Assembly opinion (adopted September 22, 1997). XXXVI International Legal Materials 1415 (1997).

16. Human Cloning Prohibition Act, H.R. 923, S.1601 (March 5, 1997).

17. Act of Oct. 4, 1997, ch. 688, 1997 Cal. Legis. Serv. 3790 (West, WESTLAW through 1997 Sess.).

18. Prohibition on Cloning of Human Beings Act, S. 1602, 105th Cong. (1998).

19. Stolberg SG. A small spark ignites debate on laws on cloning humans. New York Times. January 19, 1998:A1.

20. Gusfield J. Symbolic crusade: status politics and the American temperance movement. Urbana: University of Illinois Press, 1963.

21. Wolf SM. Ban cloning? Why NBAC is wrong. Hastings Cent Rep 1997;27(5):12.

22. Wilson JQ. The paradox of cloning. The Weekly Standard. May 26, 1997:23–7.

23. Zhang J, Grifo J, Blaszczyk A, et al. In vitro maturation of human preovulatory oocytes reconstructed by germinal vesicle transfer. Fertil Steril 1997;68:Suppl:S1. abstract.

24. Bonnicksen AL. Transplanting nuclei between human eggs: implications for germ-line genetics. Politics and the Life Sciences. March 1998:3–10.

© 1998, Massachusetts Medical Society.

Why We Should Ban Human Cloning

GEORGE J. ANNAS, J.D., M.P.H.

IN FEBRUARY THE U.S. SENATE voted 54 to 42 against bringing an anticloning bill directly to the floor for a vote.[1] During the debate, more than 16 scientific and medical organizations, including the American Society of Reproductive Medicine and the Federation of American Societies for Experimental Biology, and 27 Nobel prize-winning scientists, agreed that there should be a moratorium on the creation of a human being by somatic nuclear transplants. What the groups objected to was legislation that went beyond this prohibition to include cloning human cells, genes, and tissues. An alternative proposal was introduced by Senator Edward M. Kennedy (D-Mass.) and Senator Dianne Feinstein (D-Calif.) and modeled on a 1997 proposal by President Bill Clinton and his National Bioethics Advisory Commission. It would, in line with the views of all of these scientific groups, outlaw attempts to produce a child but permit all other forms of cloning research.[2,3] Because the issue is intimately involved with research with embryos and abortion politics, in many ways the congressional debates over human cloning are a replay of past debates on fetal-tissue

George J. Annas, J.D., M.P.H., Boston University Schools of Medicine and Public Health, *Boston, MA 02118. Used by permission of the Massachusetts Medical Society.*

transplants[4] and research using human embryos.[5] Nonetheless, the virtually unanimous scientific consensus on the advisability of a legislative ban or voluntary moratorium on the attempt to create a human child by cloning justifies deeper discussion of the issue than it has received so far.

It has been more than a year since embryologist Ian Wilmut and his colleagues announced to the world that they had cloned a sheep.[6] No one has yet duplicated their work, raising serious questions about whether Dolly the sheep was cloned from a stem cell or a fetal cell, rather than a fully differentiated cell.[7] For my purposes, the success or failure of Wilmut's experiment is not the issue. Public attention to somatic-cell nuclear cloning presents an opportunity to consider the broader issues of public regulation of human research and the meaning of human reproduction.

CLONING AND IMAGINATION

In the 1970s, human cloning was a centerpiece issue in bioethical debates in the United States.[8,9] In 1978, a House committee held a hearing on human cloning in response to the publication of David Rorvik's *In His Image: The Cloning of a Man*.[10] All the scientists who testified assured the committee that the supposed account of the cloning of a human being was fictional and that the techniques described in the book could not work. The chief point the scientists wanted to make, however, was that they did not want any laws enacted that might affect their research. In the words of one, "There is no need for any form of regulation, and it could only in the long run have a harmful effect."[11] The book was an elaborate fable, but it presented a valuable opportunity to discuss the ethical implications of cloning. The failure to see it as a fable was a failure of imagination. We normally do not look to novels for scientific knowledge, but they provide more: insights into life itself.[12]

This failure of imagination has been witnessed repeatedly, most recently in 1997,

when President Clinton asked the National Bioethics Advisory Commission to make recommendations about human cloning. Although acknowledging in their report that human cloning has always seemed the stuff of science fiction rather than science, the group did not commission any background papers on how fiction informs the debate. Even a cursory reading of books like Aldous Huxley's *Brave New World*, Ira Levin's *The Boys from Brazil*, and Fay Weldon's *The Cloning of Joanna May*, for example, would have saved much time and needless debate. Literary treatments of cloning inform us that cloning is an evolutionary dead end that can only replicate what already exists but cannot improve it; that exact replication of a human is not possible; that cloning is not inherently about infertile couples or twins, but about a technique that can produce an indefinite number of genetic duplicates; that clones must be accorded the same human rights as persons that we grant any other human; and that personal identity, human dignity, and parental responsibility are at the core of the debate about human cloning.

We might also have gained a better appreciation of our responsibilities to our children had we examined fiction more closely. The reporter who described Wilmut as "Dolly's laboratory father,"[13] for example, probably could not have done a better job of conjuring up images of Mary Shelley's *Frankenstein* if he had tried. Frankenstein was also his creature's father and god; the creature told him, "I ought to be thy Adam." As in the case of Dolly, the "spark of life" was infused into the creature by an electric current. Shelley's great novel explores virtually all the noncommercial elements of today's debate.

The naming of the world's first cloned mammal also has great significance. The sole survivor of 277 cloned embryos (or "fused couplets"), the clone could have been named after its sequence in this group (for example, C-137), but this would only have emphasized its character as a laboratory product. In stark contrast, the name Dolly (provided for the public and not used in the scientific report in *Nature*, in which she is identified as 6LL3) suggests a unique individual. Victor Frankenstein, of course, never named his creature, thereby repudiating any parental responsibility. The creature himself evolved into a monster when he was rejected not only by Frankenstein, but by society as well. Naming the world's first mammal clone Dolly was meant to distance her from the Frankenstein myth both by making her something she is not (a doll) and by accepting "parental" responsibility for her.

Unlike Shelley's world, the future envisioned in Huxley's *Brave New World* in which all humans are created by cloning through embryo splitting and conditioned to join a specified worker group, was always unlikely. There are much more efficient ways of creating killers or terrorists (or even soldiers and workers) than through cloning. Physical and psychological conditioning can turn teenagers into terrorists in a matter of months, so there is no need to wait 18 to 20 years for the clones to grow up and be trained themselves. Cloning has no real military or paramilitary uses. Even clones of Adolf Hitler would have been very different people because they would have grown up in a radically altered world environment.

CLONING AND REPRODUCTION

Even though virtually all scientists oppose it, a minority of free-marketers and bioethicists have suggested that there might nonetheless be some good reasons to clone a human. But virtually all these suggestions themselves expose the central problem of cloning: the devaluing of persons by depriving them of their uniqueness. One common example suggested is cloning a dying or recently deceased child if this is what the grieving parents want. A fictional cover story in the March 1998 issue of *Wired*, for example, tells the story of the world's first clone.[14] She is cloned from the DNA of a dead two-week-old infant, who died from a mitochondrial defect that is later "cured" by cloning with an enucleated donor egg. The closer one gets to the embryo stage, the more cloning a child looks like the much less problematic method of cloning by "twinning" or embryo splitting. And proponents of cloning tend to want to "naturalize" and "normalize" asexual replication by arguing that it is just like having "natural" twins.

Embryo splitting might be justified if only a few embryos could be produced by an infertile couple and all were implanted at the same time (since this does not involve replicating an existing and known genome). But scenarios of cloning by nuclear transfer have involved older children, and the only reason to clone an existing human is to create a genetic replica. Using the bodies of children to replicate them encourages all of us to devalue children and treat them as interchangeable commodities. For example, thanks to cloning, the death of a child need no longer be a singular human tragedy but, rather, can be an opportunity to try to replicate the no longer priceless (or irreplaceable) dead child. No one should have such dominion over a child (even a dead or dying child) as to use his or her genes to create the child's child.

Cloning would also radically alter what it means to be human by replicating a living or dead human being asexually to produce a person with a single genetic parent. The danger is that through human cloning we will lose something vital to our humanity, the uniqueness (and therefore the value and dignity) of every human. Cloning represents the height of genetic reductionism and genetic determinism.

Population geneticist R.C. Lewontin has challenged my position that the first human clone would also be the first human with a single genetic parent by arguing that, instead, "a child by cloning has a full set of chromosomes like anyone else, half of which were derived from a mother and half from a father. It happens that these chromosomes were passed through another individual, the cloning donor, on the way to the child. That donor is certainly not the child's 'parent' in any biological sense, but simply an earlier off-spring of the original parents."[15] Lewontin takes genetic reductionism to perhaps its logical extreme. People become no more than containers of their parents' genes, and their parents have the right to treat them not as individual human beings, but rather as human embryos—entities that can be split and replicated at their whim without any consideration of the child's choice or welfare. Children (even adult children), according to Lewontin's view, have no say in whether they are replicated or not, because it is their parents, not they, who are reproducing. This radical redefinition of reproduction and parenthood, and the denial of the choice to procreate or not, turns out to be an even stronger argument against cloning children than its biologic novelty. Of course, we could require the consent of adults to be cloned—but why should we, if they are not becoming parents?

Related human rights and human dignity would also prohibit using cloned children as organ sources for their father or mother original. Nor is there any constitutional right to be cloned in the United States that is triggered by marriage to someone with whom an adult cannot reproduce sexually, because there is no tradition of asexual replication and because permitting asexual replication is not necessary to safeguard any existing concept of ordered liberty (rights fundamental to ordered liberty are the rights the Supreme Court sees as essential to individual liberty in our society).

Although it is possible to imagine some scenarios in which cloning could be used for the treatment of infertility, the use of cloning simply provides parents another choice for choice's sake, not out of necessity. Moreover, in a fundamental sense, cloning cannot be a treatment for infertility. This replication technique changes the very concept of infertility itself, since all humans have somatic cells that could be used for asexual replication and therefore no one would be unable to replicate himself or herself asexually. In vitro fertilization, on the other hand, simply provides a technological way for otherwise infertile humans to reproduce sexually.

John Robertson argues that adults have a right to procreate in any way they can, and that the interests of the children cannot be taken into account because the resulting children cannot be harmed (since without cloning the children would not exist at all).[16] But this argument amounts to a tautology. It applies equally to everyone alive; none of us would exist had it not been for the precise and unpredictable time when the father's sperm and the mother's egg met. This biologic fact, however, does not justify a conclusion that our parents had no obligations to us as their future children. If it did, it would be equally acceptable, from the child's perspective, to be gestated in a great ape, or even a cow, or to be composed of a mixture of ape genes and human genes.

The primary reason for banning the cloning of living or dead humans was articulated by the philosopher Hans Jonas in the early 1970s. He correctly noted that it does not matter that creating an exact duplicate of an existing person is impossible. What matters is that the person is chosen to be cloned because of some characteristic or characteristics he or she possesses (which, it is hoped, would also be possessed by the genetic copy or clone). Jonas argued that cloning is always a crime against the clone, the crime of depriving the clone of his or her "existential right to certain subjective terms of being"—particularly, the "right to ignorance" of facts about his or her origin that are likely to be "paralyzing for the spontaneity of becoming himself" or herself.[17] This advance knowledge of what another has or has not accomplished with the clone's genome destroys the clone's "condition for authentic growth" in seeking to answer the fundamental question of all beings, "Who am I?" Jonas continues: "The ethical command here entering the enlarged stage of our powers is: never to violate the right to that ignorance which is a condition of authentic action; or: to respect the right of each human life to find its own way and be a surprise to itself."[17]

Jonas is correct. His rationale, of course, applies only to a "delayed genetic twin" or "serial twin" created from an existing human, not to genetically identical twins born at the same time, including those created by cloning with use of embryo splitting. Even if one does not agree with him, however, it is hypocritical to argue that a cloning technique that limits the liberty and choices of the resulting child or children can be justified on the grounds that cloning expands the liberty and choices of would-be cloners.[18]

MORATORIUMS AND BANS ON HUMAN CLONING

Members of the National Bioethics Advisory Commission could not agree on much, but they did conclude that any current attempt to clone a human being should be prohibited by basic ethical principles that ban putting human subjects at substantial risk without their informed consent. But danger itself will not prevent scientists and physicians from performing first-of-their-kind experiments—from implanting a baboon's heart in a human baby to using a permanent artificial heart in an adult—and cloning techniques may be both safer and more efficient in the future. We must identify a mechanism that can both prevent premature experimentation and permit reasonable experimentation when the facts change.

The mechanism I favor is a broad-based regulatory agency to oversee human experimentation in the areas of genetic engineering, research with human embryos, xenografts, artificial organs, and other potentially dangerous boundary-crossing experiments.[19] Any such national regulatory agency must be composed almost exclusively of nonresearchers and non-physicians so it can reflect public values, not parochial concerns. Currently, the operative American ethic seems to be that if any possible case can be imagined in which a new technology might be useful, it should not be prohibited, no matter what harm might result. One of the most important procedural

steps Congress should take in setting up a federal agency to regulate human experimentation would be to put the burden of proof on those who propose to undertake novel experiments (including cloning) that risk harm and call deeply held social values into question.

This shift in the burden of proof is critical if society is to have an influence over science.[20] Without it, social control is not possible. This model applies the precautionary principle of international environmental law to cloning and other potentially harmful biomedical experiments involving humans. The principle requires governments to protect the public health and the environment from realistic threats of irreversible harm or catastrophic consequences even in the absence of clear evidence of harm.[21] Under this principle, proponents of human cloning would have the burden of proving that there was some compelling contravailing need to benefit either current or future generations before such an experiment was permitted (for example, if the entire species were to become sterile). Thus, regulators would not have the burden of proving that there was some compelling reason not to approve it. This regulatory scheme would depend on at least a de facto, if not a de jure, ban or moratorium on such experiments and a mechanism such as my proposed regulatory agency that could lift the ban. The suggestion that the Food and Drug Administration (FDA) can substitute for such an agency is fanciful. The FDA has no jurisdiction over either the practice of medicine or human replication and is far too narrowly constituted to represent the public in this area. Some see human cloning as inevitable and uncontrollable.[22,23] Control will be difficult, and it will ultimately require close international cooperation. But this is no reason not to try—any more than a recognition that controlling terrorism or biologic weapons is difficult and uncertain justifies making no attempt at control.

On the recommendation of the National Bioethics Advisory Commission, the White

House sent proposed anticloning legislation to Congress in June 1997. The Clinton proposal receded into obscurity until early 1998, when a Chicago physicist, Richard Seed, made national news by announcing that he intended to raise funds to clone a human. Because Seed acted like a prototypical "mad scientist," his proposal was greeted with almost universal condemnation.[24] Like the 1978 Rorvik hoax, however, it provided another opportunity for public discussion of cloning and prompted a more refined version of the Clinton proposal: the Feinstein-Kennedy bill. We can (and should) take advantage of this opportunity to distinguish the cloning of cells and tissues from the cloning of human beings by somatic nuclear transplantation[25] and to permit the former while prohibiting the latter. We should also take the opportunity to fill in the regulatory lacuna that permits any individual scientist to act first and consider the human consequences later, and we should use the controversy over cloning as an opportunity to begin an international dialogue on human experimentation.

NOTES

1. U.S. Senate. 144 Cong. Rec. S561–S580, S607–S608 (1998).

2. S. 1611 (Feinstein-Kennedy Prohibition on Cloning of Human Beings Act of 1998).

3. Cloning human beings: report and recommendations of the National Bioethics Advisory Commission. Rockville, Md.: National Bioethics Advisory Commission, June 1997.

4. Annas GJ, Elias S. The politics of transplantation of human fetal tissue. N Engl J Med 1989;320:1079–82.

5. Annas GJ, Caplan A, Elias S. The politics of human embryo research—avoiding ethical gridlock. N Engl J Med 1996;334:1329–32.

6. Wilmut I, Schnieke AE, McWhir J, Kind AJ, Campbell KH. Viable off-spring derived from fetal and adult mammalian cells. Nature 1997;385:810–3.

7. Butler D. Dolly researcher plans further experiments after challenges. Nature 1998;391:825–6.

8. Lederberg J. Experimental genetics and human evolution. Am Naturalist 1966;100:519–31.

9. Watson JD. Moving toward the clonal man. Atlantic Monthly. May 1971:50–3.

10. Rorvik DM. In his image: the cloning of a man. Philadelphia: J.B. Lippincott, 1978.

11. Development in cell biology and genetics, cloning. Hearings before the Subcommittee on Health and the Environment of the Committee on Interstate and Foreign Commerce of the U.S. House of Representatives, 95th Congress, 2d Session, May 31, 1978.

12. Chomsky N. Language and problems of knowledge: the Managua lectures. Cambridge, Mass.: MIT Press, 1988.

13. Montalbano W. Cloned sheep is star, but not sole project, at institute. Los Angeles Times. February 25, 1997:A7.

14. Kadrey R. Carbon copy: meet the first human clone. Wired. March 1998:146–50.

15. Lewontin RC. Confusion over cloning. New York Review of Books. October 23, 1997:20–3.

16. Robertson JA. Children of choice: freedom and the new reproductive technologies. Princeton, N.J.: Princeton University Press, 1994:169.

17. Jonas H. Philosophical essays: From ancient creed to technological man. Englewood Cliffs, N.J.: Prentice-Hall, 1974:162–3.

18. Annas GJ. Some choice: law, medicine and the market. New York: Oxford University Press, 1998:14–5.

19. Annas GJ. Regulatory models for human embryo cloning: the free market, professional guidelines, and government restrictions. Kennedy Inst Ethics J 1994;4:235–49.

20. Hearings before the U.S. Senate Subcommittee on Public Health and Safety, 105th Congress, 1st Session, March 12, 1997. (Or see: http://www-busph.bu.edu/depts/lw/clonetest.htm.)

21. Cross FB. Paradoxical perils of the precautionary principle. Washington Lee Law Rev 1996;53:851–925.

22. Kolata GB. Clone: the road to Dolly, and the path ahead. New York: W. Morrow, 1998.

23. Silver LM. Remaking Eden: cloning and beyond in a brave new world. New York: Avon Books, 1997.

24. Knox RA. A Chicagoan plans to offer cloning of humans. Boston Globe. January 7, 1998:A3.

25. Kassirer JP, Rosenthal NA. Should human cloning research be off limits? N Engl J Med 1998;338:905–6.

Ethical and Policy Issues of Human Cloning

HAROLD T. SHAPIRO

THE IDEA THAT HUMANS MIGHT someday be cloned from a single adult somatic cell without sexual reproduction moved further away from science fiction and closer to a genuine possibility when scientists at the Roslin Institute in Scotland announced the successful cloning of a sheep[1] by a new technique that had never before been fully successful in mammals. The technique involved transplanting the genetic material of an adult sheep, apparently obtained from a well-differentiated somatic cell, into an egg from which the nucleus had been removed. The resulting birth of the sheep, named Dolly, on 5 July 1996, was different from prior attempts to create identical offspring because Dolly contained the genetic material of only one parent and was therefore a "delayed" genetic twin of a single adult sheep.

This cloning technique, which I will refer to as "somatic cell nuclear transfer," is an extension of research that had been going on for over 40 years with nuclei derived from nonhuman embryonic and fetal cells. The further demonstration that nuclei from cells derived from an adult animal could be "reprogrammed," or that the full genetic complement of such a cell could be reactivated well into the chronological life of the cell, is what sets the results of this experiment apart from prior work. At the same time, several serious scientific uncertainties remain that could have a significant impact on the potential ability of this new technique to create human beings.

The author is chair of the National Bioethics Advisory Commission and president of Princeton University. Princeton, NJ 08544, USA. Reprinted with permission from H. Shapiro, "Ethical and Policy Issues of Human Cloning," *Science* 277, 195 (1997).

Examples of such uncertainties include the impact of genetic imprinting, the nature of currently unknown species differences, and the effects of cellular aging and mutations.

The initial public response to this news, here and abroad, was primarily one of concern. In some cases, these concerns were amplified by largely fictional and mistaken accounts of how this new technology might dramatically reshape the future of our society. The sources of these feelings were complex, but usually centered around the basic fact that this technique would permit human procreation in an asexual manner, would allow for an unlimited number of genetically identical offspring, and would give us the capacity for complete control over the genetic profile of our children.

ETHICAL AND LEGAL ISSUES

Within days of the published report, President Clinton instituted a ban on federal funding related to attempts to clone human beings in this manner. In addition, the president asked the recently appointed National Bioethics Advisory Commission (NBAC) to report within 90 days on the ethical and legal issues that surround the potential cloning of human beings[2].

This was an unusually challenging assignment for many reasons. These issues are complex and difficult, and many scientific uncertainties remain. Conflicting values are at stake, and Americans disagree on the implications of this new technology for the social and cultural values they hold dearest. It is difficult to decide if and when our liberties, including the freedom of scientific inquiry, should be restricted. Finally, the commission was given an ambitious timetable.

Nonetheless, NBAC made every effort to consult widely with ethicists, theologians, scientists, scientific societies, physicians, and others in initiating an analysis of the many scientific, legal, religious, ethical, and moral dimensions of the issue. This included a careful consideration of the potential risks and benefits of using this technique to create children and a review of the potential constitutional challenges that might be raised if new legislation were to restrict the creation of a child through somatic cell nuclear transfer cloning.

The commission focused its attention on the new and distinctive ethical issues that would be raised by the use of this technique for the purpose of creating an embryo genetically identical to an existing (or previously existing) person that would then be implanted in a woman's uterus and brought to term. Although the creation of embryos for research purposes alone always raises serious ethical questions, these issues have recently received extensive analysis and deliberation in our country, and the use of somatic cell nuclear transfer to create embryos raises no new issues in this respect. The unique and distinctive ethical issues raised by the use of somatic cell nuclear transfer to create children relate to serious safety concerns and to a set of questions about what it means to be human; questions that go to the heart of the way we think about families and relationships between generations, our concept of individuality, and the potential for treating children as objects, as well as issues of constitutional law that might be involved in the area of procreation.

CONCERNS

In its deliberations, NBAC reviewed the scientific developments that preceded the Roslin announcement, as well as those likely to follow in its path, and the many moral and legal concerns raised by the possibility that this technique could be used to clone human beings. Although some of the initial negative response arose from fictional accounts of cloning human beings, more thoughtful concerns revealed fears about harm to the children who may be created in this manner, particularly psychological harm associated with a possibly diminished sense of individuality and personal autonomy. Others expressed concern about a degradation in the quality of parenting and family life.

In addition to concerns about specific harms to children, people have frequently expressed fears that the widespread practice of somatic cell nuclear transfer cloning would undermine important social values by opening the door to a form of eugenics or by tempting some to manipulate others as if they were objects instead of persons. These are concerns worthy of widespread and intensive debate, but arrayed against these concerns are other vitally important social and constitutional values, such as protecting the widest possible sphere of personal choice, particularly in matters pertaining to procreation and child rearing; maintaining privacy; protecting the freedom of scientific inquiry; and encouraging the possible development of new biomedical breakthroughs.

To arrive at its recommendations, NBAC also examined longstanding religious traditions and found that religious positions on human cloning are pluralistic in their premises, modes of argument, and conclusions. Some religious thinkers argue that the use of somatic cell nuclear transfer cloning to create a child would be intrinsically immoral and thus could never be morally justified. Other religious thinkers contend that human cloning to create a child could be morally justified under some circumstances but believe that it should be strictly regulated to prevent abuses.

PUBLIC POLICIES

The public policies that NBAC recommended with respect to the creation of a child by means of somatic cell nuclear transfer reflected the commission's attempt to balance the various interests at stake and to apply its best judgments about the ethics of attempting such an experiment at this time as well as its view of U.S. constitutional traditions regarding limitations on individual actions in the name of the common good. We concluded that, at present, the use of this technique to create a child would be a premature experiment that would expose the fetus and the developing child to unacceptable risks. In our judgment, this in itself might be sufficient to justify a prohibition on using this new technique to clone human beings at this time, even if such efforts were to be characterized as the exercise of a fundamental right to attempt to procreate. Beyond the issue of the safety of the procedure, however, NBAC found that concerns relating to potential psychological harm to children and effects on the moral, religious, and cultural values of society merit further reflection and deliberation. Whether upon such further deliberation our nation will conclude that the use of this new cloning technique to create children should be allowed or permanently banned is, for the moment, an open question. Fortunately, time is an ally in this regard, allowing for the accrual of further data from animal experimentation, an assessment of the prospective safety and efficacy of the procedure in humans, and a period of fuller national debate on ethical and social concerns.

The commission therefore concluded that a period of time should be imposed in which no attempt is made to create a child using somatic cell nuclear transfer.

CONCLUSIONS AND RECOMMENDATIONS

Within this overall framework, the commission's full set of conclusions and recommendations was as follows:

1) The commission concluded that at this time it is morally unacceptable for anyone in the public or private sector, whether in a research or clinical setting, to attempt to create a child using somatic cell nuclear transfer cloning. We reached a consensus on this point because current scientific information indicates that this technique is not safe to use in humans at this time. Indeed, we believe that it would violate important ethical obligations were clinicians or researchers to attempt to create a child using these particular technologies, which are likely to involve unacceptable risks to the fetus or potential child. Moreover, in addition to safety concerns, many other serious ethical concerns have been identified that require much more widespread and careful public deliberation before this technology may be used.

The commission therefore recommended the following: (i) A continuation of the current moratorium on the use of federal funding to support any attempt to create a child by somatic cell nuclear transfer. (ii) An immediate request to all firms, clinicians, investigators, and professional societies in the private and nonfederally funded sectors to comply voluntarily with the intent of the federal moratorium. Professional and scientific societies should make clear that any attempt to create a child by somatic cell nuclear transfer and implantation into a woman's body would at this time be an irresponsible, unethical, and unprofessional act.

2) The commission further recommended that federal legislation should be enacted to prohibit anyone from attempting, whether in a research or clinical setting, to create a child through cloning by somatic cell nuclear transfer. It is critical, however, that such legislation include a sunset clause to ensure that Congress will review this issue after a specified period of time (3 to 5 years) to decide whether the prohibition continues to be needed. If state legislation is enacted, it should also contain such a sunset provision. Any such legislation or associated regulation should require that at some point before the expiration of the sunset period, an appropriate oversight body will evaluate and report on the current status of somatic cell nuclear transfer technology and

on the ethical and social issues that its potential use to create human beings would raise in the light of public understandings at that time.

3) The commission also concluded that (i) any regulatory or legislative actions undertaken to effect the foregoing prohibition should be carefully written so as not to interfere with other important areas of scientific research. In particular, we believe that no new regulations are required regarding the cloning of human DNA sequences and cell lines, because neither activity raises the scientific and ethical issues that arise from the attempt to create children through somatic cell nuclear transfer, and these fields of research have already provided important scientific and biomedical advances. Likewise, research on cloning animals by this technique does not raise the same issues as attempting to use it for human cloning, and its continuation should only be subject to existing regulations regarding the humane use of animals and to review by institution-based animal protection committees. (ii) If a legislative ban is not enacted, or is enacted but later lifted, clinical use of somatic cell nuclear transfer techniques to create a child should be preceded by research trials that are governed by the twin protections of independent review and informed consent, which is consistent with existing norms of human subjects protection. (iii) The U.S. government should cooperate with other nations and international organizations to enforce any common aspects of their respective policies on the cloning of human beings.

4) The commission concluded that different ethical and religious perspectives and traditions are divided on many of the important moral issues that surround this topic. Therefore, it recommended that the federal government and all interested and concerned parties encourage widespread and continuing deliberation on these issues to further our understanding of the ethical and social implications of this technology and to enable society to produce appropriate long-term policies should the time come when present concerns about safety have been addressed.

5) Finally, because scientific knowledge is essential for all citizens to participate in a full and informed fashion in the governance of our complex society, the commission recommended that federal departments and agencies concerned with science should cooperate in seeking out and supporting opportunities to provide information and education to the public in the area of genetics and about other developments in the biomedical sciences, especially where they affect important cultural practices, values, and beliefs.

NBAC hopes that the sections of its report that outline the scientific, religious, ethical, and legal issues associated with human cloning will form a useful basis for the widespread deliberations and broad public education we believe are so essential. We believe that this kind of deliberation and education are especially critical in a society where individuals hold various religious and moral perspectives. As I have already noted, issues related to human cloning in this novel manner go to the very nature of what it means to be human and to the very heart of what people think of as their families and their individuality. These are issues worthy of intensive and widespread debate.

Once again, however, time is an ally, allowing for the accumulation of more scientific data from animal studies as well as granting an opportunity for fuller national debate on ethical and moral concerns. Through such deliberation, we can, as a society, improve not only our understanding of the scientific issues but our prospects for achieving moral agreement where that is possible, or mutual respect where such agreement cannot be achieved.

NOTES

1. I. Wilmut, A. E. Schnieke, J. McWhir, A. J. Kind, K. H. S. Campbell, *Nature* 385, 810 (1997).

2. The full report will be posted on the NBAC home page at http://www.nih.gov/nbac/nbac.htm.

Would Cloned Humans Really Be Like Sheep?

LEON EISENBERG, M.D.

THE RECENT PROOF, by DNA-microsatellite analysis[1] and DNA-fingerprinting techniques,[2] that Dolly the sheep had indeed been cloned as Wilmut et al. claimed,[3] and the report by Wakayama et al.[4] of the successful cloning of more than 20 healthy female mice are likely to reactivate discussions of the ethics of cloning humans and to provoke more calls to ban experiments on mammalian cloning altogether. From the standpoint of biologic science, a ban on such laboratory experiments would be a severe setback to research in embryology.[5] From the standpoint of moral philosophy, the ethical debate has been so obscured by incorrect assumptions about the relation between a potential human clone and its adult progenitor that the scientific issues must be reexamined in order to clarify the relation between genotype and phenotype. There are powerful biologic objections to the use of cloning to alter the human species, objections that make speculations about the ethics of the process largely irrelevant.

EXPERIMENTS IN CLONING

A clone is the aggregate of the asexually produced progeny of an individual organism. Reproduction by cloning in horticulture involves the use of cuttings of a single plant to propagate desired botanical characteristics indefinitely. In microbiology, a colony of bacteria constitutes a clone if its members are the descendants of a single bacterium that has undergone repeated asexual fission. The myriad bacteria in the clone each have precisely the same genetic complement as that of the progenitor cell and are indistinguishable from one another.

Success in cloning mammals demonstrates unequivocally that at least some of the nuclei in fully differentiated mammalian cells contain the full complement of potentially active genetic material that is present in the zygote. What distinguishes differentiated cells is the sets of genes that are turned "off" or "on." The cloning experiments in animals suggest that similar techniques might make it possible to clone humans. Such cloning would involve transferring a human ovum to a test tube, removing its nucleus, replacing it with a somatic-cell nucleus from the donor of the ovum or another person, allowing the ovum with its new diploid nucleus to differentiate to the blastula stage, and then implanting it in a "host" uterus. The resultant person, on attaining maturity, would be an identical genetic twin of the adult nuclear donor. This hypothetical outcome, although remote, has given rise to speculation about the psychological, ethical, and social consequences of producing clones of human beings. The futuristic scenarios evoked by the prospect of human cloning contain implicit assumptions about the mechanisms of human development. Examination of these underlying premises highlights themes that can be traced back to Greek antiquity, themes that recur in contemporary debates about the sources of differences between groups with respect to such characteristics as intelligence and aggression.[6]

Leon Eisenberg, M.D., Harvard Medical School, Boston, MA 02115-6019. Reprinted by permission of the Massachusetts Medical Society.

THEORIES OF DEVELOPMENT

The enigmas of human development have concerned philosophers and naturalists since people first began to wonder how plants and animals emerged from the products of fertilization.[7] Despite the fact that there is no resemblance between the physical appearance of the seed and the form of the adult organism, the plant or animal to which it gives rise is an approximate replica of its progenitors. The earliest Greek explanation was preformation—that is, the seed contains all adult structures in miniature. This ancient speculation, found in the Hippocratic corpus, was given poetic expression by Seneca.[8] "In the seed are enclosed all the parts of the body of the man that shall be formed. The infant that is borne in his mother's wombe has the rootes of the beard and hair that he shall weare one day." The theory of preformation was so powerful that 1600 years later, when the microscope was invented, the first microscopists to examine a sperm were able to persuade themselves that they could see in its head a homunculus with all the features of a tiny but complete man. Improvements in the microscope and the establishment of embryology as an experimental science made the doctrine progressively more difficult to sustain in its original form. With better microscopical resolution, the expected structures could not be seen, and experimental manipulation of embryos produced abnormal "monsters" that could not, by definition, have already been present in the seed.

The alternative view, that of epigenesis, was formulated by Aristotle. Having opened eggs at various stages of development, he observed that the individual organs did not all appear at the same time, as preformation theory demanded. He did not accept the argument that differences in the size of the organs could account for the failure to see them all at the same time. Others as well as Aristotle had noted that the heart is visible

before the lungs, even though the lungs are ultimately much larger. Unlike his predecessors, Aristotle began with the observable data. He concluded that new parts were formed in succession and did not merely unfold from precursors already present[9]:

> It is possible, then, that A should move B and B should move C, that, in fact, the case should be the same as with the automatic machines shown as curiosities. For the parts of such machines while at rest have a sort of potentiality of motion in them, and when any external force puts the first of them into motion, immediately the next is moved in actuality . . . in like manner also that from which the semen comes . . . sets up the movement in the embryo and makes the parts of it by having touched first something though not continuing to touch it. . . . While there is something which makes the parts, this does not exist as a definite object, nor does it exist in the semen at the first as a complete part.

This is the first statement of the theory of epigenesis: successive stages of differentiation in the course of development give rise to new properties and new structures. The genetic code in the zygote determines the range of possible outcomes. Yet the genes that are active in the zygote serve only to initiate a sequence, the outcome of which is dependent on the moment-to-moment interactions between the products of successive stages in development. For example, the potential for differentiating into pancreatic tissue is limited to cells in a particular zone of the embryo. But these cells will produce prozymogen, the histologic marker of pancreatic tissue, only if they are in contact with neighboring mesenchymal cells; if they are separated from mesenchyme, their evolution is arrested, despite their genetic potential.[10] At the same time, the entire process is dependent on the adequacy of the uterine environment, defects in which lead to anomalous development and miscarriage.

OUTCOMES OF HUMAN CLONING

The methodologic barriers to successful human cloning are formidable. Nonetheless, even if the necessary virtuosity lies in a more distant future than science-fiction enthusiasts suggest, one can argue that a solution exists in principle and attempt to envisage the possible outcomes.

Restricting Genetic Diversity

One negative consequence of very wide scale cloning is that it would lead to a marked restriction in the diversity of the human gene pool. Such a limitation would endanger the ability of our species to survive major environmental changes. Genetic homogeneity is compatible only with adaptation to a very narrow ecologic niche. Once that niche is perturbed (e.g., by the invasion of a new predator or a change in temperature or water supply), extinction may follow. For example, the "green revolution" in agriculture has led to the selective cultivation of grain seeds chosen for high yield under modern conditions of fertilization and pest control. Worldwide food production, as a result, is now highly vulnerable to new blights because of our reliance on a narrow range of genotypes.[11] Recognition of this threat has led to a call for the creation of seed banks containing representatives of "wild" species as protection against catastrophe from new blights or changed climatic conditions, to which the current high-yield grains prove particularly vulnerable.[12] Indeed, the loss of species (genetically distinct populations) is impoverishing global biodiversity as the result of shrinking habitats.[13]

Precisely the same threat would hold for humans, were we to replace sexual reproduction with cloning. The extraordinary biologic investment in sexual reproduction (as compared with asexual replication) provides a measure of its importance to the evolution of species. Courtship is expensive in its energy requirements, reproductive organs are elaborate, and there are extensive differences between male and female in secondary sexual characteristics. The benefit of sexual reproduction is the enhancement of diversity (by the crossover between homologous chromosomes during meiosis and by the combining of the haploid gametes of a male and female). The new genetic combinations so produced enable the species to respond as a population to changing environmental conditions through the selective survival of adaptable genotypes.

Cloning Yesterday's People for Tomorrow's Problems

The choice of whom to clone could be made only on the basis of phenotypic characteristics manifested during the several decades when the persons being considered for cloning had come to maturity. Let us set aside the problem of assigning value to particular characteristics and assume that we agree on the traits to be valued, however unrealistic that assumption.

By definition, the genetic potential for these characteristics must have existed in the persons who now exhibit them. But the translation of that potential into the phenotype occurs in the particular environment in which development occurs. Even if we agree on the genotype we wish to preserve, we face a formidable barrier: we know so little of the environmental features necessary for the flowering of that genotype that we cannot specify in detail the environment we would have to provide, both before and after birth, to ensure a phenotypic outcome identical to the complex of traits we seek to perpetuate.

Let us make a further dubious assumption and suppose the day has arrived when we can specify the environment necessary for the flowering of the chosen phenotype. Nonetheless, the phenotype so admirably suited to the world in which it matured may not be adaptive to the world a generation hence. That is, the traits that lead a person to be creative or to exhibit leadership at one moment in history may not be appropriate at another. Not only is the environment not static, it is altered by our own extraordinary impact on our ecology. The proliferation of our species changes patterns of disease[14,15]; our methods of disease control, by altering population ratios, affect the physical environment itself.[16] Social evolution demands new types of men and women. Cloning would condemn us always to plan the future on the basis of the past (since the successful phenotype cannot be identified sooner than adulthood).

THE CONNECTION BETWEEN GENOTYPE AND PHENOTYPE

For the student of biology, cloning is a powerful and instructive method with great potential for deepening our understanding of the mechanisms of differentiation during development. The potential of a given genotype can only be estimated from the varied manifestations of the phenotype over as wide a range of environments as are compatible with its survival. The wider the range of environments, the greater the diversity observed in the phenotypic manifestations of the one genotype. Human populations possess an extraordinary range of latent variability. Dissimilar genotypes can produce remarkably similar phenotypes under the wide range of conditions that characterize the environments of the inhabitable portions of the globe. The differences resulting from genotypic variability are manifested most clearly under extreme conditions, when severe stresses overwhelm the homeostatic mechanisms that ordinarily act as buffers against small perturbations.

Phenotypic identity requires identity between genotypes, which cloning can ensure, and identity between environmental interactions, which it cannot ensure. At the most trivial level, we can anticipate less similarity even in physical appearance between cell donor and cloned recipient than that which is observed between one-egg twins. Placental attachment and fetal-maternal circulation can vary substantially, even for uniovular twins housed in one uterus. Developmental circumstances will be more variable between donor and cloned recipient, who will have been carried by different women.

Postnatal Environmental Effects on the Human Brain

Let us force the argument one step further by assuming that the environmental conditions for the cloned infant have been identical to those of his or her progenitor, so that at birth the infant is a replica of the infant its "father" or "mother" was at birth. Under such circumstances (and within the limits of the precision of genetic specification), the immediate pattern of central nervous system connections and their responses to stimulation will be the same as those of the progenitor at birth.

However, even under these circumstances, the future is not predestined. The human species is notable for the proportion of brain development that occurs postnatally. Other primate brains increase in weight from birth to maturity by a factor of 2 to 2.5, but the human brain increases by a factor of 3.5 to 4. There is a fourfold increase in the neocortex, with a marked elaboration of the receiving areas for the teloreceptors, a disproportionate expansion of the motor area for the hand in relation to the representation of other parts, a representation of tongue and larynx many times greater, and a great increase in the "association" areas. The elaboration of pathways and interconnections is highly dependent on the quantity, quality, and timing of intellectual and emotional stimulation. The very structure of the brain, as well as the function of the mind, emerges from the interaction between maturation and experience.[17]

Nature and nurture jointly mold the structure of the brain. The basic plan of the central nervous system is laid down in the human genome, but the detailed pattern of connections results from competition between axons for common target neurons. Consider the steps in the formation of alternating ocular layers in the lateral geniculate bodies. Early in embryogenesis, axons from both eyes enter each of the geniculate nuclei and intermingle. How does the separation of layers for each eye, essential for vision, come about? It results from periodic waves of spontaneous electrical activity in retinal ganglion cells, because immature cell membranes are unstable. If these electrical outbursts are abolished experimentally, the layers simply do not become separated.[18] Competition between the two eyes, driven by spontaneous retinal activity, determines eye-specific lateral geniculate connections.[19] Neither the genes governing the retina nor the genes governing the geniculate specify the alternating ocular layers; it is the interaction between retina and geniculate during embryogenesis that brings it about. Furthermore, the precise targeting of projections from lateral geniculate to occipital cortex is dependent on electrical activity in the geniculate. Abolishing these action potentials with an infusion of tetrodotoxin results in projections to cortical areas that are normally bypassed and a marked reduction in projections to visual cortex.[20]

Postnatal stimulation is required to form the ocular dominance columns in the occipital cortex.[21] Both eyes of the newborn must receive precisely focused stimulation from the visual environment during the early months of postnatal life in order to fine-tune the structure of the cortex. If focused vision in one eye of a kitten or an infant monkey is interfered with, the normal eye "captures" most neurons in the occipital cortex in the absence of competition from the deprived eye. The change becomes irreversible if occlusion is maintained throughout the sensitive period. Amblyopia in humans, characterized by incongruent visual images from the two eyes, results in permanent loss of effective vision from the unused eye if the defect is not corrected within the first five years of life.

Thus, which of the overabundant neurons live and which die is determined by the amount and consistency of the stimulation they receive. Interaction between organism and environment leads to patterned neuronal activity that determines which synapses will persist.[22] Experience molds the brain in a process that continues throughout life. Myelination in a key relay zone in the hippocampal formation continues to increase from childhood through at least the sixth decade of life.[23] And recent research has provided evidence that neurons in the dentate gyrus of the hippocampus continue to divide in the adult brain.[24]

Changes in the Brain with Use

Techniques of functional brain mapping reveal marked variations in cortical representation that depend on prior experience. Manipulation of sensory inputs leads to reorganization of the cortex in monkeys[25] and humans.[26] The motor cortex in violinists displays a substantially larger representation of the fingers of the left hand (the one used to play the strings) than of the fingers of the right (or bowing) hand. Moreover, the area of the brain dedicated to finger representation is larger in musicians than in nonmusicians.[27] Sterr et al.[28] compared finger representation in the somatosensory cortex in blind persons who used three fingers on each hand to read Braille with that in Braille readers using only one finger on one hand and in sighted readers. They found a substantial enlargement of hand representation in the Braille readers who used two hands, with topographic changes on the postcentral gyrus.

If enlargement of cortical areas accompanies increases in activity, shrinkage follows loss. Within days after mastectomy, the amputation of an arm or leg, or the correction of syndactyly, the cortical sensory map changes. Intact areas have an enlarged representation at the expense of areas from which innervation has been removed.[29,30] What begins prenatally continues throughout life. Structure follows function.

BECOMING HUMAN

There is yet another level of complexity in the analysis of personality development. The human traits of interest to us are polygenic rather than monogenic; similar outcomes can result from the interaction between different genomes and different social environments. To produce another Wolfgang Amadeus Mozart, we would need not only Wolfgang's genome but his mother's uterus, his father's music lessons, his parents' friends and his own, the state of music in 18th-century Austria, Haydn's patronage, and on and on, in ever-widening circles. Without Mozart's set of genes, the rest would not suffice; there was, after all, only one Wolfgang Amadeus Mozart. But we have no right to the converse assumption: that his genome, cultivated in another world at another time, would result in the same musical genius. If a particular strain of wheat yields different harvests under different conditions of climate, soil, and cultivation, how can we assume that so much more complex a genome as that of a human being would yield its desired crop of operas, symphonies, and chamber music under different circumstances of nurture?

In sum, cloning would be a poor method indeed for improving on the human species. If widely adopted, it would have a devastating impact on the diversity of the human gene pool. Cloning would select for traits that have been successful in the past but that will not necessarily be adaptive to an unpredictable future. Whatever phenotypes might be produced would be extremely vulnerable to the uncontrollable vicissitudes of the environment.

Proposals for human cloning as a method for "improving" the species are biologic nonsense. To elevate the question to the level of an ethical issue is sheer casuistry. The problem lies not in the ethics of cloning a human but in the metaphysical cloud that surrounds this hypothetical cloned creature. Pseudo-biology trivializes ethics and distracts our attention from real moral issues: the ways in which the genetic potential of humans born into impoverished environments today is stunted and thwarted. To improve our species, no biologic sleight of hand is needed. Had we the moral commitment to provide every child with what we desire for our own, what a flowering of humankind there would be.

NOTES

1. Ashworth D, Bishop M, Campbell K, et al. DNA microsatellite analysis of Dolly. Nature 1998;394:329.

2. Signer EN, Dubrova YE, Jeffreys AJ, et al. DNA fingerprinting Dolly. Nature 1998;394:329–30.

3. Wilmut I, Schnieke AE, McWhir J, Kind AJ, Campbell KH. Viable off-spring derived from fetal and adult mammalian cells. Nature 1997;385: 810–3. [Erratum, Nature 1997;386:200.]

4. Wakayama T, Perry AC, Zuccotti M, Johnson KR, Yanagimachi R. Full-term development of mice from enucleated oocytes injected with cumulus cell nuclei. Nature 1998;394:369–74.

5. Berg P, Singer M. Regulating human cloning. Science 1998;282:413.

6. Eisenberg L. The human nature of human nature. Science 1972;176:123–8.

7. Needham J. A history of embryology. New York: Abelard-Schuman, 1959.

8. *Idem.* A history of embryology. New York: Abelard-Schuman, 1959:66.

9. *Idem.* A history of embryology. New York: Abelard-Schuman, 1959: 47–8.

10. Grobstein C. Cytodifferentiation and its controls. Science 1964;143: 643–50.

11. Harlan JR. Our vanishing genetic resources. Science 1975;188:618–21.

12. National Research Council. Genetic vulnerability of major crops. Washington, D.C.: National Academy of Sciences, 1972.

13. Hughes JB, Daily GC, Ehrlich PR. Population diversity: its extent and extinction. Science 1997;278:689–92.

14. Black FL. Infectious diseases in primitive societies. Science 1975;187: 515–8.

15. *Idem.* Why did they die? Science 1992;258:1739–40.

16. Ormerod WE. Ecological effect of control of African trypanosomiasis. Science 1976;191:815–21.

17. Eisenberg L. The social construction of the human brain. Am J Psychiatry 1995;152:1563–75.

18. Shatz CJ, Stryker MP. Prenatal tetrodotoxin infusion blocks segregation of retinogeniculate afferents. Science 1988;242:87–9.

19. Penn AA, Riquelme PA, Feller MB, Shatz CJ. Competition in retinogeniculate patterning driven by spontaneous activity. Science 1998;279: 2108–12.

20. Catalano SM, Shatz CJ. Activity-dependent cortical target selection by thalamic axons. Science 1998;281:559–62.

21. Wiesel TN. The postnatal development of the visual cortex and the influence of environment (the 1981 Novel prize lecture). Stockholm, Sweden: Nobel Foundation, 1982.

22. Nelson CA, Bloom FE. Child development and neuroscience. Child Dev 1997;68:970–87.

23. Benes FM, Turtle M, Khan Y, Farol P. Myelination of a key relay zone in the hippocampal formation occurs in the human brain during childhood, adolescence, and adulthood. Arch Gen Psychiatry 1994;51:447–84.

24. Eriksson PS, Perfilieva E, Björk-Eriksson T, et al. Neurogenesis in the adult human hippocampus. Nat Med 1998;4:1313–7.

25. Wang X, Merzenich MM, Sameshima K, Jenkins WM. Remodelling of hand representation in adult cortex determined by timing of tactile stimulation. Nature 1995;378:71–5.

26. Hamdy S, Rothwell JC, Aziz Q, Singh KD, Thompson DG. Long-term reorganization of human motor cortex driven by short-term sensory stimulation. Nat Neurosci 1998;1:64–8.

27. Schlaug G, Jancke L, Huang Y, Steinmetz H. In vivo evidence of structural brain asymmetry in musicians. Science 1995;267:699–701.

28. Sterr A, Muller MM, Elbert T, Rockstroh B, Pantev C, Taub E. Perceptual correlates of changes in cortical representation of fingers in blind multi-finger Braille readers. J Neurosci 1998;18:4417–23.

29. Yang TT, Gallen CC, Ramachandran VS, Cobb S, Schwartz BJ, Bloom FE. Noninvasive detection of cerebral plasticity in adult human somatosensory cortex. Neuroreport 1994;5:701–4.

30. Mogilner A, Grossman JA, Ribary U, et al. Somatosensory cortical plasticity in adult humans revealed by magnetoencephalography. Proc Natl Acad Sci U S A 1993;90:3593–7.

Notes

Notes for Part 1

1. For an interesting argument that there is really very little disagreement on ethical principles across cultures, see Richard Brandt, *Ethical Theory.* Englewood Cliffs, NJ: Prentice Hall, 1959. Brandt argues that the reason particular moral judgments may differ from culture to culture is because of the different factual beliefs that each group holds, not because they hold different principles. What one group believes to be good may vary considerably from the beliefs of another group, for example. So while they both follow the same principle, "do good and avoid evil," the actions that they consider to be morally acceptable may differ considerably.

2. The major ethical work of Jeremy Bentham, published in 1823, is his *Introduction to the Principles of Morals and Legislation.* (Oxford: Oxford University Press, 1948.) Mill discusses his moral views in several works. Chief among these is *Utilitarianism,* (Indianapolis: Bobbs-Merrill, 1957) first published in 1863.

3. Kant's views on ethics are developed in his *Critique of Practical Reason,* and *Fundamental Principles of the Metaphysics of Morals,* trans. Thomas Abbott. Indianapolis: Bobbs-Merrill, 1949.

4. *Fundamental Principles,* p. 9.

5. Ibid., p. 24.

6. Aristotle's views on ethics are developed in his *Nichomachean Ethics,* trans. W. D. Ross. Oxford: Oxford University Press, 1925.

7. This "do no harm" principle appears to be foundational in Buddhist ethics. As we will see, it is also more central in our moral lives than is usually acknowledged by moral philosophers.

8. Some rights do not have correlative duties. Such rights are called permissive rights. They give legal permission to do something, like marry, for example, but do not impose a duty to do so.

9. The psychologist Carol Gilligan was first to study the differences in the ways that boys and girls exhibit moral reasoning. See her *In a Different Voice: Psychological Theory and Women's Development.* Cambridge, MA: Harvard University Press, 1982.

10. Tom Beauchamp and James Childress, *Principles of Biomedical Ethics.* New York: Oxford University Press, 1994.

11. Perhaps the best statement of the principle of autonomy is to be found in the opening paragraphs of John Stuart Mill's *On Liberty,* (Indianapolis: Bobbs-Merrill, 1956) first published in 1859.

12. This idea of ranking competing rules according to their highest priorities was much discussed by W. D. Ross in *The Right and the Good.* Oxford: Clarendon Press, 1930. He distinguished between *prima facie* duties and actual duties. *Prima facie* duties are all those duties or obligations that you are subject to at any one time. Your actual duty is the one among these with the highest priority.

13. The view that virtues are simply internalized rules and that an ethics of virtue may be reduced to an ethics of principles has been defended by G. J. Warnock in *The Object of Morality.* London: Methuen, 1971.

14. This pattern of critical thinking has been introduced and developed by Richard Paul. See his *Critical Thinking.* Rohnert Park, CA: Center for Critical Thinking and Moral Critique, 1990.

Notes for Part 2

Chapter 5: Capital Punishment

1. In Part 2 new terms will be introduced in bold letters. Terms referring to matters of critical thinking will be in bold type and italics. Italics only will be used for emphasis.

2. Stephen Nathanson, *An Eye for an Eye?* New York: Roman and Littlefield, 1987.

3. Ernest van den Haag, "Deterrence and Uncertainty", *Journal of Criminal Law, Criminology and Political Science,* v. 60, no 2 (1969).

Chapter 6: Abortion

1. This view was first presented by Judith Jarvis Thomson in a very famous and often anthologized article, "A Defense of Abortion," *Philosophy & Public Affairs,* v. 1, no. 1 (1971).

2. Justice Harry Blackmun, *The Majority Opinion in Roe v. Wade.* United States Supreme Court, 410 U.S. 113 (1973).

3. Mary Ann Warren, "On the Moral and Legal Status of Abortion," *The Monist,* v. 57, no. 1 (1973).

4. John Noonan, "An Almost Absolute Value in History," from *The Morality of Abortion: Legal and Historical Perspectives.* Cambridge, MA: Harvard University Press, 1970.

5. Warren, "On the Moral and Legal Status."

6. Don Marquis, "Why Abortion Is Wrong," *Journal of Philosophy,* v. 86 (1989).

7. Thomson, "A Defense of Abortion."

8. Daniel Callahan, *Abortion: Law, Choice and Morality.* New York: Macmillan, 1970.

9. Jane English, "Abortion and the Concept of a Person," *Canadian Journal of Philosophy,* v. 5, no. 2 (1975).

10. Warren, "On the Moral and Legal Status."

Chapter 7: Physician Assistance in Dying

1. Kathleen M. Foley, M.D., "Medical Issues Related to Physician Assisted Suicide." Testimony given to the Judiciary Subcommittee on the Constitution, April 29, 1996. For Dr. Foley's full testimony see www.soros.org/death/testimony.htm

2. This medical definition of suffering is found in *The Management of Cancer Pain,* U.S. Department of Health and Human Services, *Clinical Practice Guidelines,* no. 9, March, 1994.

3. Foley, "Medical Issues."

4. James Rachels, "Active and Passive Euthanasia," *New England Journal of Medicine,* vol. 292, no. 2 (Jan. 9, 1975).

5. This is from a 1996 decision by Judge Roger J. Miner, Second Court of Appeals, New York. Judge Miner's decision in *Quill v. Vacco* struck down laws prohibiting assisted suicide in New York. It was later overturned by the U.S. Supreme Court.

6. From her article, "Helping Desperately Ill People to Die," in *Regulating How We Die,* ed. Linda Emanuel. Cambridge, MA; Harvard University Press, 1998.

7. Emanuel, "Helping Desperately Ill People," p. 13.

8. Margaret Battin, "Is a Physician Ever Obligated to Help a Patient Die?" in *Emanuel,* "Helping Desperately Ill People," p. 23.

9. Emanuel, "Helping Desperately Ill People," p. 26.

10. J. Gay-Williams, "The Wrongfulness of Euthanasia," in Ronald Munson, *Intervention and Reflection.* Belmont, CA: Wadsworth, 1993.

11. Edmund Pelligrino, "The False Promise of Beneficent Killing," in *Emanuel,* "Helping Desperately Ill People," p. 76.

12. David Orentlicher, "The Supreme Court and Physician-Assisted Suicide: Rejecting Assisted Suicide but Embracing Euthanasia," *New England Journal of Medicine,* vol. 337 (Oct. 1997), pp. 1236–1239.

Chapter 8: Affirmative Action

1. For a good discussion of the history of affirmative action see Louis Pojman, "The Moral Status of Affirmative Action," *Public Affairs Quarterly* v. 6 (1997).

2. New York: Free Press, 1994.

3. Princeton, NJ: Princeton University Press, 1998.

4. Lisa Newton, "Reverse Discrimination as Unjustified," *Ethics,* 83 (1973).

5. Justice Clarence Thomas, United States Supreme Court. 115 S. Ct. 2097 (1995).

6. Newton, "Reverse Discrimination."

7. Louis Pojman, "The Moral Status of Affirmative Action," *Public Affairs Quarterly,* v. 6 (1977).

8. Thomas, 115 S. Ct. 2097 (1995).

9. Laura Ingraham, "Testimony before the U.S. House of Representatives, April 3, 1995." Reprinted in A. E. Sadler, ed., *Affirmative Action.* San Diego: Greenhaven Press, 1996.

10. Shelby Steele, *The Content of Our Character.* New York: St. Martin's Press, 1990.

11. Arch Puddington, "What to Do About Affirmative Action," *Commentary,* 1995. Reprinted in Sadler, *Affirmative Action.*

12. Susan Estrich, "Feminism," *The Boston Globe,* Sept. 15, 2000.

13. *The New York Times,* October 30, 2000.

14. Transcript from "The NewsHour with Jim Lehrer," April 1, 1998.

15. William Julius Wilson, *The Declining Significance of Race.* Chicago: University of Chicago Press, 1987.

16. Abigail Thernstrom, "A Class Backwards Idea," *The Washington Post,* June 11, 1995.

Chapter 9: Global Justice

1. From Robert Kates, "Ending Hunger: Current Status and Future Prospects," *Consequences*, v. 2, no. 2, (1996).

2. See the United Nations publication, *Long-Range Population Projections: Based on the 1998 Revision* (ESA/P/WP.153), 1999.

3. See his "Lifeboat Ethics: The Case against Helping the Poor," *Psychology Today* (1974), and "The Tragedy of the Commons," from Garrett Hardin and John Baden, *Managing the Commons.* New York W. H. Freeman, 1977.

4. Hardin, "The Tragedy of the Commons."

5. Hardin, "The Tragedy of the Commons."

6. Hardin, "Lifeboat Ethics."

7. Hardin, "Lifeboat Ethics."

8. This article first appeared in *Philosophy and Public Affairs*, v. 1, no. 3 (1972).

9. See "The Singer Solution to World Poverty," *New York Times Sunday Magazine.* September 5, 1999.

10. Singer, "Famine, Affluence, and Morality."

11. Singer, "Famine, Affluence, and Morality."

12. As reported in the *Boston Globe,* September 7, 2000.

13. Onora O'Neill, "Ending World Hunger," eds. William Aiken and Hugh LaFollette, *World Hunger and Morality,* Upper Saddle River, NJ: Prentice Hall, 1996.

14. From the report of the Presidential Commission on World Hunger, found in *Overcoming World Hunger: The Challenge Ahead.* Washington, DC: U.S. Government Printing Office, 1980.

15. Lester Brown and Jennifer Mitchell, "Building a New Economy," from *State of the World,* eds. Lester Brown et al., Washington, D.C.: World Watch Institute, 1998.

16. Richard Watson, "Reason and Morality in a World of Limited Food," ed. Louis Pojman, *Life and Death: A Reader in Moral Problems.* Belmont, CA: Wadsworth, 2000.

17. O'Neill, "Ending World Hunger."

18. Hardin, "Lifeboat Ethics."

19. Singer, "Famine, Affluence, and Morality."

20. Singer, "Famine, Affluence, and Morality."

21. For example, see Kai Nielson, "Global Justice, Capitalism and the Third World," eds. Robin Attfield et al., *International Justice and the Third World.* New York: Routledge and Kegan Paul, 1992.

22. See this 2000/2001 *World Bank* report on hunger and poverty at the Web site: http://www.worldbank.org/poverty/data/trends/income.htm

23. See http://www.worldbank.org/poverty/data/trends/scenario.htm

24. Singer, "The Singer Solution to World Poverty."

25. Chimimba David Phiri and Barbara Huddleston, "Food Security and Food Assistance Executive Summary," *Food and Agricultural Organization Report.* See http://www.fao.org/waicent/faoinfo/economic/ESA/foodsec/fasssum.htm

26. From *The New York Times,* December 15, 2000.

27. The following are references for "Famine and Famine Relief":

ABCFM (American Board of Commissioners for Foreign Missions) (1860–1950). Archives at Houghton Library, Harvard University. ABC 16.3.12, North China Mission, 88 vols.

American National Red Cross (1929). *The Report of the Ameircan Red Cross Commission to China.* Washington, DC: American Red Cross.

Ashton, B., Hill, K., Piazza, A. & Zeitz, R. (1984). Famine in China, 1958–61. *Population and Development Review*, 10, 613–45.

Baker, J.E. (1943). *Fighting China's Famines.* Unpublished manuscript. New York: Burke Library, Union Theological Seminary.

Bernstein, T.P. (1984). Stalinism, famine and Chinese peasants: grain procurements during the Great Leap Forward. *Theory and Society*, 13(3), 339–77.

Blom, C.F. (1932). The values of famine relief work, *The Chinese Recorder*, 63(11), 696–99.

Bohr, P.R. (1972). *Famine in China and the Missionary: Timothy Richard as Relief Adminstrator & Advocate of National Reform,* 1876–1884. Cambridge, Mass.: East Asian Research Center, Harvard University.

China International Famine Relief Commission (1936). *The CIFRC Fifteenth Anniversary Book,* 1921–1936. Peiping: CIFRC.

China, National Flood Relief Commission (1932). *The Work of the National Flood Relief Commission of the National Government of China,* August 1931–June 1932. Shanghai: National Government of China.

Chopra, R. N. (1981). *Evolution of Food Policy in India,* New Delhi: Macmillan India Limited.

Edwards, D. W. (1932). The missionary and famine relief. *The Chinese Recorder,* 63(11), 689–96.

Jackson, T. (1982). *Against the Grain.* Oxford: OXFAM.

Johnson, W. R. Papers, deposited at Day Missions Library, Yale Divinity School, China Records Project, Record Group 6.

Lancaster, C. (1985). Africa's development challenges. *Current History,* April. 145–49.

Lappe, F. M. and Collins, J. (1977). *Food First: Beyond the Myth of Scarcity.* Boston: Houghton Mifflin.

Li, L. M. (1982). Introduction: Food, famine, and the Chinese state. *Journal of Asian Studies,* XLI, 687–707.

Nathan, A. J. (1965). *A History of the China International Famine Relief Commission.* Cambridge, Mass.: East Asian Research Center, Harvard University.

Presbyterian Historical Society. Philadelphia. Record Group 82. China Mission, 1890–1955. Box 20, Folders 11–12. China Famine Fund.

Sanderson, F. H. and Roy, S. (1979). *Food Trends and Prospects in India,* Washington, DC: The Brookings Institute.

Schwab, P. (1985). Political change and famine in Ethiopia. *Current History* (May), 221–23.

Sen, A. (1984). Development: which way now? In his *Resources, Values, and Development,* 485–508. Cambridge, Mass.: Harvard University Press.

Shawcross, W. (1984). *The Quality of Mercy: Cambodia, Holocaust and Modern Conscience.* New York: Simon & Schuster.

Shepherd, J. (1985a). When foreign aid fails. *The Atlantic Monthly,* April, 41–46.

Shepherd, J. (1985b). Ethiopia: the use of food as an instrument of U.S. foreign policy. *Issue,* 14, 4–9.

Stroebf, G. G. (1932). The great central China flood of 1931. *The Chinese Recorder,* 63(11), 669–80.

Tang, A. M. & Stone, B. (1980). *Food Production in the People's Republic of China.* Washington, DC: International Food Policy Research Institute.

Thomson, J. C., Jr. (1969). *When China Faced West: American Reformers in Nationalist China, 1928–1937.* Cambridge, Mass.: Harvard University Press.

White, T. H. & Jacoby, A. (1946). *Thunder Out of China.* New York: William Sloan.

Chapter 10: The Moral Status of Animals

1. Peter Singer, *Animal Liberation* New York: Random House, 1975.

2. Tom Regan, *The Case for Animal Rights.* Berkeley: University of California Press, 1983.

3. http://www.peta-online.org/mc/facts

4. Singer, *Animal Liberation.*

5. See http://www.sciam.com/0297issue/0297barnard.html. This is the *Scientific American* Web site.

6. *Scientific American* Web site.

7. See http://www.labanimal welfare.org/overwiew.htm. This is the Web site of the *Center for Laboratory Animal Welfare.*

8. *Scientific American* Web site.

9. Such an argument is presented by R. G. Frey. See his "Animal Experimentation Needs Moral Justification," in *Animal Experimentation.* San Diego: Greenhaven Press, 2000.

10. Tom Regan, "The Case for Animal Rights," ed. Peter Singer, *In Defense of Animals.* London: Blackwell, 1985.

11. Regan, *The Case for Animal Rights,* p. 236.

12. Regan, *The Case for Animal Rights.*

13. Peter Singer, *Animal Liberation.* 2nd ed. New York: Random House, 1990, p. 7.

14. Singer, *Animal Liberation,* pp. 81–82.

15. Singer, *Animal Liberation,* p. 19.

16. Regan, *The Case for Animal Rights.*

17. See Carl Cohen, "The Case for the Use of Animals in Biomedical Research," *New England Journal of Medicine,* vol. 315 (October 2, 1986).

Chapter 11: Sex, Love and Marriage

1. S. A. Sanders and J. M. Reinisek, "Would you say you 'had sex' if. . .," *Journal of the American Medical Association* U.281 (1999), 281, 275–277.

2. *U.S. News and World Report* (5/19/97).

3. See the Gallup Poll (July 25, 1998) at http://www.gallup.com/poll/releases/pr980725.asp

4. "A Statement on Homosexuality," *Journal of the American Psychological Association,* July (1994).

5. *Declaration on Sexual Ethics.* Rome: Sacred Congregation for the Doctrine of Faith, 1975.

6. Honora O'Neill, "Between Consenting Adults," *Philosophy and Public Affairs,* v. 14, no. 3 (1985).

7. Andrea Dworkin, *Intercourse.* New York: The Free Press, 1997.

8. St. Thomas Aquinas, *Summa Theologica,* XCIV, art. 2. From *The Basic Writing of Thomas Aquinas,* trans. Anton Pegis (New York: Random House, 1945).

9. Aquinas, *Summa Theologic.*

10. Alan Goldman, "Plain Sex," *Philosophy and Public Affairs,* v. 6, no. 3 (1977).

11. See Vincent Punzo, "Morality and Human Sexuality," in Vincent Punzo, *Reflective Naturalism.* Upper Saddle River, NJ: Prentice Hall, 1969. Punzo takes the position that sexual morality should be determined from a perspective of a morality of aspiration.

Chapter 12: The Censorship of Pornography

1. *The Attorney General's Commission on Pornography: The Final Report.* Washington, DC: U.S. Department of Justice, 1986. Hereafter, this report will be called the *Meese Commision Report,* after then-attorney general, Edwin Meese.

2. Helen Longino, "Pornography, Oppression, and Freedom: A Closer Look," ed. Laura Lederer, *Take Back the Night: Women on Pornography.* New York: William Morrow, 1980.

3. *U.S. News and World Report.* Find this report at http://www.usnews.com/usnews/issue/10porn.htm

4. *Meese Commision Report.* Each of the following quotes attributed to the Meese Commission are from this report.

5. Catherine MacKinnon, *Feminism Unmodified.* Harvard University Press, 1987, p. 168.

6. *Catechism of the Catholic Church.* Rome: Liberia Editrice Vaticana, 1992, paragraph 565.

7. U.S. District Court of Appeals, *American Booksellers v. Hudnutt* (1985).

8. John Stuart Mill, "On Liberty," from *Utilitarianism.* New York: Bobbs-Merrill, 1957.

9. Mill, "On Liberty."

10. Wendy Kaminer, "Feminists Against the First Amendment," from *The Atlantic Monthly,* November 1992.

11. Mill, "On Liberty."

12. See http://www.eff.org/pub/Censorship/aclu opposes porno censorship.article.

13. *Meese Commision Report.*

14. See, for example, "A Report on the Use of Pornography by Sexual Offenders," Federal Department of Justice, Ottawa, Canada, 1983; M. H. Silber and A. M. Pines, "Pornography and Sexual Abuse of Women," in *Sex Roles,* v. 10, pp. 857–868 (1984); V. B. Cline, *Pornography's Effects on Adults and Children.* New York: Morality in the Media, 1999.

15. Cline, *Pornography's Effects.*

16. J. Dobson, "Interview with Ted Bundy," Florida State Prison, 1989. See http://www.moralityinmedia.org/harmfuleffects.htm

17. Longino, "Pornography, Oppression, and Freedom."

18. Irving Kristol, "Pornography, Obscenity, and the Case for Censorship." See http://www.personal.umich.edu/~wbutler/kristol.html

19. Walter Berns, "Pornography Versus Censorship." See http://web3.infotrac.galegroup.com/itw/session/943/552/22323615w3/21!xrn_2_0_A56027257

Index